Mediterranean Encounters

Mediterranean Encounters

TRADE AND PLURALISM IN EARLY MODERN GALATA

Fariba Zarinebaf

UNIVERSITY OF CALIFORNIA PRESS

University of California Press, one of the most distinguished university presses in the United States, enriches lives around the world by advancing scholarship in the humanities, social sciences, and natural sciences. Its activities are supported by the UC Press Foundation and by philanthropic contributions from individuals and institutions. For more information, visit www.ucpress.edu.

University of California Press
Oakland, California

Library of Congress Cataloging-in-Publication Data

Names: Zarinebaf, F. (Fariba), 1959- author.
Title: Mediterranean encounters : trade and pluralism in early modern Galata / Fariba Zarinebaf.
Description: Oakland, California : University of California Press, [2018] | Includes bibliographical references and index. |
Identifiers: LCCN 2017055319 (print) | LCCN 2017058926 (ebook) | ISBN 9780520964310 (Ebook) | ISBN 9780520289925 (cloth : alk. paper) | ISBN 9780520289932 (pbk. : alk. paper)
Subjects: LCSH: Galata (Istanbul, Turkey)—History.
Classification: LCC DR737 (ebook) | LCC DR737 .Z37 2017 (print) | DDC 949.61/8—dc23
LC record available at https://lccn.loc.gov/2017055319

Manufactured in the United States of America

27 26 25 24 23 22 21 20 19 18
10 9 8 7 6 5 4 3 2 1

ILLUSTRATIONS

FIGURES

MAPS

ACKNOWLEDGMENTS

The idea for writing this book was born when I was a graduate student in Istanbul and lived in a Bohemian neighborhood (Cihangir) in Pera in 1990s. Before the gentrification of Pera, Cihangir was the residence of Europeans as well as artists, professors, and expat communities. All the European cultural and research institutes were located there as well as some major bookstores and libraries. Pera was a museum of the Ottoman Empire's European enclave since all the embassies had moved to Ankara when it became the capital during the Republican period. Back then, it was still possible to live, feel, and sense the traces of this once cosmopolitan port that had witnessed its own share of a glorious past during the Ottoman era as well as war and occupation at the end of the empire in the early twentieth century. But somehow, it was still a pole of attraction for European and American scholars and tourists, local artists, and businessmen as well as thousands of strollers from Turkey and all over the world who frequented Rue de Pera (Beyoğlu) every day, perhaps to experience the disappearing heritage of a cosmopolitan Ottoman port. I am often among them when I visit Istanbul.

My father used to visit me in Istanbul when I was a graduate student, and we would go on our own strolls in Pera. He brought with him my grandfather's account book and a box of business letters that had been exchanged between my grandfather, who had been a merchant in Tabriz, and his cousin, Haj Reza Jorabchi, who had represented the firm *Jorabchi et Frères* in Istanbul and had had a shop in Mahmud Pasha Suq. During the late nineteenth century, Istanbul had had a vibrant Iranian community of traders. My father took me on a tour of Istanbul while I was living in Pera and pointed out the importance of this place for Iranian intellectuals who had been exposed to Ottoman and European, particularly French liberal and modernist, ideas there during the late nineteenth century. Pera had been the window to Europe for Iranian and Ottoman intellectuals. I eventually coedited and coauthored a volume entitled *Les Iraniens d'Istanbul* with Thierry Zarcone, a member of the French Institute of Anatolian Studies, which had a research project on the Iranian and other cemeteries in Istanbul. This research sparked my interest in the history of Galata.

I came into close contact with the French academic community in the French Institute of Anatolian Studies, which is located in the former Palais de France, or French Embassy, after the embassy was moved to Ankara. My interest in the history of Franco-Ottoman contacts in Galata and Pera also developed as result of my earlier academic interest in French history (the Enlightenment and the French Revolution) as well as my own encounters with the French community in Pera. My own position was that of an in-between person in a borderland between the East and the West, a situation in which I felt most comfortable and thrived intellectually and personally.

I am indebted to many individuals who have inspired and supported my intellectual journey, several institutions that have funded my research, and various archives and archivists who have provided me with access to sources as well as to many friends, colleagues, and family members in Istanbul, Chicago, and Riverside who never stopped listening and offering their insights, support, and love. First, I would like to thank the readers and editors of the University of California Press, particularly Niels Hooper, whose continuing confidence and interest in my scholarship have been a major driving force for me to complete this manuscript.

Without the financial support of several institutions, this dream would not have come true. I received a senior residential grant from the Research Center for Anatolian Studies at Koç University (2011–12) in Istanbul to start this project. This grant provided me with a rare opportunity to live in Pera with an international and interdisciplinary community of scholars and to share my findings and research with them. I thank Scott Redford, my fellows at RCAC, and the kind staff for their support. The Fulbright Scholars Program (2013–14) provided me with another grant to go back to Istanbul and continue my research and writing. During my RCAC and Fulbright grant periods, I was affiliated with Boğazici University and benefited immensely from interacting with my colleague and friend Paolo Girardelli, whose insights, advice, and seminars on Ottoman ports were very important to me. I thank the Fulbright Commissions in Ankara and Istanbul for their warm support throughout the process and my Fulbright fellows for their friendship and intellectual support. At Boğazici University, I would also like to thank Edhem Eldem, Nevra Necipoğlu, Şevket Pamuk, and Ahmet Ersoy.

In addition, the American Research Institute in Istanbul (ARIT) has been my intellectual home away from home in Turkey since I was a graduate student. I received several research grants in the past from ARIT. The director, Anthony Greenwood, and staff members like Gülden Güneri and Brian Johnson have been very generous with their support and help throughout my academic career, research, and long stays there. Living in the village of Arnavutköy along the Bosphorus also inspired me to write chapter 7.

The University of Chicago granted me a visiting researcher position during the last phase of my research and writing. I would like to thank my mentor, John Woods; Frank Lewis; Hakan Karateke; Holly Shissler; Orit Bashkin; Fred Donner; David Nirenberg; and Cornell Fleischer as well as many graduate students who offered their insights and critical perspectives as well as their enthusiastic support.

As well, my colleagues in the Department of History at the University of California–Riverside have been an important source of support at various stages of my project. I received several senate grants as well as a subvention from the Dean of the College of Humanities, Arts, and Social Sciences (CHASS) for the book. I thank Randolph Head, Kiril Tomoff, and Dean Pena as well as my colleagues Georg Michels, Juliette Levy, Monte Kugel, Ray Kea, Jonathan Eacott, and Ademide Adelusi-Adeluyi, Ruhi Khan, Benjamin Liu, Susan Ossman, and Thomas Cogswell and my graduate students for their constant support and inspiration.

I owe a great debt of gratitude to the various archives and libraries but most of all to the Başbakanlık Archives and the Islamic Research Center (ISAM) in Istanbul for access and welcome support for many years. I also thank the archivists at the Chamber of Commerce in Marseille for giving me access to their valuable collection. The French Institute of Anatolian Studies, located on the grounds of the former French Embassy, has been a crucial space throughout my research years in Istanbul. I want to thank the French consul general, Muriel Domenach, and my colleague Olivier Bouquet for hosting me at several lunches and dinners at the institute and for their warm support. The Regenstein Library in Chicago has also always been a crucial place for my research, and its librarians were open and welcoming.

The Pera Museum in Istanbul and the California Museum of Photography at the University of California–Riverside as well as the Newberry Library in Chicago offered images for the book from their collections. I thank the curators Barış Kıbrıs and Fatma Çolakoğlu (Pera Museum), John Powell (Newberry), and Leigh Gleason (CMP) for their timely processing of my requests and for sharing their collections. I thank Paul Khaldjian for his wonderful and diligent renderings of the maps of Istanbul and Galata as well as of the villages along the Bosphorus. Emily Flock and Professor Alex Papadopoulos of the Department of Geography at DePaul University were very forthcoming in offering their expertise in preparing the map of Mediterranean ports. Vici Casana has been a steady source of support with her wonderful editorial assistance and her timely suggestions to make the book more accessible to the general reader. I also thank Bradley Depew and Emilia Thiuri for overseeing the final phase of production, and Brian Craig for indexing.

My late *hoca* and mentor, Professor Halil Inalcik, followed my research with great enthusiasm. I am saddened that he and my late mother did not live to see the final product. In Istanbul, Suraiya Faroqhi, Haldun Gülalp, Fikret Yılmaz, Ali Akyıldız, Gülden Sarıyıldız, Mehmet Genç, Sinan Kuneralp, Kenan Yıldız, and Faruk Bilici provided intellectual support, valuable knowledge, and critical insights. Sinan Kuneralp provided several books and insights to help with my research. Moreover, Dilek Barlas and her family have supported my research and stay with their warm hospitality and friendship. Mühiddin Eren's bookstore was always a wonderful space in Pera to hang out, drink tea, chat, and learn about new books in Ottoman studies and to meet old and new friends after a long day of research.

In the United States, the Mediterranean Studies Seminars organized by Brian Catlos and Sharon Kinoshita and the West Ottomanist workshops have provided me with an excellent forum and community of scholars to test and develop my ideas and share my findings for many years. My friends and colleagues Linda Darling, Ariel Salzmann, Richard Bea, Jo'an Schurlock, and Nasrin Qader and those in California—Nile Green, Baki Tezcan, Hasan Kayali, Ali Gheissari, Will Smiley, Matthew Herbst, and others—were always sources of great support as I moved from Istanbul to the West Coast to Chicago to work on the manuscript. Stefan Sanchev read the first chapter and offered great insights when we were both involved in an NEH workshop with a group of wonderful teachers in Istanbul.

The ongoing love of my late mother and her passion for scholarship and the endless warmth of my family and friends in Chicago and my nieces and nephew, even during very trying times, provided me with the final drive to complete the manuscript. The residents of Galata, Pera, Ortaköy, and Arnavutköy were always generous, inspiring, and interesting. I hope that the final product will not disappoint all the people who were involved in this long and enriching journey.

NOTE ON TRANSLITERATION
AND TRANSLATION

All the translations of Ottoman sources in the text and the appendix and a few French passages are my own, and I have tried to remain close to the original text as much as possible. I have also used the Ottoman renditions of Arab (e.g., *Mehmed*), non-Muslim, and European names and have used the same form of transliteration. I have used Christian calendar dates when citing documents.

For terms other than common English forms (e.g., *pasha*), I have followed modern Turkish orthography. For the English transliteration of specific Ottoman terms, I have followed Sir James Redhouse's *Turkish and English Lexicon,* New Edition, Beirut, 1987. For proper names (Arabic and Turkish), I have followed the modern Turkish orthography (e.g., *Mehmed*).

Pronunciation of modern Turkish letters that are not transliterated in English:

ç ch, as in *church*
ş sh, as in *ship*
ğ unvocalized; lengthens preceding vowel
ı as in *bird*
c j as in *jam*

Introduction

GALATA WAS THE EUROPEAN PORT of Constantinople/Istanbul and had been a crossroads of trade among Asia and Europe, the Black Sea, and the Mediterranean since medieval times. Although many books have been written on Ottoman-European trade, the port of Galata has not received much attention until very recently, partly due to a dual approach that has been taken to the history of the imperial capital.[1]

In Ottoman contemporary writing (Evliya Çelebi's *Seyahatnamesi*), Galata was described as the "sin city" and a Frankish town where the "infidel" resided.[2] In European travel writing, Galata was the enclave of European culture, Catholic Christianity, progress, and modernity, in contrast to the traditional and sleepy peninsula across the Golden Horn during the nineteenth century. This dual approach to the history of Istanbul and Galata has dominated much of the historiography to this date. In reality, the city was more integrated during the eighteenth century than it had been previously as people moved in and out of Galata and set up residence in Pera and the villages along the Bosphorus. Moreover, the diplomatic importance of Pera has been ignored in much of the scholarship. This study will focus on the European port of Galata in Istanbul and its maritime trade with the Black Sea and the Mediterranean, giving particular attention to its connectivity to the port of Marseille from the second half of the seventeenth to the early nineteenth century. Indeed, as this book demonstrates, Ottoman economic and commercial policies, the granting of *ahdnames* (commercial and diplomatic treaties) to trading nations, and the legal pluralism of this port played a crucial role in the rise and development of Galata in the early modern period.

The field of Mediterranean studies has become an exciting forum of critical debate and inquiry, with scholars from across disciplines and regions contributing to a growing literature.[3] The forthcoming volume by Brian A. Catlos, Mark Myerson, and Thomas Burman entitled *The Sea in the Middle: The Mediterranean World, 650–1650* highlights the contribution of Perso-Hellenic and Islamicate civilizations to the development of Mediterranean history and culture, emphasizing the diversity and connectivity of this region and its peripheries from the ancient to the early modern periods. Moreover, the works of scholars in the field of Indian Ocean studies have offered important analytical and critical perspectives as well as correctives on cross-cultural trade and alternative models of economic development.[4]

However, with few exceptions, the Ottoman Empire has been absent from the master narratives of the Mediterranean except when it was at war with Europe. For Henri Pirenne, the unity of the Mediterranean that existed during the Roman period was disrupted by the Germanic invasions and the rise of Prophet Muhammad and the Islamic expansion into Europe.[5] Thus, religion in its most essentialist expression became the defining characteristic of a complex and dynamic civilization that has been viewed as lagging behind the West and unable to modernize following the Western model. The failure of the Ottoman Empire to become an Atlantic maritime power and participate in the colonization of the New World in the sixteenth century is yet another aspect of this "decline paradigm."[6]

Fernand Braudel elaborated on the role of the Ottoman Empire in the Mediterranean world in his meganarrative of the sixteenth century. Braudel (1902–85) wrote his history of the Mediterranean, which was first published in 1949, from a prison camp in Germany.[7] Unlike Pirenne, he emphasized the unity of the Mediterranean in its geographical makeup and its connectivity through trade. But Braudel was still ambivalent about the role of Islam and Muslims in Mediterranean history since for him the Ottoman Empire was largely a military power and not a commercial one.[8] On the other hand, Braudel in his later writings also argued that the Ottoman Empire was not very different from the Byzantine Empire in its socioeconomic makeup and that Constantinople/Istanbul[9] bridged the two empires. He described the impact of the Ottoman Conquest of Constantinople in 1453 in the following manner:

In the early days, the Turkish conquest took a heavy toll on the subjugated peoples[,] ... but the Conqueror was not deficient in political wisdom, as can be seen from Muhammad II's concessions to the Greeks summoned to Constantinople after 1453. Eventually[,] Turkey created, throughout the Balkans, structures within which the peoples of the Peninsula gradually found a place, collaborating with the conqueror and here and there curiously re-creating the patterns of the Byzantine Empire. This conquest brought a new order, a pax Turcica.[10]

Braudel did not elaborate on the institutions of the Ottoman government, its commercial and economic policies vis-à-vis European states, due to limited research opportunities and material available to him in the Ottoman archives back then. But in his *Structures of Everyday Life,* he included Istanbul (as well as Cairo and Isfahan) as an important port in the urban and maritime networks of the Mediterranean.[11] Although Braudel privileged the Western city in its unparalleled freedom and autonomy, he also praised Istanbul for its religious diversity and commercial sophistication:

Of course[,] every town varied slightly from this pattern, if only because of its importance as a market or craft center. The main market in Istanbul, the two stone bedestans, was a town within a town. The Christian district of Pera and Galata formed another town beyond the Golden Horn.[12]

Istanbul did not completely fit the so-called model of Islamic cities due to its Greco-Roman as well as Italian heritage in the port of Galata prior to the Ottoman takeover. Some Ottomanist historians have proposed foregrounding Istanbul as the center of the Mediterranean world and have highlighted the integral role of the Ottoman Empire in the history of Western Europe in the early modern period.[13]

The legacy of Fernand Braudel and the Annales School of historiography has been particularly strong in the field of Ottoman studies, especially at its inception in Turkey with founding fathers like Ömer Lütfi Barkan, Fuad Köprülu, and Halil Inalcik. However, the exploration of Ottoman as well as European archives by scholars on the study of Ottoman institutions and their transformation has been an important corrective to the scholarship of an earlier generation of scholars who could not write beyond the paradigms of "holy war" or the "sick man of Europe," a historiography influenced by a century or more of European travel narratives on a "decaying empire."[14]

Indeed, as the heir to both the Byzantine and Seljuk Empires, Perso-Islamic and Roman civilizations, the Ottoman Empire created its own "world system," with Istanbul as the "middle ground" or bridge between East and West, a transit port with networks of trade extending into the Balkans (*via ignatia*), Iran (the Silk Route), India (the spice trade), and the Mediterranean world (the Levant trade). Its urban, commercial, and legal institutions were a blend of Roman and Perso-Islamic practices that the Ottomans developed further.

Like the Byzantine Empire, Istanbul was bound by its geography and location to serve as a bridge between the Black Sea and the Mediterranean, Asia, and Europe. The diplomatic, military, fiscal, commercial, and economic policies of the Ottoman state followed the Byzantine model but also departed from it important ways. For example, like the Byzantine state, the Ottoman state considered the provisioning of the imperial capital to be very important to its economic policies and its legitimacy. The revival of the economy of Istanbul after the conquest, the return of its former residents, and the resumption of trade with the Italian city-states were key to the policies of the Ottoman sultans. To gain control of the Black Sea trade, Sultan Mehmed II was determined to drive Genoa from her colonies such as Caffa and Chios. The next important step was to drive Venice from her colonies on the Aegean and the eastern Mediterranean (i.e., the Morea and Cyprus), thus enhancing Ottoman hegemony over the islands and ports. After the defeats of the Knights of Rhodes in 1522 by Sultan Süleyman I (1520–66) and of Cyprus by Sultan Selim II (1515–20) in 1571, the entire eastern Mediterranean fell under Ottoman state control. It was also essential for the Ottoman state to control Christian piracy to make the eastern Mediterranean safe for maritime trade.

The conquest of the Mamluk state was also driven by economic as well as by political motives. The Mamluks had kept European traders out of the Red Sea trade and confined them to Alexandria, where they could have their own consuls but had to pay higher taxes than Muslims did.[15] The Ottoman conquest of Egypt and Syria in 1517 was also crucial for the control of the Red Sea trade and the supply of grains, coffee, and sugar from Egypt to Istanbul.[16] In his fascinating book *The Ottoman Age of Exploration*, Giancarlo Casale has underscored the commercial policies of Grand Vizier Ibrahim Pasha in Egypt to revive the spice trade after the conquest in 1517 despite Portuguese attacks. Casale has also argued that Ottoman cartographers like Piri Reis had advance knowledge of trading posts on the eastern shores of Africa as well as on the Indian Ocean.[17] The Ottoman state was also trying to expand into the Persian Gulf, defeat the Portuguese strongholds in Yemen and Hormuz (on the Persian Gulf), and expand into the Indian Ocean in the sixteenth century.[18] The Ottoman-Safavid Wars were in part motivated by the control of commercial centers like Tabriz and the Silk Route as well as of Baghdad and the Persian Gulf.

However, the Ottoman expansion into the eastern Mediterranean ports and islands generated strong religious and ideological backlashes all over Europe, even among Ottoman allies like France. Although Venetian and French merchants and travelers had acquired an intimate knowledge of the Ottoman Empire and its institutions, the "Turk" nevertheless became a menace, an intrusion, and a military and economic rival that had to be defeated and driven out of Europe, particularly after the conquest of Constantinople in 1453. Thus, the search for a direct route to the Persian Gulf and India was part of the ideological as well as the commercial agenda to undermine the Ottoman Empire.

Palmira Brummett has captured the wild imagination and curiosity of Europeans about the Ottoman Empire in their mapping and collecting of information and images as well as in their narrations about the exotic kingdom.[19] The image of a "fallen Turk" and Muslim captives on a map of a fortress or port city symbolized European victory.[20] The narratives of European travelers and diplomats supplemented and reinforced these images, particularly after the Ottoman defeat at Lepanto in 1571. Cross-cultural contacts and exchanges between Englishmen and Ottoman subjects also created anxieties as well as great curiosity and interest that gave rise to their portrayal in English plays from the sixteenth to the eighteenth centuries. Moreover, the themes of captivity, conversion to Islam ("turning Turk"), and becoming renegades and entering Ottoman service created great interest in the stories of these individuals, exacerbating anti-Muslim sentiments in Europe.[21]

However, trade and diplomacy were also important aspects of Ottoman-European encounters, as reflected in the signing of commercial and diplomatic treaties (*ahdnames*) and the settlement of European communities in Ottoman ports that generated intense commercial and cultural contacts.[22] The Ottoman Empire created its own international law through the granting of ahdnames to friendly nations to boost trade despite the outbreaks of war and hostility, even by friendly nations. The ahdnames mediated peace in order to resume trade after these violent episodes on the Mediterranean. Joshua White's recent study has underscored the importance of ahdnames in regulating maritime trade and suppressing North African piracy on the Mediterranean.[23]

As a result, Mediterranean ports like Venice, Marseille, and Galata became sites of diplomacy, commercial exchange, and cultural encounters. David Abulafia has underscored the importance of studying Mediterranean ports and people who crossed the sea to trade. Ports were places where corsairs and renegades, displaced Moriscos and Marranos, and enslaved Christians and Muslims as well as converts mixed and where the identities of the local population were constantly being reshaped.[24] Julia Clancy-Smith is opposed to the binary and monolithic study of the Mediterranean (Christian versus Muslim) and instead proposes to study it as a layered zone of contact and a borderland where the movement and migration (both long-term and temporary) of people (both forced and voluntary) in ports like Tunis profoundly shaped the cityscapes and the identities of the newcomers. She is right to point out that every zone had a different trajectory of contact and interaction and that it is difficult to mark the boundaries of Europe, particularly in the nineteenth century, when the number of European residents in ports like Tunis, Algiers, and Galata multiplied by several folds.[25] Tobias Graf's recent study of European renegades (mainly Italian and German) and converts to Islam who entered Ottoman service at the elite level has also revised the binary vision of the Mediterranean, emphasizing the fluid identities and networks of these individuals during the sixteenth and seventeenth centuries.[26]

In contrast with North African ports, Istanbul was the epicenter of the Ottoman Empire, where the European countries had to play the diplomatic game to compete with each other and implement the articles of the ahdnames. In Istanbul, the size of the European communities was still limited, and they had not yet formed a settler society or a colonial cityscape, though Pera was emerging as their hub. Moreover, Galata had a different trajectory and power structure than Tunis, Izmir, and even Alexandria did, one in which Europeans (mainly the French and English) did not yet wield considerable influence in the eighteenth century. In Galata/Pera European ambassadors often had to turn to the grand vizier and dragomans drawn from local non-Muslim communities to help them navigate the complex and competitive diplomatic and commercial world of the Levant and to seek legal protection from tax collectors, bandits, and pirates as well as from merchants and producers. While Constantinople/Istanbul was a port *par excellence,* Marseille and Galata were both in perfect locations with maritime access to more than one sea that brought provisions, slaves, silks, and spices as well as colonial goods. Following the pathbreaking scholarship of Fernand Braudel and others, a comparative and critical perspective to the study of the Ottoman Empire and eastern Mediterranean cities based on the exploration of Ottoman as well as European archives has emerged.[27]

STATE AND COMMERCE IN OTTOMAN HISTORIOGRAPHY

First of all, it is necessary to reaffirm a simple truism, which has been consistently denied in the scholarly literature: Ottoman society, like all human societies throughout history, was fluid and dynamic. Moreover, it retained these qualities throughout its history, including the so-called period of decline in the seventeenth century.

RIFA'AT ALI ABOU-EL-HAJ[28]

An important research question in Ottoman studies has revolved around the role of the state in regulating economic life in its urban centers. The study of state institutions has assumed a central role in Ottoman studies, and historians have long argued that the Ottoman state considered provisioning its capital and collecting revenue its most important economic priority in the early modern period. Indeed, the Ottoman state exercised great control over the institution of landholding for a long time. It also maintained a tight control over the production and distribution of foodstuff and raw materials through guilds and imposed price ceilings on basic goods, discouraging profiteering and competition in the economy, particularly in Istanbul.[29] The state, according to this view, did not protect or promote its own merchants while it opened its markets to foreign merchants and goods, thus harming its own production and the well-being of its artisans, who had to compete with importers of Western goods. This historiography assigns the Ottoman state total control over its economy and a fixed policy that changed little over time.

Inalcik's pioneering works on the development of Istanbul and Galata after the conquest, as well as those on the history of the Black Sea trade based on archival sources that he had unearthed, have opened an exciting pathway to rigorous studies of urban life.[30] In addition, his studies of the silk trade between Bursa and Tabriz based on the Islamic court records of Bursa have underlined the importance of these sources for commercial history.[31] Like the discovery of the Cairo Geniza records by Shelomo Dov Goitein that shed great light on the activities of Jewish and Arab merchants in the Mediterranean trade during the medieval period, the exploration of Islamic court records has played a similar role in the study of Ottoman social and economic history in the early modern period.[32]

Rifa'at Abou El-Haj has warned us about essentialist arguments, abstract and moralistic approaches that assign the Ottoman state and society unique and unchanging characteristics without any comparative studies with the rest of the Mediterranean world or Western Europe.[33] He attributes the transformation of the Ottoman state structure and economy to internal conditions such as monetization, privatization of revenue collection (tax farming), and the rise of provincial magnates. He has rightly observed that the sultan as the epicenter of the state had lost much of his power to an oligarchy of civilian groups and grandees in the seventeenth century, in contrast with the rising absolutist monarchies in Europe like France.[34] Mehmet Genç has also emphasized the role of the institution of tax farming in the privatization of revenue collection during the eighteenth century. But according to him, the state still played an important role in assigning tax farms and confiscating the properties of local notables and merchants, thus preventing the accumulation of capital and merchant investment in production.[35]

Inspired by the scholarship of Genç, Ariel Salzmann's important study of the expansion of the institution of tax farming and lifetime tax farms in the eighteenth century has also underscored the commercialization of the Ottoman economy and the rise of local notables as well as the emergence of a group of janissaries and non-Muslim bankers who were based in Istanbul. This development also led to the establishment of a network of Jewish, Armenian, and Greek financiers who lent money to tax farmers and the state.[36] However, the participation of janissary-artisans, migrants, merchants, and ulema households in urban movements and rebellions in Istanbul during the eighteenth century undermined the authority and legitimacy of the sultan as the epicenter of power.[37] More recently, Baki Tezcan and Ali Yaycioğlu have also argued against the grain of the absolutist state in their scholarship on the seventeenth, eighteenth, and early nineteenth centuries.[38]

Bin Wong has observed a similar trend in Chinese historiography. According to this historiography, an autocratic and centralized state controlled the economy in the early period. Moreover, Wong has argued that scholars have highlighted the contrast between Chinese imperial policies and those of European states by focusing on the winners like England and France based on a single model of economic development.[39] Like Abou-El-Haj, Wong has argued that this type of historiography cannot trace change and the transformation of the economy, commerce, and urbanization that led to the relaxation of state control over the markets.

Francesca Trivellato's important study on the role of the Jewish trading diaspora has offered a different model based on family partnerships as vehicles of cross-cultural trade in the Mediterranean. She has also underscored the continuity of family firms and the plurality of business forms and practices despite the rise of corporate capitalism in the West.[40] This is not to deny that family firms among Jews, Armenians, and Greeks were based purely on blood ties and did not include outsiders (Europeans) as agents and creditors, which was the case in Ottoman ports. Like the Jewish and Greek trading diaspora, the Armenians of New Julfa in Isfahan formed a corporate body and assembly of merchants and enjoyed wide networks in the Levant.[41]

The Ottoman state indeed promoted the market economy and valued its merchants to achieve security and stability.[42] Perhaps we can trace this transformation better in its port cities and periphery than in the center of the empire. Moreover, ports across the Mediterranean shared certain institutions of commerce, practices, and cultures. For example, commercial partnerships (*commenda* in Latin) spread from the Islamic Middle East to Islamic Spain in the medieval and early modern periods.[43] The offices of dragoman (in Turkish, *tercuman:* interpreter) and *simsar* (broker), for example, existed in both Venice and Galata. The *şehbender* (chief of port) in Ottoman ports and cities represented the interests of merchants, as did the Venetian *bailo.* In short, Ottoman ports shared many commercial institutions and practices with western Mediterranean ports like Venice.

Gilles Veinstein has correctly warned us that our understanding of Ottoman commercial policies toward European merchants is based on limited research in the Ottoman archives.[44] Niels Steensgaard argued some time ago that Muslim merchants deliberately kept their commercial activities secret and did not leave behind much of a record about their caravan and maritime trade. But Halil Sahillioğlu's discovery of a list of caravan merchants who arrived into Aleppo in 1610 and included Iranian, Arab, Indian, and Turkish as well as European merchants underlined the importance of digging into the archival material.[45]

Furthermore, the study of cross-cultural trade following Philip Curtin's seminal work has emerged as an important topic in the recent scholarship.[46] The exploration of Ottoman and European archives has enhanced scholarship on cross-cultural trade. For example, Edhem Eldem's rigorous study of French archives has shed important light on French trade in Istanbul during the eighteenth century.[47] In the same vein, Daniel Panzac's study of French trade with the Levant also offers important insights on the role of French ships in domestic trade as well as on partnerships between Ottoman and French traders.[48] Ottomanist scholars have also carried out important studies on Cyprus, Crete, Izmir, Salonica, and other ports, emphasizing connectivity.[49] Daniel Goffman's study of Izmir in the Levant trade shows that the power of state had receded in western Anatolia during the seventeenth century.[50] Michael Talbot's recent study on diplomatic and commercial relations between England and the Ottoman Empire in the eighteenth century has underscored the shrinking role of England in the commerce of the Levant due to competition with France, the Ottoman-Iranian and Anglo-French Wars, and the diminishing importance of the Levant in English trade as compared with England's role in the East and West Indies trade.[51]

There is ongoing debate among historians on the meaning and impact of ahdnames/capitulations on the Ottoman economy.[52] Some historians have blamed them in part for the decline of the Ottoman economy during the early modern period.[53] More recently, some scholars have argued that the Ottoman plural legal system and the capitulations led to "hundreds of thousands" of Ottoman minorities taking flight from Ottoman legal jurisdiction and becoming protégés of European states. They have maintained that a coherent Ottoman bourgeoisie never came into existence. Those merchants who potentially could have been part of it preferred European protection and legal jurisdiction to Ottoman jurisdiction due to the "lack of transparency in the Ottoman legal system"; the restrictions of Islamic law concerning inheritance, which divided the property of the deceased among heirs; and the Ottoman state's "lack of interest in the local economy."[54] Thus, Islamic law and legal pluralism as well as the regime of ahdnames are viewed as the primary obstacles to the development of Western-style capitalism in the Ottoman Empire. Huri Islamoğlu has critiqued this binary vision of the world economy based on the liberal and secular Western trajectory and the peripherilization of non-Western economies due to the "Islamization" of its legal institutions.[55] She has called for a revision of the world system approach that is based on the model of European development. She is critical of the view that claims that the penetration of Ottoman markets by Western goods and the latter's divergence from the Western model of capitalism led to the underdevelopment of the non-West. Instead, she has emphasized the institutional and legal transformation of the empire that started in the eighteenth century to respond to global changes.

Furthermore, historians of Mediterranean and European ports have started exploring the Venetian, French, and English as well as the Dutch archives to shed light on commercial and cultural contacts in Ottoman ports.[56] Eric Dursteler's studies on Ottoman-Venetian trade as well as on the Venetian community in Istanbul have revised the notion of a divided Mediterranean. He has instead recognized fluidity and connectivity as important features of Mediterranean ports like Venice and Istanbul. The works of Benjamin Arbel, Natalie Rothman, and Steven Ortega have underscored the importance of the Venetian archives for the study of commercial contacts between the Ottoman Empire and Venice.[57] Similarly, the exploration of the Dutch archives has led to important findings by Alexander De Groot, Maurits van den Boogert, and Ismail Hakki Kadi on the Ottoman-Dutch trade and the legal status of Dutch traders in Galata. These studies have revised the notion of a passive state capitulating to European economic and colonial interests.[58]

Moreover, some scholars have adopted comparative studies of Ottoman ports and caravan cities, going beyond the essentialist model of the "Islamic city" provided by Max Weber and other scholars.[59] Suraiya Faroqhi and Gilles Veinstein have recently presented some of these findings in a collective volume on the activities of Ottoman merchants in Anatolia and the Balkans as well as in Europe.[60] Other scholars have suggested comparing Mediterranean ports like Barcelona and Indian Ocean ports like Bengal in the nineteenth century.[61]

My own study of Galata builds on these and other works and offers an alternative way of examining an Ottoman port through its layered history, legal pluralism, merchant networks, and connectivity. I also emphasize the unique role of Galata as a crossroads of commerce between the Black Sea and the Mediterranean, the East and the West. I argue that merchant partnerships and networks played an important role in Galata's international trade as well as in its financial institutions.

THE ORGANIZATION OF THE BOOK

The book is divided into three parts. Part 1 provides an urban context for Ottoman-European encounters in Galata and Pera while part 2 offers a legal framework through a comparative and analytical study of ahdnames (diplomatic and commercial treaties) as legal institutions of trade. As such, part 2 provides an important legal and diplomatic framework for the study of commercial and cultural encounters presented in part 3, which focuses on the domestic and international trade of Galata. Throughout this study, I use the term *ahdname* (treaty with a friendly nation) and avoid its Western usage, *capitulation* (Latin *capitula:* headings in a treaty), to emphasize the contractual and legal aspect of an institution that has been greatly misunderstood in the general scholarship. In part 3, I focus on a "thick history" of Galata's trade and merchant networks in domestic and international trade. This part also examines cultural (sexual and religious) encounters between the French and Ottoman residents in Galata and Pera as well as in villages on the European shore of the Bosphorus to shed light on the nature and limits of Ottoman pluralism.[62]

In chapter 1, I emphasize the layered history of Galata and study continuity and change from Byzantine and Genoese rule to Ottoman administration. Basing my argument on Ottoman surveys and archival and narrative sources, I contend that the Ottoman takeover of this port undermined Latin control but also left much of the old urban fabric intact since the port had been taken peacefully. However, an important priority for the sultan was the creation of a Muslim space as well as the settlement of Muslims and Marrano Jews, many of whom had arrived after their expulsion from the Iberian Peninsula in the sixteenth and early seventeenth centuries.

Chapter 2 traces the development of Pera, the suburb and necropolis of Galata outside the walls, in the seventeenth century. Due to the spread of congestion, crime, and plague in walled Galata, Pera became the diplomatic hub of the empire, with Western European embassies lining Rue de Péra (*Beyoğlu*). The role of the Tanzimat reformers as opposed to the roles of local communities and European residents in the transformation of Ottoman ports like Galata and Izmir has been at the heart of the debate on the nature of the urban transformation of Galata and greater Istanbul.[63] I emphasize the impact of fires and plague in the imposition of central control over migration, policing of the streets, and the establishment of building codes in Pera and Galata.

In part 2 (chapters 3 and 4), I examine the impact of ahdnames—or commercial and diplomatic treaties—on the status of Ottoman ports, their legal pluralism, and international trade. I trace the origins of ahdnames to the Mediterranean and Islamic states and offer a comparative analysis of a series of ahdnames granted by the Ottoman state to the Italian city-states as well as to Western European nations from the sixteenth to the early nineteenth centuries. I argue that the ahdnames/capitulations predated the Ottoman Empire and were Mediterranean and Islamic legal institutions intended to ease trade across religious divides as well as cohabitation and trade among communities of faith in port cities. I agree with Maurits van den Boogert that the ahdnames were not tools of Western European colonialism and that the Ottoman state maintained control over the implementation and revocation of their articles well into the nineteenth century.

Part 3 (chapters 5 through 7) examines the implementation of the ahdnames by focusing on domestic as well as on European trade. Contrary to the proponents of Ottoman absolutism, I argue that the Ottoman Empire practiced a combination of laissez-faire commercial policies with its allies in the Mediterranean trade while it controlled and protected domestic trade and its own merchants on the Black Sea until the late eighteenth century.[64]

Nevertheless, the state faced constant challenges from its own merchants and artisans, who were against promoting the interests of foreign merchants. Linda Darling's important study on the "Circle of Justice" has underlined the continuity of this tradition from the ancient Near East to the modern period.[65] As Marshall Hodgson keenly observed, the "unitary contractulalism of Islamdom" meant that ultimate legitimacy was not based in the autonomous and hierarchical corporative offices of the Occident but in the "egalitarian contractual responsibilities of the state."[66] Though the Ottoman state did not follow the Western model of capitalism, it developed its own responses to change and practiced a combination of laissez-faire and protectionist policies.

As I show in chapters 5 and 6, the Ottoman state paid close attention to the implementation of the articles of the ahdnames as well as to the *shari'a* through its law courts and through the process of petitioning the Imperial Council, which was open to all subjects (Muslim and non-Muslim men and women) as well as to foreigners. Thus, the Ottoman state's laissez-faire economic policy of providing opportunities for everyone to trade worked simultaneously with its protectionist policies to uphold the interests of its own merchants, producers, and consumers, depending on economic circumstances.

Chapter 6 examines the rise of France in the Levant trade from the sixteenth to the early nineteenth century. Although France enjoyed the status of most favored nation and obtained favorable ahdnames from the Ottoman Empire, French traders still faced numerous challenges in Ottoman ports from local traders and officials. This competition was best reflected in legal proceedings between French and Ottoman merchants in the Islamic courts of Galata and the process of the ambassador's petitioning the Imperial Council, which I explore.

Chapter 7 continues this critical perspective by focusing on the cultural encounters between Ottoman and French subjects in Galata and Pera. I contend that French traders had become embedded in the social life of Ottoman ports and that some had acquired fluid identities as "Levantines" through intermarriage and long residency in Ottoman ports by becoming Ottoman subjects. Despite the growing number of Europeans, particularly French subjects, in Ottoman ports in the eighteenth century, interfaith sex and conversion at the hands of Catholic missionaries generated anxieties and tensions within these communities.

The Epilogue focuses on the impact of the French Revolution in 1789 and Napoleon's invasion of Egypt in 1798 on Franco-Ottoman relations and the status of French subjects in Galata and Pera. The French Revolution and Napoleon's invasion of Egypt ended the special relationship between the two states and the old era of Levant Company monopolies. The Ottoman Empire's signing of bilateral ahdnames with France and England opened European markets up to Ottoman traders while lifting all bans on Ottoman exports and internal visas. The impact of this new set of commercial treaties led to a manifold increase in the volume of trade between the Ottoman ports and Europe (primarily England) and the incorporation of ports like Galata and Izmir into the global economy after the Crimean War. The appendix provides a sample of Ottoman documents that I have translated into English.

A central question in this book revolves around the role of Ottoman merchants in European trade. I maintain that before the rise of the Levant Companies, Muslim merchants were not absent from the European trade and had been active in Venice and Ancona since the sixteenth century, if not earlier.[67] However, due to the monopolistic policies of the English and French as well as the Dutch Levant Companies, Ottoman merchants (especially Muslims) were not welcome in European ports like Marseille and London. Bruce Masters has underscored the intolerance of European ports as well as the impact of Sunni-Shi'i rivalry and the Ottoman-Safavid Wars in the withdrawal of Muslim merchants from the Levant trade with Europe. Christian piracy in the Mediterranean was another factor in attacks on Ottoman ships. But Ottoman Armenian and Greek merchants filled the gap, as best reflected in the monopoly of Armenians in the silk trade.[68] Daniel Panzac's fascinating study of French shipping in the Ottoman Empire has shown that Muslim merchants entered into commercial partnerships with

French captains to transport their goods to European ports during the Russo-Ottoman Wars in the late eighteenth century.[69] My own research of Ottoman archival sources corroborates Panzac's findings and sheds light on the activities of a handful of Muslim merchants in Europe and the challenges that they faced.

Moreover, recent scholarship based on regional studies has shown that Ottoman merchants adjusted their portfolios and shifted to different trade routes and markets when European companies took over trade in major ports in the Levant and the Indian Ocean. Nelly Hanna is critical of scholars who have assigned a passive role to merchants, offering a static model of state control and rigid guild structure and attributing change to capitalist stimuli from the West to the declining economy of the eighteenth century. She instead argues that the Egyptian textile industry survived with large-scale exports to North Africa, Syria, and Europe through the first half of the eighteenth century. The change came when refined sugar exports from Marseille, Trieste, and Fiume replaced Egyptian sugar in the eighteenth century and led to the conversion of vast agricultural lands to cash crops like cotton destined for export.[70] Hala Fattah has also emphasized the flexibility and diversity of local merchants and their family firms in investing in regional and long-distance trade in bulky goods as well as in local textiles during the eighteenth and nineteenth centuries. She has also highlighted the resistance of local merchants and producers to European penetration of the markets as well as to local and state controls through boycott, sale of contraband, and insurrection in nineteenth-century Arabia.[71]

In a critical essay on the "quest for an Ottoman bourgeoisie," Edhem Eldem has noted historians' and social scientists' avoidance of applying the term *bourgeoisie* to Ottoman merchants. He has pointed to the problematic definition of Ottoman merchants as "comprador or dependent bourgeoisie," most of whom were members of Ottoman minority communities.[72] This tendency was in part the outcome of the nationalist historiography and the dependency theories of 1960s and 1970s and the popularity of the concept of *comprador bourgeoisie* in Turkey. Thus, the "Ottoman bourgeoisie" appear segmented along ethno-religious lines, divided into bureaucratic and commercial groups that were conflict ridden, fragile, and dependent on a Western capitalist class. This book is a corrective to the paradigm of a "fragmented and dependent bourgeoisie," underscoring deep tensions and competition between Ottoman non-Muslim and European traders in Istanbul during the eighteenth century.

Parts 1 and 2 of the book cover the long *durée* in the history of Galata from the Ottoman Conquest to the early nineteenth century, thus providing an important historical backdrop to the commercial, social, and cultural developments during the long eighteenth century. That century was an important period in the transformation of the Ottoman economy and society in Istanbul, with the rise of provincial notables and tax farmers as well as financiers. It was also an era of long wars against Russia and Iran that led to a deep economic crisis. Additionally, this period was very eventful in Western Europe, characterized by long continental wars, the Ottoman-French alliance against the partitioning of Poland, and Russia's expansion into the Black Sea. Anglo-French rivalry was also strong over the colonies in the West Indies and America as well as over trade routes in the Levant and the Indian Ocean. The French Revolution and the Napoleonic Wars intensified these developments, which had a direct impact on the lives of members of French communities in Ottoman ports and on the rise of French and English colonial projects to partition the empire.

The availability and exploration of Ottoman and European archival sources as well as of embassy accounts and travel literature have been crucial in studying the history of European trade in the Levant. For a long time, scholars of the Ottoman Empire had assumed that due to limited archival records on merchants, they had not had a strong presence and legal status in Ottoman society, unlike corporate groups like artisans and guilds. Niels Steensgaard has rightly argued that Muslim merchants kept their trade portfolios and knowledge secret and that the absence of source material does not reflect lack of activity or interest in commerce by peddling traders. Moreover, both Steensgaard and Janet Abu-Lughod have emphasized the sophistication of Muslim commercial culture and the use of bills of exchange and letters of credit.[73] Abu-Lughod has argued that too often scholars project developments that took place in the modern period, such as Western capitalism, backward. She points out that Islam was not inimical to capitalism. However, this picture is being revised since scholars now have greater access to the archives and are able to study Islamic court records for various parts of the empire.[74] Although many commercial contracts were oral, when disputes arose, the lawsuits and petitions left a paper trail in the court registers and the Imperial Council. Moreover, all merchants (Ottoman and foreign) had to register their transactions in the Islamic courts and to obtain a document that they could use in lawsuits and claims. The Islamic court records of Galata cover a long period from the early sixteenth to the early twentieth centuries.[75]

In Galata, the Islamic court records also contain lawsuits brought by European subjects. The Imperial Council had jurisdiction and a higher authority than the Islamic courts had over the implementation of the articles of the ahdnames. Europeans who lived in provincial ports and towns preferred to submit their lawsuits and petitions to the Imperial Council via their ambassador rather than to the Islamic courts due to the shari'a's preference for Muslim male witnesses. But occasionally non-Muslims also were used as witnesses in cases that involved non-Muslims.

There was busy traffic between the French Embassy in Pera and the Imperial Council after the signing of the Ahdname of 1740 that led to the expansion of trade between the two states. Every Wednesday, the ambassador and one of his dragomans traveled from Pera to the Sublime Porte in Istanbul proper to present written petitions in Ottoman translation to the grand vizier on behalf of the French nation. These documents are now kept in the Collection of Foreign Nations (*Ecnebi defterleri, ADVN.DVE collection*) and *name-yi hümayun* registers at the Başbakanlık Archives.[76] They make up more than one hundred volumes that cover foreign city-states and countries from Venice to Iran and the United States from 1567 to 1922.[77] I have focused on the study of registers for France in the eighteenth century, which begin in 1750 (vol. 100) and continue through the early nineteenth century. Several folders for each year contain around one hundred or more original documents (of one to three pages) in the form of handwritten petitions by the dragomans on behalf of ambassadors who represented French subjects. Occasionally, French subjects presented petitions directly and signed them. The state would then issue an imperial order to local officials and the kadi to look into the lawsuits in accordance with the articles of the ahdnames. A single document would contain the original petition in Ottoman translation signed by the ambassador, the report of Ottoman officials, and the imperial order in response to the petition, thus providing great insight into the legal procedure and the content of disputes as well as into the perspective of the state toward the implementation of the articles of the ahdnames (see appendix).

Many documents in this collection (several registers per year) deal with daily commercial affairs such as requests for permission for French commercial ships as well as for subjects and protégés to travel between ports. They also deal with requests from the ambassador and consuls for the issuance of imperial orders for *berats* (patents of appointment) for consuls and dragomans. As well, the files contain copies of actual berats that were issued to French subjects and protégés. In addition, summaries of these petitions, together with the imperial orders issued to local officials, were copied in bound registers for each nation (*Fransa ahkam defterleri*).[78]

Prior to the eighteenth century, the Mühimme Registers (registers of important affairs) contained summaries of petitions by European ambassadors and imperial orders in response to them. But they were sporadic and became systematic only in the eighteenth century, probably with the establishment of the Office of Chief Chancery, or the *reis ul-küttab,* which was in charge of foreign affairs (see chapter 4). Furthermore, the collection of imperial orders for Istanbul (*Istanbul ahkam defterleri*) is an important source for studying the activities of maritime traders, merchants, and artisans in Galata and greater Istanbul as well as disputes among artisans, guilds, and merchants that were submitted to the Imperial Council.[79]

Ottoman customs registers also offer details on the entry of foreign ships into Galata and their cargoes as well as on customs dues.[80] Customs revenues in Ottoman ports were farmed out to non-Muslims, mostly to Jews in Izmir and Galata. But in the eighteenth century, they were mostly farmed out to Ottoman elites (janissaries and merchants). Istanbul had several customs stations, including one in Galata. The study of Ottoman customs registers is still in a preliminary stage, but scholars have started using them to gain a better understanding of Ottoman commercial policies and an overall picture of trade not only with Europe but also with the Black Sea, India, and Iran.[81]

Correspondence between the members of the Levant Company in Ottoman ports and the Chamber of Commerce in Marseille is preserved in the archives of the Chamber of Commerce in Marseille. I have briefly explored these sources to compare them with Ottoman sources. They are invaluable documents on commercial transactions and bankruptcies of French merchants, but they do not shed much light on day-to-day activities and legal issues faced by French traders. The French ambassador also sent regular reports to the Chamber of Commerce in Marseille about the daily affairs of French subjects, most of the time regarding commercial affairs.[82] The Chamber in Marseille maintained systematic statistical data on French trade with the Levant based on the reports of the embassy in Istanbul as well as on files on the bankruptcies of merchant houses in the eighteenth century.[83] In addition, consular courts handled disputes among members of

European communities. The records of the secretariat of the embassy, the minutes of the assembly of the nation in Istanbul, and the correspondence of the ambassadors are kept in the archives of the city of Nantes.[84]

In addition, European (mostly French) embassy accounts offer great insights into the world of diplomacy in Pera while other European writers present views of life in the Ottoman Empire. The travel literature of the period has been the object of much scrutiny and critical analysis since Edward Said's seminal work on Orientalism.[85] However, this material must be approached with a great deal of caution since it often reflects the bias of European observers of the Ottoman Empire. French ambassadors and drago-mans like Antoine Galland kept official diaries about their interactions with the Sublime Porte as well as with local communities that were published later.[86] Moreover, European (primarily English) women offered an alterna-tive "gaze" on the Ottoman Empire since, due to their direct interactions with Ottoman women in the eighteenth century, their accounts were less sexualized than those of their male counterparts. However, as Mary Roberts has noted, English women had created their own "gaze" that reflected a hier-archical relationship with Ottoman women and fantastic narratives, some of which displayed a strong bias.[87] Therefore, we have to balance European nar-rative sources with Ottoman archival material to get a more accurate picture.

PART ONE

———————

The Urban Setting

THE FIRST PART OF THE BOOK will provide a historical background on
the rise of Galata as the European port of Istanbul since the Ottoman
Conquest of 1453. Galata's layered history as a Byzantine, Genoese, and
Ottoman port shaped its urban fabric as well as its social makeup and diversity. Chapter 1 will focus on the Ottoman takeover and transformation of
this port while chapter 2 will discuss the rise and development of Pera outside
the walls. Although the immediate impact of the Ottoman Conquest was
the flight of the Latin residents of Galata and the Ottoman confiscation of
their property, the sultan undertook a series of measures to rebuild Galata
and attract its population back to boost trade. At the same time, the Ottoman
state also created a Muslim space in Galata and imposed an Ottoman administration led by the *kadi* (Islamic judge). The suburb of Pera played the role of
a diplomatic as well as a commercial hub in the imperial capital as Galata
expanded to the north beyond the hills. The movement of the diplomatic
corps and European embassies to Pera was borne out of necessity as a response
to fires, plague, growing congestion, and crime in Galata inside the walls.
Pera became the center of the Ottoman modernization movement, in which
the European and Ottoman residents played a key role.

ONE

A Layered History

FROM A GENOESE COLONY TO AN OTTOMAN PORT

Galata is at the present the residence of many merchants of all nations[,] and the narrow streets are formed by shops and magazines for articles of European commerce. The circuit encloses four miles. Its pretended jurisdiction is claimed by the Venetians, whose ambassadors are styled "bailo" and whose public entrance through the gates is attended with a ceremony of presenting the keys. The lover of Gothic antiquity will discover with pleasure escutcheons of arms, and inscriptions in that character, placed against the walls. Imperfect remains only are now seen of the Genoese fort, from which the chain was drawn across to the Seraglio point, during the sieges, which happened in the reigns of Leo III, Michael II, and Constantine the last.

—JAMES DALLAWAY, *chaplain and physician to the British Embassy in Constantinople, 1797, 124.*[1]

JAMES DALLAWAY (1763–1834), THE CHAPLAIN to the English Embassy in Istanbul, described the Italian character of the European port of Galata in the late eighteenth century. He noted the pomp and ceremony in the entrance into Galata of the Venetian *bailo* (ambassador), a still-powerful figure despite the decline of Venice's influence at this time. Galata was the European port of Istanbul, the Ottoman imperial capital, and one of its four main districts: Istanbul proper, Galata, Eyüp, and Üsküdar.

The district of Galata included Galata inside the walls; Pera, on the hills outside the walls to the north; the neighborhoods of Tophane and Kasım Paşa, where the cannon foundry and the arsenal were located, and the villages along the European shore of the Bosphorus (see chapter 7). Compared with the rest of Istanbul, Galata had a distinct character as the former Genoese colony and the hub of European trade. In the popular imagination, however, it was the Frankish "sin city" with its taverns and brothels. As a

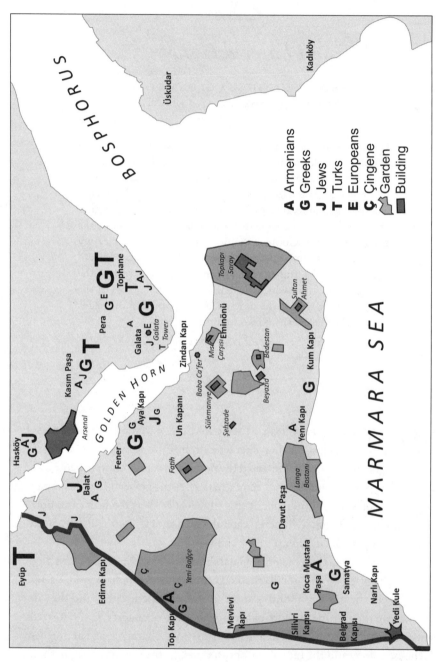

Greater Istanbul (4 Districts) and the ethnic composition of neighborhoods. Cartography by Paul Kaldjian, based on Mantran's maps of Istanbul (1962).

Antoine de Favray, *Panorama of Istanbul* (1773). Suna and Inan Kiraç Foundation Collection, © Uğur Ataç.

port, its harbor also contained the scale for oil, the customs house, the fish market, and a variety of workshops for artisans, a bedestan, *hans,* the market (loggia), and storage houses, making up the commercial district of Galata. The arsenal next door in Kasım Paşa and the cannon foundry in Tophane employed galley slaves of mostly European origins and convicts as well as sailors, artisans, and porters. Walls enclosed the town while gates shut down traffic in and of town at night. The Galata Tower, the physical symbol of the town, functioned as a storage house for wheat, a prison for indebted men, and a fire watch. It was repaired numerous times after major fires (see chapter 2).

This chapter will first briefly trace the history of Galata to the Byzantine period and the Latin Conquest of 1204 to provide some historical context and shed some light on the layered history of the town. The second part will examine continuity as well as change in the urban fabric, the district's ethno-religious makeup, and the administration of the port under Ottoman rule.

BETWEEN GENOA AND VENICE

Mediterranean ports like Galata functioned as centers of connectivity as well as conflict in the early modern period, depending on the ebb and flow of trade as well as diplomatic relations between trading nations. Since medieval times, the Byzantine as well as the Italian city-states had competed for control of ports like Constantinople proper and Galata that lay on strategic locations such as theirs at the confluence of the Black Sea and the Mediterranean. Constantinople had two major ports on both shores of the Golden Horn, one catering mainly to domestic trade and the other specializing in European trade during the early modern period.[2]

The ancient city of Byzantium was founded as a Greek city in 660 BC by Byzas, who had established a Greek colony on the first hill. The Greek city-state controlled the Bosphorus, the main crossing point that connected Asia to Europe. Roman Emperor Septimius Severus then conquered the city-state in 196 AD.[3] Later, Emperor Constantine I made it the capital of the Roman Empire in 330 AD. It became known as New Rome (Nova Roma) and was renamed Constantinople after the emperor's death in 337. Constantinople served as the capital of the Roman Empire (330–95), the Byzantine Empire (395–1204 and 1261–1453), the Latin (Roman) Empire (1204–61), and the Ottoman Empire (1453–1922). The Byzantine Empire adopted Christianity as its official religion in the fourth century and Greek as the official language in the seventh century; that situation continued with a brief Latin interregnum (1204–61) until the Ottoman Conquest in May 1453, when Islam became the official religion.

The ancient city was composed of two major settlements on the two shores of the Golden Horn, Constantinople proper and the smaller settlement of Sycae. Ancient Sycae (fig tree) was a small settlement in the fifth century located on the northern shore of the Golden Horn at its confluence with the Bosphorus, which connected it to the Black Sea to the north and the Mediterranean Sea to the south. Byzantine Emperor Justinian I renamed it Justinianopolis, or the "city of Justinian," in sixth century. He incorporated Sycae into his capital, Constantinople, as the VIII Region; enclosed it with walls (three meters in width); and gave it full rights.[4] Sycae was 37 acres in size and contained a harbor, forum, baths, theatre, and churches as well as a tower, called the Tower of Christ, which was built in 528 AD. Later in the century, Emperor Tiberius II (578–82 AD) built a fortress to protect the Golden Horn against enemy shipping.[5] The chain that closed off the Golden Horn to protect it against enemy shipping extended from Constantinople to Sycae. Sycae became known as Galata in the ninth century and was also called Pera ("beyond" in Greek). Pera was a Greek name that initially was used for the section of Galata inside the walls but later referred to the hills to the north. It became the diplomatic hub in the seventeenth century (see chapter 2).

During the High Middle Ages, the Italian city-states of Genoa and Venice dominated trade between the Christian West and the Byzantine Empire and carved out merchant colonies in the Mediterranean (Greek islands), on the Aegean Sea (i.e., Chios), and on the Black Sea coasts. The city-states vied for control of Constantinople proper and Galata as Byzantine military power declined in subsequent centuries.[6] The Italian city-states of Amalfi, Venice, Pisa, and Genoa enjoyed trading privileges in Constantinople proper on the southern shore of the Golden Horn (Eminönü) and in Galata from the mid-tenth century (944 AD) on. The Republic of Venice maintained a large and powerful fleet on the Adriatic Sea with large armed merchant galleys that could accommodate 150 tons of cargo and 200 sailors to carry merchants to Tana and Trebizond on the Black Sea.[7] In order to facilitate trade, Venice signed commercial treaties with the Byzantine Empire in 992 and in 1082 that provided the Venetian community with the exclusive privilege to trade in the main ports without having to pay customs dues. The treaty also provided the Venetians with a place to settle on the southern shore of the Golden Horn. The Venetian *bailo* resided in his own house in Bal Kapanı (Eminönü), and the Venetian community obtained the right to build churches, shops, houses, bakeries, and mills in the neighborhoods of Bal Kapanı and Tahtakale.[8] This area, which contained spice and food markets, was commercially very important. Slowly, small German, French, and Spanish communities also settled nearby. Jews were not allowed to settle in Constantinople proper and were confined to their own ghetto in Galata by Emperor Theodosius in the fifth century.[9] A small Jewish community, however, managed to settle in Eminönü (on the site of Yeni Cami) next to the Venetian community on the Golden Horn in the twelfth century. A Jewish community continued living in Galata by the Galata Tower as well.

Meanwhile, Genoese merchants had also obtained a concession from Byzantine Emperor Manuel I Comnenus (1143–80) to settle in Galata in 1155. Genoa established a colony in Galata to trade with Black Sea ports like Caffa in bulky goods like grains, dried fruits, beeswax, alum, cloth, furs, hides, spices, silks, and slaves.[10] Genoese merchants managed to negotiate with the emperor to establish an autonomous status for Galata, and they competed with Venice for control of maritime trade with the Mediterranean world.[11] Genoa and Venice were also involved in trade with the Ottoman principality as well as the principalities of Menteşe and Aydin, particularly in slaves.[12] The commercial rivalry between Genoa and Venice resulted in constant clashes and devastation to Galata and Constantinople proper. To punish Venice in

1171, Emperor Manuel Commnene (1143–80) evicted the Venetians from their quarter along the Golden Horn in Constantinople proper, where they had established themselves for a century.

In response, Venice launched attacks against Constantinople and the Greek islands and brought other Latin invaders to Constantinople and Galata during the Fourth Crusades in 1203–4. The crusaders stormed the castle of Galata in June 1203 and broke the chain that closed the entrance to the Golden Horn.[13] They set fire to parts of Galata, and the flames consumed the crowded Jewish quarter next to Galata Tower in July 1203. After this fire, Jews were forced to move from Galata back to their old quarter in Constantinople. Most Greeks from Galata were also forced to settle in Constantinople as a result of the Venetian destruction.[14] Afterward, the Venetian fleet launched a large assault on the sea walls of Constantinople in July 1203, capturing most of the defensive towers while the soldiers set fire to the houses inside the walls on the fifth hill. In August 1203, Latin forces also destroyed the Muslim quarter near the Church of St. Irene that was located between the Pisan and Venetian quarters.[15] Greek residents in turn set fire to the Pisan and Amalfian houses near the Venetian quarter on the Golden Horn.[16]

A great deal of destruction took place in both Constantinople proper and Galata as a result of these clashes as the Byzantine emperor lost his power as an autonomous ruler. After the attacks, the Latins released Emperor Isaac II from prison in August 1203 and restored him and his son Alexius IV to rule as their puppets. However, Alexius Ducas Comnenus won the throne as the legitimate ruler of the Byzantine Empire in January 1204 and ordered the Latin occupiers to leave Constantinople.

Latin forces led by Venice then attacked the city again in April 1204 and bombarded the land and sea walls, causing a fire that lasted for eight days and led to extensive damages. They began looting the abandoned houses on the fifth hill in Constantinople and burned the buildings along the Golden Horn.[17] The Latin crusaders sacked the city for three days, looting the great church of Haghia Sophia and transferring important treasures and relics to Venice and France. The fighting, the fires, and the Latin sack devastated extensive sections of Constantinople and Galata, destroying churches, monasteries, shops, markets, city walls, and private buildings. The extensive damage, the exodus of Greek residents, and the seizure of property by Latin forces halted economic life in the city as a whole from 1203 to 1204.

Once victorious, the Latins took control of the city, its governance, and its churches. Prior to the conquest, the Latin forces had agreed to divide

Constantinople and the empire (kingdom of Romans) into three major parts to be shared among the Latin emperor, the Venetians, and the other crusaders. They formed a committee of twelve and selected Baldwin of Flanders to be crowned as the Latin ruler of the empire in Haghia Sophia in May 1204. The new settlers occupied the houses that had been abandoned and converted a number of Greek Orthodox churches, including the church of St. Paul in Galata, to the Roman Catholic rite and put a Catholic patriarch in place. The Venetian *podesta,* Marino Zeno, made the Greek church of Pantokrator the seat of the Venetian administration, treasury, and judiciary after the Latin Conquest.[18] Later, the Franciscans established themselves in the city in 1220 and took over some of the Greek churches, such as St. Paul in Galata. Greek churches and monasteries had suffered extensively while their revenues and relics were transferred to churches in Venice like St. Marco. The Greek Orthodox clergy fled to Nicaea, one of the three remaining Byzantine provinces (Nicaea, Trebizond, Epirus) and did not return to Constantinople until the restoration of Byzantine rule in 1261.

When the Venetian army had left for an expedition on the Black Sea, leaving the walls undefended, a Byzantine force approached the walls of Constantinople in July 1261. They easily overcame the small Latin guard during the night and forced Baldwin II to escape on a Venetian ship. Michael VIII Palaeologus then entered the city triumphantly through the Golden Gate and marched to the Church of Haghia Sophia. He placed Arsenius on the patriarchal throne and was crowned as emperor on August 15, 1261.[19] After forcing the remaining crusading forces and residents (three thousand people) out of Constantinople, Michael VIII Palaeologus began rebuilding Constantinople and reviving the trade of Galata. He temporarily kicked the Genoese out of Galata since the podesta had been accused of cooperating with Sicily. The Genoese were settled in Constantinople proper at the Palace of Pantokrator, which the Venetians had turned into a fortress. But the Genoese eventually returned to Galata once peace had been restored.

In 1261, Emperor Michael Paleologus gave Galata as a partial grant to Genoa, with privileges once enjoyed by Venice, in return for its alliance against Venice.[20] The emperor also signed the defensive Treaty of Nymphaeum with Genoa against the common enemy, Venice, in 1261 (see chapter 4). This treaty aided the creation of Genoese commercial colonies in Galata as well as on the island of Chios on the Aegean Sea and in the port of Caffa on the Black Sea. In these ports, the Genoese traders could own markets, houses, churches, shops, and bakeries and have their own consul in Galata to oversee the affairs of Genoese colonies. From 1267 on, the Genoese became the dominant force in Galata and shaped its institutions and commercial life as well as the religious character of Galata, which almost became a "state within a state."

The Venetians managed to negotiate a similar commercial treaty in 1277, which allowed them to return to their old quarter (Bal Kapanı) on the Golden Horn in Constantinople and to own houses, shops, workshops, mills, bakeries, churches, and cemeteries.[21] The Venetian bailo continued to reside in Constantinople proper and represented the *Doge* for a term of two years. The bailo and the Council of Twelve were in charge of all the Venetian colonies in the East. They also collected taxes and settled disputes within the community. In other words, both the Genoese and Venetian colonies managed to negotiate important privileges with the Byzantine emperor and carved out important spaces across both shores of the Golden Horn. The Genoese held Galata as their chief colony.

A GENOESE ENCLAVE

Galata became a Genoese enclave, and its trade thrived in the fourteenth century. When Ibn Battuta, the North African traveler, visited Constantinople and Galata in 1334, he was impressed by the size of the harbor and diversity of Galata, which he described in the following manner:

> The second part [of Constantinople], on the western flank of the river[,] is called Galata and is reserved [for] the Frankish Christians who dwell there. They are of different kinds, including Genoese, Venetians, Romans[,] and people of France; they are subject to the authority of the king of Constantinople, who sets over them one of their own number[,] of whom they approve, and him they call the Comes. They are bound to pay a tax every year to the king of Constantinople, but often they revolt against him[,] and he makes war on them until the Pope makes peace between them. They are all men of commerce[,] and their harbor is one of the largest in the world; I saw there about a hundred galleys and other large ships, and the small ships were too many to be counted (Ibn Battuta, *Travels in Asia and Africa, 1325–54*).[22]

Ibn Battuta also noted the Italian and European residents of Galata but underlined the constant tensions between them and the Byzantine ruler, who collected an annual tribute from them. However, the old rivalry over commercial rights between the two city-states continued as Genoa and Venice got involved in new clashes in Constantinople and Galata a few decades later. The

Venetians set fire to the Genoese commercial settlements in Galata and Caffa in July 1296. To protect Galata against Venetian assaults, the Genoese obtained the right from the Byzantine ruler to construct a moat around Galata in 1303–04 but were not allowed to build fortifications.[23] The *Statuti de Pera/Genoa* (Status of Pera/Genoa) reconfirmed the autonomous status of Genoese Galata in 1304 and allowed for the building of meat and flour markets, loggia, baths, and churches in an area between Bankers' Street and Karaköy. Genoa also took possession of the island of Chios and constructed fortifications there and around Galata between 1316 and 1349. The Genoese migration to Galata increased as Genoese commercial activities grew, adding to a population of around two thousand Genoese and Greeks in the fourteenth century.[24] In addition, smaller communities of Catalans, Pisans, Florentines, and Ragusans also lived Galata.[25] The trade of Galata grew so much that it surpassed that of Constantinople by a ratio of about seven to one in the fourteenth century.[26]

The number of Latin Christians grew to several thousand in Constantinople and Galata before the Ottoman Conquest in 1453.[27] Galata acquired an Italian character and had seven Catholic churches: St. Francesco, St. Paul and St. Domenco (one church), St. Peter (or St. Pierre), St. Antonio, St. Benoit, St. Jean Baptiste, and St. Nicolas during the rule of Alexis Commnene.[28] It also had a number of Greek Orthodox churches, such as Ayios Dimitrios and Ayios Ioannis.[29] The podesta, who was appointed by the senate in Genoa every year, acted as the governor of Galata. He resided in his *Palazzo del Commune* (municipality palace), which was built in 1316 on Bankers' Street (the site of the Ottoman Bank). The Genoese expanded Galata to the northwest, constructed the Galata Tower, and enclosed the new expanded zones in 1387 and 1397, although they were prohibited from fortifying them.[30] Some of the gates bore the coat of arms of Genoa and the podesta of Galata, which survived until the second half of the nineteenth century, when the walls were torn down. The wealthy Genoese families formed the ruling class in Galata, while most of the artisans, accountants, fishermen, laborers in the arsenal, and shopkeepers in Galata were Greek.

In addition, the Genoese in Galata formed commercial ties with some Turkish principalities like Menteşe and Aydin. The rise of Turkish principalities all over Anatolia undermined Byzantine control in the fourteenth century. Genoa turned to the Turkish principalities of Menteşe in 1311 and Aydin in 1351, which controlled western Anatolia, for alliance against Venice and Rhodes. In addition, Genoa also signed a treaty of friendship with the ruler of the Ottoman principality, Sultan Murad I, in 1352 and 1387, largely dictated from its colonies in Chios and Galata.[31] In the Treaty (*ahdname*) of 1352 with the Ottoman principality, the Genoese agreed to return Turkish slaves and captives of war to the Ottomans.[32] Just as the Byzantine emperors had done, Muslim rulers signed treaties of friendship with their Christian allies that also contained commercial as well as legal rights.

Genoa refused to join an anti-Turkish alliance called for by the Pope in 1362. Therefore, Emperor John V Palaeologus declared a union of Greek and Roman churches in October 1367 to gain the support of the Papacy against the expansion of the Ottoman Turks. However, the Ottoman victory over Serbia in 1389 and Sultan Bayezid's defeat of the crusading army in Nicopolis (Bulgaria) in 1396 tipped the balance in favor of the Ottomans in the Balkans.

The successful expansion of the Ottoman principality in the Balkans changed the balance of power in the remaining Byzantine territories. The Ottoman principality had established a naval and military presence on the Bosphorus and had moved very close to the walls of Constantinople in the early fifteenth century. Sultan Bayezid I (1385–1402) built the fortress of Anadolu Hisari on the Asian side of the Bosphorus and laid siege to Constantinople in 1394.

Emperor John VIII appealed to Latin Europe for military help and began promoting Christian unity at the Council of Florence. In 1396, the Hungarian king, Sigismond, led a huge crusading army to liberate Constantinople from Ottoman siege. Bayezid I defeated the Crusaders near Nicopolis in September 1396, an outcome that forced the Byzantine emperor to make peace with the Ottoman sultan. The Byzantine emperor agreed to pay an annual tribute of 10,000 gold coins to the Ottomans and allowed the establishment of a Turkish neighborhood and an Ottoman mosque and kadi in Constantinople proper.[33]

Constantinople was the most important target of Ottoman expansion. However, Timur's defeat of Bayezid in 1402 saved Constantinople from further Ottoman incursions for half a century as the Ottoman presence in Anatolia had been weakened and the long siege lifted. After an eleven-year interregnum and civil wars among three Ottoman princes, Sultan Mehmed I (1413–20) and his son Murad II (1420–44; 1446–51) reconstituted the Ottoman state in the Balkans and conquered Salonica in 1430. After twenty years of warfare, Sultan Murad II abdicated in favor of his twelve-year-old son, Mehmed II, in 1444. But Murad II was recalled to the throne by Grand Vizier Çandarli Halil when a crusading army composed of Hungary, Venice, and Wallachia threatened the Ottoman state. Sultan Murad II defeated the crusading army in Varna in 1444 and took over the throne from his son Mehmed II in 1446 for another five years after a janissary revolt against his son.

As Byzantine power receded further, Genoa sought an alliance with the Ottoman state, which was now based in Edirne. Francesco Draperio, a wealthy member of the community who had a large commercial cartel of alum trade that spread as far as Chios, acted as the ambassador of the community in Galata to the Ottoman sultan. He had negotiated the renewal of the treaty (ahdname) with both Sultan Bayezid I and Sultan Murad II in 1446. The Genoese-Ottoman friendship was now established on stable ground and protected the commercial interests of the large merchant families in Galata. For the Ottomans, the neutrality of these merchants or their alliance in the upcoming war was very important.

THE OTTOMAN CONQUEST

When Mehmed II ascended the throne in 1451, he had reached a decision to conquer Constantinople and get rid of the Byzantine ruler, who had called for another crusade against the Ottomans. Sultan Mehmed II was determined to take Constantinople to strengthen his own position and legitimacy and to secure the future of the Ottoman state. After having invited the Byzantine emperor three times to surrender and avoid pillage and the Ottoman sacking of the city, Mehmed II decided the take the city by force when the emperor again refused his offer.[34] Grand Vizier Çandarlı Halil opposed this plan in the name of peace with the Byzantines. But the sultan's close adviser, Zaganos Mehmed Pasha, was in favor of the conquest of Constantinople. However, there was some disagreement among the Genoese in Galata regarding the policy toward the Ottomans. As the Ottoman threat to Constantinople became real, the Genoese podesta in Galata sent seventy-four Genoese merchants to Chios with money to mobilize and recruit mercenaries in May 1452.

Mehmed II started building the large fortress of Rumelı Hisari on the European shore of the Bosphorus across the Anadolu Hisari (built by Bayezid II) and placed cannons in both to prevent the passage of ships and the arrival of provisions from the Black Sea. He increased the number of janissaries from five thousand to ten thousand. His Hungarian engineer, Urban, constructed large cannons. With a fortified new fleet and heavy artillery, Mehmed II laid siege to the city with a force of seventy thousand soldiers on April 2, 1453. The siege lasted for fifty-four days until the city was taken on May 29, 1453.

The Genoese had supplied the defensive forces with soldiers and food but declared their neutrality after they had witnessed the inevitable Ottoman victory on May 29, 1453. According to Islamic law and European practice, once a city had been taken by force, its population could be reduced to slavery, and the city could be subjected to plunder for three days. Mehmed II, however, stopped the sacking of the city on the evening of the first day, having witnessed the level of destruction by the janissaries. The sultan seized all the buildings and walls (the unmovable property) and took one-fifth of the movable property.[35] The rest of the movable property was divided among the ruling class (viziers), sufi şeyhs like his mentor Şeyh Ak Şemseddin, soldiers, and the grandees who rented the properties and established charitable foundations.

Moreover, around fifty thousand residents, including women and children, had been taken as prisoners of war. The sultan freed many of the enslaved population, gave them free houses, and exempted them from taxes for one year.[36] He also ordered the execution of some members of the Byzantine aristocracy and took others under his employment. Tursun Beg, who was a secretary in the sultan's council and present during the siege, conducted a survey of all the houses and shops in Istanbul and Galata in 1455.[37] The sultan settled Turks from Anatolia in Üsküdar, Greeks from the Morea in Fener, Jews from Salonica and Safed in Hasköy, and war captives from Iran in the Mahmud Pasha neighborhood (after the Battle of Başkent in 1474).[38] He also invited many merchants from all over Anatolia to settle in the city and constructed markets and caravanserais for them to revive the economy.[39]

The fate of Galata followed a slightly different trajectory from that of Constantinople proper. While some Genoese families like the Draperios were reaching out to Mehmed II, others like the Spinola family were providing funds to the Byzantine Emperor Constantine XI.[40] Two days after the conquest of Constantinople, Podesta Angelo Lomellino sent Mehmed II the keys to Galata and sent a report to Genoa about the takeover of the city by the Ottomans in June 1, 1453.[41] There is no doubt that the report about the Ottoman takeover of the city created a panic, forcing the podesta to reach an agreement with the sultan.[42] The podesta sent two envoys to the sultan to express his cordial congratulations and to negotiate the confirmation of the treaty that the Genoese in Galata had negotiated with the Byzantine rulers (the Treaty of Nymphaeum). According to Islamic law, the Christian inhabitants of a city or town who surrendered peacefully could acquire the status of *zimmi,* Ottoman non-Muslim subjects, which required that the Islamic state protect their lives and property and allow for the free practice of their religion once they had agreed to pay the poll tax. The sultan sent his Greek minister, Zaganos Pasha, to negotiate the terms of the peace treaty (ahdname), which the latter drew up in Greek[43] (see chapter 3).

On June 1, 1453, the sultan accorded the Latin community in Galata an imperial order for the formation of the *Magnifica Communita di Pera,* followed by an ahdname/capitulation that granted them commercial, fiscal, and religious rights.[44] In the ahdname, the sultan promised not to reduce the fortress of Galata, convert its churches to mosques, take over the property, or enslave its population (see chapter 3). The ahdname was a crucial step in guaranteeing the peaceful takeover of Galata and protecting the status of most of its Latin churches.

OTTOMAN ADMINISTRATION

There is an ongoing debate about the nature of the Ottoman conquest of Galata and the policies of Mehmed II in the transformation of the former Genoese colony into an Ottoman port. While most historians have concentrated on the study of the conquest and the transformation of Constantinople proper, the Ottoman takeover of Galata has received much less attention.[45] The Ottoman administration of Galata was based on the following major principles: 1. establishing Ottoman control over Galata and the abandoned property, 2. negotiating the rights of Latin and European communities in Galata through treaties known as *ahdnames* (and as *capitulations* in the West) to revive the economy, 3. settling Ottoman subjects from all over the empire as well as Moriscos and Jews from the Iberian peninsula, 4. creating an Ottoman administrative structure, 5. converting some major Latin churches into mosques to create a Muslim space for Morisco refugees, and 6. investing in the commercial infrastructure of Galata to make it one of the most important ports of trade with the Black Sea and Europe.

On June 3, 1453, the sultan visited Galata and ordered the inhabitants to lay down their arms. The Ottoman forces then entered the houses and shops of those who had fled and confiscated the abandoned property for the state. Before returning to Edirne on June 18, he ordered that part of the land walls of Galata be demolished, leaving the sea walls intact.[46]

Lomellino stepped down from his post as the Genoese podesta but remained in charge of the community until September 1453, when he returned to Genoa.[47] He helped the sultan in inviting back the Latin community that had fled from Galata. The Genoese community, led by Tommaso Spinola, could select a steward (*kethüda*) to mediate its affairs with Ottoman officials like the kadi, according to the Ahdname of 1453. They selected Pietro de Gravaga as the new head of the community.[48] The Draperio family continued to live in the old quarter of Drapoza and became Ottoman subjects while the Spinola family maintained its ties to Genoa.

Although many Genoese had also fled in panic, the Venetian community received worse treatment at the hands of Sultan Mehmed II. The sultan ordered the execution of the Venetian bailo, Minotto, and his son for having aided the Byzantine forces.[49] Moreover, twenty-nine Venetians were taken into captivity and became part of the sultan's palace pages.[50] Bartolomeo Marcello, the new envoy of the Doge, who was very apologetic for the alliance with Byzantine forces, managed to sign an ahdname with the sultan in late April 1454 that allowed Venice to maintain an ambassador (bailo) for two years in Istanbul and allowed Venetian citizens to enjoy freedom of trade and keep their possession in Negroponte (see chapter 3).[51] The old Venetian neighborhood in Bal Kapanı in Constantinople proper became the center of the new Turkish settlement and Muslim quarters that were part of the Fatih *vakfiyye* (an Islamic charitable foundation).[52]

It is clear that the Ottoman Conquest of Constantinople and takeover of Galata ended the Latin control of Galata and imposed an Ottoman administration over it while allowing it to retain some of the commercial and legal rights of an Italian city-state. For example, the Genoese lost the extraterritorial rights that they had enjoyed under Byzantine rule. They now had to pay customs dues on imports and exports and pay the poll tax if they became Ottoman subjects. Moreover, Mehmed II ended the Genoese domination of the Black Sea trade in 1475 after he took control of Caffa. The Genoese lost their control of the island of Chios in 1566 and of Caffa in 1575.

David Abulafia may be correct in stating that the aim of Mehmed II was to restore rather than destroy the Byzantine Empire by taking Constantinople and ending the Venetian control of the Morea and the Genoese domination of Galata and the Black Sea.[53] The Ahdname of 1453 drew a distinction between two groups of Genoese, those who lived in Galata permanently and became Ottoman subjects (*reaya*) and who were liable to pay the poll tax and the Genoese merchants who did not pay personal taxes but paid customs dues. A third group made up of captives could be ransomed and freed. A core Genoese community of about two-dozen families (such as the Draperii, Fornetti, and Testa families) remained in Galata permanently as Ottoman subjects and organized the Council of Twelve that became the *Magnifica Communita*.[54] While the Spinola family had old ties to Genoa, the Draperio family lacked solid ties to the city. Many Genoese merchants like Tommaso Spinola were also active in the Bursa silk trade and on Caffa and Chios. The Council was elected from among the community and held authority over communal and religious affairs. It replaced the authority of the podesta and met regularly at the church of St. Francesco to oversee the affairs of Latin churches.[55] Dursteler has argued that although Mehmed II placed the Council under the authority of Ottoman officials, the community gained a fair degree of autonomy in its daily life.[56] Mehmed II moved all the European communities to Galata sometime between 1453 and 1499.[57]

In an attempt to gain central control over Galata, Mehmed II appointed a *voyvoda,* a *kadi* (Islamic judge), a *subaşı* (chief of day police), a *muhtesib* (market inspector), and a customs collector to oversee the social, legal, and fiscal affairs of Galata.[58] The voyvoda, who functioned like the mayor of Galata, had executive authority and worked with the kadi of Galata, who was the most important Ottoman urban and judicial official.

The Ottoman state divided greater Istanbul into four main judgeships: Istanbul proper, Galata, Üsküdar, and Eyüp. In each district, the kadi represented the most important state and urban authority and had under his jurisdiction his deputies, the chief of day police, the chief of night police, the market inspector, and the various tax collectors as well as other officials. The kadi of Galata had forty-four deputy judges under his jurisdictions who served in Tophane, Kasım Paşa, Hasköy, Beşiktaş and the villages on the European shore of the Bosphorus as well as on the islands of Marmara, Erdek, Mudanya, and Piri Paşa. He held court at the heart of the new Muslim neighborhood next to the Arab Cami'i. The kadi oversaw the affairs of the Muslim community and European diplomatic and trading communities as well as those of non-Muslim residents, their legal disputes with Ottoman subjects, and any breach of Ottoman law.[59]

All the European merchants were required to register their commercial transactions in the kadi's court and to submit any lawsuits with Ottoman subjects involving an amount below 4,000 *akçe* to the kadi's court. The kadi kept a copy of the Qur'an, the Bible, and the Old Testament in the court.[60] The kadi also oversaw the settlement of Ottoman and foreign communities in Galata and issued permission for their members to purchase property (see chapter 6).

In addition, the kadi oversaw the affairs of Ottoman merchants and guildsmen. He appointed a market inspector *(muhtesib)* to inspect prices, weights, and

The Galata Tower, Constantinople, Turkey. Keystone-Mast Collection, UCR/California Museum of Photography, University of California, Riverside.

scales in the marketplace; to ensure the timely distribution of raw materials like grains to bakers; and to prevent fraud. The chief of day police (*subaşı*) arrested criminals during the day, while the night watch (*asesbaşı*) was in charge of punishing criminals at night.[61] The *mumcu,* a special division of the janissaries, kept order in the taverns. In addition, another special division of the janissaries, together with the *subaşı* and *asesbaşı,* had several hundred armed men and was in charge of law and order day and night in crime-ridden Galata. In the seventeenth century, Galata became part of the endowments of the Sultan Ahmet I Mosque and thus fell under the jurisdiction of the Chief Black Eunuch.[62]

Sultan Bayezid II fully restored the outer walls of Galata in the late fifteenth century. Matrakçı's map of 1537 shows the inner and outer walls of Galata, which completely encircled the town.[63] Moreover, Piri Reis's map of Galata in *Kitab-i Bahriye* depicts a well-populated town with inner and full outer walls in the mid-sixteenth century.[64] Evliya Çelebi described Galata in the seventeenth century as a fortress town with inner and outer walls and numerous gates that closed at night. The Galata Tower (67 meters high and 26.45 meters wide), which had been built by the Genoese in 1348–49 to defend the town, burned several times during the great fires and was reconstructed in the seventeenth, eighteenth, and nineteenth centuries. Takiuddin, the famous Ottoman astronomer, used the upper floor of the tower as an observation point during the second half of the sixteenth century.[65] The main observatory was in Pera, where the French embassy was built. The Galata Tower also later served as a fire watchtower in the nineteenth century.

OTTOMAN SETTLEMENT POLICIES

The Ottoman sultans followed a different policy of settlement toward Galata than they did in the rest of the city since the sultan wanted to maintain and even enhance the role of Galata as a European port city. At the same time, he wanted to create a Muslim space in Galata to gain control of the port and allow the settlement of Morisco refugees. However, the process of Islamization in Galata was very gradual and more limited than it was in the rest of the city. The Ottoman surveys of 1455 and 1478 make this point very clear.

The Ottoman surveys of the city right after the Ottoman Conquest in 1455 and in the sixteenth century (1540 and 1545), *vakf* registers (1471, 1475, 1481), and Islamic court records of Galata from the sixteenth century have begun to shed some light on the demographic transformation of Galata under Ottoman rule.[66] The sultan ordered a survey of Galata and Istanbul on June 3, 1455, to determine the status of the property (empty, occupied) and the tax status (zimmi versus foreign) of the remaining residents.[67] The survey of 1455, which has survived with some missing pages, lists around 908 houses in 25 quarters and 1,108 individuals in Galata.[68] The survey also lists 23 churches, two monasteries, and one synagogue in Galata in 1455.[69]

At the same time, the sultan did not want to alter the Italian character of the former Genoese colony too much and left intact the *Magnifica Communita di Pera* (Genoese Council).[70] After the Conquest of 1453, the sultan dispatched messengers to Chios, where many Genoese had fled, inviting them to return within three months and retake possession of their property. Mehmed II provided tax exemptions for the old Latin subjects who had returned and issued several orders to the kadi of Galata on the exemption from taxes for local and foreign Latin communities who had returned or who had stayed on and had become Ottoman subjects.[71]

The Ottoman state had taken possession of some of the abandoned properties and rented them out. According to the published survey of 1455, of the total number of 908 houses listed in the 1455 survey, 89 (10 percent) had been taken over by the treasury, and 45 (5 percent) had been rented out to new occupants. Moreover, of 1,108 individuals listed as living in Galata in 1455, 352 (one-third) were exempt from the *cizye* (poll tax) due to their status as poor or because they had remained Latin subjects. Many poor men and widowed women occupied the houses and received exemption from the *cizye*. The sultan also settled by force war captives, slaves, and people from all over the empire without any religious discrimination and gave them houses to rent and exemption from paying taxes if they were poor.[72]

The Jewish quarter contained two churches and thirty-five houses of rich Jews like the physician Istori as well as Armenians and Greeks.[73] The Armenians also had their own quarter. In addition, members of the Ottoman ruling class and religious figures like Aşıkpaşazade occupied some Genoese houses and shops in Galata.[74] The treasury collected more than one hundred million akçes in rents from abandoned properties in Istanbul and Galata in 1455.[75]

As the Genoese regained their positions in Galata and reclaimed their properties, business resumed between the ports of Caffa, Galata, and Chios. According to notarial records in Galata, shortly after the conquest, many Genoese were involved in forming partnerships, conducting business transactions, trading with the three ports, establishing credit networks, resolving legal disputes, and even conducting marriage ceremonies.[76] Many were involved in the sale and purchase of their own slaves (Circassian and Russian) and those captured by the Ottoman forces during the conquest of Constantinople. The Genoese retained ownership of their shops and houses along the Loggia as well as the churches of San Francesco and San Michele. Nasuh Matrakçi's map of 1537 shows a few Latin churches and a large cathedral (possibly San Francesco) in the central ward of Galata, where the Genoese resided.[77]

Two decades after the conquest, the vakf register of 1478 shows that Galata inside the walls had 592 Greek households (39 percent), 535 Muslim households (35 percent), 332 Catholic/Latin households (22 percent), and 62 Armenians (4 percent), totaling 1,521 households. However, the size of the Latin Catholic (foreign) community shrank from 332 in 1478 to 74 in 1545.[78] Muslim settlement had grown from a handful of residents in 1455 to 535 households in 1478 that made up one-third of the population. In Istanbul proper, Muslims made up a little more than half of the population in 1478.[79]

The number of Greek households in Galata dropped from 592 households in 1478 to 77 households in 1545. But the number of Armenians grew slightly from 62 households in 1478 to 89 households in 1545. Sultan Mehmet took the Genoese ports of Amasra and Caffa in 1475, winning complete control of the Black Sea.[80] Numerous refugees (seven hundred families) fled from Caffa to Istanbul and Galata, settling around the churches of Santa Maria and St. Nicolas in a separate neighborhood called "Little Caffa." Many Karaim Jews also fled Caffa and settled in Galata in an area that became known as Karaköy (Karai village, or "black village"). The survey of 1478 did not list any Jewish households in Galata, but it listed 1,647 Jewish households in Istanbul proper. According to Inalcik, between 1477 and 1492, 390 new Jewish families, mostly from the Iberian Peninsula, had settled in greater Istanbul.[81] Moreover, the earliest sicils (Islamic court registers) of Galata show Jewish residents who had come to the court of Galata in the first half of the sixteenth century.[82] The survey of 1540 listed 22 Jewish households in Galata, and the 1545 survey listed 19.[83] The size of Jewish settlement was growing in Galata with the settlement of Marranos from the Iberian Peninsula.

ETHNO-RELIGIOUS COMPOSITION

The city has eighteen Muslim quarters, seventy quarters of Greek infidels, three of cranky Franks, one of Jews, and two of Armenians. No infidels reside in the first castle, and none at all in the second castle as far as the Arab mosque. Aside from these two castles, the two walled areas of Galata as far as Tophane are filled with Franks of the seven kings (i.e., from the Habsburg [sic] Empire) and other Christians. According to the survey of Murad Khan (IV), there are 200,000 infidels and 64,000 Muslims. May God preserve it.

—EVLIYA ÇELEBI, Seyahatnamesi, vol. 1[84]

By the mid-seventeenth century, Galata was a well-populated fortress town with complete outer and inner walls and gates that divided the town into a Muslim ward (castle) and three Christian wards.[85] In the seventeenth century, Evliya Çelebi counted seventeen Greek quarters, eighteen Muslim quarters that concentrated from the Arab Cami'i to Azap Kapı, three Latin quarters stretching from the third and fourth castle to Tophane, two Armenian quarters, and one Jewish quarter. He estimated the total Christian population of Galata at 200,000, while Muslim residents were 64,000.[86] However, this estimate (264,000 residents) may be too large for Galata intramural and may have included the population of Pera or Beyoğlu outside the walls as well.

After the normalization of the Ottoman Empire's relations with Venice and the signing of ahdnames with Venice and other Italian city-states, the size of Galata's Latin community increased to between 300 and 400 people in the sixteenth century (see chapter 3). The size of the European community at large and its embassies and staff grew in 1606 to around 3,000, most of whom settled in Pera (see chapter 2).[87] The Latin community lived in the central ward close to Galata Tower. In the seventeenth century, this ward was full of masonry houses built on checkerboard streets that stretched from Galata Tower down to the sea walls.

Greeks made up the majority of the population of Galata after the conquest.[88] According to the survey of 1455, the Greeks lived in the outer ward of Galata close to Tophane and to the north of the Karaköy and Mumhane Gates on the harbor. The Islamic law accorded the Christian and Jewish subject communities that had submitted peacefully and accepted Muslim rule certain rights as "People of the Book" that included protection, freedom of worship, and legal and religious autonomy in return for payment of the poll tax. Nonetheless, they were still second-class citizens who did not enjoy political office and were banned from the military. When Mehmed II appointed Gennadius as the patriarch of the Greek community, the community received a charter to practice its religion freely and have its own law courts under the jurisdiction of the Grand Patriarchate in return for peaceful submission and payment of the poll tax. Members of the Greek clergy enjoyed a tax-exempt status, and their religious places could acquire the status of vakf, with properties attached to them that paid taxes to the endowments. The Patriarchate basically functioned as a small kingdom within the empire with its own church council, jurisdiction over all the Greek Orthodox subjects, the right to collect taxes, and the right to enjoy considerable administrative

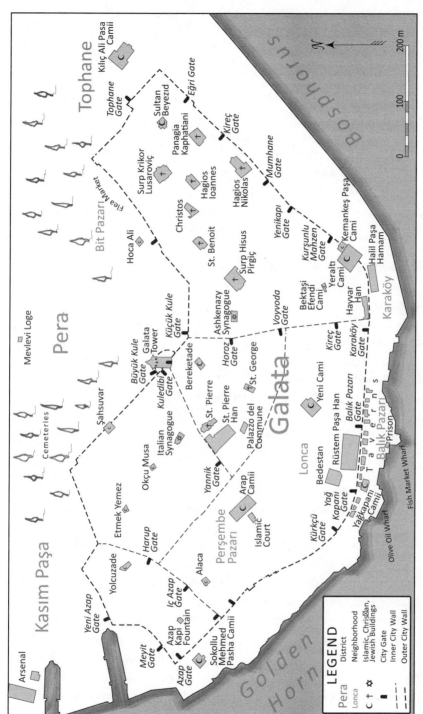

Galata in the early modern period. Cartography by Paul Kaldjian.

and legal autonomy from the central government. The chief Greek and Armenian Orthodox patriarchs as well as the chief rabbi resided in Istanbul and exercised great authority over their communities all over the empire.[89]

The Armenian and Jewish (People of the Book) communities received similar rights as non-Muslim (*zimmi*) subjects of the sultan and were placed under the spiritual and legal jurisdiction of the Armenian Orthodox patriarch and the chief rabbi, respectively. As zimmi communities, they paid lower customs taxes (4 percent) than those paid by European traders in the international trade. The Armenians were settled from Caffa and lived predominantly in the quarters next to the Jewish quarter to the east of Galata.[90] Evliya Çelebi counted three Armenian churches in Galata in the seventeenth century.[91] In 1391, the Armenians from Caffa had constructed the oldest Armenian church, that of St. Gregory the Illuminator, in Galata.[92] It burned down in the Great Galata Fire and was rebuilt in 1733 (see appendix).[93]

Galata also had had a small Romaniot Jewish community since the Byzantine period. These Jews predominantly lived near the Yüksek Kaldırım and close to the church of St. Benoit and Galata Tower. A small Romaniot Jewish community also was living near Karaköy at the time of the 1455 survey.[94] Some Jewish residents may have been forcefully transferred to the old Jewish neighborhood in Eminönü and Balat to make room for Turkish and Morisco settlers in Galata.[95] In addition, some Jewish communities from Crimea and Edirne were forced to settle in greater Istanbul later in the century.

The flow of Iberian Jews after 1492 and their settlement in Istanbul, Galata, Salonica, Izmir, and other Ottoman cities and towns enhanced the diversity of Ottoman ports in the early modern period. However, Romaniot Jews did not initially welcome Iberian Jews and closed down their synagogues.[96] In the sixteenth century, Spanish Jews settled first in the old neighborhoods on both shores of the Golden Horn, like the Eminönü area and Hasköy, while Portuguese Jews of Christian background (Marranos) settled in Galata since they were familiar with the Latin culture and spoke Ladino in the mid-sixteenth century.[97] The survey of 1545 listed 19 Jewish households in Galata and 121 households in Istanbul.[98] With an increase in the Jewish population, the state issued orders to the kadi of Istanbul in March 1566 to appoint 20 well to-do Jewish butchers in special shops to serve the community and to prevent them from slaughtering sheep in public spaces.[99] By the end of the sixteenth century, Iberian (Sephardic) Jews made up 40 percent of the Jewish population in Istanbul and were divided into their own communities, usually on the basis of their place of origin.[100] For example, the poll tax register of 1609 listed 786 Iberian Jewish residents (*nefer*) of high, middle, and low income who had come to Istanbul from Portugal (85), Aragon (93), Catalonia (50), Sicily (80), and other places.[101] The flow of Iberian Jews continued in the seventeenth century. In 1688, Sephardic Jews made up 60 percent of the Jewish population in Istanbul.[102]

Jews lived in their own neighborhoods, which were sometimes mixed, but there were no ghettos in Istanbul that confined Jews to certain quarters and imposed restrictions on their movements.[103] For example, in 1691, the majority of the 5,265 Jewish households in greater Istanbul lived in Balat and Fener (1,552), Galata and Tophane (1,229), and Hasköy (592). One-fifth of Jewish households (1,229) in greater Istanbul lived in Galata and Tophane. Of this number, 63 households had high income, 315 had middle income, and 851 households had low income.[104] Contrary to common perceptions, the majority of Jewish households in Galata and Tophane were of low income. Fewer than 20 percent of the families were listed as high income.

Galata and Tophane housed a larger number of Jews than Hasköy did. The Jewish population of the villages of Ortaköy (637 households), Beşiktaş (123 households), Kuruçesme (128 households), and Kuzkuncuk (110 households) on the European and Asian shores of the Bosphorus was growing quickly (637 households), a trend that signaled the rise of the Jewish bourgeoisie who operated as dealers of fine woolens (*çuha*), bankers, and tax farmers of customs dues in Galata. They had a wide commercial network in Mediterranean ports stretching from Istanbul, Izmir, and Salonica to Venice, Livorno, Marseille, and Amsterdam, making them indispensable as intermediaries in the East-West trade.[105] In the seventeenth century, Evliya Çelebi counted one Jewish quarter and two synagogues in Galata, one near Galata Tower and another in Karaköy. According to the author, the Jewish community kept an armed guard for fear of being attacked by Christians (Latins), possibly due to members' experiences of forceful conversion and expulsion from Spain and Portugal.[106] As well, the number of synagogues increased to six in Galata and Pera as the number of Jewish residents grew in the eighteenth and nineteenth centuries.[107]

THE CONVERSION OF LATIN
CHURCHES INTO MOSQUES

> Galata is a large enough town vis-à-vis Istanbul, from which is it separated by the port. It was a former Genoese town and quite considerable. The houses are beautiful and well built, where a good number of Greeks and Franks reside. There are five Latin/ Catholic churches in Galata: the church of Santa Maria (that belongs to the Cordeliers), and the churches of St. Francis, St. Peter (that belongs to Jacobins), St. Benoit (that belongs to Jesuits), and St. George (that belongs to Capuchins).
>
> —JEAN THÉVENOT, *L'empire du grand Turc*[108]

Jean Thévenot, a French traveler who embarked on his journey to Istanbul and the Levant after Minister Colbert's creation of the School of Oriental Languages (*école des jeunes de langue*) in Paris, left a detailed account of the government, administration, and urban institutions in Istanbul in the second half of the seventeenth century. He noted the Greek and European population of Galata and the number of Latin churches. This number had decreased from six to five due to Mehmed II's conversion of the major Cathedral of St. Domenco to a mosque.

Sultan Mehmed II followed a policy of accommodation and appeasement toward the Latin community after its peaceful submission. No doubt under pressure from more conservative forces, he had to create a Muslim presence in Galata in order to administer it more effectively. Contrary to his pledge in the Ahdname of 1453 not to convert any churches into mosques, he decided to convert the main Catholic cathedral into a mosque quite late in his rule.

As in the creation of the sacred district of Eyüp, where Şeyh Ak Şemseddin had located the tomb of one of the companions of the Prophet Muhammad (Eyüp al-Ansari), Ottoman Muslim legend had also located a mosque in Galata. According to this legend, one of the Umayyad commanders by the name of Mesleme bin Abdulmelik had built the Arab Cami'i in Galata during the siege in 716–17. The legend also held that this mosque supposedly was later converted to the Latin Church of St. Paul and St. Domenco during the Latin rule (1204–61).[109] It appears that this legend was used to justify the conversion of the Latin cathedral into a mosque to create a space for the settlement of Moriscos.[110] This legend had become quite popular by the mid-seventeenth century since Evliya Çelebi had also presented it as evidence of the origins of the Arab Cami'i in his *Seyahatname*.[111] The architecture of the Arab Cami'i is quite similar to that of a Latin church despite some additions having been made to it.

However, scholars have not found much historical evidence of the Arab takeover of Galata before the Ottoman Conquest.[112] It is certain that Muslim trading communities had lived in Istanbul proper and Üsküdar since Byzantine rulers had granted the Turks a treaty to trade and reside inside the city around their own mosque, which was later destroyed. And there had been a mosque in Constantinople that was destroyed by the Fourth Crusaders in 1204.

According to Benedetto Palazzo, the Arab Cami'i in Galata had originally been a Greek Orthodox Church devoted to St. Irene and was constructed as a Latin monastery by Dominican monks devoted to St. Paul in the first quarter of the fourteenth century.[113] Archeological excavations of the site have found many Greek reliefs and Latin tombstones and frescoes, indicating the Greek Orthodox as well as the Catholic origins of the mosque. Moreover, the survey of 1455 did not list any Muslims in Galata who had lived there before the Ottoman takeover, although Turkish traders and galley slaves must have passed through Galata since the Genoese had had a treaty with the Ottomans since 1352.

So why did Mehmed II decide to convert the Latin cathedral into a mosque? No doubt under the influence of more conservative advisers, Mehmed II converted this church into a mosque in Galata and endowed it as a vakf in 1475 to create the foci for Morisco settlement.[114] This action would have been in keeping with his policy directing the conversion of six Greek Orthodox churches, including Hagia Sophia, into mosques and a college on the historic peninsula after the Conquest. The conversion of major churches into mosques to create Muslim settlements was also part of Ottoman post-conquest policies elsewhere.

The mosque in Galata became officially known as Cami'i Kebir (the great Friday mosque) but was also called the Arab Cami'i, and the quarter around it acquired the same name. With the settlement of Moriscos by Hayrettin Barbarossa in 1533, the mosque became known as the Arab Cami'i.[115] The bell tower was converted into a minaret, and the mosque acquired a distinct Andalusian style in parts of its architecture (windows, arches) as it was repaired after many fires. The Muslim cemetery was located at the Meyit (dead) wharf nearby.[116] The Islamic court of Galata and a prison were also built close to this mosque.

After the mosque had been damaged in the fire of 1731, Saliha Sultan, the mother of Sultan Mahmud I (1730–54), renewed the mosque in the baroque style and built a fountain nearby in 1734.[117] The mosque burned down during a fire in 1807 and was rebuilt again by the women of the harem. In 1868, Adile Sultan, the sister of Sultan Mahmud II (1808–39), and her husband, Mehmed Ali Pasha, restored parts of it and built a fountain for ablution there. The mosque became the center of the Muslim neighborhood in Galata, and soon other structures were built around it.

The Latin community reestablished itself in the church and monastery of St. Peter and St. Paul, which was nearby. The podesta's *Palazzo del Commune* was also in this area. In 1600, there were twelve churches of Latin rite in greater Istanbul, mostly in Galata and Pera.[118] According to Thévenot, five Catholic churches dominated the landscape of Galata inside the walls in the second half of the seventeenth century.[119]

Most Latin churches in Galata survived; a few were converted into mosques, but no additional ones were built inside the walls after the Ottoman takeover in the fifteenth century. For example, the Benedictine monastery of St. Benoit (St. Benedetto) was built in 1427, survived the conquest and fires, and later became the royal chapel of French ambassadors. The Jesuits then took possession of the church for several centuries. The Lazarists acquired it in 1773 and established a school there in 1802[120] The Church of St. Benoit burned down a number of times in the fires of 1660, 1686, and 1731; was subsequently restored several times; and survived as a major Catholic church in Galata. Many French ambassadors were buried in the walls of this church.[121] The French embassy also had a small chapel called St. Louis, which was built in Pera in 1581.

Fires sometimes led to the confiscation of land by members of the ruling class and the conversion of churches into mosques. The Church of Santa Maria, which carried the relics of the True Cross, the ecclesiastical treasure of the *Magnifica Communita,* had patents of authority (*berats*) from the sultan and the *signoria.* Clara Drapperii, a widow of the wealthy Draperii family, gave the Church of Santa Maria Draperis to the Franciscan monks in 1584; it became the principal repository of local ecclesiastical archives.[122] After the church burned down during a major fire in 1660, the community could not get permission to rebuild it, so it constructed another church by the same name in Pera near the French Embassy in 1678.

Grand Vizier Kemanskeş Kara Mustafa Pasha converted the Church of San Antonio (built in 1390 by a Donna Marietta) in Galata into a mosque named after him in 1606.[123] An imposing Franciscan church by the same name, San Antonio of Padua, which had been built in Pera near the French

Embassy in 1725, was reconstructed in Gothic style and red brick after a fire in 1913. The Church of St. Francesco, with its monastery and nine friars, had been the focal point of Catholic religious life at the center of Galata.[124] After the church burned down in 1697, Valide Gülnuş Sultan, the mother of Ahmed III, confiscated the land where the original church had stood and built the Yeni Cami'i (or Valide Sultan Cami'i) in its place.[125] The vakf register of this complex shows that in 1739 it collected revenues from lands as far away as the island of Chios and Anatolia.[126]

The Ahdname of 1453 gave the Genoese community (through the Council of Twelve) authority over the remaining Latin churches in Galata, which the community safeguarded with great zeal against Ottoman and papal intervention. The Vatican claimed authority over Latin churches in Galata and Pera since it funded many of their activities, but the Ottoman state did not recognize its claim. The Pope established the office of Propaganda Fide in 1622 and tasked it with converting the Christian "heretics" of the eastern Mediterranean. Rome also assigned a vicar and then replaced him with a bishop to take control of the Latin churches in Galata, although no papal representative was allowed in Galata at this time.[127] The French Embassy assumed the responsibility of protecting Catholic missionaries (Jesuits and Capuchins) and negotiated their freedom of action in Galata and other ports in the Ahdname of 1673 (see chapter 4). In the late seventeenth century, the papacy, Venice, and France fought for jurisdiction over Latin churches and Catholic converts. France won control of some major churches thanks to the Capitulation of 1673. After the dissolution of the Magnifica Communita in 1682, the administration of Latin churches was left in limbo and ultimately was taken over by King Louis XIV of France. France tried to carve out a spiritual place for itself in Galata as well as in the Holy Land, thus competing with the Greek Orthodox and Armenian Patriarchates (see chapter 4).

Galata's Latin community lived next to Muslims and interacted with them on a daily basis.

CREATION OF MUSLIM SPACE AND THE SETTLEMENT OF MORISCOS

No infidels reside in the first castle [Muslim neighborhood], and none at all in the second castle as far as the Arab mosque—the inhabitants of the quarter possess a noble rescript from Mehmed the Conqueror[,] according to which no infidel is allowed in, and if they see an armed Christian [Latin], they give no quarter and kill him immediately. The majority of these inhabitants are grief-stricken Mudejars who came from Spain, driven out by infidels, in the time of Sultan Ahmed I. If they see an armed infidel in Galata, they kill him right away.

—EVLIYA ÇELEBI, *Seyahatnamesi,* Book I[128]

At the time of the survey of 1455, a handful of Muslims (twenty in 1455) lived predominantly near Galata Tower and close to the Azap Kapı, but the number grew as a result of the settlement policies.[129] The vakf register of 1496 for Galata listed twenty Muslim, thirteen Italian, eight Greek Orthodox, and six Armenian quarters in Galata.[130] Evliya Çelebi emphasized the Morisco character of the Muslim neighborhood in Galata around the Arab Cami'i in the mid-seventeenth century.

The Ottoman Conquest of Constantinople in 1453 and the Spanish Reconquista of Muslim Spain in 1492 were intimately connected and led to the expulsion of Moriscos from the Iberian Peninsula to North African and Ottoman cities. The expulsion of Moriscos from Muslim Spain was also due to the Spanish fear of a possible Ottoman fifth column (agents of a foreign country) aiding a supposed Ottoman takeover of Granada, especially during the Morisco Rebellion in the mid-sixteenth century. The flow of Moriscos and Marranos (Jews who had converted to Catholicism) from Iberia started in the late fifteenth century and continued into the early seventeenth century.[131]

Ottoman expansion into Constantinople and Mediterranean ports created a backlash against Muslims in Europe in the sixteenth century. After the breakup of the Caliphate in Cordoba in 1031, the Catholic kingdoms of Aragon and Castile began expanding into Muslim territories to launch a crusade, with the approval of the Vatican. Muslims who lived under Christian rule (*Mudéjares*) were at first protected as zimmis were under Muslim rule. But they were prevented from building mosques in Christian-controlled towns or engaging in public religious rituals in Valencia and Castile.

After the reunification of the kingdoms of Castile and Aragon with the marriage of Queen Isabella of Castile and King Ferdinand II of Aragon, the last Muslim kingdom of Granada fell in 1492. The Vatican supported a collective Catholic plan of action against all Muslims and Jews, even those in the Iberian Peninsula who had converted to Catholicism. The forceful conversion and expulsion of the Jewish and Muslim population (from Granada,

Valencia, Aragon, and Catalonia) between 1480 and 1526 led to the flow of thousands of Jewish and Muslim refugees into the Ottoman capital and other cities like Izmir, Salonica, and Edirne. They settled in North African and Ottoman cities and in new neighborhoods in Istanbul and Galata according to their places of origin.[132] The settlement of Jewish refugees from Spain in Ottoman cities has received some attention from scholars, but the study of Moriscos (Muslims who converted to Catholicism after 1501) in Ottoman cities is in a preliminary stage.[133]

The Moriscos in Spain were in regular contact with Mehmed II and Bayezid II, asking for assistance. Mehmed II received a Muslim delegation from Spain in 1477, one year before the start of the Spanish Inquisition. Undoubtedly, these contacts led to the suspicion of Muslims being foreign agents and a threat that could bring Ottoman invaders to Spain.[134] Sultan Bayezid II offered the Moriscos asylum after the fall of Granada, and many arrived in Ottoman lands with the help of Grand Admiral Hayreddin Barbarossa. According to some sources, a ship carrying 290 Moriscos from Spain landed in Istanbul in 1493.

In the kingdom of Castile, the Moors who remained were subjected to pogroms, forced conversion, and expulsion in 1502. Most of the Muslim population converted to Christianity but continued practicing Islam secretly.[135] Consequently, they were subjected to a series of laws that forbade them to marry within the community, celebrate Muslim holidays, grow a beard, wear the veil, and dress in Muslim fashion in Granada.[136] In Valencia, after a rebellion by Comuneros in Castile in 1519, Christian violence was directed against the Muslim population that supported the crown, forcing them to baptize their children as Christians and convert their mosques into churches.

The Muslims of Granada asked for help from Sultan Süleyman, describing their plight under Christian rule in their appeal and expressing their continued faith in Islam. In 1529, Süleyman ordered the head of his navy, Hayreddin Barbarossa, to evacuate between seventy and eighty thousand Muslims form Spain; many of them settled in North Africa, and some ended up in Ottoman cities.[137] Those who stayed in Spain and secretly remained Muslim faced the arm of the Inquisition and accusations of apostasy and witchcraft and of conspiring with Muslim enemies like the corsairs of North Africa and the Ottoman sultan.[138] In Granada in 1567, Moriscos were forbidden from speaking and writing in Arabic, adopting Moorish names, and celebrating their holiday on Fridays.

These measures led to a Morisco rebellion in Granada from 1568 to 1570, leading to extreme violence by both sides. Philip II ordered the expulsion of 150,000 Moriscos from Valencia (100,656) and Aragon (74,000) and a smaller number from Catalonia. Their expulsion led to the government's expropriation of their property in November 1570.[139] Eventually, King Philip III developed a plan to expel all Moriscos from Spain in 1602, using them as scapegoats for internal conflicts. An edict was issued to the agents of the crown to supervise the expulsion of 275,000 Moriscos (out of a population of 300,000 Moriscos) from Spain.

The flow of Muslim and Morisco refugees to North Africa, Galata, Salonica, and Izmir took place in several phases and peaked in 1608 and 1610 during the final expulsion. The largest settlement of Moriscos in Galata took place after their final expulsion from Spain in 1608; they moved into the quarter of the Arab Cami'i, occupying space all the way to Galata Tower.[140] After the final expulsion, most Moriscos settled in North Africa (Tunisia), speaking Spanish and having Spanish names. Some joined North African corsairs in their raids on Spanish and western Mediterranean ports and on Christian shipping (with the exception of French shipping). Some Moriscos ended up in Galata, providing information and intelligence on Spanish naval bases and the Spanish military to the Ottoman navy. Their settlement also added to tensions with the Latin population as the Moriscos carved out an important space for themselves. Consequently, the Muslim neighborhood in Galata acquired an important Andalusian character.

THE ROLE OF THE ISLAMIC VAKF IN THE CREATION OF MUSLIM SPACE

The congregational mosque complexes built by members of the Ottoman ruling class (male and female) played an important role in attracting Muslim settlements and in the development of a Muslim space in a predominantly Christian port. Halil Inalcik has emphasized the role of the Islamic *vakf* (an Islamic religious and charitable foundation) complexes in the Islamization of Constantinople and other Ottoman cities by members of the Ottoman dynasty and ruling class.[141] The grand viziers and female members of the Ottoman royal family played an active role in the building of vakf complexes in Istanbul proper, Üsküdar, Eyüp, and, to a lesser extent, Galata due to its special status as a European colony.[142] Galata, therefore, unlike the rest of

Istanbul, did not become the site of monumental mosque architecture. However, it soon did acquire a good number of Friday mosques and small neighborhood mosques.[143] The major mosque complexes were built outside the walls and in Tophane and Kasım Paşa.

By the end of seventeenth century, Galata and Pera had twelve mosques (six inside the walls).[144] The major Friday mosques in Galata were the Arab Cami'i, Sokollu Mehmed Pasha Cami'i, Yağ Kapanı Cami'i or Kurşunlu Mahzen Cami'i, Mustafa Pasha Cami'i, and Karaköy Cami'i in Pera (see map 2).[145] The Arab Cami'i remained the most important congregational mosque complex in Galata and had a market (Arab Çarşı), around which residential neighborhoods developed.[146] Gradually, many houses and shops became part of the imperial as well as the local vakf complexes of Aya Sophia, Fatih (Sultan Mehmed II), and Sultan Ahmed I.

In addition, the three grand viziers of Sultan Süleyman, Ibrahim Pasha, Rüstem Pasha, and Sokollu Mehmed Pasha, founded two small congregational mosque complexes and constructed a han in the port area near the Azap Kapı during the sixteenth century. Grand Vizier Ibrahim Pasha built the Yağ Kapanı Cami'i near the Yağ Kapanı (scale of oil) in 1536 (see map 2).

The next grand vizier of Süleyman, Rüstem Pasha, confiscated the main Cathedral of Saint-Michel (founded in 1296), destroyed it, and ordered the imperial architect, Sinan, to build the Rüstem Pasha Han (Kurşunlu Han) and mosque in 1561.[147] There were shops and storage houses next to the Rüstem Pasha Han that belonged to the Rüstem Pasha Vakf. The han was the depot for the import of hides from the Black Sea into Galata.[148] After the fire of 1660 burned the oil scale and customs house, these structures were moved to the Rüstem Pasha Han.[149] Rüstem Pasha had built a major mosque complex across the Golden Horn. The revenues of the han and shops in Galata were endowed to his mosque complex. Rüstem Pasha was a very powerful grand vizier who had married Süleyman's daughter Mihrimah Sultan, a wealthy princess. Using his wife's wealth as well as his own, he invested in the maritime trade of textiles with Europe as well as in commercial ventures in Galata.[150] He sent his agents from Galata to trade in Venice and the Mediterranean islands and ports.

Sinan also built the Sokollu Mehmed Pasha Friday Mosque, also known as the Azap Kapı Cami'i, between 1577 and 1578.[151] Sokollu Mehmed Pasha was the grand vizier of Sultan Süleyman and Sultan Selim II. In addition, Kılıç Ali Paşa, the chief admiral and former governor of Algiers, built the famous Kılıç Ali Pasha Friday Mosque and Hamam along the water in

Tophane just outside the walls of Galata. It is known that while in Algiers, Kılıç Ali Pasha had met Cervantes, who had been taken as a slave, and freed him to return to Spain.

In time, as the number of Muslim residents grew, they built more than twenty-five small neighborhood mosques in Galata and Pera, which attracted more Muslim settlers to the neighborhoods that formed around them.[152] The earliest Muslim quarters that developed around mosques were Okçu Musa and Şehsuvar, named after the military personnel who had founded them. In addition, the hamams and twenty-three fountains served the residential quarters that developed around these and smaller mosques, which were composed of small pious foundations (vakfs)[153] (see map of Galata, map 2).

Moreover, one of the viziers of Sultan Bayezid II (1481–1512), Iskender Pasha, built the Melevihane outside the walls of Galata in Pera in 1491.[154] The Mevlevi Lodge here and the one in Beşiktaş devoted to the Mevlevi dervishes became important sites of communal interaction and the patronage of male and female members the ruling class, who were members of the lodge. Some European residents of Galata also joined the lodge and converted to Islam (such as Count de Bonneval, who took the name Humbaraçı Ahmed Pasha). The female members of the Ottoman dynasty like Cududil Valide Sultan; Saliha Sultan, the wife of Mustafa II (1664–1703); and Gülnuş Sultan, the mother of Ahmed III (1703–30), built fountains and a medrese (Islamic college) in Galata. By the seventeenth century, Galata was housing a sizable Muslim community in several neighborhoods that had developed around small mosque complexes, although it is difficult to derive an exact estimate in the absence of surveys.[155] Residents were sailors, artisans, and traders. Many Muslims who found the price of property quite high in Galata moved to Tophane and Kasım Paşa, two neighborhoods that were dependencies of Galata that soon became congested with Muslims.[156]

Some Jews may have been driven from Galata and Kasım Paşa to make room for Muslim settlers. Some Sephardic Jews may have settled in Kasım Paşa since a small Jewish cemetery existed there outside the walls of Galata. But this cemetery was slowly being taken over by the growing Muslim community in the sixteenth century. For example, the residents of Kasım Paşa, led by several sea captains, came to the court of Galata demanding the construction of a mosque in their neighborhood, the Yel Değirmen quarter, in April 1603. They claimed that there were no mosques there and that they wanted to convert the former Jewish cemetery nearby, which had been closed by an imperial order, into a mosque. Halil Pasha had built a fountain there. One of the imperial admirals named Kürd Agha had endowed 100,000 akçe to build a mosque in the empty attached land (16 zira') next to the fountain. In April 1603, an imperial order was issued to the kadi of Galata to approve the project if the mosque did not infringe on anyone's land or endowed property.[157] The residents of Kasım Paşa were mostly Morisco sailors and sea captains who dressed in North African fashion, according to Evliya Çelebi. Merchants and ship carpenters were also numerous in Kasım Paşa. The tanning industry was located there, with three hundred workshops operated by between twenty and thirty artisans.[158] The chief admiral had his own court (*divan*) and oversaw the most serious crimes and lawsuits among naval officers and sailors in Kasım Paşa, where he also resided.

Similarly, in Galata the neighborhood around the Arab Cami'i was considered sacred. The government issued several bans to prevent the settlement of non-Muslims near the Arab Cami'i and in Muslim quarters in response to complaints from Muslim residents, but these bans were largely ineffective.[159] Tensions between Muslims and Christian residents sometimes ran high due to the drinking and prostitution in taverns. For example, in January 1683, Baron Chateauneuf, the French ambassador, submitted a petition to the Porte regarding the mistreatment and expulsion of French residents from the neighborhood of the Arab Cami'i, arguing that they had lived there with the permission of the former kadis and had not committed any wrongs.[160] Therefore, they wanted to continue living there. The imperial order issued to the kadi asked him to follow the shari'a and imperial orders. However, despite the involvement of the ambassador, tensions between Muslim residents and non-Muslims continued. Several years later, in July 1700, the state issued an imperial order to the kadi, chief architect, and voyvoda of Galata banning the settlement of Christians near the Arab Cami'i in Galata in response to the petition of Al-Hac Mehmed, the superintendent of the said mosque complex.[161] The latter had complained that non-Muslims and Europeans had settled near the mosque and had rented their rooms to foreigners, contrary to regulations. After a fire had burned down the houses belonging to some Christians, the state ordered the sale of those houses near the mosque to the Muslims. The imperial order also banned the construction of Jewish houses and those belonging to foreigners. Fires, thus, paved the way for the Islamization of certain parts of Galata and the clearing of non-Muslim residences and churches from these areas, while drinking in taverns led to attempts to expel Ottoman Christian and European residents from Muslim neighborhoods, pushing Europeans to settle outside the walls on the hills of Pera (see chapter 2).

SLAVES AND CAPTIVES

Due to corsair activities, many Mediterranean ports housed a good number of captives and slaves. A good proportion of Galata's European population was composed of war captives. Galata also contained a large servile population that worked in the arsenal of Kasım Paşa as galley slaves.[162] Some were European and Russian war captives, and others had been taken during pirate raids on Christian shipping in the Mediterranean. The manumission and ransoming of slaves created a steady traffic to the court of Galata, as the following case demonstrates:

> The pride of ladies, Hadice Hatun the daughter of Mahmud, sends her agent, Ihsan Çelebi son of Abdullah, to the court to free her slave, Francesco son of Francesco, whom she received from her father when he was alive. The latter is of medium height, is blue eyed with thick eyebrows, and has an injury mark on his head. The aforementioned is now free like other zimmis. He confirmed his manumission in January 1590.[163]

At times of war, the number of slaves in Galata increased, and some ended up in the households of middle-class Muslims while others served as forced labor in the galleys and in construction. The institution of slavery had existed in both the Islamic and Christian halves of the Mediterranean world since medieval times. The Genoese were active traders in trafficking Muslim as well as Orthodox Christian slaves prior to the Ottoman takeover of the Black Sea in 1475.[164] Venice and the Turkish principalities had also been involved in slave trafficking in medieval times. Slave trafficking on the Black Sea by the Crimean Tatars continued under Ottoman rule, but the Genoese were pushed out of this trade. The Crimean Tatars made their living by raiding Russian territories and then selling their captives, males and females, to Italian and later to Ottoman dealers. They also paid part of their annual tribute to the sultan in the form of white slaves (Russian, Abkhazian, and Circassian), some of whom ended up in the imperial harem (e.g., Roxelana, or Hurrem Sultan,the favorite concubine and wife of Sultan Süleyman).

In addition, captives from Europe made up an important portion of the population of Galata, especially during battles on the Mediterranean or wars with Russia and incidents of piracy. The Battle of Lepanto and the war with Venice over Cyprus between 1570 and 1571 resulted in the flow of Latin captives to Galata. European ambassadors and the Venetian bailo played an important role in the ransoming of slaves while individuals also manumitted them voluntarily or in return for a fee. The above case from the kadi's register highlights the manumission of a Latin slave by a Muslim woman, who sent her agent (a former slave himself) to the court of Galata in 1590 to free her Italian slave.

Catholic states also enslaved thousands of Muslims and used them as forced labor in the galleys during the early modern period.[165] According to an estimate, more than seven thousand Muslim captives were distributed to Spain, Venice, and the papacy.[166] The ports of Livorno and Malta were important distribution centers for the sale of Muslim captives by Latin corsairs.[167] Manumission was also an important source of income for slaveholders and traffickers. No doubt, slaves on both sides of the Mediterranean lived in miserable conditions. Being captured by Mediterranean corsairs was a constant fear and risk for sea captains and their merchant marines.

Nur Sobers Khan has identified six hundred Christian slaves in three Galata court registers (14/2, 14/4, 14/4) during the thirteen-year period from 1560 to 1572.[168] During the war with Venice over Cyprus in 1571, two thousand Christian slaves from various backgrounds were held in Galata. Of this number, five hundred were manumitted in 1581. Alvise Contarini, an Italian visitor, put the number of Christian Latin slaves in Galata alone in 1581 at between eight and ten thousand. The Senate in Venice estimated the number of Venetian captives alone in the Mediterranean at twenty-five hundred in 1588.[169] However, this figure may have underestimated the actual number since many Ottoman sea captains hid their slaves for the fear of having to release them according to the terms of the Ottoman-Venetian Ahdname, which stated that both sides should release their war captives and enslaved populations once peace had been restored.[170] According to a papal visitor in the late 1580s, even after the ransoming of many captives, five hundred freed slaves remained in Galata, and sixty more lived in Istanbul proper. Moreover, three hundred exiled convicts (*banditi*) worked in the Ottoman arsenals in 1591 as caulkers, carpenters, and other craftsmen, making up more than one-third of the 838 workers in the arsenal of Kasım Paşa.[171]

Many Muslim residents in Galata had servile origins themselves or were converts, as indicated by their surnames, such as bin/bint Abdullah (son/daughter of the slave of God).[172] Based on these records alone, it is very difficult to calculate the total number of slaves in Galata at a given time since many had been ransomed. Unlike the practice in other ports, slaves were ransomed and freed at a high speed in Galata, a situation that may have been due to Islamic law's emphasis on manumission and the slaveholders' economic need to convert their slaves into cash. The state kept vigilance over the employment of manumitted slaves in Muslim households. For example, an imperial order issued to the kadi of Galata in February 1560 commanded him to review the status of Christian, Jewish, and Frankish slaves and to prevent the sale of manumitted slaves and their employment in Muslim households.[173]

The court of Galata was very busy registering the manumission of Italian, Cypriot, Iranian Shi'i, and Russian slaves during this period. The rate of manumission also appeared to be high at this time, a condition that may have been due to the Ottoman-Venetian Ahdname's requirement that captives be freed. For example, in March 1575, Mehmed Çelebi son of Huseyn manumitted his blue-eyed, blond Italian (*efrenci*) slave, Demenko son of Cuvan (Dominico son of Giovanni), in return for seventy gold coins in the Muslim court of Galata in the presence of three Muslim witnesses.[174] At the end of the same month, Carullah son of Resul came to the court of Galata and manumitted two Italian slaves, Divenber and Cuvan Anton (Giovanni Antonio), a tall Italian man with a an injury mark on his face, in return for 110 pure gold coins in the presence of more than three Muslim witnesses.[175] It is not clear how these slaves could afford to pay to their master the hefty price in gold coins unless a wealthy relative back home or the Venetian bailo was willing to pay the ransom.

It appears that many Muslim residents of Galata owned slaves as part of their property, even though the cost of a slave was very high in the marketplace. For example, the inventory of the estate of a deceased man in Galata in March 1579 listed four Italian slaves, each valued at 10,000 akçe, and a female slave valued at 3,000 akçe. It is possible that this man had been a slave dealer who operated between Galata and Egypt since he had a boat and a shop and owed money to the customs collector of Galata.[176] Some owners sold their slaves after a time to make a living, and other ransomed them as a good deed. It is possible that the relatives of the Venetian captives were paying heavy ransoms in the court of Galata through the Venetian Embassy to get them freed. The court registers describe many Italian slaves carrying wounds on their bodies, an indication of their status as war captives, possibly from the Battle of Lepanto or the war over Cyprus in 1571.

In addition to Italian captives, the court of Galata registered the manumission of many Russian women, like Afitab daughter of Abdullah, the slave of Mustafa Çelebi, and Nazenin daughter of Abdullah, the blue-eyed slave of Turbedar Mehmed Çelebi, in May 1579.[177] In these two cases, the masters did not receive a ransom for the manumission of the female slaves and might have simply freed them out of the goodness of their hearts after the slaves had given birth to a child in order to enable them to marry as free women.

We do not know what happened to these slaves after they were freed, whether they returned home or were eventually converted to Islam and stayed in Galata. We know that many Italian captives converted to Islam and ended up in Ottoman service as naval officers and commanders, renegades, spies, translators, and ship captains. Others fled from Venetian-held Crete or were captured during the wars and pirate raids. Many Italian slaves also became traders and shop owners in Galata and Kasım Paşa. For example, the deceased sea captain Hussam Reis son of Abdullah, a former slave and resident of Kasım Paşa, left an estate valued at 216,920 akçe that included corsair captives worth 115,500 akçe, an orchard worth 40,000 akçe, a garden in Tatavla worth 3000 akçe, and shops valued at 20,000 akçe in 1590 in Galata. Three of his Russian male slaves brought a lawsuit to the court of Galata to obtain their freedom after his death in accordance with the agreement they had already made. His big house was made into a family vakf for his wife and her descendants, his freed female slave and her descendants, and his other freed slaves as primary, secondary, and third-rank beneficiaries.[178]

While a few slaves like Hussam Reis became wealthy sea captains, others with lesser skills worked as rowers on the galleys or worked in the port area. At times of peace, the number of slaves dropped dramatically from eight to a few thousand. In the decade after the war of Lepanto, the number dwindled to a few thousand in the 1590s.[179] In 1714, after the long war with the Holy League (1684–98), galley slaves numbered between four and five thousand in Galata.[180] During the Ottoman-Iranian Wars (1725–46) and the capture of Azerbaijan, many Iranian Shi'i slaves ended up in Istanbul. During the Ottoman-Iranian Wars, since the enslavement of Shi'i Iranians was considered legal by the Ottoman ulema, many ended up in Galata and Istanbul from the sixteenth to the eighteenth centuries. Iranian Shi'i female slaves were also among those who presented lawsuits to gain their freedom in the courts of Istanbul in the eighteenth century. African slaves also resided in Galata, and some were freed by their masters. Many slaves also worked in the arsenal and serviced the commercial district.

The most beautiful fish market in the world is located on the marina, on a street where fish shops occupy both sides, offering large quantities of fish of all varieties and excellence in cheap prices. The Greeks run many taverns/cabarets in Galata, where they attract many rascals who are very insolent when they are drunk, and with whom encounters can be dangerous.[181]

Thévenot elaborated on the size of the fish market in Galata in the seventeenth century and the varities of great quality fish that were available at an affordable price.[182] The port of Galata, together with the arsenal of Kasım Paşa and Tophane, were emerging as important commercial and industrial centers of Istanbul, employing a large number of sailors, sea captains, caulkers, coffeeshop attendants, cooks, tailors, tavern workers, boatmen, and porters in the seventeenth century. The port of Galata contained the custom house, the scale of olive oil, the fish market, the covered bedestan, and the loggia (*lonca*), or market area. The commercial district of Galata was also near the Arab Cami'i. Commercial shops as well as workshops related to the shipbuilding industry were located in the area between the Yağ Kapanı and the fish market, which made up the commercial area in Galata.

The port of Galata was divided into three landing stages (*iskele*) made up of the wooden structures of Azap Kapı, Karaköy, and Mumhane in the early modern period. The area between the Yağ Kapanı (oil scale) and Balık Iskelesi (the wharf for the fish market) comprised both the Genoese and the Ottoman ports, from which the Perşembe Pazarı (Thursday market) road started going uphill toward Galata Tower and Pera (see map 2, Galata).

Inside the walls, the major arteries were Voyvoda Street, the Arab Cami'i road, the Harbi road, and Kulekapı Street. Outside the walls, the Büyük Yol (Great Road) was the major artery along the harbor in the seventeenth century.[183] The Galata prison was located on the harbor near the Arab Cami'i and the gate of the scale of oil, from which prisoners used to shout to passersby for donations (see map 2).[184]

In Istanbul and Galata, each small wharf specialized in the import of certain goods. Galata imported olive oil and fish from the Aegean and the Black Sea ports into Istanbul. Galata was the final destination for the olive oil imported from all over the empire (such as the Aegean islands). The trade of olive oil and clarified butter was primarily in the hands of Muslim merchants (see chapter 5). At the fish wharf, many shops sold a variety of fish and foodstuff. All the fish had to first be taken to the tax collector of fish (*balık emini*) in Balikhane; from there it would be distributed to fish markets all over the city. In addition, European and colonial goods like coffee and sugar were imported into Galata on European ships (see chapter 5). According to the survey of 1792, Galata also housed a variety of food shops, coffeehouses, *bozahanes* (a fermented millet drink), bakeries, and mills.[185]

Sultan Mehmed II, his successors, and members of his ruling class invested heavily in the construction of major commercial infrastructures (covered bazaars) comprised of shops, markets, workshops, hans, caravansarais, mosques, and soup kitchens through the institution of vakfs (pious foundations) in all four districts of Istanbul after the conquest. These structures were part of the vakf complexes in every major city and also provided security for trade on the roads and seas.[186] The Iranian notion of the Circle of Justice required rulers to provision cities with an abundance of foodstuff and raw materials at affordable prices and to promote trade by investing in commercial infrastructures in urban centers and ports and along important trade routes. International trade produced revenue for the state and brought in bullion, provided military materiel and luxury goods for the ruling class, and brought prosperity to urban artisans and traders in urban centers[187] (see chapters 5 and 6).

In Galata, Sultan Mehmed II built the *bedestan* (covered market), a small two-story square building (20 x 20 meters) with one gate and three windows on each side and covered with twelve lead domes. The bedestan was probably damaged by fires and was later restored by Sultan Murad III (1574–95), this time with nine domes.[188] Mehmed II also built the main bedestan of Istanbul in the covered bazaar, while the one in Galata played a secondary role.[189] The existence of a bedestan, where jewelry and luxury goods were sold, usually signified the commercial importance of a city or a port. The bedesdan of Galata had all kinds of shops inside that specialized in furs, silks, and jewelry.[190] In the seventeenth century, Italian and Greek merchants operated most of the shops there.

In addition, Grand Vizier Rüstem Pasha built the Kurşunlu Han in place of St. Michel Church near the sea walls. The famous Ottoman architect Sinan built this two-story rectangular brick building (83 x 35 meters), which also contained the customhouse until the nineteenth century.[191] Traders stayed in this han after they had disembarked from the ships. The scale for olive oil and clarified butter was also located near this building since Galata was the final destination for the import of olive oil from the Aegean ports and clarified butter from the Black Sea.[192]

The survey of 1478 listed 260 shops and hans between the Karaköy gate and the Azap Kapı in Galata, most of which were owned by Genoese merchants.[193] In the seventeenth century, the port of Karaköy was developed as an important commercial district outside the sea walls by Grand Vizier Merzifonlu Kara Mustafa Pasha, who moved the customhouse and oil scale there.[194] The number of shops inside the walls increased from 260 in 1478 to 3,080 in the seventeenth century; most of these were owned by Greeks and Italians, according to Evliya Çelebi.[195]

THE RED-LIGHT DISTRICT

As trade expanded and migration increased due to wars and rebellions in Anatolia, the population (especially of single men) of Galata grew. The number of coffeehouses and food shops also increased to cater to the increasing population. In addition, Galata was the entertainment district of Istanbul, featuring Frankish bakeries, coffeehouses, taverns, sherbet shops, and brothels. The red-light district of Galata was located in the harbor area (see chapter 7). Evliya Çelebi described the European bread and colored candies made by Moriscos as well as the variety of wines served in the taverns of Galata in the following manner:

> First is the fine white Mudejar francala bread. The thousands of colored candies, flavored with musk and ambergris and worthy of padishah, in the glass jars at the confectioners' market are found nowhere else, unless it is paradise[-]scented Damascus. The Mudejars also sell spiced sweetmeats topped with decorative leaves and spiced ring bread (*simit*). As for drinks, in the taverns named *Taş Nerdüben* (stone steps)[,] *Kefeli, Manyali, Mihalaki, Kaskaval, Sünbüllu,* [and] *Kostani* ... are sold various notorious[,] forbidden ruby-dripping wines, including misket (from Bulgaria) and wines from Ancona, Syracuse, Mudanya, Erdemit, and Bozcaada (island of Tenedos).[196]

Evliya Çelebi underscored the role of Moriscos in importing European-style sugar candies, breads, and spiced sweetmeats (*pastırma*) (see chapter 5). In addition, eight beautiful markets specialized in selling fine white bread made by Moriscos, expensive sweets, special *helva*, crystal glassware imported from Venice, and European watches in the seventeenth century.[197] Many varieties of local and foreign wines were also available in more than two hundred taverns in the middle castle along the harbor, where several hundred people gathered, drank, played music, and sang every night until dawn. Sea captains returning from their travels also enjoyed social gatherings in the taverns and gardens in the villages along the Bosphorus.[198]

The sale of wine to Muslims, however, created a great deal of tension in Galata. The Islamic court records of Galata contain many cases of delinquency by the Muslim residents. For example, in August 1552, the night police arrested Iskender b. Abdullah and Cafer b. Abdullah for drinking in Galata that month. When they were asked who had supplied them with the wine, they answered, "A friend."[199] In April 1572, the Muslim notables of Galata gathered in the Islamic court and complained about the sale of wine in Galata to Muslims by non-Muslim residents. The state subsequently issued an order to the kadi of Galata to punish and imprison the wine sellers and to place a ban on the sale of wine to Muslims in Galata.[200]

From time to time, orders were also issued for the closure of tavens. Despite these complaints, the taverns reopened and even increased in number as the population of Galata grew in the seventeenth century. Nevertheless, the taverns that were near mosques always attracted the ire of Muslim residents. It appears that Kasım Paşa was more conservative than Galata since its population was less diverse. For example, when the residents of the quarter of Cami'i Kebir (in Kurd Agha mahalle) in Kasım Paşa complained about the presence of taverns and drinking during Fridays, an order was issued in July 1631 to the kadi of Galata for the destruction of those taverns.[201] However, these orders were not always effective. In January 1647, the Muslim residents of Galata came to the kadi's court and demanded the closure of a tavern near the Cami'i Şerif (Arab Cami'i) owned by a zimmi named Seraped after it had previously been closed down. An order was issued to the kadi for the punishment of Seraped and the closure of this tavern near the mosque.[202]

Since the capitulations allowed European embassies to import and store wine in their embassy buildings without having to pay taxes, there was a brisk trade in wine imported from the Aegean islands and even from as far as Marseille (see chapter 2). Galata soon acquired a reputation for delinquency as a place where wine flowed freely in European embassies and houses as well as in hundreds of taverns operated by non-Muslims and where sailors and sea captains socialized with Europeans at night (see chapter 7).

Prostitution also spread in Galata due to the presence of the port and the large numbers of sailors and traders as well as sea captains. In 1536, many lawsuits brought to the Islamic court of Galata dealt with prostitution and drinking among Muslims and non-Muslims.[203] The settlement of Moriscos may have also introduced an element of European lifestyle into Galata, and many poor refugee women and settlers may have turned to commercial sex. For example, in September 1565, a number of Muslim residents came to the Islamic court of Galata and complained about the moral misconduct of five women— Arab Fati (possibly Morisco), Tarin, Giritlu (Cretan) Nefise, Kamer, and Balatlu Atin—in their neighborhood. Arab Fati did not show up in court, but the others came and were confronted by the Muslim residents, who testified about the women's "moral misconduct," especially that of Balatlu Atin, who had a bad reputation. The accused women lashed out at the *imam* (leader of Friday prayer), making "blasphemous remarks." The kadi, imam, and *müezzin* (the man who called for prayer) then carried out an investigation in the homes of these women. As a result, Balatlu Atin and Arab Fati were caught with unrelated men in their houses. The residents subsequently demanded the women's expulsion from the neighborhood and the sale of their houses. An imperial order was then issued to the kadi of Galata for the sale of the women's houses and their removal from the neighborhood. The woman (the wife of a janissary) who had made blasphemous remarks was ordered to reconvert to Islam and was imprisoned until her husband showed up.[204]

This is a very interesting case that sheds some light on the social life of Galata and the tensions that arose as a result of the red-light district's location next to the emerging Muslim neighborhood. Moreover, some of these marginal women were Muslims themselves, and Arab Fati could have been a poor Morisco woman who had turned to commercial sex to support herself. Their houses were located next to taverns and bachelors' rooms, where the clientele, single men like sailors and traders, must have also used the services of prostitutes.

ARTISANS AND MIGRANTS

By the eighteenth century, Galata was expanding in several directions, outside the walls to the north in the direction of Pera, to the south in the direction of Karaköy, and to the villages along the Bosporus. The neighborhoods of Kasım Paşa to the east, where the imperial arsenal was located, and Tophane to the west, which housed the cannon foundry, were military industrial centers and dependencies of Galata outside the walls. Galata and these two neighborhoods housed sea captains and sailors as well as traders and a large working-class population.[205]

Artisans were organized into guilds, but membership was not open to all workers. Istanbul had more than 167 guilds, and many were religiously mixed in the eighteenth century. A survey of grocers in the district of Galata listed 91 shops in Galata inside the walls in 1731.[206] These shops were owned by Muslims and non-Muslims and rented and operated by one or two Muslim or non-Muslim tenants. As the population grew, the number of shops that were operated by guilds in Galata increased to 264 in 1761. The guilds in Galata were composed of bakers, millers, bun sellers, butchers, grocers, green-grocers, food shops, coffee sellers, coffeehouse attendants, salted-fish makers and merchants, chest makers, watchsellers, jewelers, locksmiths, seat makers, cap makers, fez sellers, fur sellers, felt makers, cloak makers, tailors, barbers, shoemakers, knife makers, tobacco sellers, snuff sellers, water carriers, boat-men, and porters. Galata also had become a center of food and wine produc-tion as well as a center for trade in fine woolen and silk textiles and luxury goods such as furs, watches, snuff, and colonial coffee and sugar.

As migration to the city peaked, guilds had to deal with new members or those who worked outside the guild structure.[207] The number of migrant workers in Galata and Kasım Paşa who had no membership in guilds had grown during the eighteenth century. A good number worked as porters in the harbors of Galata and Kasım Paşa. The elders of the bakers' and grocers' guilds in Galata complained constantly to the Imperial Council about the entry of nonmembers into their professions.[208] Women were also employed outside the guilds as textile weavers, a situation that attracted the ire of guild elders.[209] At the request of the guilds, which did not welcome migrant work-ers, the state carried out regular inspections of shops and bachelors' rooms as well as hans. Migrants and vendors who opened shops outside of guilds in Galata or worked as peddlers in Tophane and Kasım Paşa were expelled in 1731 and 1777 at the demand of the elders of the guild of grocers.[210]

A survey of 1763 carried out by the voyvoda of Galata to inspect guilds, shops, bachelors' rooms, and hans identified 5,156 artisans (single and mar-ried, Muslim and non-Muslim) who had guarantors and membership in guilds. The survey also identified 497 workers who had no guarantors and were working outside the guilds; they were thus expelled from Galata and had to return to their homes.[211] The survey of 1763 listed the names of Muslim and non-Muslim artisans and their guarantors (*kefils*) in various guilds in the port area in Galata. In greater Istanbul, the vast majority of the artisans in the eighteenth century were members of the janissary corps who had joined the guilds to supplement their shrinking salaries. They carried the title *beşe* (janissary title) next to their names and dominated the guilds of shield makers, stool makers, tanners, carpenters, chest sellers, coffeehouse attendants (a job that required no skills), and butchers in Galata and Kasım Paşa.

Since Galata had become the entertainment center of Istanbul, the number of coffeehouses in Galata had grown from 115 in 1763 to 162 in 1792 due to an increase in the population of Galata, where smoking had also become very popular. The coffeehouses were all operated by Muslim masters but had a religiously mixed group of workers.[212] Many were members of the janissary corps who had turned artisans. Coffeehouses had become important spaces of social interaction among all strata of Ottoman society except for women, for whom public baths (*hamams*) played a similar role. The six hamams in Galata employed 114 workers (see chapter 6).

In addition, Galata housed a large working-class population that serviced the arsenal as well as the port area. The survey of 1792 listed 142 porters in Karaköy (40 Muslim and 80 non-Muslim) and 55 boatmen (46 Muslim and 9 non-Muslim) in the harbor of Galata.[213] In 1768, a porter's daily wage was 5 *para* a day, which would only allow him to purchase two loaves of bread.[214] In addition, in 1763, there were 281 bachelors' rooms and hans in Galata and Kasım Paşa (110 bachelors' rooms) that were located near the arsenal and in the port area close to the gates. They housed single men like sailors and janissaries as well as traveling merchants. French merchants, Russian and Ottoman non-Muslim merchants, and money-changers (*sarraf*) stayed in the Yeni Han in Galata.[215] The large number of hans and single rooms had to do with the growing number of merchants, single men, migrant workers, and janissary-artisans who lacked a family and housing in the eighteenth century. Foreign merchants, sailors, shield makers, porters, and boatmen stayed in bachelors' rooms and hans in the congested section of Galata. Slowly, due to overpopulation as well as to a growing crime rate, the hills of Pera to the north were emerging as the diplomatic center of the empire and the residential area for European traders and their Ottoman protégés, who kept their shops in Galata.

CONCLUSION

Historians have not paid much attention to the unique history of Galata and its transformation from a medieval Genoese and Byzantine fortress to an Ottoman port during the early modern period. Moreover, the Ottoman

Conquest of Constantinople is viewed as a major turning point that led to the decline of the city and the destruction of its former urban fabric. The Ottoman Conquest of 1453 created a temporary rupture in the commerce of Galata, but soon the sultan and his grand viziers began repopulating Galata and building a commercial infrastructure on the harbor to revive its trade with Europe as well as with the Black Sea. Under Ottoman rule, Galata acquired an Ottoman administration and a Muslim space and community that had a strong Andalusian character. At this time, the hills of Pera to the north were also emerging as the Western European diplomatic hub.

TWO

―――――

The Rise of Pera

FROM NECROPOLIS TO DIPLOMATIC AND
COMMERCIAL HUB

From Galata, one climbs up to Pera, which is separated from Galata by cemeteries. It is a fine town where Christian ambassadors reside, except for those of the king[s] of Poland and Ragusa, who live in Constantinople. The French ambassador lives in a beautiful grand palace in Pera called ["]The House of the King,["] which has a beautiful view of the port area and the Topkapi Palace. The embassy in Pera is built on a hill at a higher elevation than [that of] the sultan's palace. Pera is on an elevation[,] and its houses are beautiful; only wealthy Greeks live nearby.

—JEAN THÉVENOT, mid-seventeenth century[1]

THE VINEYARDS AND CEMETERIES OF PERA outside the walls to the north of Galata became the site of embassies and diplomatic corps in the seventeenth century. Although Evliya Çelebi did not mention anything about Pera in his travelogue, possibly because it was not yet fully inhabited, French residents like Jean Thévenot left vivid impressions of life in the new suburb of Pera. The hills of Pera to the north were the original necropolis of Galata (*Grand Champs de Morts*) for the Muslim as well the non-Muslim (Greeks and Armenians) and European population. However, due to the growing population, plague, fires, and the rising crime rate, a reconfiguration of the space took place from the introverted walled city of Galata toward Pera and the shores along the Bosphorus. This chapter will focus on the rise of Pera outside the walls of Galata as a result of the expansion of trade and diplomacy with Western Europe. It also examines the impact of the plague and fires on the reordering of streets, surveillance of public spaces, and imposition of new building codes in the late eighteenth and early nineteenth centuries. The role of the state as well as that of European embassies in the transformation of Pera will conclude this chapter.

We have had a raging plague for above seven months . . . [that] has swept away incredible numbers of people of all ranks, and great numbers in the Frank quarters of Pera and Galata. I lost a Greek under-butler[,] his wife[,] and three children—poor people[—]by their own folly. But by God's great goodness[,] there was no other accident in the family.

—LADY ABIGAIL, 1733[2]

Lady Abigail, the wife of Lord Kinnoull, the British ambassador to Constantinople, wrote about the victims of the devastating plague in Galata and Pera in January 1733. Its victims included the elderly and the young, the rich and the poor. Families sometimes lost one-third to one-half of their members. Death from the plague and social dislocation from fires were constant features of life due to the density of the urban fabric, the use of coal in cooking and heating houses, the use of wood in construction in Galata and Pera as well as high winds in winter and spring and aridity during the hot months of summer.[3] European travelers and Ottoman residents underscored the daily ritual of death and loss in Pera in the eighteenth century. They were affected by death themselves, although European residents were able to flee to villages along the Bosphorus when the plague hit and during the summer when fires raged (see chapter 7). Since Ottoman authorities were late in adopting the quarantine system, the plague and cholera also struck Ottoman cities in the eighteenth and nineteenth centuries. While the plague led to demographic decline, particularly with the arrival of commercial ships in the crowded port areas, fires spread during the hot months of summer with the winds and destroyed the old commercial areas that were congested as well as poor neighborhoods, leading to further social dislocation and urban decay.

Ottoman officials, led by the kadi, kept an eye on the spread of the plague and prepared a list of the victims to oversee burials in cemeteries that dotted the city inside and outside the walls and increased in size as the death toll mounted. Galata inside the walls had a small cemetery called the *Petit Champs des Morts,* but the larger cemetery, called the *Grand Champs des Morts (Büyük Mazarlık),* was in Pera. The latter was divided into Muslim, Catholic, Protestant, Greek Orthodox, and Armenian burial grounds from 1560 until the mid-nineteenth century.[4] Christian burial grounds also became sites of gatherings and rituals in the eighteenth century. The removal

Antoine-Ignace Melling, *View of the Cemetery of Pera*. Photo courtesy of the Newberry Library, Chicago.

of cemeteries from neighborhoods inside the walls to areas outside the walls was a measure taken by the Ottoman state to prevent the spread of the plague in the port of Galata.[5] Ottoman tombstones, unfortunately, did not specify the cause of death, nor did the inventory of estates of the deceased in the Islamic court registers state how residents had passed away. But the estates of the deceased in the court registers do show that death was a regular occurrence during the early modern period.

The bubonic plague (*ta'un, veba*) spread to Ottoman cities like Istanbul and Izmir with the frequent arrival of ships and caravans from Asia and the Middle East.[6] The population density in port areas, regular human contact, and the circulation of contaminated merchandise led to rapid population losses. The death toll from the plague varied according to its severity and duration, usually lasting from the month of May to October. In Istanbul, small plagues (81 percent) occurred almost every year, with a total population loss of 1.2 percent annually, but big plagues (10 percent) also struck Ottoman cities like Istanbul (1705, 1726, and 1778), Aleppo, and Izmir, causing grave demographic losses.

The plague spread from Ottoman ports to Mediterranean ports like Marseille through maritime trade on a regular basis. In Europe, this urban disease was regarded as the symbol of Oriental decadence and absolutism in the Ottoman Empire. But in reality, the plague spread rapidly through maritime trade as urban life expanded and trade between the Levant and western Mediterranean ports increased.[7] Nükhet Varlık offers a view of the Mediterranean as a "unified disease zone" with shared medical traditions and experiences during the second pandemic following the Black Death.[8] She has argued that the plague spread with the consolidation of the Ottoman Empire, urbanization, and the expansion of caravan and maritime commercial networks from Central Asia, the Caucasus, Anatolia, Iran, the eastern Mediterranean, and North Africa. The movement of populations (merchants and pilgrims) and goods, their contact with others on caravans and ships, and their disembarkation spread disease to the ports of the Levant. Istanbul thus became the empire's plague hub, receiving and spreading the plague across the Ottoman Empire and the Mediterranean ports through maritime trade.[9]

The containment of the plague and treatment of those striken with it assumed central importance for Ottoman authorities. According to Varlık, Ottoman authorities developed measures to survey the neighborhoods that had been hit by the plague, recorded the dead, isolated the sick and the dead, and controlled burial sites in early modern Istanbul. Measures were also taken to clean the water supply, pave the streets, and control garbage collection.[10] For the earlier period (the sixteenth to eighteenth centuries), we have to rely on the reports of Ottoman judges and chroniclers who recorded deaths from the plague. For example, the kadi of Üsküdar (a district of Istanbul on the Asian side) recorded the death of Karagöz son of Abdullah, the slave of a janissary in the village of Kalburcu, from the plague in July 1519.[11] Another record tells that in December 1579, Valo son of Zado, who had been stricken with the plague, came to the court of Üsküdar and confirmed that he had settled his claim of debt (500 akçe) with Hüseyin for 200 akçe and stated that if he died from the plague, he would give up an additional 300 akçe to Hüseyin.[12]

The accounts of Europeans who lived in Pera, like Lady Mary Montagu, also reported about the plague and fires. The plague hit the foreign legations in Pera quite regularly since foreign ships carried contaminated merchants and even sick sailors, and the employees of the embassies came into regular contact with them. European embassies recorded the deaths of European residents, and French merchants reported to the Chamber of Commerce in Marseille about the plague.[13] For example, on May 4, 1701, the chief scribe of the French Embassy in Galata, Blodel, wrote to the Chamber of Commerce in Marseille about the death of two Europeans in Pera, a Venetian student of foreign languages who had died within twenty-four hours after contracting the plague and someone in the English Embassy.[14] European doctors and Jesuit missionaries took care of the sick within the community hospitals in Galata. In 1725, the Ottoman state issued orders for prayers in all mosques for the victims of the plague in Istanbul.[15]

Galata was particularly hard hit since commercial ships arriving from Red Sea and Black Sea ports were not quarantined before unloading their goods until the second half of the nineteenth century. For example, in May 1768, a fight broke out between the sailors on a Muslim commercial ship and those on a French ship in Karaköy Harbor in Galata. The dispute was taken to the kadi's court in Galata in the presence of the dragoman of the French Embassy, Carlo Fornetti. Fornetti came from an old family of dragomans who were originally Venetian. The French sailors and merchants claimed that they did not want the fifteen Muslim sailors to get close to them for the fear of contracting the plague or another contagion. The witnesses testified to having seen the fight, so the Muslim captain withdrew his lawsuit.[16] This lawsuit illustrates that French sailors were under strict orders from the Chamber of Commerce in Marseille to watch out for Ottoman ships when the plague hit and to not allow Ottoman sailors to board their ships.

The plague of 1778 started in Galata in January and gathered strength in April and May, spreading to the villages along the Bosphorus by July. It claimed one thousand dead every day during the month of July and had wiped out between fifteen and twenty thousand people, a third of the population, in greater Istanbul by November 1778.[17] While European diplomats fled to their summer houses in Büyükdere and the islands, French merchants asked for permission from the Chamber of Commerce in Marseille to return to Marseille.[18] The plague continued to strike Istanbul, Galata, and other ports like Izmir throughout the early nineteenth century. In Izmir, the plague of 1812 decimated 20 percent of the population.[19]

Ottoman historians like Cabi Ömer Efendi began reporting about the plague in Istanbul in the early nineteenth century, noting:

> Imperial orders have been issued to the judges of all three districts of Istanbul to prevent the sale of shrouds and tombs at exorbitant prices to the poor victims of the plague, whose number has risen to 2,004, according to the list of [the] customs inspector. The people of İstanbul who have survived the plague live in great fear and anxiety. (*Cabi's History,* August 1812)[20]

Cabi told of the shortage of shrouds needed to wrap the corpses before their burial in the aftermath of a plague that hit the city in August 1812.[21] That plague left 2,004 dead in Istanbul and caused inflation in the price of burial shrouds.[22] Prayers were held in major mosques in Istanbul and around the houses hit by the plague to prevent its spread in August and September 1812. The plague continued to strike Istanbul during the following year. The French ambassador, who had arrived in Istanbul in 1813, feared catching the plague and stayed on the islands and in Büyükdere for five months before returning for his reception at the Sublime Porte and assuming his embassy post in Pera in the winter.[23] In a different approach, when the Ottoman ambassador, Moralı Seyyid Ali Effendi, arrived in Marseille, he was kept in quarantine for a long time in the spring of 1797 to ensure that he was plague free.[24]

In the nineteenth century, Asian cholera, a new epidemic imported from Russia, India, and the Hijaz by pilgrims, struck Istanbul and Ottoman cities like Izmir very hard. Cholera had appeared in Arabia for the first time in 1821, possibly coming from India and the Persian Gulf via pilgrims due to poor sanitation and crowded ships. The epidemic of 1831 decimated 20,000 people in the Hijaz and quickly spread to Istanbul and other Ottoman ports. Cholera hit Istanbul and other Ottoman ports again in 1835, 1836, 1847, and 1865 (large outbreak) and from 1893 to 1895. In 1835, the cholera epidemic killed 180,000 people in Egypt.[25] In İstanbul, the epidemic of 1836 killed between 25,000 and 30,000 people, while that of of 1837 killed between 15,000 and 16,000 people.[26] French doctors in Istanbul published guidelines on food hygiene and water sanitation to fight cholera in the Ottoman journal *Takvim-i Vakayi'* in 1832, and a few quarantine stations were established on the upper Bosphorus to control ships coming from the Black Sea.[27] But these measures were not sufficient to stop this urban disease.

CLEANING THE STREETS

The modernization of the urban fabric, the control of migration, and the imposition of public order and hygiene were often responses to contagious diseases and fires in Europe as well as in the Ottoman Empire. Like its European counterparts, the Ottoman state took measures to police migration, prevent congestion and contagion, and segregate those who had been hit by the plague. The Ottoman goverment was familiar with the quarantine system that had spread to the Balkans and in places like Dubrovnik since the late seventeenthc century.[28] The government of Selim III (1798–1807) attempted to set up a *lazaretto* (quarantine station) in Istanbul, but the effort was not successful. Selim III followed the French model in modernizing the city and setting up a plague inspection regime and worked closely with French architects, engineers, and doctors.

Selim III also very closely followed Napoleon's policies in Cairo regarding the treatment of the plague (see epilogue). These ranged from the forced fumigation of victims' houses, furnishings, and clothing to the isolation of victims and establishment of hospitals for their treatment. Napoleon's brief rule in Cairo and Alexandria (1798–1801) brought about some changes in the sanitation regime in a Muslim setting or society. For example, when the sultan's tax collector arrived in Cairo by ship, Napoleon's officials, fearing he might be carrying the plague, ordered that he be confined on the ship for forty days and fumigated the ship.[29] Napoleon also set up a municipal council (*divan*) composed of local officials like the *muhtesib* (market inspector) and French military officials that issued rulings for garbage collection and fined anyone who violated the rules. In Cairo, Napoleon's officials and later Muhammad Ali's government demolished the tombs of plague victims and moved the cemeteries in Azbakiyya to pave the way for construction of new buildings, gardens, and parks.[30] Napoleon also required street lighting on all shops and houses in Cairo and fined those who did not follow his directive.[31] The French moved to the hills of Azbakiyya, demolished several mosques, expelled residents, and created a barricaded settlement, the first colonial quarter, for fear of reprisals.[32] Napoleon's reforms of the urban landscape continued under Muhammad Ali and his descendants and were later adopted in the rest of the Ottoman Empire. But these measures also faced opposition and incited a rebellion in Cairo (see epilogue).[33] The opening up of old Cairo neighborhoods was intended to control rebellions as well as the plague.[34]

Unlike France and Austria, the Ottoman state did not systematically establish a cordon sanitaire and a quarantine system in Galata until the early nineteenth century. For this reason, European states typically banned Ottoman ships and sailors from their ports before the early nineteenth century to prevent the spread of the plague. The Austrian government established a long cordon sanitaire along the Ottoman border in 1812. Sultan Mahmud II (1808–39) set up the Bureau of Sanitation with the help of Austrian and French doctors who helped establish the first quarantine in Istanbul in 1839, followed by those in other Ottoman cities like Izmir, Bursa, Aydin, Erzurum, Antalya, Konya, and Adana between 1841 and 1842.[35] Each quarantine station had a European doctor and an Ottoman Muslim director. They registered the name, age, place of birth, and cause of death of each person within fifteen days of his or her death. In Istanbul the head of each religious community and the kadi were required to report the deaths of their members from disease.[36] Delegations from every European nation, Russsia, and America were involved in the advisory staff of the Bureau of Sanitation and were notified when a European or other foreign subject had to go through quarantine upon arrival in İstanbul. The establishment of quarantines, therefore, assumed great importance in Ottoman ports and borderlands from the early nineteenth century until the end of the empire.

DISLOCATION FROM FIRES: CONTROLLING THE STREETS

Although the plague decimated a good portion of Istanbul's population, regular fires destroyed the urban fabric and caused further human dislocation. Fires also gave the state an opportunity to reshape the urban fabric, forcibly move certain groups from crowded neighborhoods around the city and seize their properties, and control crowded areas and close down and destroy bachelors' rooms on the harbor. It also issued building codes and enacted fire control measures, allowing local officials to inspect houses, shops and coffeehouses regularly and expel migrants from the city.

The port area near the Azap Kapı in Galata had become very congested during the eighteenth century with a growing number of migrant workers (porters) and sailors. Many fires started in this area and near Galata Tower and spread quickly to the rest of the town. Fires occurred due to the use of wood in the construction of houses and shops and the use of coal for heating wooden houses and shops. Coal use often caused accidents that led to fires. Smoking in coffeehouses was another cause of fire, usually during the night when accidents occurred. In addition, conditions in the industrial and commercial areas in Tophane and the arsenal triggered fires.[37] From time to time in the aftermath of fires, the state forcibly moved communities to new neighborhoods and removed shops and bachelors' rooms in dense areas. The forced removal of the Jewish community from the Eminönü area and the construction there of Yeni Cami'i by Turhan Sultan in 1651 is a perfect example of this measure.

In Galata the Great Fire of 1696 destroyed half of the district and burned down three Latin churches—St. Benoit, St. George, and St. Francesco. In 1697, the French ambassador petitioned the Imperial Council for permission to repair the damages to the two Jesuit and Capuchin churches in Galata. An order was then issued to the kadi of Galata to carefully examine the two churches and report back on the state of the damages. He was also ordered not to intervene in the restoration of the two churches.[38] The state directed the French community to move from the Bereketzade quarter in Galata intra-muros (inside the walls) to Pera. It also relocated the Church of St. Francesco that had burned down from Galata to Pera and built a mosque in its place (see chapter 1).[39]

Fires continued in Pera in the eighteenth century, damaging houses, churches, and the European embassies. According to Lady Mary Wortley Montagu, the wife of the British ambassador, who lived in Pera, the fire of 1717 burned down five hundred houses in Galata.[40] After the Great Fire of 1721, the Dominicans obtained the right to repair the three convents of St. Peter, St. George, and St. Benoit in Pera. The old Armenian church of Surp Krikor Lusaroviç in Galata had been damaged in the fire of 1733, so the community presented a petition to repair the church according to its old plan (see appendix).[41]

Fires destroyed several European embassies, greatly disrupting the activities of the diplomatic corps. The fire of 1726 demolished much of the British Embassy. A few years later, Lady Kinnoull reported that a big fire had started in Galata at 2 AM on July 10, 1731, and had continued until 3 PM, burning down three-quarters of the port. Fortunately, the magazines, which were built of masonry, where the Europeans stored their goods had survived in Pera.[42] In September 1767, a fire started in a European tailor's shop in the market of Pera and soon spread to the Sicilian, Dutch, and Russian embassies, burning down forty large and small wooden houses that belonged to Europeans.[43] The fires of 1700 and 1767 destroyed the Dutch Embassy twice.[44]

Fires led to the construction of rental properties (commercial and residential) and their sale to wealthy residents, in this case non-Muslims. For example, after a fire had burned down a building in a Muslim and Christian neighborhood in Galata, the state took possession of the land and sold it to seven dragomans of the French and English Embassies (one English and six French), dividing 3,820 meters of land into shares of between 394 and 546 meters in February 1663.[45] The dragomans then appeared in the court of Galata to register the purchase. The state also reinforced the zoning of urban residential areas and maintained control over who owned or could reside in these newly constructed homes, which required state permits, as well as over the reconstruction of churches that had been damaged (see epilogue). For example, in Istanbul proper, after a fire had destroyed a han near Gedik Pasha in 1751, the owner, a certain Abdurrahman, began constructing new shops, a new han, houses, and bachelors' rooms in its place. He built a wall around the construction area and began renting the houses to non-Muslims. Clearly, the owner had taken advantage of the destruction caused by the fire to construct rental properties. But this move was challenged by the state, which issued bans on building new structures without permits. For example, the state banned the construction of bachelors' rooms after the fire of 1782 and also banned the rental of rooms to non-Muslims.[46] In addition, the state issued bans on the construction of new structures and ordered the chief architect to tear down the illegally constructed houses and the wall and to expel the non-Muslim tenants and rent houses in Muslim neighborhoods only to Muslims.[47]

The government was also trying to promote the use of bricks and masonry in the construction of commercial buildings. To prevent fires, in the eighteenth century the government of Ahmed III (1703–30) issued building codes banning the use of wood in commercial buildings and bachelors' rooms.[48] It also limited the height of houses to two stories. Anyone who wanted to remodel or build a new house had to obtain a permit from the chief architect (*mimarbaşı*) of the city. For example, government orders were issued in 1702 to the property owners to rebuild the shops that had burned down around the bedestan in the covered Bazaar in Istanbul using masonry and to supply the owners with bricks and tiles.[49] In another series of orders issued to the judges of Istanbul, Üsküdar, and Galata in 1733, the state limited the size of houses of Muslims to 9.96 meters (12 zira') and those of non-Muslims to 7.58 meters (10 zira').[50] The government of Selim III limited the height of workshops to 4 meters and of shops to 3.79 meters and banned the use of wood in the construction of bachelors' rooms and Jewish houses.[51]

The state also issued imperial orders to the kadis of Istanbul and Galata to implement fire-control measures. For example, the state issued orders to these kadis in January 1751 to require all the imams to inspect the cleaning of ovens in houses every fifteen days.[52] Clearly, the use of coal in ovens for cooking and heating was a major cause of fires in houses, particularly during the winter. In 1796, the state issued orders to the kadi of Galata to inform residents to protect their houses against fires caused by ovens and coal used for heating houses. The imam of every quarter was also required to inspect ovens and inform residents not to put too much coal in them and to cover them when they left their houses.[53]

Crowd control was another measure undertaken by the state to prevent fires. The state carried out a wide inspection of all hans and bachelors' rooms in Galata, Kasım Paşa, and Tophane in 1763 and expelled migrants who did not have guarantors. For example, according to the report of the superintendant of Tophane, thirteen Muslim migrants were expelled from Tophane alone and were put on board ships to be taken to Iznikmid.[54] In 1769, the state issued a ban on the celebration of an Ottoman military victory on the streets of Istanbul by hundreds of children who carried lanterns due to fire hazards. In addition, the state was concerned about the potential participation of "trouble makers and rifrafs" in arson and ordered the police, parents, and schoolteachers to prevent children from appearing on the streets at night.[55] The Ottoman method for dealing with fires after they had started was to quickly demolish burning buildings before the fire could spread to others. The *baltacı* (men wearing hatchets) were in charge of quickly demolishing buildings that had caught fire and those houses that were nearby. The establishment of a fire brigade (*tulumbacı*) did not take place until the nineteenth century.[56]

Despite these preventive measures, fires continued in the nineteenth century and caused even more damage due to congestion and the continued use of wood as the main construction material. The fires of 1800, 1831, 1841, 1852, 1856, 1857, 1859, 1860, and 1870 burned down hundreds of houses and structures and destroyed entire quarters. European embassies and the houses of European merchants were heavily damaged by the fires of Galata and Pera because they had been made of wood.

In addition, the fire of 1807 burned twelve watchsellers' shops in Galata near the Perşembe Pazarı quarter, forcing the Armenian shop owners to ask the state for permission to rebuild the shops by using their own funds.[57] Later, the fire of 1841 burned down most of Pera. In Istanbul, the fire of 1841 destroyed four thousand houses and twenty-five hundred stores in the Muslim and Jewish neighborhoods. The fire of August 1852 started near the Mevlevi Lodge in Galata and continued for four and half hours, causing heavy damage to the lodge and burning down 150 shops.[58] The hot summer season, the continued use of wood in construction and coal in ovens, and overcrowding as well as aridity were some of the leading causes of major fires. The worst fire in Pera occured in 1870, reducing most of the city to ashes and leading to a major facelift on the street of embassies. The Great Fire of June 5, 1870, started in Feridiye Street near Taksim at 2 PM and, as a result of high winds coming from several directions, spread to Rue de Pera and all the way to Galatasaray.[59] It burned down between 3,500 and 4,000 houses and shops and 103 residential quarters on fifty acres of land within thirteen hours, leaving 680 people dead and thousands of families homeless.[60] In addition, the fire burned down the Luxembourg Hotel, the Naum Theatre, *bon marché* shops and magazines, the Galatasaray Police Station, and an Armenian Catholic church. It also heavily damaged the British and the American Embassies.

THE RISE OF NEOCLASSICAL ARCHITECTURE ON *GRAND RUE DE PÉRA*

With the expansion of trade and diplomacy with Europe, the vineyards of Pera became the center of the European diplomatic corps and the residential area for traders in the seventeenth century. In addition, fires resulted in the reconstruction of European embassies in new styles that lined *Rue de Péra*.

> The great suburb called Pera stretches for more than two miles along the summit of a lofty hill. The streets intersect each other, are ill paved, and [are] irregularly built. This quarter has long been assigned to the corps diplomatiques for their winter residence. (James Dallaway, eighteenth century, 125)[61]

Pera had become the new site of settlement for the European ambassadors, their staff, and rich traders as well as for the new bourgeoisie in Galata. Dallaway, the chaplain of the English Embassy, described Pera as the residence of embassies. Sarkis Hovhannesyan (1740–1805), an Armenian banker, also emphasized the presence of dragomans and Latin churches there:

> When you enter through the Karaköy gate and climb up the street slowly, pas[t] the Galata Tower gate, you arrive to the Dört Yol Street. When you stand there, Tophane is to your right, Kasım Paşa and the Arsenal to your left. Across is located a long street where European embassies, the palaces of Latin nobility[,] and the houses of their dragoman[s] and a few Latin churches here and there are located, like St. Marie, St. Antoine, and St. Trinité and others. (Sarkis Hovhannesyan, 1770s)[62]

By the late eighteenth century, the diplomatic corps in Pera included the French, Dutch, and English ambassadors; the Venetian bailo; and the envoys of Austria, Sweden, Spain, Prussia, Russia, and Naples. The French ambassador held the pride of place due to a long alliance between the Ottoman Empire and France against the Habsburg Empire dating back to the early sixteenth century (see chapter 3). Russia was the rising power in the late eighteenth century, while England became an important power and trading partner after the French Revolution (see chapter 3). The Americans were new-comers and did not establish an embassy in Pera until the second half of the nineteenth century.

The Venetian and French Embassies had been moved from the walled town of Galata to Pera in the sixteenth century. The original French, Dutch, and Venetian Embassies had been designed in the vernacular style of Turkish *konaks* (mansions) with large wooden structures, public and private halls, and a garden enclosed within a wall.[63] The Venetian bailo had first moved from Constantinople to Galata in 1499 and resided in a quarter near Galata Tower close to the Jewish neighborhood. He kept a second summer residence in Pera between 1537 and 1540 in order to escape from the summer heat and the plague. The special Venetian envoy to the Porte, however, resided in Pera.[64] For example, Bailo Alvise Gritti had a beautiful and grandiose resi-dence in Pera, where he received the grand vizier in the sixteenth century. Because he was the son of a Venetian noble, he received the title *Beyoğlu* ("son of a notable") from the Turks. Consequently, the whole neighborhood in Pera where he resided also received this name. After the war over Cyprus ended, relations resumed and the Venetian Embassy was permanently moved to Pera in 1571. In Pera, the baili had more space and freedom to move around, especially at night after the gates of Galata were closed.[65] The public rooms of the Venetian Embassy (Palazzo di Venezia) included a chancellory, a large meeting room, a banquet hall, and rooms where students studied languages to become dragomans.[66]

The Venetian Council of Twelve convened regularly in the embassy in Pera to discuss communal affairs. The baili received official visitors from the nation, who came to settle various legal, fiscal, and administrative issues, in the public reception hall. In addition, the baili regularly hosted banquets at night for guests of various backgrounds, such as European ambassadors, trad-ers, and Ottoman high officials, with whom they intermingled freely.[67] The baili gained intimate knowledge of Ottoman politics through these contacts and embassy receptions.

Soon, the French, Dutch, and English Embassies were moved to Pera for the same reasons that the Venetian baili had effected their move. The French ambassador Savary de Bréves (1589–1606) had purchased a wooded piece of land in Pera (the site of Takiuddin's observatory) and in the late sixteenth century built the French Embassy (*Maison de France*) on Tomtom Street, close to the Venetian Embassy and along the upper slopes of Tophane, with a beautiful panorama of the Sea of Marmara and the Bosphorus. The French

Germain Fabius Brest, *The French Palace in Pera* (1855–59). Suna and Inan Kiraç Foundation Collection, © Uğur Ataç.

ambassadors Henry de Gournay and Marquis de Nointel (1670–79) expanded the original building several times during the seventeenth century, possibly after major fires.[68]

The Parisian architect Vigné de Vigny in 1721 proposed a new plan in timber for the embassy that resembled Ottoman residential architecture. However, his master rejected the plan, and the existing building was instead renovated with a geometrical courtyard. The ground floor contained a wine storage, which was very important for the social life of the embassy. The first floor had offices and bureaus, and the second and third floors contained the private residence of the ambassador and his family, with salons and dining rooms for entertainment and bedrooms.[69] After the big fire of 1767, the current French ambassador, François-Emmanuel Guignard comte de Saint-Priest (1768–84), moved the embassy further away from the main street of Pera. François Baron de Tott, the French aristocrat of Hungarian origin and military adviser in İstanbul, rebuilt the structure from masonry in a neoclassical design with Ionic colonnades and pilasters between 1774 and 1777.[70] But the building had suffered badly from several fires, so the embassy had to be moved to the Venetian Embassy's building after Napoleon's takeover of Venice in the early nineteenth century. In 1815, Austria took over the Venetian Embassy, and the French Embassy moved back to its old site.

Fires also led to financial losses for the ambassadors. For example, in 1800, the English ambassador sent his dragoman to the Porte to report that since the recent fire had destroyed the papers of English merchants, they needed a loan and some extra time to pay their taxes (the poliçe tax). He requested a loan of 70,000 kuruş from the Ottoman state, which was denied because the state lacked funds and had just made a loan to the French Embassy.[71] However, the Ottoman state asked two Jewish bankers to provide a loan in several installments to the English merchants so that the latter could pay their taxes.

The fire of 1831 in Istanbul burned all of the embassies except the Austrian Embassy (the former Venetian Palazzo). However, the fire created opportunities for the embassies to be reconstructed in a new hybrid style. The design of the European embassies was subsequently transformed from that of a traditional Ottoman *konak* to a hybrid Ottoman and neoclassical style after major fires had caused extensive damages.[72]

The French Embassy building burned down completely during the fire of August 1831, after which the embassy was temporarily moved to its summer residence in Tarabya, far away from other embassies. Ambassador Albin-Rein baron Roussin (amb. 1832–39) commissioned the Parisian architect Pierre Laurésisque to begin constructing a new building in a monumental and neoclassical style in 1839. The new embassy building, which was completed between 1844 and 1847, had two courtyards, in the back and front, and contained a chapel dedicated to St. Louis des Français. Many French ambassadors were later interred in the chapel.[73] A new addition, constructed between 1873 and 1874, contained a law court, a prison, a church, a school, and stables.

After the major fires, Europeans led the trend of adopting a new building style in Pera with their embassy buildings' reconstruction that reflected the increasing power of the European and Russian embassies. The growing influence of French, English, and Russian diplomats led to the selection of the palatial and monumental neoclassical style, which Paolo Girardelli has called "the architecture of diplomacy and power," for the design of their countries' embassies. Girardelli has argued that this architecture of diplomacy was ambivalent in that it reflected the cultural identity of the country it represented as well as the local Ottoman surroundings.[74] But the monumental embassy architecture also reflected the competition for power among England, France, and Russia in the Ottoman capital. All three embassies adopted this architectural style as they competed for power in the Ottoman capital in the late eighteenth and nineteenth centuries.

After earlier European and Russian embassies had burned down several times during the fires of Galata, they were rebuilt by European architects such as the Swiss Giuseppe Fossati. The fire of 1831 had destroyed the Dutch as well as the Russian Embassies. After that fire, the reconstructed Russian Embassy established the tone for the monumental architecture of diplomacy that made the palatial embassies of Russia, France, and Great Britain centers of power and rivalry among these nations in Pera.[75] The Fossati brothers, who worked for the Russian tsar as his official architects, moved to Istanbul in 1837 to design the new Russian and Dutch Embassies. They lived in Istanbul for twenty years and also became the sultan's official architects. In 1855, the Fossati brothers restored the Haghia Sophia Friday Mosque after a fire. Giuseppe Fossati also redesigned the Dutch Embassy in 1855. His brother, Gaspare Fossati, designed the new Russian Embassy between 1837 and 1845 in the monumental style that reflected the rising power of Russia during this period.[76] It took six years to construct the Russian Embassy in an imposing neoclassical style with the help of Russian craftsmen brought from St. Petersburg and Italian artists who had been commissioned to paint the ceilings and walls. Thomas Allom, an English artist, architect, and topographic illustrator who designed many buildings in London such as St. Peter's Notting Hill and parts of the Parliament, described the changes on the street of embassies after the reconstruction of the British Embassy in 1839:

> The town of Pera occupies the elevated ridge of a high promontory between the harbor and the Bosphorus. On the spine of this eminence[,] the European natives have established their residence. The merchants, whose stores and offices are below, have their dwelling houses on this lofty and healthful elevation, to which they are seen climbing in groups every evening, when the business of the day is over. Their habitations form a strong contrast to [those] of the Turks. They are lofty, solid, and convenient, and from their height command a magnificent view of the circumjacent seas, with all their bays and islands. Here also the ambassadors of the different powers of Europe have their palaces, among which the British [Embassy], before its destruction by fire[,] was the most beautiful and conspicuous. (Thomas Allom and Robert Walsh, 1838)[77]

The British Embassy was the first embassy to be rebuilt from masonry at the beginning of the nineteenth century. The oldest hotels (the Bristol, Büyük Londra, and Pera Palace) and the oldest theatre were also located in this neighborhood (Tepebaşı) next to the British Embassy.

Antoine-Ignace Melling, *Constantinople seen from Pera*. Photo courtesy of the Newberry Library, Chicago.

LA BELLE ÉPOQUE: MUNICIPAL REFORMS IN PERA

To reconstruct their embassy buildings and part of Pera in the aftermath of the fires, European embassies also hired architects and engineers to prepare maps of Istanbul and Galata and carry out surveys of buildings. The German architect François Kauffer, a friend of the French ambassador, Marie-Gabriel-Florent-Auguste, Comte de Choiseul-Gouffier (amb. 1784–92), and Antoine-Ignace Melling (1763–1831) prepared the first series of scientific maps of İstanbul and the villages along the Bosphorus in 1784. In addition, French architects, military advisers, and engineers played an important role in the construction of embassies, modern barracks, military schools, dams, canals, and the new arsenal in the French neoclassical style in Istanbul. During the second half of the eighteenth century and the reigns of Mahmud I (1730–54) and Selim III (1789–1807), French advisers helped to build waterworks and new dams in Bahçeköy in the Belgarde Forest that distributed water through underground canals to the new quarter in Pera, Kasım Paşa, Galata, and Tophane. The distribution center, a masonry structure, was in Taksim, the highest point in Pera, where a fountain was constructed. The erection of new dams and distribution networks was completed during the reign of Abdülhamid I (1774–89) in 1784.[78]

The Tanzimat Reforms (1839–1874), which were carried out in several phases, asserted the role of the state in municipal administration, undermining the role of religious officials like the kadi and the imam in local affairs. The Rescript of Gülhane initiated the Tanzimat Reforms by Mahmud II (r. 1808–39) in 1839, and the Reform Order of 1856 promised the protection of life, property, and honor to all Ottoman subjects regardless of their religion.[79] The concept of the protection of private property by the state, which had previously been weak in the Ottoman Empire, gained ground during these reforms. Moreover, new laws allowed foreign residents to purchase property after 1856. The Tanzimat Reforms legalized private property on a large scale, undermining the vakfs' control over commercial property and leading to the commercialization of the urban fabric in Karaköy and Pera. The opening of closed quarters and dead-end streets reduced the risk of fires but at the same time undermined the roles of the community watch and the janissary corps in controlling crime. Instead, modern police stations were installed in Asmalı Mescit to monitor crime.

Reşit Pasha, the engineer of the Tanzimat Reforms and the former Ottoman ambassador in London, advocated the adoption of European technology and masonry construction to reduce the risk of fires. The English pattern of detached houses and firewalls was adopted in parts of Galata and Pera, particularly in the reconstruction of embassies. Helmuth Van Moltke, a Prussian topographic cartographer, designed a development plan in 1839 for proper street networks and width as well as for open spaces, building heights, and masonary buildings.[80]

In Galata and Pera, the existence of European communities had an important influence on the modernization projects that had already begun during the eighteenth century. In these cities, Ottoman sultans, the Tanzimat reformers such as Reşit Pasha and their European advisers, and members of the local bourgeoisie all played key roles in the modernization of the urban fabric.[81] The role of European advisers (mostly French) and architects in the transformation of Pera and greater Istanbul continued after the great fires (1831–1870) that had destroyed much of the urban landscape in Galata and Istanbul proper, paving the way for these changes.[82]

Like Paris, Istanbul was divided into fourteen municipal districts in 1856, each to be placed under the administration of a municipal council that was responsible for building reconstruction, garbage collection, street lighting, and tax collection. Thirteen districts were under the control of the mayor. A fourteenth, the Sixth District, was composed of Pera, Galata, Kasım Paşa, Taksim, and Tophane and extended all the way to Harbiye and the villages along the European shore of the Bosphorus.[83] It was directly under the control of the Prime Minister. The Municipal Council of the Sixth District was modeled after the French *Prefecture de Ville* and was made up of seven members, who had been appointed by the government; it was chaired by Kamil Bey, the Minister of Foreign Affairs and the first director of the council. Kamil Bey visited many European cities and headed the organization of the Ottoman Pavilion at the Universal Exhibition in Paris in 1856.

The Municipal Council reflected the diversity of the Sixth District and included local Ottoman, European, and non-Muslim subjects who were under European protection. Regardless of their nationality and religion, the members had to be property owners who had lived in the district for more than ten years.[84]

Although the European embassies had tried to exert control over the council, the central government eventually assumed leadership of the municipal government in the Sixth District in 1868.[85] The district was then placed under the jurisdiction of the Supreme Council of Judicial Ordinances and was headed by the mayor, Salih Pasha, who had been appointed by the Ottoman government and had to approve every plan. The Advisory Commission of the Sixth District was headed by Haci Hussam Efendi and was composed of European residents and protégés like Antoine Alleon (a real estate developer); wealthy non-Muslim bankers like Ohannes Migerdiç (an Armenian banker), David Revelaki (a Greek under British protection), and Avram Camondo (a banker and Jewish real state developer under Austrian protection); Septime Franchini and Charles Hanson, British traders; Theodore Naum, an Ottoman citizen under French protection who founded the first Opera House in the 1840s; two local Greeks; an Armenian; and two Muslims.[86] Of this group, Abraham (Avram) Camondo played the most important role in the development of Galata.[87]

The responsibilities of the Municipal Council included the preparation of a detailed cadastral survey (showing detailed information on properties and buildings for tax purposes) for the district, road construction, street widening and planning, sewer replacement, water supplying, garbage collection, the construction of sewerage, and the regulation of markets. The Sixth District had the authority to draft its own budget, collect taxes (2 percent on income from properties), and service its own buildings, powers that it retained until 1868, when a new municipal model was introduced for the whole city.[88] One of the most important tasks of the Municipal Council was to collect revenue from property owners for urban services such as street cleaning and street planning.

But European residents, who enjoyed the protection of embassies, refused to pay property taxes in accordance with the articles of the ahdnames. The government appointed four Muslim Turks to the Advisory Commission and Server Efendi, the former chief secretary of the Ministry of Foreign Affairs, as the new director in 1868. The Advisory Commission prepared development plans for reconstruction from masonry, street widening (4.5, 7.5, and 9 meters), street planning (a grid system), building heights, and public spaces. It also initiated plans to establish a modern fire department and modern policing, gas lighting, and garbage collection as well as modern transportation.[89]

However, due to financial problems, these plans remained on paper. Due to the lack of funding to even pay the salaries of the staff, the Municipal Council failed to achieve much after a few years of work, so much of the urban fabric in Galata and Pera remained traditional. This outcome was in part also due to the topography of Galata and the densely inhabited neighborhoods that made the grid plan very difficult to impose on areas that had not been leveled by fires.

In addition, the introverted city was being expanded with the demolition of the ramparts and the opening of dead-end streets. The demolition of the old Genoese walls of Galata in 1864 by the municipal office of the Sixth District (followed by similar measures in Salonica and Izmir) occurred under the supervision of a French architect who lived in Istanbul, Marie de Launay, and aimed to integrate Galata into the rest of the city. By the mid-nineteenth century, dead-end streets had started disappearing, even in the traditional neighborhoods such as Kasap Ilyas in Istanbul proper.[90] Moreover, plans were underway for the removal of cemeteries from Taksim for relocation in Şişli and for the construction of a Beaux-Arts park in their place in Taksim and a public park in Tepebaşı.[91] The construction of the Municipal Palace for administrative offices in Şişhane in 1870s highlighted the privileged positon of the Sixth District before the government assumed its administration.

By the mid-nineteenth century, Pera resembled Marseille in its architecture and Paris in its municipal organization since it was connected to the former via maritime trade and the latter through diplomacy. Rue de Pera in many ways was very similar to Rue de Canebière in Marseille with its *bon marché* shops, covered passages, arcades, patisseries, cafés, brasseries, beer gardens, masonary apartment buildings, hotels, and tramway line. Art Nouveau architecture dominated the design of commercial shops as well as new apartment buildings in Marseille and Pera. However, Marseille had undergone a major modernization in its urban environment during the eighteenth and nineteenth centuries, whereas, due to the lack of funding, the process was partial and limited in scope in Galata and Istanbul.

CONCLUSION

The rise of Pera, the old necropolis of Galata, accompanied the settlement there of European diplomats and traders from congested and crime-ridden Galata inside the walls. The plague and fires led to the establishment of central control, the surveillance and control of certain city-scapes (coffeehouses, bachelors' rooms), and the conversion of a few churches into mosques or their relocation. The great fires of Galata and Pera in the eighteenth and nineteenth centuries reduced most of the Rue de Pera to ashes, paving the way for the rise of municipal reforms during the Tanzimat era (1839–74) and modern city planning in Pera and Galata. The rebuilding of European embassies that had burned down in the fire of 1831 led the way for the adoption of neoclassical palatial and monumental design. European architects and advisers as well as the new commercial bourgeoisie played an active role in the modernization of Isanbul as a whole that can be traced back to the eighteenth century. Although Istanbul did not become a colonial city like Algiers, European finance and (French) models of urban development played a key role in the physical transformation of Pera and the rest of the city in the second half of the eighteenth and nineteenth centuries. In parts of Galata and Pera (the Sixth District), the enclosed and self-contained *mahalle* (residential quarter) was opened up by the adoption of a grid system and regular street plans.

The expansion of the marketplace, the slow dissolution of guilds, the rise of commercial institutions (banks) connected with trade, and the dissolution of traditional urban institutions began in the late eighteenth century but gained speed during the second half of the nineteenth century.[92] But in Galata and Pera, unlike in Marseille, modernization was partial, patchy, and hybrid due to limited state funds and the fragmented and layered topography of the city as well as the role of vakf properties, which made it difficult for them to be converted into new structures. But the old order based on corporate groups like guilds and public domain policies (vakf properties) was slowly giving way to a new urban regime based on the role of capital, international finance, and private property envisioned by the Tanzimat reformers, the emerging bourgeoisie, and their European advisers.[93]

PART TWO

———————

The Legal and Diplomatic Setting

AFTER THE PEACEFUL TAKEOVER OF GALATA, Sultan Mehmed II granted the Genoese community of Galata an ahdname in June 1453 that basically renewed the treaties the Genoese had received from the Byzantine state since 1261. The Ottoman state followed this legal regime and developed it further to revive trade and attract the friendly Italian and Western European traders to its ports. Both the shari'a and the kanun provided the legal foundation for the treatment and status of Christian states and local non-Muslim communities. These communities enjoyed considerable legal and religious autonomy in Galata. The second part of this book will trace the origins of this legal regime and its evolution and development in Ottoman ports like Galata. Placing these treaties in a comparative context, chapters 3 and 4 will explore the content of the treaties and their evolution as well as their limitations in the context of the changing commercial and diplomatic dynamics from the fifteenth to the nineteenth centuries. Contrary to the notion of a weak empire that surrendered its commercial interests to an aggressive West, chapter 3 will shed light on a very dynamic international order in which the Ottoman state was a major player. It formed diplomatic alliances as well as commercial partnerships not only with Catholic countries like France but also with Protestant nations like England and the Netherlands out of a sense of pragmatism. Chapter 4 will show that a close alliance with France in the eighteenth century gave her the most favored nation status in the Ahdname of 1740. This ahdname was a turning point in the regime of ahdnames that granted France important commercial rights that extended to the Black Sea. The Ottoman state, however, was losing its grip on the Black Sea and Crimea with the rise of Catherine II's colonial project. Nevertheless, the Ottoman state implemented the articles with great rigor as long as peace prevailed between it and the signatory states. However, the French Revolution and Napoleon's occupation of Egypt disrupted this process in a profound manner (see epilogue).

THREE

Ottoman Ahdnames

THEIR ORIGINS AND DEVELOPMENT IN
THE EARLY MODERN PERIOD

THE OTTOMAN COMMERCIAL REGIME WAS A MIXTURE of regulatory and laissez-faire policies that it had inherited from the Byzantine Empire as well as from Islamic states. Its economic system evolved over time in accordance with domestic needs, diplomatic relations, and global conditions. The legal regime of ahdnames regulated international trade with friendly nations and Italian city-states after the conquest of Constantinople and the takeover of Galata in 1453, although this system can be traced back to the medieval period. The origins and evolution of this legal regime in Galata and other Ottoman ports is the focus of part 2.

Eastern Mediterranean ports like Galata and Izmir shared a special social makeup and a legal system that provided a great deal of social and ethno-religious diversity during the early modern period.[1] Bruce Masters has referred to caravan cities like Aleppo where Europeans resided and enjoyed the privileges accorded by ahdnames as treaty cities. The plural legal system of Ottoman ports was in part based on a shared Mediterranean tradition of commercial and diplomatic treaties signed between Muslim states and foreign communities to facilitate international trade. This legal instrument was called a *capitulation* (heading in a treaty) in the Mediterranean West and an *ahdname* (pact or treaty of alliance) in the eastern Mediterranean and the Islamic world, with slight variations. One could easily study these documents as medieval antecedents of international commercial law as well as the components of a plural legal system. It is clear that this legal regime was part of the Byzantine tradition as well. While Europe shifted to a uniform legal system in the sixteenth century, the legal pluralism of Ottoman ports continued until the early twentieth century.

A systematic and comparative study of these treaties from the late medieval period to the early nineteenth century reveals the evolution of Ottoman commercial policies in its port cities as well as its diplomacy with the West. This chapter will trace the origins of this international legal system under the regime of ahdnames and its development in the Ottoman Empire while the next chapter (4) will explore its transformation in the seventeenth and eighteenth centuries.

AHDNAMES: COMMERCIAL TREATIES OR TOOLS OF IMPERIALISM?

There is ongoing debate among Ottomanist historians on the definition of *ahdnames* and on their impact on the Ottoman economy during the early modern period.[2] There is a tendency among some scholars to mistranslate the term *capitulation* into "submission" or "surrender" to European powers on the part of Ottoman rulers as a result of their military weakness and lack of economic vision, which led to a colonial relationship. The Latin word *capitula* meant headings or chapters in a treaty or charter that the Italian city-states acquired from Byzantine emperors and Muslim rulers.[3] Medieval forms of capitulations (treaties) also regulated commercial and diplomatic relations between Muslim Granada and the kingdoms of Aragon and Valencia. In addition, they defined the status of Muslim communities in Christian majority states.[4] In fact, the legal status of Muslim subject communities in Christian majority states in Iberia was very similar to that of *zimmi* (non-Muslim) communities in Muslim majority states in the Islamic world. In other words, this use of ahdnames was a shared legal tradition to ease cohabitation and commerce across religious divides that can be traced back to the medieval Mediterranean and Islamic worlds.

While the European states shifted to a uniform legal system in the sixteenth century after the expulsion of Moriscos and Marranos from the Iberian Peninsula, the Ottoman state built on the legal tradition of using ahdnames and expanded it with its close allies like France in its major port cities. But the Muslim bureaucrats always used the term *ahdname* (treaty), a Persian term, rather than *capitulation,* which became popular in European states. *Ahdname* in the Ottoman context meant a voluntary, temporary, unilateral, and revocable pledge of amnesty or protection given to a friendly foreign Christian community or nation as long as peace prevailed. Thus, every ahdname signed between the Ottoman and European rulers had to be approved by the head of the Muslim judiciary, the *şeyhülislam,* to conform to the *shari'a* (Islamic law), which also assigned a special status to non-Muslim communities (both local and foreign). Muslim bureaucrats never used the Latin term *capitulation,* which had a different history and trajectory in medieval Europe. While the earlier ahdnames had been reciprocal or had reciprocal articles, the later ahdnames excluded reciprocity in commerce and legal protection for Muslim communities in Europe.

THE ISLAMIC ORIGINS OF AHDNAMES

Some historians have traced the granting of capitulations to the earlier Islamic and Turkish states as well as to medieval Mediterranean states.[5] Nesim Susa has traced the origins of *extraterritoriality,* or "personality of law," in which foreign nations were subject to their own laws, to ancient Egypt, Greece, the Roman Empire, and the early Islamic states. He has described the basis of this legal system as the "personality of law," according to which foreigners carried their own laws wherever they went, a practice that was commonly recognized.[6] The concept of *territorial sovereignty* was weak in Europe and the Ottoman Empire until the sixteenth century, so foreigners could live under the jurisdiction of their own legal systems when they traveled. Daniel Goffman has defined the regime of ahdnames as the Ottoman contribution to the age of "New Diplomacy" in Renaissance Europe based on the shari'a principles in port cities where Europeans lived in their own enclaves. He has called Ottoman port cities like Galata "middle grounds" between two civilizations.[7]

In the Islamic world, non-Muslim foreign nations were divided into two categories, those from the abode of war (*dar al-harb*) and those that enjoyed peace and treaty relations (*dar al-ahd*) with Muslim states. Therefore, the shari'a promised protection and safe conduct for the lives and property of diplomats and traders from those nations that entered into peaceful relations with Muslim states.[8] After a period of warfare, Islamic law allowed Muslim states to form a truce with Christian enemy states for one year and to grant unilateral treaties (ahdnames) that would last from four months to one year to allow trade if the Muslim state was strong. It is important to emphasize the temporary nature of these treaties and their contingency on the state of peace between the signatory states. Therefore, at the ascension of a new sultan, it was highly important for European states to renegotiate and renew these treaties.

Halil Inalcik has argued that ahdnames were revocable and unilateral pledges of peace granted by the Ottoman state to friendly nations that had at the same time unwritten reciprocal privileges for Ottoman subjects.[9] In other words, they were created to facilitate trade and diplomacy and were not tools for Western domination of Ottoman markets. European states, however, were reluctant to allow Muslim traders to reside in their ports and have the same privileges that European subjects had in Ottoman ports.

Alexander De Groot has maintained that the Ottoman state also used a variety of legal terminologies like *truce, peace,* and *submission* (of Christian states like Venice) to enter into treaty relations that provided mutual protection with otherwise enemy states.[10] Inalcik has also emphasized the shari'a-based legal definition of the *ahdname* and the support of the *şeyhülislam* (chief religious figure) for these treaties with friendly Christian states. All non-Muslim foreigners were thus regarded as obedient subjects on whom the benevolent Ottoman ruler bestowed privileges as long as peace prevailed in accordance with the Ottoman Hanafi tradition. Moreover, Inalcik has rightly pointed out that the Ottoman state did not consider Western trade to be crucial to its economy, as was the case with domestic and Eastern trade. It, therefore, used the ahdname as a tool of diplomacy with some Western European countries (particularly France) against their common enemy, the Habsburg Empire, in the sixteenth century.[11]

This legal tradition, however, had existed earlier in the Islamic world. Medieval Muslim states had granted ahdnames to Italian city-states to promote trade and forge alliances, often against other Muslim states. For example, the Fatimid (909–1171) and Mamluk sultans (1250–1517) gave concessions to the merchants of Amalphi, Pisa, Venice, Florence, and France to trade in Egypt in the twelfth and thirteenth centuries.[12] These treaties were usually reciprocal and bilateral regarding commerce. They guaranteed the general security of persons and their property, freedom of worship, freedom of burial, and freedom of dress. The treaties also allowed repairs to ships and provided aid against corsair attacks. Foreign subjects could submit petitions to Muslim states and also enjoy legal access to consular courts of their own nations.[13] In addition, the shari'a allowed the subject "peoples of the book" (Christians and Jews) to practice their own religions and apply their own laws in civil matters in Islamic states as long as they paid the Ottoman poll tax and refrained from declaring war, a legal arrangement that was extended to foreigners who enjoyed protection. But foreigners were still under the jurisdiction of Islamic law and sultanic kanun as long as they lived in Muslim states.

The Ottoman Empire followed the Seljuk and Ilkhanid as well as the Byzantine traditions in granting ahdnames to Italian city-states and European nations. The Seljuk state of Anatolia (1074–1300) signed trade agreements with Venice in the thirteenth century, of which only the text of the Treaty of 1220 has survived.[14] This tradition also existed in medieval Iran. In addition, the Ilkhanid Mongol state in Iran (1250–1334) expanded the silk trade with Italian city-states in Tabriz and pursued its own policy of alliance with the Vatican and Italian city-states against the Mamluks[15] The Ilkhanid rulers also allowed Dominican and Franciscan monks to establish churches and monasteries in Tabriz, actions that created an important base for Catholic missionaries in Iran.[16]Venice established a consul in Tabriz and signed trade agreements with the Ilkhanid state in 1246, 1271, and 1320 (29 articles).[17] The Ahdname of 1320 provided Venetian merchants with freedom of trade, security of life and property, exemption from internal dues, low customs rates (2 percent), and freedom of legal and religious practice.[18] After the disintegration of the Ilkhanid state in 1334, trade declined, and in 1338 the Senate in Venice forbade her merchants from going to Tabriz. Venice then shifted her commercial activities to Western Anatolia (Bursa) and the Aegean islands.

The Ilkhanid tradition of having treaty relations with the Italian city-states continued under the Turkish principalities in Anatolia and laid the foundation for what emerged later under the Ottomans. Venice signed a series of treaties with the rising Turkish principality of Menteşe in 1318 and 1331 and with Aydin in 1337 and 1353 to import corn, rice, cattle, horses, hides, wax, gall nuts, alum, salves, and metal from Anatolia into Europe and to export wine, soap, and Italian textiles (silk, flax, cotton, and wool) to the Levant.[19] The treaties contained important reciprocal clauses on the general security of life and property of merchants, freedom of trade and worship, the protection of Turkish and Cretan merchants and their ships from piracy, aid during shipwrecks, the liberation of captives abducted from Crete and other islands that were dependencies of Crete, the extradition of slaves, the rate of customs and other dues, bans on the trade of certain goods like grains, and the duties and jurisdictions of Venetian consuls.[20] In 1390, the Ottoman sultan Bayezid I (1389–1402) granted the same privileges to Venice that were renewed by subsequent Ottoman sultans in 1403, 1406, 1411, 1419, 1430, and 1446.[21] These treaties were very similar to those granted by the Byzantine states to the Italian city-states.

BYZANTINE TRADITION: TREATY OF NYMPHAEUM, 1261

The Ottoman Empire also followed Byzantine traditions in negotiating ahd-names with the Italian city-states, but it departed from them in an important way. Since the tenth century, the Byzantine state also had granted treaties to the Italian city-states to trade freely in her ports. After the Fourth Crusade (1204–61), the Italian city-states received trading rights and privileges in Constantinople and Galata to trade and to build houses, shops, warehouses, churches, and a municipal office in the port areas (see chapter 1). The bilateral Treaty of Nymphaeum that the Genoese in Galata signed with Byzantine emperor Michael Paleologos in April 1261 pledged permanent peace with Genoa and a state of war with Venice. The emperor promised to protect Genoese possessions on land and sea (on the islands and in harbors that his nation possessed), prevent any act of piracy against her merchants, and protect the persons and property of Genoese nationals, including those who had been shipwrecked.

In addition, Genoa could establish consuls in all these places who could settle disputes between Genoese subjects in consular courts. But the Byzantine emperor settled any disputes between the Genoese and Byzantine subjects in his own court of justice, a tradition that continued under the Ottomans, as will be discussed later. The Genoese could also own property and churches in Galata, on Chios, and in all the colonies. They could export foodstuff, grains, and all merchandise and were exempt from all taxation and customs dues on imports, exports, and transit trade throughout the empire. In return, Byzantine traders could trade freely in Genoese lands and pay lower customs dues.[22] In addition, the Treaty of Nymphaeum gave the Genoese exclusive access to the Black Sea, an arrangement that ended with the Ottoman conquest of Constantinople in 1453.

In 1391, the Byzantine emperor also granted the Ottoman Turks permission to conduct trade in Constantinople, build a mosque, and establish an Islamic court with a kadi that had jurisdiction over the affairs of the small

Muslim community.[23] Turkish merchants also traded with Galata after the signing of an Ottoman-Genoese treaty in the mid-fourteenth century.

THE AHDNAME OF 1453 WITH THE GENOESE COMMUNITY IN GALATA

Following the earlier treaties granted to Ragusa in 1430 and 1442 and to Genoese-controlled Chios in 1453 as tribute-paying but autonomous ports, the Ottoman state granted a series of ahdnames to Italian city-states after the conquest of Constantinople on May 29, 1453.[24] Galata was more important than both Dubrovnik and Chios, two important treaty ports on the Aegean and the Adriatic Seas, due to its strategic location in the capital. The Genoese community had already signed a treaty of alliance with the Ottoman principality in 1352, but its aid to Byzantine forces during the siege of Constantinople had undermined its relationship with the Ottomans. Once the community had surrendered peacefully to Sultan Mehmed II, it was able to negotiate and receive an ahdname in June 1453. The text of the Ahdname of 1453 played an important role in Ottoman-Genoese commercial relations and formed a model for the subsequent treaties given to other Italian-city states:

> I [Mehmed II] in return [for their submission] agree that they [the Genoese] may follow their own customs and rites as were in force before; that I will not go against them and demolish their fortress. So I ordered that their money, provisions, properties, storehouses, vineyards, mills, ships[,] and boats, in short[,] all their possessions as well as their wives, sons, and slaves of both sexes be left in their hands as before and that nothing be done contrary thereof, nor to molest them; that they pursue their livelihood, as in other parts of my dominion, and travel by land and by sea in freedom without any hindrance or molestation and be exempt from extraordinary impositions; that I impose on them the Islamic poll tax that they pay as other non-Muslims do every year; that they keep their churches and perform their customary rites in them with the exception of ringing their church bell too loudly; that I do not take away from them their present churches and turn them into mosques, but that they do not attempt to build new churches; that the Genoese merchants come and go by sea and land for trade, pay the customs dues as required under the established rules[,] and be free from molestation by anyone. And I ordered that their sons not . . . be taken as janissaries and that no infidel be converted into Islam against his will, that they elect freely someone amongst them as *kethüda* [steward] to look after their own affairs[,] and that the inhabitants of the fortress as well as [the] merchants be free from forced labor.[25]

Like the previous treaties given to Dubrovnik and the Genoese community in Chios, this treaty provided a special status for the community in Galata. Furthermore, the treaty provided for the freedom of trade by land and sea anywhere in the empire as long as the Genoese paid the agreed-upon customs dues and remained peaceful. The Genoese community was divided into two groups, those who became Ottoman subjects and had to pay the poll tax (*cizye*) as non-Muslims if they resided in Galata longer (than one year) and those who remained Genoese subjects and had to pay customs dues. According to the shari'a, European merchants were subject to the poll tax if they stayed in Galata longer than one year. This provision was later changed to ten years and then to an indefinite time and led to disputes over the payment of the poll tax between Ottoman officials and European subjects. The treaty also granted the Genoese exemption from all extraordinary taxes and promised a measure of self-rule within the walls of Galata. In addition, the Genoese could elect a representative (*podesta*) to look into their affairs.

Inalcik has cautioned us, however, not to exaggerate the communal autonomy of the Genoese in Galata, even though they had received an ahdname.[26] The self-organization of foreign nations in Galata was very similar to the organization of non-Muslim communities in the empire.[27] But the ahdname was above all a commercial charter given to foreign merchants allowing for the freedom of trade and residence in certain ports, towns, and spaces as well as exemption from personal taxes and internal dues. Venice, Florence, and Pisa received similar ahdnames in the second half of the fifteenth and sixteenth centuries that granted their merchants rights similar to those of Genoese merchants.[28] In addition to those given to the Italian city-states, ahdnames were granted to western European allies such as France in 1569, 1581, 1597, 1604, 1673, and 1740; to England in 1580, 1583, 1601, 1616, 1624, 1643, 1666, and 1675; and to the Netherlands in 1612. Poland, Russia, and Austria also received ahdnames, and nations without one (e.g., Spain, Sicily) could trade under the flag of Great Britain and France. The ahdname formed a network of interconnected charters of rights and codified taxes and consular representation that allowed foreign merchants to reside in Ottoman ports and trade without having to become Ottoman subjects. Ahdnames were useful as instruments of international law and dispute resolution since Galata had become an important international transit port for the export of Iranian raw silk and silk textiles from Tabriz and Bursa to Italian-city states and Europe.[29]

Venice was the most powerful of the Italian city-states, with commercial colonies all over the Aegean and the eastern Mediterranean. In addition, Venice dominated the spice trade between Egypt and the Mediterranean as well as the silk trade among Iran, the Levant, and Europe until the sixteenth century. Despite many wars between the two states, Venice enjoyed the longest treaty relations with the Ottoman Empire among the Italian city-states, and the two states exchanged envoys on a regular basis during times of peace.[30] The Venetian *bailo* was the most powerful European envoy in Galata, and Ottoman temporary envoys (*çavuş*) visited Venice regularly in the sixteenth century.[31] At the same time, Venetian traders and bailos also gathered information and were most familiar with politics in the Porte and conditions of trade in the empire (see chapter 1). Venice received an ahdname from Sultan Mehmed II in April 1454 that was the confirmation of the older treaty that had concluded in Edirne with Mehmed II in 1451. It gave Venetian merchants freedom to trade all over the empire at a reduced customs rate of 2 percent. It also called for reciprocal protection of merchants, ships, and goods from piracy.[32] In return, Ottoman merchants could trade and reside freely in Venetian ports and could enjoy safety of conduct.[33]

However, Venice's relationship with the empire deteriorated with a new series of Ottoman conquests in the Morea and Aegean islands. The Ottoman conquest of the Morea in 1464 and of the prized Venetian posts of Negroponte and Limnos between 1477and 1479; Lepanto in 1499; and Navarino, Coron, and the entire Peloponnesian Peninsula by 1502 undermined Venice's commercial ascendancy in the eastern Mediterranean. Falling from its position as a major commercial power that possessed thirty-eight Aegean islands in the early fifteenth century, Venice became a secondary player in the sixteenth century. The import of grains from the thirty-eight Aegean islands it possessed was of primary importance. Although Venice had enjoyed duty-free trade under Byzantine rule, her traders had had to pay customs dues, which Mehmed II had raised to 5 percent. Venetian traders also had to compete with other Italian city-states, Dubrovnik, and Western European maritime powers that gained an important foothold in Ottoman ports after the signing of ahdnames with the Ottoman Empire in the sixteenth century.

Mehmed II also promoted the trade of Florentine merchants and gave them important privileges and an ahdname.[34] They imported woolen textiles into Galata and exported Persian raw silk, silk textiles from Bursa, spices, hides, and other goods. For example, the Florentine Giovanni Francesco Maringhi was a major trader and banker in Galata who had made fortunes from the silk trade. Florence replaced Venice as the main Italian partner during the Ottoman-Venetian Wars (1463–1500) in the late fifteenth century.

Once these wars had ended and negotiations had resulted in the drawing of new borders, Venice sued for peace and received an ahdname in return for the payment of an annual tribute in order to trade in Ottoman ports. For Venice, commercial concerns often took precedence over religious differences and even over border disputes with the Ottoman Empire. Some scholars have argued that the earlier ahdnames with Venice in 1403 and 1411 were unilateral grants, but they became reciprocal in 1419 and changed again in 1482, after which they remained unilateral.[35] Clearly, Ottoman-Venetian relations were filled with tensions, which were reflected in the language of the treaties signed between the two states. Ottoman attacks on Venetian ships were a constant thorn in the side of the Senate in Venice. Venice imposed an embargo on trade with the Ottoman Empire in 1462, even after the signing of an ahdname in 1454.[36] But Venice had to pay a tribute to the Ottoman state in order for her merchants to conduct trade safely and to receive protection for her ships, merchants, and goods in Ottoman ports. The ahdnames of 1478 and 1482 with Venice specifically stated the need for traders and ships of both states to be assured safe conduct and for peaceful interactions between Venetian and Ottoman ships in return for an annual tribute of 10,000 gold florins in 1478 and 50,000 gold florins in 1482 to be paid by Venice.[37] In other words, Venice had to protect Ottoman ships and merchants, compensate for damages inflicted on Ottoman ships on the sea, seize fugitive debtors, and protect the lives and goods of Ottoman victims of shipwrecks while the Ottomans were obligated to provided Venice with the same protections and services.[38] It goes without saying that the earlier Ottoman-Venetian treaties had also been bilateral and reciprocal.[39]

As a result of these treaties, Ottoman Muslim merchants traded in Venice on behalf of the sultan or in partnership with other traders.[40] Levantine Jews also became very prominent as traders in Venice, though they were subjected to harassment and persecution during times of war over Cyprus in 1570.[41] The *Signoria* (ruler of Venice) appointed a Venetian bailo to Galata to dispense justice and collect the estates of deceased Venetians if no heir had been found.

According to the Treaty of 1478, he was not responsible for the debts of Venetian merchants.

Venice enjoyed a long history of commercial and diplomatic relations with Muslim states and had a dominant presence in Mamluk Cairo and Aleppo as well as in Tabriz in northwestern Iran supplying Asian spices from Cairo and Persian silks from Tabriz and Bursa to Europe. Venice considered her trade in spices with Mamluk Egypt far more important for its commercial interests than her trade in the Aegean islands and the Black Sea. However, the Ottoman expansion into the eastern Mediterranean ports and islands and later into Mamluk Egypt in 1517 undermined Venice's position in the spice trade.

After the conquest of Mamluk Egypt and Syria in 1517, Sultan Selim I (1520–40) renewed the Venetian ahdname in 1513 and 1517 in return for an annual tribute of 8,000 florin from Venice. To appease Venice, the sultan did not take the island of Cyprus, which lay between the Syrian cities and the ports of Egypt. Egypt exported crucial foodstuff like grains and rice to Istanbul and the Syrian cities in the north. In return, Venice pledged not to engage in piracy against Ottoman ships from its base in Cyprus. In addition, according to the ahdname, the Venetian bailo could reside in Istanbul for three years. Although the Ottoman state did not have a permanent envoy in Venice, a temporary envoy (çavuş) traveled there from time to time to represent the interests of Ottoman Muslim and Jewish merchants when disputes broke out in Venice, a frequent occurrence.[42] Both sides also pledged to punish those traders who fled before paying their debts. If a Venetian captive fled to Ottoman lands, he would be returned to his or her owner in return for a ransom of 1,000 akçe, whether or not the captive had converted to Islam. Likewise, the Venetian authorities would treat Ottoman subjects and convicts who had fled to Venetian lands in a similar manner.[43] However, Venetian merchants had to obtain permission from the bailo to travel to Ottoman towns like Bursa and would be exempt from the poll tax if they did not permanently reside in Ottoman lands. If they died in Ottoman lands, their estates would be given to the bailo. Disputes between the Venetian and Ottoman subjects would be handled in Ottoman courts by the kadi. Ottoman subjects and North African Muslims trading in Venetian lands would be subjected to the same treatment as Venetian subjects were in Ottoman ports.

Piracy by North African corsairs and privateers like the Barbarossa brothers, Oruc and Hizir (who had been born to a mixed parent from Lesbos), on the Spanish and Italian coasts was on the rise during the sixteenth century. With the naval assistance of Sultan Selim I, thousands of Christians were taken into captivity, and hundreds of merchant ships were incessantly attacked by Tripolitan pirates. Hizir Barbarossa later became the chief Ottoman admiral and governor of Algiers during the reign of Sultan Süleyman (1540–66) and received the new first name of Hayreddin. He continued his raids with the help of Turkish corsairs, North African Berbers, and Moriscos who had escaped and offered their services and knowledge of the Spanish coast to the Ottoman navy.[44] The sultan took one-fifth of the captives of war, and many ended up in the arsenal of Kasım Paşa as rowers (see chapter 1). Some became renegades and offered their services as corsairs and spies. Thus, the Mediterranean Sea had become the center of corsair attacks by both sides during the sixteenth century, making maritime commerce a dangerous activity. The ahdnames thus emphasized the suppression of piracy by both sides and the release of captives and goods.

Sultan Süleyman renewed the ahdname with Venice in 1521, 1535, and 1540 in return for the payment of 300,000 gold florins to the Ottoman state.[45] The Ahdname of 1540 also pledged reciprocal commitment for punishing pirates and those who enslaved Ottoman and Venetian traders and allowed for the ransoming of captives, whether or not they had converted to Catholicism or Islam, in return for 1,000 akçe. It stated that Venetian subjects who traded in Ottoman ports (Istanbul, Galata, Caffa, Trabzon, Alexandria, and other Arab ports) were exempt from personal taxes (cizye) as long as they did not live in those ports permanently. As stated in previous treaties, the bailo settled any disputes among Venetian subjects, but the kadi handled disputes between Venetian and Ottoman subjects in the presence of a Venetian dragoman. Any complaints against the bailo, however, were to be heard in the Imperial Council. No one would be responsible for the debt of a Venetian merchant but himself or his guarantor (kefil).[46] The goods of any Venetian merchant who had been attacked in Ottoman lands without any provocation were to be returned to him, his heir, or his agent, and the estates of deceased merchants were to be given to the bailo instead of seized by the Ottoman treasury.[47] The Venetian Doge also pledged friendship with the most important Ottoman ally, France, and maintained a state of war with her enemies, notably, the Habsburg Empire. No doubt, the articles of the ahdname were frequently violated by both sides.

Regular correspondence between the Porte and the Doge in Venice highlights the bilateral aspect of the Ottoman-Venetian ahdname regarding the affairs of Ottoman merchants in Venice and Venetian merchants in Istanbul and other Ottoman ports like Izmir. Ottoman merchants enjoyed safe conduct in Venice and Ancona and traded there freely for a while as long as peace prevailed. In general, Venetian traders were treated far better in Ottoman ports than Ottoman merchants were treated in Venice because the bailo in Galata protected the interests of Venetian merchants.[48]

But during times of war between the two states, Muslim and Jewish merchants were subjected to abuse, arrest, and threats of expulsion. Moreover, after the incorporation of Ancona into the Papal States, Jewish and Turkish merchants were subjected to increasing hostility and expulsion after 1556. An Ottoman imperial rescript in 1564 forbade Ottoman traders from going to Ancona due to the growing violence against Muslims and the possibility of their enslavement, encouraging them to instead trade with Venice and Dubrovnik.[49]

Ottoman relations with Venice deteriorated further during the war over Cyprus in 1570–71. Venice had gained control of Cyprus in 1489 and had imposed a colonial regime over its Greek population with heavy taxes (one-third of produce) and a demand for *corvée* labor (forced labor) three days a week). In addition, Christian pirates from coastal towns on Cyprus attacked Ottoman vessels on their way from Alexandria and Syria to Istanbul laden with grains and rice from Egypt and luxury goods from Syria. When news of an alliance between Spain and Venice reached Istanbul, Sultan Selim II (1566–74) ordered a large armada of three hundred vessels led by Lala Mustafa Pasha to attack Cyprus in June 1570.[50] The Greek Cypriots treated Lala Mustafa Pasha as their liberator from Venetian hands and helped Mustafa Pasha march into the capital city of Nicosia and swiftly take over the island in August 1571. As in Chios, the Ottomans did not allow the troops to plunder the island, carried out a survey of the island in 1572, reduced taxes on the Greek population, and ended the *corvée* demand and excise tax on salt. The Ottoman state forcefully settled Muslim nomads and farmers from Anatolia and Jews from Safed and Jerusalem on Cyprus.

Benjamin Arbel's study of Venetian archives has revealed important insights into the treatment of Muslims and Jews in Venice during the war over Cyprus.[51] In 1570, anti-Jewish hostilities reached a climax in Venice after the victory against the Ottomans in Lepanto. The Senate in Venice decided to expel all Jews from all Venetian territories in an edict of expulsion. The Pope was also invited to expel Jews from Ancona. In the interest of trade, the expulsion did not take place, but many Jews had decided to leave Venice, while Muslims were turning their trade to the port of Livorno. When the Cypriot War began, Ottoman Muslim and Jewish merchants were detained in March 1570, and their goods were confiscated according to a decree issued by the Senate. According to the report of a Jewish merchant who had escaped from Venice, seventy-five Muslims and eighty-seven Jews had been arrested and imprisoned in Venice alone. The number of Muslim and Jewish captives was far greater in other Venetian-held territories like Crete. The Venetian state confiscated their properties, worth 400,000 ducats, and sold them for half their value. In addition, Levantine Jews were stoned when they passed by the Greek quarter in Venice, their storage houses in the Rialto were plundered, and their ships were attacked. Jews were described as God-killers, traitors, and enemies in various pamphlets published in Venice during this time.[52]

The ahdname between the two states was no longer in effect during times of war, so both nations disregarded it. For example, the Venetian bailo received a lawsuit on August 1593 on behalf of an Ottoman merchant, Al-Hac Hüseyn, who had died in Venice, his goods having been seized by local officials.[53] When the news of the mistreatment of Muslim traders reached Istanbul, Grand Vizier Sokollu Mehmed Pasha threatened the bailo, Barbaro, with the arrest of all Venetians in Istanbul. He pressured the bailo to arrange the release of the Ottoman prisoners in Venice. In response, the Venetian bailo in Galata submitted a petition to the Imperial Council asking for the release of the goods of Venetian captains and merchants that had been seized by Ottoman officials during the war. Consequently, in May 1571, the Ottoman state issued an imperial order claiming that the mistreatment of the Venetian merchants had not been carried out by the order of the central government at time of peace but rather was a response to the abuse suffered by Ottoman merchants in Venice, which was contrary to the terms of the ahdname.[54] The imperial order also stated that Ottoman merchants who had been taken into custody in Venice should be returned to the Ottoman borders with their goods. In return, Venetian merchants who had been arrested in Ottoman lands would be released and could return to Venice. Finally, after peace had been restored on May 16, 1571, the Ottoman merchants in Venice were transferred to the bailo's mansion and were allowed to trade in the Rialto while Venetian merchants in Galata were also allowed to resume their trade.[55]

This case clearly underscores the precarious position of Ottoman merchants in Venice and Venetian merchants in Ottoman lands and the violation by both sides of the protections granted by the ahdname during times of war (see epilogue). Interestingly, it was through the mediation of Solomon

Ashkenazi, a Jewish physician in the Ottoman court who was originally from Udine and had ended up in Istanbul in 1561, and the Venetian bailo that peace was restored between the two states in 1573. Ashkenazi also acted as an agent and spy for the bailo in Istanbul from time to time. Ottoman authorities had arrested him several times, but the grand vizier had protected him. Both Bailo Barbaro and Solomon Ashkenazi, himself a trader, had convinced the Council of Ten in Venice that the safe return of Levantine Jews was essential for the continuation of trade and peace with the Porte. Finally, the Venetian edict of expulsion was withdrawn, and Levantine Jewish merchants were compensated for their losses and returned to Istanbul.[56] Despite the resolution of this case, Venetian merchant ships were still constantly being attacked by Ottoman privateers in the Aegean (Morea), and their goods were being seized, according to the correspondence between the bailo and the Porte in 1590s.[57] Nevertheless, despite incidents of religious persecution during the Inquisition, Venice remained the only tolerant city in Europe where Ottoman Jews, Armenians, and Muslim merchants could live and conduct business until the rise of Marseille as the main trading partner of Galata in the Mediterranean.[58]

MOST FAVORED NATION AND ALLY: THE *AHDNAMES* OF 1536 AND 1569 WITH FRANCE

To expand trade and promote diplomacy against the Habsburg Empire, the Ottoman state started negotiating a series of ahdnames with France, England, and the Netherlands in the sixteenth and seventeenth centuries.[59] France, the Dutch Republic, and England vied for control of the Levant trade and slowly drove Venice out of the Levant trade by the early seventeenth century.

France emerged as the most favored nation and enjoyed a special relationship with the Ottoman state in the early sixteenth century. In addition to Venice, the port of Marseille had had a long history of trade with the Levant (primarily with the Syrian coast and Egypt since the Mamluk period) and was an important center of silk (for the silk industry in Lyon) and spice trade with the East. After the Ottoman conquest of Mamluk Egypt and Syria in 1517, French and Italian merchants tried to maintain their commercial rights in the ports of Egypt and Syria. Sultan Selim I (1512–20) renewed the concessions given by Mamluk sultans to French merchants and issued a *berat* to the

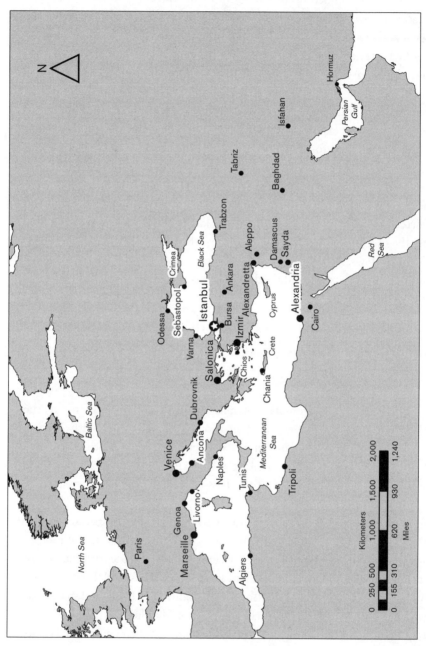

Ports and cities on Mediterranean maritime trade networks. Cartography by Emily Flock.

French community of Alexandria that contained eighteen articles on safe conduct and freedom of trade but did not grant an ahdname since no diplomatic missions had been sent to Istanbul.[60] Berats were patents of appointment issued by the Porte to friendly foreign ambassadors, consuls, merchants, interpreters, and priests that spelled out their legal rights, freedom of trade, and protection from abuse and arrest as well as their tax status.

The Ottoman Empire forged an important alliance with France. When Francis I (ruled 1515–47), the Valois king, took the French throne in 1515, he fought a series of battles with the Habsburgs over the title of the Holy Roman Empire and control of Milan, Palermo, and Nice. He got involved in the Italian wars against the Papal States in 1515 and won control of Milan. King Francis I also fought Emperor Charles V (1519–58) during the Four Years Wars (1521–26) but was defeated in the Battle of Pavia south of Milan in February 1525. King Francis I was captured and imprisoned in Madrid, from which he sent a secret envoy to Sultan Süleyman to ask for his aid. Sultan Süleyman gave an ultimatum to Charles V to release the captive king, and Francis I managed to gain his freedom a year later by signing a disastrous treaty with Charles V renouncing French claims to Naples, Milan, and Burgundy.[61]

The alliance between Francis I and Sultan Süleyman against the Habsburg Empire in 1535 and their joint naval operations to maintain French control of Nice between 1543 and 1544 formed the basis of a new relationship called the "impious alliance" in Europe. Chief Ottoman admiral Hayreddin Barbarossa aided France during these raids with his navy. This naval alliance led to the establishment of the permanent French embassy in Galata and the expansion of trade.[62] Francis I sent a second secret mission to the Ottoman Empire calling for an alliance against Charles V in another series of wars over Italy in 1535. The mission was very successful, and the French envoy, Jean-François Frangepani, was received with great ceremony at the Ottoman court. He took a positive response from the sultan back to the king in 1526. Francis I sent an official embassy led by Jean de La Forest (ambassador, 1535–37) to Istanbul to forge an alliance against Charles V, who was attacking La Goletta in Tunis, and to negotiate a commercial treaty in 1535.[63] Ambassador La Forest was accompanied by the French scholar Guillaume Postel, who was in charge of collecting Oriental manuscripts for the royal library in Paris.[64] Moreover, this alliance led to the frequent exchange of Ottoman envoys and French ambassadors among the Sublime Porte, Marseille, and Paris.[65] La Forest accompanied the sultan to Azerbaijan in a campaign against the

Safavid shah, Tahmasp, and managed to get his agreement for a treaty between the two states in 1536. He also accompanied the sultan in his campaign against Corfu in 1537 but died that year. In accordance with the agreement, Marseille then became the port of the Franco-Ottoman naval alliance against the Habsburg Empire. Ottoman military and naval aid was crucial in preventing the conquest of French territory by King Philip II. The Ottoman Empire played a key role in maintaining the territorial integrity of France and the balance of power in Europe.[66]

France obtained her own ahdname in 1536, which contained seventeen articles but was not ratified due to the untimely execution of Grand Vizier Ibrahim Pasha, who had negotiated the treaty with the French ambassador, at the order of Sultan Süleyman. The first article provided for the freedom of French subjects to travel all over the empire at will. The second article guaranteed bilateral commerce and the right of merchants of both sides to buy, sell, exchange, and transport by land and sea all unbanned goods and to pay the customary and new taxes paid by local subjects. The third article allowed the French king to establish consuls in Ottoman towns where a French community resided. Articles 3 and 9 gave legal jurisdiction to French consuls to try and judge French subjects in civil and criminal matters in accordance with French law.[67] Article 6 provided for the religious freedom of French subjects in Ottoman lands. It is clear that only the second article of this ahdname emphasized bilateral commerce while the rest of the articles defined the rights of French subjects in Ottoman lands alone. In other words, while Ottoman merchants could trade freely in French towns and ports, they did not enjoy the same legal and religious rights as French subjects did in Ottoman lands. As we will see, none of the ahdnames granted by Ottoman rulers to European states defined the religious and legal rights of Ottoman subjects in European lands.

There is an ongoing debate among historians on the date of the first formal ahdname given to France by the Ottoman state since the final text has not survived in the French archives. Some French historians (Pélissié du Rausas, Gilles Veinstein) have argued for some time that Sultan Süleyman granted the first ahdname to France in 1536; it was negotiated by the French envoy, La Forest, and Grand Vizier Ibrahim Pasha.[68] However, other historians (Nicolae Iorga and Gaston Zeller) have maintained that the bilateral treaty negotiated between the two monarchs, Francis I and Süleyman Kanuni, in 1536 was never ratified due to the untimely execution of Ibrahim Pasha.[69] According to Lamar Jensen, the published text lacked a preamble enumerating the titles and dominions of Sultan Süleyman, which was a typical component of ahdnames.[70] These historians may have assumed that it was the grand vizier and not the sultan who had the final authority to ratify these treaties.

From reviewing Ottoman sources, it appears that the Ottoman state had indeed negotiated a treaty with France in 1536 that was in effect from the perspective of both sides.[71] Although the final signing of the treaty may have been postponed due to the absence of the sultan in Istanbul, Ottoman documents in the *Mühimme defterleri* regarding relations between the two states made constant references to the 1536 ahdname, underscoring the fact that its articles were in effect. French traders received an imperial decree allowing them to trade in the empire until a formal ahdname was ratified in 1569.

Although commercial considerations were secondary, the first Ottoman-French ahdname granted French traders protection and freedom to trade, codified their rights for the first time, and opened up the markets of the Levant to French traders. French consulates were established in several ports and towns. Prior to this period, French merchants had been concentrated in the ports of Egypt (chiefly Alexandria) and Syria and had modest numbers in western Anatolian ports (Izmir) and Galata. Unlike the Genoese and the Venetians, French traders did not have their own neighborhoods in these ports and were submissive to Turkish authorities. The Ahdname of 1536 gave French merchants the opportunity to establish an independent presence in some Ottoman ports. During these negotiations, France also gained the protection of the Ottoman state for her merchants, particularly against piracy by Tripolitan states.[72]

PIRACY AND DIPLOMACY

The importance of North African corsair states to the Ottoman Empire had increased with Habsburg threats against eastern Mediterranean ports and islands. The Ottoman state incorporated the North African provinces of Tripoli, Algiers, and Tunis in 1519 and hired pirates like Hayreddin Barbarossa, who became the commander of the Ottoman navy in 1533. During the sixteenth century, Ottoman corsair activities against European shipping from naval bases in the eastern Mediterranean and later in North Africa (Algiers) interrupted European shipping and forced Europeans to seek treaty relations (ahdnames) with the Ottoman Empire to suppress piracy. The ahdnames contained important articles on the suppression of piracy by both sides. However, these articles were violated by corsairs and privateers all the time. For example, in 1568, the governor of Alexandretta in Syria submitted a report to the Imperial Council in Istanbul stating that Yasef (Joseph Nasi), the duke of the island of Naxos, had confiscated the goods of a French ship and had imprisoned the French captain and the traders, claiming they owed him a debt of 150,000 gold coins. In response, the state issued an imperial order to Nasi to return the goods of the French merchants in order not to harm French trade and the collection of state taxes from trade.[73] However, the dispute continued until 1569, when French King Henri III (r. 1551–89) sent a special envoy, Claude de Bourg, to Istanbul to demand redress from the sultan for the confiscation of French property by the Jewish entrepreneur Joseph Nasi. To avoid this type of crisis in the future, the ambassador also signed the first official ahdname with Sultan Selim II (1566–74) in 1569, which placed an important emphasis on the protection of French ships from Ottoman pirate attacks (see chapter 6).

Marrano Jews such as Nasi who had settled in the Ottoman Empire had wide networks that stretched from Galata to Izmir, Livorno, Venice, and Marseille. They formed networks of trade in the Mediterranean and partnered with Ottoman Muslim as well as non-Muslim traders.[74] Joseph Nasi (1524–79) was a rich Marrano and a member of the house of Mendes/Benveniste who had fled Spain for Portugal after Charles I had confiscated the property of the Mendes family. He left Portugal during the inquisitions in 1547 and settled first in the Netherlands and later in Venice and France.[75] Like many other Marranos, he eventually ended up in Istanbul with his aunt, Dona Garcia Mendes, in 1554 and became a close adviser to Sultan Selim II. Nasi played an instrumental role in the war between the Ottoman Empire and Venice over the island of Cyprus in 1570. In return for his services, Nasi was appointed the duke of the island of Naxos and took over the wine and beeswax trade between the Aegean islands and Poland. He also became a financier to European rulers like the king of France and lent his own money and that of many Ottoman pashas in the amount of 150,000 gold coins to king Henry II (1519–59) and French traders at an interest rate of between 12 and 16 percent. When the French defaulted on the payment of their loan, he took action with Ottoman backing by attacking French ships until he had collected his debt.[76] His action created a long diplomatic exchange between the French king and Sultan Selim II and finally led to the signing of a formal ahdname between the two states in 1569, which contained an important clause on piracy.

Marranos like Joseph Nasi and members of the Mendes family played an important role as intermediaries in diplomacy with Europe as well as in the Ottoman trade with such ports like Venice and Ancona.[77] Joseph Nasi invested his wealth in trade and tax farming as well as in finance in the Ottoman Empire and the Mediterranean. Nasi's aunt, Dona Garcia, who was the head of the Mendes family in Istanbul, was involved in several commercial ventures of her own in the trade of woolens, grain, and pepper with Europe as well as in the tax farming of customs dues in Ottoman ports.

A good proportion of the correspondence between European ambassadors and the Sublime Porte that were copied into Registers of Important Affairs (*muhimme defterleri*) as well as petitions to the Imperial Council by French sea captains and merchants dealt with pirate attacks by Tripolitan corsairs. In accordance with the articles of the ahdname, the Ottoman state tried to suppress piracy by North African ships on the Mediterranean and in 1565 issued several orders to the *beys* (commanders) of Algiers and Tunis that they not attack ships that carried the French flag and merchants near French borders. For example, in several orders issued to the beys of Algiers in response to the petition of the French ambassador to the Imperial Council in August 1565, the Ottoman state ordered the beys to cease attacking French ships and to return the goods that they had seized to the French captains in accordance with the articles of the ahdname. The beys were also ordered to prepare a list of French captives taken by North African pirates, release them, and return them to the French king in order to avoid punishment.[78] Greek ship captains from the Aegean islands also engaged in pirate attacks against European shipping.

In 1565, the French ambassador in Istanbul submitted a petition to the Porte about North African corsair attacks against French ports. The Ottoman state issued an imperial order to the governor of Algeria in August 1565 requesting protection for France against North African corsair attacks and the release of all French merchants and their goods in accordance with the ahdname with France.[79] A French-Algerian and Ottoman alliance was formed in the sixteenth century, and France established a separate consul in Algiers in 1580. Moreover, the sultan and the grand admiral, Hayreddin Barbarossa, sent envoys to Paris regularly to resolve commercial disputes and those having to do with pirate attacks. The French established consuls in Tripoli, Alexandria, Algiers, Tunis, and Fez, underscoring the importance of French trade with North African ports.

In April 1560, Francis II (r. 1559–60) sent a letter to Sultan Süleyman to renew the ahdname, which Süleyman had pledged to Francis's father, Henri

II.[80] Sultan Süleyman responded favorably in October 1560 but requested the release, protection, and safety of all Ottoman war captives before signing the treaty.[81] Similarly, the Ottoman state agreed to release the goods of French merchants who were in debt to the Ottoman state. For example, in January 1560, the Ottoman treasury had taken the estate of a French merchant who had died in Galata since he had been in debt to the state. The rest of his property was transferred to his agent, Paolo, and no one was to interfere in his estate, according to the terms of an *agreement* signed with Henry II.[82] The Ottoman sultan referred to the French king with the special title of *padishah* (monarch), which he did not confer on any other European sovereign or head of state in the sixteenth century.

The French claimed that there had been an earlier ahdname signed in 1536, but they could not find the text of it and asked Sultan Murad III (r. 1574–95) to search for a copy of it in Istanbul.[83] A copy of the Ahdname of 1536 must have existed in the Ottoman chancellery since the Ottoman scribes made constant reference to it, and it formed the basis of the 1569 ahdname. The Ahdname of 1569 was a bilateral treaty granted by Sultan Selim II to France and was modeled on the earlier agreement of 1536 and the Venetian Ahdname of 1540. It contained eighteen articles on the freedom and security of trade and travel on land and sea for both French and Ottoman merchants, mutual protection of ships from piracy, assistance in cases of shipwrecks, the release of slaves and captives by both sides. In addition, it contained articles on French subjects' exemption from the payment of *cizye* (poll tax). Other articles reconfirmed the legal jurisdiction of consuls over French subjects in internal disputes, the obligatory presence of a French dragoman during trials of French subjects at the kadi's court, and the need for the registration of all transactions at the kadi's court.[84] The Ahdname of 1569 with France contained numerous articles on the suppression of piracy and the protection of French ships and merchants. This ahdname also declared that the Ottoman state would give preferential treatment to the French ambassador over all other European ambassadors in the Porte.

In July 1581, Sultan Murad III renewed the French ahdname, which contained twenty-seven articles on safe conduct, freedom of trade, free passage of ships, the suppression of piracy and the protection of property, and the security of life and religion of French subjects in the empire. It contained an important article on the ability of European traders (English, Portuguese, Catalans, Sicilians, Anconians, Genoese, and even Venetians) who did not have any treaty relations with the Ottoman Empire to trade under the French flag in the Ottoman Empire.[85] As in the 1569 Ahdname, article 6 of the treaty provided for French subjects' freedom of worship and exemption from the poll tax and all personal taxes unless their residency exceeded ten years. The Ottoman-French ahdname was renewed again in 1597, 1604, 1618, 1673, and 1740 with additional articles.

After the signing of the Ahdname of 1569, French Ottoman trade entered a new phase. It led to an increase in Marseille's trade with the Levant. The number of ships in the French merchant fleet in the Mediterranean increased from twenty vessels in 1535 to two hundred fifty years later. The customs dues on trade in Marseille increased from 7,000 *livres* in 1570 to 19,000 *livres* (almost a threefold increase) in 1573.[86] The commercial boom in Marseille led to the establishment of a woolen cloth factory for goods destined for the markets of the Levant in 1570, a sugar refinery in 1574, and a soap factory in 1578.[87]

The French held a monopoly over the spice trade in Cairo and Aleppo, replacing Venice in the late sixteenth century. Marseille imported Indian spices from Cairo, silks of Persia from Aleppo and Izmir, grains and olive oil from the Aegean islands, and wool and hides from Anatolia.[88] England also imported Indian and Indonesian spices from the Levant, such as indigo, pepper, and exported kerseys (coarse woolen cloths), tin, and silver currency.

However, piracy continued to disrupt trade on the Mediterranean. The Ottoman state tried to suppress piracy by Christian ships on this route by taking control of Venetian-held Cyprus in 1571 and by building and repairing castles.[89] But corsair attacks on Ottoman ships continued. The sale of Muslim captives and their goods by pirates in ports like Malta and Livorno continued until the late eighteenth century. The number of Muslim slaves in the port of Livorno exceeded more than 20 percent of the total population.[90] This was an important factor in the absence of Muslim traders in European ports. In 1578, Muslims (possibly North Africans) who had been captured by Christian corsairs fled to France but were taken captive again in France. The Ottoman state demanded their release and return to their homeland in accordance with the ahdname.[91]

THE OTTOMAN-FRENCH ALLIANCE
AND THE AHDNAME OF 1604

Ottoman-French trade, however, had its own ebb and flow due to internal wars and an increase in piracy in the Mediterranean. The French Religious

Wars (1562–98) between the Roman Catholics and the Protestants (Huguenots) led to a temporary decline in French industries and trade with the Levant.[92] In addition, the civil war in Marseille between the staunch supporters of the pro-Spanish mayor and those of the French king, Henry IV of Navarre, as well as Henry III (1572–1610), who was a Huguenot and protector of Protestants, contributed to the decline in trade. However, the war with Spain continued for several years. Henry IV, however, was deemed unacceptable by the Catholic Holy League, which was composed of the Papacy and the Habsburg king, due to his Protestant ties.

The French ambassador to the Porte, Jacques Savary de Lancosme, seigneur de Brève (amb.1584–91), convinced Sultan Murad III to send a letter to the Council in Marseille threatening that he would order the ships of merchants of Marseille in Ottoman ports to be confiscated if Marseille did not end the rebellion. In 1595, the Ottoman state ordered the governor of Algeria to send a delegation to Marseille to accept the authority of the new French king, Henry IV(r.1589–1610), who was an Ottoman ally. The governor was authorized to attack the town if Marseille refused to do so.[93] The Ottoman state would boycott trade if Marseille did not switch its allegiance away from the Habsburgs. However, Marseille resisted the Turkish attempt to impose its ally, so trade with the Levant continued to decline. Finally, King Henry IV of France converted to Catholicism in July 1593 to gain the support of the Catholic League.

On April 1598, King Henry IV, having negotiated peace with Spain, signed the Edict of Nantes, confirming Roman Catholicism as the state religion of France. He also granted religious freedom to a large number of Protestants, ending forty years of religious strife in France. King Henry IV revived the economy, established the silk industry in France, and encouraged the manufacture of tapestries, glassware, cloth, and luxury items.

As a result, Marseille returned its allegiance to the French king, and de Brèves renewed the ahdname in 1597 (thirty-two articles) and again five years later in 1604 (fifty articles). Consequently, Marseille's trade with the Levant grew again.

The ahdnames of 1604 gave the French king the right of protection over holy places in Jerusalem. It also granted French subjects the right to visit the Christian holy places in Palestine and gave permission to Catholic monks to reside in Jerusalem. France had its own claims of becoming the protector of Catholics in the Levant and Christian holy places in Jerusalem, which undermined the authority of the Pope. Article 22 granted the French dragoman the same rights as those of a French subject, exempting him, his sons, and two servants from the poll tax, the slaughter tax, and other customary dues.[94] This article also required that the French dragoman be French (Frank) in ethnicity (rather than an Ottoman non-Muslim subject; see chapter 7).

The 1604 ahdname also removed the ban from the trade of contraband Ottoman commodities that the French could now import (cotton, cotton thread, morocco leather), thus leading to an increase in French imports from the Levant. The number of vessels from the coast of Provence trading with the Levant had increased to more than one thousand by the end of the sixteenth century, proving the success of French diplomacy with the Porte.[95]

However, Christian and Muslim piracy on the Mediterranean was still an important factor in disrupting trade. In 1622, Sultan Osman II (r.1618–22) issued an imperial order to the governors and kadis of Algiers and Tunis stating that noble families from Marseille were free to travel on land and sea to North African ports and settle there and that their persons, men, ships, and goods were under the protection of the ahdname he had renewed with France.[96] Local Ottoman officials were ordered not to violate the articles of the ahdnames and to guarantee the safe conduct and travel of French ships. However, North African piracy continued and even increased against European shipping into the early seventeenth century. French traders were sometimes involved in ransoming Muslim captives from corsairs in Malta as well. For example, in June 1663, a French merchant from Izmir came to the court of Galata claiming that his partner, Marchilio, had freed two Muslim merchants from the corsairs of Malta and had placed them on a French ship and delivered them to the Yağ Kapanı wharf in Galata. Their arrival had been registered in the court of Galata, according to the dragomans of the embassy, Batista son of Tomaso and Andriya son of Gabriel.[97]

The 1604 ahdname contained an important article on the suppression of piracy. The 1604 ahdname also removed England from the list of nations protected by the French ahdname since England had received its own ahdname in 1580.[98]

A PROTESTANT ALLY: THE AHDNAME OF
1580 WITH ENGLAND

Since England, as a Protestant state, was opposed to the Habsburg Empire, it gained a special position in the Ottoman Empire in the second half of the sixteenth century. Before 1570, English merchants had purchased Levantine goods in the markets of Antwerp. At that time, the Pope had placed a ban on the export of foodstuff and ammunitions to the Ottoman Empire. However, English merchants, who had been declared heretics by the Pope, felt free to supply the Ottoman Empire with cloth for uniforms, metal, tin, and lead for arms.

Before the establishment of diplomatic contacts, a few English merchants had already been trading with the Levant. Two such enterprising merchants, Anthony Jenkinson and William Harborne, initiated commercial contacts with the Ottoman state in 1553 and 1579.[99] In 1579, Sultan Murad III granted them a berat for safe conduct, freedom of trade, protection of their lives and property, exemption from consular fees, and aid during shipwrecks.[100]

Soon after these initial contacts by individual English merchants, Queen Elizabeth I (r. 1558–1603) sent an ambassador to negotiate the terms of an ahdname with Sultan Murad III in 1580.[101] The ahdname contained twenty-three articles and very closely followed those granted to Venice in 1540 and France in 1569. English ships obtained the freedom to travel to all Ottoman ports and enjoyed protection and aid during shipwrecks and a pledge for the return of all goods by Ottoman officials. Moreover, it is important to note that some of the articles of the treaty concerning the protection of merchants were reciprocal. For example, in a letter to Sultan Murad III on January 8, 1581, Queen Elizabeth I offered protection and security of travel to an Ottoman merchant, Gabriel Defrens (probably an Armenian merchant), as part of an "equal goodwill" gesture.[102]

Within a year after the signing of the ahdname, twelve English merchants received berats from Sultan Murad III to trade in Turkey for seven years and established the Turkey Company in September 1581. The Turkey Company was initially a chartered corporation of English merchants who had obtained a royal charter from Elizabeth I in 1581 that gave them a monopoly in the Levant trade for seven years. It was a joint-stock company to which Queen Elizabeth I contributed 40,000 pounds.[103] However, its charter was not renewed in 1588. In January 1592, the Levant Company (a merger of the Turkey Company and the Venice Company) was established under the directorship of William Osborne. The company had fifty-three core members and twenty merchants who paid membership fees of 130 sterling; it received a new charter from Queen Elizabeth I that gave it a monopoly in the Levant trade for twelve years. Its members pledged not to trade with the Levant on their own; in addition, they had to be wholesale merchants. The membership had grown to three hundred by the end of the seventeenth century. King James I (1603–25) renewed the company's charter in 1606 and, despite his anti-Turkish rhetoric, added new privileges. The company received an exclusive right to trade in the Levant indefinitely and was transformed from a joint stock company to a regulated corporation, operating as such until it was dissolved in 1825.[104] (see epilogue).

As a result of the establishment of this company, trade expanded and between 46 and 79 percent of all English woolen cloths were exported to the Levant between 1609 and 1619. The Levant Company had a board in London made up of a governor, vice-governor, and twelve directors, all of whom were required to live in London or its suburbs. The company also had a deputy governor in every Ottoman city where there were company merchants. The company's representative was appointed by the king to act as the ambassador to Istanbul, and he received a pension. He enforced company ordinances, negotiated ahdnames, maintained law and order, settled disputes, and collected consular fees on exports and imports from merchants.[105]

The Sublime Porte supported the legal jurisdiction of the English ambassadors over her subjects. For example, in 1697 and 1698, imperial orders issued to the kadis of Istanbul and Galata asked them to protect the trade of English merchants on land and sea in accordance with the articles of the ahdname. If English merchants had not violated any laws, the kadis were ordered not to interfere in the legal disputes among English subjects, which were under the jurisdiction of the ambassador, and to allow the merchants to submit petitions to the Imperial Council with the authorization of the ambassador.[106] In addition, European ambassadors received a salary from the Levant Company and also a daily stipend form the Ottoman government since they were official guests.

The ambassadors had a dual responsibility to the Levant Company and the Crown overseeing factories and factors (merchants). But the ambassador's power over the consuls and factors in other cities was minimal, and his authority was difficult to enforce.[107] The company had a consul in Aleppo and one in Izmir whose salaries were between 1,000 and 2,000 pounds in the eighteenth century—not enough to cover expenses. As a result, the consuls and ambassadors started selling berats to Ottoman merchants for between 2,600 and 5,500 akçes in the seventeenth and eighteenth centuries to supplement their income.[108] (see chapter 7) The Levant Company dispatched factors to strategic trading outposts like Izmir, Salonica, Aleppo, Cairo, and Algiers. Its headquarters were in Aleppo. Since the company had to fight North

African pirates as well as Spanish galleys, its merchant ships in the Levant, which numbered between twenty and twenty-five, were heavily armed.

The English ahdname was renewed in 1583, 1601, 1616, 1624, 1643, 1666, and 1675. Ambassador Lello negotiated a reduced customs rate of 3 percent in 1601, which was an important privilege that gave the English merchants an edge over other European merchants, who paid 5 percent customs dues.[109] In addition, English merchants did not pay customs dues on the import of gold and silver coins. A new charter in 1601 did not limit the Levant trade to any one city (such as London) or restrict the number of merchants but instead opened participation to others. This new liberal trade policy was the result of a long political struggle and a debate over the Levant Company's rights, leading to freedom of trade and the passing of Free Trade Laws. Membership in the company thus was opened to new merchants in 1605.

Thanks to the Ahdname of 1580, the English Levant Company became the most successful trade venture established between 1580 and 1600 before the formation of the East India Company. England exported fine and inexpensive dyed broadcloth (the amount of which tripled from 1598 to 1621) and kerseys into Istanbul, Izmir, and Aleppo. From Aleppo, broadcloth was exported to Persia.[110] England also ignored the papal ban on the export of arms, lead, and tin to the Ottoman Empire. Before the establishment of the English East India Company in the early 1600s, the Levant was the center of transit trade in spices as well as in Persian raw silk between Asia and Europe. England imported spices from the Levant, particularly pepper brought from India and Indonesia by Muslim merchants via caravan as well by as maritime routes. English imports of Persian raw silk from the Levant (mainly from Aleppo and Izmir) increased from 11,904 pounds in 1560 to 357,434 pounds in 1669.[111] By the early eighteenth century, silk made up four-fifths of the English imports from the Levant.[112] The English silk industry expanded because of the importing of Persian raw silk from the Levant. England also imported raisins, currants, wine, olive oil, cotton, and cotton yarn as well as dyes (indigo, galls) from Anatolia in the late sixteenth century.[113] Levantine dyes completely replaced those imported into England from Flemings.

However, the English Levant trade was disrupted during the English civil wars in 1640s and 1650s, a situation that affected the community in Galata, but trade boomed again after 1660.[114] The civil war also impacted English life in the Levant; the disruption revolved around the attempt by the exiled British king, Charles I (r. 1625–49), to wrest the ambassadorship in Istanbul and the consulship in Izmir away from the control of the Levant Company.

In response, Englishmen, who were divided into royalists and Levant Company sympathizers, fought on the streets of Galata, Izmir, and Aleppo. Ambassador Bendysh, who represented the Levant Company in Galata, colluded with Ottoman officials to resist the policies of the English ambassador, Sir Sackville Crow, who represented the king.

The problem within the English community involved the overlapping authority of the king and the Levant Company over the appointment of ambassadors and consuls to the Ottoman Empire. But it ultimately involved the authority of the English state over the Levant Company and its jurisdictions in the Levant. Clearly, the Ottoman state favored the Levant Company in this duel for jurisdiction. For example, Henry Hyde, the powerful English consul in the Morea, also held the position of Ottoman *voyvoda* and customs collector in Patras.[115] Hyde had established a fiefdom for himself in the Morea by purchasing these positions with company money; he was also involved in shipping dried fruits to the Levant Company.[116]

Finally, the English crown won the control of the Levant Company. The new 1661 charter signed by King Charles II (1660–85) after the restoration of monarchy endorsed the company's organization as a regulated corporation under the state's supervision, with exclusive membership of the company in London that remained in effect until the company's dissolution in 1825. Foreign trade thus became an important component of the national English economy, contributing to a favorable balance of trade, with exports exceeding imports, under beneficial treaties signed by the English ambassador and the Ottoman state.

The subsequent ahdnames that Britain signed with the Ottoman state reflected this new charter and the importance of exports over imports. The English Ahdname of 1675 granted by Sultan Mehmed IV (r. 1648–87) to the Levant Company contained seventy-five articles and included all of the privileges previously granted to Venice, Poland, France, and the Netherlands. It allowed foreigners who did not have treaty relations with the Porte (Spain, Portugal, Ancona, Sicily, Florence, Catalonia, and even Holland) to trade under her flag.[117] English merchants could buy and export all kinds of merchandise, with the exception of banned goods from the Ottoman Empire. The Ahdname of 1675 put an end to all internal taxes other than the customs dues of 3 percent on the import and export of all merchandise and raw materials except for banned goods.[118] English merchants would not be charged the scale tax and customs fees on silks from Bursa, Persia, and Georgia that they had purchased from Armenian merchants in Izmir.[119] They could purchase Angora wool or mohair directly without encountering any problems in the markets of Ankara. English merchants were required to obtain a receipt upon payment of their customs dues only once in the ports and were not to be charged again. In addition, English merchants would pay 120 *aspers* for every piece of fine or coarse woolen cloth or other fabrics manufactured in England and imported into the Levant.[120] Every ship had to pay 300 *aspers* for anchorage duty in Ottoman ports, and merchants would pay the *masdariye* tax as well. The *masdariye* tax amounted to 1.5 percent of the value of a limited number of goods collected from European and domestic merchants in Istanbul. The exemption from paying the *masdariye* tax was an important privilege that the French obtained later in 1740 and that the Dutch received in 1754.[121] However, when facing economic difficulties, the Porte later imposed new taxes on European merchants that had not been spelled out in the ahdnames.

More importantly, this treaty gave England a monopoly to conduct trade by sea between Istanbul and the ports of Egypt (Alexandria and Damietta), a right that inserted English merchants into the domestic trade of the Ottoman Empire, which had previously been closed to Europeans.[122] English ships in transit would not be subject to customs dues if they did not unload their goods in Ottoman ports (Istanbul, Alexandria, Tripoli in Syria, Alexandretta in Syria, or other ports). Thus, England gained an important foothold in the domestic trade of the empire, a right that the French and the Dutch would jealously fight for during the seventeenth century and would enable France to surpass English trade in the eighteenth century.[123] The Ahdname of 1675 also allowed English merchants to trade with Muscovy and Persia.

Since trade in Iranian silk was constantly disrupted during the Ottoman-Safavid Wars in the late sixteenth (1585–1603) and eighteenth centuries (1725–1746), the English traders tried to reach Iran through a northern route via Russia and the Caspian Sea. But the Tabriz-Bursa silk route had been shifted from Aleppo to the Tabriz-Izmir route due to the Celali rebellions in Anatolia and the Ottoman-Iranian wars during the seventeenth century. Izmir thus became the new transit center of the silk trade among Tabriz, Marseille, London, and Amsterdam and boomed from this trade in the seventeenth century.

The Ottoman-Safavid Wars of 1725 to 1746 led to the devastation of the silk-producing region of Gilan in the Caspian Sea region and the Ottoman occupation of the silk *entrepot* of Tabriz from 1725 to 1730.[124] The Afghan occupation of Iran in 1722; the triple division of western Iran and the provinces in the Caucasus among the Ottoman Empire, Russian, and Afghan forces; and the subsequent wars caused a permanent decline in the silk trade between Iran and the Levant as well as between Iran and Western Europe.[125] In addition, the development of sericulture (raw silk production) in the Ottoman Empire (in Bursa, Syria, and the Morea) and the East India Company's import of poorer quality but cheaper silk from Bengal largely replaced Persian silk.[126] However, Levantine raw silk, mainly from Syria (Antioch) and the Morea, continued to play a minor role in European imports from the Ottoman ports through the early nineteenth century.

Moreover, the English East India Company, like the Dutch East India Company, had taken over the spice trade by way of the Cape of Good Hope in 1603. The capture of the Port of Hormuz from the Portuguese after a joint Anglo-Safavid military alliance in 1622 established an English presence in the Persian Gulf and the Indian Ocean. The rise of the English and Dutch East India Companies undermined the role of Muslim as well as Venetian traders in the spice trade between the Levant and Europe.[127] The English were re-exporting spices from Asia and India to the Levant in the seventeenth century. But, despite the Portuguese and later the English and Dutch intrusions into the Indian Ocean, the spice trade across the caravan route to Basra and the Red Sea continued and was the same in volume as English imports of spices into the Levant in the mid-sixteenth century.[128]

However, the blow to the English exports of woolens into the Levant came with the improvement of French woolen textiles in Provence that matched Levantine and Persian tastes better. In the late sixteenth century, half of the French trade was with the Levant while only one-tenth of English trade was being carried out with the Levant in the early seventeenth century. Although the volume of English trade in the Levant had declined compared with that of France in the seventeenth century, the English Levant trade did not completely disappear. The English Levant Company continued to import cotton from Anatolia; mohair yarn from Ankara; gall nuts that produced dyes from Mosul and Diyarbekir; currants, raisins, and figs from western Anatolia and the Greek islands; and coffee from Egypt. The turn to cotton fabrics in English fashion was also an important factor in the decline of the silk trade in the eighteenth century.[129] Among the goods imported by an English ship to Istanbul in 1805, we come across pepper, cinnamon, sugar, English woolen textiles (londra), English cotton yarn, and lead. The exports from the Levant to England included silk textiles from Sidon (Sayda) in Syria, Cyprus, and the Aegean islands; raw silk from Bursa; Angora yarn from Ankara; and cotton and cotton yarn, candle wax, gall nuts, copper, figs, and currants.[130] However, English traders soon faced new rivals in Galata, the Dutch traders.

A SPECIAL RELATIONSHIP: THE AHDNAME
OF 1612 WITH HOLLAND

Before the establishment of Holland's formal relations with the Porte through an ahdname, a small Dutch community composed of traders and goldsmiths resided in Galata and Pera in the sixteenth century.[131] They first traded under the English and French flags in the eastern Mediterranean ports (mainly Izmir) since Dutch ships were targets of North African privateers. But soon the leaders of the Dutch revolt in the United Provinces were seeking Ottoman support against the Habsburg Empire in Spain in 1569. In this effort, Don Joseph Nasi played an important role in the establishment of Ottoman-Dutch contacts.[132] Nasi enjoyed wide contacts in Holland and Istanbul and became a mediator between Ottoman sultans (Süleyman and Selim II) and Protestant communities (Utrecht Union) in Holland and Germany. He had a mansion in Pera on the site of the Galatasaray School (see chapter 6).

Like the English traders, the Dutch residents in Galata started negotiating for an ahdname in 1610. Grand Vizier Halil Pasha, who was also the former chief of the navy, dispatched a letter with Gicamo Gishbrechti, a Dutch resident, to Holland inviting the States General to send an envoy to Istanbul. Cornelis Haga arrived as the extraordinary ambassador to Istanbul in March 1612 and stayed in Pera next to the French Embassy on Tomtom Street until 1639. The Dutch ambassador received support from the members of the Sephardic Jewish community like Joseph Nasi in Istanbul.[133] However, neither the English nor the French ambassadors were very happy about the arrival of their Dutch rivals in Pera. They tried to persuade Sultan Ahmed I (1603–17) not to grant the Dutch an ahdname since they would lose business and the consular fees that they had been collecting from Dutch traders who traded under their flags.[134]

Despite these setbacks, within a few months the Calvinist ambassador Cornelis Haga negotiated an ahdname with Sultan Ahmed I in July 1612 that contained seventy-five articles.[135] According to the text of the ahdname, the Dutch had demonstrated their friendship by freeing Muslim captives who had been taken on the Mediterranean and had refrained from attacking Ottoman ships, thus gaining the friendship of the Sublime Porte.[136] Therefore, they received an ahdname similar to the ones given to England and France that promised freedom of trade, security of life and property, and mutual protection from piracy and enslavement. In addition, the ahdname allowed the Dutch the freedom to export banned goods (cotton, cotton thread, morocco leather) from Ottoman lands, privileges that the French and English ahdnames did not contain. No duties were to be collected for Dutch silver and gold coins, nor were Dutch coins to be converted into Ottoman coins at the mint. Similar to the terms of the English ahdname, the customs dues were set at 3 percent, to be paid once, and Dutch traders were exempt from paying other local dues like the butcher tax *(kasabiye),* transit tax *(reft),* market tax *(bac),* and other dues *(yasakkuli).* However, as Ismail Hakki Kadi argues, the Dutch traders still paid local taxes like the stamp tax on silk *(mizan)* and the scale tax *(kantar)* on bulky goods. They were also liable for payment of taxes when they traded in the interior of the empire.[137]

The Ahdname of 1612 granted Dutch traders additional rights that other European merchants did not enjoy.[138] For example, Dutch ships could import salt from Cyprus at established rates and could transport the goods of Muslims from Damietta, Alexandria, and other Egyptian ports on their ships without having to pay customs dues. In addition, Dutch ships had the freedom to trade with Black Sea ports like Trabzon and Caffa, and no customs were to be collected on transit trade in Istanbul. These two provisions allowing Dutch ships to get involved in the domestic trade of the Ottoman Empire in North Africa and on the Black Sea were crucial privileges granted to Dutch traders.

Moreover, the ahdname also allowed Dutch dragomans and their servants the freedom of trade (article 27), a privilege that was an important departure from the terms of previous treaties granted to France and England. The personal goods of ambassadors, consuls, their dragomans, and their two servants were exempt from customs dues and internal dues. In addition, Dutch subjects were exempt from paying the poll tax when they married Ottoman non-Muslim women (see chapter 7). Most Dutch traders married local women and lived in Ottoman ports until they died. This practice was very different from that of French and English traders, who were forbidden by the Levant Company from marrying local women[139] (see chapter 7). The ahdname also granted Dutchmen the freedom to visit holy places in Jerusalem.

As in the terms of previous Ottoman ahdnames with other nations, internal disputes between Dutch subjects were to be handled in consular courts according to Dutch laws, but any disputes between Dutch and Ottoman subjects involving fewer than 4,000 akçes had to be taken to the kadi's court in the presence of a dragoman, and those involving larger amounts had to be submitted to the Imperial Council. Moreover, any lawsuits brought against the ambassador or consuls had to be referred to the Imperial Council. All transactions with Ottoman subjects had to be registered in the kadi's court.

This treaty was conditional upon the duration of friendship between the two states; it was renewed in 1680, its text being identical to that of the earlier one, and it remained in effect until capitulations were abolished in 1922.[140] However, unlike the French and the English, the Dutch pursued free trade policies in the Levant, and the Dutch Levant Company was not a company with a monopoly. The board of directors of the Dutch Levant Company was composed of seven members chosen from the merchants of Amsterdam who traded with the Levant. It was established by the municipality of Amsterdam but was a state institution that controlled the Levant trade policies of the Dutch state until the nineteenth century.[141] One of the most important tasks of the directorate in Amsterdam was to correspond with the ambassador in Istanbul and the consuls in the ports of the Levant and North Africa. Izmir became the center of Dutch commercial activities in the seventeenth century, while five trading firms were established in Galata and Pera in the eighteenth century.

CONCLUSION

Contrary to the commonly held view that blames the regime of ahdnames, or capitulations, for the decline of the Ottoman economy, I have argued that in fact they created an early modern international commercial legal framework in continuity with earlier Mediterranean and Islamic practices that allowed for open zones of trade in certain ports and caravan cities but also regulated commercial, legal, and political interactions and aided dispute resolutions between signatory nations. Furthermore, eastern Mediterranean ports like Galata enjoyed a special status under both Byzantine and Ottoman administrations that provided their merchant communities with a great deal of autonomy to develop maritime trade and to function as hubs of international trade. In the earlier period (from the sixteenth to the eighteenth century), they had bilateral articles on trade and mutual protection from piracy. However, these were temporary, were revocable depending on the state of peace, and had to be renewed at the accession of every sultan. They became unilateral as the relationship between the Ottoman Empire and Europe changed in the eighteenth century.

A comparative study of some these treaties and their evolution and implementation over time within the context of port cities reveals a very complex and dynamic picture that differs from the rigid portrait offered by many scholars. What emerges from a study of the texts of these ahdnames and Ottoman archival sources is a flexible legal framework based on the shari'a, kanun, and local customs to improve maritime trade, resolve disputes, and protect European merchants in Ottoman ports like Galata and Izmir. In other words, ahdnames created important legal institutions for international trade in Ottoman ports and caravan cities during the early modern period.

FOUR

War, Diplomacy, and Trade in the Seventeenth and Eighteenth Centuries

PERA, AS THE DIPLOMATIC HUB OF THE EMPIRE, gained great importance in the seventeenth century. Diplomacy became an integral aspect of Ottoman-European commercial exchanges, but sometimes wars among European nations and among the Ottoman Empire, Safavid Iran, and Russia disrupted these relations and undermined trade, even putting the lives of ambassadors and European communities at a great risk (see epilogue). This chapter will examine the change in French-Ottoman diplomacy under Minister Colbert and the signing of two major ahdnames with France that led to the expansion of French trade with the Levant in the eighteenth century (see chapter 6). Moreover, Ottoman-Iranian and Ottoman-Russian wars over the control of the Caucasus, the Crimea, and the Black Sea were important developments in the eighteenth century. France played a key role in these relations, and French ships provisioned Istanbul during wars with Russia. Embassy accounts reported on changes in Ottoman-European diplomacy at the Sublime Porte, as the following detailed statement demonstrates:

> The ambassador is then brought to a great gate near the audience, the porch of which is filled with white Eunuchs, clothed in silks and cloth of gold; farther than this, none is suffered to proceed, besides the secretary, interpreter[,] and some other persons of best quality; at the door of the Chamber of Audience is a deep silence, and the murmuring of a fountain nearby ... adds to the melancholy; and no other guard is there but a white eunuch, and there a pause is made, and they tread softly in token of fear and reverence ... so as not to disturb with the least noise the majesty of the sultan, for access to the eastern princes was always difficult.... When the ambassador comes to appear before the Grand Seignior, he is led in and supported under the arms by the two *kapıcıbaşıs* [chief of palace heraldries] before mentioned[,] who bringing him

to a convenient distance, laying their hands upon his neck, make him bow until his forehead almost touches the ground, and then raising him again, retire backwards to the farthest part of the room[;] the like ceremony is used with all the others who attend the ambassador. Only they make them bow somewhat lower than him. The ambassador at this audience has no chair set for him, but standing, informs the grand seignior by his interpreter of several demands of his Master, and the business he comes up on, which is all penned first in writing, which when read, is with the letter of credence consigned into the hands of the great vizier from whom the answer and farther treaty is to be received. (Paul Rycault, *The Present State of the Ottoman Empire)*[1]

Paul Rycault (1628–1700) served as the secretary to the English ambassador, Sir Heneage Finch, the third Earl of Winchilsea (ambassador 1660–1667), for five years and wrote an embassy report to the king about the Ottoman government, its military, and its provincial administration in the second half of the seventeenth century. Rycault also served as the English consul in Izmir for eleven years (1667–78) during a tumultuous time in the Ottoman Empire. He devoted several pages to the "barbaric" treatment of European ambassadors at the Porte during the Köprülu era.[2]

While Rycault may have held a biased view of the Ottoman government, which was typical of his era, French ambassadors and their dragomans like Antoine Galland (1646–1715) and Jean Thévenot (1633–67) were more knowledgeable about Ottoman culture and government due to their language training; thus, they became keen observers of events in the capital and life in Galata. They reported about the accession of a new sultan, the appointment of new grand viziers, changes in the government that affected the treatment of European subjects, and the renewal of ahdnames.[3] The most important mission of the ambassador was to protect Ottoman merchants and to renew ahdnames at the accession of the new sultan. The second half of the seventeenth century witnessed the rise of a series of powerful and ambitious grand viziers from the Köprülu household. In his account, Thévenot described the enormous power of the Köprülu vizier and his audience with the vizier and the sultan in the following manner:[4]

It is [he] [the grand vizier] who gives regular audiences to the ambassadors. The ambassadors receive only two receptions from the sultan, one during their arrival and another during their departure. These receptions are ceremonial in nature[,] during which one does not talk too much. He [the sultan] listens to the proposals and responds.

Thévenot was a natural scientist and botanist who also studied in the school of Oriental languages established by Minister Colbert in Paris. He traveled to Istanbul in May 1655 and stayed there until August 1655, then traveled to Alexandria, Sinai, and Cairo in 1657. From Cairo, he joined a pilgrim caravan to Jerusalem.[5] He next traveled to Alexandria for the second time in 1663 and also visited Damascus, Aleppo, and Baghdad. In August 1664, Thévenot entered Iran and visited Isfahan, Shiraz, and Bandar Abbas, where he stayed for five months. He visited India in 1665 and stayed there for thirteen months. Thévenot returned to Bandar Abbas in Iran and died in November 1667 on his way to Tabriz due to an illness. Thus, he gained a deep knowledge of the Ottoman Empire, Iran, and India. During this period, France was also interested in establishing direct contact with Safavid Iran through Isfahan and trade in silks. Thévenot's account of his first trip to the Ottoman Empire was published in Paris in 1665. It underscores the rising power and authority of the grand vizier in diplomatic affairs during the second half of the seventeenth century. It is far less biased than Rycault's account and gives a more balanced view of Ottoman society, particularly in Galata, possibly due to his training in Oriental languages and fluency in Ottoman, Persian, and Arabic. He also describes the system of justice, policing, and punishment in the imperial capital as well as the military and the harem in 1655. French travelers were often commissioned by Minister Colbert and King Louis XIV (1643–1715) to collect information on merchants, goods, prices, and trade routes in the second half of the seventeenth century.[6]

WAR AND DIPLOMACY DURING THE KÖPRÜLU ERA

Clearly, the second half of the seventeenth century was the low point of Ottoman diplomacy with Europe due to a long war against Venice (1645–69) over control of Crete and against the Holy League over control of Vienna in 1683. In addition, the Ottoman Empire fought a series of wars against Poland (1621, 1672–76) over control of the province of Podolia. This was not the golden age of Ottoman-European relations, and for the first time the Habsburg Empire, Venice, Russia, and the Polish-Lithuanian Commonwealth (the Holy League) united to defeat the Ottoman Empire before the gates of Vienna in 1683. As a result, in 1699, the Ottoman Empire had to sign the humiliating Treaty of Carlowitz with the Holy League, which led to major losses of territory in Hungary, Poland, and the Morea and undermined the legitimacy of the Ottoman sultan among his subjects. In 1703, a major rebellion led by the janissaries broke out that expressed the janissaries' anger against the Treaty of Carlowitz and the withdrawal of Ottoman troops from Vienna.[7]

The expansion of Ottoman naval power in the Mediterranean and the Venetian-controlled Greek islands started in the late fifteenth century and continued with brief disruptions (such as the Battle of Lepanto in 1570) into the eighteenth century. After the Ottoman occupation of Cyprus in 1571, Crete was considered the most important Mediterranean island for Ottoman naval and commercial expansion. Since the thirteenth century, Venice had controlled the island, which was important both commercially and strategically for maritime trade.[8] Crete, as the most important transit hub and linchpin in trade with the Levant, was the jewel of the Venetian crown. Spices from Egypt were carried to Venetian Crete, from which they were exported to Europe. Venice also imported grains, wine, and some olive oil from Crete and controlled the islands' economy very tightly. Moreover, France imported from Crete enormous quantities of olive oil, which was essential for the soap industry in Provence.

In addition to its importance to Venice, the island of Crete was also significantt both commercially and strategically for Ottoman trade and defense against Christian piracy. The Cretan War started over an act of piracy by the Maltese against Ottoman officials. In autumn 1644, some Maltese pirates attacked an Ottoman ship carrying the Chief Black Eunuch named Sünbüllü Agha and Bursali Mehmet Efendi to Egypt and Mecca (possibly taking funds to the pilgrims), killed them, and seized their enormous treasure.[9] Sultan Ibrahim (1640–48) accused the Venetian forces in Crete of giving the Maltese pirates safe haven, using the incident as an excuse to attack Venetian-controlled Crete in June 1645.

During the Cretan War (1645–69), France and England provided assistance to the Ottoman navy with eighteen warships that carried provisions to Crete that had been loaded in Çesme and Izmir in 1649.[10] But soon Ottoman-French relations entered a period of hostility during the Cretan Wars since France had also provided military assistance to Venice and considered herself the protector of the Catholic communities in the Levant. For these reasons, the Köprülu viziers displayed contempt toward the Venetian and French ambassadors and imprisoned both Bailo Molino and the French ambassador, Denis de la Hay Vantalet (1639–61), for three months in the Yedi Kule prison in 1659.[11]

Moreover, French vessels were required to transport provisions for the Ottoman army from Alexandria to Istanbul during the Cretan Wars. When French vessels were caught on their way from Alexandria to Italy instead of going to Istanbul, the French ambassador was thrown into prison for the second time in October 1669.[12] In 1667, the court of Istanbul received several lawsuits from Muslim merchants like Ibrahim and Mustafa Agha and two Jewish merchants, Mosi and Isak, who had hired French captains to transport sugar, rice, coffee, and cotton cloth from Alexandria to Istanbul. But the French captains Petro and Kiro had taken the goods to warring nations instead.[13] Furthermore, the grand vizier accused the French ambassador of also helping Count Konispolski, the general of the Polish army who had been captured during the fight with Poland, to flee from a prison on the Bosphorus to Poland.[14]

The Cretan War continued for two decades, at the end of which the Ottoman forces conquered Crete in 1669. The Cretan Wars brought about a crisis in Ottoman-Venetian and Ottoman-French relations. During this low period of Ottoman relations with Venice and France, the Venetian and French communities and ambassadors in Ottoman ports faced a myriad of challenges and abuses from local officials, judges, tax collectors, merchants, and their intermediaries. For example, the Köprülü viziers and local pashas in Cairo and Aleppo imposed *avanias* (illegal fees) on French merchants to raise revenue; the imposition of these fees, together with Maltese piracy in the Mediterranean and the disorganization of the French Levant trade, led to the decline of French trade in the second half of the seventeenth century.

The reduction of French trade with the Levant was the direct outcome of these developments as well as the Cretan Wars and the deterioration of Ottoman-French relations during the reign of King Louis XIV in the second half of the seventeenth century. Rivalry with the Netherlands and England also played an important role in the deterioration of French trade with the Levant. While the English and Dutch Levant Companies enjoyed great supremacy in the first half of the seventeenth century, French trade later fell to a tenth of what it had been 1620[15] (see chapter 6). French trade declined further due to the *Fronde* (peasant rebellions) and war with Spain, shrinking to fewer than three million *livres* in 1660. This was the lowest point in Ottoman-French trade since the early sixteenth century. By 1664, the number of French vessels trading between Provence and the Levant had dropped to thirty due to diplomatic rupture and increasing piracy on the Mediterranean by Tripolitan as well as English and Maltese ships.[16] French trade declined in the seventeenth century due to the deterioration of relations with the Ottoman Empire, the Cretan Wars, and a rise in piracy in the Mediterranean.[17]

COLBERT AND THE REVIVAL OF DIPLOMACY WITH THE PORTE

The conclusion of the Ottoman-Cretan Wars in 1669 and the appointment of Minister Colbert led to an improvement in Franco-Ottoman relations. Jean-Baptiste Colbert (1619–83) came from a merchant family in Reims and rose to the position of Controller-General of Finance in the court of Louis XIV in 1665. Having witnessed the decline of French trade in the Levant and elsewhere, his plan was to create a favorable balance of trade by raising tariffs and reviving the Levant trade in order to enable the French to compete effectively with English and Dutch traders (see chapter 6).[18]

In addition, Colbert controlled the appointment of French ambassadors to Istanbul. Under instructions from Minister Colbert, the French ambassador was given a mission to improve relations with the Porte, promote French commerce in the Levant and enable it to compete there with other European nations, protect the Catholics in the Levant, and renew existing ahdnames. To achieve these goals, France sent three special envoys to Istanbul between 1659 to 1665. King Louis XIV appointed Jean de la Haye, the son of Denis de la Hay, as ambassador to the Porte from 1665 to 1670. Jean de La Haye enjoyed special relations with the grand vizier, but he failed to renew the French-Ottoman ahdname because he was recalled to Paris in 1670 due to the large debt he had incurred as a result of his lavish lifestyle and purchasing of gifts for Ottoman officials, including those for the Chief Black Eunuch.[19]

The sultan sent Süleyman Agha Müteferrika to Paris as the Ottoman envoy in the years 1669 to 1670 to demand an explanation for the recalling of Ambassador Jean de la Haye from the Porte.[20] However, the French king refused to treat the Ottoman envoy as an ambassador and forced him to spend some time in quarantine, an experience that shocked the envoy. Nevertheless, aside from his mistreatment, the Ottoman envoy's visit to King Louis XIV generated great interest among the French in things Turkish, like coffee and coffeehouses, and produced a vogue in dress style and decoration called "La Turquerie" in Versailles.[21]

French diplomacy with the Porte was too important for Colbert to leave to incompetent ambassadors who were more interested in their own fortunes than in relations with the Porte. Colbert appointed Charles-Marie-François Olier Marquis de Nointel as the French ambassador (held office 1670–79) to the Porte in 1670. Nointel was accompanied by Antoine Galland (1646–1715), a young man aged twenty-four, as his deputy.

Galland, who had been born in a village in Picardie, had studied Greek in Paris and learned Turkish and Persian as well as Arabic in Istanbul. He studied at Collège de France in Paris and collected ancient manuscripts for the king.[22] He became the dragoman of the French Embassy in 1670, kept a diary about the daily activities of Ambassador Nointel, and wrote a travelogue about Izmir. Between 1670 and 1678, Galland made several trips to Izmir and the archipelago that he recounted in the travelogue. The embassy had a commercial, religious, and scientific mission, and Galland became one of the most well-known French *savants,* having collected and translated the Qur'an and oriental manuscripts like the *One Thousand and One Nights* from Arabic into French for the French king.

Ambassador Nointel served for nine years in Istanbul, but he encountered the same problem that the previous ambassador had had with the grand vizier, Kara Mustafa Pasha, when he requested the renewal of the French ahdname in 1670.[23] The grand vizier complained about France's foreign policy toward the Ottoman Empire, even after having received the sumptuous gifts of the French ambassador during his reception in Edirne. Ambassador Nointel, following instructions from Minister Colbert, was also trying to expand the jurisdiction of the French king over the Ottoman Catholic subjects in 1671, another highly sensitive issue. Another important mission of the French ambassador was the manumission of French slaves who had been captured by Tripolitan corsairs. Earlier, the Ottoman state had issued an order allowing the Tripolitan states to engage in piracy against enemy shipping (Habsburg, Maltese, and Venetian), but French ships were under the protection of the sultan in accordance with the ahdnames at times of peace.[24] Ambassador Nointel met several times with the grand vizier and three times with Sultan Mehmed IV (1648–87) and reported to Colbert on his progress in dealing with the situation of French merchants in Ottoman ports and the state of affairs in Istanbul.[25]

The French victory against Holland had led to the softening of Ottoman attitudes toward France, particularly at a time of Ottoman military weakness. The fifth Ottoman-French ahdname was finally signed between King

Louis XIV and Sultan Mehmed IV in June 1673.[26] The Ahdname of 1673 had seventeen articles on the status of Catholic communities in the empire and the right of the French king to protect Catholic Christians. In addition, Nointel succeeded in adding articles to this ahdname concerning French ships' freedom to trade in the Red Sea, a privilege already enjoyed by English traders.[27] More importantly, Ambassador Nointel succeeded in reducing the customs rates on imports and exports from 5 to 3 percent, to be paid once, a right that the English and Dutch merchants had already obtained in 1601 and 1612, respectively.[28] In addition, the transit taxes on silk textiles from India and Persia were abolished. The French were to pay the same amount of *masdariye* tax as Dutch and English merchants did in Istanbul and Galata. The tax was a nominal fee on imports and exports (1.5 percent) that European and local merchants had to pay. This ahdname also confirmed the French protection of merchant communities that did not have treaty relations with the Porte (such as Portugal, Ancona, Sicily, Messina, and Catalonia).

Furthermore, the 1673 ahdname gave new freedoms to French and Ottoman Catholic subjects in the Christian holy places and allowed Jesuit and Capuchin missionaries to gain a foothold in Palestine.[29] It extended diplomatic protection to French priests and monks in Galata, Izmir, Sidon, Alexandria, and wherever else a French community resided, exempting its members from the poll tax. French subjects and anyone under French protection was free to travel to holy places within and outside Jerusalem, an arrangement that added to tensions between French and Greek Orthodox monks over the control of holy places (see chapter 7). Capuchin and Jesuit monks could also reside in their two churches (St. Benoit and St. Francis) in Galata, read and teach the Gospel (to Ottoman subjects) in their hospital in Galata, and repair their churches after damages had occurred during fires. The Church of St. George was given to the Capuchins, who could repair it after fires and expel the Jews who inhabited part of the land (article 8). The French started reconstructing the Church of St. George in Pera in June 1675.[30] Although King Louis XIV wanted to become the protector of all Christians in the Ottoman Empire and wanted to place them on an equal footing with Muslims, the sultan did not confer this title on him.[31] The French king instead became the representative rather than the protector of the Catholic community for having the pride of place among Christian nations.[32]

In 1679, the French ambassador negotiated five more articles on lifting the ban on the import of Turkish silk and cotton tread. He also got the sultan to guarantee the protection of French ships from corsair attacks. However, despite his success with the signing of the ahdname, Ambassador Nointel, like his predecessor, fell out of favor with Colbert due to his extravagant lifestyle in Pera and was recalled to Paris in 1679. He took from Istanbul a collection of Islamic manuscripts and works of art that Antoine Galland had purchased with money borrowed from many merchants in Istanbul. In 1690, the new French ambassador in Istanbul, Pierre Antoine Castagnères, obtained an imperial decree from the sultan that reduced the customs rate on French-Egyptian trade as well from 10 to 3 percent, a clear victory after years of trial and failure.[33] As a result of the Ahdname of 1673, French trade with the Levant began expanding, and the number of French merchants in Izmir and Galata started rising (see chapter 6).

THE NEW AGE OF THE OTTOMAN-FRENCH ALLIANCE

After the Ottoman defeat in Vienna in September 1683, the Ottoman state turned to France as a mediator since France had not joined the Holy League alliance against the Ottoman Empire during the second siege of Vienna.[34] The crushing defeat of Ottoman forces in Vienna had led to the execution of Grand Vizier Merzifonlu Kara Mustafa Pasha in 1684. His successor, Fazil Mustafa Pasha, had a much more conciliatory attitude toward France and reestablished Ottoman-French relations after a gap of five years.

The new French ambassador, Gabriel-Joseph de la Vergne, comte de Guilléragues, obtained a reception with the sultan in November 1684 but died soon after in Istanbul from epilepsy in March 1685. From his correspondence with the French king, it is clear that war with the Tripolitan corsairs and the situation of seven hundred French captives in North Africa, which posed a great threat to French trade in the Levant, were the primary preoccupations of the ambassador.[35] Piracy by Tripolitan states in the Mediterranean targeted European ships and peaked at times of high tension between the Ottoman Empire and the Habsburg state. The conclusion of peace between France and the Tripolitan states in 1681 brought some relief to French ships and better relations between the French ambassador and the Porte. But the Porte could not always guarantee the protection of French ships from Tripolitan corsairs. The French, therefore, pursued their own diplomacy with the Ottoman provinces of Algiers and Tunis.

At the conclusion of the war with the Holy League, the Treaty of Carlowitz signed between the Ottoman state and the Holy League (Austria, the Poland-

Lithuanian Commonwealth, Venice, and Russia) in 1699 marked the first serious loss of territory by the Ottoman Empire in Hungary and Transylvania to the Habsburgs, Podolia to Poland, and the Morea and Dalmatia to Venice. Muscovy had emerged as a major power, demanding a curb on raids by the Crimean Tatars and posing a threat to the port of Azov on the Black Sea. A decade later, the Ottoman Empire defeated Peter the Great at the Battle of Pruth in 1711, driving Russian forces temporarily out of the port of Azov. The failed Ottoman siege of Vienna and the Treaty of Carlowitz had brought about not only territorial losses but also a serious economic and political crisis in the Ottoman Empire marked by janissary unrest and rebellions in Istanbul in 1703 and 1730.[36] To calm the rebels, Sultan Mustafa II (1695–1703) was forced to abdicate in favor of his brother, Sultan Ahmed III (1703–1730), in August 1703. The age of Köprülu viziers representing the war party against Europe had come to an end, and the peace party led by a new grand vizier had come to power at the Sublime Porte in 1718.

Grand Vizier Nevşehirli Ibrahim Pasha (1718–30), the son-in-law of Ahmed III, revived the age of diplomacy with Western Europe, particularly with France, an old ally and commercial partner. He was in direct contact with Ambassador Louis-Sauveur, marquis de Villeneuve (in office 1728–41) and entertained him in his mansion. Ottoman grand viziers assumed a direct role in negotiations with Western and Russian ambassadors in the eighteenth century. After the signing of the Treaty of Carlowitz in 1699, the Chancery division within the bureaucracy directed by the head of Chancery (*reisülküttab*) was appointed to lead the peace mission. The latter was responsible for foreign affairs and assumed greater importance than the grand vizier had in peace negotiations and employed his own scribes (thirty or so) and dragomans, the latter drawn from the Greek Phanariot community in Istanbul. The Greek notables who lived in the Fener neighborhood of Istanbul supplied dragomans to the Sublime Porte and governors to the two principalities of Moldavia and Wallachia.[37]

By the end of the eighteenth century, the Chancery had between 100 and 150 scribes, underscoring the importance of foreign affairs and diplomacy.[38] This office became increasingly professionalized as its job was to carry out correspondence with foreign powers, negotiate treaties with ambassadors, and handle disputes between the Ottoman and European (and Iranian) subjects. For example, Rami Mehmed Efendi became the chief negotiator at Carlowitz in 1699 and was accompanied by the chief dragoman of the Imperial Council, Iskerletzade-Alexander Mavrocordato, a member of the

Greek Phanariot community and the governor of Moldavia and Wallachia, during these negotiations. The Europeans regarded the head of Chancery as the chief of foreign affairs at the Sublime Porte.

Increasingly, the eighteenth-century grand viziers were drawn from among the heads of Chancery, who had the most experience in foreign affairs at that time. Koca Ragib Pasha, for example, who served as the chief negotiator with Nadir Shah of Iran in Tabriz in 1730, became the *reisülküttab* and grand vizier under Sultans Osman III (1754–57) and Mustafa III (1757–74). He was in charge of negotiating international treaties with Austria and Russia and kept a collection of these treaties in his archives.[39] Moreover, a copy of every *berat* (imperial decree of appointment) issued to the European ambassadors, their staffs, and merchants was kept in the archive of this division. Correspondence with European ambassadors, consuls, and subjects as well as with the boards of directors of the Levant Companies were also archived in this division, along with a copy of every ahdname (see introduction).

The French ambassadors in Pera played an important role in informing the Chamber of Commerce in Marseille and the French government in Versailles about politics as well as trade. The Chamber of Commerce in Marseille and the Ottoman treasury paid the expenses of each new ambassador and his large retinue when they arrived in Pera. The ambassadors and consuls also collected a *consulage* fee of 2.5 percent on trade from the subject merchants and received a salary of 6,000 livres from the Chamber of Commerce in Marseille.[40] The European embassies, especially the French and English, employed a large staff drawn both from back home and increasingly from the Levantine community in the Ottoman Empire. The chief dragoman of the French Embassy, who was appointed from among *les jeunes de langues* like Antoine Galland, played a key position in French foreign affairs with the Sublime Porte.[41] They were mostly drawn from members of the Levantine community of Pera like the Fonton, Fornetti, Pisani, Testa, and other families (see chapter 7). Members of the Testa family served as dragomans for the embassies of France, England, Venice, Prussia, Tuscany, and Holland in the eighteenth century (see chapter 7).[42]

The Ottoman state sent regular envoys (*çavuş*) to Europe but did not have permanent embassies in European states until 1792.[43] The first permanent Ottoman ambassadors were appointed to London (Yusuf Agha Efendi), Paris (Seyyid Ali Efendi), and Berlin (Aziz Efendi).[44] Sultan Mahmud II (1808–39) sent regular ambassadors to Paris, London, Vienna, Berlin, St. Petersburg, and Tehran. Before this period, the Ottoman state had relied on

Jean-Baptiste Vanmour, *Dinner at the Palace in Honor of an Ambassador*, 1725(?). Suna and Inan Kiraç Foundation Collection, © Uğur Ataç.

temporary envoys, networks of Moriscos and Jews, and Tripolitan corsairs as well as on its own spies, traders, and renegades to collect information on European affairs while the European states had also trained their own spies and collected information on the Ottomans.[45]

Beginning in the mid-seventeenth century, Ottoman embassy reports assumed great importance and provided political, technological, and cultural knowledge about Europe, thus becoming precursors of the modernization movement at the government level.[46] The Ottomans sent sumptuous gifts of jewels, handicrafts, and precious textiles with their embassies. The exchange of gifts and the sharing of meals were important aspects of embassy receptions at the Sublime Porte.

Jean Louis d'Usson, Marquis de Bonnac (1672–1738), the French ambassador to the Ottoman Empire from 1716 to 1724, enjoyed great favor and friendship with Grand Vizier Nevşehirli Ibrahim Pasha (1718–1730), who regarded France as a natural ally against Austria and Russia.[47] The Ottoman state gained some victory against Russia in the Battle of Pruth in 1711 and took back

Azov. It also defeated Venice and regained the Morea in 1715. Grand Vizier Ibrahim Pasha traveled to Vienna to ratify the Treaty of Passarowitz with Austria in 1718 with the mediation of ambassador Bonnac since he was well aware of the importance of international diplomacy.[48] The grand vizier dispatched Ottoman ambassadors to Vienna (Ibrahim Pasha) in 1719 and Paris (Yirmi Sekiz Çelebi Mehmed Efendi) and held receptions for European ambassadors at his palace. Yirmi Sekiz Çelebi Mehmed Efendi's mission in France was to renew the Franco-Ottoman alliance and to inform the French king that the sultan had granted him permission to repair the Church of Holy Sepulcher in Jerusalem. He also visited fortresses and factories to gather information on the means of progress, the modern military, and education.[49]

In France, the government of Louis XV (1710–40) was aiming at expanding commerce with the Levant, renewing and expanding the French capitulation with the Ottoman government. Cardinal de Fleury had made the integrity of the Ottoman Empire the pivotal point of his politics and had assigned Ambassador Villeneuve the task of mediating peace with Russia and Austria. Louis Saveur, Marquis de Villeneuve, had been born in Marseille in 1675 to a noble family. He was appointed by Cardinal Fleury as the ambassador to Istanbul in 1728 and remained in that position until 1741.

Villeneuve mediated peace negotiations between Austria, Russia, and Iran and forged a close relationship with Grand Vizier Nevşehirli Ibrahim Pasha (1718–30). This closeness was evidenced when Grand Vizier Ibrahim Pasha received Ambassador Marquis de Villeneuve in his summer residence along the Bosphorus.[50]

France was against the Russian expansion into the Black Sea and supported the Ottoman Empire. After the disintegration of the Safavid Dynasty in 1722 as a result of the Afghan occupation of Iran, the Ottoman forces moved into Azerbaijan and Western Iran in 1725 and reached a deal with Peter the Great of Russia to divide up the northern provinces. Iran was thus divided among the Afghan forces, the Ottoman Empire, and Russia, with a small province in central Iran under the control of a Safavid prince. The French ambassador mediated peace between the Ottoman state and Iran in 1725. Five years later, the new ruler of Iran, Nadir Shah, the founder of the Afshar Dynasty, defeated the Ottoman forces in 1730 and drove them out of western Iran. Ambassador Villeneuve mediated the peace treaty among Iran, Russia, and the Ottoman Empire.

The withdrawal of Ottoman forces from Tabriz led to the Patrona Halil Rebellion in September 1730.[51] The rebels targeted French subjects and

Europeans in Galata, partly due to the close relationship of the French ambassador and the grand vizier, Ibrahim Pasha, who was subsequently executed upon their demand. Non-Muslims and European traders were particular targets of the rebels, who were partly composed of artisans and small traders. The new Ottoman ruler, Mahmud I, restored order after suppressing the rebellion and entered war with Austria and Russia in 1736.[52]

Meanwhile, Russia had invaded the Ukraine and Crimea and had taken back Azov in 1736 in violation of the Peace Treaty of Pruth and was demanding the right of navigation on the Black Sea. In 1738, the Ottoman forces defeated Austria and occupied all the towns that the empire had lost in 1718. Villeneuve played a crucial role in negotiating the Treaty of Belgrade with Austria in 1739, which returned to the Ottoman Empire territories she had lost in the Treaty of Passarowitz in 1718. After the intervention of Villeneuve, Russia also agreed to return the port of Azov on the Black Sea and all the conquered territories to the Ottomans. More importantly, the Black Sea remained closed to the Russian merchant marine, so Russian merchants had to carry their trade on Ottoman ships.[53] Ambassador Villeneuve was committed to preventing the dissolution of the Ottoman Empire and keeping Russia out of the Black Sea. He also managed to negotiate the most important French ahdname with the new sultan as a result of his mediation and close contacts with the grand vizier.

THE FRENCH AHDNAME OF 1740

After his close cooperation in the Ottoman peace negotiations, Villeneuve succeeded in negotiating with Grand Vizier Mehmed Pasha on May 28, 1740, for the renewal of the French ahdname, which contained eighty-five articles and gave French subjects new rights.[54] It was the most comprehensive ahdname that had been given to any Western power since the sixteenth century. The treaty first reconfirmed the special relationship between the Ottoman sultans and the French king, the special representative of Christian kings that had existed since the time of Sultan Süleyman the Magnificent. The ahdname made a vague reference in the final article to the future status of the treaty, stating, "From now on, our successors, grand viziers[,] and pashas will protect and enforce the ahdname in its entirety."[55] It is not at all clear whether the Ottoman negotiators rescinded their right to revise or cancel any of the articles, but the sultan, as we will see, could still revoke the ahdname if peace and friendship (*amité*) no longer prevailed between the two states (see epilogue).

Clearly, the treaty basically renewed the ahdnames of 1673 and added some new articles on trade. As in the Ahdname of 1673, it gave the French ambassador special titles and priority over all the other European ambassadors in obtaining an audience with the sultan or the grand vizier at the Sublime Porte. It then provided permission for French subjects to freely visit Jerusalem and the Church of Holy Sepulcher without any hindrance, as were the terms of the 1673 ahdname. More importantly, the ahdname also confirmed that French traders could continue trading in previously banned items such as cotton and wool, cotton thread, beeswax, and hides. They were exempt from paying taxes on their gold and silver coins, and the Ottoman treasury did not have permission to convert their coins into Ottoman coins. The remaining articles can be divided into the following headings.

Freedom of Trade and Protection From Piracy

As in previous ahdnames, the first series of articles promised French traders safe conduct, freedom to trade on land and sea, and protection from Muslim piracy and from enslavement. They stated that French traders found on enemy ships would not be taken into slavery as long as they conducted their trade in peace and were not helping Christian corsair ships. If Muslim corsairs captured French traders, they were to release them and return their goods. French ships were allowed to purchase grains (previously a banned item of trade) from Muslim ships and take them to their country (but not to enemy lands). French ships would receive assistance when they landed in North African ports, but if North African pirates attacked French ships, the former would be punished. In other words, the North African governors who allowed French ships to be attacked and French traders to be taken into captivity by their corsairs would be removed from their positions. Moreover, local governors had to provide financial guarantee for the looted goods of the French merchants. This stipulation was a significant step in providing French ships with some sort of insurance against Tripolitan corsair attacks, though it could not prevent Christian (Maltese) corsair attacks on French ships. In addition, the treaty pledged that all Ottoman officials and subjects would provide aid (such as lead, sails, and gunpowder) to all French ships that sank in the rough seas and would return all their goods. The ambassador and consuls would investigate the identity of all French ships, and Ottoman authorities would not harass them for corsair activities. If Ottoman officials and subjects rented a French ship, local officials would inform the ambassador or French consuls and obtain their permission to do so. All the provincial and district governors, captains, kadis, tax collectors, and Ottoman subjects would act according to the articles of the treaty and would not allow the violation of its terms.

Freedom to Trade on the Black Sea, Export of Grains and Foodstuff, and Sale of Goods to Ottoman Subjects

The next most important series of articles dealt with new privileges for French merchants. In addition, the 1740 treaty provided French traders the much sought after freedom of trade on the Black Sea, a right that Dutch traders already enjoyed. French ships had been trying to gain access to the Black Sea to import grains since the second half of the seventeenth century.[56] French ships could now import Russian grains from the Black Sea via Istanbul to Marseille without any interference from local officials as long as they were not selling Ottoman provisions to an enemy territory. In addition, French merchants could travel to Russia and the port of Odessa on the Black Sea to sell their goods without having to pay transit dues in Istanbul (see chapter 5). Moreover, French ships could export dried fruits and walnuts from Crete once a year on their ships as long as they paid the customs taxes.

Taxes and Fees

Furthermore, as in the 1673 treaty, the customs dues on the import and export of all goods, including French woolens, were reduced from 5 to 3 percent, to be paid once in the empire. This lower customs rate was the most important article of the 1673 treaty that was renewed in 1740 with the new provisions. In addition, French merchants were exempt from paying sales tax when they sold their goods in local markets as well as other customary taxes (*kasabiye, reft, bac, yasak kolu* and *selamlık*). For example, when French merchants imported a cap called a *fez* into Izmir or Tunisia, they would not have to pay the customs tax if they were unable to sell the caps in Izmir. However, they would pay the customs tax when they sold the fez in Ottoman markets like Galata. French merchants would pay the same amount of *masdariye* taxes as English merchants would. They would pay customs on silk exports from the Ottoman Empire only once. This new set of articles considerably reduced the number of local taxes to be paid by French merchants.

It is interesting to note that this ahdname acknowledged the fact that Ottoman merchants were allowed to carry their merchandise on French ships since the Levant Company banned Ottoman subjects from trading directly with Marseille and other French ports. However, Ottoman subjects who transported their goods on French ships were also subject to the payment of consular dues of 2.5 percent on exports. This was an important provision that Ottoman merchants obviously resisted. French ships on their way to Galata would pay transit taxes once in Boğazhisar or Gelibolu. The ahdname also stated that no taxes would be charged on bills of exchange or promissory notes (*poliçe*) on French merchants. French merchants accumulated a great deal of cash from imports and engaged actively in drawing up bills of exchange and giving loans to Ottoman state officials (see chapter 6).

In addition, the French merchants' gifts (to the Sublime Porte), personal clothing, food, and wine were exempt from customs dues and sales tax. French consuls, their dependents, their dragoman, French merchants, and French priests had permission make wine at their homes and to import it without any harassment. Moreover, they would not be charged any wine tax by local tax collectors. This provision exempted French subjects from the wine tax and removed the ban on wine trade, which was issued from time to time (see chapter 7). In addition, French subjects would be able to sell any goods in Ottoman markets without the interference of the authorities. This provision also gave French subjects who resided in Ottoman lands the right to travel anywhere in the interior with official permission (internal visas) and to dress in their own garb while they moved around (see chapter 6). These provisions gave French merchants direct access to Ottoman markets and sources of supply without any need for Ottoman intermediaries, although they did have to apply for internal visas. Previously, French merchants had been restricted to ports like Galata and certain neighborhoods in other towns and ports (see next chapter [5]).

As stated in previous treaties, French subjects (consuls, traders, dragoman, artisans, priests, and monks) who lived in Ottoman ports were exempt from payment of the poll tax, as were their dragomans and protégés (see chapter 7). This article did not place a time limit on French residents before they were liable for the payment of the poll tax. As in previous ahdnames, the allies of the French king (Catalan, Portuguese, Sicilian, and Anconan merchants) had the right to trade under the French flag and were to be treated like French subjects by customs collectors in Ottoman ports.

Settlement of Legal Disputes

As in previous treaties, legal disputes among French subjects were to be handled by French consular courts under their own laws, but those between Ottoman and French subjects were to be taken to the kadi court (disputes under 4,000 akçe) and to the Imperial Council if they involved more than 4,000 akçes (see chapters 6 and 7). When a French subject committed murder or any other crimes, the lawsuit could only be heard in the presence of the French consul. Any legal disputes between Ottoman and French subjects in the kadi courts could only be heard in the presence of their dragoman, and if the dragoman was not present, the kadi would have to wait until he showed up (see appendix). French subjects were free to take their disputes to the Imperial Council when they were not happy with the decisions of the kadi courts (see chapter 6). Any disputes between the consuls and merchants of European nations would be referred to the consular courts, and Ottoman authorities could not interfere or hear those cases unless the parties to the dispute allowed it. Any lawsuits by Ottoman and French subjects against ambassadors and consuls would be taken to the Imperial Council. These articles allowed parties to any legal disputes to forum shop and present their disputes, even if they involved French subjects, to the Imperial Council. Thus, the Ottoman Imperial Council functioned as a last resort and like a Supreme Court. It is important to note that the Ottoman shari'a and kanun held equal jurisdiction, if not a higher position, as French laws did over French subjects. French subjects in Istanbul, however, preferred to submit their lawsuits to the Imperial Council through the ambassador since they did not like the second-class status that the shari'a accorded to zimmis and foreigners.

Legal documentation, however, was required from Ottoman as well as from French subjects before their disputes could be heard in the courts. French subjects were obliged to register any financial and commercial transactions in the kadi courts and to obtain receipts and documentation that would be required in legal disputes. The kadi would not prosecute any disputes without proper documentation and trustworthy witnesses. Any undue violence or oppression against French subjects would be punished. Their debts would not be collected from innocent Frenchmen. When a French merchant declared bankruptcy, and it was proven, his debts would be paid off from the sale of his remaining goods, with ample legal documentation. The French ambassador, consuls, and dragoman would not be harassed to stand as guarantors for the debt of French merchants who had defaulted. No forceful entry was allowed into the residence of French subjects without the permission of the ambassador and consuls (see chapter 6).

Affairs of Consuls, Dragomans, and Brokers

France had the right to set up consulates anywhere that a French community resided in the Ottoman Empire. French consuls could fly the French flag wherever they resided and could hire guards from among the janissaries to protect their consulates. French ambassadors and consuls also could hire anyone as their dragomans, and no one could impose any decisions on them regarding this matter (see chapter 7). French dragomans who represented the ambassador and consuls could not be questioned, harassed, or imprisoned while they were properly carrying out their duties. If they committed any wrongs, the consuls and ambassador would punish them through their own laws and courts. French dragomans would be exempt from paying personal taxes like the poll tax as well as from paying other customary taxes to the Ottoman government. They would enjoy the same exemptions that French subjects did. These provisions were very significant in providing tax exemptions to the non-Muslim subjects (mostly Greeks and Armenians) of the Ottoman Empire who became the dragomans of French embassies and consulates but engaged in trade most of the time. No one would interfere in the affairs and selection of brokers, whatever their backgrounds, who represented the French merchants in commercial transactions. Most brokers were Ottoman non-Muslim subjects such as Jews.

Visits and Pilgrimages to the Holy Places and
Freedom of Religious Practice

Religion continued to play an important role in French policy in the Levant. The 1740 treaty renewed all the articles in the 1673 treaty that dealt with freedom of religious practice for French subjects and those under French protection. They were free to visit holy places in Palestine based on the treaty of 1673. In addition, as in that treaty, all French priests and (Catholic) monks from any religious order would be able to conduct their rites and practice their religion freely in Ottoman lands and to visit the Church of the Holy

Sepulcher and other Christian holy places in and outside Jerusalem. No one was allowed to forcefully enter their sacred places and demand the poll tax (see chapter 7). If their disputes were not settled locally, they would be referred to the Imperial Council. The Jesuit and Capuchin monks in Galata could repair their two churches after damages caused by fires with permission from the kadi and would not be charged money by Ottoman authorities. They would also be able to recite the Bible in their hospital in Galata, as was stated in the 1673 treaty.

Articles 84 and 85 made the 1740 ahdname the most comprehensive textual corpus that contained all the previous articles as well as the new ones that would apply to the most favored nation in Istanbul and all other ports. As mentioned previously, it vaguely referred to the binding and perpetual nature of this ahdname upon the succeeding sultans.[57] However, French ambassadors took this article for granted and demanded the application of the 1740 ahdname when the Ottoman state tried to impose new restrictions on the permitted number of dragomans and to demand new taxes.

What is more significant is that the French government did not recognize the principle of reciprocity to provide Ottoman merchants with the same rights to trade in France as those granted to the French in the Ottoman Empire until the nineteenth century and basically after the dissolution of the Levant Company following the French Revolution. Nor did France recognize the rights of Ottoman merchants to exclusive control in domestic trade and insisted on getting rid of monopolies by the guilds of cloth sellers and grocers while the Levant Company maintained its own monopoly vis-à-vis Ottoman merchants in Marseille.[58] Therefore, while French merchants were gaining new freedoms to trade in the Black Sea and in the interior of the Ottoman Empire (domestic trade), Ottoman merchants were still excluded from Marseille and other French ports. Clearly, this treaty did not close the door on future negotiations and revisions, as we shall see. French trade expanded considerably, and France gained the top place in the Porte's foreign trade with Europe until the opening of the Black Sea to Russian navigation (see chapter 6).

THE FRANCO-OTTOMAN ALLIANCE
AGAINST RUSSIA

For the Ottoman Empire, the eighteenth century was a period of long wars against Iran and Russia, resulting in serious economic crises in the second half of the century.[59] The rivalry over control of the Black Sea and Poland brought France and the Ottoman Empire together against Russia and Austria. England sided with the latter since France was her biggest enemy and rival. For the Ottoman Empire, Russia emerged as the most important threat on the Black Sea and gained steady ground in the late eighteenth century.

France played a key role in Ottoman-Russian relations, and French ambassadors like Villeneuve were assigned important tasks to mediate between these two countries. The initial French policy was to encourage the Porte to go to war with Russia in order to protect Poland, but the subsequent Franco-Russian and Franco-Austrian alliances brought about a change in this policy in 1756, a situation that angered the Porte. As a result, Franco-Ottoman relations faced some challenges during the embassy of Louis Bonneville de Marsangy le Chevalier de Vergennes (ambassador 1755–68) due to the French alliances with Russia and Austria in 1756.[60]

France and the Ottoman Empire had supported Poland against Russian and Austrian designs to partition it. However, the French policy in Poland had failed as the newly elected king was backed by Russia in 1762. The reign of Catherine the Great (1762–96) renewed the Russian efforts to control Poland and gain access to the Black Sea. Ambassador Vergennes was recalled from Istanbul to France in 1768 due to his reluctance to obey Minister Etienne-François duc de Choiseul's demand that he encourage the Ottoman Empire to declare war on Russia. Vergennes was a Turcophile and tried to promote the interests of the Ottoman Empire against Russia, as had long been the French policy. Another reason for his recall was his marriage to his former mistress and beloved, Annette de Viviers, or Madame Testa, a Levantine widow of a French doctor in Pera, in 1767 (see chapter 7).[61]

Taking advantage of the growing weakness of the Polish-Lithuanian Commonwealth, Russia, Austria, and Prussia formed the Triple Alliance to partition Poland among themselves and carried out the effort three times— in 1772, 1793, and 1795.[62]

The Russian navy, having gained access to the Aegean Sea, dealt a heavy blow to the Ottoman fleet at the Battle of Çeşme in 1770 during a Greek rebellion in the Morea. Moreover, the Russian threat to Crimea took a serious turn as well in the second half of the eighteenth century.[63] Like the Polish Commonwealth, the Crimean Khanate had fallen into full disarray over rivalry between various Tatar clans for leadership after the death of Kirim Giray Khan in 1769. Russia occupied Crimea in 1770, an action that led to Selim Giray Khan's abdication and escape to the Ottoman Empire. The new khan, Sahib Giray Khan, was Catherine II's lieutenant and no longer considered himself a close ally of the Ottoman Empire. He declared independence from the Ottoman Empire under Russian protection in 1771.

The ensuing war between the two states (1768–74) led to an Ottoman defeat and the signing of the Treaty of Küçük Kaynarca in 1774 (27 articles). The treaty restored peace between the two states and recognized Crimean independence under Russian protection and the withdrawal of Ottoman forces from Crimea, which was opposed by the Tatar khan in Istanbul. Russia pledged to return to the Ottoman Empire all of Besserabia; the ports of Akkerman, Kilia, and Ismail; and the forts of Bender as well as the two principalities of Wallachia and Moldavia, together with all the fortresses, ports, towns, and islands of the archipelago that it had occupied. The loss of Crimea and the subsequent Russian expansion into the Black Sea and southern Ukraine were major blows to Ottoman control of the Black Sea and an important loss of a Muslim territory to Russia. In addition, this treaty provided Russia the freedom to establish a merchant marine in Ottoman seas—including the Black Sea, the Straits (the Bosphorus and the Dardanelles), and the Danube—and to import and export all kinds of goods, which could not be unilaterally revoked by the Ottomans. The treaty also provided for mutual freedom of trade and for the security of the subjects of both states. Russia also received the right to establish an embassy in Istanbul as well as consuls all over the empire. All Russian subjects and pilgrims were allowed to visit holy places in Jerusalem and Palestine and to enjoy the same exemption from dues and taxes as other European subjects did. The Ottoman Empire agreed to pay a war indemnity to Russia over three years.[64] Russian had clearly gained an important diplomatic and commercial footing in the Ottoman Empire (see chapter 2).

The treaty also made vague references to the Russian protection of the Greek Orthodox subjects of the Ottoman Empire (particularly in the principalities of Moldavia and Wallachia) while making the sultan the authority over Muslims in Crimea. This clause (Russian protection of the Greek Orthodox) has been subject to varying interpretations by both sides. But ultimately it led to Catherine II's Greek Project and interference in the internal affairs of the Greek subjects in the Ottoman Empire. To return Crimea, the Ottoman Empire declared war on Russia in 1787 and suffered a humiliating defeat in 1789.

The opening of the Black Sea trade was the next important change in the international trade of the Ottoman Empire. The Black Sea had been a closed Ottoman lake since the conquest of Constantinople in 1453. It played a very important role in the provisioning of Istanbul with grains and other food-stuff, which was under the control of Muslim *kapan* (provisioning) merchants and sea captains (see chapter 5).[65] Russia built its own ports, such as Odessa, on the Black Sea, established Russian consulates in Ottoman cities, and received all the commercial and legal rights that the subjects of England and France enjoyed in Ottoman lands.

Catherine II also aimed at liberating the three Ottoman principalities of Wallachia, Moldavia, and Besserabia and gaining total control over the Crimea. In 1783, Russia annexed the Crimea and insisted on receiving a full ahdname (eighty-one articles) similar to the ones given to France and England. Consequently, the Ottoman state recognized the full annexation of Crimea by Russia in the Treaty of Jassy in 1792.[66] Russia was allowed to build a church of Orthodox rite in Pera in 1784.[67] As a result of the important privilege that Russia had gained on the Black Sea, England obtained access to the Black Sea in 1799, France formally received it in the Treaty of Paris in 1802, and Prussia gained it in 1806.[68] The Ottoman Empire was only able to assert its right to prevent warships from passing though the Straits in the Treaty of the Dardanelles signed with England in January 1809.[69] The Treaty of Bucharest in 1812 opened the Black Sea to Russian and European navigation, freeing the supply of grains and corn from Odessa to Istanbul and to western Mediterranean ports like Marseille (see chapter 5). The Ottoman capital was potentially exposed to possible Russian naval attacks as the Black Sea opened up to international commercial shipping.

CONCLUSION

While the first series of ahdnames had bilateral articles, the second group became unilateral since they were usually granted after major wars and during peace negotiations. However, the wars of the second half of the seventeenth century and growing piracy on the Mediterranean caused economic crises for both the Ottoman Empire and France. The second (1650–1774) series of capitulations were granted to France and Russia after the conclusion of the Cretan Wars and the revival of Ottoman-French diplomacy under Minister Colbert. A series of able ambassadors like Villeneuve implemented French policies when the Ottoman Empire opened up to closer diplomatic, cultural, and commercial contacts with France during the Tulip Age (1703–30). The Ahdnames of 1673 and 1740 with France included new provisions for French merchants and monks, giving them an important position in the affairs of Catholic communities as well as the holy places in Jerusalem. The new ahdnames lifted bans on some Ottoman exports and granted French merchants new rights in domestic shipping and trade on the Black Sea. But Ottoman-Russian wars led to the defeat of the Ottoman Empire, the annexation of Crimea, the signing of the Ottoman-Russian ahdname, and the opening of the Black Sea to Russian trade in 1784, thus impacting the traders of Galata who were in charge of provisioning Istanbul.

PART THREE

Commercial and Cultural Encounters

WHILE THE AHDNAMES CREATED A LEGAL FRAMEWORK for the conduct of diplomacy and trade, their implementation faced constant challenges from Ottoman officials and European traders as well as from residents of port cities. As European traders got involved in domestic trade, they faced strong resistance from local producers, artisans, and merchants. Part 3 of the book will focus on commercial, legal, and cultural encounters between Ottoman and European communities, with a focus on the French community in Galata. Chapter 5 will underscore the role of Galata in domestic trade and in feeding Istanbul as a port on the Black Sea as well as part of the Mediterranean trade. The state played a key role in provisioning Istanbul, but it turned to private merchants and even to foreigners at times of war and shortages, undermining its provisioning policies and the monopoly of local traders in domestic trade. Chapter 6 will focus on the evolution of maritime trade between Galata and France, with a focus on the eighteenth century. Chapter 7 will shed light on the social, cultural, and religious aspects of Ottoman-European encounters as the number of European residents in Galata and its suburbs increased. The epilogue will examine the impact of the French Revolution and Napoleon's invasion of Egypt on Franco-Ottoman diplomacy and trade, the revocation of the Ahdname of 1740, and the dissolution of the French Levant Company.

FIVE

Feeding Istanbul

THE MERCHANTS OF GALATA AND THE
PROVISIONING TRADE

The Harbor of Galata, being an extremely fine one, is protected
from the eight winds, and in winter time 1,000 ships lay anchor
there without fear.

The people of Galata are in (———) categories: The first are
sailors, the second merchants, the third craftsmen of various
sorts, and the fourth joiners and caulkers. Most of them wear
clothing of Cezayir [the Aegean Archipelago] because they are
mainly mariners. They are fabulously rich captains, among them
Elvan Kapudan. The Greeks are tavern keepers. The Armenians
are sellers of pressed meat (*pastırma*) and wealthy merchants.
The Jews are intermediaries in the marketplace.

EVLIYA ÇELEBI, *Seyahatname*, vol.1, part 2[1]

MEDITERRANEAN AND BLACK SEA PORTS like Galata played an
important role in the provisioning trade. The provisioning of cities with
foodstuff was an important aspect of the commercial policies in medieval
and early modern Mediterranean states. Riots were usually triggered by a rise
in the price of basic foodstuff like bread due to economic crises, droughts,
and wars that disrupted trade. The supply of affordable foodstuff, particularly grains, formed an important element in the policies of states regarding
maritime trade. Consequently, provisioning merchants and ship captains,
many of whom lived in Galata, enjoyed great wealth, prestige, and government support. Provisioning big cities like Venice and Paris was also an important government task. Fernand Braudel underscored the importance of
provisioning grain in Mediterranean cities:

> The trinity of grains, flour, [and] bread is to be found everywhere in the his-
> tory of Europe. It was the major preoccupation of towns, states, merchants,
> and ordinary people[,] for whom life meant "eating one's daily bread."[2]

Galata had been a center of provisioning trade, particularly with the Black Sea, since the Genoese times. The port of Galata was the second most active port of Constantinople that connected the Mediterranean to the Black Sea ports.[3] The number of ships anchoring in the harbor of Galata had increased from one hundred at the time when Ibn Battuta had visited Galata in the mid-fourteenth century to one thousand when Evliya Çelebi wrote his account in the mid-seventeenth century.

Evliya Çelebi's description of the inhabitants of Galata underscores the role of sea captains and traders as well as their wealth and prestige in Ottoman society. Wealthy traders and sea captains of all backgrounds resided permanently in mansions in Kasım Paşa and Galata. Many wealthy sea captains, according to Evliya Çelebi, were from the eastern Mediterranean and the Black Sea ports and enriched themselves through the provisioning trade in olive oil, cheese, honey, spices, coffee, and wine.

The Ottoman capital, with a population of almost half a million, was the largest port *par excellence*, a consuming imperial capital, and a center of redistribution and connectivity in the early modern Mediterranean.[4] The two shores of the Golden Horn were the most commercially active ports of Istanbul that catered to the provisioning of a fast-growing city with a population of between 300,000 and 500,000 residents in the late eighteenth century.

Istanbul was the biggest consumer of grains in the empire due to its large and growing population. Istanbul consumed 200 tons of grains daily in the eighteenth century.[5] In 1758, Istanbul imported 181,000 tons of wheat, of which 85.8 percent came from the Black Sea and the Sea of Marmara while 14.2 percent was imported from Thrace and the eastern Mediterranean ports like Crete and Alexandria.[6] Every year between 3,000 and 4,000 ships arrived in Istanbul and Galata delivering bulky foodstuff like grains, rice, olive oil, clarified butter, wine, sugar, spices, and coffee and other goods such as hides, timber, hemp, and coal from the Black Sea and Egypt as well as from the Aegean islands. Ships carrying grains unloaded them across from the port of Galata in Un Kapanı on the southern shore of the Golden Horn.[7] The public scale for wheat was located in Eminönü, where all ships carrying grains had to bring their cargoes and pay taxes before distributing them among retailers. The public scale for oil (*yağ kapanı*) was located in Galata on the opposite shore of the Golden Horn while scale for honey (*bal kapanı*) was near the Egyptian market in Eminönü.

Galata was also the center of the production of food like pressed meat (*pastırma*) as well as of the sale of European confections, colonial coffee, and colonial sugar from the West Indies.[8] *Francela* bread, a special high quality white bread, was also made in the bakeries of Galata for European consumption. During food shortages, the state imposed limits on its production due to price hikes.

This chapter will focus on the activities of the provisioning traders in Galata, the role of state in regulating this trade, and the entry of France into this trade in the late eighteenth century. Whereas chapters 3 and 4 offered the legal framework for Ottoman commercial policies in port cities, this chapter will examine the impact of these policies on domestic trade through the lens of Ottoman narrative sources, court documents, documents related to urban and economic issues, petitions and lawsuits brought by traders and artisans, imperial orders, and consular correspondence. We will also be able to test some of the theories put forward by Ottoman economic historians on the "Ottoman economic mind" and the role of domestic merchants in the transformation of Galata during the long eighteenth century.

OTTOMAN MERCHANTS AND THE HISTORIOGRAPHY OF THE COMMAND ECONOMY

> Merchants (traveling and local) were the only group in Ottoman society [that was] free of guild controls and regulations and [that] could amass wealth without any restrictions and become capitalists. Merchants possessed the necessary characteristics for the development of merchant capitalism in the Middle East.[9]

The Ottoman economy was part of the Mediterranean maritime as well as the overland caravan trade networks of Eurasia that can be traced back to the ancient Mediterranean and the Near East.[10] There is an ongoing debate among Ottomanist social scientists and historians about the nature of the Ottoman economic mind, the role of the state in regulating economic life, and the political and ideological impediments of the rise of merchant capitalism in contrast to the emerging mercantilist states in Europe. While social scientists have been drawn to economic models based on the Western experience, historians have revised these models, relying on archival sources and comparative studies across time and space with the rest of the Mediterranean world.

For a long time, the study of classical institutions dominated Ottoman historiography, according to which the state was considered the most important player in regulating and commanding economic life. In two important articles and several book chapters in his earlier writings, Halil Inalcik argued that, combined with the ethical principles of Islam and the Persian tradition of the *Circle of Justice,* an Ottoman welfare system commanded the economy.[11] The Circle of Justice, borrowed from the ancient Iranian tradition of statecraft, linked a strong state to a strong army that depended on a strong treasury. A strong treasury relied on taxes from tax-paying subjects. The welfare of the tax-paying subjects in turn depended on the justice of the king. Therefore, justice made up the most important aspect of the political culture of the premodern Middle East.[12] An important responsibility of a "just king" was to guarantee the abundance of basic foods and raw materials at fair prices. To achieve this end, the state, rather than feudal lords, owned much of the grain-producing land in the Ottoman Empire.

In his earlier writings, Inalcik also pointed out that the state's control over the economy such as state-owned agricultural land (*miri*), taxation, and production remained primordial in the classical era (1500–1600).[13] He added that, unlike the mercantilist West, the Ottoman state did not believe in the balance of trade and promoted imports over exports by granting ahdnames to friendly European nations. It only banned the export of grains and important war and raw materials like cotton, silk, raw wool, and hides. Inalcik believed that the Ottoman state had failed to adopt protectionist policies by opening up its markets to European goods and controlled the production and distribution of basic necessities like foodstuff and raw materials to provision the army, the palace, and the capital.[14]

It is important to note that Inalcik emphasized these government policies regarding the provisioning of Istanbul with basic necessities like grains and meat from 1500 to1600. He believed that the state loosened its control over the economy in the subsequent period with the expansion of tax farming in the eighteenth century. Due to chronic revenue shortfalls, the state farmed out important sources of revenue from rural as well as urban production to private individuals who provided ready cash in regular bids to purchase the right to collect taxes and make a profit (between 10 and 20 percent). Tax farms were granted for a period of one to two years, but some were lifetime grants that were hereditary. The institution of tax farming led to the rise of provincial notables who collected taxes from agricultural production for the state and assumed an important place in the provincial administration, thus weakening the control of the central state. It also led to the commercialization of agriculture in the eighteenth century. Many urban revenues like customs dues were also farmed out to private individuals. For example, in Galata and Izmir the customs taxes were usually farmed out to wealthy Jewish subjects as well as to janissaries. The Greeks farmed out the wine tax.

Moreover, Inalcik revised his earlier position on the Ottoman economic mind and elaborated further on the role of long-distance merchants, arguing that traveling merchants (*bezirgans*) enjoyed greater freedom than retail traders and artisans did since they were not subject to the same guild rules and state controls during the early modern period. They were allowed to make a high profit, were free to trade anywhere in the empire, and did not pay taxes on overland trade. In addition, the state allowed Muslim merchants in particular greater freedom to trade at low customs rates of between 2.5 and 3 percent while non-Muslim Ottoman merchants paid 4 percent, and European merchants paid 5 percent dues (later reduced to 3 percent) in international trade prior to the eighteenth century.[15]

In his later writings, Inalcik continued to emphasize that the Ottoman state did indeed protect its own merchants and promoted their interests vis-à-vis foreign traders, particularly in the Black Sea and Red Sea trade. He further elaborated on the role of merchants in Middle Eastern and Ottoman economies, highlighting their contribution to the commercial economy as free agents.

In the major ports and caravan cities like Bursa, Aleppo, Izmir, and Galata, merchants accumulated capital, often in the form of cash; engaged in *commenda* partnerships to share risks and profits; lent money with interest, and (a few) became tax farmers, thus investing in the rural and urban economies, particularly in the eighteenth century. Cash vakfs functioned like informal banking institutions in the Ottoman Empire. Since interest was banned in Islam, cash vakfs were established by wealthy Muslim individuals as charitable endowments to provide loans and credit at low interest rates (between 5 and 10 percent) in the Ottoman Empire.[16]

Mehmet Genç, the prominent economic historian of the Ottoman Empire, elaborated further on the Ottoman state's role in the economy during the classical era that, according to him, lasted from 1500 to 1800, a periodization that was two hundred years longer than the one offered by Inalcik. He developed a model for the Ottoman economy composed of three economic principles—1) provisionism, 2) traditionalism, and 3) fiscalism—that, according to him, changed very little until the nineteenth century.[17] Following Inalcik, he believed that the most important principle of the Ottoman economic model was provisionism, or the supply of cheap, abundant, and high quality goods for the palace, the army, and the residents of the capital.

According to Genç, the Ottoman state followed a traditional approach to the economy for a long time, thus safeguarding the interests of organized groups like guilds and its own fiscal needs rather than promoting the interests of merchant groups.

Both Inalcik and Genç emphasized the principle of state ownership of agricultural land and the weak development of private property in the Ottoman Empire as important features of the command economy. According to Genç, in commerce, the Islamic as well as the Sufi principles (the *ahi* tradition) of egalitarianism, equity, and cooperation rather than competition prevailed. Inalcik and Genç both believed that the state tried to maintain a balance between production and distribution and prevented profiteering among producers and guilds and the accumulation of capital among merchants. When merchants and tax farmers got too rich, the state could confiscate their goods, according to Genç. It also promoted moderation in consumption for fear of shortages that could lead to riots and political crisis. However, it is not clear how the state could control the consumption patterns of the population at large or the elites in Istanbul and the provinces. Moreover, many historians like Inalcik and Genç believed that by promoting imports (particularly of fine textiles) at low customs rates through the granting of ahdnames to European traders, the state failed to protect its own merchants and industries, unlike the policies of mercantilist Europe, until the early eighteenth century. However, local industries met the demands of the population at large while imports were largely consumed by the elites. Genç also believes that these policies remained fixed for several centuries and that the state prevented any changes in the basic economic structure or ideological principles and punished those who violated these principles through the guilds, which had internalized these principles and controlled their application. We therefore need larger studies of consumption patterns not only of the residents of Istanbul but also of the residents of other cities to make these conclusions.

However, although the state may have initiated policies from time to time to prevent the accumulation of merchant capital and investment in production, it took the lead in protoindustrial development. After 1709, the state began investing in woolens and silk workshops that it established in Istanbul. It also increased production of sailcloth for the navy due to the growing demand for it during the Russo-Ottoman Wars.[18] But in essence, Genç argues, the state was anticapitalist for a long time, and the only stimulus for change came from the West during the nineteenth century.[19] This attitude was best reflected in state policies toward traders, who could not accumulate capital and raise their profits beyond certain margins (between 10 and 15 percent). Both Inalcik and Genç emphasized the cultural aspects of the Ottoman economic mind such as the ancient and Islamic notions of the Circle of Justice and the Anatolian Sufi tradition. We lack sufficient studies of merchant groups across time and space and their wealth formation and investment patterns to reach any definite conclusions.

Building on the arguments of Inalcik and Genç, Murad Çizakça has offered a comparative analysis of Ottoman economic policies and those of Western Europe and the transformation of Ottoman policies over time. He states that Ottoman merchants operated within specific institutional frameworks that determined their relative efficiency while other options were certainly open to them.[20] Çizakça defined the Ottoman economy as "proto-pseudo-socialist" rather than protocapitalist because of its strong guild and provisionist culture. The absence of a well-developed banking and public finance sector led to weak credit networks based on cash vakfs that loaned small amounts of money with low interest rates (between 5 and 10 percent). He has compared the *kapan* merchants (see below), who were an organized group of private but state-licensed merchants in charge of provisioning Istanbul from the Black Sea region, to regulated European companies.[21]

Şevket Pamuk, another leading economic historian, has argued that the longevity of Ottoman economic and state institutions had to do with their flexibility in response to economic changes. Like Inalcik, Genç, and Çizakça, he believes that the state was a major player in the economy but that it also responded to change.[22] Pamuk and Çizakça have emphasized the transformation of the Ottoman economy during the so-called "decline period" that started in the late sixteenth century and lasted through the eighteenth century. Both Çizakça and Pamuk have pointed out that cultural explanations offered by scholars like Timur Kuran that emphasize the role of Islam in holding back economic development in the Middle East are essentialist arguments that do not take into account the regional differences and the internal dynamism and changes over time in each region stretching from Egypt to Anatolia and the Balkans.[23] Although Kuran has offered a fascinating study of Islamic and Ottoman economic institutions to explain the absence of joint-stock companies and corporations in the Ottoman economy, his emphasis on the role of Islam gives his study a more cultural approach rather than one based on archival sources and adequate research-based studies.

Pamuk has convincingly argued that a large section of the urban population in Istanbul and other major cities was already part of the monetary economy, the credit networks (despite Islamic bans on usury and interest), and the market by the sixteenth century.[24] He has argued that the state moved away from provisionism to "selective intervention" at times of food shortages and crises, but it lifted bans due to its limited resources for controlling the economy. Pamuk has rightly pointed out that all early modern states in Europe practiced some level of provisionism as well. But he agrees with Genç and Çizakça that the divergence between the Ottoman and European economies emerged with the rise of mercantilism in Western Europe. Pamuk also believes that merchants and their ideas did not play a significant role in the policies of the Ottoman state.[25] However, it is not clear how long these policies prevailed without any changes and whether the state had equal control over the economy in the capital and those in the peripheries of the empire. A closer reading and an analysis of Ottoman narrative and archival sources provide a more nuanced picture of the activities of Ottoman merchants, their networks, and their collaboration and competition with European merchants based on a range of systematic archival studies and shed light on the policies of the state concerning merchant groups in a changing economy.

PROVISIONING TRADE IN GALATA

> Following the procession of the Mediterranean Sea captains, the butchers were supposed to pass, according to imperial decree. But all the great Egyptian grain merchants, including dealers in rice, hemp, and Egyptian reed mats, coffee[,] and sugar[,] gathered together and began quarreling with the butchers. Finally[,] they went before the sultan [Murad IV] and said, "My Padishah, our galleons are charged with transporting rice, lentils, coffee, and hemp. They cannot do without us, nor we without them. Why should these bloody and tricky butchers come between us? Plagues have risen from cities where they shed their sheep's blood, and for fear of this, their stalls and shambles in other countries are outside the city walls. They are a bloody and filthy band of ill omen. We, on the other hand, always make Istanbul plentiful and cheap with grains of all sorts."
>
> —EVLIYA ÇELEBI, *Seyahatname*, vol. 1[26]

In his important and colorful account of the parade of guilds and corporate groups like butchers and provisioning merchants in Istanbul before Sultan Murad IV (1623–40) in 1638, Evliya Çelebi offered a detailed description of the merchants and sea captains who traded with the Black Sea and the Mediterranean, two groups he considered the most important in provisioning Istanbul. His lively account of the encounter between Egyptian merchants and sea captains in charge of importing rice, sugar, coffee, hemp, and henna from Egypt into Istanbul and butchers who supplied meat underscores the importance of domestic merchants and ship captains in the society of Istanbul.

From Çelebi's detailed account, we also learn that provisioning merchants were an organized group and had their own hierarchy in Istanbul. In the lively debate between the elders of each group with Sultan Murad IV about the importance of each in provisioning Istanbul, the butchers claimed a higher place of honor. In response, the Egyptian merchants claimed that they produced customs revenue on their galleons in the amount of 550,000 akçe annually (1,100 *kese*), thus enriching the state coffers in addition to importing better quality rice and sugar to provision the city. Having heard both sides, the sultan finally decided in favor of the Egyptian merchants and sea captains, who then marched before the butchers, after whom the furriers displayed their wares. This passage underscores not only the competition among provisioning merchants and butchers but also the corporate identity of each group. The state clearly considered them both crucial to the everyday life of Istanbul as well as to its fiscal needs and thus protected their statuses.

The provisioning of Mediterranean cities with grains and other foodstuff had been the most important maritime activity since ancient times. The Roman, Byzantine, and Ottoman states had regulated the provisioning of grains and other important foodstuff for major cities. For example, ancient Athens, with a population of more than 300,000 residents, imported 100,000 tons of grains annually during the fourth and fifth centuries BC. The provisioning merchants established small partnerships composed of a sea captain, a ship owner, a moneylender, and a wholesaler who provided small capital. The shipper used a chartered vessel, contracted with a captain, and took capital from investors to pay for the cargo and freight charges and fees. The merchants relied on written contracts and guarantors. They operated between four and five months a year and traveled as far as Marseille and Byzantium (ancient Istanbul) in one journey per year, a slow, one-way trip and shorter return trip after the cargo had been unloaded. The ships also brought cargo from southern Russia and Egypt to Athens. The investors rather than the ship owner assumed total responsibility for all losses that resulted from piracy and bad weather.[27] Although the operations remained private, the government of Athens passed certain laws to provision the city, banned Athenians from exporting grains, and allowed only one-third of the grain that entered the city to be exported by foreigners. When the ships arrived, each wholesaler could distribute a certain amount of grain to mills and bakeries. This system of provisioning basically continued with some changes for a long time in the eastern Mediterranean.

Grains had been the most important item of trade between Anatolia and the Mediterranean cities before the Ottoman takeover of Constantinople in 1453. Early modern states regulated the domestic trade in grains and other important foodstuff and paid special attention to the provisioning of their capital cities with abundant grains to prevent shortages and bread riots. The Ottoman state followed both the Byzantine and Islamic traditions in provisioning the capital with plentiful and affordable grains and other foodstuff like meat, cheese, olive oil, and clarified butter and placed a price ceiling on basic foodstuff, particularly during times of drought and food shortages. Like the Byzantine state, it banned the export of provisions (grains, wine, and olive oil) as well as strategic goods like iron, cotton for sailing ships, arms, and raw silk and punished smugglers.[28]

In their important study of the Mediterranean Sea, Peregrine Horden and Nicholas Purcell have rightly pointed out the continuation of exchange and trade between the Christian and Muslim halves of the Mediterranean world and the similarities and continuity in commercial institutions and practices from the medieval to the early modern period.[29] They have also emphasized the impact of geography and climate in addition to the effects of war and piracy on commerce by Muslims and Christians.[30] Moreover, they have deemphasized the role of the state in the command economy of the Mediterranean since political authority remained fragmented and decentralized in the western Mediterranean most of the time.[31]

The provisioning of Istanbul had been a major maritime activity since medieval times. Prior to the Ottoman takeover of Constantinople and the Black Sea ports, Genoese and Venetian merchants had played an important role in the trade of bulky foodstuff like grains, alum, wine, beeswax, butter, and hides as well as slaves with Turkish principalities and the Byzantine Empire. Kate Fleet has argued that the Ottoman takeover of Constantinople did not end the role of Genoese traders in Galata since after a short period of looting of their houses and shops by Ottoman forces, Genoese traders returned and resumed trade in Galata and Chios until 1566 (see chapter 1).[32]

The Ottoman state practiced partial control of the trade of the Black Sea after 1453. Sultan Mehmed II (1444–46, 1451–81) established state monopolies on various goods like grains, timber, and soap.[33] He raised customs dues on imports from 2 to 4 percent ad valorem (on the value of goods) for Ottoman subjects and 5 percent for foreigners. But these rates were subject to modification and varied in each customs zone and on each good.[34] However, provisions for the army were exempt from taxes.

In reviving the trade of Galata, Mehmed II also aimed at ending the domination of Genoese merchants in the Black Sea trade after he took the control of the port of Caffa in 1475. But the Genoese presence in the Black Sea trade and in Galata continued until the mid-sixteenth century.[35] Considerable maritime activity by Ottoman traders took place on the Black Sea, which was closed off to foreign shipping until the late eighteenth century.[36] Moreover, Polish-Lithuanian and Cossack raids against Muslim inhabitants and shipping eventually led to an Ottoman naval military presence on the Black Sea since the borders were not clearly demarcated and thus subject to contestation. The Cossacks were the pirates or raiders of the Black Sea in the seventeenth century.[37] Shipwrecks due to high winds were also a recurring factor in disrupting trade.

KAPAN, OR PROVISIONING, MERCHANTS

Many ports on the Black Sea and the Aegean catered to the provisioning of the capital with grains, meat, cheese, fat, honey, flax seed, hazelnuts, hides, tallow for candle making, and timber. The Plain of Thrace, the Danubian Basin, Bulgaria (the port of Burgaz), and the steppe region around the Black Sea from Dobruja to the Don River exported grains to Istanbul from the ports of Tekirdağ, Kilia, Akkerman, Azov, and Caffa on the Black Sea. In addition, grains were imported from the plains of Thessaly in western Anatolia as well as from Egypt (the ports of Damietta and Alexandria) into Istanbul.[38] As a result, large farms, or *çiftliks,* emerged in the eastern Balkans, Salonica and its surroundings, Romania, and Bulgaria.[39] In addition, Izmir and its hinterland provisioned Istanbul with raisins, figs, honey, olive oil, other fruits, almonds, and dried fruits in the sixteenth century.[40] Olive oil and soap production were also very important in Syria, particularly in Nablus, and this significance led to the rise of merchant networks and the commercialization of agriculture in the eighteenth century.[41]

The state's control over the provisioning trade varied in time and space, and the state adopted different policies in response to droughts and shortages and during times of war and high piracy. The Black Sea region supplied hides for the tanners of Istanbul while sheep from the Balkans provided meat for Istanbul.[42] The Ottoman economy was self-sufficient except for a few goods, whereas European states had to import cereals; raw materials such as silk, mohair, and later cotton; and foods such as olive oil, raisins, honey, beeswax, spices, and butter from Ottoman ports.

The Black Sea maritime trade was under the control of domestic sea captains and merchants. The customs registers of the port of Caffa show that ship owners operating on the Black Sea were both official and private and that the majority (two-thirds) were Muslim in the late fifteenth century. Many famous sea captains such as Sinan Pasha and Mesih Pasha, who were important admirals during the reign of Bayezid II, were involved in commercial shipping on the Black Sea when they were not fighting for the navy.[43] Greeks made up the second largest group in the shipping of bulky goods from the Black Sea to Istanbul and used large, medium-sized, and small vessels that traveled six weeks per year from mid-August to the end of September.

Due to the importance of the Black Sea trade in the provisioning of the capital, the state selected merchants to be in charge of provisioning (*kapan* merchants) and issued them licenses to purchase grains from certain districts selected by the government, load them onto ships, and import grains and foodstuff into Istanbul (Un Kapanı) and Galata (Yağ Kapanı). Galata was the final destination for all the olive oil imports from the Aegean ports and islands like Crete. Consequently, the court of Galata received many lawsuits from sea captains as well as from merchants over unpaid shares from the profits that they earned from this trade.[44]

State officials like the kadi and his staff were responsible for distributing grains to the bakers and mills once they had arrived at Un Kapanı. They also calculated the price of bread and other foodstuff based on supplies and the recommendations of the bakers' guilds.[45] Suraiya Faroqhi believes that official prices were not that different from market prices and depended on supplies, weather conditions, and shipwrecks. Prices rose when supplies shrank, and artisans suffered greatly during the wars with Russia that disrupted the Black Sea trade during the eighteenth century.[46] Provisioning merchants received support from the state and clearly had a corporate identity; they were divided into groups and had a master who was elected and represented their interests before the state. Ottoman merchants dominated domestic and maritime trade with the Black Sea as well as with Egypt, Iran, and India. Domestic trade made up the bulk of commercial activities and was an enormous source of wealth in the Ottoman Empire until the nineteenth century.[47]

Historians have divided the provisioning merchants in Istanbul into two groups, those who imported grains (*un kapanı tüccar*) and those who imported olive oil, clarified butter, fat, cheese, honey, and beeswax (*yağ kapanı* and *bal kapanı tüccar*) from Thrace, southern Russia, the Black Sea, the Aegean islands and the Morea.[48] According to Evliya Çelebi, merchants trading with the Black Sea region numbered 3,000 and owned 1,000 large armed galleons with storage, 600 medium-sized ships, and 2,000 small ships in the mid-seventeenth century.[49] Galleons were used in both transportation and war, and they were increasingly used to transport grain supplies.[50] These merchants were mostly Muslim, although some were Greek. Their patron saint was the prophet Noah. They paraded before the sultan clad in expensive clothing lined with furs and bore arms. Some even had their own militias and guards[51]

Evliya Çelebi's description also shows that traders were a corporate group and members of guilds. Some were very wealthy, although others did not earn large profits (less than 20 percent). Long-distance traders, however, were free agents and could make as much profit as they wished. For example, merchants dealing in maritime trade with the Mediterranean and Egypt numbered around 11,000 and operated 6,000 storage houses in greater Istanbul in the mid-seventeenth century. The wealthiest among them was Hacı Kasım, who operated in Bal Kapanı in Istanbul and owned seven storage houses in the mid-seventeenth century. His wealth amounted to twenty-five million akçe (50,000 kese). Other prominent Mediterranean maritime *bezirgans* were Hacı Envar, Hacı Ferhad, and Hacı Nemutullah, who owned ten galleons and seven hans. One Ali Agha was the superintendent of customs; others who were extremely wealthy had agents in India, Yemen, Iran, Arabia, and Europe.[52] Evliya Çelebi divided the merchants of Egyptian goods into rice sellers (40 shops, 300 individuals), henna sellers, (15 shops, 55 traders), Egyptian linen sellers (105 shops, 208 traders), Egyptian mat sellers (45 members), sugar sellers (70 shops, 100 traders), and mocha coffee dealers (200 shops, 300 dealers). They had a *şehbender* (master of the port) who resided around Bal kapanı. The *bezirganbaşı* (chief of *bezirgans*) was elected from among the wealthy and reputable merchants and represented their interests before the government and local officials like the kadi.[53] Although long-distance merchants were not organized into guilds, they did elect a representative from among themselves to oversee their affairs before government authorities. For example, when a certain Ibrahim Reşid b. Ali, the head of merchants in Galata, died without an heir, the government appointed Ali Riza b. Hafiz Ibrahim, who had been elected by the merchants as their trusted representative, and issued a berat for him in 1816.[54]

The provisioning of Istanbul also involved all kinds of traders who formed private partnerships. Some received licenses from the government to trade in foodstuff as kapan merchants. Kapan merchants had priority in purchasing grains, the amount of which was specified in the license each received. They transported grains on special ships that could carry 76.8 tons of grains, but they could not take grains outside of Istanbul.[55] The state did not allow foreign merchants to participate in the trading of foodstuff until the late eighteenth century when ships were needed for the military. The government commissioned a consortium of fifty-six ship owners to make 658 voyages on 118 ships to deliver grains to Istanbul in the seventeenth century.[56]

The needs of the capital led to the expansion of commercial agriculture in the grain-producing regions. For example, the voyvodas of the Romanian provinces of Wallachia and Moldavia had to provide a fixed amount of grains at fixed prices annually to provision Istanbul. The state also placed bans on the export of grains, but contraband trade by members of the cavalry, janissaries, and local governors to Italian city-states continued from western Anatolia and Albania due to high prices paid there, a practice that caused long-term shortages in Anatolia.[57]

Trade with Egypt was also very important, so the state protected merchant ships from pirate attacks. Armed galleons departed Alexandria through the port of Damietta with their cargoes of rice, sugar, and coffee on a single voyage that lasted from three to six months and called on northern Syria, Rhodes, Chios, Tenedos, Samos, and Lesbos before entering the Dardanelles to arrive in Istanbul. The Ottoman navy did not have a sufficient number of ships for maritime trade; therefore, it used military ships as well as private and European ships in maritime trade with Egypt and the Red Sea.[58]Many Ottoman merchants made great fortunes in the trade of Egypt.

There is an ongoing debate about whether all kapan merchants were under the control of the Ottoman state and used government-owned ships and credit to finance their operations. Çizakça has argued that provisioning merchants acted like a regulated company since they had to obtain licenses from the government and had their own guilds and rules. However, they never grew into joint-stock companies since they had to sell at maximum prices set by the government and could not make high profits (a 10 to 15 percent margin). Therefore, a provisioning merchant's appointment usually brought him financial ruin since he could hardly cover his finances and also make any profits.[59] Other scholars, however, have argued that kapan merchants were private but licensed merchants who used their own capital and ships, but obtained credit from the government only during times of shortages. The government supported them and provided them with capital to prevent food shortages during times of drought.[60]

Although the state controlled the production and distribution of grains through its ownership of state land and price fixing, it eventually loosened its monopoly and resorted to more flexible and liberal methods in allowing market forces to determine prices. Moreover, although the government could exert more control over production and exports in the Marmara Sea and Black Sea regions, it was unable to prevent contraband on the Aegean. For example, in 1767, a group of Muslim kapan merchants and their agents petitioned the state, complaining that other Muslim merchants had imported ropes for ships into Galata and sold them at higher prices at the Kurşunlu Han than they had, thus causing harm to their business. They asked the state to prevent the other Muslim merchants' activities and to allow the petitioners to sell their wares at a higher price because they also had to deal with competition from smugglers and a hike in transportation fees, customs, and other dues.[61] This and other cases demonstrate the flexibility of the government in allowing market forces to determine the prices of strategic goods during times of shortages. This case also illustrates the merchants' refusal to follow the regulations of the government.

Private merchants and ships from Galata got involved in the trade of the Black Sea due to the growing demand of a rising population in the capital for provisions and wars during the eighteenth century. In 1782, 146 Ottoman vessels transported 742,799 kile (1 kile/24.215 kg) of grain from Black Sea ports to Istanbul.[62] The majority of the captains of these ships (93 percent) were Muslim. A good proportion of these traders were wealthy Muslim merchants.[63] The Black Sea trade was completely controlled by private merchants in this period, the number of whom rose to 56 major merchants and 110 agents between 1779 and 1781. The sea captains and merchants formed partnerships and pooled their capital to import provisions from the Black Sea ports as well as from the Aegean islands. For example, the customs registers of Galata list the ships, the names of captains and merchants, and the amounts of their cargoes of clarified butter that entered the oil scale in Galata in August 1800. They also show that seventeen ships imported 16,109,137 kg of clarified butter from the Black Sea ports into Galata in less than a month.[64]

Every ship transported the goods of several merchants. For example, the ship of Osman Reis carried the goods of four Muslim merchants and one Greek merchant who imported 319,619 kg of clarified butter from the Black Sea into Galata in late August 1800. A few days later, the ship of Mehmed Reis imported 3,548,180 kg of clarified butter that belonged to thirty-seven Muslim merchants from the port of Ismailiye into Galata. Also, the chief admiral was bringing 652,266 kg of refined oil into Galata. The vast majority of the sea captains (fifteen out of seventeen) were Muslims while two were Greeks, and all were from either Istanbul or Black Sea towns. Greeks, however, played an active role in the import of provisions from the Aegean islands into Istanbul. For example, a register dating from February 1802 listed the names of nine Muslim kapan oil wholesale merchants (*bezirgan*) as well as six Greek wholesale kapan merchants such as Yani Acı, Dimitri Acı Panayod, and Hiristo Acı Panayod (probably brothers) and their partners, who were retail merchants. The wholesale oil kapan merchants who imported olive oil from the island of Mytilene into Istanbul and sold it to their partners had the same religious affiliation, with the exception of one merchant.[65] They carried out a portion of their provisioning trade on imperial galleons. Olive oil was mainly imported from the island of Mytilene, Edremid, and Athens.[66] The composition of provisioning merchants, however, changed from time to time. For example, according to Fatih Gedikli, in Istanbul, twenty-two out of twenty-five Bal Kapanı merchants were Muslims, and only three were zimmis, while all of the thirty-eight Yağ Kapanı merchants in Galata were Muslims in 1894.[67] It is possible that in the late nineteenth century, Greeks had lost their position in provisioning olive oil in Galata due to rising tensions with this community.

Domestic merchants did not leave much trace behind in the historical records; therefore, it is very difficult to gauge their activities. When merchants and sea captains died, an inventory was made of their estates by the kadi or his scribe, who compiled an inventory in special registers to allow the heirs and debtors to claim their shares. These are rich sources, understudied by historians, that shed great light on the wealth, investment, commercial partnerships, consumption patterns, and credit history of a good proportion of a cross-section of the population, mostly Muslims. For example, when Al-Hac Mehmed son of Mahmud, a resident of Kasım Paşa, died on a ship in the Mediterranean, his estate was registered in the court of Galata in

1606.[68] It was divided into his commercial cargo, his personal belongings, his properties, his debts, and the loans he had taken from individuals as well as from institutions. Among the contents of his estate, we can identify various kinds of sugar (hard and powdered); a variety of spices like pepper, cumin, and saffron; coffee; dyes; beeswax; herbal essences and oils, and rosewater estimated at 19,158 akçe. His personal belongings included two copies of the Qur'an, two European watches, fine woolen cloaks with fur linings, other clothing, prayer rugs, mats, bedding, kitchenware, plates and cups, a coffee ewer, a washing bowl and pitcher, a candlestick, copper utensils, and three silver daggers with covers. He also had an investment in a spice shop worth 14,437 akçe and another investment in a shop in Kasım Paşa worth 60,000 akçe, and he owned an orchard in Kasım Paşa near Fındıklı worth 40,000 akçe. His personal goods, investments, and properties were valued at 188,8074 akçe. In addition, he had a sugar shop in Galata worth 60,000 akçe; a *bozahane*, where fermented drinks were sold, in Eyüp worth 24000 akçe; a vakf spice shop outside the Yemiş wharf in Istanbul worth 120,000 akçe; and a storage house near Rüstem Pasha mosque worth 12,000 akçe, amounting to a total value of 216,000 akçe. His total estate was valued at 394,074 akçe.

We also learn from the inventory of his estate that many people owed him money, the amount of which was unknown, and had given him their personal goods, for example, a mother-of-pearl box worth several hundred akçe, as collateral. He also had borrowed money from two cash vakfs amounting to 120,000 akçe. In addition, he owed a certain Hasan Bey 15,000 akçe and owed his own wife 3,000 akçe as her bride price. His total debts were 143,250 akçe, so his remaining estate was worth 44,823 akçe, which was divided among his wife (5,603 akçe), his one son, (19,610 akçe), and two daughters (9,805 akçe each).[69] His sugar shop, spice shops, *bozahane* shop, and storage house were also divided among his son and two daughters equally (72,000 akçe each). From his estate, it is clear that Al-Hac Mehmed was a merchant from Kasım Paşa who owned two spice shops in Eyüp and in the commercial district of Istanbul and a sugar, or confectionary, shop in Galata. He traded with Egypt in spices, dyes, mocha coffee, and sugar as well as in medicinal herbs and essences, which a typical spice dealer would offer. Among his personal belongings, fine woolen textiles as well as two European watches stand out the most. From his debts, it appears that he had taken large loans from two cash vakfs and had probably been involved in a partnership with a government official, a certain Hasan Bey. He also had loaned money and taken collaterals. From his personal belongings and the total value of his estate, investments, and properties, it appears that he was a wealthy spice merchant of some means with a diverse commercial portfolio that included long-distance trade, retail, investment in commercial properties, and informal banking. He might have died from the plague on a ship on its way from Egypt to Istanbul. He left behind a wife, a minor son, and two older daughters. We do not find any evidence of state involvement in his trade in the form of capital investment. His portfolio of commercial activities was very similar to those of the merchants described by Evliya Çelebi who were involved in Egyptian trade and the provisioning of Istanbul.

COMMERCIAL PARTNERSHIPS

Commercial partnerships were important economic institutions in Islamic societies. Ottoman law recognized the formation of a contract partnership in a company with property as capital and labor as credit. Ottoman companies were mainly divided into *mudaraba, inan,* and *vucuh* partnerships. A mudaraba partnership was an Islamic and Mediterranean (*commenda*) institution that prevailed in Mediterranean cities like Venice as well as in Istanbul. Mudaraba, or commenda, partnerships were widespread in maritime trade and among provisioning merchants and ship owners in Galata and Istanbul.[70] They were also prevalent among silk merchants in Bursa. Mudaraba partnerships were formed by Muslims as well as non-Muslims in Galata, and members came from all walks of life. Women also invested in this kind of partnership. Ship captains dominated this kind of partnership in Galata.[71]

In the mudaraba form of partnership, the principal party provided the capital, and the other partner (the agent) provided labor and usually carried out trade over long distances.[72] The agent returned the principal and an agreed-upon share of profits (usually split 50–50) to the investor once the voyage had been completed and the goods unloaded and sold. The investor paid for all losses if accidents or pirate attacks occurred, an arrangement that made these partnerships sometimes last for a long time. A guarantor was usually required for mudaraba partnerships. In the mid-eighteenth century, Un Kapanı merchants who formed mudaraba partnerships carried out 91.8 percent of the grain trade, while the state organized 8.6 percent of this trade.[73] This ratio was also true for Yağ Kapanı and Bal Kapanı merchants in Galata and Istanbul. Due to the economic capacity of partners and in order to lower the risk, the amount of capital usually remained small or medium in mudaraba partnerships that only lasted for a short duration.[74] Mudaraba was the most widespread form of partnership among provisioning merchants in Galata.

The second type of partnership was called *inan*. In an inan partnership, the principal of equality was not stipulated, and the profits were divided according to prearranged shares. The partners sought greater profit in this kind of partnership by contributing more capital than those in mudaraba partnerships did. Inan partnerships were practiced widely among the Yağ Kapanı and Bal Kapanı merchants as well as in the silk trade. Inan was small in scale while mudaraba was used in the export trade and provisioning, production, and service sector. Inan partnerships were partly based on property (shops, taverns) as well as on labor and were used in the manufacturing of textiles and shoes.[75]

A third form of Islamic/Ottoman partnership, which was called *vucuh,* was for poor partners with small capital and labor who had established a good reputation in business. This kind of partnership involved capital formation by borrowing it from individuals and informal institutions.[76] As in an inan partnership, the profits were divided according to shares in the principal provided by each partner. Sometimes this form of partnership led to accumulation of capital since it involved a larger capital pool through borrowing and trading with multiple partners.[77] There are very few examples of this kind of partnership in the records of Galata for the eighteenth century.

Scholars have argued that while in Western Europe, mudaraba, or commenda, partnerships evolved into joint-stock companies in the sixteenth century, they remained stagnant and hardly evolved in the Islamic world. Çizakça has argued that, although powerful merchants supplied capital to multiple partners who provided labor, sometimes up to twenty persons to carry goods from Istanbul to Egypt, they did not evolve into public ventures or joint-stock companies.[78] But the many forms of merchant partnerships for merchants with varying amounts of capital, their freedom from company rules and monopolies, and their evolution across Ottoman societies have not received much attention from historians since most of these agreements remained private and were not registered in the Islamic courts.[79]

The inventories of the estates of deceased merchants and sea captains recorded in the Islamic court registers, however, shed great light on their wealth and partnerships. For example, a sea captain, Mahmud Reis son of Şaban, had died in a neighborhood outside the walls of Galata in 1606 and left a small estate worth 26,000 akçe.[80] It included personal clothing, small furnishings, and a female slave. But he owed 34,000 akçe to fifteen Muslim men in the form of loans (*deyn-i musbet*) ranging from 1,000 to 2,000 akçe due to each. A total number of forty-nine individuals, who could have been his mudaraba partners, had invested sums of between 1,000 and 2,000 akçe on average, totaling 91,400 akçe, in his maritime trade. Among the partners, a good number appear to have been merchants; eight others were sea captains. All but two were Muslim men; the other two were Muslim women. His heirs included a wife and a female slave who was the mother of his two sons. Mahmud Reis was clearly a man of modest means, but he had been involved through his labor and his ship in partnerships with forty-nine merchants that added up to a large amount of capital. Unfortunately, the record does not provide any clues to the nature of his commercial activities. The inventory had been compiled for the benefit of his heirs and claimants. After the death of one partner, other partners came to the court and claimed their shares from the estate of the deceased partner. Even though Ottoman merchants did not form formal corporations like the Levant Company, research into the Islamic court records of Galata shows that partnerships outside the family between merchants and ship captains and among Muslims and non-Muslims sometimes expanded to twenty persons whose investments were added to create a substantial amount of capital.[81]

Since many partnerships were based on credit, the number of disputes increased over the payment of loans. The Islamic court of Galata and Istanbul proper recorded many disputes arising out of mudaraba partnerships among sea captains and merchants. For example, Al-Hac Şaban son of Halil, a resident of Galata, presented a lawsuit to the court of Galata against a ship captain, Yorgi Reis son of Kiryako, in May 1663. He claimed that he had provided his ship and 36,000 akçe to Yorgi in return for 10,000 akçe profits from each voyage. But Yorgi had paid him only 29,000 akçe and had claimed a loss of 7,000 akçe from the sale of goods (not specified in the record). After many lawsuits, they finally settled for the payment of 2,000 akçe that Yorgi pledged to pay within thirty days to Al-Hac Şaban, the ship owner who gave up the remaining 5,000 akçe that he had claimed earlier.[82] Clearly, this was a small partnership between a ship owner who had provided capital and his ship and a ship captain who had provided labor, transported and sold the goods, and split the profits, but the loss was born by the investor, Al-Hac Şaban. They had also settled to cut their losses.

Other disputes arising from partnerships were submitted to the court of Galata. For example, in March 1769, a certain oil merchant, Yağcı (oil seller) Süleyman Beşe, presented a lawsuit to the court of Istanbul against an oil merchant in Galata, Al-Seyyid Ali, claiming that he had paid 190 kuruş to him in advance for the purchase of oil, but Ali had not honored the deal. Süleyman Beşe was thus claiming 190 kuruş from Ali. However, the latter claimed that he had sold the oil and had provided Süleyman Beşe with the money, and he brought forth several witnesses to prove his claim.[83] This case appears to be an example of a small mudaraba partnership in which Süleyman Beşe had provided a small amount of capital, and Ali had been expected to provide labor, load oil and bring it to Galata, sell it, and then split the profits. But Ali may have smuggled the oil instead of bringing it to the oil scale, thus avoiding the payment of taxes and making a profit for himself.

In another lawsuit presented by the oil seller Süleyman Beşe Al-Hac Cafer to the court of Istanbul in March 1769 against Al-Seyyid Ali, the oil kapan merchant from Galata, the former claimed 190 kuruş from the latter. Süleyman Beşe had given an advance to Al-Seyyid Ali to purchase olive oil for him, possibly in a mudaraba partnership. Ali provided two Muslim witnesses for his claim that he had purchased the oil and handed it to Süleyman Beşe, and the court determined that Süleyman should end his lawsuit since he could not prove his claim.[84] The courts clearly took these disputes very seriously and protected merchants who invested capital as well as those who provided labor.

In another case, Sino son of Istimat, one of the two partners in a *francela* bakery, sued his partner, Vasil son of Dimitri, claiming 89 kuruş since their partnership in the shop had ended. But since Vasil was unable to pay the full amount, they settled for the payment of 50 kuruş. Vasil was unable to pay that amount, either, so they finally settled for the payment of 25 kuruş in October 1798.[85] This was probably an inan type of partnership in which each side supplied an equal amount of capital and labor, and the partners split the profits according to an agreed-upon sum. But the bankruptcy or default of one partner may have led to the annulment of the partnership in this case. This case also underscores the flexibility of partnerships in Galata, their small size, and the small amount of capital that was involved in the service sector, such as the funds needed to set up bakeries. It also sheds light on the economic difficulties faced by the average residents of Galata at the end of the eighteenth century and the use of a settlement (*sulh*) in paying debts through the Islamic court of Galata (see chapter 6).[86]

Due to rough weather, clouds, and high winds as well as to pirate attacks, accidents took place on the Black Sea regularly during the winter and spring seasons, and sea captains often lost their cargoes. For example, in 1759, fifteen oil kapan merchants from Galata—Isma'il Beşe, Ibrahim, Hacı Ibrahim, Hacı Ömer, Seyyid Ibrahim, Kuçuk Mulla Süleyman, Ahmed Hoca, Al-Hac Hasan, Hacı Mehmed, and others—submitted a petition to the Porte claiming that their partner, Oğuzoğlu Huseyin, had loaded clarified butter, honey, beeswax, candle wax, hides, and other provisions. But the ship had been involved in an accident on its way from the Black Sea to Istanbul, and the port authorities in Kumceğiz had confiscated its cargo. The merchants had sent an agent and were requesting an imperial order to recover their goods.[87] Cases such as this one underscore the risk of maritime trade due to environmental factors and the role of the state in providing some relief and in preventing the total bankruptcy of provisioning merchants in the absence of maritime and company insurance. The state also helped cover some of the merchants' losses when accidents or pirate attacks occurred.

Many sea captains completely lost their cargoes in these accidents. We learn a great deal about the cargoes of these ships from reports that were submitted to government officials to recover goods. For example, the ships of three Galata oil kapan merchants who imported oil, honey, and other provisions from the Black Sea into Istanbul were involved in an accident in 1800. The merchants submitted a petition to have their cargoes shipped to Istanbul without being charged transit taxes by port authorities. An imperial order was subsequently issued to that effect.[88]

In another example, in January 1747, a group of merchants from Galata, Haci Ahmed, Seyyid Ali, Usküdari Hacı Ömer, Hacı Mustafa, Hammamcizade Ibrahim, and others, submitted a petition to the Imperial Council. They claimed that the ship of their partner, Hacı Feyzioğlu Mustafa, which had been carrying clarified butter, oil, honey, *pastırma* (pressed meat), wheat, barley, and hides, had been involved in an accident due to encountering rough weather in Podima and that its cargo had been confiscated by port authorities. The state then issued an imperial order to the said port authority and sent an agent appointed by the superintendent of customs in Galata to recover their cargo and have it sent to them at the port of Galata.[89] This case illustrates a commercial partnership among several merchants in Galata who were involved in provisioning Istanbul. It also underscores the risks of maritime trade and the support the state provided in protecting provisioning merchants so that they would not suffer complete losses as a result of shipwrecks and the abuse of port authorities.

In another case, in March 1764, Huseyin Reis, a sea captain, had established a partnership with five or six merchants who had each provided capital of more than 15,000 akçe for each voyage to import grains from Egypt into Istanbul. But his ship had sunk on its way to Istanbul, and his partners were demanding their principal capital in addition to interest, amounting to 20,926.5 kuruş. He submitted a petition to the Imperial Council about the accident that had led to his bankruptcy. The state then issued an imperial order to the kadi of Istanbul stating that Huseyin Reis had pledged to pay his debt on time after the completion of each voyage and to sell the provisions without interest. He also pledged to pay 2,500 akçe to each partner.[90] This case illustrates the private nature of a commercial partnership between a Muslim sea captain and a number of merchants who had invested in trade between Egypt and Istanbul. It also emphasizes the risks of maritime trade and the way in which merchants could lose their investment as a result of an accident on the rough seas or pirate attacks. The state often came to the aid of sea captains who formed such private partnerships. Clearly, the involvement of the courts in enforcing the articles of these partnerships was also very important.

GOVERNMENT BANS AND INSPECTIONS

Although the Ottoman government considered the provisioning of Istanbul the most important aspect of its economic policies during the classical period, ample evidence suggests that government bans were constantly violated regarding price ceilings and the export of grains. From time to time, the state tried to arrest smugglers and placed bans on European ships transporting grains.

Sometimes merchants were accused of hoarding foodstuff until prices rose so that they could make a higher margin of profit. They sometimes negotiated for better deals with retailers and buyers outside the guilds they were assigned to supply. For example, in 1631, the grocers in Galata submitted a petition to the Imperial Council against food shops and tavern owners who had illegally purchased clarified butter, olive oil, honey, and rice, which were traditionally sold by the grocers, from kapan merchants. Accordingly, an imperial order was issued in November 1631 to the kadi of Galata to prevent the tavern operators and food shops from interfering in the business of the grocers.[91] This case clearly illustrates the kapan merchants' attempt to sell to taverns and food shops at a higher price and profit margin than the price ceiling imposed by the state. It also illustrates that even kapan merchants violated the rules set by the state.

These violations increased during times of food shortages and sometimes led to the punishment of officials as well as smugglers. Recent studies have shown that Ottoman provisionist policies might have been in effect in the capital, as was the case in France,[92] particularly during times of drought, food shortages, and economic hardship, when the state intervened actively in the marketplace to ensure the supply of grains and other foodstuff.[93] The amount of grains distributed to bakers in Istanbul increased from 5,012,505 kg in 1755 to 12,063,458 kg in 1762, more than doubling in less than a decade.[94] For example, in 1712, the state ordered the delivery of 55,176 kg of wheat per day to forty-three bakeries in Istanbul proper at the price of 50 akçe per kile from state granaries in the arsenal for fifteen days (827,640 kg) due to shortages.[95] But shortages of wheat, barley, and meat continued due to the harsh winter in Anatolia and led to the dismissal of the kadi of Istanbul, Zulali Hasan Efendi, for failing to enforce price ceilings on these goods in 1728.[96] The government feared social unrest, especially after two major rebellions in Istanbul in 1703 and 1730 that had led to the overthrow of the governments of Mustafa II and Ahmed III.[97]

The populace regarded ensuring the supply of affordable foodstuff, especially bread, as an important duty of the government during the early modern period. The price of a loaf of bread (110 *dirhem,* or 374 grams weight) remained at one akçe from the seventeenth to the eighteenth century, although the weight and purity of the flour varied during times of shortages.[98] The market inspector controlled the weight, quality, and price of bread. The state severely punished bakers who sold light bread (374 grams) with low-quality mixed grain or above the price ceiling (1 akçe) by sentencing them to forced labor in the galleys.[99] For example, a report by the market inspector Mehmed Şerif al-Seyyid to the government stated that a *börek* seller near the Islamic court of Galata had sold *börek* and *boğaca* (sweet rolls) at the current price of 2 *para*[100] but at 8-*dirhem* lower weight than the standard. He requested the punishment of the baker, a certain Mehmed, by imprisoning him in a fortress on the Bosphorus in April 1819.[101]

Due to the growing population and the demand for affordable food, the number of itinerant sellers had increased in the city, causing competition with the guilds in the eighteenth century. At the request of the guilds, the government carried out regular inspections of bakeries, workshops, hans, and bachelors' rooms to evict rural migrants, marginal men and women who lacked guarantors and membership in the guilds (see chapter 2). The government rounded up these itinerant sellers and expelled them to their villages. It also closed down the shops outside guilds in Galata and Kasım Paşa in 1731, 1763, and 1792.[102] For example, in response to the petition of the guild of grocers against the interference of outsiders in their business, the state carried out a survey of grocery shops in 1731 in Galata, Kasım Paşa, and Tophane. The survey also banned the interference of outsiders in selling foodstuff (wheat, barley, oil, olive oil, candle fat, cheese, dried grapes, figs, nuts, and dates) above the government-imposed price ceiling.[103] But several similar orders that were issued in 1754, 1757, and 1776 demonstrate that these bans were violated constantly due to the increasing population and the growing demand for food sold at market prices.[104] Although in each case, the state supported the claims of corporate groups like guilds, clearly the state was unable to reinforce its provisionist policies, even in Istanbul and Galata.

The inspections were also a measure of surveillance to control marginal populations and certain spaces that they inhabited, such as bachelors' rooms, at times of social unrest and economic crisis. The market inspector, the kadi, and the voyvoda of Galata led these inspections and prepared surveys in 1763 and 1792 during times of shortages and economic crises.[105] They targeted bakeries in particular and controlled the quality and weight of bread as well as its price. Those who violated the rules were sentenced to forced labor in the galleys or were physically disciplined and imprisoned, and some were even executed during the nineteenth century. For example, the survey of 1792 listed 11 braided cake sellers' shops, 73 groceries operated by non-Muslims, and 140 coffeehouses operated mostly by Muslims and janissary-artisans in Galata.[106] The number of bakeries in greater Istanbul that belonged to guilds was also an important concern of the government. The number of legal bakeries in Galata was sixty-five in 1763, four of which belonged to Muslims, while non-Muslims owned the rest. Moreover, the activities of nonguild members in selling bread were strictly prohibited during times of shortages. So the survey of shops that provisioned the city aimed at reinforcing guild controls and the activities of itinerant sellers who operated outside the guilds.

At times of drought and shortages, the quality and weight of bread dropped, and the flour was often mixed with low-quality grains and impure material. The state tried to limit the number of bakeries that sold special white bread (*francela*) during times of shortages.[107] For example, in an order to the kadi of Istanbul proper, the state limited the number of bakeries selling *francela* bread in all four districts of Istanbul to twenty-five and ordered the closing of others during Ramazan in January 1768.[108] Only nine bakeries in Galata and four in Pera were allowed to make *francela* bread, and the rest were to be closed. European embassies had to petition the state to reopen the bakeries that supplied them with *francela* bread. For example, the state reduced the number of bakeries selling *francela* and *hass* (pure) bread that used better quality flour for the embassies in Pera to four during a period of shortages in April 1797. In response to this ban, the chief dragoman of the English Embassy, Anton Dane, presented a petition to the state asking for permission to open another bakery for the European residents and embassy staff near the English Embassy in the neighborhood of Asmalı Mesjid quarter, where the embassy was located in Pera. He claimed that the kapan merchants and the guild of bakers had tried to close down their *francela* bakery and mill in November 1792. He therefore asked for permission to purchase wheat from European ships instead of from kapan merchants and to hire a French baker by the name of Averyal since the quality of bread in regular bakeries was bad, and the wheat sold by them was mixed and impure. As a result, in December 1792, the state issued an order to the voyvoda and kadi of Galata to prevent the bakers from interfering in the affairs of the European bakeries and mills.[109]

Wars, piracy, and bad weather conditions also caused disruptions in the supply of grains and shortages in Istanbul. The state sometimes came to the rescue of bakers and delivered flour from its own granaries during these times. Due to another drought around the Black Sea in 1800, an official in charge of provisioning the city was ordered to oversee the delivery of 2,420,000 kg of grains to Istanbul at the official price of 110 para per kile (24.2 kg). But he claimed that the prices had risen due to the shortages and that grain merchants had gone to Izmir to sell the grains there at a higher price, so it was difficult to attract them back. He also claimed that the cost of transportation had gone up. Therefore, he suggested a 10 *para* price hike per kile in order to attract the merchants back to deliver the grains to Iznikmit and from there to Istanbul.[110] In 1793, the bakers of Istanbul presented a petition to the Islamic court of Istanbul stating that since the provision of grains from the Black Sea had been reduced, the action had caused shortages in Istanbul. They were asking the state to release and distribute 1,210,750 kg of grains (847,350 kg of wheat and 363,150 kg of barley) to the bakers. The state then issued an order to the head of the storage house in the arsenal to release 1,210,750 kg grains at a total cost of 73,156 kuruş to the bakers in response to the petition.[111]

In addition, the war economy caused great distress to the population of Istanbul, and guilds contracted and lost control over supplies and pricing as well as over their membership in the late eighteenth century.[112] The supplying of olive oil and soaps from the Aegean islands (Crete) and Izmir to Istanbul was crucial during shortages in 1795. For example, the state issued an order to the guild of soap sellers in Izmir to send 332 *kantar* of soap with merchant Selanikizade Hac Ahmed on the ship of Mustafa Reis to Istanbul in 1795.[113] However, the shortages continued in Istanbul, and in 1798 and 1804, the state placed a ban on the exporting of olive oil on European ships from the Morea due to shortages and issued an order to punish those who violated the ban and exported olive oil to Europe.[114]

There was also a great deal of smuggling going on, so Ottoman officials had to relax maximum prices and regulations from time to time to discourage the smuggling of wheat to Europe, a practice that was most widespread among Greek captains in the islands of the Aegean. The slow disappearance of price ceilings on goods other than basic foodstuff and the loosening of the guilds' monopoly over the supplying of raw materials (not foodstuff) were some of the consequences of the growing internal demand due to the population increase.

FRENCH SHIPS IN THE PROVISIONING TRADE

Ottoman policies regarding the provisioning of Istanbul remained flexible and responded to supply and demand or market forces as well as to wartime needs in the eighteenth century. Several bans were inserted into the articles of the ahdnames to prevent foreign ships from getting involved in provisioning trade. At the same time, European nations like France had constantly been trying to remove these bans and enter into the domestic provisioning trade, especially on the Black Sea, in their negotiations for the renewal of ahdnames since 1673. The French Ahdname of 1740 removed many of these bans on the export of cotton yarn and hides (see chapters 3 and 4).

Moreover, during times of war and the shortage of ships in the navy, piracy, and insecurity on the Mediterranean and the Black Sea, the Ottoman Empire relied on French ships in its provisioning trade in the second half of the eighteenth century. In February 1772, Ambassador Saint-Priest obtained permission from the Ottoman government to allow French ships to provision Istanbul due to the presence of Russian ships on the Black Sea, which threatened Ottoman commercial shipping.[115] The number of ships bringing wheat from the Levant to Marseille fluctuated, depending on internal needs in the Levant and bans placed by Ottoman authorities.

Daniel Panzac's pioneering research and publications have shed important light on the partnership between Ottoman and French merchants and the role of French ships in Ottoman domestic trade during the eighteenth century.[116] Since the Ottoman navy lacked a sufficient number of ships, during times of war (the Russo-Ottoman Wars of 1768 and 1787), the state allowed friendly European nations like France to get involved in importing grains and other foodstuff from the Black Sea and North Africa into Istanbul. In 1770, according to the report of the French ambassador, Vergennes, a French captain purchased 22,230 kg of state wheat on behalf of the Ottoman state in Salonica and carried it to Istanbul with proper documentation in accordance with an imperial order.[117] French ships could also provision Istanbul and export formerly banned goods like grains and cotton yarn. For example, in 1725, 205 vessels transported wheat from the Levant to Marseille.[118] Clearly, there were no shortages in Istanbul at this time.

During the Russo-Ottoman wars over the control of Crimea (1768–1774), the provisioning of Istanbul assumed tremendous importance. The Ottoman-Russian Wars (1768–74 and 1787–92) led to severe economic problems in the Ottoman Empire that were characterized by chronic budget deficits, inflation, and food shortages. The Black Sea was no longer the main center for provisioning Istanbul due to a state of war. The number of French ships transporting grains from the Levant to Marseille dropped from ninety-five in 1768 to two in 1771.[119] Instead, French ships became the only vehicle for provisioning trade with Istanbul and received exemption from French taxes from 1763 to 1773. A total of twenty-four French vessels that belonged to twelve trading houses in Istanbul that were escorted by four armed ships delivered grains to Istanbul between March and July in 1772. A total of 185 French vessels supplied provisions (including 1,200 tons of grains) from the Aegean ports, Syria, Crete, Greece, and Macedonia to Istanbul from 1789 to 1790.[120] In addition, 178 French vessels delivered 44,160 tons of grains from the Black Sea ports to Istanbul during the same period.[121] The capacity of French vessels on the Black Sea was two times higher than that of Ottoman ships. Galleons of between 250 and 300 tons dominated French shipping with

Istanbul, and the majority of these ships (eleven out of thirteen) conducted trade between Istanbul, Izmir, Damietta, Alexandria, Salonica, Kavala, Aleppo, Jaffa, and Beirut.[122]

The shortage of provisions in Istanbul was a serious concern for the Ottoman government. The state issued an order to the kadi of Istanbul in 1775 to organize thirty-five kapan merchants in Istanbul and three oil kapan merchants in Galata to import grains from Boğdan into Istanbul after the signing of a peace treaty with Russia. An order was also sent to the voyvoda of Boğdan for the safe conduct of the merchants.[123] The state placed several bans on the export of grains. Nevertheless, the shortages continued, and the presence of European ships in the grain trade from the Black Sea to their ports made the situation worse. In 1788, the Ottoman state issued several orders to the kadis of Silistre, Varna, and Rodosçuk to load grains, oil, and honey only on kapan ships and to prevent the ships of European merchants from transporting grains to Istanbul since the state then lost control over pricing.[124]

Despite these bans, European states were trying to gain a foothold in the Black Sea trade. France established consuls in the Crimea and other ports and entered into direct negotiations with Crimean khans in the seventeenth century. The Khanate of Crimea played a crucial role in organizing the grain trade between southern Russia and Istanbul, assuring the transportation, pricing, and timely delivery of grains on private ships. The foreign policy of France toward Crimea as well as toward Poland had an important commercial motivation to gain access to the Black Sea ports and markets. France's merchant marine aimed at making great profits by exporting goods like wine to Crimea as well as by importing grains from southern Russia (see chapter 4). Crimea also supplied Istanbul with great quantities of furs since it was the habitat of animals like the fox, wolf, jackal, rabbit, lamb, and sheep. It exported these furs through the ports of Azov and Kherson, where Greeks from Yeniköy, a village along the European shore of the Bosphorus, were very active.[125] But in the eighteenth century, with the growing demand for furs and other luxuries from a new class of urban rich men and women, the guild of furriers lost their monopoly over the importing of furs into Istanbul.[126]

The Treaty of Küçük Kaynarca ended the Ottoman control of Crimea and opened up the Black Sea to Russian commercial shipping in 1774 (see chapter 4). The number of French ships trading between the Black Sea port of Kherson (now in the Ukraine) and Marseille increased from two in 1782 to twenty-five in 1787.[127] The port of Kherson imported from Marseille wine, textiles like French silks, sugar, French olive oil and soap, wine, spices, coffee, perfumes, and furniture. However, the most important item imported from the Black Sea to Marseille was wheat.

The French ambassador in Istanbul played an active role in mediating the relationship between Russia and the Ottoman Empire and in obtaining permission for French ships to transport provisions to Istanbul. For example, Yustinian a French merchant who resided in Galata, received an imperial order to transport wheat from North African ports to Istanbul in December 1773. He pledged not to take the wheat to any other place and to pay the government a fine of 10,000 kuruş if he sold it to others for a higher price. If his ship were to run into an accident, he pledged that he would try to bring the goods to Istanbul and to provide witnesses if he was unable to do so. Once he had arrived in Istanbul, he could sell the wheat at market prices since he had purchased it with his own capital.[128] In another imperial order, the state issued permission to French merchants to import grains into Istanbul in 1788 and 1789 with the guaranty of the French ambassador.[129] In 1788, the French ambassador reported to the Sublime Porte that, in accordance with the request and permission of the grand vizier, French ships would be transporting 2,420,000 kg of wheat from the Black Sea ports of Ibra'il and Isma'iliye to Istanbul in two voyages.[130] French ships obviously were not bound by guild rules and price ceilings.

Moreover, French ships also got involved in transporting the goods of Ottoman merchants, sometimes in partnership with them within the empire. For example, in 1774, the French ambassador requested permission for French merchants to purchase 145,2000 kg of wheat from Algeria to transport to Istanbul.[131] Antoine Martin, a French captain, transported the goods of Muslim merchants from Trablusşam (Tunis) to Istanbul, and the kadi made an announcement to protect the ship from corsair activities.[132] In 1775, out of a total of 1,172 ships trading with Alexandria, 620 belonged to Ottoman captains, and 552 belonged to European trading houses that were involved in domestic trade and trade with Europe.[133] In 1788, 234 French ships delivered wheat from the Levant, and 93 ships delivered it from North Africa into Marseille.[134] Grain exports from North Africa and the Levant into Marseille had also increased, causing further hikes in prices.

French ships were still subject to North African pirate attacks as well as to mistreatment at the hands of Ottoman naval officers. For example, in a petition submitted by the French ambassador, Vergennes, to the Porte in 1763, he claimed that an imperial sea captain, Hasan Agha, had harassed the ship of French captain Roberto on the island of Tenedos while it was carrying wheat to Istanbul. He asked for protection of the French merchants who were passengers on the ship.[135] Ambassador Vergennes also submitted a petition to the Porte in October 1770 stating that Reyno, a French captain, had been transporting tin, soap, lead, cotton yarn, and woolens from Izmir to a French merchant in Salonica. But the ship had been involved in an accident on an island near Çamlıca, and its goods had been seized by the voyvoda of the island. Vergennes was requesting an imperial order to have the goods transported to the French merchant in Salonica.[136] Moreover, war between France and England led to attacks on each other's ships in the Mediterranean and to shortages of rice, sugar, and coffee in 1779. The Ottoman government tried to maintain its neutrality and ordered governors in western Anatolia to return the goods of ships of both nations when they attacked each other and pulled into their ports for safety.[137] With the opening of the Black Sea to Russian and European merchant marines, Galata gained more importance as a center of transit trade between Russia and Europe. Ottoman Greek merchants gained an important position in this trade in the nineteenth century, and many settled in Odessa.

CONCLUSION

Early modern Mediterranean states considered the provisioning of their capital city with abundant and affordable foodstuff, particularly grains, the most important aspect of their economic policies in order to prevent political upheavals and bread riots. The Ottoman Empire followed both Islamic and Byzantine traditions but asserted its control over the supply zones of the Black Sea and gave a near monopoly to provisioning Muslim merchants and sea captains after 1475. Kapan merchants received commercial licenses from the Ottoman government and functioned like regulated companies, but most were private merchants. Kapan merchants and sea captains formed mudaraba partnerships in Galata and Istanbul and enjoyed state support, with some becoming very wealthy. Once the Kapan merchants had delivered the provisions to the ports of Istanbul and Galata, the state regulated the purchase, distribution, and pricing of grains and basic foodstuff through its officials like the market inspector and the kadi in greater Istanbul. But during times of war and shortages, it allowed all kinds of merchants and captains, including foreign ships, to get involved in temporarily provisioning Istanbul and removed some of the bans and regulations. Moreover, during severe shortages, price ceilings were ineffective and were subject to supply and demand as well as to hoarding and smuggling. The opening of the Black Sea to Russian and European ships undermined the control of the Ottoman state and guilds over the provisioning trade. The paradigm of an ever-present Ottoman command economy is now being revised, with more research being conducted in the Ottoman and European archives that challenges the theory of a fixed and rigid economic system frozen in time and space or of ever-dominant European merchants in the markets of the Levant.[138]

SIX

Between Galata and Marseille

FROM SILKS AND SPICES TO COLONIAL
SUGAR AND COFFEE

THE HISTORY OF OTTOMAN-EUROPEAN TRADE has been usually written from a Western perspective based largely on the exploration of European (Levant Company) archives, with the assumption that Ottoman archives did not contain much information on trade and traders. The Islamic court documents as well as petitions submitted by European residents through their ambassadors to the Imperial Council contained in the collection of *ecnebi defterleri* (Registers of Foreign Nations) as well as customs registers and other financial records show that the commercial world of Ottoman port cities such as Galata was complex and posed numerous challenges to European traders and diplomats, even when they enjoyed close diplomatic relations with the Porte. The patterns of trade changed as European traders established a direct link with Persia, India and Asia, but they were still involved in the trade of the Levant in other capacities as bankers, importers of colonial goods, ship captains, and exporters of other cash crops like cotton. For example, with the growing involvement of French traders in the economic life of Ottoman port cities, the number of lawsuits and petitions presented on behalf of French traders involving insolvency and even bankruptcy began to grow, a situation that is reflected in hundreds of petitions in the collection of the *ecnebi defterleri* that cover the period from the second half of the eighteenth to the early nineteenth century.[1]

This chapter will examine the evolution of Ottoman-French trade, the activities of French traders after the reforms of Minister Colbert, and the rise of Marseille as the major port of Levant trade. In other words, while chapters 3 and 4 focused on the legal regime of international trade created by the ahdnames in Ottoman ports, this chapter will focus on the implementation of the commercial articles of the French ahdnames until the dissolution of the French Levant Company after the French Revolution.

SETTLEMENT OF DEBTS

Due to difficult economic conditions as a result of the Russo-Ottoman Wars during the second half of the eighteenth century, many cases brought to the Islamic court of Galata by European traders dealt with unpaid debts, as the following example illustrates:

> In May 1769, the dragoman of the French embassy (Tomtom) appeared in the Islamic court of Istanbul in the company of two Jewish witnesses (Kumal son of Mihal and Mordehay son of Avram) and five French merchants. He submitted a lawsuit on behalf of the French ambassador against Konorot son of Avram, the guarantor of a group of Jewish merchants. In the petition, the French ambassador (Comte de Saint-Priest) stated that nine Jewish merchants, who were absent from the court, had purchased French goods from the afore-mentioned French merchants but had fled before paying their debt of 15,000 *kuruş*. Consequently, the court sealed off their shops and storage houses in the Mahmud Pasha Suk until they paid their debt. Finally, some of the Jewish merchants agreed to settle for the payment of 4,000 *kuruş* in installments of 1,000 *kuruş* every four months over a year. After this agreement, the court removed the seal from the shops of two Jewish merchants, Sabatay and Haim[,] in the presence of the dragoman of the French embassy. The guarantor of the Jewish merchants then paid the first installment of 1,000 *kuruş* to the French merchants. The court forwarded a report to the Imperial Council.[2]

The above case is drawn from the Islamic court register of Istanbul and illustrates the close economic and legal entanglements between a group of French traders who resided in the port of Galata and some Ottoman Jewish traders involving an outstanding debt. The Jewish merchants had defaulted on their payment of 15,000 *kuruş* to the French traders, who lived in Galata, possibly over the purchase of French goods (woolens, coffee, or sugar) and had fled, leaving their guarantor (*kefil*) to deal with the French traders. These and other similar cases involved local merchants who sometimes acted as agents and brokers for European traders who themselves were agents of French trading houses in Marseille. After the testimony of Jewish witnesses in favor of the French merchants in the court, the judge sealed off the shops of the Jewish merchants, thus forcing them to settle for the payment of one-fourth of the debt.

The case entry does not shed any light on the nature of transaction—whether it was a purchase made by the Jewish merchants from the French merchants on credit, a loan given by the French merchants on interest, or a mudaraba/commenda partnership between the Jewish and French traders (see chapter 5). The lawsuit also involved the French ambassador, Comte de Saint-Priest (amb. 1768–84), who wrote the petition on behalf of the French merchants; the dragoman of the embassy, who translated the petition into Ottoman and represented the French merchants in the court; the Jewish witnesses; and a guarantor. The courts allowed non-Muslim witnesses when Europeans submitted lawsuits, although they preferred the testimony of Muslims. The Jewish guarantor, on the other hand, represented the Jewish merchants and was liable in the case of default by the merchants. He acted like a form of insurance for transactions on credit. Guarantors were usually trade partners or relatives of the person or persons whom they were pledging to support. The legal proceeding followed the articles of the applicable ahdname (1740 in this case), which required the presence of the dragoman of the embassy, while the court required guarantors for commercial transactions, documentation, and witnesses (see chapters 3 and 4).[3]

The kadi of the district of Istanbul as well as Galata enforced the articles of the ahdnames when lawsuits between Ottoman and European subjects involved fewer than 4,000 akçe. If the lawsuit involved an amount higher then 4,000 akçe, it would be submitted to the Imperial Council by the dragoman (see chapters 3 and 4). However, this case involved a higher amount (15,000 *kuruş*) and was still submitted to the kadi's court, showing that the courts played an important role in resolving disputes between Ottoman and European subjects in the eighteenth century. A summary of each lawsuit and its resolution were copied down in the registers of the kadi's court, and a copy was sent to the Imperial Council when foreigners were involved. If the case had only involved European subjects, the consular courts would have prosecuted the case in most instances.[4] Fleeing the authorities and creditors to avoid justice was yet another choice for defendants attempting to avoid payment, as was the case here. Sometimes the fear of angry creditors forced the ambassadors and consuls to smuggle their nationals who had defaulted onto a ship back home at night before the Islamic court initiated legal proceedings. This type of conduct, however, caused problems for consuls and ambassadors.

The Imperial Council was the final court of appeal if the parties were not happy with the decision of the Islamic or consular court. It even held higher jurisdiction than the consular courts, and even foreigners could submit lawsuits involving their own nations. It appears that settlement (*sulh*) had become a widespread practice in cases of outstanding debts and defaults in the courts of Galata and Istanbul.[5] Islamic law (the Hanafi School) promoted settlement in cases of default and delayed payment. Settlement was a common form of resolution in the court of Galata for these types of lawsuits that involved debt. As this case demonstrates, settlement in the court over the payment of debts was quite widespread in the second half of the eighteenth century, possibly due to economic difficulties.[6] For example, Al-Şeyh Agha, a merchant in Valide Han in Istanbul, sued Istavraki for failing to pay 75 kuruş from a total debt of 300 kuruş in February 1769. Since Istavraki was unable to pay the whole amount, the parties settled for the payment of two kuruş per month until he completed the payment. A certain Nikoli stood as guarantor, and the case was registered in the court.[7] Some cases were settled outside the court, but disputes over payment brought the parties to the court. In this way, the courts avoided imposing the harsher punishments of imprisonment and total bankruptcy and gave both parties a chance to negotiate a settlement.

THE RISE OF MARSEILLE IN THE LEVANT TRADE

Trade among Marseille, the Levant, and North Africa had always been very important for the economy of France as well as for that of the Ottoman Empire. Iranian raw silk became highly popular in the Ottoman Empire as well as in Europe during the sixteenth and seventeenth centuries. Silk workshops in Bursa, Venice, Provence, and England depended on the import of Iranian raw silk from the Levant in the early modern period.

As a result of the Ottoman-Safavid Wars that lasted from the sixteenth to the mid-eighteenth centuries, the silk trade through the Levant had been disrupted several times. Trade routes shifted from the Tabriz-Aleppo (war front) route to the Tabriz-Izmir route, and Armenian traders gained a monopoly due to the abuses of Iranian *shi'i* merchants and their subsequent captivity and enslavement in Ottoman lands during periods of war. The silk-growing regions of Gilan in northern Iran and Gence in the Caucasus also suffered from war and occupation. The Safavids were gradually shifting the silk trade with Europe from Anatolia and Azerbaijan to the Persian Gulf. Moreover, the English and Dutch traders had managed to establish direct contact with Safavid Iran in the seventeenth century through the port of Hormuz on the Persian Gulf, and England had received an ahdname from the shah in 1616. The English helped Shah Abbas defeat the Portuguese and expel them from the port of Hormuz and Qishm in 1622. In return, the shah agreed to wave customs dues on English exports from Hormuz.[8] They also received the right to collect half of the customs revenue in Hormuz, although local tax collectors opposed these privileges that had been given to the British traders. The Dutch East India Company established direct trade through the signing of its own ahdname from the Safavid shah in 1623 and soon dominated the Persian Gulf trade, ousting the British East India Company from the silk trade.[9] The importing of silk and cotton contributed to expansion of the English silk and cotton industries during this period, while French trade with the Levant experienced a decline during the Cretan Wars (see chapter 4).[10]

At the end of these wars, the reforms of Minister Colbert and his diplomatic efforts with the Porte improved the situation of French traders in Marseille during the second half of the seventeenth century (see chapter 4). Marseille, which had long been the center of commerce with the Levant, maintained a degree of autonomy from the central government in Paris. The Marseille Chamber of Commerce, the first of its kind in France, had already been established in 1599. But in 1660, King Louis XIV effectively took control of Marseille, a city that had been resisting royal interference into its affairs for some time. He gave Minister Colbert the authority to manage its commercial affairs. Colbert believed in mercantilism, which was an economic practice in Europe from the sixteenth to the eighteenth century that promoted government regulation of the economy to increase state power at the expense of local groups.

Following this school of thought, Colbert believed that the enrichment of the country could be achieved through commerce and better manufacturing, especially of woolen textiles in Languedoc, and through central regulation and governance. The balance of trade was an important part of this model, and exports were favored over imports to protect the local industry. Colbert wanted to also end the flow of currency and gold to the Levant and ordered that ships on their way there be inspected regularly, an action that brought the crown into conflict with local merchants. He thought that a company with great capital could improve the lot of merchants, provided that it did not act out of self-interest and followed the ordinances of the Crown for the public good.[11] He got the support of King Louis XIV behind the Levant

Company and established a fund for the Chamber of Commerce in Marseille, from which the merchants could borrow.[12]

Thanks to Colbert's efforts, the French Levant Company received a royal monopoly in the Levant trade in 1660. The Chamber of Commerce organized the Levant trade as well as trade with the Barbary Coast and also became involved in the organization of the American trade and trade with Spain, Italy, and Northern Europe. The Chamber of Commerce in Marseille was composed of an oligarchy of wealthy merchants and was closed to outsiders like Protestants until 1779. From 1700 to 1792, it had 450 members.[13] After 1685, the Chamber of Commerce in Marseille limited the number of trading houses in each port. Colbert abolished taxes on international traders in 1669 and made Marseille a duty-free port with a monopoly over France's trade with the Levant, which previously had been open to other ports such as Lyon.

Colbert regulated and centralized the Levant Company and created a commercial code by which all merchants had to abide. The code regulated imports and exports and aimed at establishing a balance of trade for France and improving and protecting French manufacturers and their export to the Levant.[14] Anyone outside of Marseille who traded with the Levant had to pay export taxes of 20 percent. To avoid paying this tax, all French merchants from Provence had to bring their merchandise to Marseille to load it on ships for the Levant. But the Chamber of Commerce opposed the creation of a duty-free port for fear of loss of revenue and income and of the takeover of the port by foreign merchants.[15] Slowly, various royal taxes were imposed on duty-free goods like olive oil in 1727.

Colbert also improved the state of French manufacturing (of cloth and glass) in Provence and Lyon and reformed the Levant Company and the French East India Company so that they could compete more effectively with the English and Dutch Levant Companies. Colbert strengthened the French woolen textile industry in Provence by making French woolens more competitive in the markets of the Levant. Thanks to government subsidies to manufacturers and Colbert's reforms, French woolens replaced English woolens in the Levant in the eighteenth century. By 1785, 57,000 pieces of cloth worth 8,250,000 *livres* had been sent from Languedoc to the Levant.[16] The government also protected the cloth, soap, and leather industries as well as the tanneries of Marseille. Bans were placed on the importing of Indian cotton cloth and foreign hides to protect the cloth and leather industries of Provence.[17] But contraband trade in these goods continued by local merchants who defied the center.

To improve trade and diplomacy and end the corruption of local consuls, Colbert reformed the consulates in the *échelles* in the Levant by bringing all consuls under his control.[18] Consuls were to be appointed by the king for a fixed time period and could collect a consular fee of 2.5 percent from the cargo of every ship. French merchants in the Levant elected members of assemblies of the nation who participated in decision making. Moreover, every ambassador and consul had to send reports on commerce to the Chamber of Commerce in Marseille and maintain a paper trail of all transactions and shipments.

However, after the death of Colbert, mercantilism came under attack regarding monopolies and regulations on the grain trade (domestic and foreign). In Paris in 1700, the government began controlling trade through the creation of the Council of Commerce, which included deputies from chief commercial centers.[19] Some deputies attacked Marseille's monopoly in the Levant trade as well as high tariffs on imports and exports from other ports and protective policies. They opposed the 20-percent duty on imports from the Levant into ports outside Marseille. Some deputies, such as those from Rouen, wanted every trading city to be free of government regulations. Some advocated for more freedom in the Levant trade while the deputy of Marseille defended the monopoly.

Despite these objections and attacks on Colbertism, the revival of trade with the Levant had led to prosperity for Marseille's urban dwellers. The population of Marseille had grown from 30,000 in 1550 to 50,000 in 1650 and 75,000 in 1695. It rose further to 100,000 before the plague of 1720.[20] Like Galata, Marseille was a diverse port in the seventeenth century. Armenian traders from Iran and the Levant had already established themselves in Marseille in 1636 when Cardinal Richelieu invited them to settle in French towns with their merchandise of silk. Many Catholic Armenians began settling in Marseille after Colbert's Edict of 1669 invited Levantine Armenians and Jews to settle in Marseille, with the prospect that they could become French subjects. By 1670, around four hundred Armenian merchants, artisans, and priests from Livorno and Isfahan had settled in Marseille, playing a crucial role in establishing the silk workshops of Provence and trading in South Asian textiles and calicos.[21] The anti-Ottoman policies of the French government during the Cretan Wars led to the favoring of the Julfa Armenian merchants from Iran during this period as well.[22] The Armenians had their own neighborhood in Marseille, and many had already converted to Catholicism in Isfahan since the Shah was very open to the activities of Catholic missionaries. They opened the first coffeehouse in Marseille.[23]

Ottoman Jewish traders also settled in Marseille when it became an open port. Moriscos and Marranos had taken refuge in Marseille after their expulsion from Iberia in the fifteenth century. The new arsenal in the Old Port in Marseille also brought many Muslim galley slaves, including Turks, to the port. But a general atmosphere of hostility as well as Catholic anti-Muslim, anti-Jewish, and anti–Armenian Orthodox (Christian) feelings prevailed from time to time.[24] After Colbert's death, Armenians were subjected to similar exclusions and prohibitions in Marseille since the silks they imported from Persia threatened to undermine the French silk industry in the eighteenth century.[25]

The revocation of the Edict of Nantes in 1685 by the staunch Catholic king Louis XIV led to the expulsion of Armenians and Jews as well as Protestants from Marseille. The number of Armenians in Marseille dropped from four hundred to twenty, then rose to twenty-five between 1669 and 1695.[26] This edict may have also led to the conversion of many Armenians to Catholicism in order to remain in Marseille. Moreover, the networks of Levantine Jews threatened the Marseille Chamber of Commerce as rivals in the Levant trade.[27] In 1682, King Louis XIV expelled the Jews from Marseille for illegally opening a synagogue. In 1697, the French government revoked letters of naturalization for foreign subjects who had homes abroad. Later, a royal ordinance in 1711 decreed freedom of commerce only to Catholics in France, promoting the king's goal of "one king, one law, and one faith" and excluding non-Catholics and those who were not French subjects from this trade. Moreover, Muslims and Jews were blamed for corsair attacks by Tripolitan pirates on French ships.

FRENCH TRADE IN THE EIGHTEENTH CENTURY

Thanks to Colbert's efforts in reviving Ottoman-French trade and diplomacy, the reign of Sultan Ahmed III (1703–30) and the tenure of Grand Vizier Nevşehirli Ibrahim Pasha witnessed a warming of relations between France and the Ottoman Empire[28] (see chapter 4).

French trade with the Levant and Europe expanded considerably, enriching urban life in France during the eighteenth century. Marseille, Bordeaux, and Nantes had become the most important ports in France. They imported silks, spice, olive oil, dried fruits, coffee, and wines from the Levant. The Levant trade also counted for a third of France's exports.[29]

In his excellent study, Edhem Eldem has shown that French trade with the Ottoman Empire had expanded considerably, despite some ups and downs due to wars and the plague, in the eighteenth century.[30] Thus, French imports (largely woolen textiles) from the Levant into Marseille increased from 7.3 millions *livres* in 1671 to 23.3 million *livre* in 1714, reflecting a three-fold rise in forty years or so. Moreover, the number of ships coming from the Levant and entering into the port of Marseille (excluding those that carried wheat) increased from 63 in 1710 to 253 in 1714.[31]

However, the Great Plague of May 1720 in Marseille arrived on a ship from the Levant with contaminated merchandise. Due to the delayed quarantine in Marseille, the disease soon spread to warehouses in the Vieux Port.[32] The Chamber of Commerce, the Bureau of Health, and public officials denied the existence of the plague for a while out of fear of hurting commerce and refused to do anything. It soon spread to poor neighborhoods and led to a large number of casualties followed by great violence, looting, and pillaging from July to October.[33] From Marseille, the plague spread to other towns in Provence. By August, 300 people were dying every day, eventually leading to the loss of one-third of the population of Marseille (between 40,000 and 50,000 people).[34] Public health measures had failed, and the state was refusing to admit the gravity of the contagion. Moreover, the Plague of 1720 caused a large setback to the economy of Marseille and disrupted commerce with the Levant for two years. The number of vessels coming from the Levant into Marseille dropped from 167 in 1720 to 75 in 1722, largely due to the plague and the resulting economic decline as a consequence of the French ban on trade with the Levant. As a result, many trading houses declared bankruptcy in Marseille.

The early eighteenth century was also a period of urban violence and rebellions in Istanbul and Izmir, partly as a result of the long wars with Iran that had caused economic crises. During the Patrona Halil Rebellion, the French community in Galata was the target of hostile attacks by the rebels in August 1730 since the French ambassador had mediated peace with Iran.[35] The wars with Iran (1725–48) also interrupted the silk trade and caused a setback to the Ottoman and Safavid economies.[36] After the plague of 1720, trade between the Levant and France soon resumed in 1723, and the number of vessels coming from the Levant increased from 75 in 1722 to 130 in 1723.[37] France carried out three-fifths of the trade between Europe and the Ottoman

Empire from 1763 to 1773, while England carried out only one-third of this trade during this period. Half of the Ottoman Empire's trade with Europe in the eighteenth century was carried out with Marseille.[38] French traders established themselves in Izmir, Alexandria, Sidon, Salonica, and the Greek archipelago and set up consuls in Modon, Coron, Chios, and Milos.[39] Due to its location, Izmir emerged as the most important port in western Anatolia, handling about 45 percent of the commercial traffic with Marseille. One-quarter of the ships from Marseille called into Izmir in the eighteenth century.[40]

Istanbul ranked fifth in importance in the trade of Marseille, while Izmir, ports in Syria, Egypt, and later Crete ranked higher. But the enormous size of Istanbul (between 300,000 and 500,000 people in the eighteenth century) and its ruling class's needs for luxury goods made it an important port. By the mid-eighteenth century, French trade in Istanbul was two-thirds of all Western trade with the capital. Istanbul controlled 34.4 percent of all French imports to the Levant and only 7.7 percent of all exports in the eighteenth century.[41] In 1773, the number of ships from Marseille that traded with the Levant was 143 (23.3 million *livres*), and 13 (9 percent) of these ships carried out trade with Istanbul, amounting to 1.3 million *livres* in 1772. The maritime distance from both Marseille and Venice to Istanbul was between 30 and 60 days. From Marseille, ships usually departed in mid May and arrived in Istanbul in July. They stopped in Istanbul for between 60 and 80 days and then left at the end of October through December, not undertaking voyages in winter. Livorno and Sicily were gathering points for ships before they stopped in Malta, Modon, Coron, and the Cyclades Islands. French ships also stopped in Tinos and the Dardanelles and then arrived at Istanbul. In the Dardanelles (Boğaz Hisar), French ships had to pay local taxes and consular fees and receive crossing authorization to enter Istanbul (see map 3).[42]

The registers of foreign nations in the Ottoman Empire contain many requests by French ambassadors for permission for French ship captains to travel from Ottoman and Black Sea ports to Marseille. Some indicate the names of the captain and his ship and its cargo, while others just list the name of the captain, the ship, the point of origin, and the destination (e.g., the Mediterranean, the Black Sea) as the following case demonstrates:

> In August 1770, the French ambassador (Sieur LeBas) requested travel permissions for sixty French ship captains from the Imperial Council in Istanbul to return from Galata to Marseille. The ambassador pledged that they had

delivered their merchandise, [had] loaded up their ships[,] and had paid the customs dues and obtained a receipt of payment. Travel permissions were issued[,] and the kadi of Boğaz Hisar was notified not to prevent the passage of the ships.[43]

As French trade with the Levant expanded, the Porte issued berats (patents of appointment) that listed the rights of French traders and their exemption from taxes in accordance with the ahdnames. It also issued travel permissions in response to the requests of ambassadors and consuls to protect the lives and property of French and other European subjects when they traveled outside the ports if they were trading legally in the empire and had paid their taxes. The travel permissions were like internal visas that provided legal protection for European subjects who were allowed by the terms of the ahdnames to travel freely within the empire. The following travel permission also underscores the rise of French trade between the Black Sea ports and Marseille, especially in grains (see chapter 5):

> Antoine Muniye, a French captain, has received permission to travel from Russian ports to the Mediterranean Sea, transporting 193,600 kg of wheat in September 1838.[44]

In addition, the dragomans, their sons and servants, priests, and the dependents of the French subjects also received *berats* (patents of appointment) and enjoyed protection as well as exemption from personal taxes. But from time to time, Ottoman officials violated the articles of the current ahdname and charged illegal taxes. For example, in 1770, the French ambassador, Saint-Priest, submitted a petition to the Imperial Council stating that a naval officer, a certain Hasan, had forcefully charged French traders on the island of Rhodes with the poll tax, contrary to the articles of the ahdname, after beating them up. The ambassador was calling for the refund of the poll tax. Consequently, an imperial order was issued demanding the return of the poll tax to the merchants and clarification that French ambassadors, consuls, dragomans, and traders were exempt from paying the poll tax.[45] In the same year, the ambassador asked for travel permission and protection for two French monks, Flippo and Mavro, who were traveling to Ahıska.[46]

The French ambassador was a representative of the Chamber of Commerce in Marseille as well as of the government, handling commercial affairs and representing French traders in the Sublime Porte and the Islamic courts. In return for his services on behalf of the traders, the ambassador collected consular dues of 2.5 percent from every ship that left Levantine ports. He had to be present when ships arrived with their cargoes or left the port of Galata, and he registered their cargoes. He also presented a report to the Sublime Porte about the names of ship captains, the names of ships, and their cargoes to obtain permission for them to travel. For example, in 1770, the French ambassador submitted a petition to the Imperial Council stating that a French captain, Eligoti, had loaded 145,200 kg of wheat that belonged to a certain Isma'il Efendi and that another French captain, Royan, had loaded 135,520 kg of his wheat in Kilyos on the Black Sea. The ambassador was asking for permission for the ships to travel into Istanbul.[47] This case also illustrates French ships' involvement in transporting grains from Black Sea ports to provision Istanbul (see chapter 4).

Moreover, customs officials at each port of call also registered the arrival of European ships and their cargoes and collected customs dues and other fees. Istanbul had several customs regions in three major areas: the Marmara Sea (Tekirdağ, Aynoz, Edirne, and the Gelibolu ports), the Aegean Sea (Izmir, Chios, and Foça), and the Black Sea (Sinop, Samsun, Inebolu, Erğeli, and Bartin). The ports of Galata and Eminönü on the two opposite sides of the Golden Horn were the two major customs stations for the maritime trade of Istanbul. Customs dues on overland trade with Istanbul were collected in Edirne and Üsküdar.[48] The Ottoman government followed the Byzantine policies of taxing imports and exports. Ottoman Muslim and non-Muslim subjects paid 4 percent in the ports of Galata and Istanbul, while foreign merchants paid 5 percent on imports and exports, which was later reduced to 3 percent in the ahdnames granted to England, the Dutch Republic, and France in the seventeenth century (see chapter 4).

The earlier ahdnames had not specified the customs rates because the rates were flexible and varied in each station and on each good. They were collected ad valorem on the basis of the value of each type of merchandise or in accordance to its weight.[49] The customs rate on the import of bulky foodstuff (based on weight) was much lower than that on luxury goods such as silk. Customs dues on some goods like wine or paper were collected per cask or glass. For example, foreign traders importing cloth paid a 3 percent customs rate in Bursa but 5 percent in Istanbul. They also paid a host of other dues and market fees. In addition to customs dues on imports and exports, the Ottoman government collected a modest sales tax from importers and sellers when the goods were sold.[50] The stamp tax on cloth was collected per load or bale.[51] However, bulky goods (foodstuff) that were destined for the military and the palace were exempt from customs taxes.

The Ottoman government farmed out the collection of customs dues to private individuals but issued regulations for each province that listed customs and sales taxes. Tax farmers earned between 10 to 20 percent profit from collecting customs dues and market taxes in Istanbul and other ports.[52] Jewish tax farmers were prominent in Izmir and Istanbul in the sixteenth and seventeenth centuries. For example, Ilyas, Yaku, and Musa were prominent Jewish tax farmers in Istanbul and Galata in the late sixteenth century.[53] However, as the economic conditions of Jews deteriorated, they were no longer able to bid for the tax farms in Istanbul. In 1730, the tax farmers of the customs revenues of Galata were mostly Muslim men (janissaries) like Isma'il Agha, Yeğen Mehmed Agha, Mehmed, and Hasan.[54] The tax farms were divided into shares and auctioned to different tax farmers for their lifetime, a process that produced greater income for the government than the regular tax farms did.[55] The revenue from the customs of Istanbul and Galata supported the pensions of government employees and members of the ulema.[56] No ship could load goods or leave the ports without the permission of the customs collector or tax farmer.

Smuggling as well as cheating, however, was widespread since merchants viewed tax farmers as rapacious individuals out to make a profit for themselves. Ottoman customs officials sometimes violated the articles of the current ahdname and collected taxes several times form French ships, contrary to conditions stipulated in the ahdnames. To prevent cheating and smuggling, the government required the presence of officially appointed *dellal* (brokers) during the sale of precious commodities such as silk at the bazaars. A broker had to register all sales immediately and report any misconduct. He put goods on auction, trying to get a good price for them. He received a fee for his services from both the seller and the buyer and could not engage in any commerce of his own. All brokers in a particular bazaar were organized under the leadership of a *simsar* (head broker) who had received an official appointment or *berat* (diploma of appointment) from the government. He supervised the activities of the other brokers. All the porters served the head broker and could not transport goods without his permission.[57] This system also existed in Venice, where Ottoman merchants had their own brokers.

French traders had their own brokers, who were often Jews, to protect their commercial transactions. For example, after Aslan son of Avram, a broker of French merchants, had died in the Bereketzade quarter in Galata, his son Elya presented a lawsuit in April 1750 in the court of Galata against Konorot and Hayim sons of Isak claiming 250 kuruş from brokerage charges as well as a partnership debt that they owed his father.[58] The parties settled for the payment of 20 kuruş, and Elya gave up his claim against Konorot and Hayim. This case recounts the interaction of the Jewish broker of French traders in Galata with other Jewish merchants, demonstrating the role of Ottoman Jews in the commercial activities of French merchants as brokers and dealers, especially of woolen textiles.

In the eighteenth century, French traders were involved in the importing of all kinds of goods from Marseille as well as from French colonies in the West Indies and India. French traders imported fine-quality woolen textiles from Provence into Istanbul, colonial goods such as coffee and sugar from the West Indies, and dyes and spices from the East Indies. For example, French importing of sugar doubled and that of coffee increased by five fold between 1768 and 1789.[59] French traders imported Persian silks from Izmir, Angora wool from Ankara, coarse wool from Anatolia and Crimea, olive oil, wheat, and cotton from Syria and the Levant into Marseille.[60] In the late seventeenth century, the Iranian silk trade shifted from the Tabriz-Aleppo route to Izmir due to lower tolls and the safety of this caravan route despite its longer distance.[61] Izmir became the major transit center for the silk trade among Iran, Amsterdam, and Marseille. Iranian raw silk made up the bulk of the merchandise that French traders imported from Izmir into Marseille in 1691.[62] Each year, French traders imported between 400 and 500 bales of raw silk from Izmir into Marseille. The Chamber of Commerce in Marseille recorded the continuing arrival of Iranian silk from Izmir into Marseille during the early eighteenth century. But the Afghan occupation of Iran, followed by the disintegration of the Safavid Dynasty in Iran in 1722 led to the disruption and total collapse of the silk trade between Iran, Anatolia, and France. The Ottoman state occupied western Iran (1725–30) to take control of the silk-producing areas in Shirvan and the Caspian Sea region.[63] The long wars with Iran (1725–1747) caused further setbacks to the silk trade with Anatolia and Syria. Silk trading between Iran and Aleppo dropped to 160 tons in 1725, and local silk produced in Anatolia and Syria replaced Iranian silk.

With the disruption of Persian silk imports into Anatolia in the eighteenth century, French traders imported raw silk from Syria, the Morea, and Anatolia. But silk imports from the Levant into Marseille dropped by 15.7 percent from the period 1700–59 to 5.9 percent during the period 1777–89 due to competition from Italy as well as lower demand. The import of raw silk from the Levant into England also dropped by 77 percent from 1699 to 1765.[64] Italian silk had largely replaced Persian and Levantine silk in France in the late eighteenth century. However, France continued to import small quantities of silk as well as spices and Indian shawls from Istanbul in the nineteenth century.[65]

THE COTTON AND ANGORA TRADE

Cotton was slowly replacing silk as the most important item of trade with Europe because of a change in fashion in the eighteenth century. The Ottoman government also lifted the ban on the importing of cotton yarn in the Ahdname of 1740 with France. From Istanbul French traders imported sheep's wool, mohair yarn, raw animal hides for the tanneries of Marseille, processed leather, alum used in dying textiles and treating hides, hare skins, wool, cotton, silk textiles, beeswax used in making candles, spices, and herbal medicine as well as wheat when Ottoman authorities lifted the bans.[66] French traders also imported a variety of manufactured Turkish woolen and cotton textiles from Aleppo, Diyarbekir, and Gaziantep as well as from Iran into Marseille in the eighteenth century.[67] France outrivaled England in the importing of cotton and woolen textiles from the Levant into Europe. It is important to note that the Ottoman Empire exported its own cotton textiles to Europe via Marseille in the eighteenth century.

To obtain raw materials like cotton and angora, it was important for French traders to gain access to the interior of Anatolia. In the 1740 ahdname, French merchants acquired the right to trade freely anywhere in the empire and to purchase goods like cotton directly from Ottoman producers and traders. They became very active in the interior of the empire, established partnerships with local merchants, and traveled widely to reach direct producers. For example, in 1777, the French chargé d'affairs, Sieur de Lebas, requested permission for Martel, a French merchant from Galata, to travel with his two Ottoman servants to Ankara, probably to purchase angora wool, without any interference or harassment. An imperial order was accordingly issued to grant him travel permission.[68] A year later in 1778, Sieur de Lebas, requested another travel permission, this one for Yani Istamo, an Ottoman Greek subject and the servant of one of the dragomans, to travel to Narda for business.[69]

But sometimes French traders had to deal with far more organized local actors, their acts of fraud, and default. Moreover, during times of war, the Ottoman state placed bans on the export of strategic goods like cotton since it was used in sailcloth. For example, in May 1769, the guild of cotton (*bez*) textile weavers complained about the loss of business due to war (with Russia) and provisions they had had to sell to the army at low prices.[70] They probably preferred to sell to foreign merchants and got involved in selling contraband. For example, in 1778, a group of French merchants in Galata sent their brokers (*simsars*), Ağop and Mihail, to a place called Kırk Ağaç to obtain cotton for them. They requested travel permission and protection for the two brokers in accordance with the ahdname. The imperial order subsequently granted stated that brokers who traveled on behalf of French merchants should not be harassed and were under the protection of the ahdnames.[71] In the same year, two French doctors, Liopold and Solini, applied for permission to travel from Istanbul to Diyarbekir and Mosul, probably to purchase cotton, under the protection of the ahdname.[72] During this period, cotton had replaced silk as the most important export from the Levant (western Anatolia and Syria) into Marseille (and London), increasing from 15,280 *quintals* in the years 1700–02 to 127,920 *quintals* in the years 1786–89.[73] In Izmir, too, the cultivation and export of cotton to Europe assumed greater importance than silk did during this period. The export of cotton from Izmir to Europe rose by three folds from 1788 to 1820.[74] Ottoman textile industries relied heavily on the supply of cotton and sheep's wool as well as silk, so the Ottoman state had to impose bans from time to time on the export of these raw materials to Europe to protect its own industry.

FRENCH TRADERS IN GALATA

With the expansion in French-Ottoman trade, the number of French residents in Ottoman ports increased. For example, 175 French subjects lived in Galata in 1719.[75] However, after the Plague of 1720 in Marseille, trade between Istanbul and Marseille came to a standstill, and the number of French residents decreased. After the resumption of trade between the two ports, the number of French men, women, and children and their protégés (mostly from Geneva) in Galata rose to 343 individuals in 1723.[76] Of this number, 82 single men were part of the household of the ambassador in Pera. French traders numbered 35, in addition to 12 wives and 16 children (a total of 63 individuals). In addition, traders had 12 clerks, who were single men. French artisans in Galata numbered 43 men with 27 wives and 59 children (a total of 129 individuals). The 1723 census of the French nation in Galata also listed 42 priests and seven surgeons with three wives and 15 children.[77]The number of French traders and their clerks in Galata increased from 35 in 1731 to 60 in 1755.[78] By 1769, the number of French residents in Galata had increased to 217 individuals, a number that included 31 individuals in the household of the ambassador, 12 dragomans and students, 12 traders, 32 clerks, and 40 artisans and that excluded 90 physicians. Galata had the largest French community in the Levant (a total of 1,211 subjects).[79]

To limit competition among French traders in the Levant, the Chamber of Commerce in 1743 restricted the number of trading houses to 12 in Istanbul, 12 in Izmir, 17 in northern Syria, 14 in southern Syria, 16 in Egypt, 6 in the archipelago, and 8 in Crete.[80]In Istanbul, the number of trading houses from Marseille rose to 16 in 1764 and dropped to 7 at the end of the eighteenth century. This drop reflected the decline of French trade in the Levant.

Ottoman sources do not provide any information on the connections of French traders to trading houses in Marseille. However, the Chamber of Commerce in Marseille kept files on trading houses in the Levant, particularly when they went bankrupt, as the Rémuzat trading house did.[81] Eldem provides a list of the major trading houses in Marseille that were present in Galata, such as the Magy family, which traded with Galata from 1672 until its bankruptcy in 1766.[82] The Maynard family was also active in Galata from 1683 until it went bankrupt in 1742, after which it established a new house in 1765. The Magallons first established themselves in 1731 and remained in business until the late eighteenth century. Likewise, the Rémuzat family set up a partnership with Guys and maintained a strong presence in Galata from 1728 until the late eighteenth century. All these trading houses operated like family firms in which the principal traders were based in Marseille, and the agents were sent with a small amount of capital to the ports in the Levant and North Africa. The Chamber of Commerce in Marseille controlled the number of trading houses that did business with each port in the Levant, a situation that meant that not every merchant could set up business in these ports. Furthermore, the agents had no control over the capital or the types of goods to be purchased and followed the directives of the trading houses and the Chamber of Commerce. They collected a 2 percent commission on sales and 3 percent on purchases, and a few carried out their own business and got involved in banking. The agents had established their own networks in Ottoman ports and cities that included protégés who were Ottoman subjects. Some had married Ottoman Christian women (Greek and Armenian) from very wealthy families and had become "Levantines," cutting their ties from Marseille (see chapter 7).[83]

VIOLENCE AGAINST FRENCH TRADERS

To protect themselves from banditry and robbery, all French residents and their agents had to obtain travel permission to move outside designated areas to protect their lives, property, and tax-exempt status. When French traders left coastal towns and ports, they became liable to pay higher taxes and even the poll tax. For example, in 1762, Ambassador Vergennes submitted a petition about the tax collector of the Morea's illegal demand that a French merchant named Gutiye pay the poll tax, contrary to the terms of the ahdname. Vergennes requested that the money be returned to the French merchant upon an imperial order, which was issued to the tax collector in July 1762.[84]

Violence against French traders also increased outside the main ports and during times of trouble, economic crisis, and wars in the second half of the eighteenth century. In 1763, Ambassador Vergennes submitted another petition to the Porte stating that a French trader, Ligho, and his servant had been attacked in Edirne by a group of Greek bandits known as Zorbaoğulları who had taken 420 kuruş from them. He was requesting that an imperial order be issued to the kadi and the commander of Edirne for the arrest and trial of the bandits in the court of Edirne.[85]

French ships were often subject to pirate and bandit attacks and looting on the Aegean islands. When a French ship had gotten involved in an accident near Rhodes in 1774 and had to pull into a small island nearby, its cargo had been seized by the French consul, Dophine, and placed in a storage house. But when Dophine left his house at night, several bandits attacked him, attempting to murder him and take the goods. The consul was then rescued by a number of Muslims who took possession of the cargo and investigated the matter. When it became clear that the bandits were the men of a certain Yorğaki, they fled and took refuge with a local notable, Hacı Kadiroğlu. The latter had sent two people to arrest and imprison the French consul, and they had taken 1,200 kuruş from him. Ambassador Saint-Priest submitted a petition on behalf of the consul, Dophine, asking that an imperial order be given to the commander of Rhodes to arrest Hacı Kadiroğlu. After the legal proceedings, an imperial order was issued in 1774 to arrest and punish Hacı Kadiroğlu and to reclaim the property of the French consul from Yorğaki and send a report to Istanbul.[86] In this instance, even the French consul was not safe from robbery and attacks by local Greek and Turkish bandits.

All of these three cases demonstrate the challenges French merchants faced when conducting trade in Morea as well as on the Aegean islands and dealing with local traders, bandits, and officials. Contributing to the general insecurity of travel in the countryside, the shrinking power of the central government and the rise of local notables did not necessarily provide security and safe conduct for European traders. The ambassadors were well aware of the abuses of local officials, bandits, and pirates, but they could not do much to stop them, even if they wanted to help merchants carry on their trade, and they themselves collected dues from French ships. The distance between the local courts and Istanbul was also a factor in the difficulty of enforcing the articles of the ahdnames. The consuls lacked jurisdiction to arrest and punish local bandits and had to instead rely on the support of local officials who sometimes colluded with the bandits and local actors. Baron de Tott noted the degree of extortion that French traders had to deal with and underscored the role of bribery used by parties to win their cases in the courts, even the ones in Istanbul, during the late eighteenth century.[87]

Moreover, tensions between French traders and local producers and traders were on the rise during the second half of the eighteenth century. It is clear that the lifting of bans on the exporting of raw materials like cotton and sheep's wool and the French penetration of local markets in the interior caused stress. For example, Ambassador Saint-Priest submitted a petition to the Imperial Council on behalf of some French merchants in Galata who had sent agents to Selanik (Salonica) to purchase sheep's wool from four Muslim merchants, Mustafa, Isa, Mulla Ibrahim, and Memiş, in 1778. The French traders had made an advance payment of 10,000 kuruş to the Muslim merchants. The latter had then distributed 3,000 kuruş to a certain Şehbenderoğlu Abdulrahman to purchase wool from villages in the district. But Abdulrahman had kept the money, refusing to purchase the agreed-upon amount of wool. Therefore, the ambassador was requesting that the four merchants return the money since the deal had been broken. After proceedings in the court in April 1780, an imperial order was issued to the kadi of Selanik to that effect.[88] From this lawsuit we learn that French traders in Galata made commercial agreements with Muslim merchants to purchase raw materials and that these merchants then subcontracted with local traders to purchase raw materials from producers.

By the late eighteenth century, French woolen cloth had lost its dominant position in the markets of Levant to better quality British cloth, which had made a comeback. However, as Marseille began turning to the West and East Indies for the bulk of its commerce, the Levant trade declined from 40 percent at the end of the seventeenth century to 25 percent at the end of the eighteenth.[89] The number of French vessels coming from the Levant into Marseille dropped from 226 in 1747 to 140 in 1780.[90] The French had turned to trade in colonial goods like coffee and sugar.

TRADE IN COLONIAL GOODS: COFFEE AND SUGAR

Istanbul became a center of trade in colonial goods from the Atlantic world as well as from Asia due to the needs of its ruling class (the imperial kitchen) and its growing population. What was unique about its trade is that these goods (spices, dyes, coffee, and sugar as well as cotton textiles) continued arriving via the old maritime and caravan routes as well as from the New World. The history of coffee in Yemen—its consumption and trade from Aden to Cairo (1510); from there to Istanbul (1517), Damascus, and Aleppo (1532); and then to Marseille and Paris—sheds an important light on the diffusion, consumption, and cross-cultural significance of this beverage.

Egypt had traditionally supplied Mocha coffee from Yemen and sugar to Istanbul, and both Egyptian and Anatolian merchants and sea captains made fortunes in this trade (see chapter 5). Coffee had been an important beverage in Ottoman cities since the sixteenth century. The importing of Mocha coffee from Yemen by Arab traders played an important role in the economy of Cairo as well as that of Istanbul.[91] Muslim merchants like Isma'il Abu Takiyya made large fortunes by trading in coffee and sugar in Cairo in the seventeenth century.[92] He invested in the cultivation of sugar cane in Upper and Lower Egypt, production and refinement of sugar, and construction of coffeehouses in Cairo.

The popularity of coffeehouses among the lower-class residents caused anxiety among state elites. From time to time religious rulings (*fetvas*) were issued against the drinking of coffee, especially during the Kadizadeli era in the second half of the seventeenth century. The state also regularly issued orders to close down coffeehouses at times of urban upheavals.[93]

Despite these bans, the consumption of coffee and sugar became very widespread among the masses as well as the ruling class in Istanbul. Istanbul

Antoine-Ignace Melling, *A Public Coffeehouse in Tophane.* Photo courtesy of the Newberry Library, Chicago.

imported 600 tons of coffee a year in the early eighteenth century. This amount increased to 983 tons a year in 1765.[94] The estates of many residents of Galata contained at least one coffeepot during the second half of the eighteenth century, illustrating that coffee consumption was not limited to coffeehouses but was also conducted privately in homes.[95] French ambassadors also reported about the serving of coffee when they visited the Topkapi Palace.[96]

Jean Thévenot, when visiting Istanbul during the second half of the seventeenth century, was disgusted by the aromatic taste of coffee, which was largely unknown at that time in France.[97] However, the beverage soon did become popular in Europe. Coffeehouses spread from Istanbul to European cities like Vienna, London, and Marseille in the seventeenth century. Coffee arrived from Istanbul into Venice in 1615, Paris in 1634, Marseille in 1644, and London in 1651. Armenian traders opened the first coffeehouse in Marseille in 1672.[98] A Turkish envoy introduced coffee to his guests in Paris in 1669, and it soon became a popular drink as a remedy for some illnesses. Armenians dressed as Turks and carrying trays, cups, and coffeepots became the first peddlers and owners of coffeehouses in Paris and Marseille during the second half of the seventeenth century.[99] By the eighteenth century, Paris had six or seven hundred cafés. These establishments, such as the famous Café Procope, became rendezvous destinations for the bourgeoisie and the idle as well as for intellectuals like Diderot and Rousseau.

France imported 12,700 *quintals* (1 quinatl is 100 kg) of coffee every year from Cairo into Marseille.[100] By the eighteenth century, the consumption of coffee had tripled in France, but the nation had started importing the bulk of its coffee and sugar from Brazil, Java, the Bourbon Islands, and the islands of Cayenne and Martinique rather than from Cairo. In 1787, France imported 38,000 tons of coffee, much of it coming from the West Indies.[101] The merchants of Marseille imported coffee from Martinique into the Levant as well, a trade that acquired great significance and created large fortunes.

The consumption of sugar also increased in Europe and the Ottoman Empire due to the growing consumption of coffee in the seventeenth century. Sugar had originated in China and had spread to Persia and Egypt by the tenth century. The Arabs introduced it in Sicily and Valencia, and the crusaders imported it from Syria into Cyprus in the thirteenth century. Traditionally, sugar had been imported from Egypt as well as from Cyprus into Istanbul, but the available quantity was limited. Sugar reached the New World and Brazil in the early sixteenth century.[102] From Brazil, the Dutch brought it to Santo Domingo and Martinique, where it was produced in great quantities in the seventeenth century. Sugar consumption had become a fad in eighteenth-century Europe, although its production was slow and labor intensive. The Parisians consumed 5 kg of sugar per person per year before the French Revolution.[103]

Istanbul had two hundred Mocha coffee-sellers' shops (three hundred guild members) and seventy sugar-sellers' shops (guild members) that were organized into powerful guilds in the mid-seventeenth century.[104] Only five shops in the Egyptian market sold colonial coffee.[105] The number of coffeehouses in Galata alone had increased from 115 that employed 171 janissary-artisans in 1763 to 162 in 1792 (see chapter 1).[106] In addition, peddlers sold coffee on the streets.

However, tribal rebellions in Yemen disrupted the spice and coffee trade from the Red Sea and Egypt.[107] The shortage of coffee coming from Egypt led to price hikes in Istanbul. For example, when in January 1756 bad weather had caused interruptions in the importing of coffee from Cairo to Istanbul, merchants raised its price. The government then took possession of the existing supplies of coffee and distributed them among coffee sellers at a fixed price. When the flow of coffee resumed, the guild of coffee roasters (all Muslim) pledged at the court of Istanbul in January 1766 to sell coffee that they had purchased from importers at 64 para for 70 para per *kiyye* (1.28 kg), adding 6 para for the cost of roasting.[108] It is clear that the availability and price of coffee were important for the provisioning of Istanbul during this period.

Due to coffee shortages and increasing consumption, the government allowed the importing of colonial coffee from the French colonies in the West Indies (the Caribbean islands). Since the government promoted abundant supplies of coffee to keep prices low, it did not matter whether coffee was coming from Yemen or from the Atlantic world via Marseille.[109] French importing of colonial coffee into Istanbul increased two-fold from 1734 to the 1770s. French traders imported between 250 and 300 tons of colonial coffee worth half a million livres into the Levant in 1770s and 1780s; this coffee made up one-sixth of the total French imports into Galata during this period.[110]

An important aspect of French trade with the Levant was the importing of sugar from Brazil, which was refined in Marseille during the eighteenth century. Marseille had become a middle port among the Atlantic sea-borne trade, the Levant, and North Africa. America became the source of cheap coffee, tobacco (Virginia), and sugar, which were imported from the West Indies and Brazil by English and French ships into Europe and the Levant.[111] French refined sugar made up 2.5 percent of the imports from Marseille into Istanbul in the eighteenth century.[112] The consumption of refined sugar imported from Marseille into Istanbul increased from fifty tons in the 1720s to eight hundred tons by the end of the eighteenth century.[113]

Many European traders were involved in importing colonial coffee and sugar into Galata. For example, in April 1755, a French captain sent a petition to the Imperial Council stating that his ship transporting a cargo of woolen textiles, sugar, coffee, pepper, indigo, and gall nuts from Marseille to Istanbul had been stopped by English ships near Chios due to the state of war between France and England. But he had managed to sneak the ship away at night and make it to Salonica and then Istanbul despite constant harassment by English ships (see appendix).[114] In another recorded case, in 1787, a French merchant asked for permission from the ambassador to import 128 kg (100,000 *vukiye*) of coffee into Galata.[115]

It appears that Jewish dealers purchased colonial coffee from French importers in Galata. For example, in April 1785, the dragoman of the French Embassy presented a lawsuit to the court of Galata on behalf of French merchants Rigolof and Ari against a Jewish merchant, Matatya son of Yasef. The dragoman claimed that Matatya owed the French merchants 7,660 kuruş from the sale of coffee. Three Jewish witnesses, Yasef, Aron, and Yako sons of Musa, testified in favor of the French merchants[116] (see appendix).

In 1795, ships coming from Genoa, Livorno, Venice, and England imported 106,686 kg of colonial coffee into Galata.[117] Due to the growing demand, Istanbul's share of the import of colonial coffee from Marseille increased from between 100 and 150 tons in the 1740s to between 250 and 300 tons in the 1770s and 1780s (20 percent of total coffee imports).[118] American coffee imported from the Bourbon Islands and Martinique was of lower quality and price than mocha coffee imported from Yemen. However, the introduction of American coffee from the West Indies via Marseille into Istanbul, Izmir, Salonica, and other ports undermined the position of Mocha coffee imported from Yemen via Cairo into Istanbul and other ports.

The Seven Years' War (1756–63) between England and France over control of the colonies in America caused a serious disruption in French trade with the Levant (see chapter 5). The disruption led to a hike in the prices of French imports like woolens as well as in the prices of colonial goods in Ottoman ports.[119]

The sale of coffee was clearly a profitable business given the large number of coffeehouses in Galata and the increasing consumption of the beverage. Local coffee sellers kept pressuring the state to ban the importing of colonial coffee. For example, Ambassador Saint-Priest presented a petition to the Imperial Council in 1798 on behalf of French merchants importing sugar and spices into Istanbul. He stated that the guild of sherbet sellers and spice sellers in the Yeni Çarşı in Pera wanted to monopolize the sale of their goods at fixed prices, whereas according to the ahdnames, the French traders had the right to sell their goods to anyone at any price that they wished.[120] This case demonstrates competition among guilds over the purchase of French sugar and spices and the attempts of French importers to sell their goods at market prices. Clearly, the provisionist policies of the state were upheld by the guilds, which resented competition from the French importers. But the state had to allow a certain degree of competition to boost supplies.

The state sometimes issued bans on the import of colonial coffee. For example, in May 1799, the state banned the importing of Frankish coffee by Russian merchants into Istanbul. The Russians were newcomers in the trade of Istanbul and thus did not enjoy as much state support. The guild of coffee sellers constantly complained about the importing of colonial coffee undercutting their business. In response to these complaints, the state tried to limit the sale of colonial coffee to only certain shops in Galata. In 1763, an imperial order allowed French sugar and coffee to only be sold by Muslim guilds in special shops in Yeni Çarşı in Pera.[121]

But French traders also exerted pressure on the Ottoman state to expand their markets. In 1766, the French ambassador, Vergennes, submitted a petition to the Imperial Council on behalf of the French traders asking for permission for them to be able to sell colonial coffee in two shops in addition to the five existing shops where they currently could sell it in Galata and to sell it in shops outside Galata, a practice that was banned. He stated that demand for colonial coffee by janissaries, non-Muslims, and Europeans who frequented coffeehouses in Galata was on the rise. The imperial order issued to the kadi of Galata stated that French traders had imported 2,560 kg of colonial coffee into Galata in 1763. But in response to the petition of the coffee sellers in the Egyptian market, the Council decided that the French traders would not be allowed to sell coffee anywhere other than the five shops in Galata. However, an imperial order was issued in June 1766 to allow the sale of French coffee in two more shops in Galata since the practice would not harm the business of local traders who sold Mocha coffee in the Egyptian market in Istanbul.[122]

Despite the resistance of local traders, French ships continued importing coffee into Galata. For example, in 1770, a French ship carrying coffee, sugar, and lead was attacked and looted on its way from Izmir to Istanbul, according to a petition of the French ambassador.[123] From these cases, it is clear that French traders were increasingly importing colonial goods into Galata in the last decades of the eighteenth century. In 1797, the head of the guild of porters in Galata brought a lawsuit against French traders to the court of Galata in the presence of the dragoman of the embassy, Francesco Frangini. He stated that the porters had drawn up a contract with French merchants in 1791 listing the wages they were to be paid to transport the cargo of French ships to storehouses in the customs station in Galata. For the cost of transporting specific items of cargo, they charged different rates. The cargo of the French ship included colonial coffee, Mocha coffee, powdered sugar, spices like pepper, gall nuts, indigo, sherbets, spirits, almonds, woolen textiles, tin, lead, iron, and a variety of paper from Genoa and France. Obviously, the market share of woolen textiles had drastically dropped and had been replaced by colonial goods from the West (coffee, sugar) and East Indies (spices, dyes, sherbets) as well as by goods from Europe (tin, lead, paper, spirits). Like England, France had largely become an importer of colonial goods into Istanbul. The organized action of the guild of porters in Galata and their demand for specific wages for every item of cargo that they transported for French traders also reflect the growing power of the working-class people who worked for wages when servicing European traders in Galata who imported colonial goods at the end of the eighteenth century.[124]

However, domestic traders continued to import Mocha coffee from Egypt into Istanbul. For example, in 1799, a ship belonging to two Ottoman non-Muslim merchants, Karabet and Dimitri, had been transporting 5,337 kg of coffee, 3,810 kg of sugar, 2,709 kg of cotton, and 226 kg of cotton yarn from Alexandria to Istanbul when it became involved in an accident with imperial galleons.[125] In a petition submitted to the court of Rhodes, the owners of the ship and goods, Karabet and Dimitri, claimed that the ship had barely made it to Chios after the accident and that some of the goods put in storage in Aynoz had gone bad, and the rest could not be sold. They stated that they could not find a ship to transport the remaining goods to Istanbul in time to salvage them. An imperial order was then issued for the goods of said merchants to be carried to Istanbul since provisioning the capital with coffee and sugar was of utmost importance to the authorities.[126] The state, however, had to protect the interests of its own merchants before opening its markets to European traders and goods, a situation that was becoming increasingly more difficult.

We still lack empirical studies to compare the importing of Mocha coffee into Istanbul with that of colonial coffee. It is not clear whether the average Istanbul resident outside Galata consumed colonial coffee and how the different coffee beans and prices affected consumption. Nelly Hanna's pioneering work on the activities and wealth of a Muslim merchant family, the Abu Taqiyya family, in Cairo in the seventeenth century has revised the picture of the decline of the Red Sea region during the European expansion in trade and the continuity of Muslim commercial networks in Cairo.[127] Clearly, the guild of coffee sellers resisted the domination of European coffee and tried to restrict its sale and consumption to Galata for some time. The provisionist policies of the state did not always coincide with the interests of local dealers. After having faced the resistance of local traders, European traders had to turn to other activities to make money.

INFORMAL BANKERS TO PASHAS: BANKRUPTCIES
AND OUTSTANDING DEBTS

Due to a shortage of cash and the draining of silver coins from Ottoman ports to Iran and India, Ottoman traders largely operated on credit. In addition, money lending had become widespread in Ottoman ports due to expansion of tax farming. The state resorted to internal borrowing through the institution of tax farming while tax farmers themselves borrowed from Ottoman Armenian and Jewish money changers and French traders to purchase tax farms or to pay taxes to the government. The records of estates of many Ottoman traders and sea captains in Galata and Istanbul show a great deal of money-lending activities as well as transactions based on credit.[128] In addition, many lawsuits presented to the Islamic court of Galata involved outstanding claims brought by merchants. Almost everyone with a small amount of cash, including women, became an informal banker or borrowed money in the Ottoman Empire.[129] However, informal banking networks depended on trust and legal protection. The use of guarantors for financial transactions that used credit was also very important, and defaults led to lawsuits in the courts. Cash vakfs had a stronger legal foundation as charitable institutions than informal bankers did and charged lower interest rates of between 5 and 10 percent, while non-Muslim money changers (*sarrafs*) could charge as high as 20 percent. At times of economic crisis, defaulting also became widespread, so the courts had to promote settlement even between Ottoman and European traders to prevent total bankruptcy. Elena Frangakis-Syrett has pointed out two recurring monetary problems in Ottoman markets: the shortage of specie (coins) and currency volatility due to the shortage of liquidity and currency debasement during the eighteenth century.[130]

In the Ottoman Empire, merchant credit was largely based on informal financial networks that were based on trust and stretched from Ottoman to European ports. For example, French traders and diplomats in Istanbul who had a surplus of cash (because they imported more than they exported from Istanbul) were involved in a variety of activities to make money in the Levant, although their ventures were not always successful. When Ambassador Vergennes arrived in Pera in May 1755 to begin his tenure, one of his important tasks was to set the financial affairs of the French community in order. He went over the archives of the embassy and reviewed the personal papers of his predecessor, Rolland Puchot Comte de Alleurs, who had been the French ambassador from 1747 to 1754. Comte de Alleurs had married a Polish aristocratic woman and led an expensive lifestyle in Pera. He died from epilepsy in a state of bankruptcy in Pera in 1754 and was buried in the chapel of St. Louis at the French Embassy.[131] He had accumulated a debt of 140,000 *écus* owed to the French nation in addition to 50,000 *écus* owed to Ottoman traders in Pera. From the reviewing the inventory of Comte de Alleurs's estate, Vergennes discovered that the previous ambassador had spent 50,000 *écus* acquiring furniture and luxury goods for himself and his family. In addition he had spent 70,356 *livres* giving sumptuous gifts like gold watches, silver bowls, chandeliers, torchlights, chinaware, porcelain wares, silk fabrics, and tapestries to Sultan Osman III (1754–57), his grand vizier, the chief naval officer, and other officials.[132] He had also been involved in the grain trade and speculation and had lost his investment when he shipped low-quality grain from the Levant to Marseille in 1752. In addition, the delay in the ship's arrival in Marseille had caused a price drop. The difference in the prices of wheat in the Levant and in Marseille and the low quality of the grain led to a big commercial disaster and Comte de Alleurs's bankruptcy. His bankruptcy underscores the involvement of French ambassadors in trade as well as their overspending to maintain expensive lifestyles in the late eighteenth century.

The giving of lavish gifts to the sultan, his grand vizier, and all kinds of other officials in order to renew the ahdnames had also become a big financial burden for the French and other European ambassadors. Ambassador Vergennes himself had to provide expensive gifts for the palace when he negotiated the renewal of the Ahdname of 1740. The expenses of the embassy in the eighteenth century had also increased to cover the cost of housing the ambassador's family as well as secretaries, dragomans, and servants. The French Embassy housed seventy-eight people, including Ottoman dragomans and janissaries who guarded the embassy.[133]

The ambassadors had to meet the expenses of maintaining a large staff, a luxurious lifestyle, and a rich social life. The French Embassy frequently hosted large dinner parties for other ambassadors in Pera and Ottoman officials. In addition, the ambassador had to use some funds from the nation to aid bankrupt French merchants from time to time and to pay fines to Ottoman authorities. Therefore, getting involved in money lending as well as in selling berats to Ottoman subjects became a trend among all European ambassadors in Pera.[134]

Transactions conducted on credit had become widespread in Ottoman ports due to people's economic difficulties and the shortage of cash. Money lending even among average men and women for daily needs had become the norm.[135] European traders became involved in lending money since they had a surplus of cash. For example, in 1776, Yasef Baruh, the scribe of the French Embassy, defaulted on the payment of his debt to an English merchant, William Jackson. He was then imprisoned at the Swedish Embassy at the request of Jackson. Baruh pledged to pay his debt to Jackson by transferring

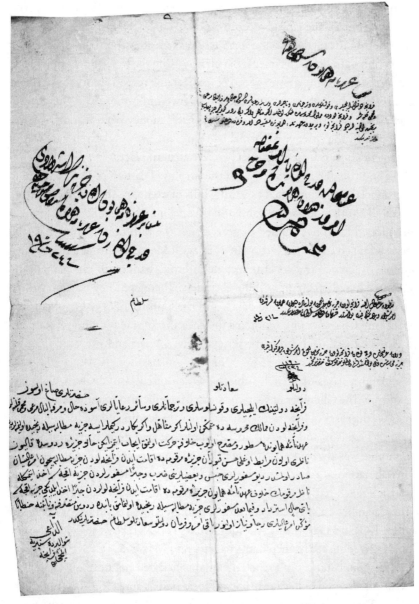

Petition submitted by Ambassador Saint-Priest to the Imperial Council regarding the charging of poll tax on French subjects in Rhodes in 1776. Courtesy of the Başbakanlık Archives, Istanbul.

it to those individuals who owed him money, a certain Tahir Agha, who owed him 1,037 kuruş, and a certain Zonana, who owed him 17,177 kuruş. Baruh submitted five documents to Jackson regarding these debts for collection.[136] In lieu of payment, Baruh was using the well-known practice of *havale,* or employing a letter of credit transferring responsibility for payment of his debt through proxy to others who owed him money.[137] The government also used the *havale* system to transfer money from distant areas to Istanbul. In the absence of formal banking, this was a relatively safe way of paying debts or transferring cash between distant places.

In addition, French traders used the surplus of cash in ports like Istanbul in financial operations such as issuing bills of exchange that they drew from Istanbul to other ports like Izmir and became informal bankers to Ottoman grandees. Eldem has studied in great detail the bills of exchange that connected French traders in Ottoman ports with Marseille through these transactions.[138] French traders also became informal bankers to tax farmers and operated based on credit with local traders. Therefore, they became vulnerable to defaults, outstanding debts, and the bankruptcies of Ottoman subjects. The Chamber of Commerce in Marseille kept files on houses of commerce that had declared bankruptcy in the Levant and prepared detailed inventories and lists of claims.[139] French ambassadors had to handle the bankruptcy cases of French subjects, which often also involved Ottoman creditors. The Chamber of Commerce in Marseille also contained numerous files on the cases of French merchants from the leading houses of commerce (such as Le Roy and Gazan) in Istanbul that had gone bankrupt.[140] The Chamber was always worried about the consequences of bankruptcies on the French nation as a whole and the imposition of extraordinary taxes (*avanias*) on the French nation by Ottoman authorities and angry Turkish creditors. The Chamber established a commission to look into the affairs of the house of Le Roy and Gazan in 1751, liquidate its goods to pay the creditors, and obtain freedom for its merchants to return to Marseille.

The circumstances of French merchants had deteriorated considerably in Syria and Egypt due to the rapacity of local pashas and governors. For example, in December 1750, the French ambassador, Rolland Alleurs (1747–54), and some French merchants had lent 37,500 kuruş to Seyyid Ahmed Pasha, the district governor of Sidon in Syria.[141] The governor had pledged to repay the loan within 121 days, but he had refused to pay the debt for three years despite several requests. In a petition to the Imperial Council, the French ambassador stated that, since the governor was a close friend of the vizier and had been in dire straits, he and the French merchants had tried to help him out. But the unpaid debt had accumulated interest of more than 12,500 akçe in three years. Meanwhile, the governor had died, and Ambassador Alleurs was now claiming that he was owed the debt by petitioning the Imperial Council. It is not clear from the petition whether the ambassador was able to collect the money from the heirs of the governor.

Meanwhile, the circumstances of French merchants in Sidon continued to deteriorate. The local Azmzade family had become very powerful as governors of Syria in the eighteenth century. A year after the previous petition, in 1751, the district governor of Sidon in Syria, Mehmed Pasha Azmzade, had forced the brokers of French merchants to purchase silk from him, charging them 10,500 akçe. But when the brokers were unable to pay that amount, he imprisoned them and had them beaten.[142] Consequently, the French consul in Sidon submitted a petition to the Porte about the governor's abuse of the French brokers. The pasha refused to free the brokers before he collected 4,250 kuruş from their steward and their guards. An imperial order was then issued to the district governors of Sidon and Damascus to follow the shari'a and respect the terms of the ahdname. These two cases of default and extortion by two different district governors of Sidon, one involving the default of payment of a large debt for three years and another having to do with extortion and violence against French brokers, illustrate the extent to which French merchants were being mistreated in Sidon in 1755. These cases also underscore how weak the French consul's ability to enforce the articles of the ahdname had become and the inability of the Ottoman central government to persuade local pashas and governors in Syria to protect European merchants and pay their debts.

Despite their occasional mistreatment, French traders were involved as informal bankers to leading merchants in Syria as well. Economic conditions in Syria also played a role in the defaulting of local traders. For example, in 1792, a French merchant named Kulovini claimed that he was owed 7,500 kuruş by Shaykh Muhammad Azhari, the head of merchants (reis ul-tüccar), in Latakia. The shaykh was also indebted to the customs collector of tobacco in Latakia in the amount of 52,300 kuruş as well as to two customs collectors in Istanbul in the amounts of 52,000 kuruş and 26,000 kuruş (a total of 78,000 kuruş) from the dues of cotton. He was clearly involved in the trade of tobacco and cotton and had defaulted on paying French traders as well as customs collectors. Shaykh Muhammad was subsequently arrested and imprisoned in Latakia and was forced to pay his debt to the government. The

French merchant was demanding priority for the payment of his claim of funds due to him from Shaykh Muhammad according to the terms of the French ahdname.[143]

The conditions of French traders in Syria and Egypt had deteriorated considerably in the eighteenth century due to local conditions (see epilogue). Bankruptcies among European traders and even among consuls had become an important risk of doing business in the Levant. As mentioned, in 1740, the French House of Le Roy and Gazan had declared bankruptcy in Galata, and the proceedings continued into 1765.[144] One of its members, Jean Pere, owed 14,000 *piastres* to the tax collector of the Morea. After his death in December 1730, his sons turned to the Istanbul branch to pay the debt so that the French nation would not be subject to a penalty (*avania*).[145] In the same year, the French House of Boisson and Company went bankrupt in Salonica. English consuls in the Syrian port of Latakia and the Palestinian town of Acre also went bankrupt in 1758 and 1768, respectively.[146] The vicious cycle— namely, the financial involvement of French ambassadors, traders, and consuls in the economic activities of Ottoman elites and traders—exposed French traders to the ups and downs of the Ottoman economy. As traders they were only involved with brokers and upper-class consumers, but as financiers they were increasingly exposed to disruptions in the economic cycles of the Ottoman economy due to wars, local rebellions, and environmental disasters as well as fraud and default.

The petitions and lawsuits of French traders illustrate that in their day-to-day commercial activities, they were often unable to collect outstanding debts from local traders and had to settle for lower payment after taking a case to court. Moreover, much commercial activity was carried out on credit, and guarantors often had to be involved to underwrite a deal and act as a form of insurance. Although the kadi of Galata often encouraged settlement of outstanding debts involving Ottoman and European traders, it appears that when bankruptcies only involved European subjects, the Chamber of Commerce and the ambassadors became involved, as the actions of Ambassador Vergennes in the case of former Ambassador Comte de Alleurs demonstrate.

In a petition in December 1777 presented by the French *chargé d'affairs* to the Imperial Council, he stated that Dovire, a French merchant from Galata, had traveled to Edirne for business. Dovire claimed that a fez seller named Mehter Odabaşı owed him 1,987 kuruş. But the latter had refused to pay the debt, probably after purchasing the products from Dovire. Dovire and Dinar, another French merchant from Galata, were also claiming that a janissary in Edirne, Ibrahimoğlu Emin Agha, owed them 650 kuruş, possibly also from the sale of fez. The French ambassador was asking that an imperial order be issued to the kadi and *bostancıbaşı* of Edirne for payment of the debts in accordance with the shari'a.[147] Again, it is clear that French fez sellers from Galata had been involved in sales to a trader and janissary in Edirne and were unable to collect their debts. In another petition presented by the French ambassador in December 1810, he stated that a French merchant in Istanbul named Petro Jinkerya had been owed 90,134 kuruş by the district governor of Eflak (Wallachia, now in Romania), Kostantin, for seven years. The ambassador had sent several requests and letters trying to obtain payment, but the governor had refused to pay the debt. The ambassador was asking for an imperial order to collect the debt owed to the French merchant.[148]

Sometimes, members of the French nation sued each other for outstanding debts and took their cases to the Imperial Council. For example, in May 1795, a certain Vincent, representing Floranvil, a French merchant in Galata, claimed that a certain French merchant who resided in Aleppo owed Floranvil 1,883.5 kuruş and for eight months had refused to pay the amount upon request. Vincent was asking that an imperial order be issued to the governor and kadi of Aleppo to bring the French merchant to court and to force him to pay the debt to Floranvil's agent in accordance with the shari'a. An imperial order was issued to the kadi of Aleppo accordingly.[149] It is interesting that in this case, a French merchant from Galata was claiming that an outstanding debt was due him from a French merchant in Aleppo by submitting a petition to the Imperial Council rather than to the French consul in Aleppo. It is possible that the fees involved in presenting the case to the French consul might have been too high or that the French consul lacked the authority to claim these debts. Moreover, the kadi court in Aleppo rather than the consular court was in charge of collecting the debt of the French merchant in Galata from another French merchant. In another example, in May 1795, the agent of a French merchant in Marseille who lived in Istanbul submitted a petition to the Imperial Council claiming 25,000 kuruş from a French merchant in Izmir who had refused to pay the debt on time.[150]

Normally, these types of lawsuits involving any French subjects would have been submitted to consular courts, in this case, the one in Izmir. But it is possible that the consular courts could not resolve the issue, so the merchant in Marseille decided to forward it to the Imperial Council via his agent in Istanbul. Clearly, the plural legal system in Ottoman ports allowed Ottoman and European subjects to forum shop, and the Imperial Council held higher jurisdiction than the consular courts did.

French traders had also established an important commercial presence in the Morea and had become informal bankers to local notables. Both Muslim and Greek subjects and notables borrowed money from the French consuls and provided guarantors. In a petition to the Imperial Council, this one in 1763, Mehmed Elçi Paşzade, a resident of Eğriboz (the island of Euboea in present-day Greece) and the guarantor of a group of residents from Kızıl Hisar and Athens, stated that seven *reaya* (all Muslim subjects) and eight Greek *koçabaşıs* (local notables) had come to Eğriboz in 1750. They had borrowed 4,500 kuruş from two French consuls in Eğriboz and Athens and 2,000 kuruş from the dragoman of the French consul (Anton) to use the money for the affairs of their district. Mehmed Elçi Paşazade had stood as guarantor to them, but they had refused to repay the funds within the sixty-one days on which they had agreed. Mehmed, the guarantor, was asking for an imperial order directing the district governor of Eğriboz, Mustafa Pasha, to force the Turks and Greeks to pay the debt. The French ambassador had also presented a petition to the Imperial Council regarding this case. As a result, in August 1763, an imperial order was issued to Mustafa Pasha to make the fifteen men pay the full 6,500 kuruş to the French consuls.[151] It is interesting that in this case, it was the Muslim guarantor who submitted the petition against the fifteen debtors who had defaulted on their payment to the two French consuls and their dragoman for thirteen years. We learn from this case that the French consuls and their dragoman were acting as informal bankers to local Muslim residents as well as to Greek local notables, using a local Muslim guarantor as a surety.

Muslim notables also borrowed from French residents in the Morea. For example, In 1790, Isma'il Bey, the son of deceased vizier Çatalçalı Ali Pasha, had borrowed a sum of money from the dragoman of the French consul in the Morea, a certain Hayim Goufini.[152] Isma'il Bey owed an outstanding debt of 19,340 kuruş to the dragoman. Together with his friend Abdulğefur Bey, he later had taken another loan of 20,000 kuruş to purchase a lifetime tax farm (*malikane*) in Arkadiye, a district of the Morea. But Isma'il Bey had not paid any of his outstanding debt to the dragoman, even after he had been recalled to Istanbul. The dragoman had subsequently traveled to Istanbul to seek redress from Ambassador Choiseul-Gouffier. This case nicely illustrates the informal banking activities of French consular agents and the financial transaction between a French dragoman and a Muslim local notable and tax farmer in the Morea and the latter's subsequent defaulting on the loan in the late eighteenth century.[153]

The potential for collusion among the local tax collectors, local traders, and judges against Europeans was higher in the provinces than it was in Istanbul. For example, when French merchants from Galata were planning to travel to Bursa and Balıkesir, the French ambassador, Saint-Priest, submitted a petition asking for permission for them to travel that guaranteed protection of the life and property of the French merchants. He also wanted any lawsuits that might arise from their travel to be heard in the Imperial Council if they involved an amount higher then 4,000 akçe rather than in the Islamic court for fear of collusion between the kadi and local residents. An imperial order was issued to the kadi of Bursa and the deputy judge of Balıkesir accordingly in 1774.[154] Clearly, in provincial towns French merchants felt more vulnerable due to the distance between these towns and the port cities, where a sizable French community resided and a consul could represent their interests.

French merchants were certainly not getting rich from their commercial activities and financial transactions as informal bankers to Ottoman pashas. In fact, sometimes claiming outstanding debts put them at great risk. For example, in 1815, a French merchant named Bon Fort had been murdered by a local Greek man, Anaştaş Paskali, in a village in Büyük Çekmeçe, a dependency of Istanbul. It is possible that the French trader had gone to claim an outstanding debt from a Greek trader, an action that had led to a brawl and the Frenchman's death from a bullet wound. The villagers had reported his death to the authorities. The meager items in his estate included a horse, a used shirt and cloaks, a used shawl, a tobacco bag, a tin spoon and fork, a linen bag, a pipe, an umbrella, a Circassian knife, an old cloak, a cup and dish, a rain cloak, an umbrella, a pair of boots, a snuff box, a watch, eighty-four quarter gold coins, one Egyptian gold coin and ten paras (sixty para equaled an akçe), and forty-four receipts and documents in a bag.[155] Although by the early nineteenth century, French trade had resumed in the Levant, the man's modest belongings stood in sharp contrast to the luxurious lifestyles of the ambassadors and their large households in Pera.

The Ottoman state practiced a combination of trade polices until the end of the eighteenth century: 1) laissez-faire policies in the Mediterranean trade ports like Galata and 2) protectionist policies in domestic trade on the Black Sea and the Red Sea. In provisioning the capital city with foodstuff and raw materials, the Ottoman Empire practiced protectionist policies as well as created monopolies in the trade of foodstuff on the Black Sea and the Red Sea until the late eighteenth century. As I have shown in chapter 5, the state placed bans on the exporting of strategic goods and raw materials such as hides, cotton yarn, raw silk, lead, and iron as well as on the exporting of olive oil to protect the local textile, leather, arms, and soap industries.

French traders also had to deal with the actions of local guilds and traders, who did not welcome competition with European goods. Their activities also resulted in tensions among their local agents and other guilds. In a 1795 petition to the Imperial Council, the guild of Jewish dealers who imported European shawls stated that a certain Isma'il Agha, the steward of the guild of woolen textile (*sof*) dealers, was demanding two rolls (*top*) of shawl per ten rolls that the Jewish dealers sold.[156] Isma'il Agha also was claiming that the Jewish shawl sellers were part of his guild. The head of the Jewish guild added that his members were already paying the woolen textile dealers' guild twenty kuruş per month (240 kuruş per year), but the steward was demanding more payment in kind from them, claiming jurisdiction over them. After the hearing, an imperial order was issued to stop the woolen textile dealers from interfering in the business of the shawl sellers and from charging them a single kuruş.[157] In this case, the state supported the free trade of European shawls and rejected protectionism.

The case also demonstrates that Jewish dealers played a prominent role in the sale of European textiles in Galata. The state divided the rights to sell local and European woolens among different guilds and shops. Although in some cases the guilds in charge of distributing local textiles had great power and influence, in this case the state supported the Jewish dealers who were importing European shawls to maintain the division between the two guilds and to protect local traders importing European goods. In the late eighteenth century, the state allowed twenty-four Jewish stores to sell European shawls in Istanbul and Galata. Thus, the distribution and sale of European imports were also divided among guilds.

The Ottoman state also practiced protectionism in the manufacture of luxury items like silk textiles and placed bans on the export of raw silk. To meet the growing local demand for silk textiles, the Ottoman state continued to import raw silk from Iran during the eighteenth century. The local silk production expanded in Bursa, Aleppo, Chios, Istanbul, and Antioch in order to meet the demands of a growing middle-class population. French silk textiles claimed a marginal share (less than 10 percent) in Ottoman markets.[158]

The Ottoman ruling class consumed a variety of silk textiles, woolens produced locally and imported from abroad (Iran, Venice, India, France), shawls, and furs. The estates of Ottoman elites like Grand Vizier Halil Pasha contained great quantities of woolens and shawls as well as silks.[159] The patterns of consumption among the residents of Galata included a good variety of local products. For example, the estate of a deceased Ottoman man, Ali Beşe b. Süleyman, who had died in Beşiktaş, a dependency of Galata, in 1765, included among other things a variety of woolen textiles and shawls from Iran and North Africa.[160] In another case, in May 1766, the court of Galata made an inventory of the goods of furrier Vasil son of Mihal, who had died in the quarter of Sultan Bayezid in Galata. Vasil had not been a rich man, but he was typical of the small traders in Galata. His estate included a variety of woolen garments, furs, a Persian sash, kitchenware, and bedding. The total cash value of his estate amounted to 6,580 akçe, which was divided among his widow, son, and two daughters.[161]

The state set up textile workshops in Istanbul to meet the demands of a growing population by bringing weavers from Bursa, Chios, and Salonica in 1703, 1720, and 1777. These two workshops, which had sixteen looms, were located in Fenerkapi in Tahtakale.[162] Another textile workshop was located near Mahmud Pasha in Istanbul proper. The stamp tax on the three silk workshops in Istanbul, which was 180,000 akçe per year in 1721, increased by 120,000 akçe and reached 300,000 akçe in 1740. It was farmed out to Mustafa and Ahmed, sons of Ali Efendi.[163] In 1741, the tax farm of the stamp tax on the woolen and silk workshops had increased from 300,000 akçe to 783,560 akçe, more than doubling. It was then farmed out as a *malikane* (lifetime tax farm) to the same Muslim men.[164] This increase may have been due to an increase in production as well as a rise in the amount of the tax farm's value. It appears that due to this large increase in the stamp tax, the guild of silk sellers was trying to have the silk woven outside the designated workshops in order to avoid paying the stamp tax to the tax farmers, according to Mustafa's petition.

In 1744, 1745, and 1762, journeymen from the guild of embroiderers presented a petition to the Imperial Council stating that putting-out merchants were hiring unskilled Jewish and Armenian men and women to dye, twist, and embroider low-quality silk textiles in their homes. The putting-out merchants hired unskilled men and women outside the guilds, sometimes in villages, to pay them lower wages than what artisans would have demanded to do the work. These men and women worked from their homes and were not under the control of guilds that could also demand a host of dues. The journeymen also complained about the imposition of new taxes by their guild masters in 1763.[165] According to Julia Pardoe, all the silk embroiderers in Istanbul in 1835 were Armenian women, who were not members of guilds.[166]

Julia Pardoe, an English resident in Istanbul, described the high demand for Bursa silks as late as 1835 in the grand bazaar of Istanbul in the following manner:

> The Broussa silk [textiles] occupy a very considerable street, as the produce in the celebrated looms of the city is greatly esteemed by the Turks, both for the pattern and texture.[167]

To protect its own silk industry in Istanbul and Bursa, the Ottoman state placed bans on the export of raw silk to Europe in the nineteenth century. For example, in 1804, the state placed a ban on the sale of raw silk produced around Bursa to foreign merchants. A certain Yalamaoğlu Al-Hac Mile who had violated this ban was punished and expelled to Bozca Ada (island of Tenedos).[168] Another imperial order banned the sale of raw silk to European merchants in 1804 in Bursa and Aleppo.[169] Raw silk produced in the district of Pazar Köy around Bursa had to be supplied to Istanbul to meet the demands of the populace in 1804.[170]

It is not clear whether wealthy merchants also invested in establishing textile workshops in Istanbul. Although the state provided the initial investment, it farmed out these workshops to private individuals. But the state faced serious challenges in operating and collecting dues from the textile workshops that it had farmed out to local businessmen. For example, in 1720, the state provided 47,408 kuruş of capital to a certain Mişu (a zimmi) to set up a woolen textile workshop in Istanbul as a tax farm. Mişu had farmed out each loom for 300 kuruş a year, but he had failed to pay a single akçe to the state, thus accumulating the state taxes in his own possession. The state then established a supervisor to collect the dues and provided more capital upon request. But according to the report of the supervisor, Mişu refused to pay the state taxes, thus wasting state funds. The chief of merchants, a certain Huseyn Agha, then took over the workshop with all the tools. The number of looms increased from six to sixteen in two years, demonstrating the demand for local woolens produced by the workshop and the success of the new manager in expanding operation and production.

Clearly, the chief of merchants' investment in the workshop was a success story. But the support of the state in supplying the workshop with affordable raw materials and initial funds was also crucial. The state issued orders for the supplying of raw wool as well as dyes from villages in Anatolia and Rumelia. The state also established guilds of weavers, dyers, and textile printers (*basmacı*) that were attached to the workshop.[171]

In 1723, the state issued orders for the supplying of sheep's wool from villages in Anatolia and Rumelia at a fixed price of six akçe per 1.28 kg for the workshop in Istanbul and placed a ban on the sale of sheep's wool to European merchants.[172] The state played an important role in the investment, operation, and supplying of raw materials to this workshop in Istanbul. It practiced a level of protectionism to ensure the supply of cheap raw materials.

However, despite the existing bans, French merchants continued purchasing sheep's wool from villages in Anatolia and Rumelia. For example, in September 1777, a French merchant from Galata traveled to the town of Bandırma near Mihaliç to purchase sheep's wool and loaded it onto his ship to transport it to Istanbul. But due to a storm, the ship had to pull into Eregli and unload the wool before it got spoiled. The commander of the port had taken possession of the wool (12,656 kg), claiming customs dues for the second time. As a result, the French chargé d' affairs was requesting that an imperial order be issued to the commander to return the wool to the French merchant without asking him to pay customs dues again, in accordance with the current ahdname.[173]

Clearly, there were profits to be made by French merchants in importing sheep's wool to Istanbul to supply local workshops or to export it to Marseille. France imported about 1,100 bales of woolen textiles into Istanbul in the 1720s, driving out higher quality English and Dutch woolens.[174] By 1760, French woolen imports into Istanbul had reached 1,900 bales per year. But this trade collapsed during the last decades of the eighteenth century, largely due to Anglo-French conflicts (1756–63) and the Russo-Ottoman Wars that caused an economic crisis in Istanbul. The collapse may have also been the result of competition with locally produced woolens. During the Anglo-French War in 1755, the price of French woolen textiles had increased by 30 akçe per *zira*[175], according to the French ambassador's report to the Imperial Council, due to a 20 percent increase in the cost of transportation and insurance.[176] Local competition might have played a role as well since the price of French woolens might have been too high for the vast majority of Istanbul's residents. Nevertheless, French woolens were in great demand among the elites, and profits could still be made from their trade. For example, in September 1784, a French merchant, Kuzinary, loaded three horse loads (*deng*) of woolens onto the boat of a certain Ali Captain in Izmir to send them to his partner in Istanbul. But the chief of police (*subaşı*) of Sadd al-Bahr, a castle on the Dardanelles, confiscated the cargo of woolens on its way to Istanbul. When the French consul in Boğaz Hisar demanded the woolens, the police chief claimed that 22 *pastav* (715 meters) were available, but the rest (15 *pastav*/487 meters) of the woolens had been stolen.[177]The ambassador was demanding the rest of the 15 bales of woolens by petitioning the Imperial Council for their return. An imperial order was then issued to respect the articles of the ahdname regarding the safety of French merchants and their goods but also stating that during the Russo-Ottoman Wars, safe conduct for European ships on their way to Istanbul was not always possible. However, despite their high quality, European woolens could never achieve the same level of demand and consumption as domestic textiles had in Istanbul.[178] Eldem has pointed out the decline in the importing of French manufactured goods such as woolen cloth during the last decade of the eighteenth century and the turn to the importing of colonial coffee and sugar as well as raw materials such as dyes (indigo and cochineal) for the growing local textile industry in Istanbul and Anatolia. He has also underscored the inability of French silk textiles to claim a share larger than 10 percent in Ottoman markets due to competition from local silk textiles as well as from those from Persia and Venice.[179] Therefore, the penetration of French and English textiles into Ottoman markets outside the big cities did not take place until the late nineteenth century.

English and French merchants switched from importing woolen textiles to importing colonial goods from India and the Caribbean. Indian textiles, especially muslins, which were used in making turbans, were always very popular in Istanbul. England also imported cheap Indian cotton, calicoes from Gujerat, and muslins into Europe and the Levant. Calicoes had become two-thirds of the English East India Company's imports into Europe by 1700.[180] In 1816, French traders were importing Indian goods such as shawls, fine cotton textiles, and muslin into Istanbul.[181]

In addition to English and French merchants' imports, local traders imported Indian cotton textiles into Galata. These imports caused tensions among local producers and guilds. For example, in 1772, a group of local merchants in Galata who imported Indian textiles like cotton faced the intervention of the guild of muslin sellers.[182] In a petition the merchants submitted to the Imperial Council, they stated that they had already paid the customs dues on the imports from India but that the guild of muslin sellers was demanding illegal dues from them, claiming them as part of their guild. Upon the merchants' refusal to pay the dues, the guild of muslin sellers had boycotted their merchandise, causing losses for them and for the customs revenue. The merchants were demanding an imperial order to stop the guild of muslin sellers from intervening in their business. Upon receiving an imperial order, the superintendant of customs of Galata, Al-Hac Emin, invited the head of the muslin-sellers guild and some guild members to the customs house to investigate the lawsuit. He ordered the head of the muslin-sellers guild to stop interfering in the affairs of the merchants importing Indian textiles.

In this case, the local muslin sellers were obviously trying to undermine the traders who imported textiles from India by forcing them to pay dues to their guild, but the state supported the importers since their merchandise was in high demand and thus produced customs dues for the state coffers. The state was clearly concerned about the abundance of muslin and in this instance did not practice protectionism, as was the case with the European shawl sellers, despite the monopolistic attempts of the other guilds.

Moreover, in the nineteenth century the export of local cotton textiles overtook that of Indian and English woolens. Although the local production of cheaper cotton textiles continued and offered important competition for English and Indian textiles, English cotton yarn and textile imports continued to grow by several folds during the nineteenth century. In fact, the importing of cheaper and better quality English yarns by local producers rose after 1790 and tripled during the first quarter of the century. Most town dwellers and villagers in Anatolia consumed locally manufactured cotton textiles made with English yarn, while the rich wore European cotton textiles and woolens in the first half of the century.[183] But English cotton textiles were quickly spreading to the Anatolian countryside due to the lifting of bans on imports, leading to the decline of local textile production. By the second half of the nineteenth century, Turkey had become the chief supplier of raw cotton to English manufacturers due to the American Civil War, which interrupted cheap cotton production in the plantations in the South of America.

An important question in Ottoman economic history has been discovering the reason for the long absence of Ottoman Muslim traders (other than those from Bosnia) from Europe and the lack of reciprocity in the ahdnames since the late sixteenth century. Ottoman merchants claimed a very small place in European trade since they faced great challenges in most European ports. The Levant Companies barred Ottoman merchants from trading in London, Amsterdam, and Marseille, and the ahdnames were not reciprocal during the seventeenth and eighteenth centuries. Moreover, the Ottoman government did not have embassies and consular representation in European capitals and ports to defend the rights of its merchants until the late eighteenth century. European ports such as Marseille were closed to Ottoman merchants, in contrast with Galata and Izmir, which were open ports.

Benjamin Arbel and Eric Dursteler have studied the activities of Ottoman Muslim and Jewish merchants in Venice in the sixteenth century. Arbel has convincingly shown that the atmosphere of anti-Ottoman sentiments during the war over Cyprus in 1571 led to the expulsion of Ottoman Muslim and Jewish merchants and the confiscation of their property (see chapter 3). After the termination of these hostilities, some of these merchants, mostly non-Muslims, seem to have returned to Venice. Although some Ottoman Muslim merchants may have also returned later and settled in their own Fondaco dei Turchi in Venice in the seventeenth century, strict rules were imposed on their activities and movement. Even in France, despite a close Franco-Ottoman alliance, anti-Turkish feelings prevailed among the Catholic populace at large.[184]

When some Ottoman Muslim merchants traveled to European cities, they faced arrest and even enslavement. For example, in 1759, port officials in Trieste arrested a merchant named Salih who was on his way to Péc to trade in Austria. The officials claimed that he was indebted to Venetian merchants and confiscated his merchandise composed of 25,690 kg of sheep's wool, among other things, and put it in a storage house for fourteen months. Consequently, some of his goods and those of other merchants that he had been transporting had decayed in the storage house. The remaining goods were then auctioned off at a low price (8 to 30 kuruş per *kantar*) like the goods of a bankrupt merchant. The port authorities in Trieste had taken the cash from the sale of his goods without providing any documentation showing that he was indebted to the Venetian merchants. Salih had appealed to the Austrian emperor, who had promised to look into his case but had failed to redress his complaint. As a result, he had also submitted a petition to the Sublime Porte requesting that it issue an order to the Austrian ambassador in Pera to look into the illegal action of the officials in Trieste since he was not in debt to Venetian traders. Moreover, Salih requested that the Venetian Embassy in Pera carry out an investigation based on the documents he had submitted with his petition. In his petition to the Sublime Porte, Salih claimed that he had fallen into poverty and had lost his good reputation while living away from his family in a strange land for fifteen months and had become hungry and destitute. Having become destitute, Salih was asking for the sultan's mercy in the five petitions he had submitted to the Sublime Porte to free him from the captivity of the infidel king for the sake of Prince Selim, four Caliphs, and twelve imams, following the shari'a, so that he could return to his home and family.[185]

This case involves a rare petition by a Muslim merchant, possibly from the Balkans, who traded in Trieste, a free port in northern Italy that had been open to Ottoman Muslim merchants since the early modern period.[186] Salih had appealed to the Austrian emperor as well as to Sultan Mustafa II (1757–74) several times within fifteen months and had fallen into poverty and destitution. Even though Ottoman merchants frequented the port of Trieste quite regularly, the case underscores the insecurity of trade for Muslim merchants in European ports. It also exposes the serious absence of Ottoman commercial and consular authorities in European ports as late as 1759 to look into these kinds of disputes.

Even though the ahdnames stipulated the legal procedure for European merchants to follow when seeking redress in Ottoman courts, they lacked similar provisions for Ottoman merchants like Salih, who appeared to have been abused by port authorities in Trieste. For example, in 1762, the goods of another Muslim merchant, Isma'il, worth 8,000 kuruş had been confiscated in Crackow, Poland, and he and his servant, who knew some Polish, had been imprisoned by the commander of the city. Isma'il had petitioned the Porte demanding the return of his goods, and the Porte subsequently issued an imperial order to the Polish ambassador to return the confiscated goods to Isma'il, punish the general, and act according to the terms of the ahdname between the two states. It appears that the Austrian government granted permission for Ottoman traders (Muslim and non-Muslim) to trade in Vienna (where an Ottoman quarter developed) and Austrian towns following the signing of an ahdname between the two states that contained reciprocal provisions for Ottoman merchants. The Ottoman government could send envoys with a large delegation to Vienna to settle the disputes of its own merchants on a temporary basis.[187]

The earlier ahdnames, particularly with those with Venice, had reciprocal clauses and protected Ottoman ships, goods, and traders from piracy and captivity but did not spell out a legal procedure to look into such affairs when Ottoman ships were involved. Ottoman envoys traveled to Venice from time to time to settle the disputes of its merchants, but these efforts did not lead to the establishment of a permanent embassy there. Moreover, the Ottoman government did not appoint permanent ambassadors and consuls to Western European ports until the late eighteenth and early nineteenth centuries. For these and other reasons, such as lack of security and the monopolistic policies of the Levant Companies, Ottoman Muslim merchants who wanted to trade in Western European ports like Marseille and London were forced to enter into partnerships with non-Muslim traders and use Jewish merchants as their agents.

Chartering European ships to transport their goods to Western European ports was thus a better option for Muslim merchants. Part of the reason for this practice was that the French Levant Company banned Ottoman ships and traders from Marseille during the eighteenth century. This was also the practice of the English Levant Company, while the Dutch Levant Company was more open in allowing Ottoman merchants into Amsterdam.[188] Many Ottoman minority merchants became honorary dragomans of the embassies and purchased berats at a high price from the ambassadors that gave them, their sons, and two servants exemption from paying the poll tax and the right to pay lower customs dues (3 percent as opposed to 5 percent) when they traded with Europe (see chapter 7). The protection system, however, was closed to Ottoman Muslim merchants.

Ottoman Muslim merchants entered into partnerships with European merchant captains to bypass this ban, but they had to pay 2.5 percent consular fees to the French ambassador. During the Seven Years' War (1756–63) between France and England, trade in the Mediterranean became very insecure. English ships constantly attacked French ships and vice versa. Thus, Ottoman Muslim merchants trading with Marseille turned to Dutch and Swedish ships to transport their goods from one port to another. For example, the Swedish ambassador claimed in a petition to the Imperial Council that a certain merchant named Sa'id b. Hamza from Tunis had drawn up a contract at the Swedish Embassy to transport his goods from Galata to Barcelona and then to Marseille on the ship of a Swedish captain after paying the rent of 4,000 kuruş and the consular dues at the beginning of 1750. But Sa'id had failed to pay the rent to the captain and had gotten into a fight with him. Therefore, the captain had refused to transport his goods from Barcelona to Marseille. The ship had ended up in Livorno for unknown reasons, and the Swedish ambassador was making a report to the Sublime Porte.[189] In Livorno, the Swedish captain had sued Sa'id and had won the case, taking possession of the cargo, which he sent to Marseille. Sa'id could not find a guarantor in Marseille due to his low credibility and had finally found a Jewish merchant in Livorno named David Martel, who had agreed to pay his debt of 4,689 kuruş to the Swedish captain. Mantel, however, had also taken possession of the 158,046 kg of grain and sold it at the market price through a French merchant named Louici in Marseille and Livorno. Sa'id was disturbed by Mantel's transaction and brought a lawsuit against him, but he failed to win it due to his bad reputation, according to the Swedish ambassador. It is possible that Sa'id, a Tunisian merchant trading in grains with Marseille, had originally planned to transport his merchandise to Marseille on a French ship, but due to the Anglo-French tensions, he had changed his plans and hired a Swedish captain and had drawn up a contract at the Swedish Embassy to take his goods to Barcelona instead. But due to insecurity in Barcelona, he may have decided to instead take his goods to the port of Livorno, which was close to Marseille. He obviously had been unable to sell the grain and pay off the captain, who had taken possession of his cargo. Finally, Sa'id had found a Jewish guarantor to pay off his debt, but the guarantor had taken possession of Sa'id's cargo as well, leaving Sa'id with very little. Sa'id did not have any access to Ottoman consular representatives in Livorno since there were none to help him defend his case in the court. If a French trader had faced a similar problem in Galata or any other Ottoman port or town, the dragoman of the embassy or the consulate would have helped him in the court.

During the Seven Years' War (1756–63) and the British navy's blockade of Marseille, Italian ports like Trieste and Livorno as well as Dutch ports became important destinations for French and Ottoman traders from Galata, Izmir and elsewhere.[190] Clearly, Ottoman Muslim merchants lacked their own networks in European ports and used those of Jewish and Armenian merchants when the need arose. Elena Frangakis-Syrett believes that the Seven Years' War was a turning point for Ottoman non-Muslim merchants, who established themselves in Dutch ports like Amsterdam and Trieste.[191]

During the first of the Russo-Ottoman Wars (1768–1774), both French and English ships got involved in shipping provisions to Istanbul as well as transporting the goods of Muslim merchants from Alexandria to ports like Izmir, Crete, Salonica, and Galata since Ottoman ships were needed for the military (see chapter 5). Western ships transported provisions from Alexandria to Istanbul, taking a long route.[192] But sometimes those ships ended up smuggling provisions from Alexandria and the Aegean ports to European ports. In 1760, the Ottoman state issued orders to the kadis and port authorities of Alexandria and Damietta to prevent the transportation of provisions from Alexandria to Istanbul on European ships since they could end up in European ports. Egyptian merchants were to be prevented from carrying their goods on European ships and had to pledge and provide guarantors to ensure that cargoes of rice, sugar, and coffee would be sent to Istanbul on Muslim ships to prevent shortages instead of to Europe.[193] Every ship, including European ships, and its cargo had to be registered by the port authorities in Alexandria and Damietta, and European ships had to also register at their consulates and provide guarantors who would assure that they would bring the goods to Istanbul instead of to European ports. However, these bans did not last long and were seldom effective since the military support offered to Ottoman commercial shipping by the Ottoman state was too weak to protect ships from pirate attacks.

French ships were very active in the domestic trade of the Ottoman Empire during the eighteenth century due to the shortage of Ottoman commercial ships.[194] Panzac has shown that Muslims (Turks and Arabs) were the majority of traders who chartered French ships in domestic coastal trade among Alexandria, Greece, Crete, Syria, and Istanbul from 1779 to 1781.[195] In 1754, Muslim merchants in Alexandria drew up 130 contracts with French ships to transport their goods to coastal towns on the Aegean, Istanbul, Thrace, Crete, the Greek archipelago, the Maghreb, Cyrus, and Syria.[196] After Egyptian merchants were banned from carrying their goods on European ships, the number of contracts dropped to 21 in 1761 but rose to 92 five years later.[197]

Moreover, despite the Ottoman government's bans on smuggling, French ships from time to time imported grains from the Aegean islands and North African towns into Marseille. For example, from 1713 to 1722, 419 vessels arrived in Marseille from Izmir. Of this number, 170 vessels had transported wheat, and 100 had transported olive oil from Izmir to Marseille.[198] However, most European ships that transported the goods of local merchants were involved in domestic trade in the Ottoman Empire.

From time to time, disputes broke out between French captains and Ottoman merchants. For example, in September 1784, Ambassador Saint-Priest petitioned the Porte about the refusal of two Muslim merchants from Alexandria, Kasım b. Hüseyn and Hacı Şaban, who had rented a French ship to transport their goods, to pay the captains according to the terms of their agreement.[199]

The French Revolution and the Napoleonic Wars eventually ended security of trade for French ships in the Mediterranean, and French trade declined compared with that of Great Britain.

CONCLUSION

Many economic historians have blamed the Ottoman state for failing to create joint-stock companies and to practice mercantilism modeled after its commercial partners England, France, and the Dutch Republic. The Ottoman state instead followed a combination of laissez-faire and protectionist policies in its international and domestic trade. Its trade with Europe still remained marginal compared with its internal trade and trade with Iran and India. Moreover, the Ottoman traders formed networks of their own based on family firms as well as on a variety of partnerships across religious and national boundaries. Family firms and merchant networks criss-crossed the Mediterranean from Galata to Marseille. Ottoman traders also formed partnerships with French traders and transported their goods on French ships to Europe in the late eighteenth century when the French Levant Company became more flexible toward such partnerships.

French trade with the Levant ebbed and flowed during the early modern period, although France was the closest diplomatic ally of the Ottoman Empire until the Napoleonic Wars. The deep involvement of French traders in the economic life of Ottoman ports and towns created opportunities as well as challenges for French traders. They got involved in money lending as well as importing colonial goods and chartering their ships to local merchants to make a living. They continued facing growing challenges to their trade in Syria, the Morea, and even Galata due to a variety of reasons such as corruption, fraud, economic difficulties, wars, and the resistance of local guilds and producers. The court of Galata received many lawsuits from French traders regarding unpaid debts and insolvencies. French traders were able to shift the pattern of their activities and get involved in informal banking and money lending to Ottoman grandees, activities that exposed them to the power and corruption of local notables. However, the French Revolution led to the dissolution of the Levant Company and the Ahdname of 1740.

SEVEN

Sexual and Cultural Encounters in Public and Private Spaces

I live in a place that very well represents the Tower of Babel: In Pera they speak Turkish, Greek, Hebrew, Armenian, Arabic, Persian, Russian, Slavonian, Walachian, German, Dutch, French, English, Italian, [and] Hungarian, and what is worse, there are ten of these languages spoken in my home. My grooms are Arabs[;] my footmen French, English[,] and Germans; my nurse is Armenian; my housemaids Russians[;] half a dozen other servants Greeks; my steward, an Italian; my janissaries, Turks; so that I live in a perpetual hearing of this medley of sounds, which produces a very extraordinary effect upon the people that are born here[,] for they learn all these languages at the same time[,] and without knowing any of them well enough to write or read in it . . .

The suburbs of Pera, Tophane[,] and Galata are collections of strangers from all countries of the universe. They have so often intermarried[,] and this forms several races of people the oddest imaginable. There is not one single family of the natives that can value itself on being unmixed. You frequently see a person whose father was born a Grecian, the mother an Italian, the grandfather a Frenchman, the grandmother an Armenian[,] and their ancestors English, Muscovites, Asiatics, etc.

—LADY MARY MONTAGU,
Turkish Embassy Letters, 1717[1]

OTTOMAN PORT CITIES REMAINED VERY MIXED as the size of European communities grew due to the expansion in trade and diplomacy. In her *Turkish Embassy Letters*, Lady Mary Wortley Montagu described the ethnic mix and the diversity of Pera as the Tower of Babel. Although she found life in Pera infinitely interesting, she described the "Levantines" as an "odd and strange mix." Lady Montagu and other European residents like Dallaway enjoyed the "picturesque" social life of Ottoman ports but found the hybrid identities of its "Levantine" residents strange and confusing at best. John-Paul Ghobrial has underscored the impact of everyday encounters between a small circle of European residents and Ottomans in the information flow among Istanbul, London, and Paris and the spread of print culture that produced knowledge (ports, trade, goods and manufactures, customs and manners, and government as well as exotica) in Europe about the Ottoman Empire in the seventeenth century. Printed *Turcica* offered European ambassadors and merchants important information about life in Istanbul and other ports in the Levant.[2] Lady Mary Montagu was following an established tradition by reporting about everyday life in Pera and the lives of women in the Ottoman Empire in her letters.

This chapter focuses on the fluid identities of the residents of Galata; their daily encounters across confessional, gender, and social boundaries; and the anxieties of cohabitation and limits of pluralism in Galata based on a study of Islamic court records, European travelogues, imperial orders, and French royal edicts. Sexual interactions between European men and Ottoman women form the backdrop to study the evolution of intercommunal relations and the change in state policies in reinforcing communal boundaries, particularly at times of political and economic crises. I also examine the role of intermediaries who defied these rules, intermarried across communal boundaries, and assumed an important place in the liminal spaces of Ottoman ports as "go in-betweens" or as "Levantines." The term *Levantine* referred to the descendants of the original Genoese, Venetian, and French Catholic communities who had lived in the ports of the Levant since medieval times and intermarried with local Christian women. Unlike Ottoman Orthodox Christian communities, they did not have a legal status as a community until the early nineteenth century, when the Catholic community was recognized as a *millet* (religious community) with a formal legal status like the Greek Orthodox, Armenian Orthodox, and Jewish communities had.

DANGERS OF INTERFAITH SEX

Although Lady Montagu resided in Pera, most European ambassadors did not bring their families to the Levant, and many traders chose to marry local Christian women. Eric Dursteler has underscored the composite, fluid, relational identities of the residents of Mediterranean ports in the pre-modern era. Boundary crossing as well as boundary marking took place at different periods in reaction to socioeconomic as well as political conditions.[3]

However, marriage and sexual interactions between European men and Ottoman women were subject to the approval of communal leaders and the community watch since conversion to Islam was always a concern. From time to time, tensions broke out as a result of sexual liaisons between Europeans and Ottomans.[4] Despite the pluralism of Ottoman ports like Galata, from time to time interfaith sex generated anxieties and led to the punishment of those who crossed communal boundaries at particular moments of political and social tensions during the eighteenth century. Contrary to the assumption of the notion of collaboration between Ottoman non-Muslim communities and the West, the religious divide between the Orthodox and Catholic communities remained deep and filled with tensions.

Franco-Ottoman relations also entered a moment of crisis and complete breakdown between the French Revolution and Napoleon's invasion of Egypt in 1798 (see the epilogue). Pera became the scene of intercommunal tensions as well as diplomatic intrigues. The Islamic court of Galata received numerous lawsuits from the residents about illicit sexual relationships between the local residents and European men during this time period, as the following case illustrates:

> In October 1798, the residents of the Kamer Hatun quarter in Pera (Beyoğlu), Mahmud Efendi son of Ramazan, Ağob son of Gabriel, Luka son of Petro, and other non-Muslim men as well as some Orthodox Christian women like Yakut daughter of Kirkor presented a collective lawsuit to the court of Galata against Dimitri son of Panayod, a Greek resident of the same quarter. They stated that Dimitri, his wife Tarsiye, and his mother in-law Kira, who were absent from the court, were in the habit of bringing unknown foreign men and women to their house at night, committing all kinds of "illicit activities." The residents stated that they had reproached the couple several times [,] but the latter had failed to pay any heed. Finally, the residents had found five bandits in the couple's home and had turned them in to the *voyvoda* [mayor] of Pera three days earlier. They demanded the expulsion of the couple and the mother-in-law from the neighborhood since their illicit activities disturbed the peace of the residents.[5]

The above case, drawn from the Islamic court register of Galata, involved a collective lawsuit by predominantly Christian and a few Muslim residents of a quarter in Pera (Beyoğlu) against a Greek couple who were accused of turning their house into a brothel and serving foreign men and women as well as "bandits." The residents had been unable to stop the couple's illicit activities, so they had turned the bandits in to the mayor of Galata. They demanded that the court expel Dimitri and his family from the neighborhood. This case underscores the impact of the community watch and social control in a neighborhood in Pera and the involvement of the Islamic court in policing the sexual activities of non-Muslim communities.[6] Even though non-Muslim communities usually policed and disciplined their own members and reported breaches of morality to their religious leaders for them to issue punishment, this case might have gone beyond the control of the community watch since "bandits and European men" were involved. What might have triggered the residents' determination to expel the family from the neighborhood after several interventions were the backgrounds of the clients, i.e., foreigners and bandits. It is not clear who precisely the foreigners and bandits were, but members of the French community had been the targets of surveillance and arrest in Pera and other Ottoman ports since Napoleon's invasion of Egypt in July 1798 (see epilogue).[7] It is possible that the foreigners and bandits were Frenchmen who were hiding in the couple's house since the state had issued orders for the arrest of all Frenchmen in Pera and Galata in September 1798. The revocation of the French ahdnames was a serious turning point in French-Ottoman relations, undermining the security of European residents in Ottoman ports (see epilogue).

In his fascinating studies of interfaith sex in medieval Spain, David Nirenberg has emphasized the importance of studying how communities of faith defined themselves sexually.[8] At times of social and political crisis, women became the repositories of both honor and shame in Mediterranean societies. The physical appearance and sexual conduct of Jewish, Christian, and Muslim women formed an important marker of identity, while miscegenation could lead to intercommunal violence. While Muslim men in Muslim majority states had access to the sexual services of Christian concubines and could marry them, Muslim women were banned from forming sexual relations and even from marrying non-Muslim men unless they converted to Islam. Except in special cases, the Ottoman state did not encourage mass conversion to Islam because it meant the loss of revenue from the poll tax. However, in Muslim majority states the conversion of Muslims to Christianity meant apostasy and could lead to death. Christian missionaries, therefore, concentrated their efforts on converting Orthodox Christians (Armenians and Greeks) rather than Muslims in the Levant. The fear of conversion always created anxieties about such interfaith relations, and the state had to reinforce and redraw sexual and communal boundaries. Interfaith marriage among Muslims, Christians, and Jews was rare outside concubinage, and many slave women eventually converted to Islam once they had married Muslim men or given birth to a child.[9] A few Christian women also converted to Islam to obtain divorce, while forum shopping was also widespread among Christian women who frequented Islamic courts to claim properties left them by their deceased parents.[10]

Whereas some scholars have emphasized the porous intercommunal boundaries and fluid identities of the inhabitants of eastern Mediterranean ports in the early modern period, the transformation of communal identities during the transitional eighteenth century has received less attention.[11] Moreover, it appears that the hardening of communal identities was often a response to economic, political, and social changes.[12]

In Ottoman ports, sexual interaction between Ottoman Muslim women and European men had its own risks. European men had to be particularly careful when they formed sexual liaisons with Ottoman Muslim women. Antoine Galland, the dragoman of the French Embassy, commented on the risks of sexual liaisons (conversion or death) between European men and Muslim women in the late seventeenth century (see chapter 4). European men had to either marry Ottoman non-Muslim women or get involved with "disreputable" non-Muslim Ottoman women. He commented on scandals caused by French merchants as a result of their nocturnal activities in Izmir, which had led to the imposition of fines by Ottoman officials during the second half of the seventeenth century. While it was common for Venetian and French merchants to contract temporary marriages with local Christian women or take slaves as concubines in Ottoman ports, sometimes these relationships were considered "illicit" when children were involved and inheritance disputes broke out after the death of the European men.[13] English merchants like Dudley North also remarked on the illicit affairs of Englishmen with local non-Muslim women in Galata, Izmir, and Aleppo.

Galata, as the red-light district of Istanbul, offered more possibilities than the rest of the city did for sexual adventures for men and women from all kinds of backgrounds. Prostitution among Muslim and non-Muslim women spread all over Istanbul during the second half of the eighteenth century due to economic difficulties, migration, and an increase in the number of single men and women.[14] The red-light district of Galata had traditionally been located inside the walls along the harbor, where hundreds of taverns and brothels served sailors, janissaries, single men, and European traders (see chapter 1).[15]

The growing number of Europeans in Galata and Pera created tensions among their neighbors, especially concerning the Europeans' private conduct and sexual encounters with local women. The size of the French community in Galata had grown considerably to two hundred men, women, and children and included sixty prominent merchant families and more than thirty-five watchmakers (see chapters 4 and 6). The French community also included Capuchin and Jesuit priests, dragoman families, sailors, bakers, and artisans.[16]

The French community concentrated in certain neighborhoods, such as the Bereketzade quarter inside the walls in Galata. This quarter also housed Ottoman Muslim and non-Muslim residents. The Bereketzade quarter had become notorious for illicit activities and was the target of scrutiny by the neighborhood watch. For example, in May 1789, the residents of the Bereketzade quarter presented a lawsuit to the court of Galata stating that a certain Hafez Mustafa Efendi had converted his house in the quarter into a brothel with ten rooms and had placed Maria Francesca, Santiye, and Katerina, all Christians, and possibly one Italian women there with unrelated men such as Konstantin, Louis (who possibly was French), and others. After a fire in the house, its inhabitants were arrested upon the report of the neighborhood watch. The neighbors wanted all of them expelled from the quarter.[17] In this case, a Muslim man had been operating a private brothel where local Christian and European women serviced local Christian and European clients. We meet Katerina (possibly the same person mentioned in the above case) in an earlier document, where she is described as a well-known prostitute who had been punished several times. Court records show that she was in the habit of bringing wealthy non-Muslim traders into her house in Orta Kapı, claiming that they were her husbands. She was exiled to Bursa after the collective testimony of her neighbors against her in March 1775.[18]

In another inspection, Lokisro daughter of Nikola, who was a well-known prostitute in the Sultan Bayezid quarter of Galata, was called into court by two night police officers on behalf of the mayor of Galata in September 1798. She had been caught with a zimmi sailor, Paolo (possibly Italian), who was not a relative, in her house at 3:00 AM. When they were questioned, they confessed to their illicit relations, so the court ordered their punishment.[19] The timing of this break-in is also interesting since it may have coincided with the surveillance of and search for Frenchmen who had gone into hiding after orders for their arrest had been issued. Many Frenchmen in Galata were sailors who probably were single and targets of surveillance. What is interesting about all these cases is the use of private residences in Galata as brothels, the intervention of the community watch in reporting such cases to the police, and the role of the Islamic court in punishing non-Muslim offenders.

As Muslims settled in Galata and Pera, they invited greater scrutiny of women's sexual conduct because there were stricter codes of social conduct for Ottoman women than for non-Muslim women. The Muslim quarters were considered private spaces and the extension of houses where women and children could freely intermingle with their neighbors and sit outside while their children played. The residents, led by the *imam,* were the "ears and eyes" of the state and agents of social disciplining.

Sexual misconduct was tolerated in Galata as long as Muslim women were not involved. For example, in May 1786, the residents of the Cami'i Kebir (Arab Cami'i) neighborhood, led by the subaşı (chief of day police) Mustafa Beşe, the *imam* (the leader of the Friday prayer), and three night guards, presented a lawsuit against Ayşe bt. Abdullah and her friend Fatma bt. Ömer, residents of the At Meyadanı neighborhood (Hippodrome) in Istanbul proper, to the court of Galata. They stated that they had caught these women with Isma'il Beşe, who was not related to them, at his house in the Cami'i Kebir quarter of Galata. The women then confessed to the activity and were to be punished accordingly.[20] Isma'il Beşe may well have been a janissary-artisan, one of the many single men who lived in Galata and brought prostitutes to their houses, who finally attracted the attention of the residents and the night watch. But he got away, even though he had been caught with these women, because the court decided to punish the women.

Women also suffered when they gave birth to illegitimate children who were then left on their own. We learn from the petitions to the Imperial Council presented by some of these homeless minor children like Fatma that they were destitute. For example, in 1811, Fatma sent a petition to the state asking for a daily stipend since she had been left homeless after the police had arrested her mother, who was a prostitute. In this case, the state established a daily stipend of ten akçe for her, putting her up in the house of the imam in January 1811 since she was underage.[21]

False accusation, however, could lead to the punishment of the accuser. For example, Kamile bt. Mehmed, a Muslim woman, brought a lawsuit to the court of Galata against a bread seller, Kara Mustafa b. Hasan, for calling her a prostitute in a Muslim quarter of Galata in October 1798. She was demanding proof and the punishment of Kara Mustafa for making a false accusation. Kara Mustafa was unable to bring forth witnesses and had to promise not to harass Kamile anymore if she dropped the lawsuit.[22] Accusations of prostitution and illicit sexual activity required four morally upright Muslim eyewitnesses to the actual act, according to the shari'a. Otherwise, false accusation could lead to eighty lashes. This case demonstrates that false accusations in the absence of four respected Muslim eyewitnesses could lead to punishment and that presenting the collective testimony of neighbors was often the best way of ensuring the punishment and expulsion of the accused. Expulsion from the neighborhoods and the city had become the norm for punishing women's sexual misconduct in the eighteenth century.[23] The surveillance of certain urban spaces like parks, bachelors' rooms, taverns, and market areas along the harbor at night had also become more prevalent (see chapter 1).[24]

To guard the honor of Muslim women during religious holidays, the government issued bans on the public visibility of women in the markets and streets in the districts of Galata and Istanbul. The kadi of Galata received imperial orders to prevent the appearance of women during the religious holidays at the end of the holy month of Ramazan and during the Feast of Sacrifice for four days in July 1750. They had to stay at home, and if they violated the ban, the kadi and the imams of the residential quarters were ordered to arrest them and bring them to the court. In addition, in March 1770, imperial orders were issued to the kadi and imams of Istanbul to ban the presence of women on the streets and in other public places during the religious festival at the end of the month of Ramazan.[25] Similar orders were issued to the kadi of Galata and the imams to prevent women from appearing in the streets and markets and between quarters during religious holidays in February (Ramazan) 1797.[26] The state policed the presence of women in public places and their sexual conduct as well as their dress during the eighteenth century. An imperial order was issued in 1750 to the judges of Galata and Üsküdar as well as to the chief of police, all of whom were in charge of protecting the villages along the Bosphorus, stating that bandits had entered the ranks of the boatmen who transported women and other residents of Istanbul, committing robberies and murder and seducing women. From now on, all boatmen had to provide guarantors and had to be registered with their names and places of origin. Those without guarantors were to be expelled from the boatmen's guild.[27] But certain spaces in the city, like the street of taverns in Galata, were free of police intervention since non-Muslims had the right to open taverns and consume alcoholic beverages, and women (other than prostitutes) were restricted from entering this area.

This city [Galata], because of its delightful climate, is famous
for its darling boys and girls. Its blessings are abundant for rich
and poor alike. All the people are impertinent lovers of dervish
temperament. They are famous for their salons in wintertime.
When the grand ship captains return from their voyages, they
take all their friends in their *faluccas* and frigates to the vineyards
in Boğazhisarı and have intimate gatherings.[28]

EVLIYA ÇELEBI,
Seyahatnamesi

While during the day Galata was the center of maritime trade and diplomacy (Pera), the nightlife transformed the port into an entertainment district,
a change that also led to a spike in the crime rate. Evliya Çelebi provided a vivid
account of nightlife in Galata, recounting its famous taverns and the variety of
wines that drove Muslim clients to bankruptcy as well as into a life of "sin."
Ports typically catered to the lifestyles of sailors and traveling merchants. Both
Kasım Paşa and Tophane, located next to Galata, also housed a large working-
class population that worked in the navy and the military. Bachelors' rooms and
hans provided housing, while taverns and coffeehouses were public spaces of
social interaction (see chapter 1). Although coffeehouses were legal, taverns had
a more conspicuous status and could be shut down if things got out of control
and Muslim neighbors complained about rowdy conduct. Indeed, drinking was
an important pastime and social activity among members of the European
communities in Pera and Izmir. Galland observed that the English and French
communities in Izmir competed in drinking bouts and that some Englishmen
had died at the age of forty from excessive drinking (see chapter 4).[29]

The ahdnames allowed European ambassadors, consuls, and traders to
purchase and consume limited quantities of wine without having to pay taxes
(see chapter 4). Despite the small size of European households, the ahdnames
allowed European subjects to purchase fixed quantities of tax-free wine,
which they consumed and sometimes even traded to Ottoman clients. The
embassies often had their own wineries and storage houses and imported
large quantities of wine and also purchased some locally.

English and French embassies guarded this allowance carefully since
embassies were sites of social interactions and frequent parties where wine
flowed freely. For example, in response to the request of the French ambassador, Vergennes, an imperial order was issued to the kadi of Galata in
September 1750 to allow Vergennes to purchase 80,500 kg (7,000 *medre*) of

wine from Istanbul and other ports for his household and dependents every year with exemption from taxes. Another imperial order allowed a French notable household in Galata to purchase 17,250 kg (1,500 *medre*) wine from the port and to transport it freely without having to pay taxes and dues every year.[30] Similarly, an imperial order was issued in the same month to the kadi of Galata in response to the English ambassador's request to allow English traders to purchase 46,000 kg of wine (4,000 medre) every year without having to pay taxes and dues. It is interesting that ambassadors and traders received an allowance for duty-free wine every year in Galata.

However, in mixed neighborhoods, drinking in taverns could cause problems. Taverns were places of social interaction among men of diverse backgrounds as well as sites of illicit activities.[31] Sometimes nocturnal activities, loud singing, and brawls raised the ire of local residents. In a lawsuit in May (Ramazan) 1786, more than fifty Christian residents (mostly Armenians) of the Bereketzade quarter, where many Europeans resided, demanded that the court of Galata close a tavern and some sweet beverage shops (*şerbethane*) where many "riffraff" gathered and disrupted the peace of the neighbors.[32] It is possible that the Armenian residents wanted to avoid trouble from Muslim neighbors during the month of Ramazan by demanding the closure of the tavern themselves.

Bans on drinking and the frequent closures of taverns led to the opening of beverage shops in Galata. In April 1816, Galata had forty-three beverage shops that paid 1,550 kuruş in taxes every month to the vakf of the Arab Cami'i and the wine tax collector. But according to the petition presented by the guild of şherbet sellers, European captains and sailors had illegally opened up their own shops in Karaköy, thus harming the businesses of guild members and affecting the revenues of the vakf and the wine tax. The guild was demanding the closure of the illegal shops and bans on the sale of wine and *arak or raki* (an unsweetened anis-flavored alcoholic drink) in groceries, houses, and illegal sherbet shops.[33] An imperial order was then issued to that effect in April 1817. It appears that in Galata, in addition to taverns, beverage shops served alcoholic drinks as well as sherbets and paid regular taxes to the vakf of the Arab Cami'i as well as the wine tax. But the number of illegal beverage shops that were operated by the Europeans in Karaköy had also increased by the early nineteenth century. During religious holidays, the state became more vigilant about monitoring drinking. An order was issued to the voyvoda of Galata during the same period to ban the sale of alcoholic drinks and close down taverns around mosques in Galata for four days.[34]

Nevertheless, despite these bans, Galata remained the center of drinking due to its large non-Muslim and European population, and the semilegal status of its taverns and brothels made it attractive to men from all walks of life and religious backgrounds.

VIOLENCE IN GALATA

Despite the many places of entertainment, Galata was still largely a male space and had a rough culture. Fights and brawls occurred regularly on the streets during the day, and drinking and illicit sexual activities at night made the streets unsafe for the residents. The violation of the night curfew after the evening prayer led to the night watch's punishing of strollers. Before the adoption of gas lighting in the late nineteenth century, the narrow alleys of Galata and Pera became scenes of crime at night. This development was partly due to the wars waged during the second half of the eighteenth century and the ensuing economic crisis due to the long wars with Russia. Brawls, assault, injury, and even murder were crimes that had particularly high occurrences in Galata during the eighteenth century.[35]

Women, minorities, and foreigners were especially vulnerable during these times, and sexual encounters across religious boundaries could trigger acts of violence. Economic motives could also lead to violence against foreigners (see the epilogue). For example, in April 1786, the scribe of the court of Galata was called in to examine the body of a sherbet seller, Tuhani son of Angeli, who had been shot to death by a bullet.[36] He might have been the victim of robbery. But everyday violence was also on the rise in Galata. In the same month, the scribe of the court of Galata was called in by the head of the seventy-first division of the janissary corps to examine the body of a janissary who had been shot to death near bachelors' rooms outside the Azap kapı in Galata in October 1798.[37] This area where many sailors lived in bachelors' rooms and frequented taverns and brothels was particularly prone to violence and nocturnal activities. We can only imagine how many fights must have broken out at night among those who frequented the taverns.

Women also became targets of sexual harassment and violence in Galata. For example, Zoyi, the daughter of Istati, who lived in the quarter of Sultan Bayezid in Galata, presented a lawsuit to the court of Galata against her son, Ali b. Abdullah, who was present at the court in March 1752. She complained that Ali beat her up every night because of the money he owed her in the amount of 450 kuruş. She subsequently settled in the court, giving up her claim of 450 kuruş since he was unable to pay it on the condition that he pledge that he would not beat her up every night.[38] This case underscores the violence that could be perpetrated within a family due to economic pressures, many residents' inability to pay their debts, and the settlement of some debts in the courts.

Moreover, often a whole family would become the target of violence due to economic pressures. In October 1798, Eryal son of Durdani, a resident of Pera, sued Ohanes son of Manas for assaulting his wife and mother in Kasım Paşa and asked the court to prevent Ohanes from inflicting further violence.[39] In the same month, Mariam daughter of Kirkor presented a lawsuit in the court of Galata about the physical assault of Artin and his friend Kevork against her. But since the men had denied the charge, and she had been unable to provide eyewitnesses, they were set free, and she had to drop her lawsuit. In March 1798, Hadice bt. of Mehmed, a resident of Okçu Musa quarter in Galata, sued her tenant, Al-Seyyid Halil, b. Ahmed, who rented a room in her house. Al-Seyyid, a sea captain, had assaulted her and taken 50 kuruş from her. But since Hadice was unable to provide two eye-witnesses, she had to drop the case.[40] Clearly, when women were assaulted, they could not always get a conviction for the attacker, particularly when witnesses were not available. But nevertheless, they sued their assailants in the court of Galata.

BANS ON INTERFAITH MARRIAGE AND ENSUING LEGAL PROBLEMS

In addition to the efforts of the community watch in the neighborhoods, the Ottoman state guarded the sexual boundaries of its subjects by discouraging interfaith marriage. The ahdnames granted to France did not have any provisions concerning the status of spouses and the offspring of such marriages, particularly in regard to inheritance. Moreover, communal authorities did not consider such marriages (between Catholics and Orthodox) legal.

The Köprülü viziers issued edicts in 1670 that considered these French Catholic men who married non-Catholics their own (Ottoman) subjects and imposed the poll tax on them despite the protests of the French ambassador. Moreover, after the death of a French or European spouse, the state could confiscate the couple's goods.[41] For example, when an English merchant, Samuel Pentlow, who had married a Greek woman in Izmir, died in 1678, the

Ottoman state confiscated his estate worth 17,000 pounds, claiming him as its subject, and prevented the settlement of his family in England. His wife, Ann, who had traveled to Istanbul to petition the sultan after the efforts of Ambassador Finch had failed, was finally awarded the house and garden as well as some money for living expenses.[42] In response to this case and the Edict of 1677, the English Levant Company took steps to prohibit the marriage of Englishmen to Ottoman women in the Levant. English company agents were even required to take an oath not to marry Ottoman women.

Similarly, the French government issued edicts in 1670 stating that those Frenchmen who married Ottoman women would lose consular protection.[43] For example, on August 11, 1716, the French king, Louis XIV, issued edicts to the Chamber of Commerce in Marseille, to Ambassador Bonnac in Istanbul, and to the French consuls in the Levant and on the Barbary Coast banning intermarriage between the sons (those under thirty years old) of French subjects in the Levant and on the Barbary Coast and local women who were subjects of the grand sultan. The edict stated that such marriages brought dishonor to the families and the French nation. French merchants in the ports of the Levant and the Barbary Coast who contracted marriage with local women were to be excluded from all administrative and public positions and assemblies of the nation.[44] For example, on July 20, 1726, another royal edict composed of three articles banned intermarriage between French and Ottoman subjects as well as marriage with French subjects born in the Levant. Furthermore, the edict demanded that those who had violated the Edict of 1716 be returned to France. The fear of their having sexual liaisons with Ottoman men and converting to Islam placed French women in the Levant under scrutiny. The edict also ordered the return of all daughters of French subjects to France, banning their residency in the Levant. French subjects of all ranks were banned from marrying Ottoman and foreign women and men as well as French women born in the Levant who had become Ottoman subjects. Those who violated these rulings were to be returned to France.[45]

When French men married Ottoman Christian women (Greeks and Armenians), it took a while for such marriages to be certified by the Chamber of Commerce in Marseille since the Catholic Church considered these women to be heretics. If they converted to Catholicism, which was often the case, they faced stiff opposition from their families and communities. For example, the Chamber of Commerce in Marseille received a report on March 21, 1731, about the marriage of a French man to a Greek woman in the Levant. The man was then ordered to return to France and to never set foot in the

Antoine de Favray, *Portrait of the Countess of Vergennes in Turkish Attire*, 1768. Suna and Inan Kiraç Foundation Collection, © Uğur Ataç.

Levant again.[46] After Ambassador Vergennes married Madame Testa, a member of a Levantine family of dragomans, in 1767, he was recalled to France.[47]

Despite these bans, intermarriage between European men and Ottoman women continued in Ottoman ports and cities and led to legal problems in the eighteenth and early nineteenth centuries. For example, a French trader who had died in Tekirdağ in 1796 had left behind his Greek wife. She had to collect a debt of 500 kuruş from a certain Foti and had to turn for help to the French ambassador, who petitioned the Imperial Council and obtained an imperial order to collect the debt through the Islamic court.[48] In another case, in 1816, Maria, a Greek resident of Ortaköy, presented a petition to the sultan stating that her husband, Daniel, an English merchant, had fled and that the Ottoman state had confiscated their goods in their home and in a shop in Galata. She and her children had been left destitute, and she was requesting the return of her husband's goods to her. The kadi of Galata then made an inventory of his goods, which were composed of personal and household items, and the voyvoda of Galata returned them to the wife in the presence of the Danish dragoman, in accordance with an imperial order that had been issued to the kadi.[49] The document states that due to a state of war between the two states, trade with England was forbidden, and English merchants were to be arrested.

Anglo-Ottoman relations entered a period of crisis when England formed an alliance with Russia against the Ottoman Empire in 1807. The new British ambassador, Charles Arbuthnol, had tried to pressure the Ottoman Empire not to attack Russia, but an English fleet had arrived in the Dardanelles in 1807, prompting the breach of the ahdname with England and the Porte's threat of violence against English subjects.[50] As a result, in January 1807, The British Embassy placed English merchants living in Istanbul on a ship, and the ambassador fled, leaving the embassy deserted. The Ottomans subsequently won the war, and the English signed an ahdname with the Ottoman Empire based on the one that had been granted in 1675. It is possible that Daniel's goods had been confiscated by the kadi earlier but were returned to his wife after the restoration of the ahdname between the two states and since she and her children were Ottoman subjects.

Moreover, when local Christian women married European men, they also faced the opposition of their community and religious leaders. For example, in February 1836, Grigorios, the Greek patriarch, sent a petition to the Imperial Council reporting that a certain Anton, who resided in Fener, was planning to illegally marry his daughter to an English merchant. The patriarch had approached Anton to try and change his mind, but Anton had already secretly married his daughter to the Englishman in Pera, violating religious principles and the will of the sultan. The patriarch was demanding that Anton be exiled to Tekirdağ and that an order be issued to the voyvoda of Tekirdağ to not release him. An imperial order was thus issued for Anton's expulsion to Tekirdağ.[51] This case demonstrates the Greek Orthodox Church's opposition to intermarriage between Greek Orthodox women and European men. It also illustrates the Ottoman state's support in maintaining the sexual boundaries of its Christian communities by punishing interfaith marriage during this period. The fear of conversion on the part of Greek woman to either Catholicism or Protestantism and the future status of any offspring must have been behind the patriarch's concern.

French and English ambassadors did not usually bring their families from home to Pera prior to the eighteenth century.[52] Some, like Ambassador John Murray and Ambassador Ainslie, never married. In Aleppo, most of the English and French merchants were also unmarried since there were few suitable European women available before the mid-eighteenth century.[53] One solution for preventing mixed marriages was to allow European men to bring their wives and families to the Levant in the eighteenth century. But French women had to apply for travel permits to travel from Marseille to the Levant to join their husbands and relatives and to return from the Levant to Marseille. French documents show that a French woman named Anne Raspaille applied for funds from the Chamber in Marseille to travel to Sayda (Sidon) in Syria in July 1721.[54] The French consul in Crete then issued her a certificate of residence. Many French women wanted to travel to Syria to visit their families and to go to Jerusalem on pilgrimages. For example, a certain Elizabeth Gobala, a native of Toulon, applied for permission from the Chamber of Commerce in Marseille to travel to Jerusalem in 1713.[55]

However, a few French women also got involved in illicit activities in Ottoman ports and towns, actions that created scandals within the community. For example, the Chamber of Commerce in Marseille received reports in June 1774 from the French consul in Aleppo that the wife of a French merchant had been involved in extramarital activities in Alexandretta. The Chamber issued orders in July 1774 for the woman to return to Marseille for fear of reprisals by Ottoman authorities, who, according to the consul, were aware of her marital status and illicit activities.[56] Marrying local Christian women was thus borne out of necessity since finding single European women in the Levant was almost impossible, and participating in illicit activities could endanger the status and lives of European residents.

Turning to prostitutes was always a convenient and less costly option for European traders in Ottoman ports. But sexual contact with prostitutes could lead to contagion and was strictly forbidden when the plague hit. The plague caused great fears and forced some members of the community to leave for Marseille. For example, in March 1779, the wife of a French merchant in Rosetta applied for travel permission to return to Marseille, her place of origin, because she was ill.[57] It is possible that she had been exposed to the plague in Rosetta. In another case, in 1720, a French woman who lived in the port of Sidon in Syria requested travel permission to go to Marseille since her mother had died there six months earlier from the plague. She stated in her letter that she had no means for survival by herself in Marseille and wanted to return to Sidon, where her brother was a merchant.[58] Exposure to disease and contagion as a result of contact, both commercial and sexual, often led to fears of divine punishment and anxiety about death.

EMBASSY ENCOUNTERS: DRAGOMANS AND THE PROTECTION SYSTEM

Intermarriage between Ottoman and European subjects also produced a class of hybrid "Levantines" who assumed important functions in the embassies. Every European embassy employed a number of Ottoman non-Muslim subjects as dragomans (interpreters) in accordance with the ahdnames since ambassadors and consuls did not typically know Ottoman Turkish and lacked familiarity with Ottoman laws and customs. Although the Venetians and French also trained their own subjects in Oriental languages and hired them to work in their embassies, they increasingly favored hiring Ottoman non-Muslim subjects who had intermarried with Europeans since they did not have to invest in their training and upkeep in addition to providing a long residency in the Levant and worrying about the possibility of their intermarrying with locals. In every Ottoman port, certain Levantine families, like the Pisanis and the Fontons in Pera, held a monopoly over the dragoman positions. James Dallaway elaborated on this system:

> Of the dragomans stationary in Pera, most are descendants of Venetian families, who have been so employed from the earliest establishment of the embassies. The German and the French (under the old government) have established a seminary for young men (*Giovani di lingua*) of their own country ... to supply vacancies as they may happen [and] plan which candour must allow to be replete with beneficial effects. It is truly singular with what precision many of them can command fluency in seven or eight languages; and Pera may well be compared with the Tower of Babel for number, and sometimes for confusion[,] of tongues. (James Dallaway, *Constantinople Ancient and Modern*)[59]

The institution of dragoman, or interpreter (the Italian derivative of the Arabic *terjuman*), was an old Mediterranean tradition that had developed as result of diplomatic and commercial exchanges between European and

Muslim states. Dragomans played key roles in negotiating international treaties and corresponding with state officials. They were cultural brokers and diplomatic intermediaries who had to be skilled in several languages and navigate different cultures and legal traditions. European states established their own office of dragoman as part of their *corps diplomatique* in their embassies. Venice invented the tradition of training dragomans in Oriental languages at a young age and sending them to serve as the interpreters of the bailo in Pera. Venice also employed dragomans in the Senate since commercial traffic between Venice and the Levant was quite regular, and Ottoman envoys often visited the lagoon to represent the affairs of Ottoman merchants.[60]

In France Minister Colbert established a language school, *Les Jeunes de Langues,* for the training of dragoman in Paris in 1670. He ordered that every three years, six young boys from Marseille, known as *enfants de langue,* be sent to the Capuchin convents in Galata and Izmir to learn Levantine languages and serve the consuls with their newly acquired language skills.[61] The Chamber of Commerce in Marseille paid for the education and expenses of these students at a Capuchin college in Pera.

Antoine Galland, the chief dragoman of the French Embassy in Istanbul in 1672, had been trained in Oriental languages in Paris and knew Arabic, Ottoman, and Persian quite well. He was commissioned by Colbert to collect Oriental manuscripts in Istanbul for Colbert's library in Paris and spent a good part of his time in Istanbul acquiring these manuscripts and translating a few, such as the *One Thousand and One Nights,* from Arabic into French. According to Galland, the French consul in Izmir employed two dragomans, one a Jewish subject of the sultan who received 100 *écus* per year and interpreted for the merchants.[62] The other was a Frenchman who had been sent as a *jeune de langues* from France to learn Turkish in Istanbul and who received 300 écus yearly. There were also five more dragomans in the French consulate in Izmir who had no specific title but enjoyed the protection of the ambassador. They were probably honorary, or *beratlı,* merchants.

The Chamber of Commerce in Marseille issued certificates of employment and residence for these dragomans. For example, in January 1722, L. A. Bourbon applied to the Chamber of Commerce for employment as a language student in the Levant. The fear of dragomans converting to Islam was one important concern, and the fear of their intermarrying with local woman was another in hiring local minorities for this position. For example, in January 1672, Galland reported the conversion of the scribe of the French consul in Edirne, Sieur Magdelaine, to Islam. In July 1672, Galland recorded in his diary that a language student had converted to Islam out of fear of punishment while he was drunk and probably had been caught earlier with a woman. Apparently, the student was later sent back to France.[63]

As time went on, European embassies began hiring local Ottoman non-Muslim traders, who had intermarried with members of their nations and had formed networks of their own, as dragomans. The French, English, and Dutch Embassies hired Ottoman Latins, Greeks, and Armenians who could navigate several cultures and languages. According to Ottoman regulations, Europeans who had lived more than ten years in Ottoman lands became Ottoman subjects and became liable for paying the poll tax. The interpretation of this unwritten rule was subject to constant tension and friction between Ottoman officials and the embassies, which claimed jurisdiction over their subjects. As we have seen, many Latins became Ottoman subjects after the conquest of Galata in 1453, and in time those Europeans who had lived in the Levant for several generations were also considered Levantine Ottoman subjects (see chapter 1). Some had intermarried with Ottoman Greeks and Armenians and paid the poll tax. But unlike the Orthodox Christians, the Catholics did not form an official Ottoman community until 1826 (see chapter 2). These local families of mixed background came to be known as "Levantines" (Latin Christians who were Ottoman subjects) and developed a distinct identity and even a distinct appearance. They were multilingual, as Dallaway observed, but spoke Italian in their professional activities as interpreters. They had wide networks in Ottoman ports since members of some families, like the Pisanis, were employed as dragomans by several embassies in Pera.[64] According to Oliver Jens Schmitt, they had an intermediary legal status as Ottoman subjects who enjoyed European protection while they were under the legal jurisdiction of the Ottoman state as well as that of their own communities. The dragomans had a lucrative income, and their position became very desirable among Ottoman subjects.

In addition, embassies also employed honorary dragomans who were drawn from the ranks of Ottoman non-Muslim subjects and received *berats* from the Ottoman state that gave them, their sons, and two servants exemption from the poll tax and extraordinary taxes as well as consular protection. The protection system became very widespread in the eighteenth century, and soon every major European embassy and consul had an array of Ottoman non-Muslim subjects under its protection. Ottoman non-Muslim subjects purchased berats from the ambassadors and consuls at exorbitant prices (between 2,500 and 4,500 kuruş) and passed them on to their sons and servants.

The Imperial Council issued berats at the request of the ambassadors after the payment of fees that spelled out the rights of dragomans, exempting them, their sons, and two servants from paying the poll tax, extraordinary taxes, and import dues.[65] In addition, when they traded as *beratlı,* or protected, merchants, they paid the same customs rates that Europeans did, 3 percent, as opposed to the 5 percent that the zimmis paid. In other words, the ambassadors and the Ottoman state charged fees for issuing berats to Ottoman non-Muslim subjects that allowed them to trade under the protection of European embassies. These *protégés* were still Ottoman subjects, but they were also under the legal jurisdiction of the consular and Ottoman courts, a condition that created a degree of confusion and even chaos from time to time.[66]

While some scholars may consider this situation legal chaos, Olivers Schmitt refers to it as a fluid legal status that may have reflected the plural legalism of Ottoman ports.[67] An honorary dragoman became a lucrative position as some dragomans became involved in trade and began amassing their own fortunes. French ambassadors also employed them as their agents in commerce in the interior of the empire. For example, in April 1784, Ambassador Saint-Priest applied for travel permission for Avanes, who was an honorary dragoman and had a berat that allowed him to travel from Istanbul to Edirne safely and under the protection of the French Embassy.[68] In another case, in March 1785, Ambassador Gouffier applied for travel permission for Isak, the servant of Şukru, the dragoman of the consul in Aleppo, to travel for business to Istanbul, Yenişehir, and Salonica.[69]

The number of Ottoman subjects who became protected merchants and honorary dragomans increased in the second half of the eighteenth century. Dallaway reported that each embassy employed up to thirty dragomans, many of whom were Greeks who lacked the qualifications needed for such a position and who had purchased the diplomas for exemption from Ottoman taxes and access to legal immunities.[70] He also noted the English ambassador's abuse of the system by filling the posts of consuls in the archipelago from the ranks of local Greek subjects and protégés. Dallaway also remarked on the steps taken by the Ottoman government to end the protégé system.

But the embassies resisted these restrictions since the protection system was an important source of income for ambassadors and consuls, although they were also violating the rules of the Levant Company. For example, the

English ambassador, John Murray, who was underpaid and could not make ends meet, earned a lucrative income from the sale of berats, earning 2,000 to 3,000 pounds every year in 1760s.[71] Toward the end of the eighteenth century, French ambassadors regularly submitted requests to the Porte for the renewal of berats for Ottoman non-Muslim dragomans when the positions became vacant or when a new sultan ascended the throne.[72] Clearly, these ambassadors were making a good income even from renewing these berats.

Every *beratlı* merchant could pass these rights on to his sons and to two servants. Although the ambassadors received these berats after paying some fees to Ottoman officials to hire dragomans, in reality they were selling protection to Ottoman non-Muslim merchants under the guise of dragoman employment. In 1783, Ambassador Saint-Priest applied for a berat to replace one of the dragomans of the French Embassy, Serabyos son of Petros, who had left his service with Avanes son of Kevork. An imperial order was then given to issue Avanes a berat, and an order was sent to the kadi of Galata regarding the exemption of Avanes, his sons, and two servants from the poll tax.[73] What is abundantly apparent from the Ottoman documents is that most of these men did not function as dragomans but instead acted as agents of French merchants in order to trade within the interior of the empire. The document did not, however, mention how much the ambassador paid the Ottoman scribe for issuing the berat.

While many historians have exaggerated the number of *beratlı* merchants that each embassy employed and the embassies' legal jurisdiction over these protégés, Ottoman sources shed new light on their number. Based on Ottoman surveys of protected merchants, Boogert estimated the total number of *beratlı,* or protected, merchants, at 1,174, of whom 463 were under French protection, 440 were under British protection, and 271 were under Dutch protection during the entire eighteenth century.[74] He estimated the total number of *beratlı* merchants for the entire Mediterranean to be 2,500 in the eighteenth century, a number far lower than what has been used by many scholars.[75] In 1789, France issued 46 berats; Great Britain, 43; and the Dutch Republic, 34 to Ottoman non-Muslim subjects. In 1789, the number of berats issued by the French Embassy was 14 in Istanbul, 6 in Izmir, and 5 in Aleppo.[76]. The number of French protégés in Istanbul was 63, of whom only 5 were actual interpreters, 6 were their children, and 14 were servants of dragomans. The rest (38) did not have a status and were probably protected traders.[77]

These numbers are a far cry from the thousands of protégés claimed by some Ottomanist historians, although they do not include *beratlı* merchants under Ottoman protection. It seems that more than trading under European protection, most of the *beratlı* merchants were seeking exemption from the poll tax for themselves and their sons and servants. These berats had to be renewed at the accession of each sultan and were not necessarily hereditary.

As European governments tried to gain political and religious influence over Ottoman communities, the government of Selim III (1789–1807) initiated a policy to restrict the European embassies' and consulates' abuse of the protection system in the late eighteenth century.[78] The government placed bans on the commercial activities of dragomans and revoked their berats if dragomans were found to be engaged in trade. Increasingly, French traders came to resent the competition from and the wide networks of the protégés and complained to the Chamber of Commerce in Marseille. They blamed the untrustworthy character of the protégés and the Levantines for the reduction of their income from the trade in the Levant.[79]

Like the Ottoman state, the Levant companies were concerned about the ambassadors' abuses of the protégé system and constantly complained about it to both the ambassadors and the Ottoman state. The companies did not welcome competition from well-placed Greek, Armenian, and Jewish merchants in the Levant and were often opposed to the protection system. The directors of the English Levant Company wrote to the Porte about its own concerns about the ambassadors' abuse of the protégé system in the mid-eighteenth century and tried to reform the system.[80] In other words, as Boogert notes, granting berats was neither a state policy nor an "instrument of imperialism," nor was the activity supported by the directors of the Levant Companies.[81] Granting berats was simply a method created by ambassadors and consuls as a way to make money and supplement their incomes.[82]

The Ottoman state also relied on non-Muslim subjects as interpreters. It hired members of the Greek Phanariot community like the Mavrogordato and Ghika families as its dragomans (see chapter 4).[83] In Istanbul, the position became hereditary among the Greek Phanariot families, making them exempt from the payment of the poll tax. After having served as dragomans in the Porte, members of the Phanariot families were appointed as princes and governors (*voyvodas*) of one of the Danubian principalities. They formed an aristocracy of their own and enjoyed great influence and prestige in foreign affairs at the Porte. During the Greek Rebellion, the Ottoman government stopped hiring the Phanariots since a Greek dragoman had been implicated in the rebellion in 1821. The government of Mahmud II began training Muslim bureaucrats like Yahya Efendi and non-Phanariot Greeks as interpreters and employed them in the Bureau of Translation during the second half of the nineteenth century.[84]

However, the abuse of this system by some European ambassadors during the nineteenth century and the compliance of Ottoman authorities led to tensions and backlashes. Contrary to the perceptions of some scholars, the protégés remained Ottoman subjects and were under Ottoman legal jurisdiction. When they intermarried with European subjects, the legal status of the children of protégés created a great deal of confusion and tension between the consular and local courts. Ottoman imperial orders to prevent this abuse were therefore issued to European ambassadors. For example, the Porte issued an order to all embassies in 1837 about establishing its own brokers for European traders, a pronouncement that led to the protest of the French ambassador, who wanted to retain the freedom to appoint brokers for the embassy's own merchants.[85] Furthermore, in 1839, all foreign governments had to appoint their consuls and dragomans in the Ottoman Empire from among their own subjects.[86] The Ottoman state also attempted to stop foreign merchants from being involved in domestic trade.

Despite these measures, the embassies continued selling these berats in larger numbers to Ottoman minorities in the late eighteenth and nineteenth centuries. For example, in 1784, the tax collector of Salonica complained that he could not collect the poll tax from many subjects in the Kara Karye district because they claimed European jurisdiction and kept switching from the protection of one consulate to another to avoid paying the poll tax, contrary to the terms of the ahdname. The tax collector was asking for an imperial order to the district governor and the kadi of Salonica to collect these taxes and to only provide exemptions to the actual dragomans, their sons, and their servants.[87]

Conversion to Catholicism was another means of becoming a French protégé and obtaining a berat and exemption form the poll tax.

RELIGIOUS ENCOUNTERS: COHABITATION
AND CONVERSION

The right of religious worship was an important aspect of life among non-Muslim communities, including Europeans, that had treaty relations with the Ottoman Empire. The religious pluralism of Galata and other Ottoman ports (as well as some cities) gave rise to great interaction among communities of faith. Although the construction of new churches was banned, Christian communities could repair churches after major fires or earthquakes with official permission from the state as long as they followed the old plan and did not expand or add new parts. The French community sought official permission in accordance with the ahdname to celebrate Easter in Galata in April 1756, as the following petition demonstrates:

> Next Sunday will be the festival of Paskalya (*kızıl yumurta[,]* or Easter). Following our old tradition, we would like to carry out our ritual around our Latin church (St. Benoit?) with candles at hand from Friday night until Sunday night in Galata. We are hereby informing the Sublime Porte via our dragoman about our upcoming festival.

> Imperial order to the voyvoda of Galata: They should carry out their festival according to their tradition.[88]

Due to the historical presence of Catholic churches and a Catholic community in Galata since the Genoese times in the thirteenth century, Catholics' rites and festivals acquired an important place in the religious landscape of Galata and Pera. After the rise of Pera, new Catholic, Protestant, and Greek Orthodox churches were constructed since Pera was not subject to the restrictions of the Treaty of 1453. The French Embassy had its own chapel, but the Church of St. Benoit in Galata became the center of French religious activities.

In addition, the Dutch and English communities built their own Protestant churches in Pera, adding to the diversity of Christian communities in Galata and Pera. Therefore, the religious landscape of Galata and Pera was quite diverse, and major Christian denominations were present as well. Many neighborhoods remained mixed, and cohabitation among practitioners of different faiths influenced religious rites and practices, created porous boundaries, and sometimes led to intermarriage and conversion. Muslims attended mass during Christmas in the Church of St. Antoine in Pera, and Muslim women went there to pray to St. Mary and seek healing for the sick.[89] The figure of the Virgin Mary acquired a special position as a female saint in Muslim religious rites, and a *surah* (chapter) in the Qur'an (the *surah* of Mary) is devoted to her and to the immaculate birth of Jesus Christ. At the same time, some Europeans took part in the Mevlevi rituals in Galata, and some renegades like Count de Bonneval (Humbaracı Ahmed Pasha) joined the lodge, converted to Sufi Islam, and were later buried there.[90]

The Ahdnames of 1673 and 1740 provided freedom of worship to French priests, monks, and missionaries as well as exemption from the poll tax. The Ahdnames of 1673 and 1740 also allowed French Catholic missionaries to carry out their activities in Galata, towns, and other ports where a sizable French community resided. Additionally, the ahdnames between France and the Ottoman Empire (1673 and 1740) contained special articles on the protection of French monks (Jesuits and Capuchins), their churches, and two monasteries in Galata and elsewhere and guaranteed the monks' freedom to travel to the holy places in and around Jerusalem (see chapter 4).

In Galata French Jesuit and Capuchin communities resided near the churches of St. Benoit and St. George. The Latin Church of St. Benoit was the center of French Jesuit missionaries as well as the spiritual center of the French nationals. Christmas ceremonies were held there every year.[91] The Latin Church of St. Peter in Galata was also very important for the community, especially for baptism and marriage.[92] In Izmir, the French community built a Capuchin church (St. Polycarbe) across from the French consul's residence in the seventeenth century. The church was grand and open to Greeks, Armenians, and other Christians when there was no plague. When the plague hit, the church was only open to the French and other Europeans for fear of contagion (see chapter 4).[93]

The papacy and the French government each claimed jurisdiction over the remaining Catholic churches in Galata and elsewhere and those that had been built recently in Pera, Izmir, and other ports. After the Vatican established the office of *Propaganda Fide* in 1622 to promote conversion among the Christian subjects of the sultan, Roman Catholic priests and missionaries began converting them, acting as guardians of the holy places in Palestine.[94] The French king, Louis XIV, considered himself the intermediary between the Pope and the sultan and maintained an interest over the Catholic holy places and Catholic subjects of the sultan (see chapter 4).[95] The plan was to bring the sultan's Christian subjects under the authority of the Pope before they were converted to the Protestant faith by English missionaries. Antoine Galland described the regular contacts between the French ambassador and the Greek and Armenian Catholic patriarchs in Istanbul while he was the dragoman of the French Embassy in 1670s.[96] Galland also collected Greek Orthodox religious texts and visited the Patriarchate regularly. The French ambassador, Nointel, was opposed to the Calvinist propaganda that the Dutch priests disseminated among the Greek Orthodox Christians and was putting pressure on the latter to reject the doctrine.

Moreover, French monks who attempted to convert local Christians, in particular, Armenian communities, faced resistance from local church leaders. For example, in April 1783, Ambassador Saint-Priest asked for an imperial order to protect French Capuchin monks while they carried out their rites in Diyarbekir and anywhere they went, in accordance with the ahdname. He asked that an imperial order be issued to the kadis of Diyarbekir and Amid to not harass the French monks.[97] From this petition, it becomes clear that French Capuchin missionaries had become active as far afield as Diyarbekir in eastern Anatolia and that local Muslim clerics were concerned about their activities. Catholic missionaries, however, were aware of the dangers of trying to convert Muslims and instead concentrated their efforts on converting Orthodox Greeks and Armenians.

Tensions erupted from time to time among the French monks and local Christian communities and led to violence and the intervention of Ottoman authorities. For example, in January 1751, the French ambassador, Vergennes, complained to the Porte about the mistreatment of French traders and monks by local Greek residents on the island of Chios. The local residents claimed that the French had converted several Greeks who were consular protégés to Catholicism, kidnapping them on French ships to Europe. Furthermore, the Greeks had broken into the houses of the French monks, consul, and traders and had used threats of violence to prevent any Greek from working for the French.[98] The ambassador claimed that the Greek residents had harmed the trade of the French nation on Chios with their assaults, acting contrary to the terms of the ahdname. Since France was an old and trustworthy ally of the Sublime Porte, the ambassador was asking for an end to this state of affairs and for punishment of the three Greek ringleaders. Meanwhile, the leader of the Greek community on Chios also presented a petition to the Islamic court of Chios concerning the conversion of some Greeks to Catholicism by the French monks, who then placed the Greeks on a ship to send them to France. The Greeks also claimed that their wives and sons had converted to Catholicism, bringing about the breakdown of their families. The Greek Orthodox patriarch was demanding that the Ottoman state punish any Greeks who had converted to Catholicism by sending them to the galleys. The Ottoman state subsequently did adopt this policy toward converts to Catholicism in the eighteenth century.

This is a fascinating case of the collapse of religious harmony between the local Greeks and the French monks and traders in Chios, which may also reflect economic tensions. The tensions brewing between the French residents of Chios, including the French missionaries, and the local Greek Orthodox residents who resisted them invited the intervention of the Ottoman state. The French ambassador defended the rights of the French missionaries in accordance with the ahdnames while the Greeks called on the sultan to protect the boundaries of their community and families against conversion by French missionaries. The situation had gotten out of control, leading to violence, kidnapping, and the decline of trade as well as punishment of the converts. The Ottoman state was in an ambivalent position, trying to protect its own Christian communities while also upholding the articles of the ahdname. The French ambassador protected the French missionaries while the Ottoman state increasingly opted to punish converts to Catholicism by sentencing them to forced labor in the galleys in accordance with the demand of the Orthodox patriarchs.[99]

The French ambassador also tried to expand his jurisdiction over the holy sites in Jerusalem and its surrounding areas and supervised the activities of Jesuit and Capuchin priests in Palestine, Izmir, and Galata. The growing influence of the French Catholic church in the Holy Land led to tensions among various Christian communities that held jurisdictions over the holy sites. French monks had to compete with the Greek Orthodox priests in Jerusalem over jurisdiction of holy places, and the growing tensions led to the arrest of five Capuchin priests by Ottoman officials during this period. The French priests had been accused of breaching the articles of the capitulations and constructing new churches, violations for which they had to pay fines.

Although French missionaries faced stiff resistance from the Greek Orthodox community opposed to their activities, they did succeed in converting a good number of Armenian Orthodox Christians to Catholicism in the eighteenth century. French missionary activities peaked during the late seventeenth century, particularly among the Orthodox Armenian communities in Galata, Izmir, and Aleppo. By the end of the seventeenth century, three-quarters of the Christian community in Aleppo had converted to Catholicism, and many Armenians in Pera had begun converting as well.[100] It is difficult to point to a single factor in the mass conversion of Armenians to Catholicism while the Greeks resisted it more successfully. Conversion may have provided better opportunities for commerce for the Armenian communities in Marseille, Livorno, and Venice as well as providing exemption from paying the poll tax and paying lower customs dues (3 percent as opposed to 5 percent) in international trade. Many had also converted to Catholicism in Iran, which was also open to the Catholic missionaries during the Safavid era (reign of Shah Abbas I).

The Armenian Orthodox Patriarchate opposed conversion that led to the loss of revenue from its flock and exerted pressure on the Ottoman state to punish the converts. In the eighteenth century, imperial orders were issued to sentence many Armenian Catholics to forced labor in the galleys while others were imprisoned.[101] For example, a certain Karabet was arrested in front of a Catholic church in Galata and was sentenced to the galleys in June 1706. During the same month, two Armenian patriarchs from Istanbul and Jerusalem, two Armenian priests, and three community leaders were sentenced to the galleys for promoting conversion to Catholicism and causing division within the community in Galata.[102] Five Armenian priests and eight converts were arrested in a Catholic church in Istanbul later that month and were also sentenced to the galleys. Most of the Armenian converts who were listed in the galley registers were from Istanbul and Galata, but some were also from Aleppo and Jerusalem. One Ağob (Akob) Hachador, a priest, had been held prisoner in the Patriarchate in the Armenian neighborhood of Samatya in Istanbul proper before an imperial order was issued to sentence him to the galleys. Another Ağob from Galata, who had converted to Catholicism while his daughter was engaged to an Armenian Orthodox, was arrested and turned in by the Armenian patriarch.[103] In another case, a certain Hizir was arrested for taking women and children to Catholic churches in Pera to study, thus creating much trouble for Armenian families, according to the petition of the Armenian Orthodox patriarch. Even though Hizir had been punished several times, he had continued his conduct and was denounced by the Armenian patriarch. An imperial order was issued sentencing him to forced labor in the galleys in 1706.[104] Many priests and even their wives were accused of converting the wives and daughters of Armenians to Catholicism, while another Armenian was accused of converting his daughter, who was engaged to an Armenian Orthodox.[105]

The French ambassador took up the cause of the Armenian Catholics and pressured the Ottoman government to release them. For example, in 1750, the French ambassador submitted a petition via the chief dragoman to the Imperial Council asking for the release of three Armenian priests (probably Catholic) and two French captives from the prison of the arsenal. They had been imprisoned due to the complaint of the Armenian Patriarch, possibly because the French priests had been trying to convert the Armenians.[106] In Pera, the Jesuits and Lazarists were in charge of converting the Armenians and Greeks to Catholicism in the Church of St. Benoit. The Jesuits managed to convert thousands of Armenians in Istanbul and Galata.[107] The government prevented the Armenian Catholics from setting up their own church, forcing them to pray at home secretly or attend Catholic churches in Galata and Pera (St. Antoine). Many Armenian Catholics frequented the Church of St. George in Galata.

These actions led to a deep division within the Greek as well as the Armenian communities.[108] The excesses of the French missionaries in their conversion efforts, the pressure exerted by Rome on French king Louis XV to support missionary activities in the Levant, and the ensuing violence and tensions with the Ottoman Christian communities undermined the position of the French ambassador in Pera. Ambassador Vergennes was opposed to the activities of the Catholic missionaries in Ottoman lands. When the papacy exerted pressure on Vergennes to obtain permission from the sultan to build a new Catholic church in Pera, he rejected the idea for fear of inciting violence from Muslims and damaging the relationship between the two states.[109] He instead advocated for moderation in missionary activities in order to maintain peace with the Muslim community. Vergennes also believed that the religious protection of the French king over the Catholic community accorded to him in the Ahdname of 1673 only extended to the French community and excluded the subjects of the sultan.[110] He was probably correct since the Ottoman state guarded the communal boundaries of its subjects in collaboration with the heads of these communities since they were officially recognized as millets. It is difficult to ascertain the social makeup of the Armenian Catholic community during the eighteenth century, but they clearly had closer ties to the French trading community and many traded with Marseille. As Armenian Catholics, they could become French protégés, intermarry with French subjects, and enjoy exemption from the poll tax, but the risks sometimes far surpassed the privileges. After the recognition of the Catholic millet under the pressure of the French government, it was given the same rights as those enjoyed by the other non-Muslim communities in the early nineteenth century. Many Catholic communities moved to villages along the Bosphorus like Ortaköy and established their churches there to enjoy greater freedom than was available to them in the rest of the city.

Violence, fires,plague, and overcrowded spaces in Galata and Istanbul proper forced members of the royal dynasty (particularly princesses), Europeans, and some members of the non-Muslim bourgeoisie to move to the villages along the Bosphorus. Taverns and pleasure gardens also spread to these villages, which had mixed inhabitants in the eighteenth century. Baron de Tott observed that while it was difficult for Ottoman women to get involved in illicit relations in the city, the villages along the Bosphorus provided them with ample opportunities to escape and enjoy greater freedom in their activities.[111] Sometimes women got into trouble while seeking adventures in these villages. In November 1751, according to the report of the kadi of Galata, two boatmen took a group of Muslim women on a boat ride to Ortaköy. They tried to kidnap these women and forcefully take them to the islands. However, the screams and cries of the women attracted the attention of another boat's passengers, who came to their aid and caught one of the boatmen while the other fled. An order was then issued to the boatmen's guild directing it to only hire boatmen with guarantors, expel those who lacked them, and register all boatmen in the four districts of Istanbul.[112]

Moreover, sexual interactions in these villages were also under the scrutiny of the neighborhood watch and invited intervention by the state since the Ottoman elite also resided there. Sometimes residents took collective action when predatory men threatened women's honor in the neighborhood. The community watch system was in place to report breaches of the moral code by men and women, Muslims and non-Muslims. For example, in March 1786, more than 165 Greek, Armenian, Jewish, and Muslim residents of the village of Ortaköy, led by their community leaders, presented a lawsuit against the steward of the guild of *hamam* (public bath) workers, a certain Isma'il Efendi, to the court of Galata. They stated that the workers of the Çifte Hamam (possibly the Hüsrev Kethüda Hamam built by Sinan in 1550) had to be selected from the ranks of trustworthy people to protect the honor of the women who attended the hamam. According to the petition, the manager of the Çifte Hamam in Ortaköy, Mehmed Emin, and some of the workers were of dubious backgrounds and had been employed without presentation of any guarantors. The petition stated that the workers constantly fought

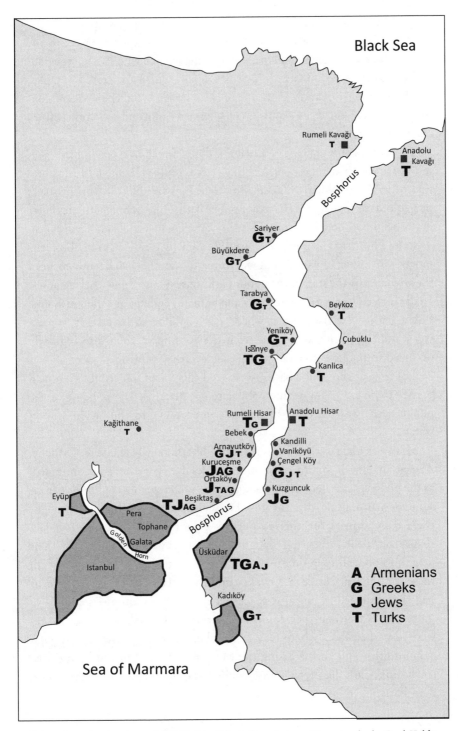

Villages along the Bosphorus Identified by Ethnic Populations. Cartography by Paul Kaldjian, based on Mantran's maps of Istanbul (1962).

amongst themselves and that the manager was also a womanizer. The residents said that he was in the habit of frequenting a shop next to the entrance of the women's hamam and harassing women who entered the public bath. They also complained that this hamam, which also served notables, had become corrupt and unsafe due to the manager's and the workers' conduct. They demanded the expulsion of Mehmed Emin and the workers from the hamam.[113]

This is a fascinating case of a neighborhood watch in a very mixed community in which members of the ruling class as well as Ottoman Muslim and non-Muslim individuals resided. The moral misconduct of working-class people and the manager of the major public bath, Çifte Hamam, in the center of the neighborhood, had united Muslim, Armenian, Greek, and Jewish residents and brought them to the court of Galata. This case was not about the moral misconduct of women but was instead about the sexual harassment of these women by the staff of the public bathhouse. It also shows that members of all these communities used the same hamam, perhaps at different hours. Public baths were risky places where men could break in, assault women, steal, and watch naked women from the rooftop.[114] Theft also regularly occurred in public baths and mosques. Nevertheless, women spent a great deal of time at the public baths, socialized there, and sometimes even held parties there for young women about to get married. The policing of the public baths was therefore of primary importance to the neighborhood watch.

Moreover, Ortaköy had become the neighborhood where Greek, Catholic, Armenian, Jewish, and Muslim communities lived together and comingled, as the previous case demonstrates. Ottoman princesses also built waterfront summer mansions nearby. The moral misconduct of a Muslim man brought these communities together to present a petition to the kadi of Galata to protect their wives and daughters from sexual harassment in their neighborhood. The community watch system included the heads of all these communities of faith. Ortaköy and the villages along the Bosphorus had thus emerged as pluralist spaces where these communities could live in greater peace than they could in the rest of the Galata. These villages were also the places where female members of the dynasty, the foreign communities, and an increasing the Muslim and non-Muslim bourgeoisie (including Catholic Armenians) rubbed shoulders and interacted on a daily basis.

The movement of members of the ruling class and the Europeans from the
walled districts of Galata to the fishing villages along the Bosphorus gave rise
to a new age of leisure and pleasure. These villages were part of the district of
Galata and were similar in their social makeup. In the eighteenth century,
members of the royal dynasty set up waterfront summer mansions in
Beşiktaş, Ortaköy, and Bebek. European embassies also had their summer
residences in some of these villages, such as Büyükdere. Paolo Girardelli has
argued that the summer residences of the French, British, and Russian
Embassies were not monumental in contrast with the embassy buildings in
Pera but rather followed the Ottoman vernacular palatial design in the villages along the Bosphorus.[115] The embassies' summer residences provided
Europeans access to the Ottoman ruling class, who lived in their waterfront
palaces in Beşiktaş and Bebek from the months of May to November. Thus,
during the summer months, the Ottoman Dynasty, along with the major
European diplomatic corps, moved to the villages along the Bosphorus,
where life was more relaxed and seeking pleasure was easier than it was
in Galata.[116]

The waterfront mansions of Ottoman princesses were also spaces for
encounters between European men and women and Ottoman ruling-class
women. Ottoman princesses accumulated great wealth and enjoyed great
prestige during the eighteenth century. They enjoyed greater freedom than
the queen mothers and princes had and married Ottoman elite men who led
monogamous lives. Princess Fatma Sultan, the daughter of Ahmed III, developed a close friendship with Ambassador Villeneuve's wife. Lady Mary
Wortley Montagu, the wife of the British ambassador, John Montagu, also
enjoyed close contacts with Ottoman princesses during her stays in Edirne
and Istanbul (1717–18).[117]

Following the tradition set by Lady Montagu, European travel literature,
especially accounts written by British women, offers great insights into the
social scene and life in these villages. However, many accounts also exhibit
strong biases and reflect some authors' lack of knowledge about Ottoman
culture. More importantly, this literature exposes the state of the mind of the
European "voyeur," the growing curiosity about and interest in Ottoman
society and culture exhibited by European men and women.

The travel literature written by European visitors like Jean Thévenot to Istanbul gave rise to the writings of the French Enlightenment figures on the harem as a place of oppression and confinement, although Ottoman society and the role of women within it were changing in the eighteenth century.[118] Ottoman princesses were at the forefront of these changes. Moroever, the increasing interaction between Ottoman elite women and European women in their salons had become a feature of social life in the villages along the Bosphorus during the eighteenth and nineteenth centuries. The harem had always been a favorite subject of study for European travelers and diplomats since the early modern period. Since most European men did not have actual access to a harem, they imagined what one was like and wrote a combination of fantasy and heresay about life in a harem. For example, Jean Claude Flachat, a French manufacturer, had moved to İstanbul in 1740 and resided there and in Izmir. He was fluent in Turkish and became very close to the Chief Black Eunuch in the imperial harem. Flachat, who became the chief merchant of the palace, installed mirrors in the palace that King Louis XV had presented to Sultan Mahmud I (1730–54). Flachat thus gained access to the harem in the Topkapi Palace and observed life within its walls. Upon his return to France in 1766, he published his observations on the commerce and arts of the Ottoman Empire as well as on life in the harem.[119]

French culture was in vogue in the courts of the Ottoman sultans in the late eighteenth century. There is ongoing debate about whether one of the concubines of Sultan Abdulhamid I (1774–89), Nakşidel, was a French captive by the name of Marthe Aimée-Rose du Buc de Rivéry, the daughter of a French owner of a wealthy plantation in Martinique and the cousin of Josephine Bonaparte, Napoleon's wife.[120] She was born in the French Caribbean colony of Martinique and had been captured by Algerian pirates while she was on her way to Nantes to enroll in the Convent of the Dames de la Visitation in 1776. She apparently had been sold into the harem of Abdulhamid I and might have given birth to Sultan Mahmud II.[121] Her presence in the harem would have been very beneficial for French influence in the court of Abdulhamid I and Selim III(1789–1807).

Moreover, European painters like the Flemish Jean-Baptiste Vanmour (1671–1737), the French Antoine-Ignace Melling (1763–1831), and the French Antoine de Favray (1706–91) were commissioned by Dutch and French ambassadors in the eighteenth century to illustrate panoramas of Istanbul and Galata, villages along the Bopshorus, embassy receptions, Byzantine and Ottoman monuments, portraits of Ottoman officials, and harem scenes as well as the male and female denizens of Istanbul in domestic and street scenes, coffeehouses, and waterworks.[122]

In addition, European architects played an important role in designing the palaces of Ottoman princesses. Kuban has emphasized Melling's role in the spread of French classical architecture, which also included Ottoman elements.[123] Melling (1763–1831) became the royal architect of Selim III and his sister, Hadice Sultan, the daughter of Sultan Abdulhamid I and the sister of Sultan Selim III. He was born in Lorraine in 1763 and had been trained in painting, sculpture, and classical architecture in Paris.[124] Melling traveled in Europe and the Levant, visiting Izmir and Egypt. In 1784, at age 20, he accompanied the French ambassador's retinue to Istanbul. He first worked under the patronage of the Russian ambassador, Yakov Ivanovic Bulgakov. Melling lived in Istanbul for eighteen years (1784–1803), during which he designed the garden and interior of the waterfront palace of Princess Hadice Sultan in Defterdar Burnu in Ortaköy, which displayed strong European neoclassical rococo influences in a wooden structure.[125] In 1793, he also designed the princely pavilion of Neşatabad for Selim III on the European shores of the Bosphorus, which was an extension of Hadice Sultan's palace.[126] In addition, Melling consulted with François Kauffer, a cartographer, in drawing up the plan of İstanbul in 1776. Kauffer had accompanied the French ambassador, Gouffier, to Pera. Melling was also close to Gouffier and lived in Pera before and after the French Revolution. He was the royal architect to the sultan and Hadice Sultan and a painter of eighteenth-century Istanbul.

Melling became closely involved with Hadice Sultan.[127] He visited the sultana in her mansion, taught her the Latin alphabet, and purchased furniture and clothing for her in Paris.[128] He also learned Turkish but wrote his letters in the Latin alphabet. He and the sultana exchanged several letters regarding his purchase of furniture, silk textiles, jewelry, and furnishings for her.[129] Hadice Sultan addressed Melling in a very familiar manner, calling him "my architect Melling," while Melling kept a very respectful tone in his letters. It is possible that the two enjoyed intimate relations since he stayed at her husband's apartment when the husband was away. Hadice Sultan also built a small hotel for Melling next to her palace.

Melling learned a great deal about the lives of Ottoman princesses through his interactions with Hadice Sultan. He observed that every Ottoman princess exercised great sovereign power in her harem, unlike the princes, whose lives were confined. He noticed that there was a great difference between the

Antoine-Ignace Melling, *The Palace of Hadice Sultan at Defterdar Burnu.* Photo courtesy of the Newberry Library, Chicago.

lives of women like the princesses, who had been born free, and those of the concubines. Hadice Sultan had married a rich pasha, the governor of Erzurum, who was very obedient in complying with her wishes and who could not visit her without her permission. He followed Hadice Sultan's orders and showered her with gifts. She was also very close to her brother, Sultan Selim III, who visited her regularly in her waterfront palace.[130]

European ambassadors used Melling to gain access to Hadice Sultan's garden. They offered her gifts of luxurious silks and Indian textiles. Hadice Sultan also entertained French and English women (the wives of ambassadors and the sister of the French Consul in Izmir) in her palatial residence in Ortaköy. The sultana received the French Consul's sister, about whom she was very curious, in her palace and communicated with her through Melling.

Hadice Sultan also helped Melling gain access to her brother, Selim III (1789–1807), who had been tutored in the French culture. Sultan Selim III commissioned Melling as the court architect to design part of the Çirağan Palace in Beşiktaş. Melling was also planning to build a palace in the French style in Saray Burnu, a project that never came to fruition due to Napoleon's invasion of Egypt in 1798 (see epilogue).

Following Napoleon's invasion of Egypt in 1798 and the subsequent war between France and the Ottoman Empire, Melling left for Paris in 1803. He

Antoine-Ignace Melling, *View of Constantinople from Büyükdere*. Photo courtesy of the Newberry Library, Chicago.

published his album of more than forty-eight magnificent engravings of Istanbul, Galata, and the villages along the Bosphorus in 1819, with corresponding texts written by Barbie de Bocage.[131] Some of these engravings depict the interior and exterior of the palace of Hadice Sultan, waterfront mansions and social life in the villages along the Bosphorus, and the presence of European men and women in villages such as Büyükdere along the European shore of the Bosphorus. In one of these paintings (above), Melling depicts himself sitting in one of the villages along the Bosphorus with his canvas and brush in hand.

According to Melling, the village of Büyükdere was the most popular among the European residents due to its charm and natural beauty. The Europeans built waterfront mansions in different architectural styles. Melling praised the summer mansions of the Danish and Russian ambassadors for their elegance. The French lived in their own quarter close to Sariyer, which was the most beautiful part of Büyükdere. They hosted picnics in the open fields where French women interacted with French men. The picnics also attracted the attention of Ottoman women, who were equally curious about the private lives of French women.[132]

The English, French, Dutch, and Russian ambassadors also had residences in the Belgrade Forest and held picnics, hunting expeditions, and parties there during the hot summer months in the eighteenth cetury. Sometimes the sultan would pass by the village during his visits to the acqueducts and receive gifts of sweet meats and sherbets from the ambassadors.[133] Baron de Tott's wife visited the palace of Ottoman princess Esma Sultan (1726–88), the daughter of Sultan Ahmed III (1703–30) and the sister of Sultan Mahmud I (1730–54), along the Bosphorus in the late eighteenth century and reported the details of the palace, dress, servants, reception, dinner, and entertainment to her husband.[134] Baron de Tott described his wife's visit with Esma Sultan in the following manner:

> Under the reign of Sultan Mahamout, this princess, yet young, and induced by the example of her brother [Sultan Mahmud I] ... to a sort of predilection in favor of the Franks, desired to have a conversation with some European women. My wife's mother, though born in Turkey, was sufficient to satisfy her curiosity, and with her daughter was invited to her palace, where the Intendant of the Exterior was ordered to receive them ... and conduct them to the sultana [Esma Sultan].[135]

Ottoman princesses like Fatma Sultan, Hadice Sultan, and Esma Sultan developed friendships with European women and invited them to their palaces, which functioned like salons. The princesses were as equally curious about European women as the Europeans were about them since the Europeans were interested in their mysterious lifestyles.[136] The Turkish women were very intrigued by English customs and the intermingling of the sexes. When English men and women bathed in the Bosphorus and danced together at balls in Tarabya, they were called "the crazy English" by their Turkish observers from behind their windows. When Edward Montagu, the son of Lady Mary Wortley Montagu, appeared in Istanbul in September 1767 wearing a long beard and a turban, he must have been the subject of much curiosity in Pera and among his Turkish as well as his European neighbors. John Murray, the English ambassador in Pera who had to host him at the embassy for seven months (1767–68), complained in his private letters about Edward's eccentric conduct and sexual polygamy. Edward Montagu had married a third wife, Catherine Dormer, in Alexandria.[137] Murray wrote in a letter to Edward Hayes in England:

> I imagine he [Montagu] is unwilling to let me know that he is going to meet his Fair one, as he has denied it to me, though I was pretty sure it was his intention, he having bought an infinite number of women's Baubles. He was angry at me for not calling her his wife.[138]

Cultural cross-dressing by European men and women had become a leisure activity as well as a way of gaining more freedom in public spaces. Lady Mary Montagu wore Turkish dress to gain access to Muslim neighborhoods outside Pera in Istanbul proper and to visit the harems of Turkish princesses.[139] The father of the famous French Enlightenment figure Jean Jacques Rousseau resided in Pera as a watchmaker for seven years in 1720s and continued to wear Ottoman clothing when he returned to Geneva.[140] Ambassador Vergennes and his wife, Madame Testa, also dressed in Turkish costume. Indeed, many French and English men and women had become part of the social map of Galata and villages along the Bosphorus as denizens of the Levant and adopted the Ottoman culture and way of life with great ease without having to give up their own. They had acquired hybrid identities.

CONCLUSION

Ottoman ports were sites of commercial, cultural, sexual, and legal encounters between the growing European community and the Ottoman communities. Yet communities of faith guarded the sexual and religious boundaries and punished those who crossed them. The Ottoman state reinforced these boundaries on behalf of its own Muslim and non-Muslim communal leaders. Moreover, European states also discouraged marriage between their men and Ottoman women, although the number of these marriages increased and gave rise to a "Levantine community." Can we define these men and women as the products of a cosmopolitan culture in Ottoman ports? Edhem Eldem argues that the term *cosmopolite* was used first by a certain French traveler, Théophile, to describe the *Republic of Turks* in 1529.[141] Ian Coller has described the hybrid social mix of Istanbul as "vernacular Eurasian cosmopolitanism," in which daily practices among the *marchant Franc* varied from hybrid dress to intermarriage and even to conversion to Islam in the eighteenth century.[142] As Ottoman ports became more diverse and "cosmopolitan" during the nineteenth century, the term *Levantine,* which once applied to the cosmopolitan residents of the Levant, became a negative term (meaning "superficial, untrustworthy, and tricky") for the Latinized Ottoman non-Muslim subjects and converts to Catholicism who had intermarried with the Europeans. The term was also used to describe the long-term European residents of Ottoman ports who had turned "Turk." In other words, although a few Europeans may have converted to Islam, others had intermarried with members of local Ottoman Christian communities. Whether they were European Levantines or local Latinized bourgeoisie, their hybrid identities became the subject of scrutiny, resentment, and even distrust among both the Europeans and Ottoman intellectuals who were turning to nationalism as an ideology.

No doubt, Ottoman pluralism did not mean legal equality among Muslim and non-Muslim subjects or multiculturalism in the western modern sense of the word. The millet system that recognized the legal status of Ottoman non-Muslim communities was contingent on the second-class status of non-Muslims and their submission to Muslim rule until the Tanzimat era reforms in 1839 that granted equality to all Ottoman citizens regardless of religion. Edhem Eldem has argued that before these reforms the Ottoman state was better able to absorb the "other" at the elite level, where there was a great deal of upward mobility among foreigners through conversion to Islam, as well as at the low end of society among the poor residents of port cities (renegades, merchants, and transnational subjects), than at the middle-class level. He is right to point out that while at both ends individuals were allowed to cross the communal boundaries, a cosmopolitan and pluralistic consciousness did NOT develop among the vast majority of the population, even as late as the nineteenth century. Thus, the pluralism of Ottoman ports became fragile and subject to rupture during times of economic and political crises as well as to the spread of ethno-religious nationalism in the Balkans during the nineteenth century. Napoleon's invasion of Egypt in 1798 and the resulting tensions and the role of European and Russian states as protectors of Catholic (France) and Greek Orthodox communities that had been granted to them in the ahdnames exacerbated the situation. Ethno-religious tensions broke out in Ottoman ports and cities like Izmir and Salonica that had once been pluralist spaces.

Perhaps a "cosmopolitan culture" had more potential to develop in villages along the European shores of the Bosphorus than in the districts inside Galata's walls.

Epilogue

THE UNRAVELING OF THE FRENCH
REVOLUTION IN PERA

The unraveling of the French Revolution in 1789, the revolutionary wars (1792–1801), and Napoleon's invasion of Egypt in 1798 had a major impact on Ottoman-French trade and diplomacy as well as on the lives of French communities in Ottoman ports.[1] Although the government of Selim III (1789–1807) initially recognized the French revolutionary government in Paris and continued diplomatic relations with France, Napoleon's invasion of Egypt in 1798 disrupted this relationship in a profound manner and breached the state of peace between the two states. Moreover, this brief but important occupation was the beginning of French colonial projects in North Africa, although as a result of a joint Ottoman-English campaign, Napoleon was forced to evacuate Egypt with his forces within three years.[2] This disruption did not last long, and peace between the two states was eventually restored in 1802 (Treaty of Amiens).[3] But the French Revolution marked the end of a long era of peace, the Ahdname of 1740, and the dissolution of the French Levant Company.

THE FRENCH COMMUNITY UNDER ARREST

In the aftermath of the French Revolution and the subsequent invasion of Egypt a decade or so later, the lives of the French communities in Ottoman ports and cities were disrupted in a serious and violent manner. For example, in September 1798, the Ottoman government declared war on France and arrested the French *chargé d' affaires,* Pierre-Jean Ruffin (amb. 1742–1824), and the embassy staff and imprisoned them in Yedi Kule Prison until 1801 (for three years). Ruffin had been born to a dragoman family in Salonica in 1742, received his education in Marseille in Oriental languages, and then joined the embassy of Vergennes in Istanbul in 1758.[4] Subsequently, he joined Baron de Tott, the consul in Crimea in 1767, and became consul there in 1770. Ruffin was imprisoned by the Russian forces for seven months in 1771, no doubt due to Baron de Tott's role in the defense of the Dardanelles against the Russian navy. Ruffin returned to Istanbul in 1772 and served as dragoman in the French Embassy. In 1774, he was recalled to France and became a professor of Turkish and Persian languages in the College de France. After the French Revolution, he was sent to the embassy in Istanbul in 1795 as the chief secretary-interpreter and was named *chargé d'affaires* in 1798. Ruffin's term coincided with Napoleon's invasion of Egypt on July 2, 1798, which affected his life and the lives of his staff in a dramatic way.

After the imprisonment of Ruffin and the confiscation of his goods by Ottoman officials, the treasurer of the French ambassador submitted a petition to the Imperial Council via the Flemish ambassador and dragoman requesting a receipt for the trunk that Ottoman officials had confiscated from the French Embassy in September 1798. In response, the government of Selim III sent the following response to the Flemish ambassador in May 1799:

> French forces invaded Egypt, the gate to the holy cities, without any notice or provocation, thus breaching the ahdname [of 1740] between the two states. Moreover, the Ottoman ambassador to France, Seyyid Ali Efendi, was taken hostage in Paris. Therefore, the French ambassador, Ruffin, and the embassy staff have been detained in the Yedi Kule prison. Since the French had arrested Muslim and non-Muslim merchants who were not war captives in Alexandria, confiscating their properties, the Ottoman state has issued orders for the arrest of all French subjects in Istanbul and all over the empire and the confiscation of their property in response to the French conduct. We hereby issue a receipt to the Flemish ambassador for having received a trunk that belongs to the French embassy.[5]

Although this letter was written to the Flemish ambassador almost nine months after the French invasion of Egypt in July 1798, it reflected a radical change in the perspective of the Ottoman government toward Napoleon's aggression and the French government. The arrest of the Ottoman ambassador, Seyyid Ali Efendi, in Paris in 1798 was also viewed as a breach of the peace that had existed between the two states. Therefore, the government of Selim III revoked the ahdname between the two states and discontinued its protection of the French ambassador, consuls, and subjects in the Ottoman Empire after almost three hundred years of peace and close alliance.

Soon French communities in Pera and in other Ottoman ports and towns became targets of arrest, imprisonment, and confiscation of their property, regardless of their sentiments toward the revolutionary government in Paris. The Ottoman government issued imperial orders to Ahmed Agha, the voyvoda of Galata, for the arrest of the rest of the embassy staff and French residents in Galata and Pera[6] (see appendix). Frenchmen were rounded up and put in prison while their property and goods were confiscated. Furthermore, an imperial order was issued to the kadi and voyvoda of Galata to collect all the guns from the French Embassy.[7] The voyvoda conducted a thorough inspection of the embassy and collected about twenty-six muskets and guns (see appendix). They then registered and placed the guns in a storage house in the han of watchsellers in Galata in September 1798. Ottoman officials also discovered several other trunks belonging to the embassy in the Spanish Embassy and turned them over to the voyvoda, who registered their contents.

The French community also sought the aid of other embassies during these inspections and the growing violence against Frenchmen by mobs in Pera and other ports. According to a report by the voyvoda of Galata, many Frenchmen had taken refuge in European embassies, paying money for protection. For example, two French royalist merchants sought protection from Ambassador Ainslie in the British Embassy. Despite their royalist sentiments, these merchants wore the tricolor cockade, which was a symbol of republicanism, since their families and property in France could be targets of the revolutionary government. But when Napoleon invaded Egypt in July 1798, the British Embassy revoked its protection of these two merchants at the request of the Ottoman government. The Ottoman state then imprisoned the merchants and confiscated their goods because of their revolutionary appearance.[8] The English ambassador made several requests to the Porte for the release of the two merchants, their servant, and their goods through Smith, the dragoman of the embassy.[9] The Ottoman government claimed that the men were revolutionaries and had been caught wearing the tricolor cockade. The Liberty Tree and the tricolor cockade (blue, white, and red) had become important symbols of the French Revolution, and about sixty thousand Liberty Trees had been planted all over France in 1792.[10] The government of Selim III had initially allowed the wearing of the cockade and the celebration of revolutionary festivities despite the objections of Austrian and Russian ambassadors, demonstrating its indifference to the revolutionary sentiments of French residents.

Shortly after the French invasion of Egypt, Ottoman officials also began inspecting all French houses in Pera and seized the French Embassy. Imperial orders were issued for all brokers to announce that any Frenchmen who tried to enter the French Embassy for five days would be arrested as thieves.[11] Furthermore, those who hid Frenchmen and did not turn them in were to be arrested, and Frenchmen who gathered in the French Embassy would be sent to fortress prisons. No one was allowed to enter the French Embassy except Ottoman officials and guards who had been placed around the embassy to prevent the entry of Frenchmen.[12] The Ottoman state released a royalist French merchant and member of the French assembly and the revolutionary club, Floranville, who had been imprisoned in the French Embassy, and turned him over to the dragoman of the embassy of Sicily in March 1799. This move on the part of the Ottoman government indicates the growing Ottoman sympathy for the royalists, in contrast to its earlier position of neutrality. Shortly after, several orders were issued to the kadi and voyvoda of Galata and to Ottoman officials in other ports to imprison French consuls and residents all over the empire and confiscate their goods.[13]

Some Frenchmen also became targets of violence and theft after government orders had been issued for their arrest and imprisonment. Some residents of Pera took the law into their own hands by denouncing Frenchmen and trying to take advantage of their desperate situation. For example, we learn from the Galata court register that a French painter named Reno was murdered in the house of a certain Avanes (an Armenian) outside Galata in October 1798.[14] The court entry does not provide further information on the motives for the murder or the background of the murderer. The date of this murder coincides with the date of the orders for the arrest of Frenchmen in Galata and Pera. Robbery, a brawl after drinking, or a claim of debt owed could well have been the backstory for the act of murder, given the deep involvement of Frenchmen in the economic, religious, and cultural life of Ottoman ports. This crime might have also been due to a state of emergency that precipitated the arrest and harassment of all French subjects in Galata and Pera, a condition that provided ample opportunities for the French to be mistreated by average people to whom they might have owed money or who simply wanted to claim a piece of property that belonged to a Frenchman.

THE FRENCH COMMUNITY IN PERA BETWEEN THE
CROWN AND THE REPUBLIC

Although the immediate impact of the French Revolution in the Levant was not felt among many Ottoman subjects, it did cause an economic crisis, a division, and deep tensions within the French and European communities in Ottoman ports and towns. Initially, the government of Selim III upheld the terms of the 1740 ahdname during the French Revolution, but tensions had been building between the two states and in the ports and cities where French communities lived. Moreover, the embassies of Austria, England, and Russia were putting pressure on the Ottoman state to curtail the activities of French revolutionaries in Pera.

But the situation on the ground was changing as the French Revolution took a radical turn after the execution of the king in January 1793 and the subsequent Reign of Terror from September 1793 to July 1794. Furthermore, the French revolutionary wars and the British blockade of the port of Marseille undermined trade and led to the bankruptcy of French merchants in Marseille and the dissolution of the French Levant Company. The number of ships entering the port of Marseilles dropped from 700 prior to the revolution to 30 in 1793 (see chapters 4 and 6).[15]

Pascal Firges's study of the period between 1789 and 1795, based largely on French sources, sheds important light on this chaotic period in Istanbul in great detail and the global turn of the French Revolution in the Levant. He has defined the situation of the French community in the Levant until 1792 (the fall of the monarchy) as a "revolution on silent feet."[16] Firges has argued that, although French community in Pera was divided between the royalists and the revolutionaries, the French government tolerated this division and did not use force to punish the royalists. The revolutionary government used propaganda rather than terror to persuade its citizens in the Levant to join its ranks. Moreover, Firges has shown that French diplomacy with the Ottoman Empire was based on pragmatism since France had lost most of its allies and only maintained embassies in three countries—the Ottoman Empire, Switzerland, and the United States—in 1792 and 1793. But Firges does not extend his study to Napoleon's colonial project and invasion of Egypt in 1798, which created a violent backlash against the French communities in the Ottoman Empire. Napoleon's plan to invade Egypt, punish the Mamluk beys, and cut the British off from the trade of India received strong support among French diplomatic circles in Paris, Egypt, and the Levant.

Moreover, Firges shows that the civil war in France played out on the streets of Galata and Pera as the community became divided between the republicans and the royalists.[17] Since French traders in Ottoman ports had suffered financially as a result of the drop in trade, many sympathized with King Louis XVI. Traders abandoned their shops and participated in revolutionary politics, some for the Republic and others against it.[18] The Ottoman government tolerated the activities of the French revolutionaries in Pera for a while and allowed their propaganda, celebrations, and festivals on the occasion of the fall of the monarchy in August 1792 and the inauguration of the French Republic in September 1792.[19]

However, as the revolution entered a violent phase during the Reign of Terror from 1793 to 1794, the French community members in Pera and other ports began fighting and clashing over their sympathies and opposition to the revolution. The revolutionary majority in Pera, composed of French, Dutch, and some English sympathizers known as Jacobins, deposed the French ambassador, Choiseul Gouffier (amb. 1784–1792), for his royalist ties and elected a dragoman, Antoine Fonton, as chargé d'affaires in Istanbul in October 1792.[20]

The French Republic accepted the new appointment in 1792 in the midst of a serious crisis within the community.[21] But Antoine Fonton resigned from his position in 1793 because he could not impose his authority and opted for Russian diplomatic protection. The rest of the Fonton family, like Pierre Fonton, and the legation's staff joined the Russian Embassy as dragomans. Like England, Russia was emerging as a protector of French royalists.

Ambassador Gouffier, who was a royalist, was recalled to France by the republican government due to his plans to cooperate with the brother of the king and the Russian, Prussian, and Austrian governments against the revolutionary government. Gouffier also put pressure on the Ottoman government to not recognize the new French envoy. He refused to return to Paris for fear of execution since his property there had been confiscated.[22] He lived under siege in the embassy for one year and then immigrated in 1792 to Russia, where Catherine II named him the director of the Academy of Arts and Imperial Public Library. Gouffier returned to France in 1802 in a state of poverty after Napoleon had granted amnesty to exiled nobles. In Paris, Gouffier published his three-volume work, *Voyage Pittoresque dans l'empire Ottomane et de la Grèce*, in 1809.[23]

The government in Paris then appointed Étienne-Felix Hénin as the second chargé d'affaires in Istanbul in May 1793, although the Ottoman government did not approve the appointment in accordance with the ahdname. Hénin had been sent by the foreign minister, Le Brun, to introduce the new ambassador, Semonville, because the French special envoy to Istanbul, Maries-Louis-Henri Descorches, had been imprisoned in April 1793 in Bosnia.[24] Hénin, who was very close to Robespierre, represented the more radical face of the French Revolution and viewed most French residents in Pera, including Descorches, as royalists.[25] He founded a Jacobin club called the Republican Society of Liberty and Equality in August 1793 and initiated a series of surveillance measures directed at the French nation in Pera, which was composed of two hundred people, to test its revolutionary sentiments.

In October 1793, Hénin issued a ruling for all French residents of Pera to wear the tricolor cockade, although many were against doing so for fear of alienating other Europeans with whom they traded and instigating reprisals from the Ottoman government.[26] Hénin was in contact with the Committee of Public Safely in Paris and reported on the former envoy, Maries Louis-Henri Descorches (1793–94), calling him an aristocrat and soft on the royalists. Jacobin crowds also occupied the French Embassy to destroy all the symbols of the monarchy. They planted a Tree of Liberty on the embassy terrace, an action that was followed by singing and dancing and a ball on January 21, 1793.[27] Cannons from a French ship in the harbor fired shots to celebrate the anniversary of the execution of the king. A large crowd of residents of Pera watched the scene from their windows and rooftops. The name of the French Embassy was changed from *Palais de France* to the *Maison Nationale*.[28] Furthermore, the Jesuits had been routed from the Church of St. Benoit and had been replaced by the Lazarists, who had placed themselves under Austrian protection earlier.

The Ottoman government had received complaints from the royalists as well as from other Europeans in Pera about the Jacobins, who had established their own club in Pera under the leadership of Hénin. The activities of the Jacobins, their festivals, and their nocturnal gatherings disturbed the Austrian, English, and Russian ambassadors. In April 1793, the Prussian, Austrian, and Russian Embassies sent notes to the Sublime Porte complaining about the French who had "killed their king" and their excessive rowdy conduct at night in Pera. They demanded the removal of the Liberty Tree from the embassy terrace and a ban on the wearing of the tricolor cockade by Frenchmen in Pera.

The Ottoman government responded to the Prussian, Austrian, and Russian governments' demands by saying that the French were guests in the

Ottoman Empire and could dress in any fashion that they wanted.[29] The Ottoman government did, however, prohibit the celebration of Bastille Day (July 14, 1793) at the French Embassy since the behavior of the revolutionaries had gotten out of control. The French Embassy was also suffering from internal chaos and lack of funds as a result of the British blockade of trade and the disruption of regular correspondence with Paris. Many French merchants had emigrated when the French revolutionary staff arrived.[30] The Reis Efendi complained to Citizen Dantan, who was the only one of the five dragomans left in the embassy in Spring 1793, about the French Republicans' disorderly conduct that was disturbing the tranquility of the residents of Pera at night. The festivities subsequently were moved to the French Inn in Pera and ended at 6 PM. According to Firges, between 77 and 250 men (women were excluded) attended these festivals at the French Inn and at the French Embassy and delivered toasts to the prosperity of the French Republic and to Sultan Selim III. To impose order in Pera, the Ottoman government issued orders for the disarming and expulsion of French sailors from Pera in October 1794.[31] On the anniversary of the execution of the French king Louis XVI on January 21, 1795, a banquet and ball were held at the embassy that gathered two hundred guests, while the royalists also held a memorial service with officers from the embassies of Austria, Spain, and Naples.[32] Strict decorum and order dominated these festivities, and no Ottoman subject was allowed to join in for the fear of reprisals from the government.

Despite these events, French diplomacy with the Ottoman Empire continued, and the Ottoman Empire eventually recognized France's revolutionary government in 1795. French authorities in the Levant had to tolerate the divergence of sentiments within the French community and discouraged the propagation of French revolutionary ideals among Ottoman subjects for fear of alienating the Ottoman government.[33] But the Ottoman state refused to ally itself with France against Russia when the latter invaded Poland, ending its independence in 1794.[34] As an ally of France, the government of Selim III sent Raşid Efendi to London to mediate peace between France and all the Great Powers. But London and Vienna did not respond warmly to this initiative, while France welcomed the idea of a triple alliance with the Ottoman Empire and Sweden against the expansionist policies of Catherine II. Upon the arrival of Raymond Verninac in Istanbul as the special envoy and successor to Descorches in April 1795, Hénin was recalled to France after the fall from power of his patron, Robespierre, from the Committee of Public Safety.[35]

Franco-Ottoman relations experienced yet another serious crisis a few years later. General Napoleon Bonaparte (the future Emperor Napoleon I), working for the Directory of the French Republic, invaded Egypt in July 1798, dealing a heavy blow to Ottoman-French relations. His action violated the Ahdname of 1740 and led to the adoption of anti-French policies after the rise of a conservative party at the Sublime Porte and the reaction of the ulema and populace in Istanbul.[36] Angry mobs threatened the lives of French subjects in Istanbul. On September 12, the Müfti (chief jurisconsult) of Istanbul issued a fetva for a holy war against France, and the sultan declared war on France for having invaded Egypt, the gate to the holy cities of Mecca and Medina. The government also ordered the arrest and imprisonment of the French ambassador and his staff as well as members of French communities in Pera and elsewhere.

Ambassador Choiseul-Gouffier; François Baron de Tott (1733–93), a French officer of Hungarian origins; Minister Tallyrand; and the French consuls in Egypt had been promoting the invasion of Egypt for several years. Baron de Tott had earlier traveled to Istanbul in the service of his uncle, Ambassador Vergennes, to learn Turkish and to investigate the situation of the Ottoman Empire in 1755. Baron de Tott, who became the French consul to Crimea in 1767, functioned as a spy, using his government position to assess the state of the Crimean khanate and to incite rebellions against Russia there. He also played a key role in the Russo-Ottoman War in 1768–74 and was in charge of defending the Dardanelles against Russian forces. He traveled widely around the empire, Egypt, and Syria promoting the construction of a canal from Suez on the Red Sea to the Mediterranean. His memoir and account of the Ottoman Empire, which was published in 1785 in Paris, played an important role in Napoleon's invasion of Egypt.[37]

The French consul in Alexandria, Charles Magallon, was also in favor of Napoleon's invasion of Egypt. Ambassador Vergennes, on the other hand, opposed it and promoted the territorial integrity of the Ottoman Empire. However, the internal crisis within the French government after the fall of Robespierre, the disagreements within the Directory, and the continuing British menace in the Mediterranean made a colonial project in North Africa inevitable.[38] Moreover, after the loss of Martinique, France needed a colony for sugar plantations. Thus, the conquest of Crete and Egypt was viewed as compensation for losses in America, even though France maintained diplomatic relations with the Sublime Porte. In addition, the growing weakness of the Ottoman Empire had convinced the revolutionary French government to take action before England and Russia divided the empire. Additionally, interest in Greek classical history and antiquities and in the Orient had been on the rise among French Enlightenment thinkers as well as among members of embassy circles since the reign of Louis XIV. Napoleon's Egyptian and Oriental project had been on the horizon of diplomats in the prerevolutionary government, but revolutionary sentiments, Napoleon's ambitions, and the war intensified support for it.

Before the invasion, the Porte sent Moralı Seyyid Ali Efendi to Paris as ambassador in March 1797 to seek French support against Russia. He first arrived in Marseille and was kept in quarantine for some time; he then traveled to Paris, where he lived for three years and reported on the impact of the French Revolution on Paris in his embassy account.[39] While in Paris, he also learned about the upcoming invasion of Egypt, which Minister Charles-Maurice Tallyrand Périgord (1754–1838), a bishop under the old regime and now a diplomat under the Directory, was promoting. Tallyrand had convinced General Napoleon to join the project.

Napoleon defined his role as the liberator of Egypt from the Mamluk beys and an ally of the Ottoman sultan, Selim III.[40] In a proclamation to the soldiers on June 28, 1798, he stated:

Soldiers!
You are about to undertake a conquest whose effects on the world civilization and trade are incalculable.

You will inflict upon England a blow which is certain to wound her in her most sensitive spot, while waiting for the day when you can deal her the death blow.

We shall make some worrisome marches; we shall fight a few battles; we shall succeed in all our enterprises; destiny is for us.

The Mamluk beys, who exclusively favor English trade, who have oppressed our merchants with vexations, and who are tyrannical over the unhappy people of the Nile valley, will cease to exist a few days after our landing...[41]

This proclamation spells out the aims of France and Napoleon against Great Britain in India and the Mamluk beys. The protection of French trade in Egypt is stated as another motivation for Napoleon's invasion. It goes on to command the soldiers to respect Islam and Muslim women and to show the same tolerance toward them that they would extend toward Jews since

Roman legions used to protect all religions. Napoleon wanted to revive the empire of Alexander the Great and to carve out a piece of the Ottoman Empire (Egypt and Syria) as well as part of Persia for the French before the old rivals, England and Russia, got there.[42] Although Napoleon showed respect for Islam and had great knowledge of it, historically, French kings had been advocating for the presence of French Catholic monks and missionaries in the Levant and the Holy Land for quite a while, a right that they had received in the Ahdnames of 1675 and 1740. In addition, some French traders and consuls in Cairo and Alexandria, like Charles Magallon, also supported Napoleon's scheme in hopes of enhancing their profits from a trade that had been declining for a long time. The rapaciousness of the Mamluk beys provided the perfect excuse for the intervention of Napoleon, who claimed to be an ally of Sultan Selim III and a friend of Muslims.

To learn more about Egypt and the Orient, Napoleon carried a library on his ship and read widely in the travel literature on Egypt and the Holy Land, books about Islam, the Bible, and the Qur'an. Every night after dinner, he held discussions, or "institutes," with savants on politics, government, religion, economics, and physics on the deck of his ship, *L'Orient*.[43] For example, he discussed Rousseau's *Discourse on the Origin of Inequality*. Although Napoleon was an opportunist, he and his colleagues believed that they could bring Western civilization to Egypt, spread the ideals of the French Revolution, and revive Egypt's ancient glory as a colony of the French republic.[44]

After capturing Malta, Napoleon landed in Alexandria on July 1, 1798, with 13 ships, 1,026 cannons, 42 frigates, 17,000 troops, as many sailors and marines, 100,000 rounds of ammunitions, 567 vehicles, 700 horses, and 170 scholars and artists.[45] He ordered all the Egyptians in Alexandria to wear the tricolor cockade, while the ulema had to wear the French sash.[46] After Napoleon's invasion of Egypt, the Porte closed its ports to French ships, revoked the Ahdname of 1740, and canceled all the berats that had been issued to the French Embassy and consulates. The Ottoman state was no longer under any obligation to uphold the Ahdname of 1740 since peace between the two states had ended, and they had entered a state of war.[47] Ambassador Morali Ali Efendi was imprisoned in Paris, but he was later released after peace had been restored between the two states.

However, Alexandria was a disappointment for the French in terms of its riches and antiquities. In addition, the shortage of drinkable water, the summer heat, and the plague made the desert the grave of many French soldiers. Mamluk beys and Bedouins were able to attack Napoleon's troops and take some of them hostage. The march toward Cairo on July 21, 1798, was equally challenging as Napoleon's army of 25,000 men faced 33,000 men mobilized by the Mamluk beys at the Battle of Pyramids. Eventually, after the massacre of Mamluk soldiers, Napoleon was able to defeat the Mamluks, march to Cairo, and prevent English ships from taking over.[48]

In Cairo, Napoleon set up an elected governing council, or *divan,* composed of six Muslim notables, six Coptic Christians, and his own officials, who received a stipend and salary. He also established a mixed commercial court and a director of trades to collect taxes. The commander also divided Cairo into eight administrative districts for tax purposes but kept the traditional administration of the quarters under the *shaykhs* (religious figures) to collect taxes and maintain law and order.[49]

Despite the efforts of Napoleon and his team to improve urban life in Cairo, especially regarding the plague, the activities of his troops in Alexandria, Rosetta, and Cairo and the imposition of new taxes created deep tensions between them and the Mamluk rulers, the ulema, and local notables.[50] Constant Bedouin raids, the plague, other diseases, and the drought led to major losses of French soldiers. The conduct of Napoleon himself and that of his soldiers also alienated the ulema. According to Napoleon's secretary, Louis-Antoine Fauvelet de Bourienne (1769–1834), Napoleon had ordered that a group of beautiful Egyptian women be brought to him, but when they appeared, he did not show much interest in them due to their obesity.[51] Moreover, he must have known that crossing sexual boundaries could generate opposition. He instead had an affair with Madame Fourés, the French wife of one of his lieutenants.[52] It was very difficult for twenty thousand Frenchmen in Cairo to find sexual partners since there were very few French women there, though some French women who worked on the ships resided in Egypt. Thus, they turned to local prostitutes and concubines, who had to cater to the growing demand for their sexual services. The local notables were keen observers of the decline of moral standards. According to Abd al-Rahman Al-Jabarti (1753–1825), the Egyptian cleric and chronicler who provided the best eyewitness account of Napoleon's rule in Cairo, the commander's soldiers established a brothel in Cairo with singers, dancers, and prostitutes and started inviting the locals to attend during a festival, then charged them a fee for services.[53]

Moreover, Napoleon's policies, particularly the new taxes, led to a major rebellion in Cairo in October 1798. Al-Jabarti provided an unbiased account of the ensuing rebellion and blamed both sides. He blamed the rebellion on the actions of the *divan* that had imposed new taxes on the populace under pressure from the French administrator.[54] The ensuing rebellion, which had initially been led by the guild of Blind men in the al-Husayn quarter, artisans, merchants, and the ulema and shaykhs, soon attracted the mob from other neighborhoods and resulted in much violence being perpetrated against Frenchmen. The rebellion gained thousands of followers who incited the religious sentiments of the populace against French solderis.[55] However, according to Al-Jabarti, many ulema and the chief kadi refused to join the rebels for fear of reprisals, and some residents barricaded themselves in their houses. Nevertheless, the pleas of the local notables did not stop the mob from committing violence and even looting some local houses and raping the women. In response, French soldiers started using their cannons from the citadel against the rebels in the Al-Azhar quarter, where they had gathered. The rebellion led to a backlash from Napoleon himself, who hunted down the rebels. His soldiers looted houses and markets and forcefully entered the Al-Azhar Mosque in Cairo. According to Al-Jabarti, the soldiers looted the mosque, destroyed books, and smashed their wine bottles in the courtyard.[56] In addition, Napoleon ordered the execution of twenty-five *shaykhs* and imposed high taxes on the city. According to some estimates, between three hundred and as many as two thousand people and twenty-five shaykhs were beheaded in the citadel at the order of Napoleon on October 23.[57] The rebellion also led to tensions between Muslims and some Christian residents from Syria and Greeks who had been accused of collaborating with the French.

No doubt, Ottoman officials in Cairo were reporting the French soldiers' mistreatment of Egyptians to the Porte on a regular basis. When Sultan Selim III read the collective complaint of the ulema of Egypt about the violence and looting of French troops and was pressured by the ulema in Istanbul, he had to take action. The Ottoman state mobilized its own army under Jazzar Pasha and formed an alliance with Great Britain and Russia to attack Egypt and the Adriatic islands, which had been taken over by France, in July 1799. Ottoman forces managed to halt Napoleon's advance into Syria (Acre) as the plague spread among his troops. Finally, Ottoman and English forces occupied Egypt and defeated Napoleon. Napoleon then fled Egypt in August 1799, leaving behind his commander, Kléber, who was subsequently assassinated by a Syrian man after another insurrection in Cairo in June 1800. Finally, a joint Anglo-Ottoman offensive defeated the French army at the Battle of Alexandria in 1801. The British navy seized some of the antiquities, including the Rosetta Stone, from the French ships as they began departing Egypt in haste. Napoleon's Oriental fantasy had turned into a nightmare, exposing the lives of Egyptians and Frenchmen in the Levant to much violence and creating an unprecedented level of anti-French sentiment.

Despite this military and diplomatic fiasco, the Ottomans were still willing to sign a peace agreement with France. After a series of meetings between the Ottoman envoy, Ali Efendi, and Napoleon's minister, Talleyrand, in Paris, an initial peace treaty was signed in 1801 stipulating the evacuation of all French forces from Egypt. After France, the Ottoman Empire, and Great Britain signed the Treaty of Amiens in March 1802, the war between France and the Ottoman Empire officially ended. The two states signed a separate treaty in Paris in 1802 that recognized the territorial integrity of the Ottoman Empire.[58] France signed a new ahdname with the Porte in 1812.

The Ottoman state agreed to return the captives and their goods, or their equivalent value in cash, that had been seized during the war. Ruffin was released from Yedi Kule Prison and played an important role in the French negotiations with the Ottoman Empire. Selim III then recognized Napoleon's government, and the two states exchanged ambassadors.[59] Commercial relations between the two states, however, had changed profoundly.

THE DISSOLUTION OF THE FRENCH AND
ENGLISH LEVANT COMPANIES

The French Revolutionary Wars (1789–1801) and Napoleonic Wars (1803–1815) undermined Franco-Ottoman trade in the Levant from 1790 to 1840. The French Revolution led to the dissolution of the French Levant Company and the English blockade of Marseille, which halted trade for more than twenty years.[60] French traders, having faced arrest, the confiscation of their property, and imprisonment in Ottoman ports and towns, were no longer representatives of a most favored nation.[61] The Levant trade between Izmir and Marseille dropped from 40 percent to 1 percent in 1801, compared with Trieste's and Ancona's trade with the Levant, which had risen to 70 percent.[62] Italian ports like Trieste and Ancona replaced Marseille in the Levant trade.

After peace had been restored, the Ahdname of 1811 provided reciprocal rights to Ottoman merchants in international trade in the nineteenth century.[63] The ahdname was composed of ten articles and basically renewed the Treaty of 1740 in its entirety. In addition, it gave French traders all of the privileges that had been accorded to other states like England, especially the right of French commercial ships to navigate on the Black Sea. In return, Ottoman merchants and ships received reciprocal rights to trade in French ports and towns (article 2). This was an important change providing Ottoman merchants access to French ports.

After the normalization of relations in the early nineteenth century, French ships again began arriving in Istanbul in 1816. The reciprocal aspect of this treaty initiated a new phase in Ottoman-French relations and trade, albeit on a lower scale than had been the case from 1535 to 1789. In 1816, after trade had resumed with France, French traders imported all kinds of European textiles and colonial and Russian goods into Istanbul.[64] They imported spices and dyes from Asia and India, powdered sugar and coffee from the West Indies, French woolen textiles, English cotton textiles, Indian muslins and fine cottons, and Indian cotton yarn into Istanbul. Furthermore, from the Black Sea they imported Russian coarse cotton textiles, Russian iron, tin, hides, and furs. French traders also exported cotton yarns from Istanbul; Angora wool, candle wax, opium, wool, and woolen textiles from Ankara; dyes, raisins, figs, currants, hides, saffron, cotton, and raw silk from Rumelia, Sidon, and Cyprus; shawls from Istanbul; gum mastic; and Indian shawls that they imported into Istanbul and from there to France.[65] With the lifting of bans and dissolution of the monopolies, French traders were involved in importing all kinds of colonial goods from the Atlantic world and India, as well as from Europe into Istanbul.[66]

Moreover, French and Greek captains again began transporting the goods of Ottoman merchants between Ottoman and European ports. The resumption of French trade and the importing of raw materials such as silk, coarse wool, and Angora wool from Galata into Marseille underscore the continuing importance of Istanbul in French trade in the early nineteenth century. Cotton became the most important cash crop and export from Anatolia to France in the late eighteenth and early nineteenth centuries. It made up between 60 and 70 percent of the share of exports from Izmir and Salonica in 1788.[67] The commercialization of agriculture around Salonica, Izmir, and the Morea was another direct impact of the expansion of trade in cash crops like cotton.

With the dissolution of the French Levant Company after the French Revolution in 1789, the dissolution of the English Levant Company in 1825, and the conclusion of bilateral free-trade agreements, the Ottoman Greek, Armenian, and Jewish merchants began taking a very active role in European trade as Ottoman subjects and eventually dominated this trade between

Ottoman and European ports. The Greeks became very prominent in the international trade of Izmir and Salonica in the nineteenth century, while Jewish, Greek, and Armenian merchants continued to play an important role in the international trade of Galata.[68]

Even before the end of the Levant companies, the age of monopolistic policies and companies was coming to an end after the repeal of the British Navigation Acts in 1780 and 1797, allowing Ottoman ships to import goods from the ports of the Levant into England. Furthermore, in 1799, the English Levant Company extended trading privileges to Ottoman merchants considerably (Greeks and Armenians).[69] Trade partnerships between English freemen (nonmembers) and Ottoman Greek, Armenian, and Jewish merchants offered new opportunities for both sides. However, Anglo-Ottoman diplomatic relations were disrupted by war between the two states in 1807–8 and by the resulting violence against British traders in Istanbul. The Levant Company had already reduced much of its commerce with the Levant before its dissolution in 1825.[70]

In response to the developments previously discussed, particularly the opening of the Black Sea to Russian, English, and French trade, the Ottoman state tried to guarantee the reciprocal rights of its own merchants both by inserting terms to that effect in the new series of ahdnames and by creating a new category of state-protected Ottoman merchants to trade with Europe (*Avrupa* merchants) and with Iran and India (*Hayriye* merchants). In 1805, the Ottoman state created its own "European merchants" by selling berats directly to non-Muslim merchants in return for a fee of 1,500 akçe to be paid directly to the Ottoman treasury. The berats provided Ottoman non-Muslim merchants and their two servants the same rights that had already been given to European protected merchants, such as a 3 percent customs rate on imports and exports.[71] But the Ottoman merchants would remain Ottoman subjects and pay the poll tax in accordance with their incomes. This policy was an important departure from the terms of earlier ahdnames that had provided tax exemptions to the protégé merchants. Moreover, the *Avrupa* merchants could appoint two agents (*vekils*) to represent their interests in Istanbul before the Ottoman government. Ottoman merchants no longer needed to purchase these berats from European embassies for a stiff price and now could pay a lower fee to the government to enjoy some of the same rights that other traders already had. However, some zimmi merchants still turned to European embassies for protection and the right to trade with European ports.

After the Anglo-Ottoman War of 1807, the Treaty of the Dardanelles in 1809 restored the ahdname between the two states, but article 5 gave full reciprocity to Ottoman merchants trading with England, a condition that was a very important development. Furthermore, it gave Ottoman merchants permission to establish commercial houses in London, making the city the center of Greek trade between Britain and the Levant.[72] This was a profound transformation, meaning that the age of monopolies by the English Levant Company had come to an end as the English trade was opened to nonmembers and to foreign ships, finally recognizing the need for reciprocity in foreign trade.[73]

The English textile trade with the Levant expanded considerably, and, besides London, England controlled Malta and Italian ports in the early nineteenth century. Ottoman ports like Galata, Salonica and Izmir became fully integrated into the European economy, catering to the export of cash crops like cotton and the import of colonial and manufactured goods. The French Revolution and the Napoleonic Wars had ended the old era of monopolies and led to a new era of free-trade policies and treaties as well as the opening of European ports to Ottoman merchants. The number of French and English traders, diplomats, missionaries, and visitors in Pera and other Ottoman ports increased considerably in the nineteenth century.

Archival Documents in English Translation

This sample of documents from the Ottoman archival sources translated into English by the author provides an insight into the social topography of Galata and the legal encounters between Ottoman and European communities in the court of Galata. Lawsuits to the court and petitions to the Imperial Council by a cross section of Galata's residents, including European ambassadors and residents dealing with fires, death, insolvency, and inheritance claims as well as with marital disputes and accusations of moral misconduct, provide a real window into the daily life of Galata. They also shed light on the role of the kadi in implementing the articles of the ahdnames as well as in regulating urban life and managing legal and social tensions among the residents.

DOCUMENT ONE

After major fires had damaged Christian churches, community leaders had to obtain official permission to rebuild and repair them. But they had to follow the old plan of the church after the inspection of the kadi and the chief architect, who reported to the government, as the following case demonstrates (see chapter 2).

A Petition

May our fortunate and compassionate Sultan be well (*sağ olusn*):

Your servants from the Armenian community of Galata present a petition regarding our old church, which has remained in our possession since the Conquest. Since it was burned and damaged badly during the last fire, we request an imperial order to the kadi to issue permission to repair our church in accordance with its old plan. We request that the kadi, voyvoda, and chief architect examine our church without any interference and issue permission to rebuild it. We request that after an agreement has been reached among us, no one shall interfere in the repair of the church in accordance with your imperial order. Final command belongs to the sultan.

Your servants:

The Armenian *reaya* of Galata

Imperial order: The kadi and the chief architect should carry out an inspection and report it to us.

Date: January 1733[1]

DOCUMENT TWO

Commercial partnerships were widespread in Galata, and they sometimes involved European merchants and their non-Muslim agents. Insolvency often brought the partners to the court of Galata. Many transactions were also carried out on credit and were registered in the court of Galata.

> Two French merchants, Rigolof son of Rigolof, and Ari son of Ari, submitted a lawsuit via the dragoman of the embassy in the presence of two Jewish witnesses against Matatya son of Yasef. The two French merchants claimed 7,660 *kuruş* from the sale of coffee to Matatya and submitted a document. They demanded payment and the punishment of Matatya. A report was made to the Imperial Council in May 1786.[2]

DOCUMENT THREE

The Islamic court of Galata received many lawsuits regarding the affairs of European merchants and their agents, usually dealing with commercial transactions, partnerships, unpaid debts, and inheritance claims. The following case embodies many of these issues discussed throughout the book and underscores the central role of the kadi of Galata in disputes and settlements between Ottoman and European subjects and the implementation of the articles of the ahdname (see chapter 6).

> Solomon son of Aron Karanfis, the agent of an Austrian merchant who resides in Galata, died while he was bringing Austrian goods to Galata. His wife, Rahel daughter of Elya, and two daughters, Rifka and Sara, have presented a lawsuit against the Austrian merchant, Shanbash son of Shanbash, in the presence of Timoni son of Timoni, the dragoman of the Austrian embassy, and Yasef and Aslan sons of Isak [probably their witnesses]. They are claiming their share from 42 trunks of glass and glassware, amounting to 5,000 *kuruş,* that Solomon had transported on the ship of Kostantin from Austria to Galata. The Austrian merchant has taken possession of the above-mentioned merchandise, keeping it in a storage house and shop in the Mahmud Pasha neighborhood. The Austrian merchant has claimed that Solomon was his agent and that he had purchased those goods with his [the merchant's] money. Therefore, the Austrian merchant claims that the goods in the store and the shop are his property. The heirs, who had been involved in a long legal dispute, have agreed to

settle, with the mediation of upright Muslims (*muslehun*), for the payment of 2,000 *kuruş* worth of merchandise in 17 trunks. They have registered the settlement and have given up all other claims as the heirs of Solomon to the rest of all the known and unknown goods in the two stores and shop as the property of the Austrian merchant. They also have declared that if any goods appear from Austria in the future, they belong to the Austrian merchant and that they [Solomon's heirs] have no claim over them. The settlement was registered in November 1783.[3]

Expert Witnesses: Ali bin Ahmed, Hasan Beşe Abdullah, Abdurrahman bin Mehmed, Al-Seyyid Mahmud bin Isma'il, and others.

Marginal note: The heirs pledged that if any claimants appeared later, the heirs would pay the debt of Solomon and that the Austrian merchant had no responsibility for paying future claims.

DOCUMENT FOUR

The religious boundaries of Ottoman ports remained very fluid, and religious conversion occurred quite regularly for various reasons (such as marriage, divorce, ransoming, and opportunism). The kadi usually registered the conversion of Christian men and women to Islam and noted the new name of the convert, as the following case demonstrates (see chapter 7).

Agusto son of Shastu, a Venetian resident of Pera (Beyoğlu) outside Galata, came to the court of Galata and claimed that he had left the false religion [Christianity] and had accepted Islam. He asked to be named *Mehmed* in May 1784.[4]

DOCUMENT FIVE

Forum shopping was widespread in Ottoman ports due to the legal pluralism of Galata (see chapter 7). In accordance with the ahdname, the French and other Europeans could bring lawsuits against their own compatriots to the courts in the embassies, but lawsuits against Ottoman subjects were presented to the kadi's court or to the Imperial Council. Sometimes French merchants presented their petitions against other French subjects to the kadi's court or the Imperial Council (the highest court of appeal), as the following case demonstrates.
A Petition:

A French resident of Marseille, Kari, presented a petition against another French merchant, Aydın [a French protégé?] from Izmir, claiming he was owed 25,000 *kuruş* from the latter. Kari had tried to collect the debt from his compatriot in Izmir, but the latter had failed to pay it. The Islamic court has called in the said merchant, demanding the full payment of the loan to the agent of the merchant in Marseille, who is a French merchant resident in Izmir. Kari is demanding that an imperial order be issued to the kadi and voyvoda of Izmir to enable him to obtain his rights. The final command belongs to my fortunate sultan.

Signature:

The agent of French merchants in the Morea

Imperial order: The case should be adjudicated in the local Islamic court.

Date: November 1794[5]

DOCUMENT SIX

Ottoman non-Muslim as well as Muslim subjects held the tax farm of the customs dues in Galata and other ports. Jewish subjects occupied a prominent position in farming out shares in the collection of customs dues in Galata and Izmir, as the following case demonstrates (see chapter 6).[6]

The petition of a servant:

The collection of customs dues in Galata, a dependency of Istanbul, had been given with a *berat* to the Jewish Sitay, who has passed away. The position is now vacant and should be given to the former shareholder, Yohi son of Isak, with an imperial diploma [*berat*]. We demand an imperial order to that effect. The final command belongs to the fortunate sultan.

Signature:

The Emin of Customs of the imperial city, Al-Seyyid [?]

Imperial order: The request should be granted

Date: December 1795[7]

DOCUMENT SEVEN

Accusations of moral misconduct often happened when fights broke out among male and female residents of Galata, but according to the *shari'a,* false accusations in the absence of four upright eyewitnesses could lead to punishment of eighty lashes. Some women confronted their accusers in the court of Galata. The following case demonstrates sexual tensions in Galata (see chapter 7).

Sherife Kamile bint Mehmed, a resident of the quarter Al-hac A'mi, presented a lawsuit to the court of Galata against Çorekçi (bun seller) Kara Mustafa bin Hasan in his presence. She stated that Kara Mustafa had been calling her a prostitute on the street, causing her distress, and that she had demanded an explanation. But since Kara Mustafa [had subsequently] pledged not to harass her anymore, she was dropping her lawsuit. Their statements were registered in the court of Galata in October 1798.[8]

DOCUMENT EIGHT

Crime was an important aspect of daily life in Galata, and theft and robbery made up a significant proportion of the convictions that were recorded in the registers of the Imperial Arsenal in Kasım Paşa, a dependency of Galata.

Mehmed Mustafa from Istanbul broke into the storage house of caulker al-Hac Mehmed in Galata and stole his goods worth 10,000 *akçe*. His crime was proven, and he was sentenced to forced labor on the imperial galleys, according to the report of the kadi. He is kept in the prison of the arsenal.

Date: October 1700[9]

DOCUMENT NINE

French ambassadors, consuls, merchants, and captains submitted petitions to the Imperial Council to obtain permission for their ships to land or depart. During the Seven Years' War between France and England, clashes took place between their ships on the Mediterranean, and trade with the Levant was disrupted, as the following petition by a French captain demonstrates. These petitions and the imperial commands were collected in the Registers of Foreign Nations (Ecnebi Defterleri) (see chapter 6).

The petition of a French captain on this Thursday of February 1756 to the Imperial Council:

This captain loaded woolen textiles, sugar, coffee, pepper, indigo, and red dyes on a merchant ship in Marseille twenty-five days ago to bring them to Istanbul. But when I arrived at Chios, I learned that English ships that were traveling in the Mediterranean waters had intercepted and stopped six French ships near the island of Chios (Değirmenlik) and had taken possession of their merchandise. So once I heard the news, I left Chios and moved toward Salonica. I managed to sail away from the English ship and arrived at Boğazhisar on the Bosphorus and in Istanbul safely. These events took place due to the war between England and France, whereas prior to the war, English ships used to conduct trade with Marseille in peace.[10]

During Napoleon's invasion of Egypt in 1798, the Ottoman government revoked the Ahdname of 1740 with France. All Frenchmen were then subject to arrest and imprisonment. Imperial orders were issued to local judges in Pera and elsewhere to conduct a survey of French residents and their properties. After peace had been restored in 1802, the prisoners were released, and their goods were returned (see epilogue).

An imperial order,

The houses of all Frenchmen should be in inspected in the neighborhood of Tatavla [in Pera] with a religious ruling from the Islamic court, and their names, professions, and property should be listed in the court register of Galata.[11]

Date: October 1798

GLOSSARY

AHDNAME: a Persian term meaning book of peace or a covenant. Known in the West as *capitulations/capitula* (headings in a treaty), ahdnames were both bilateral and unilateral diplomatic and commercial treaties granted by Ottoman sultans to friendly nations for a limited time period. They were revocable and renewable by each sultan.

AKÇE: Ottoman silver coin; also known as *asper*

ALACA: striped textiles of cotton and silk in mixed colors

AMAN: protection of life and property at times of peace

AMIL: a tax farmer

ARAK: unsweetened anis-flavored alcoholic drink

ARZ: petition

ASES: night police

ASESBAŞI: chief of night police

ATTAR: druggist; grocer

AVANIA: fines assessed on European merchants

AVARIZ: extraordinary dues assessed on some households

AVRUPA MERCHANT: licensed Ottoman merchants who traded with Europe in the nineteenth century

AZAP/AZAB: unmarried young man; a fighting man in the navy or an auxiliary footman

BAILO: Venetian ambassador in Pera

BAL: honey

BAL KAPANI: scale for honey and foodstuff imported into Istanbul; located in Eminönü

BALIK PAZARI: Fish market

BANDITI: Italian term meaning "exiled convicts"

BASMACI: Textile printer

BAZAAR/PAZAR: market

BEDESTAN: covered market where the trade of precious commodities took place

BERAT: Imperial patent of appointment or diploma issued to foreign ambassadors, consuls, dragomans, and merchants that contained their legal rights and tax exemption status

BERATLI: protected merchants who purchased *berats* from the European embassies

BEŞE: military title used by artisans who were of janissary background

BEY: title used for commanders; administrative unit, like a province

BEZIRGAN: traveling merchant

BEZIRGANBAŞI: purveyor of the palace; head of traveling merchants

BIN: son of

BINT: daughter of

BIT PAZARI: Flea market

BOĞACA: sweet rolls

BÖREK: flaky pastry containing thin layers of cheese or other fillings

BOSTANCIBAŞI: chief of palace guards who policed palaces along the waterfront

BOZA: fermented drink

BOZAHANE: a place where fermented drinks were sold

CAPITULATION: derived from Latin word *capitula*; headings in a treaty. See *ahdname.*

CARAVANSERAI: a place on caravan routes where traveling merchants stayed and stored their goods

CHARGÉ D'AFFAIRES: official placed in charge of diplomatic affairs during the temporary absence of the ambassador or minister

CIZYE: poll tax paid by Ottoman non-Muslim heads of households

ÇAVUŞ: herald; messenger

CAVUŞBAŞI: imperial chief messenger

ÇIFTLIK: large farms

ÇIVID: indigo

ÇÖREK: sweet braided bread

CORSAIRS: pirates

ÇUKA/ÇUHA: fine woolen textiles

ÇUVAL: Unit of measurement: 112.898 kg

DAR AL-AHD: treaty states

DAR AL-HARB: abode of war (non-Muslim states)

DELLAL: broker

DENG: horse load

DIRHEM: unit of measurement: 3.4 grams

DESTAR: a length of Muslin

DIVAN: council; governor's council

DIVAN-I HÜMAYUN: Imperial Council; the highest court of appeal

DOGE: the elected chief magistrate of the former republics of Venice and Genoa

DRAGOMAN/TERCUMAN: Derived from the Arabic *terjuman* (Turkish *tercuman*); interpreter

ECHÉLLE: Ottoman cities and ports where a French community resided

ECNEBI DEFTERLERI: registers of foreign nations

ÉCU: French gold or silver coin

EKMEK: regular bread

EMIN: superintendent; comptroller

FETVA: religious ruling

FRANCELA: European pure white bread

FERENG: a term used by the Ottomans for Roman Catholic and Protestant Europeans

FUHUŞ: prostitution

GRAND VIZIER: Chief minister

GÜMRÜK: customs taxes

HAMAM: public bath

HAN: guesthouse usually located near or inside markets where goods are stored

HANE: household; unit of taxation

HASS: special; imperial domain

HAVALE/POLIÇE: letter of credit; transfer of a debt or payment to another person by proxy

IMAM: leader of Friday prayer

IMARET: Imperial endowments, like a soup kitchen

IRSALIYE: provision or money sent to the government

ISKELE: wharf

KADI: Islamic judge

KANTAR: unit of measurement: 56.449 kg

KAPAN: scale (flour, oil)

KAPAN TÜCCAR: provisioning merchants in charge of supplying Istanbul with grains, oil, and other foodstuff

KAPI: gate

KAPIÇIBAŞI: head of palace guards and ushers

KAPUDAN: ship captain

KAPUDAN PASHA: the grand admiral of the fleet

KEFIL: moral and financial guarantor

KERBAS: coarse cotton; linen; hemp

KESE: bag of 500 *akçe*

KETHÜDA: steward

KILE OF ISTANBUL: unit of measurement: 24.215 kg

KIYYE/VUKIYYE/OKKA: 1.28 kg

KIZIL YUMURTA: Easter festival

KOCABAŞI: elder of community (Greeks)

KÜRK: fur; animal skin

KURUŞ: a *piaster*; large silver coin

KUTNI: mixed silk cloth and cotton used to make light cloaks

LEVANT: Eastern Mediterranean coastal area stretching from Galata to Alexandria

LEVANTINES: Latin Christians in the Levant of Genoese or Venetian origins who had become Ottoman subjects. Many had intermarried with Ottoman Greeks and Armenians who had converted to Catholicism.

MAHALLE: quarter; neighborhood

MAHKEME: Islamic court

MASDARIYE: a nominal tax on imports and exports (1.5 percent)

MEDRE: unit of measurement for wine: 11.5 kg

MEDRESE: Islamic college

MILLET: religious community (people of the book) with defined legal rights

MIRI: state-owned land

MORISCOS: Muslims in the Iberian Peninsula who converted to Catholicism after 1501

MUDAREBE: a form of commercial partnership in which profits were split equally

MUDÉJARES: Muslims who lived under Christian rule

MÜEZZIN: the man who calls for prayer from the minaret of the mosque

MUHTAR: neighborhood warden

MÜHTESIB: market inspector

MUMCU: a special division of janissaries who kept order in taverns

MURUR TEZKIRESI: internal passport

MUSLEHUN: upright/upstanding Muslims

MÜSTEMEN: protected foreign subjects who were under the jurisdiction of ahdnames

NARH: price ceiling or official maximum price imposed by the government on bread and other basic necessities

PARA: unit of money; 60 *para* equal one *akçe.*

PASTAV: unit of measurement: 32.5 meters

PASTIRMA: pressed meat

PIASTER: silver coin; *akçe*

PODESTA: Genoese governor of Galata appointed by the Senate

POLIÇE: Bills of exchange

PROTÉGÉS: Ottoman subjects protected by European embassies under the *berats*

QUINTAL: 100 kg

REAYA: Tax-paying subjects who were not part of the ruling class

REIS: ship captain

REIS ÜL-KÜTTAB: Chief officer of the Chancery

ŞAL: shawl

SARRAF: Money-changer; informal banker

ŞEHBENDER: head of merchants' guild

ŞERBETHANE: sweet beverage shops

SHARI'A LAW: Islamic law based on the Qur'an; the sayings and deeds of the Prophet Muhammad (*hadith*) and the interpretation and consensus of the *ulema*

SICIL (PLURAL *SICILS*): Islamic court register

SIMIT: Turkish pretzel

SIMSAR: broker

ŞIRKET: partnership

SOF: woolen textile

SUBAŞI: chief of day police

SULH: settlement

SULTANA: princess

TACIR: merchant

TERCUMAN/DRAGOMAN: interpreter

TEREKE DEFTERS: inventory of the estate of a deceased man or woman registered in the Islamic court.

TOP: unit of measurement for textiles. Every top is 13 meters.

TÜCCAR: merchants

ULEMA: Muslim religious scholars

UN: flour

UN KAPANI: flour scale

TEZKIRE: any kind of certificate including pay certificate

VAKF: a religious and charitable endowment normally exempt from taxation

VAKFIYYE: Islamic charitable foundation

VALI: governor

VALIDE SULTAN: Queen mother

VEKIL: representative; agent

VOYVODA: mayor or governor of a province; Slavic title used for prince; financial agent

VUKIYYE/KIYYE: unit of measurement equivalent 1.28 kg

YAĞ: oil; olive oil

YAĞ KAPANI: oil scale

YALI: waterfront mansion

YOL HÜKMÜ: travel permission for ships and individuals

ZABTIYE: police department

ZAHIRE: provisions (grains)

ZIMMI: Ottoman non-Muslim subjects

ZIRA': Unit of measurement for masons and textiles: 0.758 meter

NOTES

INTRODUCTION

1. Halil Inalcik published the first study of Galata after the Ottoman takeover based on surveys of the port. Halil Inalcik, "Ottoman Galata," in *Essays in Ottoman History,* ed. Halil Inalcik (Istanbul: Eren, 1998), 275–376. For a more recent study of the port after the conquest, see Kerim Ilker Bulunur, *Osmanlı Galatası (1453–1600)* (Istanbul: Bilge, Kültüre, Sanat, 2014).

2. Seyit Ali Kahraman and Yücel Dağlı, *Evliya Çelebi Seyahatnamesi: Istanbul,* vol. 1, pt. 2 (Istanbul: Yapı Kredı Yayınları, 2003), 394.

3. Monique O'Connel and Eric Dursteler, eds., *The Mediterranean World: From the Fall of Rome to the Rise of Napoleon* (Baltimore: Johns Hopkins University Press, 2016). For an analysis and critique of Braudel's conceptual framework by Ottomanist historians and others, see Gabriel Piterberg, Teofilo Ruiz, and Geoffrey Symcox, eds., *Braudel Revisited: The Mediterranean World, 1600–1800* (Toronto: University of Toronto Press, 2010). See also Brian A. Catlos, Thomas Burman, and Mark Myerson, *The Sea in the Middle: The Mediterranean World, 650–1650* (Berkeley: University of California Press, forthcoming).

4. See K. N. Chaudhuri, *Trade and Civilization in the Indian Ocean: An Economic History from the Rise of Islam to 1750* (Cambridge: Cambridge University Press, 1993); Chaudhuri, *Asia Before Europe: Economy and Civilization of the Indian Ocean from the Rise of Islam to 1750* (Cambridge: Cambridge University Press, 1994). On Islamic mapping, see the excellent work of Karen C. Pinto, *Medieval Islamic Maps: An Exploration* (Chicago: University of Chicago Press, 2016).

5. Henri Pirenne, *Mohammad and Charlemagne,* trans. from French by Bernard Miall (London: G. Allen and Unwin, 1954). For a critique of Pirenne's work, see Adnan A. Husain and K. E. Fleming, eds., *A Faithful Sea: The Religious Cultures of the Mediterranean, 1200–1700* (Oxford: Oneworld, 2007), 1–27.

6. Svatopluk Soucek, "Naval Aspects of the Ottoman Conquests of Rhodes, Cyprus, and Crete," *Studia Islamica* 98, no. 99 (2004): 219–61.

7. Fernand Braudel, *The Mediterranean and the Mediterranean World in the Age of Philip II,* trans. Sian Reynolds, vol. 2 (New York: Harper Colophon Books, 1976).

8. Ariel Salzmann, "The Moral Economies of the Modern Mediterranean: Preliminaries to the Study of Cross-Cultural Migration during the Long Sixteenth Century," in Vera Costantini, "Old Prayers and New in the Transition of Cyprus to Ottoman Rule," in *Living in the Ottoman Ecumenical Community: Essays in Honour of Suraiya Faroqhi,* ed. Vera Costantini and Markus Koller (Leiden: E.J. Brill, 2008), 453–78.

9. The name *Constantinople* usually refers to the Byzantine era of the city while *Istanbul* is used for the Ottoman period. Europeans, however, continued to refer to the city as Constantinople during the Ottoman era.

10. Braudel, *The Mediterranean,* 2:665.

11. Fernand Braudel, *The Structures of Everyday Life: Civilization and Capitalism, 15th–18th Centuries,* vol. 1 (New York: Harper and Row, 1981).

12. Braudel, *Structures of Everyday Life,* 2:507–9.

13. Daniel Goffman, *The Ottoman Empire and Early Modern* Europe (Cambridge: Cambridge University Press, 2002), 6; Palmira Brummett, "Visions of the Mediterranean: A Classification," *Journal of Medieval and Early Modern Studies* 37 (Winter 2007): 9–54.

14. For a recent critique of this scholarship, see Goffman, *Ottoman Empire,* 1–23; and Piterberg, Ruiz, and Symcox, *Braudel Revisited.* See also Linda Colley, *Captives: Britain, Empire, and the World, 1600–1850* (New York: Anchor Books, 2004), 125–34. Colley argues that the image of the violent and sodomite Turk and North African man changed to the lustful heterosexual Muslim man in the eighteenth century.

15. Janet L. Abou-Lughod, *Before the European Hegemony: The World System 1250–1350 ad* (Oxford: Oxford University Press, 1991), 241–42.

16. Braudel, *The Mediterranean,* 2:668.

17. Giancarlo Casale, *The Ottoman Age of Exploration* (Oxford: Oxford University Press, 2010), 36–44. Casale notes the contrast between the Portuguese policies of preventing free trade and Ottoman protection of free trade.

18. Ibid., 34–83.

19. Palmira Brummett, *Mapping the Ottomans: Sovereignty, Territory, and Identity in the Early Modern Mediterranean* (Cambridge: Cambridge University Press, 2015), 3–5. See also Jerry Brotton, *The Sultan and the Queen: The Untold Story of Elizabeth and Islam* (New York: Penguin Books, 2017), 82–102.

20. Brummett, Mapping the Ottomans, 226–32. See also Daniel J. Vitkus, *Turning Turk: English Theatre and Multiculturalism in the Mediterranean, 1570–1630* (London: Palgrave MacMillan, 2003), 77–78; Tobias P. Graf, *The Sultan's Renegades: Christian-European Converts to Islam and the Making of the Ottoman Elite, 1575–1610* (Oxford: Oxford University Press, 2017), 1–28. Vitkus points out that Englishmen were more isolated in London than they were in the Levant, where they were exposed to the multicultural world of port cities.

21. Vitkus, *Turning Turk,* 77–78.

22. I use the Ottoman term *ahdname,* which is derived from Persian (meaning "the text of a treaty"), throughout this book since the European term *capitulation* has been mistranslated and misused as a word meaning to "capitulate." For a recent study of the use of ahdnames to regulate maritime trade and suppress piracy, see Joshua M. White, *Piracy and Law in the Ottoman Mediterranean* (Stanford, CA: Stanford University Press, 2017).

23. Ibid.

24. David Abulafia, *The Great Sea: A Human History of the Mediterranean* (Oxford: Oxford University Press, 2011), 483. See also Faruk Tabak, *The Waning of the Mediterranean, 1550–1870: A Geohistorical Approach* (Baltimore: Johns Hopkins University Press, 2008). For a critique of the scholarship on the Mediterranean, see Adnan A. Husain and K. E. Fleming, eds., *A Faithful Sea: The Religious Cultures of the Mediterranean, 1200–1700* (Oxford: Oneworld, 2007).

25. Julia Clancy-Smith, *Mediterraneans: North Africa and Europe in an Age of Migration, c. 1800–1900* (Berkeley: University of California Press, 2011), 1–22.

26. Graf, *Sultan's Renegades,* 1–28. On English captives in North Africa, see Colley, *Captives.*

27. See Bruce Masters, *The Origins of Western Economic Dominance in the Middle East: Mercantilism and the Islamic Economy in Aleppo, 1600–1750* (New York: NYU Press, 1998); Daniel Goffman, *Izmir and the Levantine World, 1550–1650* (Seattle: University of Washington Press, 1990); Edhem Eldem, *French Trade in Istanbul in the Eighteenth Century* (Leiden: E. J. Brill, 1999); Elena Frangakis-Syrett, *The Commerce of Smyrna in the Eighteenth Century, 1700–1820* (Athens: Center for Asia Minor Studies, 1992); and Ismail Hakki Kadi, *Ottoman and Dutch Merchants in the Eighteenth Century: Competition and Cooperation in Ankara, Izmir, and Amsterdam* (Leiden: E. J. Brill, 2012).

28. Rifa'at Ali Abou-El-Haj, *Formation of the Modern State: The Ottoman Empire, Sixteenth to Eighteenth Centuries* (Albany, NY: Syracuse University Press, 2005), 52.

29. Halil Inalcik, "Capital Formation in the Ottoman Empire," *Journal of Economic History* 24, no. 1 (1989): 97–140; Mehmet Genç, *Osmanlı Imparatorluğunda Devlet ve Ekonomi* (Istanbul: Ötüken, 2003).

30. Inalcik, "Ottoman Galata," 275–376; Halil Inalcik, "Istanbul: An Islamic City," in *Essays in Ottoman History,* ed. Halil Inalcik, 247–71 (Istanbul: Eren, 1988); Inalcik, "Imtiyazat," in *Islam Ansiklopedisi (IA)* (Istanbul: Diyanet Vakfı, 2000), 22: 282–88; Inalcik, *The Survey of Istanbul, 1455* (Istanbul: Türkiye Iş Bankası Yayınları, 2012).

31. Halil Inalcik, *An Economic and Social History of the Ottoman Empire,* vol. 1, *1300–1600* (Cambridge: Cambridge University Press, 1997).

32. Shelomo Dov Goitein, *A Mediterranean Society: The Jewish Communities of the Arab World as Portrayed in the Documents of the Cairo Geniza,* 3 vols. (Berkeley: University of California Press, 1967).

33. Abou-El-Haj, *Formation of the Modern State,* 1–23.

34. Ibid., 52; Gilles Veinstein, *"Les marchands étrangers dans l'empire Ottoman (XVI–XVIII siècles),"* in *Merchants in the Ottoman Empire,* ed. Suraiya Faroqhi and Gilles Veinstein (Paris: Peeters, 2008), 47–55.

35. Genç, *Osmanlı*, 43–67.

36. Ariel Salzmann, *Tocqueville in the Ottoman Empire: Rival Paths to the Modern State.* Leiden: E. J. Brill, 2004), 106–18.

37. Fariba Zarinebaf, *Crime and Punishment in Istanbul, 1700–1800* (Berkeley: University of California Press, 2010), 51–69.

38. Baki Tezcan, *The Second Ottoman Empire: Political and Social Transformation in the Early Modern World* (Cambridge: Cambridge University Press, 2010); Ali Yaycioglu, *Partners of the Empire: The Crisis of the Ottoman Order in the Age of Revolutions.* Stanford, CA: Stanford University Press, 2016).

39. R. Bin Wong, *China Transformed: Historical Change and the Limits of European Experience* (Ithaca, NY: Cornell University Press, 1997), 79–83.

40. Francesca Trivellato, *The Familiarity of Strangers: The Sephardic Diaspora, Livorno, and Cross-Cultural Trade in the Early Modern Period* (New Haven: Yale University Press, 2009), 132–47.

41. Ibid., 149–50.

42. Wong, *China Transformed*, 145–50.

43. Olivia Remie Constable, *Trade and Traders in Muslim Spain: The Commercial Realignment of the Iberian Peninsula, 900–1500* (Cambridge: Cambridge University Press, 1996), 68–77.

44. Veinstein, "*Les marchands*," 47–55.

45. Niels Steensgaard, *The Asian Trade Revolution of the Seventeenth Century: The East India Companies and the Decline of Caravan Trade* (Chicago: University of Chicago Press, 1973), 22–23; Halil Sahillioğlu, "*Bir Tüccar Kervani*," *Belgelerde Türk Tarihi Dergisi* 9 (1968): 63–69.

46. Philip D. Curtin, *Cross-Cultural Trade in World History* (Cambridge: Cambridge University Press, 1984); Sebouh David Aslanian, *From the Indian Ocean to the Mediterranean: The Global Networks of Armenian Merchants from the New Julfa* (Berkeley: University of California Press, 2011); Trivellato, *Familiarity of Strangers*.

47. Eldem, *French Trade.*

48. Daniel Panzac, *La Caravane maritime: Marins Européens et marchands Ottomans en Mediterranée (1680–1830)* (Paris: CNRS Éditions, 2004).

49. Molly Greene, *A Shared World: Christians and Muslims in the Early Modern Mediterranean* (Princeton, NJ: Princeton University Press, 2000); Clancy-Smith, *Mediterraneans.*

50. Goffman, *Izmir and the Levantine World.*

51. Michael Talbot, *British-Ottoman Relations, 1661–1807: Commerce and Diplomatic Practice in Eighteenth-Century Istanbul* (Woodbridge, UK: Boydell Press, 2017).

52. Bahadir Apaydın, *Kapitülasyonların Osmanlı-Türk Adli ve Idari Modernleşmesinde Etkisi* (Ankara: Adalet Yayınevi, 2010); Turan Kayaoğlu, *Legal Imperialism, Sovereignty, and Extraterritoriality in Japan, the Ottoman Empire, and China* (Cambridge: Cambridge University Press, 2010). For a critique of this paradigm among Turkish scholars, see Fikret Yılmaz, *Geçmişten Günumüze Levantenler* (Izmir: Izmir Ticaret Odası , 2011), 50–59.

53. For a critique of this historiography, see Eldem, *French Trade,* 2–4.

54. Timur Kuran, *The Long Divergence: How Islamic Law Held Back the Middle East* (Princeton, NJ: Princeton University Press, 2011), 94. See also Kuran, "The Economic Ascent of the Middle East's Religious Minorities: The Role of Islamic Plural Legalism," *Journal of Legal Studies* 33 (June 2004): 475–515.

55. Huri Islamoğlu, "A Proposal for Global Economic History: Beyond the Histories of Stagnation and Deficiencies to 'Living' Histories of Possibilities," in *History from Below: A Tribute in Memory of Donald Quataert,* edited by Selim Karahasanoğlu and Deniz Cenk Demir (Istanbul: Bilgi University Press, 2016), 190–91.

56. Kate Fleet, *European and Islamic Trade in the Early Ottoman State: The Merchants of Genoa and Turkey* (Cambridge: Cambridge University Press, 1999); Eric Dursteler, *Venetians in Constantinople: Nation, Identity, and Coexistence in the Early Modern Mediterranean* (Baltimore: Johns Hopkins University Press, 2006).

57. Natalie Rothman, *Brokering Empire: Trans-imperial Subjects between Venice and Istanbul* (Ithaca, NY: Cornell University Press, 2012). See bibliography for Arbel and Ortega.

58. On excellent studies of Ottoman-Dutch trade based on the Dutch archives, see Alexander H. De Groot, *The Netherlands and Turkey: Four Hundred Years of Political, Economic, and Cultural Relations* (Istanbul: ISIS Press, 2009); Maurits H. van den Boogert, *The Capitulations and the Ottoman Legal System: Qadis, Consuls, and Beratlis in the Eighteenth Century* (Leiden: E. J. Brill, 2005); Kadi, *Ottoman and Dutch Merchants.*

59. Edhem Eldem, Daniel Goffman, and Bruce Masters, *The Ottoman City between East and West: Aleppo, Izmir, and Istanbul* (Cambridge: Cambridge University Press, 1999).

60. Suraiya Faroqhi and Gilles Veinstein, eds., *Merchants in the Ottoman Empire.* Paris: Peeters, 2008).

61. Nile Green, "Maritime Worlds and Global History: Comparing the Mediterranean and Indian Ocean through Barcelona and Bombay," *History Compass* 11, no. 7 (2013): 513–23.

62. On Ottoman cosmopolitanism, see Suraiya Faroqhi, "Did Cosmopolitanism Exist in Eighteenth-Century Istanbul? Stories of Christian and Jewish Artisans," in *Urban Governance under the Ottomans,* edited by Ulrike Freitag and Nora Lafi (London: Routledge, 2014), 21–37; Edhem Eldem, "(A Quest for) the Bourgeoisie of Istanbul: Identities, Roles, and Conflicts," in *Urban Governance under the Ottomans,* edited by Ulrike Freitag and Nora Lafi (London: Routledge, 2014), 159–87. Faroqhi has argued that before the Greek Rebellion, religiously based conflicts among Istanbul artisans remained low-key, and disputes brought to the court were not based on religious affiliations.

63. Murat Gül, *The Emergence of Modern Istanbul: Transformation and Modernization of a City* (London: I. B. Tauris, 2012); Cem Behar, *A Neighborhood in Ottoman Istanbul: Fruit Vendors and Civil Servants in the Kasap Ilyas Mahalle* (New York: SUNY Press, 2003).

64. Murad Çizakça, "The Ottoman Government and Economic Life: Taxation, Public Finance, and Trade Controls," in *Cambridge History of Turkey 1453–1603*, vol. 2, edited by Suraiya N. Faroqhi and Kate Fleet (Cambridge: Cambridge University Press, 2013), 260–61.

65. Linda T. Darling, *A History of Global Justice and Political Power in the Middle East: The Circle of Justice from Mesopotamia to Globalization*. London: Routledge, 2013), 127–57.

66. Marshall G. S. Hodgson, *The Venture of Islam: Conscience in a World Civilization*, vol. 2 (Chicago: University of Chicago Press, 1977), 346–47.

67. Benjamin Arbel, *Trading Nations: Jews and Venetians in the Early Modern Eastern Mediterranean* (Leiden: E.J. Brill, 1995).

68. Masters, *Origins of Western Economic Dominance*,73–75.

69. Panzac, *"La caravane maritime."*

70. Nelly Hanna, *Making Big Money in 1600: The Life and Times of Isma'il Abu Taqiyya, Egyptian Merchant* (Syracuse, NY: Syracuse University Press, 1998), 6.

71. Hala Fattah, *The Politics of Regional Trade in Iraq, Arabia, and the Gulf, 1745–1900* (New York: SUNY Press, 1997), 9–10. See also Beshara Doumani, *Rediscovering Palestine: Merchants and Peasants in Jabal Nablus, 1700–1900* (Berkeley: University of California Press, 1995).

72. Eldem, "(Quest) for the Bourgeoisie," 159–87.

73. Steensgaard, *Asian Trade Revolution*, 22–27; Abu-Lughod, *Before the European Hegemony*, 216–36. Abu-Lughod traces banking to Sasanid Iran.

74. For a quantitative analysis and discussion of these sources, see Metin Coşgel and Boğaç A. Ergene, *The Economics of Ottoman Justice: Settlement and Trial in the Shari'a Courts* (Cambridge: Cambridge University Press, 2016).

75. The Islamic Research Center in Istanbul (ISAM) holds 9,895 registers for greater Istanbul and 999 volumes for Galata dating from 1536 to 1925. I have used a random sampling method for the second half of the eighteenth century. Every volume covers a few years and is between 70 and 150 folios long on average. While some volumes are devoted to lawsuits and registration of civil cases (marriage, divorce, inheritance) and economic transactions, others are devoted to imperial orders and the inventory of estates of deceased persons (*kassam defterleri*).

76. Frédéric Hitzel and Abderrahim Ben Hadda, *"Les relations Franco-Ottomanes à travers les Name-i Hümayun du Başbakanlık Arşivi,"* Anatolia Moderna 35 (1992): 247–60.

77. Goffman, *Izmir and the Levantine World,* 148–54.

78. For an analysis of these records, see Goffman, *Izmir and the Levantine World,* 148–54.; BBA, *Fransa Ahkam Defterleri*, ADVN.DVE.d 29/4, 30/5, 35/2, 31/6, 32/7.

79. See Istanbul Ahkam Registers that contain imperial orders in response to petitions by sea captains and merchants to the Imperial Council.

80. R. Paris, *Histoire du commerce de Marseille,* vol. 5, *de 1600 à 1789, Le Levant,* (Paris: Plon, 1957); Charles Carrière, *Négociants Marseillais,* vol. 2, 1039–51; Eldem, *French Trade,* 29–33. For Ottoman customs registers, see C.HR 19/30,ADVN. NMH 39/1, D.MMK.IGG.d 23607, MAD 456, MAD 1107/1695, MAD 1238.

81. For an analysis of these registers, see Halil Inalcik, *Sources and Studies on the Ottoman Black Sea*, vol. 1, *The Customs Registers of Caffa, 1487–1490* (Cambridge, MA: Harvard University Ukrainian Research Institute, 1996); Linda T. Darling, "Ottoman Customs Registers *[Gümruk Defterleri]* as Sources for Global Exchange and Interaction," *Review of Middle East Studies* 49 (2015): 3–22; Saim Çağrı Kocakaplan, "Istanbul Gümrüğü (1750–1800): Teşkilat ve Ticaret" (PhD diss., Istanbul University, 2014).

82. See ACCM, J series, "Affairs of the Levant and the Barbary Coast."

83. For statistics on trade, see ACCM, Series I, 1–33. For an excellent evaluation of French sources, see Eldem, *French Trade,* 4–11.

84. For the catalogue, see *Ministère Des Affaires Étrangères, Centre des Archives Diplomatique de Nantes: Répertoire numérique des registres rapatriés de la Chancelleries Consulaire de l'ambassade puis consulat de France à Constantinople-Istanbul,* Séries A, 1599–1973.

85. Edward Said, *Orientalism* (New York: Vintage Books, 1979).

86. François-Emmanuel Guignard Saint-Priest, Comte de; Charles Henri Auguste Schefer, *Mémoire sur l'ambassade de France en Turquie, 1525–1770* (Paris: Philo, 1974); Albert Vandal, *Une ambassade Française en Orient sous Louis XV: La mission du Marquis de Villeneuve, 1728–1741* (Paris, 1887); Louis Bonneville, de Marsangy le Chevalier de Vergennes, *Son ambassade a Constantinople,* 2 vols. (Paris, 1894,); and ACCM, Series J. For an excellent study of information flows to the English Embassy in Istanbul in the late seventeenth century, see John-Paul Ghobrial, *The Whispers of Cities: Information Flows in Istanbul, London, and Paris in the Age of William Trumbull* (Oxford, Oxford University Press, 2013).

87. Mary Roberts, *Intimate Outsiders: The Harem in Ottoman and Orientalist Travel Literature* (Durham, NC: Duke University Press, 2007), 59–79.

CHAPTER ONE

1. James Dallaway, *Constantinople, Ancient and Modern, with Excursions to the Shores and Islands of the Archipelago and to the Troad* (London, 1797), 124.

2. I am grateful to the comments of my colleague Stefan Stanchev on the rise of Genoese Galata.

3. John Freely and Brendan Freely, *A Guide to Beyoğlu* (Istanbul: Art and Archeology Publications, 2006), 1–2; Hillary Summer-Boyd and John Freely, *Strolling through Istanbul: A Guide to the City* (Istanbul: Sev Matbaacılık, 2000), 436–37.

4. Summer-Boyd and Freely, *Strolling through Istanbul,* 427.

5. Semavi Eyice, "Galata," in *Islam Ansiklopedisi (IA),* vol. 3 (Istanbul: Türkiye Ekonomik ve Toplumsal Tarih Vakfi, 1994), 348. Zeynep Çelik, *The Remaking of Istanbul: Portrait of an Ottoman City in the Nineteenth Century* (Seattle: University of Washington Press, 1986), 17–18.

6. Abulafia, *Great Sea,* 354–55. For a recent study, see Nevra Necipoğlu, *Byzantium between the Ottomans and the Latins: Politics and Society in the Latin Empire* (Cambridge: Cambridge University Press, 2009).

7. Abulafia, *Great Sea,* 379.

8. Tommaso Bertelé, *Venedik ve Kostantaniyye, Tarihte Osmanli ve Venedik Ilişkileri,* trans. Mahmut H. Şarkioğlu (Istanbul: Yayınkitabevi, 2012), 38–39; Aygül Ağir, *Istanbul Eski Venedik Yerleşimi ve Dönüşümü* (Istanbul: Istanbul Araştıımaları Enstitüsü, 2009).

9. Çelik, *Remaking of Istanbul,* 21.

10. Fleet, *European and Islamic Trade,* 22–36.

11. Curtin, *Cross-Cultural Trade,* 8, 7.

12. Fleet, *European and Islamic Trade,* 37–58.

13. John Freely, *Istanbul: The Imperial City* (New York: Viking, 1996), 144–45.

14. David Jacoby, "The Urban Evolution of Latin Constantinople (1204–61)," in *Byzantine Constantinople: Monuments, Topography, and Everyday Life,* ed. Nevra Necipoğlu (Leiden: E.J. Brill, 2001), 282.

15. Ibid., 278.

16. Ibid., 278–80.

17. Freely, *Istanbul: The Imperial City,* 147.

18. Jacoby, "Urban Evolution of Latin Constantinople," 290–91.

19. Freely, *Istanbul: The Imperial City,* 151–53.

20. Jacoby, "Urban Evolution of Latin Constantinople," 282–83.

21. Bertelé, *Venedik ve Kostantaniyye,* 34–38.

22. Ibn Battuta, *Travels in Asia and Africa, 1325–1354* (London: Routledge and Kegan Paul, 1983), 160. See also Evliya Çelebi's account on the prosperity of Galata under the Genoese in Kahraman and Dağlı, *Evliya Çelebi Seyahatnamesi,* vol. 1., pt. 2: 387.

23. Fleet, *European and Islamic Trade,* 9–10.

24. Michel Balard, *"La société pérote aux XIV-XVe siècles: Autour des demerode et des draperio,"* in *Byzantine Constantinople: Monuments, Topography, and Everyday Life,* ed. Nevra Necipoğlu (Leiden: E.J. Brill, 2001), 302–3.

25. Eric Dursteler, "Latin-Rite Christians in Early Modern Istanbul," in *Osmanlı Istanbulu,* vol. 1, ed. Feridun M. Emecen and Emrah S. Gürkan (Istanbul: Büyükşehir Belediyesi Yayınları, 2013), 138–39.

26. Abulafia, *Great Sea,* 354–55; Fleet, *European and Islamic Trade,* 37–58; Balard, *"La société pérote,"* 299–311.

27. Dursteler, "Latin-Rite Christians," 138. Dursteler estimated the number of Latin-rite Christians in Istanbul as tens of thousands before 1453. They had thirty-five churches in the city as a whole.

28. Robert Mantran, *Histoire d'Istanbul* (Paris: Fayard, 1996), 124.

29. Galata had ten Greek Orthodox churches in 1578, most of which burned down in the fire of 1660. In 1683, there were nine Greek Orthodox churches in Galata, including Ayios Nikolas, Ayios Ioannis, and Ayios Dimitrios.

30. Louis Miller, "The Genoese in Galata," *IJMES* 10 (1979): 73; Halil Inalcik, "Ottoman Galata," 348; Çelik, *Remaking of Istanbul,* 22. See also F. Özden Mercan, "The Genoese of Pera in the Fifteenth Century," in *Living in the Ottoman Realm: Empire and Identity, Thirteenth to Twentieth Centuries,* ed. Christine Isom-Verhaaren and Kent F. Schull (Bloomington: Indiana University Press, 2016), 42–54.

31. Fleet, *European and Islamic Trade,* 10–12.

32. Mantran, *Histoire d'Istanbul,* 173; Charles Schefer, ed., *Bertirandon de La Broquiere'in Denizasiri Seyahati,* trans. Ilhan Arda (Istanbul: Eren Yayıncılık, 2000), 207.

33. Halil Inalcik, "The Conqueror, the Conquest, and the Reconstruction of Constantinople," in *Istanbul, World City,* ed. Afife Batur (Istanbul: Tarih Vakfı Yayınları, n.d.), 23–24.

34. Halil Inalcik, "The Policy of Mehmed II toward the Greek Population of Istanbul and the Byzantine Buildings of the City," *Dumbarton Oaks Papers* 23 (1969–70): 230.

35. According to Evliya Çelebi, whose grandfather had been present during the siege, the sultan took seven churches in addition to Aya Sofia, 3,000 mansions, 7,000 shops, two covered markets (*bedestans*), and 3,800 slaves from among 8,000 captives. He also took 20,000 bags of gold coins. Kahraman and Dağlı, *Evliya Çelebi Seyahatnamesi,* vol. 1, chap. 10. Christine Isom-Verhaaren argues that the story of a French woman who was taken into Mehmed II's harem was created by several Ottoman historians to justify the Ottoman-French alliance in the 1530s. See Christine Isom-Verhharen, "Royal French Women in the Sultan's Harem: The Political Uses of Fabricated Accounts from the Sixteenth to the Twenty-First Century," *Journal of World History* 17, no. 2 (2006): 159–96.

36. Inalcik, "Policy of Mehmed II," 233; Michael Kritovoulos, *The History of Mehmed the Conqueror,* trans. Charles T. Riggs (Princeton, NJ: Princeton University Press, 1954), 82–83. According to Kritovoulos, who had been the governor of the island of Imbros and had been commissioned by the sultan to write his history, fifty thousand men, women, and children had been taken into captivity, but many were eventually freed, were settled in abandoned houses, and received provisions for living. See also Halil Inalcik and Rhoads Murphey, *History of Mehmed the Conqueror by Tursun Beg* (Minneapolis: Bibliotheca Islamica, 1978), 53a–53b.

37. Inalcik and Murphey, *History of Mehmed,* 14–17; Halil Inalcik, *The Survey of Istanbul, 1455* (Istanbul: Türkiye İş Bankası Yayınları, 2012). Tursun Beg wrote his history after he had retired in 1488 following forty years of service to Bursa; he presented it to the new sultan, Bayezid. Tursun Beg was critical of some of the sultan's policies.

38. Uriel Heyd, "The Jewish Communities of Istanbul in the Seventeenth Century," *Oriens* 6, no. 2 (Dec. 1953): 299–314.

39. Inalcik and Murphey, *History of Mehmed the Conqueror,* 53b.

40. Mercan, "The Genoese of Pera," 46–47.

41. Franz Babinger, *Mehmed the Conqueror and His Time,* ed. William C. Hickman, trans. Ralph Manheim (Princeton, NJ: Princeton University Press, 1978), 101.

42. Steven Runciman, *The Fall of Constantinople, 1453* (Cambridge: Cambridge University Press, 1965), 162. For the Greek and Turkish texts of the Treaty of 1453, see Inalcik, "Ottoman Galata," 336–41.

43. Runciman, *Fall of Constantinople,* 162; Inalcik, "Ottoman Galata," 281–83. Evliya Çelebi believed that Galata had previously been conquered, along with

Constantinople, by Muslim forces before 1453. Kahraman and Dağlı, *Evliya Çelebi Seyahatnamesi,* vol. 1, pt. 2: 2, 388.

44. Babinger, *Mehmed the Conqueror,* 101–2; Inalcik, "Ottoman Galata," 336–41 (Turkish and Greek texts of the Treaty of 1453).

45. Ottoman sources include Mehmed II's letter to the Mamluk ruler of Egypt declaring the peaceful takeover of Galata. See Inalcik, "Ottoman Galata," 345; Inalcik and Murphey, *History of Mehmed,* 53b–55b; Runciman, *Fall of Constantinople,*192–98; Kritovoulos, *History of Mehmed;* Babinger, *Mehmed the Conqueror,*101–7; Kerim Ilker Bulunur, *Osmanlı Galatası: 1453–1600)* (Istanbul: Bilge, Kültür, Sanat, 2014), 55–67; Çiğdem Kafesçioğlu, *Constantinoplolis/Istanbul: Cultural Encounters, Imperial Vision, and the Construction of the Ottoman Capital* (University Park: Pennsylvania State University Press, 2009)

46. Inalcik, "Ottoman Galata," 285.

47. Runciman, *Fall of Constantinople,* 162. Runciman claims that he also destroyed the Tower of Christ.

48. Mercan, "Genoese of Pera," 50.

49. Runciman, *Fall of Constantinople,* 161–62; Babinger, *Mehmed the Conqueror,* 111.

50. Ağır, *Istanbul Eski,* 93.

51. Babinger, *Mehmed the Conqueror,* 111.

52. Ağır, *Istanbul Eski,* 99–105.

53. Abulafia, *Great Sea,* 385. For Cyprus, see Ronald C. Jennings, *Christians and Muslims in Ottoman Cyprus and the Mediterranean World, 1571–1640* (New York: NYU Press, 1993), 132–68.

54. Dursteler, "Latin-Rite Christians," 139. Some were the Draperii, Fornetti, Fortis, Galante, Navoni, Negri, Oliveri, Orlandi, Salvago, Silvestri, and Testa families, among others. On the Draperio and Spinola families, see Mercan, "Genoese of Pera," 43–47.

55. Dursteler, *Venetians in Constantinople,* 142.

56. Dursteler, "Latin-Rite Christians," 139.

57. Dursteler, *Venetians in Constantinople,* 25.

58. Zarinebaf, *Crime and Punishment,* 26.

59. The first surviving sicil of Galata dates from 1536. See Islam Araştırmaları Merkezi (ISAM), Galata Sicil 14/1.

60. Dallaway, *Constantinople, Ancient and Modern,* 79, 125.

61. Zarinebaf, *Crime and Punishment,* 26; Kahraman and Dağlı, *Evliya Çelebi Seyahatnamesi,* vol. 1 pt. 2 392.

62. Kahraman and Dağlı, *Evliya Çelebi Seyahatnamesi,* vol. 1, pt. 2: 392.

63. Matrakçi Nasuhu's-Silah, *Beyani-i Sefer-i Irakeyn-i Sultan Süleyman Han* (Ankara: TTK, 1976), 9a–8b.

64. Cevat Ulkesul, *Piri Reis ve Türk Kartograflarının Çizgileriyle XVI, XVII, ve XVIII: Yüzyıllarda Istanbul* (Istanbul: Boyut, 2013), 80; Pinar Emiralioğlu, *Geographical Knowledge and Imperial Culture in the Early Modern Ottoman Empire* (London: Ashgate, 2014), 84, 94–102.

65. J. Freely and B. Freely, *A Guide to Beyoğlu*, 88–89.

66. Inalcik, "Ottoman Galata," 289–363; Inalcik, *Survey of Istanbul*. See Mehmet Öz, "1455 Tahriri ve Istanbul'un Iskan Tarihi Bakımından Önemi," in *Osmanlı Istanbulu*, vol. 1, ed. Feridun M. Emecen and Emrah S. Gürkan (Istanbul: 29 Mayıs Universitesi Yayınları, 2013), 107–15. The numbers of households and quarters provided by Öz do not overlap with the numbers provided by Inalcik, *Survey of Istanbul*, tables I and II, p. 116.

67. Inalcik, *Survey of Istanbul*, 217–493. Since the survey is missing some pages, these numbers must be viewed with some caution. The survey of the quarter of San Neferzo is incomplete. For a complete survey, see "Istanbul," Topkpi Saray Archives, D. 2203: 272–336. I am grateful to Padriac Rohan for bringing this document to my attention.

68. Inalcik, "Ottoman Galata," 375–76.

69. Ibid., 375–76, table 1.

70. Goffman, *Ottoman Empire*, 172–73.

71. ISAM, Galata Sicil 14/17, folio 190–91; Bulunur, 63–64. The sicil also contains the Ottoman text of the Ahdname of 1453.

72. On the origins of Muslim settlers in Istanbul in 1453, see Öz, "1455 Tahriri," 118–23, table 4; Doğan Kuban, *Istanbul: An Urban History* (Istanbul: Economic and Social Foundation of Turkey, 1996), 200–201; Mantran, *Histoire d'Istanbul*, 196–201.

73. Topkapi Saray Archives, D. 2203: 288–89.

74. Inalcik, *Survey of Istanbul*, 586.

75. Inalcik and Murphey, *History of Mehmed*, 32–37.

76. Geo Pistarino, "The Genoese in Pera-Turkish Galata," *Mediterranean Historical Review* 1, no. 1 (1986): 63–86.

77. Nasuh Matrakçı, *Beyani-i Sefer-i Irakeyn-i Sultan Süleyman Han* (Ankara: TTK, 1976), 9a.

78. Inalcik, "Ottoman Galata," 363.

79. Ibid., 363, 301–10.

80. Ibid., 275–376. See also Inalcik, *Survey of Istanbul*, 217–93.

81. Miller, "Genoese in Galata," 76; Halil Inalcik, "Foundations of Ottoman-Jewish Cooperation," in *Jews, Turks, Ottomans: A Shared History, Fifteenth Century through the Twentieth Century*, edited by Avigdor Levey. (Syracuse, NY: Syracuse University Press, 2002), 6.

82. Bulunur, *Osmanlı Galatası*, 163.

83. BBA, TT 210 and 240; Mark Alan Epstein, *The Ottoman Jewish Communities and Their Role in the Fifteenth and Sixteenth Centuries* (Freiburg, Germany: K. Schwarz, 1980), 178; Stéphane Yerasimos, "*La communauté Juive d'Istanbul a la fin du XVI siècle*," *Turcica* 27 (1995): 109 [101–30]; Yerasimos wrongly dates TT 240 to 1525 on table 1, pp. 109–11. It should be dated to 1545.

84. Kahraman and Dağlı, *Evliya Çelebi Seyahatnamesi*, vol. 1, pt. 2: 391

85. The gates were the Azap Kapı, Kürkçü Kapı near the Arab Cami'i, Yağkapanı Kapısı (scale of olive oil gate), Balıkpazarı Kapısı (fish market gate), Karaköy Kapısı, Kurşunlu Mahzen Kapısı, Mumhane Kapısı, Domuz Kapı, and Kireç Kapı (see map 2).

86. We must treat these numbers with some caution. Kahraman and Dağlı, *Evliya Çelebi Seyhatnamesi*, vol. 1, pt. 2: 391–92; Robert Dankoff and Sooyong Kim, *An Ottoman Traveler: Selections from the Book of Travels of Evliya Çelebi* (London: Eland, 2010), 18–19; Bulunur, *Osmanlı Galatası*, 163. See also Zarinebaf, *Crime and Punishment*, 24–28.

87. Inalcik, "Ottoman Galata," 350. For the archives of the church of St. Peter, see Arturo Bernal Palacious, OP, "Fr. Benedetto (Giovanni) Palazzo OP (1895–1955) and His Catalogue of the Conventual Archives of Saint Peter in Galata (Istanbul)," *Dominican History Newsletter* 11 (2002): 215–50. The archives contain correspondence between the papacy and the church in addition to imperial orders from the sultan dating back to the early seventeenth century.

88. Halil Inalcik, "Policy of Mehmet II," 229–49.

89. Zarinebaf, *Crime and Punishment*, 18–21.

90. Inalcik, "Policy of Mehmet II," 236–39.

91. Kahraman and Dağlı, *Evliya Çelebi Seyatnamesi*, vol. 1, pt. 2: 392.

92. Miller, "Genoese in Galata," 90.

93. Celal Arseven As'ad, *Eski Galata ve Binalrı* (Istanbul: Şefik Matbaası, 1989), 46.

94. Inalcik, *Survey of Istanbul*, 505–7. Mehmed II transferred and settled many Jews from Istanbul and Macedonia in the neighborhood of Balat, which had the oldest Synagogue (Ohrida).

95. Minna Rozen, *A History of the Jewish Community in Istanbul: The Formative Years, 1453–1566* (Leiden: E. J. Brill, 2002), 56–57.

96. Caroline Finkel, *Osman's Dream: The History of the Ottoman Empire* (New York: Basic Books, 2005), 88.

97. Rozen, *History of the Jewish Community*, 60.

98. BBA, TT.D 240: 12. See Epstein, *Ottoman Jewish Communities,* appendix I, on the surveys of Jewish households in the empire in the sixteenth and early seventeenth centuries.

99. Ismet Demir, 5, *Numaralı Mühimme Defteri* (973/1565–1566) (Ankara: Devlet Arşivleri, 1994), 278, 348, 463.

100. Rozen, *History of the Jewish Community*, 50–56.

101. BBA, MAD 14932. This register divides the Iberian Jews who arrived in the early seventeenth century into three income groups and lists their Iberian place of origin.

102. Rozen, *History of the Jewish Community*, 54.

103. Zarinebaf, *Crime and Punishment*, 18–21. For Jewish neighborhoods in France, see Rosa Alverez Perez, "Next-Door Neighbors: Aspects of Judeo-Christian Cohabitation in Medieval France," in *Urban Space in the Middle Ages and the Early Modern Age,* ed. Albrecht Classen (Berlin: Walter de Gruyter, 2009), 309–29. In Paris, Jews resided in a few quarters, narrow and dark streets that were closed off at night. In 1182, every expulsion was accompanied by the confiscation and sale of Jewish property. In France, a royal decree in 1289 forced the Jews to live in certain administrative units in cities as serfs of the king. In the thirteenth century, the Jews reestablished themselves as two communities, one oriented toward trade on the

Right Bank of the Seine and the other on the Left Bank, which was the domain of the intellectuals.

104. MAD 1276 and 3661: 1–59. According to MAD 1276, an earlier *cizye* register dating from 1690, the total number of Jewish households in greater Istanbul was 8,235. Of this number, 545 households had high income, 3,469 had middle income, and 4,221 had low income. In 1691, the majority of the Jewish households (3, 928) in Istanbul and Galata had low income while one-fifth (1,043) had middle income.

105. Haim Gerber, "Jews and Money-Lending in the Ottoman Empire," *Jewish Quarterly Review,* n.s., 72, no. 2 (Oct. 1981): 100–18.

106. Kahraman and Dağlı, *Evliya Çelebi Seyahatnamesi,* vol. 1, pt. 2: 392.

107. B. Freely and J. Freely, *Guide to Beyoğlu,* 76.

108. Jean Thévenot, *L'empire du grand Turc vu par un sujet de Louis XIV* (Paris: Galmann-Lévy, 1965), 75–76.

109. Kahraman and Dağlı, *Evliya Çelebi Seyahatnamesi,* vol.1, pt. 2: 387–88. Evliya Çelebi believed that Muslims had laid siege to Constantinople and Galata ten times before 1453. As'ad, *Eski Galata,* 46–47. However, Semavi Eyice believes that the legend is inaccurate and that the Arabs never built a mosque in Galata. Semavi Eyice, "Arap Cami'i," in *Dünden Bugüne Istanbul Ansikopedisi,* vol. 1 (Istanbul: Kültür Bakanlığı va Tarih Vakfı, 1993), 294–95.

110. Halil Inalcik, "Galata, Osmanlı Dönemi," in *Dünden Bugüne Istanbul Ansiklopedisi,* vol. 3 (Istanbul: Kültür ve Tarıh Vakfı, 1994), 350–52.

111. Kahraman and Dağlı, *Evliya Çelebi Seyahatnamesi,* vol.1, pt. 2: 387–88; Bulunur, *Osmanlı Galatası,* 179–88.

112. Eyice, "Arap Cami'i," 294; P. Benedetto Palazzo, OP, *Arap Cami'i veya Galata Saint Paul Kilisesi* (Istanbul: Bilge Karınca, 2014), 50–56, 77–83; Ozkan Eroğlu, *Suriçi Galata* (Istanbul: Tekne Yayınları, 2015), 68–69.

113. P. Benedetto Palazzo, OP, *L'Arap Djami ou Eglise Saint Paul à Galata* (Istanbul: Hachette, 1946), 57–65.

114. Inalcik, "Galata, Osmanlı Dönemi," 349–54.

115. As'ad, *Eski Galata,* 46–50. As'ad believes that it is hard to determine the Islamic or Latin origins of this mosque.

116. Sarkis Sarraf Hovhannesyan, *Payitaht Istanbul'un Tarihçesi,* trans. Elmon Hançer (Istanbul: Tarih Vakfı Yurt Yaınları, 1997), 38.

117. Kahraman and Dağlı, *Evliya Çelebi Seyahatnamesi,* vol.1, pt. 2: 387, 390.

118. The major Latin churches in Galata and Pera were St. Benoit (Jesuit; burned in 1660, 1686, and 1731), St. Louis Chapel of the French Embassy, Santa Catarina (built in 1387), Santa Chiara, St. Clement, St. Francesco (burned in 1696 and converted into a mosque), St. George (Capuchin), St. Giovanni Battista (burned in 1660), Santa Maria Draperis, St. Michel, San Antonio, and Sts. Peter and Paul (burned in 1660 and 1730). Eric R. Dursteler, *Venetians in Constantinople: Nation, Identity, and Coexistence in the Early Modern Mediterranean* (Baltimore: Johns Hopkins University Press, 2006), 13.

119. Thévenot, *L'empire du Grand Turc.* For a comprehensive map and location of these churches, see A. M. Schneider and M. Is. Nomidis, *Galata: Topographisch-*

Archaeologischer Plan mit Erlauterndem Text (Istanbul: N.p., 1994), 22–25; As'ad, *Eski Galata,* 41.

120. Summer-Boyd and Freely, *Strolling through Istanbul,* 448–49.

121. J. Freely and B. Freely, *A Guide to Beyoğlu,* 134.

122. Miller, "Genoese in Galata," 87–89.

123. Ibid., 90.

124. Dursteler, *Venetians in Constantinople,* 143–44.

125. Inalcik, "Galata, Osmanlı Donemi," 352.

126. MAD 1152: 1–8.

127. Dursteler, *Venetians in Constantinople,* 142–44; Molly Greene, *Catholic Pirates and Greek Merchants: A Maritime History of the Early Modern Mediterranean* (Princeton, NJ: Princeton University Press, 2010), 100–109.

128. Kahraman and Dağlı, *Evliya Çelebi Seyahatnamesi,* vol.1, pt. 2: 391; Dankoff and Kim, *An Ottoman Traveler,* 18–20.

129. Many Moriscos who settled in Galata served in the navy. The new Muslim quarters in Galata were called Kapudan Bali Reis, Iskandıl Kasim Reis, Kemal Reis, Azepler, Okçu Musa, Abdi Fakih, Şehsuvar, Bereketzade, and Haci Ağver, according to the *vakfiye* of 1496; Kafesçioğlu, *Constantinopolis/Istanbul,* 1–15.

130. Inalcik, "Galata, Osmanlı Dönemi," 352.

131. Ibid.

132. Epstein, *Ottoman Jewish Communities.*

133. Inalcik, "Ottoman Galata," 325; Andrew C. Hess, *The Forgotten Frontier: A History of the Sixteenth-Century Ibero-African Frontier* (Chicago: University of Chicago Press, 1983), 127–55. For a recent article, see Miguel Angel Extremera Extremera, "A Forced Migration: Spanish Moriscos in Ottoman Lands (16th–18th Centuries)," *Turcica* 45 (2014): 61–77; 152–53; Abulafia, *Great Sea,* 470–76. On the treatment of Muslim women after 1492, see Mary Elizabeth Perry, *The Handless Maiden: Moriscos and the Politics of Religion in Early Modern Spain* (Princeton, NJ: Princeton University Press, 2005), 65–87.

134. Perry, *Handless Maiden,* 36.

135. Hess, *Forgotten Frontier,* 136. For an excellent study on the role of prophecies in the Morisco Rebellion, see Mayra T. Green-Mercado, "Morisco Apocalypticism: Politics of Prophecy in the Early Modern Mediterranean" (PhD dissertation, University of Chicago, 2012). See also Green-Mercado, "The Mahdi in Valencia: Messianism, Apocalypticism, and Morisco Rebellions in Late Sixteenth-Century Spain," *Medieval Encounters* 19, nos.1–2 (2013): 193–220. See also Brian A. Catlos, *Muslims of Medieval Latin Christendom, 1050–1614* (Cambridge: Cambridge University Press, 2014).

136. Hess, *Forgotten Frontier,* 138.

137. Hess, *Forgotten Frontier,* 136–38; Extremera, "Forced Migration," 63. We have to be careful with some of these numbers.

138. Hess, *Forgotten Frontier,* 143.

139. Ibid., 146–47.

140. Inalcik, "Galata Osmanlı Dönemi," 349–54.

141. Halil Inalcik, " Istanbul: An Islamic City," in *Essays in Ottoman History,* ed. Halil Inalcik (Istanbul: Eren, 1998), 247–71; Sherine Hamadeh, *The City's Pleasures: Istanbul in the Eighteenth Century* (Seattle: University of Washington Press, 2008).

142. Pinar Kayaalp, "The Role of Imperial Mosque Complexes (1543–1583) in the Urbanization of Üsküdar," in *Urban Space in the Middle Ages and the Early Modern Age,* ed. Albrecht Classen (Berlin: Walter de Gruyter, 2009, 650–57.

143. For the Islamization in Istanbul proper, see Kafesçioglu, *Constantinopolis/ Istanbul,* 130–42.

144. Eldem, *French Trade,* 151–52.

145. Inalcik, "Galata, Osmanlı Dönemi," 352.

146. Bulunur, *Osmanlı Galatası,* 98–99.

147. Miller, 89; Gönul Çantay, "Kurşunlu Han," *Dünden Bugüne Isltanbul Ansiklopedisi,* vol. 5 (Istanbul: Kültür ve Tarıh Vakfı, 1994), 126.

148. Bulunur, *Osmanlı Galatası,* 99.

149. Ibid., 84.

150. See the dissertation of Zahit Atcil, "State and Government in the Mid-Sixteenth Century Ottoman Empire: The Grand Vizierates of Rüstem Pasha (1544–1561)" (PhD diss., University of Chicago, 2014), 270–91.

151. See the map of Galata by Piri Reis in Cevat Ülkekul, *Piri Reis ve Türk Kartograflarının Çizgileriyle XVI, XVII, XVIII Istanbul* (Istanbul: Boyut Yayınları, 2013), 81.

152. As'ad, *Eski Galata,* 103–4; Schneider and Nomidis, *Galata,* 28–34. Other smaller mosques in Galata and Pera included the Bereketzade Mosque, built by the first voyvoda of Galata; the Şah Kulu Mosque, built by Mehmet Çelebi, the boon companion (intimate friend) of Sultan Mehmed III (who ruled from 1595 to 1603); and the Müeyyidzade, formerly known as the Yazıcı, Mosque, built in 1582 by kadi Müeyyidzade Mehmed Efendi inside the walls. Additional mosques were Alaca Mescid (early sixteenth century), Bektaş Efendi (early sixteenth century), Bereketzade Mescidi, Etmek Yemez Mescidi (1590), Haci Agvar, Kemankeş Mustafa Pasha Cami'i (seventeenth century), Kürkçiler Mescidi, Manastir Mescidi (late fifteenth century), Okçu Musa Mescidi, Sultan Bayezid Han Mescidi, Şehsuvar Mescidi, Yeni Cami'i (1697), Yolcuzade Mescidi, Ali Hoca Mescidi, Azap Kapı Mescidi (1577), Bozacı Sokak Mescidi, Eski Yağ Kapanı Cami'i (1536), Hendek (1742), Karabaş Tekkiyesi Mescidi (1530–31), Karanlık, Kurşunlu Mahzen Cami'i, Mevlevihane Mescidi, Meyit Iskelesi Mescidi, Nişancı Mescidi, Palamut Mescidi, Şahkulu Mescidi (1770), Tophane Cami'i (1580), Yağ Kapanı Cami'i (1683), Yazıcı Cami'i (d. 1582), and Yelkenci Han Mescidi.

153. Inalcik, "Ottoman Galata," 352; J. Freely and B. Freely, *Guide to Beyoğlu,* 68.

154. Ekrem Isin, "Galata Mevlevihanesi," in *Istanbul Ansiklopedisi,* vol. 3 (Istanbul: Kültür Bakanlığı ve Tarih Vakfı, 1993), 362–64; Baha Talman, "Mimari," in *Istanbul Ansiklopedisi,* vol. 3 (Kültür Bakanlığı ve Tarih Vakfı, 1993), 364–67.

155. Some historians claim that Islamization was the state policy in Galata. See Tijana Krstic, "Moriscos in Ottoman Galata, 1609–1620s" in *The Expulsion of*

Moriscos From Spain: A Mediterranean Diaspora, ed. Mercedes Garcia-Arenal and Gerard Wiegers (Leiden: E J. Brill, 2014), 269–86.

156. Bulunur, *Osmanlı Galatası,* 187. Dursteler, *Venetians in Constantinople,* 154–56.

157. Mühimme Defteri 75: 199. For Kasım Paşa and Tophane, see Kahraman and Dağli, *Evliya Çelebi Seyahatnamesi,* book 1, pt.1: 376–86; book 1, pt. 2: 2, 395–408.

158. Kahraman & Dağlı, *Evliya Çelebi Seyahatnamesi,* vol. 1, pt. 2, 382–83.

159. Ahmed Refik, *Onikinci Asr-i Hicri-de Istanbul Hayatı (1689–1785)* (Istanbul: Enderun Kitabevi, 1988), 30–31.

160. Ibid., 10–11.

161. Ibid., 30–31.

162. Zarinebaf, *Crime and Punishment,* 164–68; Nida Nebahat Nalçacı, *Sultanın Kulları: Erken Modern Dönem Istanbul'unda Savaş Esirleri ve Zorunlu Istihdam* (Istanbul: Verita Kitap, 2015).

163. Galata Mahkemesi 15 Numarali Sicil, 154.

164. Fleet, *European and Islamic Trade,* 37–58.

165. Ariel Salzmann, "Migrants in Chains: On the Enslavement of Muslims in Renaissance and Enlightenment Europe," *Religions* 4 (2013): 391–411.

166. Ibid., 394–95.

167. Greene, *Catholic Pirates,* 78–98.

168. See also Nur Sobers Khan, "Slaves without Shackles: Forced Labour and Manumission in the Galata Court Registers, 1560–1572" (PhD diss., Pembroke College, 2012), 34; Sobers Khan, *Slaves without Shackles: Forced Labour and Manumission in the Galata Court Registers, 1560–1572* (Berlin: Klaus Schwartz Verlag, 2014).

169. Dursteler, *Venetians in Constantinople,* 73.

170. Ismet Binak, *3 Numaralı Mühimme Defteri (966–968/1558–1560)* (Ankara: Başbakanlık Devlet Arşivleri Genel Müdürlüğü, 1993), 83: 206.

171. Dursteler, *Venetians in Constantinople,* 76.

172. R. Günalan, T. Mert, and C. Yılmaz, eds. *Istanbul Kadı Sicileri, Galata Mahkemesi 15 Numaralı Sicil (H. 961–1000/M. 1573–1591)* (Istanbul: Isam, 2012); Mehmet Akman and Akıf Aydın, eds., *Galata Mahkemesi 5 Numaralı Sicil (H.983–984/M. 1575–1576)* (Istanbul: Isam Yayınları, 2011).

173. *3 Numaralı Mühimme Defteri,* 257: 744.

174. Günalan, Mert, and Yılmaz, *Galata Mahkemesi 15 Numaralı Sicil,* 51. See also Khan, *Slaves without Shackles.*

175. *Galata Mahkemesi,* 66.

176. Ibid., 67.

177. Ibid., 62–63

178. Ibid., 159–64.

179. Dursteler, *Venetians in Constantinople,* 73.

180. Halil Inalcik, "Ottoman Galata, 1453–1553," in *Première rencontre internationale sur l'empire Ottoman et la Turquie modern,* ed. Edhem Eldem. (Istanbul: Isis Press, 1991), 104.

181. Thévenot, *L'empire du grand Turc,* 76. Translated into English by the author.

182. Ibid.

183. Kahraman and Dağlı, *Evliya Çelebi Seyahatnamesi,* vol. 1, pt. 2: 393.

184. Hovhannesyan, *Payitaht Istanbul'un Tarihçesi,* 39.

185. BBA, NFS.d (Nüfus Defteri) 6, 11: 21–22, 24; A.DVN.d 832: 12–15, 23, 29.

186. André Raymond, " The Ottoman Conquest and the Development of the Great Arab Towns," *International Journal of Turkish Studies* 1 (1980): 84–101. For Ottoman construction of commercial structures in Cairo, Damascus, and Aleppo, see pages 92 to 97.

187. For the commercial policies of Sultan Mehmed II and the customs rate on imports and exports by foreign and local merchants, see Robert Anhegger and Halil Inalcik, *Kanunname-I Sultani ber Muceb-i Orf-i Osmani* (Ankara: TTK, 1956), 73–76.

188. Bulunur, *Osmanlı Galatası,* 98.

189. Halil Inalcik, "The Hub of the City: The *bedestan* of Istanbul," *International Journal of Turkish Studies* 1 (1980): 1–17; Çantay, "Kurşunlu Han," 126.

190. Semavi Eyice, "Galata Bedesteni," in *Dünden Bugüne Isltanbul Ansiklopedisi,* vol. 3 (Istanbul: Kültür ve Tarıh Vakfı, 1994), 355–56; Halil Inalcik, "Galata, Osmanlı Dönemi, 348–54.

191. Wolfgang Muller-Wiener, *Bizanstan Osmanlı'ya Istanbul Limanı,* trans. Erol Özbek (Istanbul: Tarih Vakfi Yurt Yayınları, 2003), 56–57.

192. Inalcik, "Galata, Osmanlı Dönemi," 353.

193. Inalcik, "Ottoman Galata, 1453–1553," 97.

194. Bulunur, *Osmanlı Galatası,* 99–100.

195. Kahraman and Dağlı, *Evliya Çelebi Seyahatnamesi,* vol.1, pt. 2: 392–93.

196. Dankoff and Kim, *An Ottoman Traveler,* 19–21.

197. Kahraman and Dağlı, *Evliya Çelebi Seyahatnamesi,* vol.1, pt. 2: 392–93.

198. Ibid., 395.

199. ISAM, Sicil 14/1: 279.

200. Ismet Binark, ed., *12 Numaralı Mühimme Defteri,* 620.

201. BBA, *Mühimme Defteri* (MD)185: 182.

202. Mertol Tulum, *Mühimme Defteri 90* (Istanbul: Türk Dünyasi Araştırmaları vakfi, 1993), 413; Zarinebaf, *Crime and Punishment,* 100–105.

203. Tulum, *Muhimme Defteri 90,* 240, 264, 265, 272. See Zarinebaf, *Crime and Punishment,* 100–105.

204. Ismet Binark and Osman Yıldırım, eds., *5 Numaralı Mühimme Defteri* (973/1565–66), *Başbakanlık Devlet Arşivleri Genel Müdürlüğü,* 1994, 121.

205. Kahraman and Dağlı, *Evliya Çelebi Seyahatnamesi,* vol. 1, pt. 2: 393–94.

206. BBA, MM (*Maliyeden Müdevver Defteri*) 10324.

207. Suraiya Faroqhi, "Understanding Ottoman Guilds" and "Ottoman Craftsmen: Problematic and Sources with Special Emphasis on the Eighteenth Century," in *Crafts and Craftsmen of the Middle East: Fashioning the Individual in the Muslim Mediterranean,* ed. Suraiya Faroqhi and Randi Deguilhem (Cambridge: Cambridge University Press, 2005), 3–41, 90–93.

208. Zarinebaf, *Crime and Punishment,* 43–44.

209. Fariba Zarinebaf, "The Role of Women in the Urban Economy of Istanbul," *International Labor and Working-Class History* 60 (Fall 2001): 141–52.

210. BBA, MM 10324.

211. Zarinebaf, *Crime and Punishment,* 40–51; Cevdet Muallim 1: 1–25.

212. BBA, ADVN.D 832: 39.

213. ADVN.D 832: 30–33, 38–39.

214. Istanbul Sicil series, 1/32: 9a.

215. Cevdet Muallim, 1: 26.

CHAPTER TWO

1. Jean Thévenot, *L'empire du Grand Turc vu par un sujet de Louis XIV* (Paris: Galmann-Lévy, 1965), 76–77.

2. Nigel Webb and Caroline Webb, *The Earl and His Butler in Constantinople: The Secret Diary of an English Servant among the Ottomans* (London: I.B. Tauris, 2009), 22–23.

3. Lady Mary Wortley Montagu, *Turkish Embassy Letters,* ed. Malcolm M. Jack (London: Virago Books, 1994), 107–8. She claimed that five hundred houses had been burned down in a fire due to the use of coal in heating in January 1718.

4. Brian Johnson, "Istanbul's Vanished City of the Dead," in *Efsanelerden Günumüze Istanbul: Seçme Yazılar 1: Myth to Modernity, Selected Themes,* ed. Nezih Başgelen and Brian Johnson (Istanbul: Arkeoloji Sanat Yayınları, 2002), 93–104.

5. Edhem Eldem, *Death in Istanbul: Death and Its Rituals in Ottoman-Islamic Culture* (Istanbul: Ottoman Bank Archives and Research Centre, 2005), 16 (map of major cemeteries in Istanbul and Galata), 20, 72–73.

6. Zarinebaf, *Crime and Punishment,* 28–32; Daniel Panzac, *La peste, 1700–1850* (Leuven: Editions Peeters, 1985).

7. Junko Thérèse Takeda, *Between Crown and Commerce: Marseille and the Early Modern Mediterranean* (Johns Hopkins University Press, 2011), 106–7.

8. Nükhet Varlık, *Plague and Empire in the Early Modern Mediterranean World: The Ottoman Experience, 1347–1600* (Cambridge: Cambridge University Press, 2015), 160–84. See also Varlik, ed. *Plague and Contagion in the Islamic Mediterranean: New Histories of Disease in the Ottoman Society* (Newark, NJ: Rutgers University, 2017).

9. Varlık, *Plague and Empire,* 185–87.

10. Ibid., 253–59, 277–82.

11. ISAM, Üsküdar sicil series 2/2, 160a; 5/3, 76a.

12. ISAM, Üsküdar sicil series 51/8, 281a. To this date, no registers of plague victims have been found in the Turkish Archives. The cemeteries have not been studied to establish trends from the years when the plague hit the hardest.

13. Panzac, *La peste,* 49–53.

14. ACCM (Chamber of Commerce Archives in Marseille), J series, no. 177.

15. ISAM, Istanbul sicil series 24/21, 40a.

16. ISAM, Galata sicil series 14/392, 17a–18a.

17. ACCM, J series, no. 177; Panzac, *La peste,* 58–62.

18. See ACCM, LIX 710; Panzac, *La peste,* 59.

19. Sibel Zandi-Sayek, *Ottoman Izmir: The Rise of a Cosmopolitan Port, 1840–1880* (Minneapolis: University of Minnesota Press, 2012), 81.

20. Cabi Ömer Efendi, *Cabi Tarihi,* ed. Mehmet Ali Beyhan, vol. 2 (Ankara: Türk Tarih Kurumu, 2003), 902.

21. For an excellent study of Jewish cemeteries, see Minna Rozen, "Metropolis and Necropolis: The Cultivation of Social Status among the Jews of Istanbul in the 17th and 18th Centuries," in *Living in the Ottoman Ecumenical Community: Essays in Honour of Suraiya Faroqhi,* ed. Vera Costantini and Markus Koller (Leiden: E.J. Brill, 2008), 105–7. Rozen found many tombstones in Ortaköy from 1751, when the plague struck Istanbul.

22. Cabi Efendi, *Cabi Tarihi,* 2:902, 908, 910–11, 1037.

23. Ibid., 943.

24. Faik Reşit Unat, *Osmanlı Sefirleri ve Sefaratnameleri* (Ankara: Türk Tarih Kurumu, 1992), 179–81. Morali Seyyid Ali Efendi provided a detailed description of Marseille, Toulon, Lyon, and Paris, which he visited in summer 1797.

25. André Raymond, *Cairo,* trans. Willard Wood (Cambridge, MA: Harvard University Press, 2000), 300.

26. Nuran Yıldırım, *14. Yüzyıldan Cumhuriyet'e Hastalıklar, Hastaneler, Kurumlar* (Istanbul: Tarih Vakfı Yürt Yayınları, 2014), 71.

27. Ibid., 55. For Ottoman and Russian state policies on the Black Sea and the Balkans, see Andrew Robarts, *Migration and Disease in the Black Sea Region: Ottoman-Russian Relations in the Late Eighteenth and Early Nineteenth Century* (London: Bloomsbury Academic, 2017), 120–37.

28. Zarinebaf, *Crime and Punishment,* 32–34.

29. Shmuel Moreh, trans. *Napoleon in Egypt: Al-Jabarti's Chronicle of the French Occupation of Cairo, 1798* (Princeton, NJ: Markus Wiener, 1993), 63.

30. Raymond, *Cairo,* 302–11.

31. Moreh, *Napoleon in Egypt,* 117–18.

32. Ibid., 93–99.

33. Raymond, *Cairo,* 297–98; Moreh, *Napoleon in Egypt,* 63.

34. Moreh, 83–101; Raymond, 297–99.

35. Osman Nuri Ergin, *Mecelle-i Umur-i Belediye,* vol. 6 (Istanbul: Büyükşehir Belediyesi Yayınlarn, 1995), 3062–226; Musa Çardırçı, *Tanzimat Döneminde Anadolu Kentleri'nin Sosyal ve Ekonomik Yapıları* (Ankara: Türk Tarih Kurumu, 1991), 304–12.

36. Kenan Yıldız, "1782 Istanbul Yangını: Kadi Sicilerinden Tespit, Çikarı ve Yorumları," in *Osmanlı Istanbulu, II,* ed. Feridun Emecen, Ali Akyıldız, and Emrah S. Gürkan. (Istanbul: 29 Mayıs University Yayınları, 2014), 707–22.

37. Cem Behar, *A Neighborhood in Ottoman Istanbul: Fruit Vendors and Civil Servants in the Kasap Ilyas Mahalle* (New York: SUNY Press, 2003), 58–63. In Istanbul proper, the Great Fire of July 24, 1660, which started in a timber shop in

Ayaspaşa, spread to the rest of Istanbul and continued for two days, burning thousands of houses and shops and hundreds of mosques, churches, markets, and palaces.

38. Timur Kuran, ed., *Social and Economic Life in Seventeenth Century Istanbul: Glimpses from Court Records,* vol. 1 (Istanbul: Turkiye Iş Bankası, 2010), 913–17.

39. Zarinebaf, *Crime and Punishment,* 31; Eldem, *French Trade,* 232–33.

40. Zarinebaf, *Crime and Punishment,* 32; Montagu, *Turkish Embassy Letters,* 42.

41. Cevdet Adliye 85/5092.

42. N. Webb and C. Webb, *Earl and His Butler,* 21. The inventory of the embassy listed a hundred meters of Algona wine (valued at 400 dollars), 600 meters of red wine made in the Embassy Palace (valued at 600 dollars), and seven chests of brandy (valued at 60 dollars) as well as champagne, burgundy, Hungarian cyprus, and other foreign wines worth 390 dollars.

43. Çeşmi-Zade Mustafa Reşid, *Çeşmi-zade Tarihi* (Istanbul: Istanbul Fethi Cemiyeti, 1993), 58. See Yıldız, "1782 Istanbul Yangını," 707–22.

44. B.J. Slot, "The Fires in Istanbul of 1782 and 1784[,] according to Maps and Reports by Dutch Diplomatic Representatives," *Güney Doğu Avrupa Araştımaları Dergisi* 4–5 (1975–76): 48. In İstanbul, the Great Fire of 1782 started in Aksaray and caused significant destruction and displacement of residents.

45. ISAM Galata sicil series 14/90: 55.

46. ISAM, Istanbul sicil series, 1/32: 8a.

47. ISAM, Istanbul sicil series 1/32: 8a.

48. Zarinebaf, *Crime and Punishment,* 32–33.

49. Ahmed Refik, *Onikinci Asr-i Hicri'de Istanbul Hayatı (1689–1785)* (Istanbul: Enderun Kitabevi, 1988), 35–36.

50. BBA, Cevdet Belediye, 6961.

51. Ahmed Refik, *Onüçüncü Asr-i Hicri'de Istanbul Hayatı (1786–1882)* (Istanbul: Enderun Kitabevi, 1988), 9.

52. Sicil series 14/319: 88b.

53. ISAM, Galata sicil series 14/535: 84a.

54. BBA, CZ 245: 1–6.

55. ISAM, Istanbul sicil series 1/32: 8a.

56. Thévenot, *L'empire du Grand Turc,* 73.

57. BBA, Cevdet Iktisat 426.

58. Nur Akın, *19. Yuzyılın Ikinci Yarısında Galata ve Pera* (Istanbul: Literatür Yayınları, 2011), 330–36.

59. Ibid., 335–37; Murat Gül, *The Emergence of Modern Istanbul: Transformation and Modernization of a City* (London: I.B. Tauris, 2012, 47; see also Zeynep Çelik, Diane Favro, and Richard Ingersoll, eds., *Streets: A Critical Perspective on Public Spaces* (Berkeley: University of California Press, 1994), 64.

60. The estimates for burned buildings vary from between 4,000 and 10,000, with *La Liberté* providing the highest number. Gül, *Emergence of Modern Istanbul,* 47.

61. James Dallaway, *Constantinople, Ancient and Modern, with Excursions to the Shores and Islands of the Archipelago and to the Troad* (London, 1797), 125. For Ottoman ambassadors in Europe, see Faik Reşit Unat, *Osmanlı Sefirleri ve Sefaratnameleri* (Ankara: TTK, 1992).

62. Thévenot, *L'empire du grand Turc,* 76; Sarkis Sarraf Hovhannesyan, *Payitaht-Istanbul'un Tarihçesi,* trans. Elmon Hançer (Istanbul: Tarih Vakfı Yurt Yaınları, 1997), 40. He identified nine gates along the harbor in Galata and stated that the kadi of Galata had two courts, the main one next to the Arab Cami'i and a small one next to the Kireç Gate.

63. Paolo Girardelli, "Ottoman Roots, European Developments: Comparing the French and Venetian Palaces in Beyoğlu," in *The 14th International Congress of Turkish Art Proceedings,* ed. Fédérick Hitzel (Paris: College de France, 2013), 357–59; N. Webb and C. Webb, *Earl and His Butler,* 20–21.

64. Tommaso Bertelé, *Venedik ve Kostantaniyye: Tarihte Osmanlı ve Venedik Ilişkileri,* trans. Mahmut H. Şarkioğlu (Istanbul: Yayınkitabevi, 2012), 99; Eric R. Dursteler, *Venetians in Constantinople: Nation, Identity, and Coexistence in the Early Modern Mediterranean* (Baltimore: Johns Hopkins University Press, 2006), 25–27.

65. Dursteler, *Venetians in Constantinople,* 25–26.

66. Ibid., 26–27.

67. Eric R. Dursteler, "A Continual Tavern in My House: Food and Diplomacy in Early Modern Constantinople," in *Renaissance Studies in Honor of Joseph Connors,* ed. M. Israel and L. Waldman, 2 vols. (Cambridge, MA: Harvard University Press, 2013), 170–71.

68. P. Pinon, "Résidence de France dans l'empire Ottoman: Notes sur l'architecture domestique," in Les Villes dans l'Empire Ottoman: Activitees et societées, ed. Daniel Panzac (Paris: CNRS Éditions, 1994), 47–84; Aksel Tibet, "Fransa Elçiliği Binası," in Dünden Bugüne Istanbul Ansiklopedisi, vol. 3 (Istanbul: Kültür Bakanlığı ve Tarih Vakfi, 1993), 331–32; Girardelli, "Ottoman Roots, European Developments," 356.

69. Tibet, *"Fransa Elçiliği Binası,"* 331.

70. Girardelli, "Ottoman Roots," 359.

71. BBA, Hatt-i Hümayun 267/15572.

72. Paolo Girardelli, "Power or Leisure? Remarks on the Architecture of the European Summer Embassies on the Bosphorus Shore," *New Perspectives on Turkey* 50 (2013): 33–36.

73. Tibet, *"Fransa Elçiliği Binası,"* 332; Girardelli, "Ottoman Roots, European Developments," 361 (see plans of the Venetian and French palaces on page 362); Akın, *19. Yuzyılın Ikinci Yarısında Galata* 207.

74. Girardelli, "Power or Leisure?" 29–57.

75. Ibid., 35–36.

76. Ibid., 33–36.

77. *Constantinople and the Seven Churches of Asia Minor,* Illustrations by Thomas Allom, descriptions by Robert Walsh and J. C. M. Bellew, edited and introduced by Mark Wilson (NJ: Gorgias Press, 2006), 2.

78. Hovhannesyan, *Payitaht-i Istanbul'un Tarihçesi,* 42; Doğan Kuban, *Istanbul: An Urban History* (Istanbul: Economic and Social Foundation of Turkey, 1996), 352.

79. For the text of the Gülhane Rescript, see Halil Inlacik and Mehmet Seydancıoğlu, *Tanzimat, Değişim Sürecinde Osmanlı Imparatorluğu* (Istanbul: Türkiye Iş Bankası Kültür Yayınları, 2008), 13–16; for the 1856 imperial reform order, see pages 19 to 25, and for an analysis by Inalcik, see pages 31 to 56.

80. Gül, *Emergence of Modern Istanbul* 26–34.

81. On modern reforms in Istanbul, see Steven Rosenthal, "Foreigners and Municipal Reform in Istanbul: 1855–1865," *IJMES* 11 (1980): 227–45; Zeynep Çelik, *The Remaking of Istanbul: Portrait of an Ottoman City in the Nineteenth Century* (Seattle: University of Washington Press, 1986); Kuban, *Istanbul: An Urban History;* Gül, *Emergence of Modern Istanbul;* Alan Duben and Cem Behar, *Istanbul Households: Marriage, Family, and Fertility, 1880–1940* (Cambridge: Cambridge University Press, 1991); Sherine Hamadeh, "Ottoman Expression of Early Modernity and the 'Inevitable' Question of Westernization," *Journal of the Society of Architectural Historians* 63, no. 1 (March 2004): 32–51; Edhem Eldem, "Istanbul as a Cosmopolitan City: Myths and Realities," in *A Companion to Diaspora and Transnationalism,* ed. Ato Quayson and Girish Daswani (London: Blackwell, 2013), 212–30; Ariel Salzmann, "Islamopolis, Cosmopolis: Ottoman Urbanity between Myth and Postmodernity," in *Cosmopolitanisms in Muslim Countries: Perspectives from the Past,* ed. D. N. MacLean and S. K. Ahmed (Edinburgh: Edinburgh University Press, 2013), 68–91.

82. On sanitation and healthcare regulations, see Osman Nuri Ergin, *Mecelle-i Umur-i Belediyye,* vol. 6 (Istanbul: Büyükşehir Belediyesi, 1995); Musa Çadırçı, *Tanzimat Döneminde Anadolu Kentleri'nin Sosyal ve Ekonomik Yapıları* (Ankara: TTK, 1991); Kuban, *Istanbul: An Urban History,* 378–83.

83. Kuban, *Istanbul: An Urban History,* 383–84.

84. Gül, *Emergence of Modern Istanbul,* 45–46; Rosenthal, "Foreigners and Municipal Reform, " 231–33.

85. Sharon Ketering, "State Control and Municipal Authority in France," in *Edo and Paris: Urban Life and the State in the Early Modern Era,* ed. James L. McLain, John M. Merriman, and Ugawa Kaoru (Ithaca, NY: Cornell University Press, 1994), 86–97. In French cities, the sale of offices (intendants, tax collectors) by the crown and venality undermined the authority of elected members of city councils in the eighteenth century.

86. Başak Ergüder, *Galata Hanları (1868–1945)-Paranin Serüveni* (Istanbul: SAV, 2011), 210–15.

87. Nora Seni, "The Camondos and Their Imprint," *IJMES* 26, no. 4 (Nov. 1994): 665–75; Steven Rosenthal, "Foreigners and Municipal Reform in Galata, 1855–1865," *IJMES* 11 (1980): 227–45.

88. Gül, *Emergence of Modern Istanbul,* 46.

89. Ibid., 26–39.

90. Behar, *Neighborhood in Ottoman Istanbul,* 85.

91. Gül, *Emergence of Modern Istanbul*, 47.

92. Lewis Mumford, *The City in History: Its Origins, Its Transformation, and Its Prospects* (San Diego: Harcourt Brace Jovanovich, 1961), 410–14.

93. See Huri Islamoğlu and Peter C. Perdu, eds., *Shared Histories of Modernity: China, India, and the Ottoman Empire* (London: Routledge, 2009).

CHAPTER THREE

1. For a comparison with Marseille and Livorno, see Junko Thérèse Takeda, *Between Crown and Commerce: Marseille and the Early Modern Mediterranean* (Baltimore: Johns Hopkins University Press, 2011); Trivellato, *Familiarity of Strangers*. For a recent discussion on France and the Early Mediterranean as a contact zone, see the special issue of *French History* 29, no.1 (2015) edited by Megan C. Armstrong and Gillian Weiss. See also joint-stock company to Pascal W. Firges, Tobias P. Graf, Christian Roth, and Gülay Tulasoğlu, eds., *Well-Connected Domains: Towards an Entangled Ottoman History* (Leiden: E.J. Brill, 2017).

2. Nasim Susa, *The Capitulatory Regime of Turkey: Its History, Origin, and Nature* (Baltimore: Johns Hopkins University Press, 1933); Halil Inalcik, "Imtiyazat," in *Encyclopedia of Islam* (EI), new ed., vol. 3 (Leiden: E.J. Brill, 1971), 1179–89; Inalcik, "Imtiyazat," in *Islam Ansiklopedisi* (IA), vol. 22 (Istanbul: Türkiye Diyanat Vakfı, 2000), 242–52; Ali İhsan Bağış, *Osmanlı Ticaretinde Gayri Müslimler, 1750–1839* (Ankara: Turhan Kitabevi, 1983); Daniel Goffman, "The Capitulation and the Question of Authority in Levantine Trade, 1600–1650," *Turcica* 10 (1986): 155–61; Murat Çizakça, *Comparative Evolution of Business Partnerships: The Islamic World and Europe, with Specific References to Ottoman Archives* (Leiden: E.J. Brill, 1996); Maurits H. van den Boogert, *The Capitulations and the Ottoman Legal System: Qadis, Consuls, and Beratlis in the Eighteenth Century* (Leiden: E.J. Brill, 2005); Bahadir Apaydın, *Kapitülasyonların Osmanlı-Türk Adli ve Idari Modernleşmesine Etkisi* (Ankara: Adalet Yayınevi, 2010); Turan Kayaoğlu, *Legal Imperialism, Sovereignty, and Extraterritoriality in Japan, the Ottoman Empire, and China* (Cambridge: Cambridge University Press, 2010); Muhammet Emin Külünk, *Kapitülasyonların Kaldırılması* (Istanbul: Yeditepe, 2011); Edhem Eldem, "Capitulations and Western Trade," in *The Cambridge History of Turkey, 1603–1839*, ed. Suraiya Faroqhi (Cambridge: Cambridge University Press, 2006), 31; Timur Kuran, *The Long Divergence: How the Islamic Law Held Back the Middle East* (Princeton, NJ: Princeton University Press, 2011), 198–209; Kuran, "The Economic Ascent of the Middle East's Religious Minorities: The Role of Islamic Plural Legalism," *Journal of Legal Studies* 33, no. 2 (June 2004): 475–15. For a critique of this paradigm among Turkish scholars, see Fikret Yılmaz, *Geçmişten Günumüze Levantenler* (Izmir: Izmir Ticaret Odası, 2011), 50–59. See also Huri Islamoğlu, "A Proposal for a Global History: Beyond the Histories of Stagnation and Deficiencies to 'Living' Histories of Possibilities," in *History from Below: A Tribute to the Memory of Donald Quataert,* ed. Selim Karahasanoğlu and Deniz Cenk Demir (Istanbul: Bilgi

University Press, 2016), 189–96; Ali Yaycioğlu, "A Reply to Timur Kuran," *International Journal of Middle Eastern Studies (IJMES)* 48, no. 2 (May 2016): 433–35.

3. Susa, *Capitulatory Regime*, 24–25.

4. Brian A. Catlos, *Muslims of Medieval Latin Christendom, c. 1050–1614* (Cambridge: Cambridge University Press, 2014), 360–99. For copies of some of these treaties, see J. C. Hurewitz, *The Middle East and North Africa in World Politics: A Documentary Record*, vol. 1, *European Expansion, 1535–1914* (New Haven: Yale University Press, 1975).

5. Susa, *Capitulatory Regime*; Elizabeth Zachariadou, *Trade and Crusade: Venetian Crete and the Emirates of Menteşe and Aydin (1300–1415)* (Venice: Hellenic Institute of Byzantine and Post-Byzantine Studies, 1983); Alexander H. De Groot, "The Historical Development of the Capitulatory Regime in the Ottoman Middle East from the Fifteenth to the Nineteenth Centuries," *Oriente Moderno*, n.s. 22, vol. 83, no. 3 (2003): 575–606.

6. Susa, *Capitulatory Regime*, 12, 33. Daniel Goffman, "Negotiating the Renaissance State: The Ottoman Empire and the New Diplomacy," in *The Early Modern Ottomans: Remapping the Empire*, ed. Virginia H. Aksan and Daniel Goffman (Cambridge: Cambridge University Press, 2007), 62–63, 73–74.

7. G. Pelissie du Rausas, *Le régime des capitulations dans l'empire Ottoman* (Paris, 1902), 212; Daniel Goffman, "Negotiating the Renaissance State," 72.

8. Susa, *Capitulatory Regime*, 38–42. Goffman rejects the notion of "extraterritoriality" in the ahdnames and argues that the autonomy, accommodation, and the religious freedom of foreigners were the extension of the same shari'a principles applied to the non-Muslim subjects (*zimmis*). However, the Europeans did not recognize the same principles toward Muslims. Goffman, "Negotiating the Renaissance State," 72.

9. Inalcik, *Economic and Social History*1:189; Halil Inalcik, *Osmanlı Idare ve Ekonomi Tarihi* (Istanbul: Isam Yayınları, 2011), 146–47.

10. De Groot, "Historical Development," 576.

11. Inalcik, *Economic and Social History*, 189.

12. De Groot, "Historical Development," 577–78.

13. J. Wantserbrough, "Imtiyazat," *Encyclopedia of Islam (EI)*, vol. 3 (Leiden: E. J. Brill, 1971), 1178–79.

14. Zachariadou, *Trade and Crusade*, 3.

15. Luciano Petech, *"Les marchands Italiens dans l'empire Mongol,"* *Journal Asiatique* (1962): 549–74; Fariba Zarinebaf, "Tabriz under Ottoman Rule, 1725–30" (PhD diss., University of Chicago, 1991), 148–50.

16. Bertold Spuler, *The Mongols in History* (London: Pall Mall Press, 1971), 42–43; Spuler, *Iran Moğollari, Siyaset, Idare ve Kültür Ilhanlılar Devri, 1220–1350* (Ankara: Türk Tarih Kurumu Basımevi (TTK), 1957), 468–74.

17. Şerafettin Turan, *Türkiye-Italya Ilişkileri* (Istanbul: Metis Yayınları, 1990), 132–39.

18. Ibid., 135.

19. For the Italian texts of the treaties concluded between the Venetian Dukes of Crete and the Emir of Menteşe in 1331, 1337, 1358, 1375, and 1403 and the Emir of

Aydin in 1337 and 1353, see Zachariadou, *Trade and Crusade,* 187–218. On the import and export of commodities, see 150–73.

20. Zachariadou, *Trade and Crusade,* 178–79.

21. See also Maria Pia Pedani, *Inventory of the' Lettere e Scritture Turchesche' in the Venetian State Archives* (Leiden: E. J. Brill, 2009), xiii–xv.

22. Philip P. Argenti, *The Occupation of Chios by the Genoese and Their Administration of the Island, 1346–1566* (Cambridge: Cambridge University Press, 1958), 21–25.

23. De Groot, "Historical Development of the Capitulatory Regime," 577.

24. Alexander H. De Groot, *The Netherlands and Turkey: Four Hundred Years of Political, Economic, and Cultural Relations* (Istanbul: ISIS Press, 2009), 95–127; De Groot, "Historical Development," 575–604.

25. Halil Inalcik, "Ottoman Galata," in *Essays in Ottoman History,* ed. Halil Inalcik (Istanbul: Eren Yayınevi, 1998), 275–77.

26. Halil Inalcik, "Ottoman Galata," 1991, 58.

27. Halil Inalcik, "Imtiyazat," *IA,* 282–88.

28. Susa, *Capitulatory Regime,,* 53.

29. Yusuf Oğuzoğlu ed., *Halil Inalcik' in Bursa Araştırmaları* (Bursa: Bursa Büyükşehir Belediyesi, 2012), 302–3. Marseille imported 3,000 bales of Iranian raw silk, Venice imported 1,500 bales, and England imported 600 bales in the 1630s.

30. Tommaso Bertelé, Venedik ve Kostantaniyye, Tarihte Osmanlı ve Venedik Ilişkileri, trans. Mahmut H. Şarkioğlu (Istanbul: Yayınkitabevi, 2012), 47.

31. Daniel Goffman, *The Ottoman Empire and Early Modern Europe* (Cambridge: Cambridge University Press, 2002), 137–49; Serap Mumcu, *Venedik Balyosunun Defterleri,* the Venetian Baylo's Registers (1589–1684), in *Hilal: Studi Turchi et Ottomani* 4, no. 648 (Venice: Edizioni Ca'Foscari, 2014). This publication contains a catalog of correspondence (940 documents) exchanged among Ottoman sultans, the Venetian bailo in Istanbul, and the *Doge* in Venice. Many documents are about Ottoman merchants in Venice.

32. M. Tayyib Gökbilgin, "Venedik Devlet Arşivindeki Vesikalar Kulliyatında Kanuni Sultan Süleyman Devri Belgeleri," *Belgeler* 1 (1964): 119–20.

33. Robert Mantran, *Histoire d'Istanbul* (Paris: Fayard, 1996), 199; Susa, *Capitulatory Regime,* 52–53.

34. Oğuzoğlu ed., *Halil Inalcik' in Bursa,* 286–302.

35. Suraiya Faroqhi, " Before 1600: Ottoman Attitudes towards Merchants from Christendom," *Turcica* 34 (2002): 75; Suraiya Faroqhi, "The Venetian Presence in the Ottoman Empire," *Journal of Ottoman Economic History* 15 (1986): 345–84; Dursteler, Venetians in Constantinople, 161–74; Pedani, ed., Inventory of the' Lettere; Suraiya Faroqhi and Gilles Veinstein, eds., Merchants in the Ottoman Empire (Paris: Peeters, 2008).

36. On Venetian-Ottoman relations after the conquest, see Stefan Stanchev, "*Devedo:* The Venetian Response to Sultan Mehmed II in the Venetian-Ottoman Conflict of 1462–79," *Mediterranean Studies* 19 (2010): 43–66; Stanchev, "Inevitable Conflict or Opportunity to Explore? The Mechanics of Venice's Embargo

against Mehmed II and the Problem of Western Ottoman Trade after 1453," *Mediaevalia* 32 (2011): 155–96.

37. Diana Gilliand Wright and Pierre A. MacKay, "When the *Serenissima* and the *Gran Turco* Made Love: The Peace Treaty of 1478," *Studi Veneziani* 53 (2007): 261–77; M. Tayyib Gökbilgin, *"Venedik Devlet Arşivindeki Vesikalar Kulliyatında Kanuni Sultan Süleyman Devri Belgeleri," Belgeler* 1 (1964): 41–42.

38. Inalcik, "Imtiyazat," *EI*, 3: 1180. See the text of the ahdname given by Sultan Suleyman in Gökbilgin, *"Venedik Devle,"* 121–28.

39. V.L. Ménage, "The English Capitulation of 1580: A Review Article," *IJMES* 12 (1980): 376. For the Ottoman texts of earlier ahdnames, see Feridun Beg, *Münşeat-i Selatin* (Istanbul, 1858).

40. Cemal Kafadar, "A Death in Venice (1575): Anatolian Muslim Merchants Trading in the Serenissima," *International Journal of Turkish Studies* 10 (1986): 208–10; Eric R. Dursteler, "Commerce and Coexistence: Veneto-Ottoman Trade in the Early Modern Era," *Turcica* 34 (2002): 105–133; Benjamin Arbel, *Trading Nations: Jews and Venetians in the Early Modern Eastern Mediterranean* (Leiden: E.J. Brill, 1995). See also Stanchev, "Inevitable Conflict," 155–96; Stanchev, *"Devedo,"* 43–66. Stanchev argues that until 1453, Ottoman expansion into Anatolia and the Balkans did not pose a threat to the commercial interests of Venice as long she continued to trade with Mamluk Egypt, Syria, and Crete.

41. Arbel, *Trading Nations;* see also Steven Ortega's recent study, *Negotiating Transcultural Relations in the Early Modern Mediterranean: Ottoman-Venetian Encounters* (London: Ashgate, 2014).

42. Arbel, *Trading Nations,* 66–72; Goffman, *Ottoman Empire.*

43. For a case of commercial dispute between an Ottoman Jewish trader and Venetian traders in 1576, see Benjamin Arbel, "Maritime Trade and International Relations in the Sixteenth-Century Mediterranean: The Case of the Ship *Girarda* (1575–1581)," in *Living in the Ottoman Ecumenical Community: Essays in Honour of Suraiya Faroqhi,* ed. Vera Costantini and Markus Koller (Leiden: E.J. Brill, 2008), 391–408.

44. Roger Crowley, *Empires of the Sea* (New York: Random House, 2008), 26–43.

45. Gökbilgin, *"Venedik Devlet,"* 147.

46. Ibid., 125–26.

47. Ibid., 126.

48. Arbel, *Trading Nations,* 65–76.

49. Molly Greene, *Catholic Pirates,* 28–29.

50. Goffman, *Ottoman Empire,* 156–558.

51. Arbel, *Trading Nations,* 65–67.

52. Ibid.

53. Mumcu, *Venedik Balyosu'nun Defterleri,* 396.

54. *12 Numaralı Mühimme Defteri (978–979/1570–1572)* (Ankara: T.C. Başbakanlık Devlet Arşivleri Genel Müdürlüğü, 1996), 258.

55. Arbel, *Trading Nations: Jews and Venetians,* 70–76.

56. Ibid., 87–94.

57. Mumcu, *Venedik Balyosu'nun.* See summaries of documents, 385–90. For example, in 1632, the Venetian bailo claimed 2,000 *kuruş* from two Jews in Izmir and seized seventy sacks of cotton from their storehouse to force payment. Ibid., 275.

58. Arbel, *Trading Nations,* 158–62; Nathalie Rothman, *Brokering Empire: Trans-Imperial Subjects between Venice and Istanbul.* (Ithaca, NY: Cornell University Press, 2012).

59. Fikret Yilmaz, *Izmir'de 400 Yıl* (Izmir: *Kültür, Sanat ve Tarih Yayınları,* 2012), 42–43.

60. The text of this *berat* has not survived. De Groot, *Netherlands and Turkey,* 118–19.

61. Rausas, *Le régime des capitulations,* 1: 4–6; Finkel, *Osman's Dream,* 122.

62. For a recent analysis of the early phase of the Ottoman-French alliance, see Christine Isom-Verhaaren, *Allies with the Infidel: The Ottoman and French Alliance in the Sixteenth Century* (New York: I. B. Tauris, 2011), 114–41. See also Pascale Barthe, *French Encounters with the Ottomans, 1510–1560* (London: Routledge, 2016).

63. De Lamar Jensen, " The Ottoman Turks in Sixteenth-Century French Diplomacy," *Sixteenth Century Journal* 16, no. 4 (1985): 455.

64. Clarence Dana Rouillard, *The Turk in French History, Thought, and Literature (1520–1660)* (Paris: Boivin & Cie, 1940), 113–61; Jean-Louis Bacqué-Grammont, Sinan Kuneralp, and Frédric Hitzel, *Représentants permanents de la France en Turquie (1536–1991)* (Istanbul: Editions ISIS, 1991), 111–15.

65. Rouillard, *Turk in French History,* 113–61.

66. Louis Rousseau, *Les Relations diplomatiques de la France et de la Turquie au XVIIe siècle, Tome premier (1700–16),* vol. 1 (Paris, 1908), vii–viii; Jensen, "Ottoman Turks," 451–70.

67. Rausas, *Le Régime des capitulations,* 6–7.

68. Rousseau, *Les Relations diplomatiques,* vols. 1–4 ; Rausas, *Le Régime des capitulations,* 31–32; Susa, *Capitulatory Regime,* 54–55; E. Charrière, *Négociants de la France dans le Levant,* vol. 1 (Paris, 1848); Jensen, "Ottoman Turks," 455.

69. Nicolae Iorga, *Points de vue sur l'histoire du commerce de l'Orient a l'époque modern* (Paris: Gamber, 1925); Gaston Zeller, *"Une légende qui a la vie dure: Les Capitulations de 1535,"* *Revue d'histoire modern et contemporaine* 2 (1955): 127–32. For a discussion of this historiography, see Gilles Veinstein, *"Les capitulations Franco-Ottoman de 1536 sont-elles encore controversables?"* in *Living in an Ottoman Ecumenical Community,* ed. Vera Costantini and Markus Koller (Leiden: E. J. Brill, 2008), 71–88.

70. Jensen, "Ottoman Turks," 456.

71. Rausas, *Le Régime des capitulations,* 3; Veinstein, *"Les capitulations"* 74–75.

72. Paul Masson, *Marseille et la colonization Française,* 2nd ed. (Paris: Libraire Hachette, 1912), 68–69. For a recent study of North African piracy, see Joshua White, *Piracy and Law in the Ottoman Mediterranean* (Stanford, CA: Stanford University Press, 2017).

73. BBA, MD (Mühimme Defteri) 7: 2695.

74. See Arbel, *Trading Nations,,* on the activities of Jewish entrepreneurs in Venice.

75. On the network of Jewish traders in the Mediterranean, see Trivellato, *Familiarity of Strangers.* On Nasi's trade networks in the Ottoman Empire, see Halil Inalcik, "Foundations of Ottoman-Jewish Cooperation," in *Jews, Turks, Ottomans: A Shared History, Fifteenth Century through the Twentieth Century,* ed. Avigdor Levey. Syracuse, NY: Syracuse University Press, 2002), 8–11.

76. Halil Inalcik, *Devlet-i Aliyye,* vol. 1 (Istanbul: Türkiye Iş Bankası Kültür Yayınları, 2014), 283–84.

77. Emrah Sefa Gürkan, "Touting for Patrons, Brokering Power, and Trading Information: Trans-Imperial Jews in Sixteenth-Century Istanbul," in *Detras de las apariencias Informacion y espionaje* (siglos XVI–XVII), ed. Emilio Sola Castano and Gennaro Varriale (Alcala, Spain: Universidad de Alcala, 2015), 127–53. Gürkan emphasizes the role of Jewish trans-imperial brokers in Ottoman-European diplomacy as well as in warfare and espionage. See also Dursteler, *Venetians in Constantinople,* 105–12.

78. *5 Numaralı Mühimme Defteri* (973/1565–1566) (Ankara: T. C. Başbakanlık Devlet Arşivleri Genel Müdürlüğü, 1994), 94: 257.

79. *5 Numaralı Mühimme Defteri* (Ankara: T. C. Başbakanlık Devlet Arşivleri Genel Müdürlüğü, 1994), 94: 215.

80. *3 Numaralı Mühimme Defteri* (Ankara: T. C. Başbakanlık Devlet Arşivleri Genel Müdürlüğü 1993), 378:1121.

81. Ibid., 553: 1622.

82. Ibid., 276: 805.

83. See the text of the letter written by Henri III to Murad III on January 6, 1581, in S. A. Skilliter, *William Harborne and the Trade with Turkey* (London: British Academy, 1977), 139–42. For the Ahdname of 1535, see Rausas, *Le Régime des capitulations,* 6–10.

84. For the text of this treaty, see Charrière, *Négociants de la France*; Skilliter, *Harborne and the Trade,* 170–73, 273–74; De Groot, *Netherlands and Turkey,* 120–23.

85. Other articles dealt with the legal status of French subjects, requiring that all civil cases among French subjects be tried in French consular courts and that those between Ottoman and French subjects be tried in Ottoman courts in the presence of a dragoman. Criminal cases, however, would be heard in the Imperial Council.

86. Jensen, "Ottoman Turks," 464.

87. Ibid.

88. Ibid., 461; Paul Masson, *Marseille et la colonisation,* 70. England had a negative balance of trade with the Levant in the late sixteenth century.

89. Ronald C. Jennings, Christians and Muslims in Ottoman Cyprus and the Mediterranean World, 1571–1640 (New York: NYU Press, 1993), 353–59.

90. Geene, *Catholic Pirates,* 78–109; see also White, *Piracy and Law.*

91. BBA, MD 19, no. 205.

92. Ralph Davis, "English Imports from the Middle East, 1580–1780," in *Studies in the Economic History of the Middle East, from the Rise of Islam to the Present,* ed. Michael A. Cook (London: Oxford University Press, 1970), 203.

93. Emrah Safa Gürkan, "Mediating Boundaries: Mediterranean Go-Betweens and Cross-Confessional Diplomacy in Constantinople, 1560–1600," *Journal of Early Modern History* 19 (2015): 137–38.

94. Boogert, *The Capitulations,* 65–66.

95. Jensen, "Ottoman Turks," 469–70.

96. ACCM, J series.

97. Galata sicil series 14/90: 255–56.

98. The Ottoman texts of the ahdnames of 1597, 1614, and 1618 have not been published. Fortunately, the text of the 1604 ahdname has survived in Ottoman in Feridun Beg's *Munşeat üs-Selatin* and was widely circulated.

99. Anthony Jenkinson, a young English trader, reached Aleppo in 1553 and received a berat from Sultan Süleyman, who had stopped there during his campaign to Persia, to trade freely in any port or town in the empire, enjoying the same privileges that the Venetian and French merchants did. See Skilliter, *Harborne and the Trade,* 6–7; Despina Vlami, *Trading with the Ottomans: The Levant Company in the Middle East* (London: I. B. Tauris, 2015), 14–15.

100. For the Ottoman texts of these imperial orders and their English translations, see Skilliter, *Harborne and the Trade,* 14–19, 55–68, and 211–16. See also J. C. Hurewitz, *Diplomacy in the Near and Middle East,* vol. 1(Princeton, NJ: D. Van Nostrand, 1956); For the Anglo-Ottoman trade in the later period, see Mubahat Kütükoğlu, *Balta Limanı'na Giden Yol, Osmanlı-Ingliz Iktisadi Munasebetleri (1580–1850)* (Ankara: TTK, 2013).

101. For the Ottoman text in the original and the English translation, see Skilliter, *Harborne and the Trade,* 86–89, 232–36. For a concordance of the articles of the French and English ahdnames, see 91. See also Brotton, *Sultan and the Queen,* 90–95. Brotton emphasizes the diplomatic and religious (Protestant) as well as the commercial alliance between Elizabeth I and Sultan Murad III against the Habsburg Empire based on the letters exchanged between the two rulers. He argues that much of the tin exported to the Ottoman Empire was taken from the bells of Catholic churches in England. He also underscores the reciprocal aspect of the English-Ottoman commercial agreement in 1579–80.

102. For the text of the letter, see Skilliter, *Harborne and the Trade,* 142–43.

103. Vlami, *Trading with the Ottomans,* 6–7; Christine Laidlaw, *The British in the Levant: Trade and Perceptions of the Ottoman Empire in the Eighteenth Century* (London: I. B. Tauris, 2010). See also Michael Talbot, *British-Ottoman Relations, 1661–1807: Commerce and Diplomatic Practice in Eighteenth-Century Istanbul* (Bridgewood, UK: Boydell Press, 2017).

104. M. Epstein, The *Early History of the Levant Company* (London, 1908); Alfred C. Wood, *A History of the Levant Company* (London: Oxford University Press, 1935); Vlami, *Trading with the Ottomans,* 13.

105. Vlami, *Trading with the Ottomans,* 6–7.

106. Ahmed Refik, *Onikinci Asr-i Hicri'de Istanbul Hayati (1689–1785)* (Istanbul: Enderun Kitabevi, 1988), 26–27.

107. Laidlaw, *British in the Levant,* 40.

108. Ibid., 38–40.

109. Daniel Goffman, *Britons in the Ottoman Empire, 1642–1660* (Seattle: University of Washington Press, 1998), 15.

110. Inalcik, *Economic and Social History,* 370; Goffman, *Izmir and the Levantine World, 1550–1650* (Seattle: University of Washington Press, 1990), 75–76; Goffman, *Britons in the Ottoman Empire,* 53–55; Bruce Masters, *The Origins of Western Economic Dominance in the Middle East: Mercantilism and the Islamic Economy in Aleppo, 1600–1750* (New York: NYU Press, 1988), 11–35.

111. Inalcik, *Economic and Social History,* 372.

112. Ralph Davis, "English Imports from the Middle East, 1580–1780," in *Studies in the Economic History of the Middle East, from the Rise of Islam to the Present,* ed. Michael A. Cook (London: Oxford University Press, 1970), 195.

113. Inalcik, *Economic and Social History,* 370–71.

114. Goffman, *Britons in the Ottoman Empire,* 123–24; Davis, "English Imports," 195.

115. Goffman, *Britons in the Ottoman Empire,* 5.

116. Ibid., 52–53.

117. De Groot, *Netherlands and Turkey,* 124–25; Hurewitz, *Middle East and North Africa,* 1: 25–31; Linda T. Darling, "Capitulations," in *The Oxford Encyclopedia of the Modern Islamic World* (Oxford: Oxford University Press, 1995), 258. It provided exemption from personal taxes (*cizye*) for the English dragoman, his sons, and his servants.

118. Inalcik, "Imtiyazat," *IA,* 22: 248–49. Article 75.

119. Hurewitz, *Middle East and North Africa,* 1: 32. It appears that English merchants had had this exemption in the past as a mark of special friendship and perhaps were given it in an effort to redirect the Persian-English silk trade from the Caucasus to Anatolia.

120. Ibid., 1:31.

121. Ismail Hakki Kadi, *Ottoman and Dutch Merchants in the Eighteenth Century: Competition and Cooperation in Ankara, Izmir, and Amsterdam* (Leiden: E.J. Brill, 2012), 286–87.

122. Inalcik, "Imtiyazat," *IE,* 1185.

123. Gülay Web Yılırmak, *XVIII. Yüzyılda Osmanlı-Ingiliz Tiftik Ticareti* (Ankara: Türk Tarih Kurumu Basımevi [TTK], 2011), 26–28.

124. Zarinebaf, *Tabriz under Ottoman Rule,* 157–66. The import of raw silk from Tabriz into Erzurum continued into the early eighteenth century. This situation was also true of coffee from Yemen.

125. Masters, *Origins of Western Economic Dominance,* 30–33. By 1725, the English consul reported that no Iranian silk was reaching Aleppo. English exports of broadcloth to Iran via Aleppo also declined due to competition from cheaper and better quality French woolens.

126. Davis, "English Imports," 199. The English import of raw silk from India and China rose from 1,000 pounds in 1663 to 116,000 pounds in 1741. English traders imported 145,000 pounds of raw silk from the Levant while imports from Italy amounted to 294,000 pounds in 1741. Most of the silk from the Levant was coming from Antioch in Syria after 1730.

127. Goffman, *Izmir and the Levantine World*, 64–65. Goffman also attributes the decline of Venetian trade in the Levant to the attacks by English ships, the growing piracy in the Mediterranean, and the decline of the shipbuilding industry in Venice as well as to the Thirty Years' Wars. We must also add the deterioration of Ottoman-Venetian relations during the war over Cyprus (1570–73) and the Cretan Wars (1645–69). See Arbel, *Trading Nations*.

128. Inalcik, *Devlet-i 'Aliyye*, 1: 314.

129. Davis, "English Imports," 195–202. See table on English imports from the Levant.

130. BBA, C.HR 19/30.

131. De Groot, *Netherlands and Turkey*, 25–26.

132. Mehmet Bulut, *Ottoman-Dutch Economic Relations in the Early Modern Period, 1571–1699* (Amsterdam: Hilversum Verloren, 2001), 112; G. R. Bosscha Erdbrink, *At the Threshold of Felicity: Ottoman-Dutch Relations during the Embassy of Cornelis Calkoen at the Sublime Porte, 1726–1744* (Ankara: Türk Tarih Kurumu Basımevi, 1975).

133. De Groot, *Netherlands and Turkey*, 27.

134. Bulut, *Ottoman-Dutch Economic Relations*, 117. See also Alastair Hamilton, Alexander H. de Groot, and Maurits H. van den Boogert, eds., *Friends and Rivals in the East: Studies in Anglo-Dutch Relations in the Levant from the Seventeenth to the Early Nineteenth Century* (Leiden: E. J. Brill, 2000).

135. For the text of the 1612 ahdname, see De Groot, *Netherlands and Turkey*, 129–52; Bulut, *Ottoman-Dutch Economic Relations*, 117–20. See also Kadi, *Ottoman and Dutch Merchants*, 145–54.

136. Boogert, *The Capitulations*, 19–26.

137. Kadi, *Ottoman and Dutch Merchants*, 274–88.

138. Bulut, *Ottoman-Dutch Economic Relations*, 54, 110.

139. De Groot, *Netherlands and Turkey*, 36–37. See also Ian Coller, "East of the Enlightenment: Regulating Cosmopolitanism between Istanbul and Paris in the Eighteenth Century," *Journal of World History* 21, no. 3 (Sept. 2010), 447–70.

140. Boogert, *The Capitulations*, 16–17.

141. Kadi, *Ottoman and Dutch Merchants*, 154–55.

CHAPTER FOUR

1. Paul Rycault, *The Present State of the Ottoman Empire* (London, 1668), 85–87; The civil war in England had a great impact on polarizing the English community and ambassadors (Sir Sackville Crow and Sir Thomas Bendysh) between the

royalists and the parliamentarians in Istanbul and Izmir in the 1640s. See also Daniel Goffman, *Britons in the Ottoman Empire*, 113–24; Alison Games, *The Web of Empire: English Cosmopolitans in an Age of Expansion, 1560–1660* (Oxford: Oxford University Press, 2008), 147–79. Games argues that English ambassadors and consuls had a sensitive job of representing the crown as well as the Levant Company and protecting merchants from violence and rapacious local officials while they imposed company rules.

2. On the English ambassador's interaction with the Sublime Porte, see Goffman, *Britons in the Ottoman Empire*, 16–43, 109–10; Laidlaw, *British in the Levant*; Vlami, *Trading with the Ottomans*. See also Michael Talbot, *British-Ottoman Relations, 1661–1807*, 17–71. Talbot is right to emphasize the contested status of the Mediterranean and the role of piracy in the disruption of trade.

3. On the reception of the Venetian *bailo* in the mid-sixteenth century, see Goffman, *Ottoman Empire*, 93–97.

4. Thévenot, *L'empire du Grand Turc*, 176–209. See also his description of the janissary rebellion in 1655, 209–19. Thévenot also published a medieval Arabic document, the *Ahidname of Muhammad,* which claims that the Prophet gave protection to the monks of Saint Catherine's Monastery in Egypt.

5. Thévenot was captured by corsairs twice on his way to Palestine, but he managed to get free.

6. Michele Longino, *French Travel Writing in the Ottoman Empire: Marseilles to Constantinople, 1650–1700* (London: Routledge, 2015).

7. Zarinebaf, *Crime and Punishment*, 51–54.

8. For Venetian and Ottoman wars and administrations of Crete and its trade, see Kate Fleet and Svetla Ianeva, *Ottoman Economic Practices in Periods of Transformation: The Cases of Crete and Bulgaria* (Ankara: TTK, 2014), 68.

9. Molly Greene, *A Shared World: Christians and Muslims in the Early Modern Mediterranean* (Princeton, NJ: Princeton University Press, 2000), 14–15.

10. Ibid., 31–32.

11. Thévenot, *L'empire du Grand Turc*, 10; Takeda, *Between Crown and Commerce*, 38–39.

12. Jean-Louis Bacqué-Grammont, Kuneralp, and Hitzel, *Représentants,* 19–20. See also Rycault, *Present State of the Ottoman Empire*, 93, on Ottoman-French relations.

13. Rifat Günalan, *Istanbul Kadi Sicilleri, Bab Mahkemesi 3 Numarali Sicil (H. 1077/M. 1666–1667)* (Istanbul: ISAM Yayınları, 2011), 475–80.

14. Rycault, *Present State of the Ottoman Empire*, 86.

15. Inalcik, "Imtiyazat," *EI*, 3:1185.

16. Rouillard, *Turk in French History*, 158–59.

17. Inalcik, "Imtiyazat," *EI*, 3:1185.

18. Takeda, *Between Crown and Commerce*, 20–38; Paul Masson, *Histoire de commerce Français dans le Levant au XVIIIe siècle* (Paris: Librarire Hachette, 1911), 20–34, 77–81.

19. Rycault, *Present State of the Ottoman Empire*, 86–87.

20. Bacqué-Grammont, Kuneralp, and Hitzel, *Représentants Permanents*, III–12.

21. Adile Ayda, *Une diplomate Turc aupres du Roi Soleil*: Association des études Française Kongresidne 4 Eylül 1956 da okunan bir tebliğ (Istanbul: Print Book 1956); Faik Reşit Unat, *Osmanlı Sefirleri ve Sefaretnameleri* (Ankara: TTK, 1992, 1987).

22. Frédéric Bauden, ed., *Une Voyage a Smyrne: Un manuscript d'Antoine Galland (1678)* (Paris: Chandeigne, 2000), 14.

23. Robert Mantran, *"Monsieur de Guilléragues, ambassadeur de France à Constantinople, et le commerce Français au Levant (1679–1684),"* in *L'Empire Ottoman, la République de Turquie et la France,* éd. Hamit Batu and Jean-Louis Bacqué-Grammont, Varia Turcica III, Paris-Istanbul ed. (Paris: Isis, 1986), 59–72. "; Archives Nationales, *Correspondance consulaire des ambassadeurs de France a Constantinople, 1668–1708.* Paris: Centre Historique des archives nationales, 1999, 34–35.

24. De Groot, *Netherlands and Turkey*, 153–64.

25. Archives Nationales, *Correspondance consulaire*, 38. On North African piracy and attacks on French ships, see also Antoine Galland, *Istanbul'a Ait Günlük Anılar (1672–75),* trans. Nahid Sirri Örik, vol.1 (Ankara: TTK, 1998).

26. Takeda, *Between Crown and Commerce*, 40–41. Takeda states that according to this ahdname, Ottoman courts could not prosecute French nationals. However, this was the case only in disputes among French subjects, whereas those between French and Ottoman subjects had to be tried in the kadi's court or the Imperial Council.

27. Archives Nationales, *Correspondance consulaire*, 42–43. For the French text of the ahdname, see CCM, J series, no. 1.

28. De Groot, *Netherlands and Turkey*, 122.

29. Rausas, *Le regime des capitulations*, 62–66. For the French text, see ACCM, J series, no. 1.

30. Archives Nationales, *Correspondance consulaire*, 43.

31. Rausas, *Le regime des capitulations*, 70.

32. Bruce Masters, *Christians and Jews in the Arab World: The Roots of Sectarianism* (Cambridge: Cambridge University Press, 2001), 80; De Groot, *Netherlands and Turkey*, 122.

33. Inalcik, "Imtiyazat," *EI*, 3:1185.

34. Finkel, *Osman's Dream*, 285–89.

35. Archives Nationales, *Correspondance consulaire*, 67–69.

36. Finkel, *Osman's Dream*, 318–24; Zarinebaf, *Crime and Punishmen,*, 51–54.

37. Alexander H. De Groot, "Dragoman's Careers: The Change of Status in Some Families Connected with the British and Dutch Embassies at Istanbul, 1783–1829," in *Friends and Rivals in the East,* ed. Alexander H. DeGroot et al. (Leiden: E.J. Brill, 2009), 237–39.

38. Virginia H. Aksan, *An Ottoman Statesman in War and Peace: Ahmed Resmi Efendi, 1700–1783* (Leiden: E.J. Brill, 1995), 20–21.

39. On the rise of the scribal class in the eighteenth century, see ibid., 7–8, 12–20.

40. See BBA, Cevdet Hariciye Collection as well as the Duvel-i Ecnebiye Collection (Registers of Foreign Nations).

41. Antoine Galland, *Voyages inédit: Smyrne ancienne et modern*, tome 1 (Paris: Honoré Champion, 2001), 134–37. Galland provides a rare description of Izmir; its physical layout, especially the market area; and its social makeup, particularly the trading communities.

42. De Groot, "Dragoman's Careers," 239–45.

43. Unat, *Osmanlı Sefirleri ve Sefaratnameleri*, 14–23.

44. For Ottoman embassy reports, see Unat, *Osmanlı Sefirleri ve Sefaratnameleri*, 47–218. For the Ottoman embassy to London, see Mehmet Alaadin Yalçınkaya, *The First Permanent Ottoman Embassy in Europe: The Embassy of Yusuf Aghah Efendi to London (1793–1797)* (Istanbul: Isis Press, 2010). On Ottoman-English diplomacy see Talbot, *British-Ottoman Relations*, 141–73.

45. Emrah Safa Gürkan, "Mediating Boundaries: Mediterranean Go-Betweens and Cross-Confessional Diplomacy in Constantinople, 1560–1600," *Journal of Early Modern History* 19 (2015): 107–28.; On the role of Joseph Nasi, a Marrano from Portugal, in Ottoman foreign policy and the conquest of Cyprus during the reign of Selim II, see Arbel, *Trading Nations*, 55–76. See also Greene, *Catholic Pirates*, 92–99.

46. Ahmet Dönmez, *Osmanlı Modernleşmesinde Ingliz Etkisi: Diplomasi ve Reform(1833–1841)* (Istanbul: Kitapyayınevi, 2014); Mehmed Efendi, *Le paradis des infidels: Un ambassadeur Ottoman en France sous la régence* (Paris: François Maspero, 1981), 21–24; Bedriye Atsız, ed., *Ahmet Resmi Efendinin Viyana ve Berlin Sefaretnameleri* (Istanbul: Tercuman, 1980). See also Fatma Müge Göçek, *East Encounters West: France and the Ottoman Empire in the Eighteenth Century* (New York: Oxford University Press, 1987); Norman Itzkowitz and Max Mote, trans. and anno., *Mubadele: An Ottoman-Russian Exchange of Ambassadors* (Chicago: University of Chicago Press, 1970), 2–14. About forty Ottoman *Sefaratnames*, or embassy accounts, have been preserved.

47. Marquis de Bonnac, *Mémoire Historique sur L'ambassade à Constantinople* (Paris, 1894), 275–82; Suraiya Faroqhi, *Another Mirror for Princes: The Public Image of the Ottoman Sultans and Its Reception* (Istanbul: ISIS Press, 2008), 154–55.

48. Finkel, *Osman's Dream*, 342.

49. Göçek, *East Encounters West*, 7–23; M. Efendi, *Le paradis des infidels;* Unat, *Osmanlı Sefirleri ve Sefaratnameleri*, 53–58.

50. Finkel, *Osman's Dream*, 342. Unat, *Osmanlı Sefirleri ve Sefaratnameleri*, 53–58. Bacqué-Grammont, Kuneralp, and Hitzel, *Représentants Permanents*, 31–32; Albert Vandal (1853–1910), *Une ambassade Français en Orient souls Louis XV: La Mission du Marquis de Villeneuve, 1728–1741* (Paris: Libraire Plon, 1887). Villeneuve died in Marseille in 1747, where there is a street named for him.

51. Zarinebaf, *Crime and Punishment*, 54–61.

52. Ibid.

53. Rausas, *Le regime des capitulations*, 72–77. Finkel, *Osman's Dream*, 335–36. The Ottoman state supported the Swedish King Charles XII in his fight against Russia in the Great Northern War over access to the Baltic Sea from 1714 to 1721.

54. For the Ottoman text of the 1740 treaty, see BBA, ADVNE.DVE 29/4, *Fransa Ahkam ve Nişan Defteri* (d. 1280/1863), 5–35; for the printed French translation, see ACCM, J series, no. 1:1–22; Francois Emmanuel Guignard, comte de Saint-Priest, *Memoire sur l'ambassade de France en Turquie, 1525–1770* (Amsterdam: Philo Press, 1974), 475–520, and Rausas, *Le regime des capitulations,* 77–84.

55. BBA, ADVNE.DVE Fransa, 29/4:5–37. ACCM, J series, no. 1:22. The French translation was made in Istanbul by the chief dragoman of the French Embassy, Sieur Deval, in 1761 and printed in Marseille.

56. Faruk Bilici, *La politique Française en Mer Noire, 1747–1789* (Istanbul: Les Éditions ISIS, 1992), 77–94.

57. BBA, A.DVN.DVE 29/4, p. 32; Saint-Priest, *L'ambassade de France,* 522–23; Eldem, *French Trade,* 278.

58. Ibid., 280–81.

59. France fought the War of the Polish Succession in the 1730s, the War of the Austrian Succession (1739–48) with England and Spain, and the Seven Years' Wars (1755–63) against England over the colonies in the Americas. France was also involved in the Russo-Ottoman War of 1760s over the partitioning of Poland and the American War of Independence against England.

60. Louis Bonneville de Marsangy le Chevalier de Vergennes, *Son ambassade a Constantinople* (Paris, 1894), 1:149–51.

61. Munro Price, *Preserving the Monarchy: The Comte de Vergennes, 1774–1787* (Cambridge: Cambridge University Press, 1995), 7–9. Vergennes was subsequently appointed as ambassador to Sweden in 1771 and became foreign minister to King Louis XVI in 1774.

62. Aksan, *Ottoman Statesman,* 118–20; Virginia Aksan, *The Ottoman Wars, 1700–1870* (London: Pearson, 2007), 135–37.

63. Inalcik, "Imtiyazat," *EI,* 3:1186. The Ottomans were able to stop the Russian expansion at the Battle of Pruth in 1711 and regain the port of Azov that they had lost to Russia in 1718 in the Treaty of Belgrade in 1738. Finkel, *Osman's Dream,* 374–75.

64. J.C. Hurewitz, *Diplomacy in the Near and Middle East,* vol. 1 (Princeton, NJ: Van Nostrand, 1956), 54–61. Finkel, *Osman's Dream,* 377–79.

65. Salih Aynural, *Istanbul Değirmenleri ve Fırınları: Zahire Ticareti (1740–1840)* (Istanbul: Tarih Vakfı Yurt Yayınları, 2001), 52.

66. Boogert, *The Capitulations,* 78–79, 103–4. Boogert rightly points out that the treaty did not make Russia the representative of the Greek Orthodox Church in Istanbul, a position that was held by the Patriarchate.

67. Inalcik, "Imtiyazat," *EI,* 3:1186; Linda T. Darling, "Capitulations," in *Oxford Encyclopedia of the Modern Islamic World* (Oxford: Oxford University Press, 1995), 259. Finkel, *Osman's Dream,* 380–83.

68. For English trade on the Black Sea, see Vlami, *Trading with the Ottomans,* 119–31. For French trade on the Black Sea, see Bilici, *La politique Francaise.*

69. Nasim Susa, *Capitulatory Regime,* 61. The Ottoman sovereignty over the Straits was reconfirmed in the Treaty of Paris in 1856 and in the Treaty of London of 1871.

CHAPTER FIVE

1. Dankoff and Kim, *An Ottoman Traveler,* 19–20; Kahraman and Dağlı, *Evliya Çelebi Seyahatnamesi,* vol.1, pt. 2, 393–95. See chapter 1 on the commercial district in Galata.

2. Braudel, *Structures of Everyday Life,* 1:143–45.

3. Robert Mantran, *Istanbul dans la seconde moitié du XVIIe siècle* (Paris: Libraire Adrien Maisonneuve, 1962), 90.

4. On the role of exchange and maritime commerce in Mediterranean ports, see Peregrine Horden and Nicholas Purcell, *The Corrupting Sea: A Study of Mediterranean History* (Oxford: Blackwell, 2000), 395–97. For a recent discussion on France and the Early Mediterranean as a contact zone, see the special journal issue of *French History* 29, no. 1 (2015) edited by Megan C. Armstrong and Gillian Weiss.

5. Inalcik, *Economic and Social History,* 180.

6. Panzac, *La caravane maritime,* 201–202.

7. Halil Inalcik, *The Ottoman Empire during the Classical Age: 1300–1600.* (London: Phoenix, 2000), 121–45.

8. Braudel, *Structures of Everyday Life,* 137–38.

9. Halil Inalcik, *Devlet-i 'Aliyye,* 2:257.

10. On the ancient period, see Lionel Casson, *The Ancient Mariners: Seafarers and Sea Fighters of the Mediterranean in Ancient Times,* 2nd ed. (Princeton, NJ: Princeton University Press, 1991), 101–2.

11. Inalcik, *Economic and Social History,* 1:44–48; Halil Inalcik, "Capital Formation in the Ottoman Empire," *Journal of Economic History* 24, no. 1 (1989): 97–140; Şevket Pamuk, "Institutional Change and the Longevity of the Ottoman Empire, 1500–1800," *Journal of Interdisciplinary History* 35, no. 2 (2004): 228.

12. Linda T. Darling, *A History of Social Justice and Political Power in the Middle East: The Circle of Justice from Mesopotamia to Globalization* (New York: Routledge, 2013).

13. Inalcik, *Economic and Social History,* 1:48.

14. Ibid.,1:48–49. See also Inalcik, *Ottoman Empire during the Classical Age,* 144–45.

15. Inalcik, *Economic and Social History,* 44–48; Inalcik, "Capital Formation," 97–140; Halil Inalcik, *Sources and Studies,* 1:92–95.

16. Inalcik, *Devlet-i 'Aliyye,* 2:256–65.

17. Mehmet Genç, *Osmanlı Imparatorluğunda Devlet ve Ekonomi* (Istanbul: Ötüken, 2003), 43–52. Edhem Eldem, "Capitulations and Western Trade," in *The Cambridge History of Turkey, 1603–1839,* vol. 3, ed. Suraiya Faroqhi (Cambridge: Cambridge University Press, 2006), 283–336.

18. Mehmet Genç, "Ottoman Industry in the Eighteenth Century: General Framework, Characteristics, and Main Trends," in *Manufacturing in the Ottoman Empire and Turkey, 1500–1950,* ed. Donald Quataert (New York: SUNY Press, 1994), 74–82. See also Donald Quataert, "Ottoman Manufacturing in the Nineteenth Century," in *Manufacturing in the Ottoman Empire,* 87–121.

19. Genç, "Ottoman Industry," 66–77.

20. Murat Çizakça and Macit Kenanoğlu, "Ottoman Merchants and the Jurisprudential Shift Hypothesis," in *Merchants in the Ottoman Empire,* ed. Suraiya Faroqhi and Giles Veinstein (Paris: Peeters, 2008), 195–96.

21. Ibid., 195–213; Murat Çizakça, *A Comparative Evolution of Business Partnerships: The Islamic World and Europe, with Specific References to the Ottoman Archives* (Leiden: E. J. Brill, 1996), 128–30.

22. Şevket Pamuk, "Economic History, Institutions, and Institutional Change," *IJMES* 44 (2012): 532; Pamuk, "Institutional Change," 225–47.

23. Pamuk, "Economic History, Institutions," 533; Timur Kuran, *The Long Divergence: How Islamic Law Held Back the Middle East* (Princeton, NJ: Princeton University Press, 2011).

24. Pamuk, "Institutional Change," 231–32.

25. Şevket Pamuk, *A Monetary History of the Ottoman Empire* (Cambridge: Cambridge University Press, 2000), 12–14.

26. Dankoff and Kim, *An Ottoman Traveler,* 24–25.

27. Casson, *Ancient Mariners, Seafarers,* 102–3.

28. Inalcik, *Sources and Studies,* 94.

29. Horden and Purcell, *Corrupting Sea,* 24–25, 143–72.

30. Ibid., 157.

31. Ibid., 178–79.

32. Fleet, *European and Islamic Trade,* 122–26.

33. Ibid., 131–33.

34. Inalcik, *Sources and Studies,* 95–96.

35. Darius Kilodziejczyk, "Inner Lake or Frontier? The Ottoman Black Sea in the Sixteenth and Seventeenth Centuries," in *Enjeux politiques, économiques et militaires en Mer Noire (XIVe–XXIe Siecles),* études à la memoire de Mihail Guboglu, ed. Faruk Bilici, Ionel Candea, and Anca Popescu (Braila: Musée de Braila, 2007), 125–39.

36. Daniel Panzac, *La marine Ottomane, de l'apogée a la chute de l'empire (1572–1923)* (Paris, CNRS Éditions, 2009), 80–81.

37. Kilodziejczyk, "Inner Lake or Frontier?" 134–35.

38. Inalcik, *Economic and Social History,* 180–81. Izmir was transformed into the hub of European trade in western Anatolia in the seventeenth century and exported considerable quantities of foodstuff like raisins, olive oil, Persian and local silks, cotton, and Angora wool on ships (8–9) destined to Marseille as well as to London (7–8), Venice (4–5), and Livorno (2–3). On the trade of Izmir with France, see Galland, *Voyage inédit,*182. See also Goffman, *Izmir and the Levantine World,* 138–46.

39. See also Faroqhi, *Artisans of Empire,* 108–9.

40. Daniel Goffman, *Izmir and the Levantine World, 1550–1650* (Seattle: University of Washington Press, 1990), 33–35.

41. Beshara Doumani, *Rediscovering Palestine: Merchants and Peasants in Jabal Nablus, 1700–1900* (Berkeley: University of California Press, 1995), 182–232. See the list of merchant families involved in soap production in the nineteenth century, 211–14. Cotton was another important cash crop exported to France.

42. Faroqhi, *Artisans of Empire,* 108–9.

43. Inalcik, *Sources and Studies,* 1:113–15.

44. ISAM, Sicil series 14/388, 5, 11, 29.

45. According to official prices, wheat was 110 *para* per *kile,* meat was between 8 and 25 *para* per *kiyye,* and unroasted coffee was 77 *para* per *kiyye* in the mid-eighteenth century.

46. Faroqhi, *Artisans of Empire,* 109–10. According to the kadi registers, the price of lamb was 15 *para* per *kiyye* (1.28 kg); milk, 15 *akçe* per *kiyye;* yogurt, between 15 and 18 *akçe* per *kiyye;* and different varieties of cheese, between 42 and 54 *akçe* per *kiyye* in 1796. ISAM, Sicil series 14/535, 83b.

47. Suraiya Faroqhi and Giles Veinstein, eds., *Merchants in the Ottoman Empire* (Paris: Peeters, 2008); Eldem, "Capitulations and Western Trade," 304–8.

48. See Fatih Gedikli, "Ottoman Companies in the 16th and 17th Centuries," in *The Great Ottoman-Turkish Civilization,* vol. 2, ed. Kemal Çiçek (Ankara: 2000), 185–95; Gedikli, "16. Ve 17. *Asır Osmanlı Şer'iyye Sicillerinde Mudarebe Ortaklığı: Galata Orneği*" (PhD diss., Marmara University, Istanbul, 1996).

49. Kahraman and Dağlı, *Evliya Çelebi Seyahatnamesi,* vol.1, pt. 2, 507–13.

50. Idris Bostan, *Osmanlı Bahriye Teşkitaltı: XVII. Yüzyılında Tersane-i Amire* (Ankara: TTK 1992), 88–89, 94–96.

51. Kahraman and Dağlı, *Evliya Çelebi Seyahatnamesi,* vol.1, pt. 2, 507–13.

52. Ibid., *Ancient Mariners: Seafarers,* 511–12.

53. Kahraman and Dağlı, *Evliya Çelebi Seyatnamesi,* vol. 1, pt., 2, 512–13.

54. BBA, Cevdet Belediye (CB) 47/12327.

55. Salih Aynural, *Istanbul Değirmenleri ve Fırınları* (Istanbul: Tarih Vakfi, 2002), 52–54.

56. Inalcik, *Economic and Social History,* 182.

57. Ibid., 184–85.

58. Panzac, *La marine Ottomane,* 84–85.

59. Murat Çizakça, "The Ottoman Government and Economic Life: Taxation, Public Finance, and Trade Controls," in *The Cambridge History of Turkey,* vol. 2, *The Ottoman Empire as a World Power, 1453–1603,* ed. Suraiya Faroqhi and Kate Fleet (Cambridge: Cambridge University Press, 2013), 263–64.

60. Aynural, *Istanbul Değirmenleri,* 52–54; Gedikli, "Ottoman Companies," 188–94.

61. BBA, Istanbul Ahkam Defteri, vol. 8, 49.

62. Daniel Panzac, *La caravane maritime,* 203.

63. Ibid., 203–4.

64. BBA, D.BŞM.d 06870.

65. BBA, C. IKS (Cevdet Iktisat) 7/310.

66. Inalcik, *Economic and Social History,* 187.

67. Aynural, *Istanbul Değirmenleri,* 23; Fatih Gedikli, *Osmanlı Şirket Kültürü: XVI–XVII: Yuzyıllarda Mudarebe Uygulaması* (Istanbul: Iz Yayıncılık, 1998); Gedikli, "Ottoman Companies," 185–95.

68. Mehmet Akman, ed., *Istanbul Kadi Sicilleri, Galata Mahkemesi 32 Numaralı Sicil* (H. 1015–1016/M. 1606–1607) (Istanbul: ISAM Yayınları, 2011), 59–71.

69. Ibid., 69–70.

70. Çizakça, *Comparative Evolution*, 66–77, 89–93.

71. Gedikli, *Osmanlı Şirket*, 98–120, 138–47.

72. Çizakça, *Comparative Evolution*, 72–73; Inalcik, *Economic and Social History*; Kuran, *Long Divergence*.

73. Gedikli, "Ottoman Companies," 187.

74. Gedikli, *Osmanlı Şirket*, 264.

75. Gedikli, "Ottoman Companies," 189–93.

76. Çizakça, *Comparative Evolution*, 84–85.

77. Ibid., 79–85.

78. Ibid., 127–31.

79. For examples of these contracts in the sixteenth century, see Gedikli, *Osmanlı Şirket*, 276. The court records of Galata contain many cases of disputes regarding these partnerships.

80. Akman, *Galata Mahkemesi 32 Numaralı Sicil,* 73–74.

81. Timur Kuran, ed., *Social and Economic Life in Seventeenth-Century Istanbul: Glimpses from Court Records,* vols. 1–2 (Istanbul: Türkiye Iş Bankası Kültür Yayınları, 2010). See the case of Mustafa Reis in Galata, who formed partnerships with twenty-five people and died in debt (161,750 *akçe*) to thirty-two individuals.

82. Galata sicil 14/90, 223.

83. Istanbul sicil 1/32, 9.

84. Istanbul sicil 1/32, 9b.

85. Galata sicil 14/542, 56.

86. Işık Tamdoğan-Abel, "*Sulh* and the 18th-Century Ottoman Courts of Üsküdar and Adana," *Islamic Law and Society* 15 (2008): 55–83.

87. Ahmet Kal'a, *Istanbul Ahkam Defterleri: Istanbul Ticaret Tarihi,* vol. 1, *1742–1779* (Istanbul: Istanbul Araştırmaları Merkezi, 1997), 140.

88. BBA, C.IKS 8/380.

89. Kal'a, *Istanbul Ahkam Defterleri,* 1:39–40.

90. Ibid., 1:34.

91. BBA, MD (Mühimme Defteri) 85, 178.

92. In France, the provisioning of Paris with grains was considered the most important economic issue to prevent "subsistence insurgency" in the eighteenth century. Steven L. Kaplan, " Provisioning Paris: The Crisis of 1738–1741," in *Edo and Paris: Urban Life and the State in the Early Modern Era,* ed. James L. McClain, John M. Merriman, and Ugawa Kaoru (Ithaca, NY: Cornell University Press, 1994), 179–81.

93. Suraiya Faroqhi et al., *An Economic and Social History of the Ottoman Empire, 1600–1914*, vol. 2 (Cambridge: Cambridge University Press, 1997), 237–38.

94. Aynural, *Istanbul Değirmenleri,* 79. One *kile* of Istanbul was 24.215 kg.

95. BBA, CB 1207, 1–3. See the list of forty-three bakeries.

96. Mehmed Raşid, *Tarih-i Raşid,* vol. 6 (Istanbul, 1865), 615.

97. Zarinebaf, *Crime and Punishment,* 51–61.

98. Mübahat S. Kütükoğlu, *Osmanlılarda Narh Müessesi ve 1640 Tarihli Narh Defteri* (Istanbul: Enderun Kitabevi, 1983), 91; Yaşar Yücel, *Es'ar Defteri (1640 Tarihli)* (Ankara: TTK, 1992), 29. The varieties of bread included *ekmek, çörek, simit, börek,* and *francela.* Zarinebaf, *Crime and Punishment,* 82–83.

99. Zarinebaf, *Crime and Punishment,* 82–83. The government of Selim III ordered the execution of two Albanian bakers at a time of bread shortages in 1790 and also ordered their expulsion from the guild.

100. Unit of money: 60 *para* equaled one *akçe.*

101. BBA, CB 5087.

102. BBA, Nüfus Defeteri (NFS.d) 6, 7; Bab-i Asefi Divan-i Hümayun Kalemi (A.DVN.d 832); BBA, Cevdet Muallim, 1. See also Zarinebaf, *Crime and Punishment,* 41–50.

103. BBA, Maliyeden Müdevver (MM) 10324, 1–12. The document listed 110 legal grocers in Galata, 59 in Kasım Paşa, 47 in Tophane, 21 in Beşiktaş, 5 in Ortaköy, 3 in Kuruçeşme, 12 in Arnavutköy, and 8 in Rumeli Hisar (a total of 265 in Galata and its dependencies).

104. BBA, MD 85, 162. See also Ahmed Refik, *Onikinci Asr-i Hicri'de Istanbul Hayatı (1689–1785)* (Istanbul: Enderun Kitabevi, 1988), 4–5.

105. NFS.d 6: 1–30 and 7: 1–36, A.DVN.d 832: 1–52, MM 10324:1–13.

106. NFS.d 6. This was also the case in Paris, where the comptroller general and the police inspected bakeries and kept an official register of bakers. Kaplan, "Provisioning Paris," 202–4.

107. Faroqhi, *Artisans of Empire,* 111–12.

108. ISAM, Istanbul sicil series, 1/32, 3a.

109. BBA, Cevdet Hariciye (CH) 147/7312.

110. BBA, CB 950.

111. CB 141/676.

112. Ahmet Kal'a, *"Osmanlı Esnaf Sisteminin Oluşması ve Yeniden Yapılması Açisindan Istanbul Esnaf Birlikleri,"* in *Istanbul Imparatorluk Başkentinden Megakente,* ed. Yavuz Köse (Istanbul: Kitab Yayınevi, 2011), 250–55.

113. BBA, CB 25/1124.

114. CB 21/1016 and 20/970.

115. Panzac, *La caravane maritime,* 204–5.

116. Daniel Panzac, *"Les affréteurs de navires a Istanbul dans la seconde moitié du XVIIIe siècle,"* in *Merchants in the Ottoman Empire,* ed. Suraiya Faroqhi and Giles Veinstein (Paris: Peeters, 2008), 165–77.

117. BBA, ADVNE.DVE, Fransa, vol. 105: 65.

118. E. Carrière, *Négociants Marseillais au XVIIIe siècle,* vol. 2 (Marseille: Institut Historique de Provence, 1973), 1045.

119. Ibid.. These numbers exclude ships coming from North Africa into Marseille.

120. Panzac, *La caravane maritime,* 200–206. The majority of French ships transported grains from the Greek archipelago and Macedonia.

121. Ibid., 206–7.

122. Ibid. The other two types of ships were Polacre (130–180 tons) and Tartane (50–100 tons).

123. BBA, CB 109/5420.

124. BBA, C.IKS 2/81.

125. Markus Koller, "The Istanbul Fur Market in the Eighteenth Century," in *Living in the Ottoman Ecumenical Family: Essays in Honour of Suraiya Faroqhi,* ed. Vera Costantini and Markus Koller (Leiden: E.J. Brill, 2008), 117–19. Valide Han in Istanbul proper was the center of the fur trade.

126. Ibid., 121–27. The poor used fox furs while the rich wore sable and ermine. Furs became a status symbol for female members of the palace.

127. Bilici, *La politique Française en Mer Noire,* 69–104. See also appendices 8 and 9, pp.159–64, on French imports from Kherson into Marseille and exports from Marseille into Kherson.

128. BBA, AG.SABH.I 168/11251.

129. BBA Hat 189/9076; ADVN. DVE 125:45.

130. BBA, Hat 205/10749. See also ADVN.DVE, Fransa, vol. 125, on the involvement of French ships in transporting grains from the ports of Bergos and Samsun to Istanbul.

131. BBA, C.HR 147/7308.

132. C.HR 147/7311.

133. Panzac, *La caravane maritime,* 213–14.

134. Carrière, *Négociants Marseillais au XVIIIe Siècle,* 2:1047.

135. BBA, ADVNE.DVE, Fransa, 102: 48.

136. BBA, ADVN.DVE, Fransa, 105:34; ADVN.DVE 115.

137. BBA, MD 176, 142.

138. Mehmet Genç, "Ottoman Industry in the Eighteenth Century," 62–63; · Faroqhi et al., *Economic and Social History,* 696–97.

CHAPTER SIX

1. Registers of Foreign Nations (*ecnebi defterleri*) cover thirty-two nations (from Venice to America) from 1567 to 1922. Those covering France, however, start in the second half of the eighteenth century. See Goffman, *Izmir and the Levantine World,* 147–54.

2. ISAM (Islamic Research Center in Istanbul), Sicil 1/32, 15.

3. On the institution of guarantors, see Zarinebaf, *Crime and Punishment,* 132–33.

4. For insolvencies among Dutch merchants, see Boogert, *The Capitulations,* 207–56.

5. For cases from Istanbul and Galata, see, Nejdet Ertuğ, *Istanbul Mahkemesi 121 Numaralı Şeriyye Sicil (1231–1232/1816–1817)* (Istanbul: Sabancı Universitesi Yayınları, 2006), 51, 52, 81.

6. For a study of settlement cases in Üsküdar (a district of Istanbul) and Adana in the eighteenth century, see Işık Tamdoğan, "*Sulh* and the 18th-Century Ottoman Courts of Üsküdar and Adana," *Islamic Law and Society* 15 (2008): 55–83. She argues that settlement cases fell under the jurisdiction of the Imperial Council, which assigned them to the kadi. The amount of the settlement usually was half of the original debt. Sometimes the parties settled out of the court to avoid court fees. See also Coşgel Metin and Boğaç A. Ergene, *The Economics of Ottoman Justice: Settlement and Trial in the Shari'a Courts* (Cambridge: Cambridge University Press, 2016), 65–146.

7. Sicil series, 1/32, 5b.

8. Fariba Zarinebaf-Shahr, "Tabriz under Ottoman Rule, 1725–1730" (PhD diss., University of Chicago, 1991), 153.

9. Ibid., 154–55; Mathee, *Politics of Trade,* 23–26. The Dutch gained a monopoly in the spice trade between India and Iran. They also chartered their ships to Iranian merchants traveling between the Persian Gulf and the Indian Ocean.

10. Davis, *English Overseas Trade,* 31.

11. Masson, *Histoire du commerce,* 178.

12. Ibid., 137–39.

13. Carrière, *Négociants Marseillais,* 1:227–35.

14. Rausas, *Le Régime des capitulations,* 41–42.

15. Takeda, *Between Crown and Commerce,* 33–34.

16. Cole, *French Mercantilism,* 124–26. See table 5.

17. Masson, *Histoire du commerce,* 106.

18. Takeda, *Between Crown and Commerce,* 36–38.

19. Cole, *French Mercantilism,* 229–67.

20. Carrière, *Négociants Marseillais,* 1:198–99; Takeda, *Between Crown and Commerce,* 97; Masson, *Histoire du commerce,* 4–7, 24.

21. Takeda, *Between Crown and Commerce,* 97–99; Takeda, "French Mercantilism and the Early Modern Mediterranean: A Case Study of Marseille's Silk Industry," *French History,* vol. 29, no. 1 (2015): 12–17..

22. Aslanian, *From the Indian Ocean,* 75–77.

23. Takeda, *Between Crown and Commerce,* 99.

24. Ibid., 95–105.

25. Ibid., 102–3.

26. Aslanian, *From the Indian Ocean,* 76. Aslanian believes that the number of Julfa Armenian merchants in Marseille never exceeded thirty-eight.

27. Takeda, *Between Crown and Commerce,* 99–101.

28. Ismail Hakkı Uzunçarşılı, *Osmanlı Tarihi, XVIII Yüzyıl,* vol. 4., pt. 2 (Ankara: TTK, 2003), 203–15.

29. George Rudé, *Europe in the Eighteenth Century: Aristocracy and the Bourgeois Challenge* (Cambridge, MA: Harvard University Press, 1972), 38–40. The most lucrative and competitive trade of France and England was in the West Indies, Latin

America, and the English colonies. Both states imported precious metals from Spanish America; gold and coffee from Brazil; and ginger, sugar, coffee, and indigo from the West Indian Islands and North America. In return, they imported their own manufactures and African slaves into American plantations. The volume of this trade was one-third of all British operations by 1789.

30. Eldem, *French Trade*; see also Daniel Panzac, *Histoire économique et sociale de l'empire Ottoman et de la Turquie (1326–1960)* (Paris: Peeters, 1995), 290–91.

31. Carrière, *Négociants Marseillais*, 2:1046, 1051.

32. Takeda, *Between Crown and Commerce*, 126–28.

33. Masson, *Histoire du commerce*, 228–32.

34. Carrière, *Négociants Marseillais*, 1:200.

35. Zarinebaf, *Crime and Punishment*, 51–59.

36. Masters, *Origins of Western Economic Dominance*, 30–31.

37. Carrière, *Négociants Marseillais*, 2:1046.

38. Elena Frangakis-Syrett, *Trade and Money: The Ottoman Economy in the Eighteenth and Early Nineteenth Centuries* (Istanbul: ISIS Press, 2007), 134.

39. On the trade of Izmir with Europe, see the excellent studies of Elena Frangakis-Syrett, *Trade and Money*, 131–50. On French imports from Izmir in the seventeenth century, see also Antoine Galland, *Le Voyage à Smyrne: Une manuscript d'Antoine Galland (1678)*, ed. Frédéric Bauden (Paris: Chandeigne, 2000), 152–55. According to Galland, Armenians from Iran imported Persian silk to Izmir.

40. Frangakis-Syrett, *Trade and Money*, 134.

41. Eldem, *French Trade*, 23.

42. Robert Mantran, *La vie quotidienne à Istanbul au siècle de Soliman le Magnifique* (Paris: Hachette, 1990), 186–88. Venetian ships used the Ragusa–Corfu or Zante route to Modon, Coron, and crossed the Cyclades Islands to Istanbul.

43. BBA, ADVN. DVE, Fransa, 105: 4.These files contain between seventy and one hundred loose documents for a given year that are petitions by ambassadors and requests for *berats* and travel permits written in Ottoman (translated by the dragoman) on commercial affairs. On the same document, they contain imperial orders in response to these petitions as well as reports from local officials in the margins. Sometimes the petitions of merchants are also enclosed. Translated from French by the author.

44. A.DVNE.d 31/6, 327.

45. BBA, ADVN.DVE, Fransa, 113:48.

46. BBA, ADVN.DVE, Fransa, 113:46.

47. BBA, ADVN.DVE, Fransa, 113:83.

48. Halil Inalcik, *Sources and Studies*,1:95–97; Saim Çağrı Kocakalpan, "İstanbul Gümrüğü (1750–1800): Teşkilat ve Ticaret" (PhD diss., Marmara University, 2014), 34–35.

49. Inalcik, *Sources and Studies*, 95–96; Inalcik, *Economic and Social History*, 199–202.

50. Inalcik, *Economic and Social History*, 204–5. The sales tax on wool was four *akçe* per cart in the sixteenth century. The rates varied from two to four *akçe* per load, cask, or piece on most goods.

51. Linda Darling, "Ottoman Customs Registers (*Gümrük Defterleri*) as Sources for Global Exchange and Interaction," *Review of Middle East Studies* 40, no. 1 (February 2015): 7–8.

52. Genç, *Osmanlı Imparatorluğunda Devlet ve Ekonomi*, 127–39.

53. BBA, MAD.d 451 (d. 1598).

54. BBA, *Kamil Kepeci Defteri* (KK.d) 5521, MAD.d 18383 & 23203 & 2250.

55. Çizakça, *Comparative Evolution of Business Partnerships*, 179–92.

56. BBA, MAD. D 1383 (d. 1098/1686), D.BŞM.IGE.d 17170 and 17214.

57. Inalcik, *Sources and Studies,* 97–98; Inalcik, *Economic and Social History,* 202–4.

58. Galata sicil 14/314, 10a.

59. Rudé, *Europe in the Eighteenth Century,* 40. Most of the ships returning from the West Indies docked in Bordeaux (292) while the rest landed in Marseille (133) and Nantes (131) or in Rouen and Le Harve (108).

60. Daniel Panzac, *Commerce et navigation dans l'Empire Ottoman au XVIIIe siècle* (Istanbul: Les Éditions Isis, 1996), 26–27.

61. Ibid., 161–66. On the silk trade between Izmir and Marseille, see the excellent dissertation of Serap Yilmaz, *"La soie dans les relations commerciales entre la France et l'empire Ottoman au XVIIIe siècle (1700–1789)"* (PhD diss., Université de Paris, 1985).

62. Matthee, *Politics of Trade,* 224–25.

63. Zarinebaf-Shahr, *Tabriz under Ottoman Rule,* 157–58, 166–72.

64. Panzac, *Commerce et navigation,* 198–99.

65. See the long list of imports and exports by French traders in the Tariff Register (*tarife defteri*) 31/6 for the nineteenth century.

66. See customs registers like A.DVN.DVE.d 31/6; Eldem, *French Trade,* 90–112. Eldem provides statistical data for these exports based on French sources.

67. Halil Inacik, *Studies in the History of Textiles in Turkey* (Istanbul: Türkiye Iş Bankası Kültür Yayınları, 2011), 106–7.

68. ADVN.DVE 114:48.

69. AVND.DVE, Fransa, 114:44.

70. Sicil series, 1/32, 13b.

71. ADVNE.DVE, Fransa, 114:54.

72. ADVNE.DVE, Fransa, 114:64.

73. Panzac, *Commerce et navigation,* 199.

74. Elena Fragakis-Syrett, "The Trade of Cotton and Cloth in Izmir: From the Second Half of the Eighteenth Century to the Early Nineteenth Century," in *Landholding and Commercial Agriculture in the Middle East,* ed. Çağlar Keyder and Faruk Tabak (New York: SUNY Press, 1991), 97–98.

75. Paul Masson, *Marseille et la colonization Française,: Essai d'histoire colonial,* 2nd ed. (Paris: Libraire Hachette, 1912), 87.

76. Eldem, *French Trade,* 205–6. See also ACCM, J 192.

77. Eldem based these figures on censuses carried out for the Chamber of Commerce in Marseille and the parish records of the Church of St. Peter and St. Paul in

Galata. See also Edhem Eldem, "The French Nation of Constantinople in the Eighteenth Century as Reflected in the Saints Peter and Paul Parish Records, 1740–1800)," in *French Mediterraneans: Transnational and Imperial Histories,* ed. Patricia M. E. Lorcin and Todd Sheppard (Lincoln: University of Nebraska Press, 2016), 144–45 (tables 5.7 and 5.8).

78. Vergennes, *Le chevalier de Vergennes,* 1:165–67.
79. Eldem, "French Nation of Constantinople," 144.
80. Carrière, *Négociants Marseillais,* vol. 2:976.
81. ACCM, J series.
82. Eldem, *French Trade,* 208–11. On the files of some of these merchant houses and their correspondence with the Chamber of Commerce in Marseille, see ACCM, L IX: 703, 704, 705, 706, 707, 708, 709, 710, 711, 713, 714; J series 212, LIX, LXI. On the residence of French merchants in the Levant, see J series 102–4 (1726–88), J 94 on artisans in the Levant (1711–78).
83. Eldem, "French Nation of Constantinople," 142.
84. ADVN. DVE, Fransa, 102:29.
85. ADVN.DVE, Fransa, 102:46.
86. ADVNE.DVE, Fransa, 110: 20.
87. Baron de Tott, *Memoirs of Baron de Tott,* vol. 2 (New York: Arno Press, 1973), 192–95.
88. ADVN.DVE 115:34.
89. Eldem, *French Trade,* 68–84.
90. Carrière, *Négociants Marseillais,* 1:224.
91. On the history of coffee as a beverage and its spread from Yemen to Hijaz, Egypt, Syria, and Istanbul, see Ralph Hattox, *Coffee and Coffeehouses: The Origins of a Social Beverage in the Medieval Near East* (Seattle: University of Washington Press, 1985); Hanna, *Making Big Money,* 79–81.
92. Hanna, *Making Big Money,* 80–84.
93. Zarinebaf, *Crime and Punishment,* 126–28.
94. Faroqhi, *Artisans of Empire,* 125.
95. ISAM, Sicil 14/542. See estates of residents of Galata.
96. Vergennes, *Le chevalier de Vergennes,* vol. 1.
97. Thévenot, *L'empire du grand Turc,* 19.
98. Takeda, *Between Crown and Commerce,* 99.
99. Braudel, *Structures of Everyday Life,* 256–60.
100. Eldem, *French Trade,* 75.
101. Braudel, *Structures of Everyday Life,* 1:260.
102. Ibid., 224–27.
103. Ibid., 227.
104. Kahraman and Dağlı, *Evliya Çelebi Seyahatnamesi,* vol.1, pt. 2, 512–13; BBA, Cevdet Muallim 1, 26; ADVN.DVE, Fransa, 832, 29.
105. Ahmet Kal'a, *Istanbul Ahkam Defterleri: Istanbul Esnaf Tarihi,* vol. 2 (Istanbul: Istanbul Araştırmaları Merkezi, 1997), 342–43.
106. Zarinebaf, *Crime and Punishment,* 125–30.

107. C.HR 156/7760.

108. BBA, CB 11/520. The price of coffee was 64 *para* per *kiyye* in Istanbul in 1765. Roasted coffee was 77 *para* per 320 *dirhem*.

109. On Ottoman administration of Yemen, see Inalcik, *Economic and Social History*, 331–35.

110. Eldem, *French Trade*, 77.

111. Davis, *English Overseas Trade*, 35.

112. Eldem, *French Trade*, 68–70. Three-quarters of the French imports into Galata in the eighteenth century, according to Eldem, were composed of manufactured goods such as woolen textiles. The rest were colonial goods such as coffee and sugar. French sugar was of three different qualities, ranging from the best and most expensive loaves to intermediate powdered sugar.

113. Eldem, *French Trade*, 69.

114. ADVN.DVE, Fransa, 100:49.

115. ADVN.DVE.d 30/5:105.

116. Galata sicil 14/479, 17b.

117. BBA, C.IKTS, 7/342.

118. Eldem, *French Trade*, 76–78.

119. ADVNE.DVE, Fransa, 100:52.

120. ADVNE.DVE.d 30/5:57.

121. C. HR 60/2964. See also Eldem, *French Trade*, 70–73.

122. ADVNE.DVE, Fransa, 105:64.

123. ADVNE.DVE, Fransa, 105:38.

124. ISAM, Sicil 14/542, 11.

125. BBA, C.IKTS, 7/314.

126. BBA, C.IKTS, 7/314.

127. Hanna, *Making Big Money*, 4–14.

128. See sicils of Galata and Istanbul.

129. Fariba Zarinebaf, "From *Mahalle* (Neighborhood) to the Market and the Courts: Women, Credit, and Property in 18th-Century Istanbul," in *Women on the Margins: Gender, Charity, and Justice in the Early Modern Middle East,* ed. Fariba Zarinebaf (Istanbul: Isis Press, 2014), 69–81. See also Çağlar Keyder, "Perspectives on Merchant Credit," in *History from Below: A Tribute in Memory of Donald Quataert,* ed. Selim Karahasanoğlu and Cenk Demir (Istanbul: Bilgi University Press, 2016), 301–11.

130. Elena Frangakis-Syrett, "The Ottoman Monetary System and Early Banking in the Ottoman Empire," in *History from Below,* 317.

131. Vergennes, *Le chevalier de Vergennes,* 1:174–81.

132. Ibid., 1:363–66. For patterns of cons umption among the Ottoman state elite like Grand Vizier Halil Hamid Pasha (1736–85) in Istanbul, see Olivier Bouquet, *"Un grand vizier dans sa maison, edition de trois inventaires après décès* (1785)," *Turcica* 47 (2016): 185–234.

133. Boogert, *The Capitulations,* 77. The English Embassy had fifty-five members, and the Venetian Embassy had ninety-eight.

134. On the sale of *berats* to *protégés,* see the excellent analysis of Boogert, *The Capitulations,* 79–84.

135. Zarinebaf, "From *Mahalle* (Neighborhood)," 69–81.

136. C.HR 14/689.

137. Inalcik, *Economic and Social History,* 208–9.

138. Eldem, *French Trade,* 120–47.

139. ACCM, J series, 102, 103, 104 (1766–88), bankruptcies in the Levant and the Barbary Coast. For cases of bankruptcies among Dutch traders, see Boogert, The Capitulations,, 207–62.

140. ACCM, J series, nos. 102–3 (1743–66).

141. ADVNE.DVE, Fransa, 100:34.

142. ADVNE.DVE, Fransa, 100:47.

143. BBA, C.IKTS 131.

144. ACCM, J series, 103. This file contains forty-two documents.

145. ACCM, J series, 102.

146. Boogert, *The Capitulations,* 207.

147. ADVN.DVE, Fransa, 114:46.

148. BBA, C.HR 146/7265.

149. BBA, C.HR 1/37.

150. BBA, C.HR 3/106.

151. ADVNE.DVE, Fransa, 100:31.

152. ADVNE.DVE, Fransa, 113:84.

153. For tax farming in the Morea, see Fariba Zarinebaf, John Bennet, and Jack L. Davis, *A Historical and Economic Geography of Ottoman Greece: The Southwestern Morea in the 18th Century* (Princeton, NJ: American School of Classical Studies in Athens, 2005), 32–40.

154. ADVN.DVE, Fransa, 110:40.

155. BBA, *Fransa Akham Defteri* 31/6: 377.

156. *Top* is a unit of measurement for textiles. Every top was thirteen meters.

157. C.BLD 22/1057.

158. Eldem, *French Trade,* 60–62.

159. See the excellent study of Bouquet, *"Un grand vizier,"* 185–234.

160. Sicil 14/382, 7. His estate also included a house worth 12,000 *akçe,* two gardens worth 36,000 *akçe* each, 15,810 *akçe* in cash, another garden worth 300,000 *akçe,* a watch, and a coffee pot.

161. ISAM, Galata Sicil 14/382, 5a.

162. Ismail Hakkı Uzunçarsılı, *Osmanlı Tarihi,* vol. 4, *18th Century* (Ankara: TTK, 2003), 569–72. Silk textiles were also produced in Bursa, Ankara, Damascus, Hama, and Chios.

163. BBA, C.IKTS 33/1633.

164. BBA, C.IKTS 33/1633.

165. Fariba Zarinebaf, "The Role of Women in the Urban Economy of Istanbul, 1700–1850," in Fariba Zarinebaf, *Women on the Margins: Gender, Charity, and Justice in the Early Modern Middle East* (Istanbul: Isis Press, 2014), 63–64.

166. Julia Pardoe, *The Beauties of the Bosphorus: Illustrated in a Series of Views of Constantinople and Its Environs* (London, 1843), 33.

167. Julia Pardoe, *Beauties of the Bosphorus: Constantinople and its Environs* (London, 1855), 33–34.

168. BBA, C.IKTS 6/285.

169. BBA, C.IKTS 7/307 (d. 1804), 8/399.

170. C.IKTS 5/158.

171. C.IKTS 10/454.

172. C.IKTS 565.

173. ADVN.DVE, Fransa, 114:32.

174. Eldem, *French Trade*, 41–44.

175. Unit of measurement for masonry and textiles, 0.758 meter.

176. BBA, ADVNE.DVE, Fransa, 100:53.

177. ADVNE.DVE, Fransa, 118:78.

178. Eldem, *French Trade,* 56–58.

179. Ibid., 54–67.

180. Davis, *English Overseas Trade,* 34.

181. A.DVN.DVE.d 31/6, 361. On India trade, see Inalcik, *Economic and Social History,* 315–63.

182. BBA, C.IKTS 33/1633.

183. Inalcik, *History of Textiles,* 129–31.

184. Pascale Barthe, *French Encounters with the Ottomans, 1510–1560* (London: Routledge, 2016), 54–77.

185. BBA, C.IKTS 3/135.

186. On the networks of Bosnian Muslim merchants based on a review of their estates, see Markus Koller, "Some Remarks on a Merchant Family in Eighteenth-Century Bosnia," in *Merchants in the Ottoman Empire,* ed. Suraiya Faroqhi and Giles Veinstein (Paris: Peeters, 2008), 179–92.

187. C.H. 96/4763. On Muslim merchants in Vienna see, David Do Paço, "Eighteenth-Century Central Europe in Transnational Trade: The Trading Company of Molla Mustafa and the Viennese Conscription of 1767," in *Economy and Society in Central and Eastern Europe: Territory, Population, Consumption,* papers of the International Conference Held in Alba Iulia (April 25–27, 2013), ed. Daniel and Valer Morga, 31–42. Ottoman Jews and Greeks were more prominent in trade with Vienna than Muslims.

188. Ismail Hakki Kadi, *Ottoman and Dutch Merchants in the Eighteenth Century: Competition and Cooperation in Ankara, Izmir, and Amsterdam* (Leiden: E.J. Brill, 2012), 198–234. On the activities of Ottoman Greek merchants from Izmir in coastal trade and trade with Europe, see Frangakis-Syrett, *Trade and Money,* 109–30.

189. BBA, C.IKTS *3/136.*

190. Frangakis-Syrett, *Trade and Money,* 140–41.

191. Ibid., 141.

192. Ibid., 135–36.

193. BBA, C.BLD 7/312.

194. Frangakis-Syrett, *Trade and Money,* 136.

195. Panzac, *La caravane maritime,* 139–45.

196. Ibid., 146. These statistics are based on 809 contracts that were drawn up between Muslim merchants and French captains that Panzac studied.

197. Ibid., 145.

198. Ibid., 213–14.

199. ADVNE.DVE 118/74.

CHAPTER SEVEN

1. Lady Mary Wortley Montagu, *Turkish Embassy Letters,* ed. Malcolm M. Jack (London: Virago Books, 1994), 111–12.

2. John-Paul Ghobrial, *The Whispers of Cities: Information Flows in Istanbul, London, and Paris in the Age of William Trumbull* (Oxford: Oxford University Press, 2013), 15–18, 31–32.

3. Eldem, "French Nation of Constantinople, 144–47. Eric Dursteler, *Venetians in Constantinople,* 103–5.

4. Fariba Zarinebaf, "Policing Morality: Crossing Gender and Communal Boundaries in an Age of Political Crisis and Religious Controversy in Seventeenth-Century Istanbul," in *Living in the Ottoman Realm: Everyday Life and Identity from the 13th to the 20th Century,* ed. Christine Isom-Verhaaren and Kent Schull (Bloomington: Indiana University Press, 2016), 194–208.

5. ISAM, Galata sicil series 14/542, 57a. *Beyoğlu* is the Turkish name of Pera.

6. Zarinebaf, *Crime and Punishment,* 130–33.

7. Christopher J. Herold, *Bonaparte in Egypt* (South Yorkshire, UK: Pen and Sword, 1962), 64–70.

8. David Nirenberg, *Neighboring Faiths: Christianity, Islam, and Judaism in the Middle Ages and Today* (Chicago: University of Chicago Press, 2014), 91. See also Nirenberg, *Communities of Violence: Persecution of Minorities in the Middle Ages* (Princeton, NJ: Princeton University Press, 1996).

9. Zarinebaf, *Crime and Punishment,* 94–97.

10. Zarinebaf, "Intercommunal Life in Istanbul during the Eighteenth Century," *Review of Middle East Studies* 46, no. 1 (Summer 2012): 79–85. See the case of Fatima Hatun in Eric Dursteler, *Renegade Women: Gender, Identity, and Boundaries in the Early Modern Mediterranean* (Baltimore: Johns Hopkins University Press, 2011), 1–33. Dursteler emphasizes the frequency of conversion from Christianity to Islam among renegade women and men.

11. Dursteler, *Venetians in Constantinople*; Karen Barkey, *Empire of Difference: The Ottomans in a Comparative Perspective* (Cambridge: Cambridge University Press, 2008).

12. Zarinebaf, "Policing Morality," 195–96. Dursteler believes that interfaith relations were common in the border regions and that conversion to Islam among

Christians from Venice and Calabria was widespread from 1500 to 1650 due to better opportunities for employment for the poor as well as for renegades in the Ottoman Empire. Many Venetian renegades served in high positions in high government office in the Sublime Porte. Dursteler, *Venetians in Constantinople,* 12–129.

13. Antoine Galland, *Voyages inédit,* 140–47. Dursteler, *Venetians in Constantinople,* 95–98.

14. See Cevdet Zabtiye (CZ) collection: CZ 3709, 3662; 2557; Cevdet Maliye 6147; D.BŞM.IGE 14/18, D.BŞM.IGE 20/62. See also Zarinebaf, *Crime and Punishment,* 90–100.

15. Zarinebaf, *Crime and Punishment,* 26–28.

16. Hitzel, "Étienne Felix Héhin," 37. See also Eldem, "French Nation of Constantinople," 131–68.

17. Galata sicil series 14/479, 26a.

18. BBA, D.BŞM.IGE 23/1.

19. Galata sicil series 14/542, 58a.

20. Galata sicil series 14/479, 13b.

21. Cevdet Maliye 6147.

22. Galata sicil series 14/542, 57b.

23. Zarinebaf, *Crime and Punishment,* 107–11.

24. BBA, CZ 3662. During one such inspection, fifteen streetwalkers were arrested in Istanbul and were then banished to Mudanya in 1818.

25. Galata sicil series 1/32, 92b.

26. Galata sicil series 14/535, 83a

27. Galata sicil series 14/319, 90a.

28. Dankoff and Kim, *An Ottoman Traveler.*

29. Galland, *Voyage inédit,* 142–47.

30. Each *medre* was 11.5 kg. Sicil series 14/314, 96a–96b.

31. Zarinebaf, *Crime and Punishment,* 100–101.

32. Galata sicil series 14/479,18b.

33. BBA, CB 1407.

34. Galata sicil series 14/314, 89b.

35. Zarinebaf, *Crime and Punishment,* 112–21.

36. Galata sicil series 14/479, 14a.

37. Galata sicil series 14/542, 56a.

38. Galata sicil series 14/319, 15a.

39. Galata sicil series 14/542, 55a,.

40. Galata sicil series 14/542,55a, 12a.

41. Laidlaw, *British in the Levant,* 168–69.

42. Ibid., 169–99.

43. Ibid., 166–67.

44. ACCM, J series, no. 98.

45. Ibid..

46. ACCM, J series, dossier no. 98.

47. Vergennes, *Son ambassade a Constantinople,* 1:363–66.

48. BBA, C.HR (Cevdet Hariciye) 94/4652.

49. C.HR 4881.

50. Talbot, *British-Ottoman Relations,* 206–8. Talbot also found a document about the confiscation of the goods of another English trader, Smith, who lived in Galata.

51. BBA, Cevdet Adliye (C.ADL), 2/83.

52. Laidlaw, *British in the Levant,* 179–85.

53. Ibid., 192–93.

54. ACCM, J series, no. 95 (1698–1790): *Residence des Français en Levant et Barbarie.*

55. Ibid.

56. Ibid.

57. Ibid.

58. Ibid.

59. Dallaway, *Constantinople, Ancient and Modern,* 126–27, 138.

60. Stephen Ortega, *Negotiating Transcultural Relations in the Early Modern Mediterranean* (London: Ashgate, 2014), 35–42.

61. Takeda, *Between Crown and Commerce,* 38. For more information on the training of these students in a Capuchin monastery in Pera, see ACCM, J series.

62. Antoine Galland, *Istanbul'a Ait Günlük Anılar (1672–1675),* trans. Nahid Sirri Örik, vol. 1 (Ankara: TTK), 1998), 159.

63. Ibid., 41, 156.

64. Olivers Jens Schmitt, *Les Levantines: Cadres de vie et identite's d'un groupe ethno-confessionel de l'empire Ottoman au "long" 19 siècle* (Istanbul: ISIS Press, 2007), 129–51. On dragomans in the English Embassy (from the Perone, Andreassi, and Testa families) in the seventeenth century, see Ghobrial, *Whispers of Cities,* 102–09. Ghobrial underscores the networks and linguistic abilities of these dragoman families who were perpetually in motion. Not all dragomans knew Ottoman and European languages well, so the embassies also hired Ottoman Muslim scribes.

65. ADVN.DVE Fransa 114: 44.

66. Maurits H. van den Boogert, "European Patronage in the Ottoman Empire: Anglo-Dutch Conflicts of Interest in Aleppo (1703–1755)," in *Friends and Rivals in the East,* ed. Alastir Hamilton, Alexander H. De Groot, and Maurits H. van den Boogert (Leiden: E.J. Brill, 2000), 210–12.

67. Schmitt, *Les Levantines,* 131–33.

68. ADVNE.DVE Fransa, 118:65.

69. ADVN.DVE Fransa, 119:66.

70. Dallaway, *Constantinople, Ancient and Modern,* 126.

71. Laidlaw, *British in the Levant,* 39–40.

72. See ADVNE. DVE 136.

73. ADVN.DVE Fransa, 118:41.

74. Boogert, *The Capitulations,* 87–88. England had 440 and the Dutch Republic had 271 protégés (for a total of 1,174 for the three powers) in the eighteenth century. Russia was not included in the Ottoman survey of *beratlı* merchants.

75. Ibid., 92.

76. Ibid., 85–89.

77. Eldem, *French Trade*, 281.

78. Enver Ziya Karal, *Selim III'ün Hatt-i Hümayunları, Nizam-i Cedid, 1789–1807* (Ankara: TTK, 1988), 141–45.

79. Eldem, *French Trade*, 248–51.

80. See the letter of the governor of the English Levant Company to the Porte in 1760 in Boogert, *The Capitulations*, 98–99.

81. Ibid., 92–93.

82. For the protégé system in Izmir, see Zandi-Sayek, 57–63.

83. Alexander H. De Groot, "Dragoman'sCareers: The Change of Status in Some Families Connected with the British and Dutch Embassies at Istanbul, 1783–1829," in *Friends and Rivals in the East*, 237–39; J. H. Kramers, "Terdjuman," in *Encyclopedia of Islam*, vol. 4 (Leiden: E. J. Brill, 1934), 725–26; Cengiz Orhonlu, "Tercuman," in *Islam Ansiklopedisi*, vol. 12, pt. 1 (Istanbul, 1974), 175–81.

84. Orhonlu, "Tercuman," 178.

85. BBA, ADVN. DVE Fransa 137/59.

86. BBA, Cevdet Hariciye 14/668.

87. BBA, ADVN.DVE Fransa 118:73.

88. ADVN.DVE Fransa 100:54.

89. Dursteler, *Venetians in Constantinople*, 180–85. The visits of Muslims to the church of St. Antoine in Pera continue to this date.

90. Lela Gibson, "Ottoman Sufism, Orientalism, and German Politics, 1770–1825" (PhD diss., UCLA, 2015). See also Ghobrial, *Whispers of Cities*, 84. The English ambassador, Thrumbull, visited the *tekke* of dervishes frequently and described their rituals in his travelogues.

91. Galland, *Istanbul'a Ait*, vol. 2, 1.

92. For an analysis of the parish records of this church, see Eldem, "French Nation of Constantinople," 131–67.

93. Galland, *Voyage inédit*, 142–47.

94. Masters, *Christians and Jews*, 70–71.

95. Rausas, *Le Régime des capitulations*, 43.

96. Galland, *Istanbul'a Ait*, 1:43, 73.

97. BBA, ADVN.DVE Fransa 118:66.

98. BBA, ADVN.DVE Fransa 100:53.

99. Zarinebaf, *Crime and Punishment*, 165.

100. Masters, *Christians and Jews*, 82–84. See also Charles A. Frazee, *Catholics and the Sultan: The Church and the Ottoman Empire* (New York: Columbia University Press, 1983).

101. Zarinebaf, *Crime and Punishment*, 165.

102. BBA, Cevdet Adliye 5176:1–5.

103. This register (CA 5176: 10 folios) contains forty-two cases of Armenian converts who were sentenced to forced labor in the galleys in 1706. See also Kalemi Bahriye 5660, folios 1–7 for the cases of forty-five Armenian priests and

converts from Istanbul, Galata, and Aleppo who were sentenced to the galleys in June 1706.

104. CA 5176:4.

105. Kalemi Bahriye 5660:3–4.

106. BBA, ADVN.DVE 100:15.

107. BBA, NFS.d. 20 (Register of the Catholic *millet* in Istanbul in 1831). This register lists 280 Armenian Catholics in Istanbul proper in 1831. Many were merchants, tailors, and artisans originally from Ankara and Artvin. Frazee, *Catholics and the Sultan,* 155–60. Frazee believes that Pope Benedict XIV was keen about converting the sultan's Orthodox subjects. In Izmir, the Catholic Church of St. Polycarbe was in charge of converting Armenians and Greeks. The Jesuits were under attack in France after the death of Benedict in 1758 and were replaced by the Lazarists in Galata, Izmir, and Aleppo.

108. Frazee, *Catholics and the Sultan,* 160–62.

109. Vergennes, *Son ambassade,* 2:181–83.

110. Ibid., 178–80.

111. Baron de Tott, *Memoirs of Baron de Tott,* vols. 1 and 2 (New York: Arno Press, 1973), 4. On Esma Sultan's palace along the Bosphorus, see 70–75.

112. Sicil series 14/319, 88a.

113. Sicil series, 14/479, 9a.

114. Zarinebaf, *Crime and Punishment,* 76, 115.

115. Paolo Girardelli, "Power or Leisure? Remarks on the Architecture of the European Summer Embassies on the Bosphorus Shore," *New Perspectives on Turkey* 50 (2013): 29–57.

116. Ebru Boyar and Kate Fleet, *A Social History of Ottoman Istanbul* (Cambridge: Cambridge University Press, 2010), 226–30.

117. Zarinebaf, *Crime and Punishment,* 17; on Lady Montagu's visit to the harem of Fatma Sultan, the daughter of Sultan Ahmed III, see Montagu, *Turkish Embassy Letters,* 82–91. Ambassador Trumbull's wife, Katherine, also established relations with Sultan Mehmed IV's aunt Sultana Ummühan in July 1688. Ghobrial, *Whispers of Cities,* 119–20.

118. Charles de Secondat Montesquieu, *Les lettres Persanes* (Paris: N.p., 1931). On the role of women in Ottoman society, see Zarinebaf, *Women on the Margins.*

119. J.C. Flachat, *Observations sur le commerce et les arts d'une parties de l'Europe, de l'Asie, de l'Afrique et même des Indes Orientales* (Lyons, 1766).

120. Jacques Perot, Frederic Hitzel, and Robert Anhegger, *Hatice Sultan Ile Melling Kalfa: Mektuplar,* trans. Ela Güntekin (Istanbul: Tarih Vakfı Yurt Yayınları, 2001), 6.

121. See Christine Isom-Verhaaren, "Royal French Women in the Sultan's Harem: The Political Uses of Fabricated Accounts from the Sixteenth to the Twenty-First Century," *Journal of World History,* 17, no. 2 (2006): 160–61. Isom-Verhaaren believes that this story was fabricated by Napoleon III to enhance his prestige. But this explanation is very unlikely since there was a big falling out in

Ottoman-French relations after Napoleon's invasion of Egypt in 1798, and she may have played an important role in restoring these relations.

122. Günsel Renda, "Istanbul: The Travelers' Passion," in *Istanbul: The City of Dreams* (Istanbul: Pera Museum, 2008), 19–23.

123. Kuban, *Istanbul: An Urban History*, 366–67.

124. For his biography, see Perot, Hitzel, and Anhegger, *Hatice Sultan*, 1–4.

125. Hamadeh, *The City's Pleasures*, 124.

126. Sherine Hamadeh, "Ottoman Expression of Early Modernity and the 'Inevitable' Question of Westernization," *Journal of the Society of Architectural Historians* 63, no. 1 (March 2004): 32.

127. Kuban, *Istanbul: An Urban History*, 364–66.

128. Perot, Hitzel, and Anhegger, *Hatice Sultan*.

129. For the text of these letters, which were found in the French Archives, see Perot, Hitzel, and Anhegger, *Hatice Sultan*, 25–62.

130. Antoine-Ignace Melling, *Voyage pittoresque à Constantinople sur des rives de Bosphore, 1807–1824* (Paris, 1819), n.p.

131. Ibid.; Kuban, *Istanbul: An Urban History*, 363–64.

132. Melling, *Voyage pittoresque*, n.p. See the section on Büyükdere.

133. N. Webb and C. Webb, *Earl and His Butler*, 26.

134. Baron de Tott, *Memoirs of Baron de Tott*, vols. 1–2, 70–80. See also Fariba Zarinebaf, "The Wealth of Ottoman Princesses in the Tulip Age," in *Women on the Margins: Gender, Charity, and Justice in the Early Modern Middle East,* ed. Fariba Zarinebaf (Istanbul: Isis Press, 2014), 113–22.

135. Baron de Tott, *Memoirs of Baron de Tott*, 1:71.

136. Mary Roberts, *Intimate Outsiders: The Harem in Ottoman and Oriental Art and Travel Literature* (Durham, NC: Duke University Press, 2007), 88–90. According to Roberts, Ottoman women were interested in the gloves and corsets that English women wore and the shape of their bodies.

137. Laidlaw, *British in the Levant,* 46–49.

138. Ibid., 47.

139. Montagu, *Turkish Embassy Letters,* 69–72, 65–66.

140. Paul Dumont, *"Comment l'Europe perçoit-elle l'Émpire Ottoman a l'époque des Tulipes,"* in *L'horloger du Sérail aux sources du fantasme oriental chez Jean-Jacques Rousseau,* ed. Paul Dumanont and Rémy Hilderbrand (Paris: Maisonneuve et Larose, 2005), 19–25; Ian Coller, "East of Enlightenment: Regulating Cosmopolitanism between Istanbul and Paris in the Eighteenth Century," *Journal of World History* 21, no. 3 (2010): 466. Rousseau's uncle became a consul in Safavid Iran.

141. Edhem Eldem, "(A Quest for) the Bourgeoisie of Istanbul: Identities, Roles, and Conflicts," in *Urban Governance under the Ottomans: Between Cosmopolitanism and Conflict,* ed. Ulrile Freitag and Nora Lafi (London: Routledge, 2014), 159–69.

142. Coller, "East of Enlightenment," 447–48.

1. For a good analysis of the wars of the eighteenth century and the French Revolution, see George Rudé, *Europe in the Eighteenth Century: Aristocracy and the Bourgeois Challenge* (Cambridge, MA: Harvard University Press, 1972).

2. Namık Sinan Turan, *İmparatorluk ve Diploması* (Istanbul: Bilgi Universitesi Yayınları, 2014), 296–300.

3. On the impact of the French Revolution, see also Ali Yaycıoğlu, "Révolution de Constantinople: France and the Ottoman World in the Age of Revolutions," in *French Mediterraneans: Transnational and Imperial Histories,* ed. Patricia M.E. Lorcin and Todd Shepard (Lincoln: Nebraska University Press, 2016), 29–30. For a good analysis of Franco-Ottoman diplomacy during this period based on French sources, see Pascal Firges, *French Revolutionaries in the Ottoman Empire: Political Culture, Diplomacy, and the Limits of Universal Revolution, 1792–1798* (Oxford: Oxford University Press, 2016), 25–92.

4. Bacqué-Grammont, Kuneralp, and Hitzel, *Représentants permanents,* 44–45.

5. BBA, Hatt-I Hümayun (HH) 241/13537.

6. BBA, HH 168/8378.

7. ISAM, Galata sicil series 14/542:41b. See the list of guns.

8. BBA,HH 233/12431.

9. HH 223/12431.

10. Lynn A. Hunt, *Politics, Culture, and Class in the French Revolution* (Berkeley: University of California Press, 1984), 52–86. These symbols were drawn from the Roman Empire (the Goddess of Liberty) and from the Enlightenment, Freemasonry, and nature (the Liberty Tree). The festivals included the Festival of Reason and the reception of the free-born children in the Patriotic Altar (instead of baptism).

11. BBA, HH 249/14140.

12. BBA, HH 267/15571.

13. On the arrest and imprisonment of the French residents of Cyprus, see Ömer Faruk Bölükbaşı, "Napolyon'un Mısır'ı İşgali Sırasında Kıbrıs'ta Bir Fransız: André Benoit Astier ve Mallarının Müsaderesi," in *Bir İnsan-i Selim, Prof. Dr. Azmı Özcan'a Armağan,* ed. R. Arıkan and H. Demiryürek (Istanbul: Lotus, 2016), 555–89.

14. Sicil series 14/542, 14b.

15. Vlami, *Trading with the Ottomans,* 92–94.

16. Pascal Firges, "French Revolutionary Politics and Culture in the Ottoman Empire, 1792–1798" (PhD diss., University of Heidelberg, 2014), 287–88. See also the published version of the dissertation, Firges, *French Revolutionaries.*

17. See the list compiled by Hénin in 1794 of French residents in Pera (101) who had signed a letter of support for Descorches, the French envoy in Istanbul, dividing the residents into royalists and revolutionaries, in Firges, "French Revolutionary Politics," appendix A, pages 312–17. The community was composed of traders,

mariners, tailors, jewelers, watchmakers, bakers, doctors, and the embassy staff. The traders were mostly listed as being counterrevolutionary.

18. Eldem, *French Trade,* 293–94.

19. On French-Ottoman diplomatic relations during these years, see Ismail Soysal, *Fransız Ihtilali ve Türk-Fransız Diplomasi Münasebetleri (1789–1802)* (Ankara: Türk Tarih Kurumu Yayınları, 1999); Şenay Özdemir Gümüş, "Napolyon'un Mısır'in Işğalı Sırasında Osmanlı Topraklarındaki Fransızlar," *Tarihin Peşinde* 9 (2013): 249–78; and Enver Ziya Karal, *Fransa, Mısır ve Osmanlı Impratorluğu (1797–1902)* (Istanbul: Milli Mecmua Basımevi, 1938).

20. On correspondence between the French ambassador, Gouffier, and the Chamber of Commerce in Marseille, see ACCM, J series, nos. 170–71, entitled *Lettres de Comte de Choiseul–Gouffier (1784–92).* On the correspondence between the secretary and chief dragoman of the French Embassy in Istanbul (Antoine Fonton) and the Chamber, see ACCM, J series, nos. 172 and 177.

21. De Groot, "Dragomans' Careers," 242–43; 233.

22. Firges, *French Revolutionaries,* 26–29; Mehmet Alaadin Yalçinkaya, *The First Permanent Ottoman Embassy in Europe: The Embassy of Yusuf Aghah Efendi to London (1793–1797)* (Istanbul: ISIS Press, 2010), 82–83.

23. Marie-Gabriel-Auguste-Florent, Comte de Choiseul-Gouffier, *Voyage pittoresque dans l'empire Ottoman e Grèce, dans la Troade, les iles de l'Archipel et sur les cotes de l'Asie-mineur* (Paris, 1842).

24. The French envoys and ambassadors in Istanbul after the French Revolution were Charles-Louis Huguet Marquis, or Sémonville, 1792–93; Marquis-Louis Henri Descorches (special envoy), 1793–94; and Étienne Felix Hénin (*chargé d'affaires*), 1793–95. See Bacqué-Grammont, Kuneralp, and Hitzel, *Représentants permanents,* 40–41.

25. Frédéric Hitzel, "Etienne-Félix Hénin, un Jacobin à Constantinople (1793–1795)," *Anatolia Moderna* 33 (1991): 35–46.

26. Ibid., 43–44.

27. The monarchy had been abolished in September 21, 1792.

28. Hitzel, " Etienne-Félix Hénin," 37–38. Douard Marcère, *Une ambassae à Constantinople: La politique Orientale de la révolution Française,* 2 vols. (Paris: F. Alcan, 1927).

29. Eldem, *French Trade,* 295–96.

30. Firges, "French Revolutionary Politics," 62–69, 180–81.

31. Ibid., 187–88.

32. Ibid., 291.

33. Ibid., 308–10.

34. Ibid., 87–88.

35. Hitzel, "Étienne-Felix Hénin," 46. Firges, *French Revolutionaries,* 187–90.

36. Juan Cole, *Napoleon's Egypt: Invading the Middle East* (New York: St. Martin's–Griffin, 2008), 154–56.

37. Baron de Tott, *Memoires of Baron de Tott*. On Napoleon's administration of Cairo, see André Raymond, *Cairo*, trans. Willard Wood (Cambridge: Cambridge University Press, 2000), 291–308.

38. For a good analysis of the historical and regional contexts, see Cole, *Napoleon's Egypt*.

39. Unat, *Osmanlı Sefirleri*, 179–81.

40. J. Christopher Herold, *Bonaparte in Egypt* (South Yorkshire, UK: Pen and Sword, 1962), 1–38; Unat, *Osmanlı Sefirleri*, 179–81.

41. Herold, *Bonaparte in Egypt*, 56–57.

42. Cole, *Napoleon's Egypt*, 12–16.

43. Herold, *Bonaparte in Egypt*, 52–53. Paul Strathem, *Napoleon in Egypt* (New York: Bentham Books, 2009), 5–6.

44. Cole, *Napoleon's Egypt*, 16.

45. Herold, *Bonaparte in Egypt*, vi. According to some estimates, the size of Napoleon's army in Egypt was somewhere between 35,000 and 40,000. According to Strathen, there were 300 women on board the ships; some were workers, and others were spouses who had been smuggled aboard while dressed as men. Strathem, *Napoleon in Egypt*, 1–2.

46. Cole, *Napoleon's Egypt*, 29.

47. Boogert, *The Capitulations*, 26–27.

48. Herold, *Bonaparte in Egypt*, vi–vii.

49. Raymond, *Cairo*, 293–94.

50. Herold, *Bonaparte in Egypt*, 315; Cole, *Napoleon's Egypt*, 196–202. Cole offers an excellent analysis of Napoleon's policies in Egypt and the subsequent rebellion.

51. Herold, *Bonaparte in Egypt*, 205. Shmuel Moreh, trans., *Napoleon in Egypt: Al-Jabarti's Chronicle of the French Occupation of Cairo, 1798* (Princeton, NJ: Markus Wiener, 1993), 155.

52. Cole, 192–93.

53. Moreh, *Napoleon in Egypt*, 107; Cole, *Napoleon's Egypt*, 189–90.

54. Moreh, *Napoleon in Egypt*, 83–85.

55. Ibid., 101–5; Cole, *Napoleon's Egypt*, 198–200.

56. Moreh, 93–94.

57. Raymond, *Cairo*, 297–98; Cole, *Napoleon's Egypt*, 202–14.

58. For diplomacy between the two states in this period and the embassy of Muhib Efendi, see Bekir Günay, *Paris'te Bir Osmanlı: Seyyid Abdurrahman Muhib Efendi'nin Paris Seferliği ve Büyük Sefaratnamesi* (Istanbul: Kitabevi, 2009), 5–19. See also Unat, *Osmanlı Sefirleri*, 181–83.

59. On Ottoman embassy accounts to France, see Unat, *Osmanlı Sefirleri*, 183–203. The embassy accounts had a major impact on the reform movement in Istanbul.

60. Panzac, *Le caravane maritime*, 214–20.

61. Bölükbaşı, "Napolyonun İşğalı Sırasında Bir Fransız," ed. R. Arıkan and H. Demiryürek (Istanbul: Lotus Yayınevi, 2016), 555–88.

62. Panzac, *Le caravane maritime*, 141–42.

63. BBA, Fransa Nişan Defteri, 29/4, 23.

64. BBA. A.DVN.DVE. d, Fransa, 31/6, pp. 356–70. See also D.BŞM.d 41870. There are tariff registers for France.

65. BBA. A.DVN.DVE. d, Fransa, 31/6, 311.

66. ADVN.DVE, Fransa, 130; 132; 134; 136: 6, 10, 17; 137.

67. Frangakis-Syrett, "The Trade of Cotton and Cloth," 98–99.

68. Elena Frangakis-Syrett, *Trade and Money:* 155–60.

69. Vlami, *Trading with the Ottomans*, 162–63.

70. Talbot, *British-Ottoman Relations*, 102–3.

71. BBA, ADVN.TCR.1. The full text on the privileges of Avrupa merchants is available here. See also Bruce Masters, "The Sultan's Entrepreneurs: The Avrupa Tuccars and the Hayriye Tuccars in Syria," *IJMES* 24 (1992): 579–97.

72. Vlami, *Trading with the Ottomans*, 171–72; Frangakis-Syrett, *Trade and Money*.

73. Vlami, *Trading with the Ottomans*, 276–79.

APPENDIX

1. BBA, Cevdet Adliye 85/5092. The church was probably Surp Krikor Lusaroviç (*Çirçis* in the document) in the Sultan Bayezid quarter. The document also contains the report of the kadi regarding the inspection of the church in the presence of the chief architect; the superintendent of the church, Artvin; the community leader, Kirkor; and the head monk as well as a group of Muslims and a government official. The report found damages to one room, a window, and a storage house of the church.

2. ISAM, Galata sicil series 14/479, 17b.

3. ISAM, Galata sicil series 14/469, 8a.

4. ISAM, Galata sicil series 14/469, 78a.

5. BBA, Cevdet Hariciye 3/106.

6. See Goffman, *Izmir and the Levantine World*, 87–89. Jews dominated the collection of customs dues in Izmir in the seventeenth century.

7. BBA, Cevdet Dahiliye 25/1229.

8. ISAM, Galata sicil series 14/542, 57b.

9. Register of Convicts in the Imperial Arsenal, D.BŞM.d 965, 2.

10. BBA, ADVN.DVE 100: 49.

11. ISAM, Galata sicil series 14/542, 56a.

BIBLIOGRAPHY

ARCHIVAL SOURCES

Başbakanlık Arşivi, Istanbul

Registers of Foreign Nations for France:
ADVN.DVE, Fransa (Bab-i Asafi Divan-i Hümayun Düvel-i Ecnebiye Kalemi) (Registers of Foreign Nations, France): vols. 100–137 (37 registers; each contains between 75 and 120 loose documents from 1750 to 1837); 438 (1794); 445 (1810); 455.

A.DVNE.d: (Bab-i Asafi Divan-i Hümayun Düvel-i Ecnebi Defterleri/Fransa Akham Defteri) (Registers of Imperial Orders in response to petitions from the French nation): (d. 1740–1816), 21/8, 29/4 (contains the French Ahdname of 1740), 29/4 (Fransa Nişan Defteri), 30/5, 31/6, 32/7, 34/9, 34/11, 35/2, 37/59, 39/5, 342/11.

Registers of Avrupa Merchants:
A.DVNE.TCR (Bab-i Asafi Divan-i Hümayun Avrupa Tüccar Defterleri), vols. 1–10 (1802–1817).

Cevdet Collection:
Cevdet Adliye (Judicial Affairs), CA, no./series 2/83, 1/79, 85/5092, 5176.

Cevdet Belediye (Municipal Affairs): CB, no./series 7/310, 7/312, 11/520, 11/523, 11/550, 11/528, 12/582, 11/598, 14/676, 15/582, 15/732, 15/738, 20/970, 21/1016, 22/1057, 25/1239, 25/1124, 47/1227, 950, 109/5420, 111/5514, 1207, 141/676, 1407, 5087, 6961.

Cevdet Hariciye (Foreign Affairs): C.HR, no./series 1/37, 3/106, 6/420, 11/5514, 12/585, 12/594, 14/668, 14/671, 14/689, 19/30, 26/1275, 60/2964, 82/4079, 82/4088, 94/4652, 96/4763, 96/4796, 97/4805, 97/4826, 98/4881, 98/4899, 99/4912, 99/4933, 99/4935, 100/4963, 101/5003, 101/5039, 102/5017, 102/5025, 102/5052, 102/5059, 103/5144, 103/5144, 103/5147, 103/5149, 104/5147, 105/5059, 121/6012, 145/7202, 146/7260, 146/7265, 146/7267, 146/7292, 147/7308, 147/7311, 147/7312, 155/7744, 156/7760, 156/7798, 157/7808.

Cevdet Iktisat (Financial and Economic Affairs): C.IKS, no./series 1/30, 2/56, 2/75, 2/81, 2/399, 2/735, 2/1075, 3/115, 3/118, 3/124, 3/129, 3/135, 3/136, 3/484, 3/1243, 4/187, 5/136, 5/158, 5/216, 5/222, 5/238, 6/252, 6/256, 6/268, 6/285, 6/291, 7/307, 7/310, 7/313, 7/314, 7/342, 7/344, 1622, 1633, 7/307, 7/309, 7/314, 7/342, 8/380, 8/384, 8/393, 8/396, 8/399, 9/426, 10/454, 10/454, 10/565, 11/530, 12/565, 12/594, 13/624, 20/110, 32/1594, 33/1633, 131, 426, 565.

Cevdet Maliye (Financial, Commercial, and Guild Affairs): CM, no./series 2/76, 3/74, 6147.

Cevdet Muallim: 1 and 3.

Cevdet Zabtiye (Police Collection): CZ, nos. 245, 556, 1747, 1833, 2557, 3199, 3365, 3662, 3709.

Baş Muhasebe Defterleri (Registers of Finance Department): vols. BŞM.d 06870, 41870.

Hatt-i Hümayun (Imperial Orders): Hat no./series 168/8378, 189/9076, 205/10749, 223/12431, 241/13537, 249/14140, 262, 267/15571, 267/15572..

Istanbul Ahkam Defterleri (Registers of Imperial Orders regarding Istanbul): vols. 8, 49.

Kalem-i Bahriye (Bureau of Naval Affairs): 5660.

Mühimme Defterleri (Registers of Important Affairs) MD: vols. 2, 3, 7, 19, 73, 74, 75, 85, 144, 149, 185.

Maliyeden Müdevver Defterleri (Registers of Financial Affairs): MAD.d 276, 451, 456, 2250, 3661, 1152, 1276, 1383, 2250, 10324, 11238, 14932, 18383, 23203, 110, 1152.

Nüfus Defterleri (Survey of artisans, shops and hans in Galata and Istanbul): NFS.d 6, 7, 14.

NFS.d 20 (List of Catholics in Galata, d. 1831): 54 (Muslim residents of villages on the European shore of the Bosphorus).

A.DVN.d (Survey of artisans in Galata and their guarantors): 832.

Tapu Tahrir Defterleri (Cadastral Surveys): TT.D vols. 210, 240, 889, 799.

Kamil Kepeci Defterleri (Kepeci Collection on surveys of population and migrants in the district of Galata): KK.d vols. 456, 2712.

KK 6290 (Survey of Greek and Armenian migrants into greater Istanbul), 6565, 5521, 1238.

KK (wine tax): 5170, 5221, 5228, 5482, 5483.

Customs Registers of Istanbul: A.DVN.DVE.d. 31/6. See also D.BŞM.d (Istanbul Baş Muhasebe Defteri) 4187; D.MMK.IGG.d. (Istanbul Gümrük Emini Defteri), series/no. 1232/1816; D.BŞM.IGE.d, 2062, 17170, and 17214; ADVN. NMH (Bab-i Asefi Mektubi Kalemi) 39/1.

AE. SAH.I no./series 168/11251.

AG.SABH.I no./series 168/11251.

A.AMD (Amedi Kalemi) 64/53 (Commercial Council).

A.DVN.MHM (Divan-i Hümayun Mühimme Kalemi) 31/32.

A.DVN.NMH (Bab-i Asafi Mektubi Name-yi Hümayun Kalemi): series/no. 43/7.

A.MKT.MHM (Bab-i Asafi Sadarat Mektubi Mühimme Kalemi): series/no. 347/53, 347/53.

A.MKT: 22/2.

A.MKT.MV (Bab-i Asafi Sadarat Mektubi Meclisi Vala Kalemi): series/no. 28/71.

A.MKT.UM (Bab-i Asafi Sadarat Mektubi Kalemi Umum Vilayat Kalemi): series/no. 161/3.

A.MKT (Bab-i Asafi Sadaret Mektubi Kalemi) 22/2.

D.BŞM.IGE 14/18, 20/62, 23/1.

DH.MKT (Dahiliye Mektubi Kalemi) series/no. 2239/10.

D.MMk.IGE.d (Istanbul Gümrük Emini Defteri): no. 23607.

I.HR (Irade Hariciye): series/no. 36/1648, 179/2892.

I.E. HR (Irade Hariciye): series/no. 10/1012.

MVL (Meclisi Vala), nos. 472/36, 871/21; I.MVL, 528/23718, 528.

Y. PRK. ŞH: (Yıdız Şehremaneti Muruzatı) series/no. 6/33, 6/40; Y.HUS 257/63.

Türkiye Diyanet Vakfı Islam Araştırmaları Merkezi (Islamic Research Center), Istanbul

Ser'iye Sicilleri (Islamic Court Records)
Istanbul series: 1/3, 1/24, 2/25, 2/126, 1/27, 1/30, 1/32, 1/43, 24/21.
Galata series: 14/1, 14/17, 14/90, 14/225, 14/249, 14/273, 14/249, 14/259, 14/267, 14/273, 14/274,14/275, 14/286, 14/314, 14/319, 14/337, 14/338, 14/343, 14/344, 14/378, 14/380, 14/381, 14/382, 14/384, 14/388, 14/390 14/391, 14/392, 14/393, 14/394, 13/395, 14/404, 14/407, 14/410, 14/432, 14/474, 14/479, 14/488, 14/450, 14/542, 14/535; 14/542, 14/544.
Üsküdar series: 2/2, 51/8.

Les archives de la chambre du commerce, Marseille, Provence (ACCM)

LIX series (files of letters from merchant houses in the Levant and from the Chamber), nos. 703, 704, 706, 707, 708, 710, 711, 712, 713, 714, 716, 718, 719, 720.
J series (files of embassy correspondence in Pera with the Chamber), nos. 1, 2, 3, 4, 22, 94, 95, 98, 102, 103, 104, 170, 171, 172, 173, 177, 180–211, 212, 177.

ABBREVIATIONS USED

EI: Encyclopedia of Islam
IA: Islam Ansiklopedisi
IJMES: International Journal of Middle Eastern Studies
ISAM Islam Araştırmaları Merkezi (Islamic Research Center in Istanbul)
TTK: Türk Tarih Kurumu

PUBLISHED TURKISH ARCHIVAL SOURCES

3 Numaralı Mühimme Defteri (966–968/1558–1560). Tıpkı Basım. Ankara: T.C. Başbakanlık Devlet Arşivleri Genel Müdürlüğü, 1993.

5 Numaralı Mühimme Defteri (973/1565–66).). Tıpkıbasım. Ankara: T.C. Başbakanlık Devlet Arşivleri Genel Müdürlüğü, 1994.

12 Numaralı Mühimme Defteri, 989–979/1570–1572.). Tıpkıbasım. Ankara: T.C. Başbakanlık Devlet Arşivleri Genel Müdürlüğü, 1996.

Akman, Mehmet, ed. *Istanbul Kadi Sicilleri, Galata Mahkemesi 32 Numaralı Sicil* (H. 1015–1016/1606–1607). Istanbul: ISAM Yayınları, 2011.

Akman, Mehmet, and Akıf Aydın, eds. *Galata Mahkemesi 5 Numaralı Sicil* (H. 983–984/M.1575–1576). Istanbul: ISAM Yayınları, 2011.

Aykut, Şevki Nezihi, ed. *Istanbul Mahkemesi 121 Numaralı Şer'iyye Sicili (1231–1232/1816–1817).* Istanbul: Sabancı Universitesi, 2006.

Coşkun, Yılmaz, T. Mert, and R. Günalan, eds. *Istanbul Kadı Sicilleri, Galata Mahkemesi 15 Numaralı Sicil (H. 961–1000/M. 1573–1591).* Istanbul: ISAM Yayınları, 2012.

Ertuğ, Nejdet. *Istanbul Mahkemesi 121 Numaralı Şeriyye Sicil (1231–1232/1816–1817).* Istanbul: Sabancı Universitesi Yayınları, 2006.

Günalan, Rifat. *Istanbul Kadi Sicilleri, Bab Mahkemesi 3 Numaralı Sicil (H. 1077/M. 1666–1667).* Istanbul: ISAM Yayınları, 2011.

Kal'a, Ahmet. *Istanbul Ahkam Defterleri, Istanbul Ticaret Tarihi, 1742–1779.* 2 vols. Istanbul: Istanbul Araştırmaları Merkezi, 1997.

———. *Istanbul Ahkam Defterleri, Istanbul Esnaf Tarihi.* 2 vols. Istanbul: Istanbul Araştırmaları Merkezi, 1997.

Tulum, Mertol. *Mühimme Defteri 90.* Istanbul: Türk Dünyası Araştırmaları Vakfi, 1993.

PUBLISHED WORKS AND DISSERTATIONS

Abulafia, David. *The Great Sea: A Human History of the Mediterranean.* Oxford: University of Oxford Press, 2011.

Abu-Lughod, Janet L. *Before the European Hegemony: The World System ad 1250–1350.* Oxford: Oxford University Press, 1991.

Ağır, Aygül. *Istanbul Eski Venedik Yerleşimi ve Dönüşümü.* Istanbul: Istanbul Araştırmaları Enstitüsu, 2009.

Agoston, Gabor. "Information, Ideology, and Limits of Imperial Policy: Ottoman Grand Strategy in the Context of Ottoman-Habsburg Rivalry." In Aksan and Goffman, *Early Modern Ottomans,* 75–103.

Akarlı, Engin. "Punishment, Repression, and Violence in the Marketplace: Istanbul, 1730–1840." In Faroqhi, *Bread from the Lion's Mouth,* 237–56.

Akın, Nur. *19. Yüzyılın Ikinci Yarısında Galata ve Pera.* Istanbul: Literatür Yayınları, 2011.

Aksan, Virginia. H. *An Ottoman Statesman in War and Peace: Ahmed Resmi Efendi, 1700–1783*. Leiden: E.J. Brill, 1995.

———. *Ottomans and Europeans: Contacts and Conflicts*. Istanbul: ISIS Press, 2004.

———. *Writing the Ottomans into World History*. Istanbul: Isis Press, 2016.

Aksan, Virginia H., and Daniel Goffman, eds. *The Early Modern Ottomans: Remapping the Empire*. Cambridge: Cambridge University Press, 2007.

Akyıldız, Ali. *Tanzimat Dönemi Osmanlı Merkez Teşkilatında Reform (1836–1856)*. Istanbul: Eren Yayıncılık, 1993.

Allom, Thomas, and Robert Walsh. *Constantinople and the Scenery of Seven Churches of Asia Minor, Illustrated by Thomas Allom*. London: Fisher and Son, 1839.

Anhegger, Robert, and Halil Inalcik. *Kanunname-i Sultani ber Muceb-i Orf-i Osmani*. Ankara: TTK, 1956.

Arbel, Benjamin. "Maritime Trade and International Relations in the Sixteenth-Century Mediterranean: The Case of the Ship *Girarda* (1575–1581)." In Costantini and Koller, *Ottoman Ecumenical Community*, 391–408.

———. *Trading Nations: Jews and Venetians in the Early Modern Eastern Mediterranean*. Leiden: E.J. Brill, 1995.

Archives Nationales. *Correspondance consulaire des ambassadeurs de France à Constantinople, 1668–1708*. Paris: Centre Historique des Archives Nationales, 1999.

Argenti, Philip P. *The Occupation of Chios by the Genoese and Their Administration of the Island, 1346–1566*. 2 vols. Cambridge: Cambridge University Press, 1958.

Artan, Tülay. "Arnavutköy." In *Dünden Bugüne Istanbul Ansiklopedisi*. Vol. 1, 313–14. Istanbul: Kültür Bakanlığı ve Tarih Vakfı, 1993.

———. "Beşiktaş." *Dünden Bugüne Istanbul Ansiklopedisi*. Vol. 1, 137–46. Istanbul: Kültür Bakanlığı ve Tarih Vakfı, 1993.

———. "The Palaces of the Sultanas." *Istanbul Dergisi* 2 (January 1993): 87–97.

Artunç, Cihan. "The Price of Legal Institutions: The Beratlı Merchants in the Eighteenth-Century Ottoman Empire." *Journal of Economic History* 75, no. 3 (2015): 720–48.

As'ad, Celal. *Eski Galata ve Binaları*. Istanbul, 1329/1911.

Aslanian, Sebouh David. *From the Indian Ocean to the Mediterranean: The Global Networks of Armenian Merchants from the New Julfa*. Berkeley: University of California Press, 2011.

Atcıl, Zahit. "State and Government in the Mid-Sixteenth Century Ottoman Empire: The Grand Vizierates of Rüstem Pasha (1544–1561)." PhD diss., University of Chicago, 2014.

Atsız, Bedriye, ed. *Ahmet Resmi Efendinin Viyana ve Berlin Sefaretnameleri*. Istanbul: Tercuman, 1980.

Avcıoğlu, Nebahat. *"Turquerie" and the Politics of Representation. 1728–1876*. London: Ashgate, 2011.

Aynural, Salih. *Istanbul Değirmenleri ve Fırınları*. Istanbul: Tarih Vakfi, 2002.

Babinger, Franz. *Mehmed the Conqueror and His Time*. Edited by William C. Hickman. Translated by Ralph Manheim. Princeton, NJ: Princeton University Press, 1978.

Bacqué-Grammont, Jean-Louis, Sinan Kuneralp, and Frédéric Hitzel, *Représentants Permanents de la France en Turquie (1536–1991) et de la Turquie en France* (1797–1991). Istanbul: ISIS Press, 1991.

Bağış. Ali. *Osmanlı Ticaretinde Gayri Müslimler*. Ankara: Turan Kitabevi, 1983.

Balard, Michel. *"La société pérote aux XIV–XVe siècles: Autour des demerode et des draperio."* In *Byzantine Constantinople: Monuments, Topography, and Everyday Life*, edited by Nevra Necipoğlu, 299–311. Leiden: E. J. Brill, 2001.

Barkey, Karen. *Empire of Difference: The Ottomans in a Comparative Perspective*. Cambridge: Cambridge University Press, 2008.

Baron de Tott. *Memoirs of Baron de Tott*. 2 vols. New York: Arno Press, 1973.

Barsoumian, Hagop. *"The Dual Role of the Armenian Amira Class in the Ottoman Government and the Armenian Millet (1750–1850)."* In *Christians and Jews in the Ottoman Empire: The Functioning of a Plural Society*, edited by Benjamin Braude and Bernard Lewis, 171–83. New York: Holmes and Meier, 1982.

Barthe, Pascale. *French Encounters with the Ottomans, 1510–1560*. London: Routledge, 2016.

Başdaş, Begüm. "Old Buildings/New Faces: Urban and Social Change in Galata, Istanbul–Turkey." Masters thesis, University of California–Riverside, 2001.

Bashkin, Orit. *The Other Iraq: Pluralism and Culture in Hashemite Iraq*. Stanford, CA: Stanford University Press, 2008.

Batu, Afife. "Ortaköy." *Dünden Bügüne Istanbul Ansiklopedisi*. Vol. 6, 141–43. Istanbul: Kültür Bakanlığı ve Tarih Vakfı, 1994.

Batu, H., and Jean-Louis Bacqué-Grammont. *L'Empire Ottoman: La Republique de Turquie et la France*. Istanbul: Éditions ISIS, 1986.

Baudin, Féréderic, ed. *Une Voyage a Smyrnie: Un manuscript d'Antoine Galland (1678)*. Paris: Chandeigne, 2000.

Behar, Cem. *A Neighborhood in Ottoman Istanbul: Fruit Vendors and Civil Servants in the Kasap Ilyas Mahalle*. New York: SUNY Press, 2003.

Benton, Lauren. *Law and Colonial Cultures: Legal Regimes in World History, 1400–1900*. Cambridge: Cambridge University Press, 2002.

Bertelé, Tommaso. *Venedik ve Kostantaniyye: Tarihte Osmanlı ve Venedik İlişkileri*. Translated by Mahmut H. Şarkioğlu. Istanbul: Yayınkitabevi, 2012.

Beydilli, Kemal. *Recognition of the Armenian Catholic Community and the Church in the Reign of Mahmud II (1830)*. Cambridge, MA: Department of NELC, Harvard University, 1995.

Bilici, Faruk. *La politique Française en Mer Noire, 1747–1789*. Istanbul: Éditions Isis, 1992.

———. *"L'Islam en France sous l'Ancien Régime et la Révolution: Attraction et repulsion."* *Rives Méditerranénnes* 14 (2003): 17–37.

———. *"Navigation et commerce en mer Noire pendant la guerre Ottomano-Russe de 1787-1792."* *Anatolia Moderna* 35 (1992): 261–77.

Bölükbaşı, Ömer Faruk. *"Napolyonun Işğalı Sırasında Bir Fransız: Benoit Astier ve Mallarının Müsaderesi."* In *Bir Insani-i Selim, Prof. Dr. Azmi Ozcan'a Armağan*, edited by R. Arıkan and H. Demiryürek, 555–88. Istanbul: Lotus Yayınevi, 2016.

Bonnac, Marquis de. *Mémoire Historique sur L'ambassade de France a Constantinople.* Paris, 1894.

Boogert, Maurits H. van den. *The Capitulations and the Ottoman Legal System: Qadis, Consuls, and Beratlis in the 18th Century.* Leiden: E. J. Brill, 2005.

———. "European Patronage in the Ottoman Empire: Anglo-Dutch Conflicts of Interest in Aleppo (1703–1755)." In Hamilton, De Groot, and van den Boogert, *Friends and Rivals* 187–221.

———. "Redress for Ottoman Victims of European Privateering." *Turcica* 33 (2001): 91–118.

Booth, Marylyn, ed. *Harem Histories: Envisioning Places and Living Spaces.* Durham, NC: Duke University Press, 2007.

Bostan, Idris. *Osmanlı Bahriye Teşkitaltı: XVII. Yüzyılında Tersane-i Amire.* Ankara: TTK 1992.

Bouquet, Olivier. *"Un grand vizier dans sa maison: Edition de trois inventaires après décès* (1785)." *Turcica* 47 (2016): 185–234.

Boyar, Ebru, and Kate Fleet. *A Social History of Ottoman Istanbul.* Cambridge: Cambridge University Press, 2010.

Braudel, Fernand. *The Mediterranean and the Mediterranean World in the Age of Philip II.* Translated by Sian Reynolds. 2 vols. New York: Harper Colophon Books, 1976.

———. *The Structures of Everyday Life: Civilization and Capitalism, 15th–18th Century.* 2 vols. New York: Harper & Row, 1979.

Brotton, Jerry. *The Sultan and the Queen: The Untold Story of Elizabeth and Islam.* New York: Penguin Books, 2017.

Brummett, Palmira. *Mapping the Ottomans: Sovereignty, Territory, and Identity in the Early Modern Mediterranean.* Cambridge: Cambridge University Press, 2015.

Bulunur, Kerim Ilker. *"II. Mehmed Tarafından Galatalılara Verilen 1453 Ahıdnamesi ve Buna Yapılan Eklemeler Hakkında Yeni Bilgiler."* *Tarih Dergisi* 50 (2009/2): 59–85.

———. *Osmanlı Galatası (1453–1600.)* Istanbul: Bilge, Kültür, Sanat, 2014.

Bulut, Mehmet. *Ottoman-Dutch Economic Relations in the Early Modern Period, 1571–1699.* Hilversum, The Netherlands: Veloren, 2001.

Cabi, Ömer Efendi. *Cabi Tarihi.* 2 vols. Ankara: TTK, 2003.

Çadırçı, Musa. *Tanzimat Döneminde Anadolu Kentleri'nin Sosyal ve Ekonomik Yapıları.* Ankara: TTK, 1991.

Canbakal, Hülya. *Society and Politics in an Ottoman Town: 'Ayntab in the Seventeenth Century.* Leiden: E. J. Brill, 2007.

Çantay, Gönül. *"Kurşunlu Han."* In *Dünden Bugüne Isltanbul Ansiklopedisi.* Vol. 5, 126–27. Istanbul: Kültür ve Tarıh Vakfı, 1994.

Carrière, Charles. *Négociants Marseillais au XVIIIe Siècle.* 2 vols. Marseille: Institute Historique de Provence, 1973.

Casale, Giancarlo. *The Ottoman Age of Exploration*. Oxford: Oxford University Press, 2010.

Casson, Lionel. *The Ancient Mariners: Seafarers and Sea Fighters of the Mediterranean in Ancient Times*. 2nd ed. Princeton, NJ: Princeton University Press, 1991.

Catlos, Brian A. *Infidel Kings and Unholy Warriors: Faith, Power, and Violence in an Age of Crusade and Jihad*. New York: Farrar, Strauss, and Giroux, 2014.

———. *Muslims of Medieval Latin Christendom, 1050–1614*. Cambridge: Cambridge University Press, 2014.

———. *The Victors and the Vanquished: Christians and Muslims of Catalonia and Aragon, 1050–1300*. Cambridge: Cambridge University Press, 2004.

Çelik, Zeynep. *Displaying the Orient: Architecture of Islam at Nineteenth-Century World's Fairs*. Berkeley: University of California Press, 1992.

———. *Empire, Architecture, and the City: French-Ottoman Encounters, 1830–1914*. Seattle: University of Washington Press, 2008.

———. *The Remaking of Istanbul: Portrait of an Ottoman City in the Nineteenth Century*. Seattle: University of Washington Press, 1986.

Çelik, Zeynep, Diane Favro, and Richard Ingersoll, eds. *Streets: Critical Perspectives on Public Space*. Berkeley: University of California Press, 1994.

Çesmi-Zade, Mustafa Reşid. *Çeşmi-zade Tarihi*. Istanbul: Istanbul Fethi Cemiyeti, 1993.

Çetinkaya, Haluk. "Arap Camii in Istanbul: Its Architecture and Frescoes." *Anatolia Antiqua* 18 (2010): 169–88.

Charrière, E. *Négociants de la France dans le Levant*. 4 vols. Paris: Impriméries Nationale, 1848.

Chaudhuri, K. N. *Asia Before Europe: Economy and Civilization of the Indian Ocean from the Rise of Islam to 1750*. Cambridge: Cambridge University Press, 1994.

———. *Trade and Civilization in the Indian Ocean: An Economic History from the Rise of Islam to 1750*. Cambridge: Cambridge University Press, 1993.

Choiseul-Gouffier, Marie-Gabriel-Auguste-Florent, Comte de. *Voyage pittoresque dans l'empire Ottoman en Grèce, dans la Troade, les iles de l'Archipel et sur les cotes de l'Asie-mineur*. Paris, 1842.

Çizakça, Murat. *Comparative Evolution of Business Partnerships: The Islamic World and Europe, with Specific References to Ottoman Archives*. Leiden: E. J. Brill, 1996.

———. "The Ottoman Government and Economic Life: Taxation, Public Finance, and Trade Controls." In *The Cambridge History of Turkey, 1453–1603*. Vol. 2, *The Ottoman Empire as a World Power, 1453–1603*, edited by Suraiya N. Faroqhi and Kate Fleet, 195–213. Cambridge: Cambridge University Press, 2013.

Çizakça, Murat, and Macit Kenanoğlu. "Ottoman Merchants and the Jurisprudential Shift Hypothesis." In Faroqhi and Veinstein, *Merchants in the Ottoman Empire*, 195–213. Paris: Peeters, 2008.

Clancey-Smith, Julia. *Mediterraneans: North Africa and Europe in an Age of Migration, c. 1800–1900*. Berkeley: University of California Press, 2011.

Cole, Charles Woosley. *French Mercantilism, 1683–1700*. New York: Columbia University Press, 1943.

Cole, Juan. *Napoleon's Egypt: Invading the Middle East.* New York: St. Martin's–Griffin, 2008.

Coller, Ian. "East of Enlightenment: Regulating Cosmopolitanism between Istanbul and Paris in the Eighteenth Century." *Journal of World History* 21, no. 3 (2010): 447–69.

Constable, Olivia Remie. *Trade and Traders in Muslim Spain: The Commercial Realignment of the Iberian Peninsula, 900–1500.* Cambridge: Cambridge University Press, 1996.

Constantinople and the Seven Churches of Asia Minor. Illustrations by Thomas Allom. Descriptions by Robert Walsh and J. C. M. Bellew. Edited and introduced by Mark Wilson. NJ: Gorgias Press, 2006.

Cora, Yaşar Tolga. "A Muslim Great Merchant (*Tüccar*) Family in the Late Ottoman Empire: A Case Study of the Nemlizades, 1860–1930." *International Journal of Turkish Studies* 19, nos. 1–2 (2013): 1–29.

Coşgel, Metin, and Boğaç A. Ergene. *The Economics of Ottoman Justice: Settlement and Trial in the Shari'a Courts.* Cambridge: Cambridge University Press, 2016.

Costantini, Vera, and Markus Koller, eds. *Living in the Ottoman Ecumenical Community: Essays in Honour of Suraiya Faroqhi.* Leiden: E. J. Brill, 2008.

Crowley, Roger. *Empires of the Sea.* New York: Random House, 2008.

Curoing, Jonathan. *Edward Wortley Montagu, 1713–76: The Man in the Iron Wing Biography.* London, 1854.

Curtin, Philip D. *Cross-Cultural Trade in World History.* Cambridge: Cambridge University Press, 1984.

Dallaway, James. *Constantinople, Ancient and Modern, with Excursions to the Shores and Islands of the Archipelago and to the Troad.* London, 1797.

Dankoff, Robert. *An Ottoman Mentality: The World of Evliya Çelebi.* Leiden: E. J. Brill, 2004.

Dankoff, Robert, and Sooyong Kim. *An Ottoman Traveler: Selections from the Book of Travels of Evliya Çelebi.* London: Eland, 2010.

D'Arcier, A. F. *Les oubliés de la liberté: Négociants, consuls, et missionaires Français au Levant pendant la Révolution, 1784–1798.* Bruxelles: PIE, Peter Lang, 2007.

Darling, Linda T. "Capitulations." In *The Oxford Encyclopedia of the Modern Islamic World,* 257–60. Oxford: Oxford University Press, 1995.

———. *A History of Global Justice and Political Power in the Middle East: The Circle of Justice from Mesopotamia to Globalization.* London: Routledge, 2013.

———. "Ottoman Customs Registers (*Gümrük Defterleri*) as Sources for Global Exchange and Interaction." *Review of Middle East Studies* 40, no. 1 (February 2015): 3–22.

Davis, Ralph. "English Imports from the Middle East, 1580–1780." In *Studies in the Economic History of the Middle East: From the Rise of Islam to the Present,* edited by Michael A. Cook, 193–206. London: Oxford University Press, 1970.

Davis, Ralph. *English Overseas Trade, 1500–1700.* London: Macmillan, 1973.

De Groot, Alexander H. "The Development of the Capitulatory Regime in the Ottoman Middle East from the Fifteenth to the Nineteenth Centuries." *Oriente Moderno*, n.s., 22 (83), no. 3 (2003): 575–604.

———. "Dragoman's Careers: The Change of Status in Some Families Connected with the British and Dutch Embassies at Istanbul, 1783–1829." In Hamilton, De Groot, and van den Boogert, *Friends and Rivals*, 223–46. Leiden: E.J. Brill, 2009.

———. *The Netherlands and Turkey: Four Hundred Years of Political, Economic, and Cultural Relations*. Istanbul: ISIS Press, 2009.

Demirtaş, Mehmet. *Osmanlıda Fırıncılık*. Istanbul: Kitab Yayınevi, 2008.

Dönmez, Ahmet. *Osmanlı Modernleşmesinde İngliz Etkisi: Diplomasi ve Reform (1833–1841*. Istanbul: Kitabevi Yayınları, 2014.

Do Paço, David. "Eighteenth-Century Central Europe in Transcontinental Trade: The Trading Company of Molla Mustafa and the Viennese Conscription of 1767." In *Economy and Society in Central and Eastern Europe: Territory, Population, Consumption: Papers of the International Conference Held in Alba Iulia, April 25–27, 2013*, edited by Daniel Dumitran and Valer Moga, 31–42. Berlin: Lit Verlag, 2013.

———. "Trans-Imperial Familiarity: Ottoman Ambassadors in Eighteenth-Century Vienna." In *Practices of Diplomacy in the Early Modern World, c. 1410–1800*, edited by Tracey A. Sowerby and Jan Hennings, 166–84. London: Routledge, 2017.

Doumani, Beshara. *Rediscovering Palestine: Merchants and Peasants in Jabal Nablus, 1700–1900*. Berkeley: University of California Press, 1995.

Duben, Alan, and Cem Behar. *Istanbul Households: Marriage, Family, and Fertility, 1880–1940*. Cambridge: Cambridge University Press, 1991.

Dunn, Ross E. *The Adventures of Ibn Battuta, a Muslim Traveler of the 14th Century*. Berkeley: University of California Press, 2005.

Dursteler, Eric R. "Commerce and Coexistence: Veneto-Ottoman Trade in the Early Modern Era." *Turcica* 34 (2002): 105–33.

———. "A Continual Tavern in My House": Food and Diplomacy in Early Modern Constantinople." In *Renaissance Studies in Honor of Joseph Connors*, edited by M. Israel and L. Waldman. Vol. 2, 166–71. Cambridge, MA: Harvard University Press, 2013.

———. "Fearing the 'Turk' and Feeling the Spirit: Emotions and Conversion in the Early Modern Mediterranean." *Journal of Religious Studies* 39, no. 4 (December 2015): 484–505.

———. "Latin-Rite Christians in Early Modern Istanbul." In *Osmanlı Istanbulu*, edited by Feridun M. Emecen and Emrah S. Gürkan. Vol. 1, 127–46. Istanbul: Büyükşehir Belediyesi Yayınları, 2013.

———. *Renegade Women: Gender, Identity, and Boundaries in the Early Modern Mediterranean*. Baltimore: Johns Hopkins University Press, 2011.

———. *Venetians in Constantinople: Nation, Identity, and Coexistence in the Early Modern Mediterranean*. Baltimore: Johns Hopkins University Press, 2006.

Eldem, Edhem. *Bankalar Caddesi: Osmanlı'dan Günümıze Voyvoda Caddesi*. Istanbul: Osmanlı Bankası, 2000.

———. "Capitulations and Western Trade." In *The Cambridge History of Turkey, 1603–1839*, edited by Suraiya Faroqhi. Vol. 3, 283–336. Cambridge: Cambridge University Press, 2006.

———. *Death and Its Rituals in Ottoman-Islamic Culture.* Istanbul: Ottoman Bank Archives and Research Centre, 2005.

———. "The French Nation of Constantinople in the Eighteenth Century as Reflected in the Saints Peter and Paul Parish Records, 1740–1800." In Lorcin and Shepard, *French Mediterraneans,* 131–68. Lincoln: Nebraska University Press, 2016.

———. *French Trade in Istanbul in the Eighteenth Century.* Leiden: E.J. Brill, 1999.

———. *A History of the Ottoman Bank.* Istanbul: Ottoman Bank, 1999.

———. "Istanbul as a Cosmopolitan City: Myths and Realities." In *A Companion to Diaspora and Transnationalism,* edited by Ato Quayson and Girish Daswani, 212–30. Oxford: Blackwell, 2013.

———. "Istanbul: From Imperial to Peripheralized Capital." In Eldem, Goffman, and Masters, *Ottoman City,* 188–94. Cambridge: Cambridge University Press, 1999.

———. "(A Quest for) the Bourgeoisie of Istanbul: Identities, Roles, and Conflicts." In Freitag and and Lafi, *Urban Governance,* 159–87.

Eldem, Edhem, Daniel Goffman, and Bruce Masters, eds. *The Ottoman City between East and West: Aleppo, Izmir, and Istanbul.* Cambridge: Cambridge University Press, 1999.

Emiralioğlu, Pinar. *Geographical Knowledge and Imperial Culture in the Early Modern Ottoman Empire.* London: Ashgate, 2014.

Epstein, Mark Alan. *The Ottoman Jewish Communities and Their Role in the Fifteenth and Sixteenth Centuries.* Freiburg, Germany: K. Schwarz, 1980.

Epstein, Mortimer. *The Early History of the Levant Company.* London: George Routledge and Sons, 1908.

Erdbrink, Bosscha. *At the Threshold of Felicity: Ottoman-Dutch Relations during the Embassy of Cornelis Calkoen at the Sublime Porte, 1726–1744.* Ankara: TTK, 1975.

Ergin, Osman Nuri. *Mecelle-i Umur-i Belediyye.* Vol. 6. Istanbul: Büyükşehir Belediyesi, 1995.

Ergüder, Başak. *Galata Hanları (1868–1945)–Paranın Serüveni.* Istanbul: SAV, 2011.

Erkut, G., and Shirazi, R.M. *Dimensions of Urban Re-Development: The Case of Beyoğlu, Istanbul.* Berlin: N.p., 2014.

Eroğlu, Özkan. *Suriçi Galata.* Istanbul: Tekhne Yayınları, 2015.

Ersoy, Ahmet. *Architecture and the Late Ottoman Historical Geography: Reconfiguring the Architectural Past in a Modernizing Empire.* London: Routledge, 2015.

———. "Architecture and the Search for Ottoman Origins in the Tanzimat Period." *Muqarnas* 24 (2017): 116–39.

Extremera Extremera, Miguel Angel. "A Forced Migration: Spanish Moriscos in Ottoman Lands (16th–18th Centuries)." *Turcica* 45 (2014): 61–77.

Eyice, Semavi. "Arap Cami'i." In *Dünden Bugüne Istanbul Ansikopedisi.* Vol. 1, 294–95. Istanbul: Kültür Bakanlığı ve Tarih Vakfı, 1993.

————. "Galata *Bedesteni*." In *Dünden Bugüne Isltanbul Ansiklopedisi.* Vol. 3, 355–56. Istanbul: Kültür ve Tarıh Vakfı, 1994.

Faroqhi, Suraiya. *Another Mirror for Princes: The Public Image of the Ottoman Sultans and Its Reception.* Istanbul: ISIS Press, 2008.

————. *Artisans of Empire: Crafts and Craftspeople under the Ottomans.* London: I. B. Tauris, 2009.

————. "Before 1600: Ottoman Attitudes towards Merchants from Christendom." *Turcica* 34 (2002): 69–104.

————, ed. *Bread from the Lion's Mouth: Artisans Struggling for a Livelihood in Ottoman Cities.* Oxford: Berghahn Books, 2015.

————. "Did Cosmopolitanism Exist in Eighteenth-Century Istanbul? Stories of Christian and Jewish Artisans." In *Urban Governance under the Ottomans,* edited by Ulrike Freitagand Nora Lafi, 21–37. London: Routledge, 2014.

————. "The Venetian Presence in the Ottoman Empire." *Journal of Ottoman Economic History* 15 (1986): 345–84.

Faroqhi, Suraiya, and R. Deguilhem, eds. *Crafts and Craftsmen of the Middle East: Fashioning the Individual in the Muslim Mediterranean.* Cambridge: Cambridge University Press, 2005.

Faroqhi, Suraiya, Bruce McGowen, Donald Quataert, and Şevket Pamuk, eds. *An Economic and Social History of the Ottoman Empire, 1600–1914.* Vol. 2. Cambridge: Cambridge University Press, 1997.

Faroqhi, Suraiya, and Giles Veinstein, eds. *Merchants in the Ottoman Empire.* Paris: Peeters, 2008.

Fattah, Hala. *The Politics of Regional Trade in Iraq, Arabia, and the Gulf, 1745–1900.* New York: SUNY Press, 1997.

Finkel, Caroline. *Osman's Dream: The History of the Ottoman Empire.* New York: Basic Books, 2005.

Firges, Pascal W. *French Revolutionaries in the Ottoman Empire: Diplomacy, Political Culture, and the Limiting of Universal Revolution, 1792–1798.* Oxford: Oxford University Press, 2017.

————. "French Revolutionary Politics and Culture in the Ottoman Empire, 1792–1798." PhD diss., University of Heidelberg, 2014.

Firges, Pascal W., Tobias P. Graf, Christian Roth, and Gülay Tulasoğlu, eds. *Well-Connected Domains: Towards an Entangled Ottoman History.* Leiden: E. J. Brill, 2017.

Flachat, J. C. *Observations sur le commerce et les arts d'une parties de l'Europe, de l'Asie, de l'Afrique et même des Indes Orientales.* Lyons, 1766.

Fleet, Kate. *European and Islamic Trade in the Early Ottoman State: The Merchants of Genoa and Turkey.* Cambridge: Cambridge University Press, 1999.

Fleet, Kate, and Svetla Ivaneva. *Ottoman Economic Practices in Periods of Transformation: The Cases of Crete and Bulgaria.* Ankara: TTK, 2014.

Frangakis-Syrett, Elena. *The Commerce of Smyrna in the Eighteenth Century, 1700–1820.* Athens: Center for Asia Minor Studies, 1992.

————. "Implementation of the Anglo-Turkish Convention on Izmir's Trade: European and Minority Merchants." *New Perspectives on Turkey* 7 (Spring 1992): 91–112.

———. *Trade and Money: The Ottoman Economy in the Eighteenth and Early Nineteenth Centuries*. Istanbul: Isis Press, 2007.

———. "The Trade of Cotton and Cloth in Izmir: From the Second Half of the Eighteenth Century to the Early Nineteenth Century." In *Landholding and Commercial Agriculture in the Middle East,* edited by Çağlar Keyder and Faruk Tabak, 97–111. New York: SUNY Press, 1991.

Frazee, Charles A. *Catholics and the Sultan: The Church and the Ottoman Empire*. New York: Columbia University Press, 1983.

Freely, John. *Istanbul, the Imperial City*. New York: Viking Press, 1996.

Freely, John, and Brendan Freely. *Galata, Pera, Beyoğlu: Bir Biyografi*. Istanbul: Yapı Kredi Yayınları, 2014.

———. *A Guide to Beyoğlu*. Istanbul: Archeology and Art Publications, 2006.

Freitag, Ulrike, and Nora Lafi, eds. *Urban Governance under the Ottomans: Between Cosmopolitanism and Conflict*. London: Routledge, 2014.

Fuhrman, Malte. "'Western Perversions' at the Threshold of Felicity: The European Prostitutes of Galata–Pera (1870–1915)." *History and Anthropology* 21, no. 2 (June 2010): 159–72.

Fukasawa, Katsumi. *Toileries et commerce du Levant: d'a Alep a Marseille*. Paris: Édition du Centre National de la Recherche Scientifique, 1987.

Galland, Antoine. *Istanbul'a Ait Günlük Anılar (1672–1675)*. Translated by Nahid Sirri Örik. 2 vols. Ankara: TTK, 1998.

———. *Journal d'Antoine Galland pendant son séjour à Constantinople (1672–1673)*. Paris, 1881.

———. *Voyage inédit: Smyrne ancienne et modern*. Tome I. Paris: Honoré Champion, 2001.

Games, Alison. *The Web of Empire: English Cosmopolitans in an Age of Expansion, 1560–1660*. Oxford: Oxford University Press, 2008.

Garcia, Arenal, and Gerard Wiegers. *The Expulsion of Moriscos from Spain: A Mediterranean Diaspora*. Translated by Consuela Lopez-Morillas. Leiden: E.J. Brill, 2014.

Gedikli, Fethi. *Osmanlı Şirket Kültürü: XVI–XVII. Yuzyıllarda Mudarebe Uygulaması*. Istanbul: IZ Yayıncılık, 1998.

———. "Ottoman Companies in the 16th and 17th Centuries." In *The Great Ottoman-Turkish Civilization,* edited by Kemal Çiçek. Vol. 2, 185–95. Ankara: 2000.

———. "16.Ve 17. Asır Osmanlı Şeʾiyye Sicillerinde Mudarebe Ortaklığı: Galata Orneği." PhD diss., Marmara University, Istanbul, 1996.

Genç, Mehmet. *Osmanlı Imparatorluğunda Devlet ve Ekonomi*. Istanbul: Ötüken, 2003.

———. "Ottoman Industry in the Eighteenth Century: General Framework, Characteristics, and Main Trends." In *Manufacturing in the Ottoman Empire and Turkey, 1500–1950,* edited by Donald Quataert, 59–86. New York: SUNY Press, 1994.

Gerber, Haim. *Economy and Society in an Ottoman City: Bursa, 1600–1700*. Jerusalem: Hebrew University, 1988.

————. "Jews and Money-Lending in the Ottoman Empire." *Jewish Quarterly Review,* n.s., 72, no. 2 (October 1981): 100–118.

Gibson, Lela. "Ottoman Sufism, Orientalism, and German Politics, 1770–1825," PhD diss., UCLA, 2015.

Ginio, Eyal. "Piracy and Redemption in the Aegean Sea during the First Half of the Eighteenth Century." *Turcica* 33 (2001): 135–47.

Girardelli, Paolo. "Architecture, Identity, and Liminality: On the Use and Meaning of Catholic Spaces in Late Ottoman Istanbul." *Muqarnas* 22 (2005): 233–64.

————. "Between Rome and Istanbul: Architecture and Material Culture of a Franciscan Mission in the Ottoman Capital." *Journal of Mediterranean Studies* 18 (2010): 162–88.

————. "Ottoman Roots, European Developments: Comparing the French and Venetian Palaces in Beyoğlu." In *14th International Congress of Turkish Art Proceedings,* edited by Frédéric Hitzel, 357–62. Paris: Collège de France, 2013.

————. "Power or Leisure? Remarks on the Architecture of the European Summer Embassies on the Bosphorus Shore." *New Perspectives on Turkey* 50 (2013): 29–57.

Göçek, Fatma Müge. *East Encounters West: France and the Ottoman Empire in the Eighteenth Century.* New York: Oxford University Press, 1987.

————. *Rise of the Bourgeoisie, Demise of Empire: Ottoman Westernization and Social Change.* Oxford: Oxford University Press, 1996.

Goffman, Daniel. *Britons in the Ottoman Empire, 1642–1660.* Seattle: University of Washington Press, 1998.

————. *Izmir and the Levantine World, 1550–1650.* Seattle: University of Washington Press, 1990.

————. "Negotiating the Renaissance State: The Ottoman Empire and the New Diplomacy." In Aksan and Goffman, *Early Modern Ottomans,* 61–74.

————. *The Ottoman Empire and Early Modern Europe.* Cambridge: Cambridge University Press, 2002.

Goitein, Solomon. *A Mediterranean Society: The Jewish Communities of the Arab World as Portrayed in the Documents of the Cairo Geniza.* 3 vols. Berkeley: University of California Press, 1967.

Gökbilgin, M. Tayyib. *"Venedik Devlet Arşivindeki Vesikalar Kulliyatında Kanuni Sultan Süleyman Devri Belgeleri."* *Belgeler* 1 (1964): 1–151.

Graf, Tobias P. *The Sultan's Renegades: Christian-European Converts to Islam and the Making of the Ottoman Elite, 1575–1610.* Oxford: Oxford University Press, 2017.

Green, Nile. *Bombay Islam: The Religious Economy of the West Indian Ocean, 1840–1915.* New York: Cambridge University Press, 2011.

————. "Maritime Worlds and Global History: Comparing the Mediterranean and Indian Oceans through Barcelona and Bombay." *History Compass* 11, no.7 (2013): 513–23.

————. *Terrains of Exchange: Religious Economies of Global Islam.* Oxford: Oxford University Press, 2015.

Greene, Molly. *Catholic Pirates and Greek Merchants: A Maritime History of the Early Modern Mediterranean* (Princeton, NJ: Princeton University Press, 2010.

——. "The Ottomans in the Mediterranean." In Aksan and Goffman, *Early Modern Ottomans,* 104–17.

——. *A Shared World: Christians and Muslims in the Early Modern Mediterranean.* Princeton, NJ: Princeton University Press, 2000.

Green-Mercado, Mayra T. "The Mahdi in Valencia: Messianism, Apocalypticism, and Morisco Rebellions in Late Sixteenth-Century Spain." *Medieval Encounters* 19, nos. 1–2 (2013), 193–220.

——. "Morisco Apocalypticism: Politics of Prophecy in the Early Modern Mediterranean." PhD diss., University of Chicago, 2012.

Greenwood, Anthony. "Istanbul's Meat Provisioning: A Study of the *Çelebkeşan* System." PhD diss., University of Chicago, 1988.

Gül, Murat. *The Emergence of Modern Istanbul: Transformation and Modernization of a City* London: I. B. Tauris, 2012.

Gümüş, Şenay Özdemir. *"Napolyon'un Mısır'in Işğalı Sırasında Osmanlı Topraklarındaki Fransızlar." Tarihin Peşinde* 9 (2013): 249–78.

Gürkan, Emrah Safa. "Espionage in the 16th Century Mediterranean: Secret Diplomacy, Mediterranean Go-Betweens, and the Ottoman-Habsburg Rivalry." PhD diss., Georgetown University, 2012.

——. "Mediating Boundaries: Mediterranean Go-Betweens and Cross-Confessional Diplomacy in Constantinople, 1560–1600." *Journal of Early Modern History* 19 (2015): 107–28.

——. *Sultanın Casusları: 16. Yüzyılda Istıhbarat, Sabotaj ve Rüşvet Ağları.* Istanbul: Kronik Kitab, 2017.

——. "Touting for Patrons, Brokering Power, and Trading Information: Trans-Imperial Jews in Sixteenth-Century Istanbul." In *Detras de las apariencias: Informacion y espionagje (siglos XVI–XVII),* edited by Emilio Sola Castano and Gennaro Varriale, 127–53. Alcala, Spain: Universidad de Alcala, 2015.

Hamadeh, Sherine. *The City's Pleasures: Istanbul in the Eighteenth Century.* Seattle: University of Washington Press, 2008.

——. "Ottoman Expression of Early Modernity and the 'Inevitable' Question of Westernization." *Journal of the Society of Architectural Historians* 63, no. 1 (March 2004), 32–51.

Hanna, Nelly. *Making Big Money in 1600: The Life and Times of Isma'il Abu Taqiyya, Egyptian Merchant.* Syracuse, NY: Syracuse University Press, 1998.

Hanssen, Jens. *Fin de Siècle Beirut: The Making of an Ottoman Provincial Capital.* Oxford: Oxford University Press, 2005.

Hathaway, Jane. *The Arab Lands under Ottoman Rule, 1516–1800.* London: Pearson Longman, 2008.

Hattox, Ralph. *Coffee and Coffeehouses: The Origins of a Social Beverage in the Medieval Near East.* Seattle: University of Washington Press, 1985.

Hess, Andrew C. *The Forgotten Frontier: A History of the Sixteenth-Century Ibero-African Frontier.* Chicago: University of Chicago Press, 1983.

Heyd, Uriel. "The Jewish Communities of Istanbul in the Seventeenth Century." *Oriens* 6, no. 2 (December 1953): 299–314.

Hitzel, Frédéric. "*Étienne-Félix Hénin, un Jacobin à Constantinople* (1793–1795)." *Anatolia Moderna* 33 (1991): 33–46.

Hitzel, Frédéric, and Abderrahim Ben Hadda. "*Les relations Franco-Ottomanes a tracers les Name-i Hümayun du Başbakanlık Arşivi.*" *Anatolia Moderna* 35 (1992): 247–60.

Hodgson, Marshall G. S. *The Venture of Islam: Conscience in a World Civilization.* Vol. 2. London: University of Chicago Press, 1977.

Horden, Peregrine, and Nicholas Purcell. *The Corrupting Sea: A Study of Mediterranean History.* Oxford: Blackwell, 2000.

Horn, Jeff. "Lessons from the Levant: Early Modern French Economic Development in the Mediterranean." *French History* 29, no. 1(2015): 76–92.

Hovhannesyan, Sarkis Sarraf. *Payitaht-i Istanbul'un Tarihçesi.* Translated by Elmon Hançer. Istanbul: Tarih Vakfı Yurt Yaınları, 1997.

Hurewitz, J. C. *Diplomacy in the Near and Middle East.* 2 vols. Princeton, NJ: Van Nostrand, 1956.

Husain A. and K. Flemming. Eds. *A Faithful Sea: The Religious Cultures of the Mediterranean.* Oxford: Oxford University Press, 2007.

Ibn Battuta. *Travels in Asia and Africa, 1325–1354.* London: Routledge and Kegan Paul, 1983.

Inalcik, Halil. "Capital Formation in the Ottoman Empire." *Journal of Economic History* 24, no. 1 (1989): 97–140.

———. "The Conqueror, the Conquest, and the Reconstruction of Constantinople." In *Istanbul, World City,* edited by Afife Batur, 22–38. Istanbul: Tarih Vakfı Yayınları, n.d.

———. *Devlet-i 'Aliyye.* 2 vols. Istanbul: Türkiye Iş Bankası Kültür Yayınları, 2014.

———. *An Economic and Social History of the Ottoman Empire.* Vol. 1, *1300–1600.* Cambridge: Cambridge University Press, 1997.

———. "Foundations of Ottoman-Jewish Cooperation." In *Jews, Turks, Ottomans: A Shared History, Fifteenth Century through the Twentieth Century,* edited by Avigdor Levey. Syracuse, NY: Syracuse University Press, 2002.

———. "Galata, *Osmanlı Dönemi.*" In *Dünden Bugüne Isltanbul Ansiklopedisi.* Vol. 3, 348–54. Istanbul: Kültür ve Tarıh Vakfı, 1994.

———. "The Hub of the City: The *Bedestan* of Istanbul." *International Journal of Turkish Studies* 1 (1980): 1–17.

———. "Imtiyazat." *Encyclopedia of Islam.* 2nd ed. Vol. 3, 1179–89. Leiden: E. J. Brill, 1971.

———. "Imtiyazat." *Islam Ansiklopedisi.* Vol. 22, 282–88. Istanbul: Türkiye Diyanet Vakfi, 2000.

———. "Istanbul, an Islamic City." In *Essays in Ottoman History,* edited by Halil Inalcik, 247–71. Istanbul: Eren, 1998.

———. *Kuruluş Dönemi (1302–1481) Osmanlı Sultanları.* Istanbul: ISAM Yayınları, 2013.

———. *Osmanlı Idare ve Ekonomi Tarihi.* Istanbul: ISAM Yayınları, 2011.

———. "The Ottoman Cotton Market and India: The Role of Labor Cost in Market Competition." In *The Middle East and the Balkans under the Ottoman Empire: Essays on Economy and Society,* edited by Halil Inalcik, 264–306. Bloomington: Indiana University Turkish Studies, 1993.

———. *The Ottoman Empire during The Classical Age, 1300–1600.* London: Phoenix, 2000.

———. "Ottoman Galata." In *Essays in Ottoman History,* edited by Halil Inalcik, 275–376. Istanbul: Eren, 1998.

———. "Ottoman Galata, 1453–1553." In *Première rencontre internationale sur l'empire Ottoman et la Turquie modern,* edited by Edhem Eldem, 17–116. Istanbul: Isis Press, 1991.

———. "The Policy of Mehmed II toward the Greek Population of Istanbul and the Byzantine Buildings of the City." *Dumbarton Oaks Papers* 23 (1969–70): 229–49.

———. *Sources and Studies on the Ottoman Black Sea.* Vol. 1, *The Customs Registers of Caffa, 1487–1490.* Cambridge, MA: Harvard University Ukrainian Research Institute, 1996.

———. *Studies in the History of Textiles in Turkey.* Istanbul: Türkiye Iş Bankası Kültür Yayınları, 2011.

———. *The Survey of Istanbul, 1455.* Istanbul: Türkiye Iş Bankası Yayınları, 2012.

Inalcik, Halil, and Rhoads Murphey, trans. *The History of Mehmed the Conqueror, by Tursun Beg.* Minneapolis: Bibliotheca Islamica, 1978.

Iogra, Nicolae. *Points de vue sur l'histoire du commerce de L'Orient a l'époque modern.* Paris: Gamber, 1925.

Ipek, Nurhan. *Selanik ve Istanbul'da Yahudi Bankerler.* Istanbul: Yeditepe, 2011.

Isin, Ekrem. "Galata *Mevlevihanesi." Dünden Bugüne Istanbul Ansiklopedisi.* Vol. 3, 362–64. Istanbul: Kültür Bakanlığı ve Tarih Vakfı, 1993.

Islamoğlu, Huri. *Constituting Modernity: Private Property in the East and West.* London: I. B. Tauris: 2004.

———. *The Ottoman Empire and the World Economy.* Cambridge: Cambridge University Press, 1987.

———. *Ottoman History as World History.* Istanbul: ISIS Press, 2007.

———. "A Proposal for Global Economic History: Beyond the Histories of Stagnation and Deficiencies to 'Living' Histories of Possibilities." In Karahasanoğlu and Demir, *History from Below,* 189–96.

Islamoğlu, Huri, and Peter C. Perdu, eds. *Shared Histories of Modernity: China, India, and the Ottoman Empire.* London: Routledge, 2009.

Isom-Verhaaren, Christine. *Allies with the Infidel: The Ottoman Empire and the French Alliance in the Sixteenth Century.* London: I. B. Tauris, 2011.

———. "Royal French Women in the Sultan's Harem: The Political Uses of Fabricated Accounts from the Sixteenth to the Twenty-First Century." *Journal of World History* 17, no. 2 (2006): 159–96.

Isom-Verhaaren, Christine, and Kent F. Schull, eds. *Living in the Ottoman Realm: Empire and Identity, 13th to 20th Centuries.* Bloomington: Indiana University Press, 2016.

Itzkowitz, Norman, and Max Mote. *Mubadele: An Ottoman-Russian Exchange of Ambassadors.* Chicago: University of Chicago Press, 1970.

Jacoby, David. "The Urban Evolution of Latin Constantinople (1204–1261)." In *Byzantine Constantinople: Monuments, Topography, and Everyday Life,* edited by Nevra Necipoğlu, 277–97. Leiden: E. J. Brill, 2001.

Jennings, Ronald C. *Christians and Muslims in Ottoman Cyprus and the Mediterranean World, 1571–1640.* New York: NYU Press, 1993.

Jensen, De Lamar. "The Ottoman Turks in Sixteenth-Century French Diplomacy." *Sixteenth Century Journal* 16, no. 4 (1985): 451–70.

Johnson, Brian. "Istanbul's Vanished City of the Dead." In *Efsanelerden Günümüze Istanbul, Seçme Yazılar 1: Myth to Modernity, Selected Themes,* edited by Nezih Başgelen and Brian Johnson, 93–104. Istanbul: Arkeoloji Sanat Yayınları, 2002.

Jordan, David P. *Transforming Paris: The Life and Labors of Baron Haussman* New York: Free Press, 1995.

Kadi, Ismail Hakki. *Ottoman and Dutch Merchants in the Eighteenth Century: Competition and Cooperation in Ankara, Izmir, and Amsterdam.* Leiden: E. J. Brill, 2012.

Kafadar, Cemal. "A Death in Venice (1575): Anatolian Muslim Merchants Trading in the Serrinissima." *Journal of Turkish Studies* 10 (1996): 191–218.

Kafesçioğlu, Çiğdem. *Constantinopolis/Istanbul: Cultural Encounters, Imperial Vision, and the Construction of the Ottoman Capital.* University Park: Pennsylvania State University Press, 2009.

Kahraman, Seyit Ali, and Yücel Dağlı. *Evliya Çelebi Seyahatnamesi: Istanbul.* Vol. 1, pts. 1 and 2. Istanbul: Yapı Kredi Yayınları, 2003.

Kal'a, Ahmet. *"Osmanlı Esnaf Sisteminin Oluşması ve Yeniden Yapılması Açınsnndan Istanbul Esnaf Birlikleri."* In *Istanbul Imparatorluk Başkentinden Megakente,* edited by Yavuz Köse, 250–90. Istanbul: Kitab Yayınevi, 2011.

Kaplan, Steven Laurence. "Guilds, 'False Workers,' and the Fabourg Saint-Antoine." In McClain, Merriman, and Kaoru, *Edo and Paris,* 355–83.

———. "Provisioning Paris: The Crisis of 1738–1741." In McClain, Merriman, and Kaoru, *Edo and Paris,* 175–210.

Karahasanoğlu, Selim, and Deniz Cenk Demir, eds. *History from Below: A Tribute in Memory of Donald Quataert.* Istanbul: Bilgi University Press, 2016.

Karal, Enver Ziya. *Fransa-Mısır ve Osmanlı Imparatorluğu (1797–1802).* Istanbul: Milli Mecmua Basrmevi, 1938.

———. *Selim III'ün Hatt-i Hümayunlari, Nizam-i Cedit, 1789–1807.* Ankara: TTK, 1988.

Kasaba, Reşat. *A Moveable Empire: Ottoman Nomads, Migrants, and Refugees.* Seattle: University of Washington Press, 2009.

Kayaalp, Pinar. "The Role of Imperial Mosque Complexes (1543–1583) in the Urbanization of Üsküdar." In *Urban Space in the Middle Ages and the Early Modern Age,* edited by Albrecht Classen, 645–67. Berlin: Walter de Gruyter, 2009.

Kayaoğlu, Turan. *Legal Imperialism: Sovereignty and Extraterritoriality in Japan, the Ottoman Empire, and China.* Cambridge: Cambridge University Press, 2010.

Kayra, C., and E. Üyepazarcı. *Ikinci Mahmut'un Istanbul'u: Bostancıbaşı Sicilleri.* Istanbul: Istanbul Büyükşehir Belediyesi Yayınları, 1991.

Kemp, Percy. "An Eighteenth-Century Turkish Intelligence Report." *IJMES* 16 (1984): 497–506.

Kenan, Seyfi, ed. *Osmanlılar ve Avrupa: Seyahat, Karşılaşma, ve Etkileşim.* Istanbul: ISAM, 2008.

Ketering, Sharon. "State Control and Municipal Authority in France." In McClain, Merriman, and Kaoru, *Edo and Paris,* 86–97.

Keyder, Çağlar, ed. *Istanbul Between the Global and the Local.* London: Lanham, Rowman, and Littlefield, 1999.

Keyder, Çağlar, D. Özveren, and Donald Quataert, eds. *Doğu Akdeniz'de Liman Kentleri, 1800–1914.* Ankara: Tarih Vakfı Yurt Yayınları, 1993.

Kilodziejczyk, Darius. "Inner Lake or Frontier? The Ottoman Black Sea in the Sixteenth and Seventeenth Centuries." In *Enjeux politiques, économiques, et militaires en mer noire (XIVe–XXIe Siècles): Études à la memoire de Mihail Guboglu,* edited by Faruk Bilici, Ionel Candea, and Anca Popescu, 125–39. Braila, Romania: Musée de Braila, 2007.

Koçakalpan, Saim Çağrı. "Istanbul *Gümrüğü* (1750–1800): Teşkilat ve Ticaret." PhD diss., Istanbul University, 2014.

Koller, Markus. "The Istanbul Fur Market in the Eighteenth Century." In Costantini and Koller, *Ottoman Ecumenical Commmunity,* 115–29.

———. "Some Remarks on a Merchant Family in Eighteenth-Century Bosnia." In Faroqhi and Veinstein, *Merchants in the Ottoman Empire,* 179–92.

Köse, Yavuz, ed. *Istanbul Imparatorluk Başkentinden Megakente.* Istanbul: Kitab Yayınevi, 2011.

Kramers, J. H. "Terdjuman." In *Encyclopedia of Islam.* 1st ed. Vol. 4, 725–26. Leiden: E. J. Brill, 1934.

Kritovoulos, Michael. *The History of Mehmed the Conqueror.* Translated by Charles T. Riggs. Princeton, NJ: Princeton University Press, 1954.

Krstic, Tijana. "Moriscos in Ottoman Galata, 1609–1620s." In *The Expulsion of Moriscos From Spain: A Mediterranean Diaspora,* edited by Mecedes Garcia-Arenal and Gerard Wiegers, 269–86. Leiden: E. J. Brill, 2014.

———. "Subjecthood and Sovereignty in Ottoman Galata in the Age of Confessionalization: The Carazzo Affair, 1613–1617." *Oriente Moderno* 93 (2013): 422–63.

Kuban, Doğan. *Istanbul: An Urban History.* Istanbul: Economic and Social Foundation of Turkey, 1996.

Kuneralp, Sinan, and Emre Öktem, eds. *Chambre de conseillers légistes de la Sublime Porte: Rapports, avis et consultations sur la condition juridique des ressortissants étrangers, le statut des communautés non musulmanes et les relations internationals de l'empire Ottoman (1864–1912).* Istanbul: Les Editions Isis, 2012.

Kuran, Timur. "The Economic Ascent of the Middle East's Religious Minorities: The Role of Islamic Religious Pluralism." *Journal of Legal Studies* 33, no. 2 (June 2004): 50–59.

———. *The Long Divergence: How Islamic Law Held Back the Middle East.* Princeton, NJ: Princeton University Press, 2011.

———, ed. *Social and Economic Life in Seventeenth-Century Istanbul: Glimpses from Court Records.* Vols. 1–2. Istanbul: Turkiye Iş Bankası Kültür Yayınları, 2010.

Kurtaran, Uğur. *Sultan I. Mahmud ve Dönemi, 1730–1754.* Ankara: Atıf Yayınları, 2014.

Kütükoğlu, Mübahat S. *Balta Limanı'na Giden Yol: Osmanlı-Ingliz Iktisadi Münasebetleri (1580–1850).* Ankara: TTK, 2013.

———. *Osmanlılarda Narh Müessesi ve 1640 Tarihli Narh Defteri.* Istanbul: Enderun Kitabevi, 1983.

Laidlaw, Christine. *The British in the Levant: Trade and Perceptions of the Ottoman Empire in the Eighteenth Century.* London: I. B. Tauris, 2010.

Laiou, Sophia. "Christian Women in an Ottoman World: Interpersonal and Family Cases Brought before the Shari'a Courts during the Seventeenth and Eighteenth Centuries." In *Women in the Ottoman Balkans,* edited by A. Buturovich and I. Schick, 243–71. London: I. B. Tauris, 2007.

Landweber, Julia. "Leaving France, Turning Turk, Becoming Ottoman: The Transformation of Comte Claude-Alexandre de Bonneval into Humbaraci Ahmed Pasha." In Isom-Verhaaren and Schull, *Living in the Ottoman Realm,* 209–24.

Levy, Avigdor, ed. *Jews, Turks, Ottomans: A Shared History, Fifteenth through Twentieth Century.* Syracuse, NY: Syracuse University Press, 2002.

Levy, Juliette. *The Making of a Market: Credit, Henequen, and Notaries in Yucatan, 1850–1900.* University Park: Pennsylvania University Press, 2012.

Levy-Aksu, Noémi. *Ordre et désordres dans l'Istanbul Ottoman (1879–1909).* Paris: Karthala, 2013.

Lewis, Reina. *Rethinking Orientalism: Women, Travel, and the Ottoman Empire.* New Brunswick, NJ: Rutgers University Press, 2004.

Longino, Michele. *French Travel Writing in the Ottoman Empire: Marseilles to Constantinople, 1650–1700.* London: Routledge, 2015.

Mantran, Robert. *Histoire d'Istanbul.* Paris: Fayard, 1996.

———. *Istanbul dans la seconde moitié du XVIIe siècle.* Paris: Librairie Adrien Maisonneuve, 1962.

———. "Monsieur de Guilleragues, ambassadeur de France a Constantinople et le commerce Français au Levant (1679–1684)." In *L'Empire Ottoman: La République de Turquie et la France,* edited by Hamit Batu and Jean-Louis Bacqué-Grammont, 59–72. Varia Turcica III. Paris: Éditions Isis, 1986.

Marcus, Abraham. *The Middle East on the Eve of Modernity: Aleppo in the Eighteenth Century.* New York: Columbia University Press, 1989.

Marmara, Rinaldo. *La communauté Levantine de Constantinople, de l'empire Byzantine à la République Turque.* Istanbul: Éditions Isis, 2012.

Masson, Paul. *Histoire du commerce Français dans le Levant au XVIIIe siècle.* Paris: Libraire Hachette, 1911.

———. *Marseille et la colonization Française.* 2nd ed. 2 vols. Paris: Libraire Hachette, 1912.

Masters, Bruce. *Christians and Jews in the Ottoman Arab World: The Roots of Sectarianism.* Cambridge: Cambridge University Press, 2001.

———. *The Origins of Western Economic Dominance in the Middle East: Mercantilism and the Islamic Economy in Aleppo, 1600–1750.* New York: NYU Press, 1988.

———. "The Sultan's Entrepreneurs: The *Avrupa Tuccars* and the *Hayriye Tuccars* in Syria." *IJMES* 24 (1992): 579–97.

Matrakçı, Nasuh. *Beyani-i Sefer-i Irakeyn-i Sultan Süleyman Han.* Ankara: TTK, 1976.

Matthee, Rudolph P. *The Politics of Trade in Safavid Iran: Silk for Silver, 1600–1730.* Cambridge: University of Cambridge Press, 1999.

McClain, James L., John M. Merriman, and Ugawa Kaoru, eds. *Edo and Paris: Urban Life and the State in the Early Modern Era,* Ithaca, NY: Cornell University Press, 1994.

McCormick, M. *The Origins of the European Economy: Communication and Commerce AD 300–900.* Cambridge: Cambridge University Press, 2000.

Mehmed, Efendi. *Le paradis des infidels: Un ambassadeur Ottoman en France sous la Régence.* Paris: François Maspero, 1981.

Melling, Antoine-Ignace. *Voyage pittoresque à Constantinople et sur des rives de Bosphore, 1807–1824.* Paris, 1819.

Ménage, V.L. "The English Capitulation of 1580: A Review Article," *IJMES* 12 (1980): 373–83.

Mercan, Özden F. "The Genoese of Pera in the Fifteenth Century." In Isom-Verhaaren and Schull, *Living in the Ottoman Realm*

Miller, Louis. "The Genoese in Galata." *IJMES* 10 (1979): 71–91.

Montagu, Lady Mary Wortley. *Turkish Embassy Letters.* Edited by Malcolm M. Jack. London: Virago Books, 1994.

Moreh, Shmuel, trans. *Napoleon in Egypt: Al-Jabarti's Chronicle of the French Occupation of Cairo, 1798.* Princeton, NJ: Markus Wiener, 1993.

Mu'ahedat Mecmuası. Vol. 1 Ankara: TTK, 2008.

Muller-Wiener, Wolfgang. *Bizanstan Osmanlı'ya Istanbul Limanı.* Translated by Erol Özbek. Istanbul: Tarih Vakfi Yurt Yayınları, 2003.

Mumcu, Serap. *Venedik Balyosunun Defterleri.* "The Venetian Baylo's Registers (1589–1684)." In *Hilal: Studi Turchi et Ottomani* 4, no. 648 (Edizioni Ca'Foscari, 2014), 7–427.

Mumford, Lewis. *The City in History: Its Origins, Its Transformation, and Its Prospects.* San Diego: Harcourt Brace Jovanovich, 1961.

Nalçacı, Nida Nebahat. "*Erken Modern Dönem Istanbul'unda Savaş Esirleri ve Zorunlu Istihdam.*" Masters thesis, Istanbul University, 2013.

———. *Sultanın Kulları: Erken Modern Dönem Istanbul'unda Savaş Esirleri ve Zorunlu Istihdam.* Istanbul: Verita Kitap, 2015.

Neave, Dorina L. *Twenty-Six Years on the Bosphorus*. London: Grayson and Grayson, 1933.

Nirenberg, David. *Communities of Violence: Persecution of Minorities in the Middle Ages*. Princeton, NJ: Princeton University Press, 1996.

——. *Neighboring Faiths: Christianity, Islam, and Judaism in the Middle Ages and Today*. Chicago: University of Chicago Press, 2014.

Oğuzoğlu, Yusuf, ed. *Halil Inalcik'in Bursa Araştırmaları*. Bursa: Bursa Büyükşehir Belediyesi, 2012.

Orhonlu, Cengiz. "Tercuman." In *Islam Ansiklopedisi*. Vol. 12, pt. 1, 175–81. Istanbul: Türkiye Diyanet Vakfı, 1974.

Ortega, Stephen. *Negotiating Transcultural Relations in the Early Modern Mediterranean: Ottoman-Venetian Encounters*. London: Ashgate, 2014.

Öz, Mehmet. "1455 Tahriri ve Istanbul'un Iskan Tarihi Bakımından Önemi." In *Osmanlı Istanbulu,* edited by Feridun M. Emecen and Emrah S. Gürkan. Vol. 1, 107–15. Istanbul: 29 Mayıs Universitesi Yayınları, 2013.

Palacious, Arturo Bernal, OP. "Fr. Benedetto (Giovanni) Palazzo OP (1895–1955) and His Catalogue of the Conventual Archives of Saint Peter in Galata (Istanbul)." *Dominican History Newsletter* 11 (2002): 215–50.

Palazzo, P. Benedetto. *Arap Camii veya Galata Saint Paul Kilisesi*. Istanbul: Bilge Karınca, 2014.

Pamuk, Şevket. "Economic History, Institutions, and Institutional Change." *IJMES* 44 (2012): 532–38.

——. "Institutional Change and the Longevity of the Ottoman Empire, 1500–1800." *Journal of Interdisciplinary History* 35, no. 2 (Autumn 2004): 225–47.

——. *A Monetary History of the Ottoman Empire*. Cambridge: Cambridge University Press, 2000.

Panzac, Daniel. *Commerce et navigation dans l'Empire Ottoman au XVIIIe siècle*. Istanbul: Les Éditions Isis, 1996.

——. *Histoire économique et sociale de l'empire Ottoman et de la Turquie (1326–1960)*. Paris: Peeters, 1995.

——. *La caravane maritime: Marins Européens et marchants Ottomans en Mediterranée (1680–1830)*. Paris: CNRS Éditions, 2004.

——. *La marine Ottomane, de l'apogée a la chute de l'empire (1572–1923)*. Paris, CNRS Éditions, 2009.

——. *La peste dans l'empire Ottoman, 1700–1850*. Leuven: Éditions Peeters, 1985.

——. *La ville dans l'empire Ottoman: Activités et societies*. Paris: CNRS, 1994.

——. "Les affréteurs de navires à Istanbul dans la seconde moitié du XVIIIe siècle." In Faroqhi and Veinstein, *Merchants in the Ottoman Empire*, 165–77.

——. "Négociants Ottomans et captaines Français: La caravane maritime en Crete au XVIIIe siècle." In *L'Empire Ottoman: La Republiue de Turquie et la France,* edited by H. Batu and Jean-Louis Bacqué-Grammont, 99–118. Istanbul: Éditions ISIS, 1986.

Pardoe, Miss Julia. *The Beauties of the Bosphorus: Illustrated in a Series of Views of Constantinople and Its Environs*. London, 1843.

————. *Beauties of the Bosphorus: Constantinople and Its Environs*. London, 1855.

Pascale, Barthe. *French Encounters with the Ottomans, 1510–1560*. London: Routledge, 2016.

Pedani, Maria Pia. "Between Diplomacy and Trade: Ottoman Merchants in Venice." In Faroqhi and Veinstein, *Merchants in the Ottoman Empire*, 3–21.

————, ed. *Inventory of the "Lettere e Scritture Turchesche" of the Venetian State Archives Based on the Materials Compiled by Alessio Bombaci*. Leiden: E.J. Brill, 2010.

Perot, J., F. Hitzel, and R. Anhegger. *Hatice Sultan Ile Melling Kalfa: Mektuplar*. Translated by Ela Güntekin. Istanbul: Tarih Vakfı Yurt Yayınları, 2001.

Perry, Mary Elizabeth. *The Handless Maiden: Moriscos and the Politics of Religion in Early Modern Spain*. Princeton, NJ: Princeton University Press, 2005.

Petech, Luciano. "Les marchands Italiens dans l'Empire Mongol." *Journal Asiatique* (1962): 549–74.

Phillou, Christine M. *Biography of an Empire: Governing Ottomans in an Age of Revolution*. Berkeley: University of California Press, 2011.

Pinon, P. "Résidence de France dans l'empire Ottoman: Notes sur l'architecture domestique." In *Les Villes dans l'Empire Ottoman: Activitées et societées*, edited by Daniel Panzac, 47–84. Paris: CNRS Éditions, 1994.

Pinto, Karen C. *Medieval Islamic Maps: An Exploration*. Chicago: University of Chicago Press, 2016.

Pirenne, Henri. *Mohammad and Charlemagne*. Translated from French by Bernard Miall. London: G. Allen and Unwin, 1954.

Pissis, Nikolas. "Investments in the Greek Merchant Marine (1783–1821)." In Faroqhi and Veinstein, *Merchants in the Ottoman Empire*, 151–65.

Pistarino, Geo. "The Genoese in Pera—Turkish Galata." *Mediterranean Historical Review* 1, no. 1 (1986): 63–86.

Piterberg, Gabriel, Teofilo Ruiz, and Goeffrey Symcox, eds. *Braudel Revisited: The Mediterranean World, 1600–1800*. Toronto: University of Toronto Press, 2010.

Porter, David (1780–1843). *Constantinople and Its Environs in a Series of Letters Exhibiting the Actual State of Manners, Customs, and Habits of the Turks, Armenians, Jews, and Greeks by an American*. New York: Harper and Brothers, 1835.

Price, Munro. *Preserving the Monarchy: The comte de Vergennes, 1774–1787*. Cambridge: Cambridge University Press, 1995.

Prousis, Theophilus C. *British Consular Reports from the Ottoman Levant in an Age of Upheaval, 1815–1830*. Istanbul: ISIS Press, 2008.

Purcell, Nicholas. *The Corrupting Sea: A Study of Mediterranean History*. Oxford: Blackwell, 2000.

Quataert, Donald, ed. *Consumption Studies and the History of the Ottoman Empire, 1550–1922: An Introduction*. New York: SUNY Press, 2000.

————. *Manufacturing in the Ottoman Empire and Turkey, 1500–1950*. New York: SUNY Press, 1994.

————. *Ottoman Manufacturing in the Age of Revolution*. Cambridge: Cambridge University Press, 1993.

Raşid, Mehmed. *Tarih-i Raşid.* 6 vols. Istanbul, 1865.

Rausas, G. Pélissié du. *Le Régime des capitulations dans l'Empire Ottoman.* Vol. 1. Paris: Arthur Rousseau, 1902.

Raymond, André. *Artisans et commerçants au Caire XVIIIe siècle.* 2 vols. Damascus: Presses de l'Institut Français de Proche-Orient, 1973–74.

———. *Cairo.* Translated by Willard Wood. Cambridge, MA: Harvard University Press, 2000.

———. "The Ottoman Conquest and the Development of the Great Arab Towns." *International Journal of Turkish Studies* 1 (1980): 84–101.

Refik, Ahmed. *Onikinci Asr-i Hicri'de Istanbul Hayatı (1689–1785).* Istanbul: Enderun Kitabevi, 1988.

———. *Onüçüncü Asr-i Hicri'de Istanbul Hayatı (1786–1882).* Istanbul: Enderun Kitabevi, 1988.

Robarts, Andrew. *Migration and Disease in the Black Sea Region: Ottoman-Russian Relations in the Late Eighteenth and Early Nineteenth Centuries.* London: Bloomsbury Academic, 2017.

Roberts, Mary. *Intimate Outsiders: The Harem in Ottoman and Orientalist Travel Literature.* Durham, NC: Duke University Press, 2007.

———. *Istanbul Exchanges: Ottoman, Orientalists, and Nineteenth-Century Visual Culture.* Berkeley: University of California Press, 2015.

Rosenthal, Steven. "Foreigners and Municipal Reform in Istanbul: 1855–1865." *IJMES* 11 (1980), 227–45.

Rothman, Natalie. *Brokering Empire: Trans-Imperial Subjects between Venice and Istanbul.* Ithaca, NY: Cornell University Press, 2012.

Rouillard, Clarence Dana. *The Turk in French History, Thought, and Literature (1520–1660).* Paris: Ancienne Librairie Furne, 1940.

Rousseau, Louis. *Les relations diplomatique de la France et de la Tuequie au XVIIe siècle. Tome premier (1700–1716).* Paris: N.p., 1908. Reprint, Nabu Press, 2012.

Rozen, Minna. *A History of the Jewish Community in Istanbul: The Formative Years, 1453–1566.* Leiden: E. J. Brill, 2002.

———. "Metropolis and Necropolis: The Cultivation of Social Status among the Jews of Istanbul in the 17th and 18th Centuries." In Costantini and Koller, *Ottoman Ecumenical Community,* 89–115.

Rudé, George. *Europe in the Eighteenth Century: Aristocracy and the Bourgeois Challenge.* Cambridge, MA: Harvard University Press, 1972.

Runciman, Steven. *The Fall of Constantinople, 1453.* Cambridge: Cambridge University Press, 1965.

Rycault, Paul. *The Present State of the Ottoman Empire.* London, 1668.

Sahillioğlu, Halil. "Bir Tüccar Kervanı." *Belgelerde Türk Tarihi Dergisi* 9 (1968): 63–69.

Saint-Priest, Comte de François-Emmanuel Guignard, Charles Henri Auguste Schefer. *Mémoire sur l'ambassade de France en Turquie, 1525–1770.* Paris: Philo Press, 1974.

Salzmann, Ariel. "Islamopolis, Cosmopolis: Ottoman Urbanity between Myth and Postmodernity." In *Cosmopolitanisms in Muslim Countries: Perspectives from the Past,* edited by D. N. MacLean and S. K. Ahmed, 68–91. Edinburgh: Edinburgh University Press, 2013.

———. "Migrants in Chains: On the Enslavement of Muslims in Renaissance and Enlightenment Europe." *Religions* 4 (2013): 391–411.

———. "The Moral Economies of the Pre-Modern Mediterranean: Preliminaries to the Study of Cross-Cultural Migration during the Long Sixteenth Century." In Costantini and Koller, *Living in the Ecumenical Ottoman Community,* 453–79.

———. *Tocqueville in the Ottoman Empire: Rival Paths to the Modern State.* Leiden: E. J. Brill, 2004.

Schefer, Charles, ed. *Bertirandan de la Broquiere'in Denizaşırı Seyahati.* Translated by Ilhan Arda. Istanbul: Eren Yayınları, 2000.

Schmitt, Olivers Jens. *Les Levantines: Cadres de vie et identités d'un groupe ethno-confessionel de l'empire Ottoman au "long" 19 siècle.* Istanbul: ISIS Press, 2007.

Schneider, A. M., and M. Is Nomidis. *Galata: Topgraphisch-Archologischer Plan Mit Erlauterndem Text.* Istanbul: N.p., 1994.

Seni, Nora. "The Camondos and Their Imprint." *IJMES* 26, no. 4 (November 1994): 665–75.

Shaw, Stanford J. *Between Old and New: The Ottoman Empire under Selim III, 1789–1807.* Cambridge, MA: Harvard University Press, 1971.

———. "The Population of Istanbul in the Nineteenth Century." *IJMES* 10, no. 2 (May 1979): 265–77.

Shay, Mary L. *The Ottoman Empire from 1720 to 1734, as Revealed in Dispatches of the Venetian Baili.* Urbana: University of Illinois Press, 1944.

Skilliter, S. A. *William Harborne and the Trade with Turkey.* London: British Academy, 1977.

Slot, J. "The Fires in Istanbul of 1782 and 1784, according to Maps and Reports by Dutch Diplomatic Representatives." *Güney Doğu Avrupa Araştımaları Dergisi* 4–5 (1975–76): 47–52.

Smyrnelis, Marie-Carmen. *Izmir, 1830–1930: Unutulmuş bir Kent Mi?* Istanbul: Iletişim, 2008.

———. "Negociants de Smyrne aux XVIII et XIX siècle." In Faroqhi and Veinstein, *Merchants in the Ottoman Empire,* 231–41.

———. *Une ville Ottoman plurielle: Smyrne aux XVIII et XIX siècle.* Istanbul: ISIS Press, 2006.

Sobers-Khan, Nur. "Slaves without Shackles: Forced Labour and Manumission in the Galata Court Registers, 1560–1572." PhD diss., Pembroke College, 2012.

Sobers-Khan, Nur. *Slaves without Shackles: Forced Labour and Manumission in the Galata Court Registers, 1560–1572.* Berlin: Klaus Schwartz Verlag, 2014.

Soucek, S. "Naval Aspects of the Ottoman Conquests of Rhodes, Cyprus, and Crete." *Studia Islamica* 98–99 (2004): 219–61.

Soysal, Ismail. *Fransız İhtilali ve Türk-Fransız Diplomasi Münasebetleri (1789–1802)*. Ankara: Türk Tarih Kurumu, 1999.

Spuler, Bertold. *İran Mogolları, Siyaset, İdare ve Kultur İlhanlılar Devri, 1220–1350*. Ankara: TTK, 1957.

———. *The Mongols in History*. London: Pall Mall Press, 1971

Stanchev, Stefan. "*Devedo:* The Venetian Response to Sultan Mehmed II in the Venetian-Ottoman Conflict of 1462–79." *Mediterranean Studies* 19 (2010): 43–66.

———. "Inevitable Conflict or Opportunity to Explore? The Mechanics of Venice's Embargo against Mehmed II and the Problem of Western-Ottoman Trade after 1453." *Mediaevalia* 32 (2011): 155–96.

———. "Venice and the Ottoman Threat, 1381–1453." In *Reconfiguring the Fifteenth-Century Crusade,* edited by Norman Housley, 161–205. London: Palgrave, 2017.

Steensgaard. Niels. *The Asian Trade Revolution of the Seventeenth Century: The East India Companies and the Decline of Caravan Trade*. Chicago: University of Chicago Press, 1973.

Stefini, Tommaso. "Seeking Redress at the *Signoria*: Ottoman Merchants in Dispute with the Republic of Venice in the Early Modern Era." Masters thesis, Boğaziçi University, 2013.

Strathern, Paul. *Napoleon in Egypt*. New York: Bentham Books, 2009.

Summer-Boyd, Hillary, and John Freely. *Strolling through Istanbul: A Guide to the City*. Istanbul: Sev Matbaacılık, 2000.

Susa, Nasim. *The Capitulatory Regime in Turkey: Its History, Origin, and Nature*. Baltimore: Johns Hopkins University Press, 1933.

Tabak, Faruk. "Imperial Rivalry and Port-Cities: A View From Above." *Mediterranean Historical Review* 24, no. 2 (December 2009): 79–94.

———. *The Waning of the Mediterranean, 1550–1870: A Geohistorical Approach*. Baltimore: Johns Hopkins University Press, 2008.

Tagliacozzo, Eric. "*Hajj* and the Time of Pilgrim Ships and Contagion from Southeast Asia to the Red Sea." In *Global Muslims in an Age of Steam and Print,* edited by James L. Gelvin and Nile Green, 103–20. Berkeley: University of California Press, 2014.

Takeda, Junko Thérèse. *Between Crown and Commerce: Marseille and the Early Modern Mediterranean*. Baltimore: Johns Hopkins University Press, 2011.

———. "French Mercantilism and the Early Modern Mediterranean: A Case Study of Marseille's Silk Industry." *French History* 29, no. 1 (2015): 12–17.

Talbot, Michael. *British-Ottoman Relations, 1661–1807: Commerce and Diplomatic Practice in Eighteenth-Century Istanbul*. Woodbridge, UK: Boydell Press, 2017.

Talman, Baha. "Galata *Mevlevihanesi: Mimari*." In *Dünden Bugüne Istanbul Ansiklopedisi*. Vol. 3, 364–67. Istanbul: Kültür Bakanlığı ve Tarih Vakfı, 1993.

Tamdoğan, Işık. "*Sulh* and the 18th-Century Ottoman Courts of Üsküdar and Adana." *Islamic Law and Society* 15 (2008): 55–83.

Tezcan. Baki. *The Second Ottoman Empire: Political and Social Transformation in the Early Modern World*. Cambridge: Cambridge University Press, 2010.

Theunissen, Hans. *Ottoman-Venetian Diplomatics: The Ahd-Names, the Historical Background, and the Development of a Category of Politico-Commercial Instruments, together with an Annotated Edition of a Corpus of Relevant Documents. Electronic Journal of Oriental Studies of Utrecht University*. The Netherlands, n.d. Published on the Internet.

Thévenot, Jean. *L'empire du Grand Turc vu par un sujet de Louis XIV*. Paris: Galmann-Lévy, 1965.

Thomas, Smith (1638–1710). *Religion and Government of the Turks: Together with a Survey of Seven Churches of Asia*. London, 1678.

Tibet, Aksel. *Fransa Elçiliği Binası."* In *Dünden Bugüne Istanbul Ansiklopedisi*. Vol. 3, 331–32. Istanbul: Kültür Bakanlığı ve Tarih Vakfı, 1993.

Toprak, Zafer. *"Istanbul'da Fuhuş ve Zührevi Hastalıklar, 1914–1933." Tarih ve Toplum* 39 (1987): 31–40.

Tott, Baron de. *Memoirs of Baron de Tott*. 2 vols. New York: Arno Press, 1973.

Tournefort, Joseph Pitton de. *Relations d'un voyage du Levant fait par ordre du Roy*. 2 vols. Paris: Imprimé Royale, 1717.

Trivellato, Francesca. *The Familiarity of Strangers: The Sephardic Diaspora, Livorno, and Cross-Cultural Trade in the Early Modern Period*. New Haven: Yale University Press, 2009.

Turan, Namık Sinan. *Imparatorluk ve Diplomasi: Osmanlı Diplomasinin Izinde*. Istanbul: Istanbul Bilgi Universitesi yayınları, 2014.

Turan, Şerafettin. *Türkiye-Italya Ilişkileri*. Istanbul: Metis Yayınları, 1990.

Tursun Beg, *The History of Mehmed the Conqueror*. Translated by Halil Inalcik and Rhoads Murphey. Minneapolis: Biblioteca Islamica, 1978.

Ulkesul, Cevat. *Piri Reis ve Türk Kartograflarının Çizgileriyle XVI, XVII, ve XVIII. Yüzyıllarda Istanbul*. Istanbul: Boyut, 2013.

Unat, Faik Reşit. *Osmanlı Sefirleri ve Sefaratnameleri*. Ankara: TTK, 1992.

Uzunçarşılı, Ismail Hakkı. *Osmanlı Tarihi, XVIII Yüzyıl*. Vol. 4, pt 2. Ankara: TTK, 2003.

Vandal, Albert (1835–1910). *Les voyages de Marquis de Nointel (1670–1680)*. Paris: Librairie Plon, 1900.

———. *Une ambassade Français en Orient sous Louis XV: La mission du Marquis de Villeneuve, 1728–1741*. Paris: Librairie Plon, 1887.

Varlik, Nukhet. *Plague and Empire in the Early Modern Mediterranean World: The Ottoman Experience, 1347–1600*. Cambridge: Cambridge University Press, 2015.

Vatin, Nicolas. "The Ottoman View of France from the Late Fifteenth to the Mid-Sixteenth Century." *French History* 29, no. 1 (2015): 6–11.

Veinstein, Gilles. *"Les capitulations Franco-Ottoman de 1536 sont-elles encore controversables?"* In Costantini and Koller, *Living in the Ottoman Ecumenical Community*, 71–88.

Vergennes, Louis Bonneville de Marsangy. *Le chevalier de Vergennes: Son ambassade à Constantinople*. 2 vols. Paris, 1894.

Vitkus, Daniel J. *Turning Turk: English Theater and Multiculturalism in the Mediterranean, 1570–1630*. London: Palgrave MacMillan, 2003.

Vlami, Despina. *Trading with the Ottomans: The Levant Company in the Middle East*. London: I. B. Tauris, 2015.

Wantserbrough, J. "*Imtiyazat*" In *Encyclopedia of Islam*. 2nd ed. Vol. 3, 1178–79. Leiden: E. J. Brill, 1971.

Webb, Nigel, and Caroline Webb. *The Earl and His Butler in Constantinople: The Secret Diary of an English Servant Among the Ottomans*. London: I. B. Tauris, 2009.

White, Joshua. "Is it 'Halal' to Raid Them? Piracy and Law in the Seventeenth-Century Ottoman Mediterranean." In *Corsairs and Pirates in the Eastern Mediterranean, 15th–19th Centuries*," edited by David Starkey and Gelina Harlaftis, 77–94. Athens: Sylvia Ioanian Foundation, 2016.

———. "Litigating Disputes over Ships and Cargo in Early Ottoman Courts." *Quaderini Storici* 51, no. 3 (2016): 701–25.

———. *Piracy and Law in the Ottoman Mediterranean*. Stanford, CA: Stanford University Press, 2016.

Wilkins, Charles. *Forging Urban Solidarities: Ottoman Aleppo, 1640–1700*. Leiden: E. J. Brill, 2010.

Wishnitzer, Avner. *Reading Clocks: Time and Society in the Late Ottoman Empire*. Chicago: University of Chicago Press, 2015.

Wong, R. Bin. *China Transformed: Historical Change and the Limits of European Experience*. Ithaca, NY: Cornell University Press, 1997.

Wood, Alfred C. "The English Embassy at Constantinople, 1660–1762." *English Historical Review* 40, no. 160 (October 1925): 533–61.

Wright, Diana Gilliand, and Pierre A. MacKay "When the *Serenissima* and the *Gran Turco* Made Love: The Peace Treaty of 1478." *Studi Veneziani* 53 (2007): 261–77.

Yalçınkaya, Mehmet Alaadin. *The First Permanent Ottoman Embassy in Europe: The Embassy of Yusuf Aghah Efendi to London (1793–1797)*. Istanbul: ISIS Press, 2010.

Yaycioğlu, Ali. *Partners of the Empire: The Crisis of the Ottoman Order in the Age of Revolutions*. Stanford, CA: Stanford University Press, 2016.

———. "A Reply to Timur Kuran," *IJMES* 48, no. 2 (May 2016): 433–35.

———. "*Révolution de* Constantinople: France and the Ottoman World in the Age of Revolutions." In Lorcin and Shepard, *French Mediterraneans*, 21–51.

Yazıcı. Tahsin. *Osmanlı Para Vakıfları: Kanuni Dönemi Üsküdar Örneği*. Ankara: TTK, 2003.

Yerasimos, Stéphane. "Gallant, Antoine." In *Dünden Bugüne Istanbul Ansiklopedisi*. Vol. 3, 374–75. Istanbul: Tarih Vakfı Yayınları, 1994.

———. "*La communauté Juive d'Istanbul a la fin du XVI siècle*." *Turcica* 27 (1995): 101–30.

Yıldız, Kenan. "1782 *Istanbul Yangın: Kadi Sicilerinden Tespit, Çikarı ve Yorumları*." In *Osmanlı Istanbulu, II*, edited by Feridun Emecen, Ali Akyıldız, and Emrah S. Gürkan, 707–22. Istanbul: 29 Mayıs University Yayınları, 2014.

Yılırmak, Gülay Web. *XVIII. Yüzyılda Osmanlı-Ingiliz Tiftik Ticareti*. Ankara: TTK, 2011.

Yılmaz, Fikret. *Geçmişten Günumüze Levantenler.* Izmir: Izmir Ticaret Odası, 2011.

Yılmaz, Serap. *"La soie dans les relations commerciales entre la France et l'empire Ottoman au XVIIIe siècle* (1700–1789)." PhD diss., Université de Paris, 1985.

Yücel, Yaşar. *Es'ar Defteri (1640 Tarihli).* Ankara: TTK, 1992.

Zachariadou, Elizabeth. *Trade and Crusade: Venetian Crete and the Emirates of Menteşe and Aydin (1300–1415).* Venice: Hellenic Institute of Byzantine and Post-Byzantine Studies, 1983.

Zandi-Sayek, Sibel. *Ottoman Izmir: The Rise of a Cosmopolitan Port, 1840–1880.* Minneapolis: University of Minnesota Press, 2012.

Zarcone, Thierry, and Fariba Zarinebaf-Shahr, eds. *Les Iraniens d'Istanbul.* Louvain: Peeters, 1993.

Zarinebaf, Fariba. *Crime and Punishment in Istanbul, 1700–1800.* Berkeley: University of California Press, 2010.

———. "From *Mahalle* (Neighborhood) to the Market and the Courts: Women, Credit, and Property in 18th-Century Istanbul." In Zarinebaf, *Women on the Margins,* 69–81.

———. "Intercommunal Life in Istanbul during the Eighteenth Century." *Review of Middle East Studies* 46, no. 1 (Summer 2012): 79–85.

———. "Policing Morality: Crossing Gender and Communal Boundaries in an Age of Political Crisis and Religious Controversy in Seventeenth-Century Istanbul." In Isom-Verhaaren and Schull, *Living in the Ottoman Realm,* 194–208.

———. "The Role of Women in the Urban Economy of Istanbul, 1700–1850." *International Labor and Working-Class History* 60 (Fall 2001): 141–52.

———. "The Wealth of Ottoman Princesses in the Tulip Age." In Zarinebaf, *Women on the Margins,* 113–22. Istanbul: Isis Press, 2014.

———, ed. *Women on the Margins: Gender, Charity, and Justice in the Early Modern Middle East.* Istanbul: Isis Press, 2014.

Zarinebaf, Fariba, John Bennet, and Jack L. Davis. *A Historical and Economic Geography of Ottoman Greece: The Southwestern Morea in the 18th Century.* Princeton, NJ: American School of Classical Studies in Athens, 2005.

Zarinebaf-Shahr, Fariba. "Tabriz under Ottoman Rule, 1720–1730." PhD diss., University of Chicago, 1991.

Zeller, Gaston. *"Une légende qui a la vie dure: Les Capitulations de 1535."* *Revue d'histoire modern et contemporaine* 2 (1955): 127–32.

Zilfi, Madeline. *Women and Slavery in the Late Ottoman Empire: The Design of Difference.* New York: Cambridge University Press, 2010.

Zwierlein, Cornel. *Imperial Unknowns: The French and British in the Mediterranean, 1650–1750.* Cambridge: Cambridge University Press, 2016.

INDEX

164; Ismailiye, 168; Kherson, 181, 343n127; Kilia, 147, 163; not quarantined, 72; oil and fish, 60; provisioning trade, 153, 154, 162, 167, 168, 180–82, 194, 195, 196; Sinop, 196; Trabzon, 102, 106map, 123

Bonaparte, Napoleon. *See* Napoleon Bonaparte

Bonnac, Marquis de, 137, 138, 245

Bosphorus villages: Catholics, 26; cosmopolitan culture, 272; districts, 86; embassies, 80; fortresses, 33, 176; geography, 23, 43map, 83, 84; history, 23, 26, 32; Jews, 45; judgeships, 37; plagues, 68, 69, 72, 80; Ottoman princesses, 265–71; pleasure seeking, 262–64; social gatherings, 63; trade, 181, 295; violence against women, 240; wars and diplomacy, 130, 138, 147

bozahane, 61, 169

Braudel, Fernand, 2, 3, 7, 153

Brazil, 206, 207

bread: börek, 176; *francela*, 155, 173, 178; hass, 178; prices, 164, 176; restrictions on sales, 177; shortages, 342n99. *See also* bakeries

Bristol Hotel, 83

brokers, 144, 197, 198, 200, 215, 216, 255, 276

brothels, 23, 62, 237, 238, 243

Bulgaria, 32, 62, 163

Bureau of Sanitation, 74, 75

Bursa: collusion in, 219; French traders, 203; location, 106map; quarantine, 74; partnerships, 157; piracy, 129; place of exile, 238; silk, 37, 98, 100, 119–21, 170, 188, 221, 222; Venetian merchants, 95, 101; taxes, 119, 196

butchers, 44, 65, 66, 123, 160, 161

butter. *See* clarified butter

Büyükdere, 73, 73, 263map, 265, 269

Büyük Londra Hotel, 83

Büyük Mazarlık, 69

Byzantine Emperors. *See* specific emperors

Byzantine tradition, 91, 95–97, 183

Cabi Ömer Efendi, 72

cadastral surveys, 86

Caffa, 27, 29, 31, 36, 37, 40, 41, 44, 102, 123, 163, 164

Cairo: Azbakiyya quarter, 74; French merchants, 130; French Revolution, 283–85; location, 106map; plague, 74; Thévenot, 128; trade, 101, 113, 117, 204, 206, 208, 210

Camondo, Abraham, 86

cannons, 33, 64, 279

Cape of Good Hope, 121

capitulations, 35, 63, 92, 93, 123, 148, 259

Capuchins, 46, 49, 133, 257

caravan trade, 155, 157

cash crop, 185, 289

Catholic millet, 261, 355n107

Catholics: anti-Turkish feelings, 226; Armenians, 79, 191, 260–61; burial grounds, 69; Capuchins, 46, 49, 133, 257; churches and cathedrals, 31, 46, 48, 245; Cretan War, 129, 131; demographics, 41; diplomacy, 89, 133; divide with Orthodox communities, 235, 244, 245; enslaving Muslims, 57; exclusion of non-Catholics in trade, 192; festivals, 256; Franciscans, 29; French Religious Wars, 114; holy places in Jerusalem, 114, 149, 283; interfaith marriage, 244, 245, 248, 271; Jesuits, 46, 48, 49, 257, 261, 279; Levantine, 234; Marseille, 191–92; missionaries and conversion, 7, 40, 50, 95, 102, 192, 255–61; official Ottoman community, 251; protection by France, 131–33, 144, 149, 272; recognition of, 234; rites and festivals, 256; social interactions, 264

Catherine II, 89, 146, 147, 148, 278

Celali rebellions, 120

cemeteries, 43map, 47, 54, 69, 70 fig.

Chamber of Commerce in Marseille: bankruptcy reports, 214; ban on interfaith marriage, 245; French ambassadors, 136, 195; funding for language school, 250; Iranian silk reports, 198; plague reports, 71, 72; source of documents, 18; trade, 190, 191, 201, 254; travel to Jerusalem, 248

Champs des Morts, 69

charitable foundations, 34, 36, 62. *See also* vakf complexes

Charles I, 110, 118
Charles II, 119
Charles V, 107
Chios: Aegean Sea, 196; ahdnames, 96, 97, 98, 103; building Galata, 27, 29 31–33, 36, 37, 40, 49; colonial coffee and sugar, 207; tensions, 258–59; trade, 162, 166, 194, 210, 221, 295
Choiseul-Gouffier, Comte de, 84, 219, 281
cholera, 69, 73
Christians, building Galata, 30, 31, 41, 45, 51, 55; captivity, 102; commerce, 162; conversion and missionary efforts, 236, 238, 251, 257–59; piracy, 103, 140; protections, 94, 133; taverns, 242; trade, 162; treaties, 92, 94.
Church of Haghia Sophia, 28–29
Church of Holy Sepulcher, 138, 140, 145
Çifte Hamam, 262, 264
çiftliks (large farms), 163
Çirağan Palace, 268
Circle of Justice, 61, 156, 159
Çizakça, Murad, 159, 160, 166, 171
cizye. See poll tax
clarified butter, 60, 61, 154, 162, 165, 167, 168, 174, 175
Claude de Bourg, 110
coal, 77, 78, 154
coffee: colonial, 204–10, 224; Egyptian, 121, 169, 230; French traders, 130, 193, 198, 287, 292, 295; Galata, 61, 65; Kherson port, 181; Louis XIV, 131; price, 348n108; shortages, 183; trade, 154, 160, 161, 165, 166, 169
coffeehouses: inspection for fire control 75, 88; London, 205; Marseille, 192; painters' depiction of, 267; Paris, 205–6; places of social interaction, 61, 62, 66, 241; popularity, 204–6, 208, 209; profitability, 131
colonial coffee. See coffee
colonial sugar. See sugar
Colbert, Jean-Baptiste, 46, 126, 128, 131–32, 189–92, 250
Colbertism, 191
collusion, 219
command economy, 155, 158, 162, 184
commenda partnerships, 157, 170, 171, 187

Committee of Public Safety, 280
community watch, 85, 235, 236, 238, 244, 262, 264
concubines, 56, 236, 237, 266, 268, 284. See also slavery
Constantine I, 26
Constantine XI, 34
consulage, 136
consular courts, 94, 96, 123, 143, 187, 188, 217–18
consular fees, 116, 117, 122, 191, 194, 228
contraband, 166, 167, 190, 200. See also smuggling
conversion, 255, 258–62
Cornelis, Haga, 122
Cossacks, 163
cosmopolitan culture, 271, 272
cotton: ahdnames, 95, 115, 118, 121, 133, 140; Angora trade, 199–200; banned export, 156, 162; cash crop, 185, 289; Indian, 190, 224, 225; raw, 203, 220, 225; Syrian, 198; textiles, 199, 204, 224, 225, 287; trade, 130, 189, 204, 210, 215. See also yarn
Council of Florence, 32
Council of Ten, 105
Council of Twelve, 30, 37, 49, 80
courts: archival documents, 291–96; building Galata, 42, 54, 55–59, 76; coffee disputes, 206, 207, 209; consular, 94, 123, 143, 144, 187, 188, 218; distance between, 203; French traders, 115, 216, 217, 232; non-Muslim witnesses, 187; Ottoman, 105, 107, 227, 252; partnership disputes, 173, 175; sea captains, 164; sexual misconduct, 239, 240, 242–244, 262, 264. See also Imperial Council, Islamic court, kadi court
covered market, 61, 77
credit networks, 40, 159, 160
Cretan Wars, 131, 148, 189, 191
Crete: conquest, 128, 130, 281; consul, 248; naval and commercial expansion, 129; slaves, 59, 95, 104; trade, 129, 141, 154, 164, 179, 180, 194, 230; trade restrictions, 201; treaties, 95
crime: in Galata, 39, 55, 56, 66, 88, 243, 295; murder, 143, 202, 219, 240, 243, 276; police stations, 85; rate, 66, 68, 241;

prostitution, 55, 63, 64, 237–40, 248, 284, 295

Crimean Khanate, 146, 281

Crimean khans, 146–47, 181, 281

Crimean Tatars, 56, 135

cross-dressing, 271

crowd control, 77

Crusaders, 28, 29, 32, 47, 206

customs dues, 163, 189, 195, 196, 197, 223, 225, 228, 260, 294

customs registers, 164, 167, 185

Cyclades Islands, 194

Cyprus: Marrano Jews, 110; piracy, 113; slaves, 57, 58; trade, 121, 123, 206, 287; Venetian ahdname, 100, 101, 103; war with Venice, 80, 129, 226

Dalmatia, 135

Dallaway, James, 23, 79, 233, 249, 251, 252

Damascus, 106map, 128, 204, 215

Damietta, 120, 123, 163, 166, 181, 230

dellal (broker), 197. *See also* brokers

Déscorches, Maries-Louis-Henri, 279, 280

Diderot, 206

diplomats: architecture, 79, 82; cash surplus, 211; fires, 76; Napoleon, 282, 289; settlement in Galata, 25, 26, 37, 66, 67, 68, 72, 185; shari'a, 93; study of harems, 266. *See also* specific diplomats

Directory of the French Republic, 281, 282

districts of greater Istanbul: 24map, 61, 72, 85, 178, 240, 262, 265, 272. *See also* specific districts

dragoman: ahdnames, 102, 112, 114, 115, 123; berats, 195; coffee, 207; culture, 237, 238, 246, 247, 256, 257; diplomacy, 127, 132, 135, 136, 142, 199, 201, 260; plagues, 72; fires, 76, 82; French Revolution, 274, 275, 276, 278, 280; in Pera, 79; language study, 80; lawsuits, 292; merchants, 228, 229; payment, 212, 218–19; protection system, 249–55; roles, 143- 45; settlement of debts, 185, 186, 187; sexual interaction, 237, 238; trade ban response, 178

Draperio family, 34, 36, 37

dried fruit: 27, 118, 119, 121, 141, 163, 164, 193, 287, 339n38

drinking, 55, 63, 241–43, 276. *See also* taverns, wine

drought, 153, 162, 164, 167, 176, 177, 178

Dubrovnik, 73, 97, 98, 99, 103, 106map

Dursteler, Eric, 37, 226, 234

Dutch East India Company, 121, 189

dyes: colonial goods, 204, 209; merchants, 222, 223, 224; Seven Years' War, 295; trade, 118, 121, 169, 198, 287

earthquakes, 256

Easter celebration, 256

East India Company: Dutch, 121, 189; English, 118, 121, 189, 224; French, 190

ecnebi defterleri (Registers of Foreign Nations), 185, 194, 295

Edict of Nantes, 114, 192

Eldem, Edhem, 10, 15, 193, 201, 214, 224, 271, 272

embassies: accounts, 79–84; American, 79; British, 72, 79; Dutch, 76, 89; fires, 76; harems, 265; merchants, 253–54; Russian, 83, 278; Tanzimat Reforms, 85–87. *See also* French embassy in Pera

Elizabeth I, 116, 331n101

English East India Company, 118, 121, 189, 224

English Levant Company, 118; ethnic diversity, 91; French traders, 194, 198, 214, 217, 224, 229, 237, 294; goods, 163, 178, 179, 200, 208, 209; Jewish people, 110, 197; merchants, 103, 109, 113, 115, 117, 118, 119, 120, 122, 124, 125, 230; open port, 226; plagues, 70, 72, 73, 74; refugees, 51, 52; taxes, 141, 157; trade, 181, 183, 188, 286, 287, 288; violence and tensions, 193, 272; wars, 129

Esma Sultan, 270

extramarital activities, 248

extraterritoriality, 93

Evliya Çelebi: accounts of Galata, 39, 41, 42, 44, 45, 46, 50, 55, 62, 68, 241; provisioning trade, 153, 154, 160, 165, 170;

Faroqhi, Suraiya, 11, 164

Fatimid, 94

Fatma Sultan, 265, 270

Fazil Mustafa Pasha, 134

Ferdinand II, 50

fetva (religious ruling), 204, 281, 296

fez (woolen cap), 65, 141, 216, 217

fires: bedestan, 61; churches and mosques, 44, 47–49, 310n29; crusaders, 28; customs house, 53; dislocation, 75–79; embassies, 82–83; Gelata Tower, 25, 39; Genoese commercial settlements, 31; Great Fire of 1660, 322n67; Great Fire of 1782, 322n44; Islamization, 55; Lady Abigail account, 69, 71; lawsuits, 291; neighborhood watch, 238; prevention and repairs, 87, 88, 133, 145, 256, 291; quarantine, 73; relocation to Bosphorus, 262; Tanzimat Reforms, 85; use of coal as heating, 320n3

Firges, Pascal, 277, 278, 280

fiscalism, 157; repair, 256

fish market, 60, 61

Flachat, Jean Claude, 266

Florence, 94, 98, 100, 119

Fonton, Antoine, 278

Fonton family, 136, 249

foodstuff: Circle of Justice, 61; customs rate, 196; government bans and inspections, 175, 176, 177, 179; monopolies, 220; trade, 96, 101, 116, 141, 148, 153, 154, 156, 161, 162, 164, 180, 183. *See also* clarified butter, grains, honey, meat, oil, olive oil, rice, sugar, wheat

forum shopping, 237, 293

Fornetti, Carlo, 72

Fossati brothers, 83

Fourth Crusade, 28, 47, 96

Francis I, 107

Francis II, 110

fraud, 33, 199, 216, 231

francela (bread), 155, 173, 178

Franciscans, 29

Friday mosques, 47, 53, 83. *See also* Arab Cami'i

French bankers, 214–19

French East India Company, 190

French embassy in Pera: ahdname, 122; architecture, 80, 81; dragoman, 72, 132, 136, 186, 207, 250, 253, 257, 274; chapel, 48, 211, 256; establishment of, 107; fires, 82; housing and protection, 48, 212, 252;

lifestyle, 237; observatory, 39; plague, 71; protection, 48, 252; takeover by revolutionaries, 275, 276, 279, 280, 283

French nation: bankruptcies and debts; 211, 214, 216, 217; disputes, 245, 258, 279; makeup, 200; spiritual center, 257

French Religious Wars, 112–13

French Revolution: community under arrest, 273–76; dissolution of Levant Companies, 145, 232, 186, 286–89; English trade, 79; Melling, 267; Napoleon's invasion of Egypt, 90, 281–86; Pera community before Republic, 235, 277–80; security for French ships, 231; sugar consumption, 206

French revolutionary wars, 277, 286

French shipping, 52, 180

French traders: coffee, 209; Galata, 200–2; Izmir, Marseille, violence against, 202–4;

disputes, bankruptcies and debts, 214–19

French woolen cloth, 204

furs: consumption, 27, 61, 65, 165, 221; trade in, 181, 287

Galata: arsenal, 23, 24map, 25, 31, 43map, 56, 57, 59, 60, 64, 66, 75; bedestan, 24map, 25, 43map, 60, 61, 77; brothels, 32, 62; customs house, 25, 53; fish market, 25, 43map, 60; hans, 25, 61, 62, 65, 66, 77; harbor, 25, 26, 30, 42, 60–62; Latin conquest, 25, 29; loggia, 25, 31, 40, 60; origins, 23, 25–30; Ottoman conquest and administration, 33–39; scale, 25, 38, 53, 60, 61, 62; Sycae, 26; taverns, 23, 38, 55, 60, 62–64; Tower, 25, 27, 31, 38 fig., 39, 42, 43map, 44, 45, 50, 52, 60, 75, 80; walls and gate, 23, 25, 26, 28, 29, 31, 32, 39, 66

Galatasaray, 78, 79, 122

Galland, Antoine, 127, 132, 134, 136, 237, 241, 250, 251, 257

Genç, Mehmet, 8, 157–60, 280

Gennadius, 42

Genoese Council, 35, 40

Giovanni Francesco Maringhi, 100

Golden Horn, 26–28, 30, 44, 53, 154, 196

grains, 153, 154, 156, 160–67, 170, 175, 176, 178–83. *See also* rice, wheat

Robespierre, Maximilien, 279, 280, 281
Romanian principalities: Moldavia, 135,
    136, 147, 148, 166; Wallachia, 32, 135, 136,
    147, 148, 166, 217
Rosetta Stone, 285
Rousseau, Jean Jacque, 206, 271, 283,
    356n140
Ruffin, Pierre-Jean, 274, 286
Rumeli Hisarı, 33
Rue de Canebière, 87
Rue de Péra, 78, 79–83, 87, 88
Russia: adhnames, 98, 272; alliance with
    England, 247; embassy, 76, 82, 83, 265,
    277; foodstuff, 141, 180–83; Franco-
    Ottoman Alliance, 145–49; French
    Revolution, 274, 276, 278–83, 285,
    287–88; Jacobines, 279; merchants, 66;
    plague, 73; silk trade route, 120; slaves,
    40, 56–59; wars and diplomacy, 79, 126,
    128, 135–39, 200, 243, 336n53, 337n63,
    337n66; trade, 161, 164, 165, 184, 195, 200
Russo-Ottoman Wars, 158, 180, 186, 223,
    224, 230, 281
Rüstem Pasha, 53, 61
Rüstem Pasha (mosque), 169
Rycault, Paul, 127, 128

Sahib Giray Khan, 147
Saint-Priest, Comte de: French Revolution,
    252, 253, 258; moving embassy, 81; pro-
    tection for merchants, 180, 195, 202, 219,
    231; settlement of debts, 186, 187
Saliha Sultan, 47, 54
Salonica: bankruptcies, 216; cultural
    encounters, 252, 255; ethno-religious
    tensions, 272; Levant Company, 117;
    food, 163, 180, 181, 183, 208; French
    Revolution, 274, 287, 288, 289; French
    traders, 194, 203, 207, 208; location,
    106map; Russo-Ottoman Wars, 230;
    textile workshops, 221; trade with, 32,
    34, 44, 45, 51, 52, 87
sarraf (money changer), 66, 211
Savary de Bréves, 80
Safavids, 188
scale for honey, 154, 165
scale tax, 119, 123. See also kantar (unit of
    measurement)

Sea of Marmara, 80, 154, 263map
şehbender (master of the port), 165
Selim Giray Khan, 146
Selim I, 105
Selim II, 53, 103, 110, 112, 122
Selim III: ally of Napoleon, 282, 283, 286;
    canals, 84; culture, 266–68; Egyptian
    relations, 285; French Revolution,
    273–77, 280; fire prevention policies,
    77; plague response, 73, 74; policy on
    abuse of protection system, 254
Seljuk Empire, 95
settlement, 173, 188
Seven Years' War, 208, 228, 229, 295
sexual harassment, 243, 264
Seyahatname, 46, 50, 153, 160. See also
    Evliya Çelebi
şeyhülislam, 94
Seyyid Ahmed Pasha, 214
Seyyid Ali Efendi, 136, 274, 282
shari'a (Islamic law); 89, 93, 94, 98, 125, 143,
    215, 217, 227, 240, 294. See also Islamic
    court
shawls, 199, 220, 221, 287
Shaykh Muhammad, 215–16
sherbets, 209, 242, 270
Shi'i Iranians, 59
ships: captains, 59, 111, 153, 161, 170, 172,
    174, 175, 231; galleons: 160, 161, 165, 166,
    168, 180, 210; galley slaves, 56, 57, 59, 176,
    177, 192, 258, 259, 260, 295
shipwrecks: dispute settlement, 174–75;
    treaties, 95, 96, 100, 112, 116; trade, 163,
    164
Sicily, 45, 98, 119, 133, 194, 206, 276
Sidon, 121, 133, 194, 214, 215, 248, 249, 287
simsar (head broker), 197, 200
Sinan, 53, 61, 262
Şişhane, 87
Şişli, 87
silk: raw, 98, 100, 118, 121, 162, 188, 198, 220,
    222, 287, 327n29, 332n125, 333n126;
    textiles, 65, 98, 100, 121, 133, 199, 220–
    22, 224, 267, 349n162; trade, 37, 95, 99,
    100, 120, 121, 171, 188, 189, 193, 183
sin city, 23. See also red-light district
Sinop, 196
Sixth District, 85–88